TAYLOR'S
GARDEN GUIDE

Taylor's
Garden Guide

by NORMAN TAYLOR

D. VAN NOSTRAND COMPANY, INC.

D. VAN NOSTRAND COMPANY, INC.

120 Alexander St., Princeton, New Jersey
257 Fourth Avenue, New York 10, New York
25 Hollinger Rd., Toronto 16, Canada

All correspondence should be addressed to the
principal office of the company at Princeton, N. J.

PRINTED IN THE UNITED STATES OF AMERICA

PREFACE

The bringing together of the six separate books issued between 1953 and 1955, provides the garden public with a single volume designed to help the amateur. They were written, and are now issued in this form, to enable the enthusiast to get the most out of his garden and to avoid costly mistakes.

The book is not for those who know it all. Rather it is presented to those who crave the results of gardening without the drudgery of failure or the errors of judgement that lead to it. One way to get the most out of this book is to read the section on How to Use the Book. That and the table of contents, with the index, should guide any seeker to the desired goal, and make the volume what it is intended to be—a Garden Guide.

N.T.

Elmwood
Princess Anne, Maryland
New Years, 1957

HOW TO USE THE BOOK

Each of the six sections has its own directions as to their contents and where to find them. For that reason only general suggestions are made here. Reference works of large scope are listed in the bibliography (see page 492), and if one needs to go beyond what the present volume is designed for, the reader is urged to consult these more technical works.

The present one has as its main object the simplest possible directions for:

Laying out a small or even a larger garden: *The Permanent Garden*
Planting for continuous bloom: *The Everblooming Garden*
Arranging for different color schemes in the garden: *Color in the Garden*
Planting for fragrance: *Fragrance in the Garden*
Herbs, their culture and uses: *Herbs in the Garden*
Fruit trees, berries, etc.: *Fruit in the Garden*

Perhaps no one will be interested at the same time in all six of these subjects and the arrangement of the material below will guide the seeker to his field of choice, without reference to other sections that may for the moment be outside his interest.

CONTENTS

Book One: THE PERMANENT GARDEN   11

How to Lay Out a Small Place and
the Plant Materials to Use   13

Chapter I. The Garden Frame   15

Chapter II. Accents and Vistas   36

Chapter III. The Small Place   48

Chapter IV. Trees for Shade, Color and Fragrance   55

Chapter V. Evergreens for Winter Effects   69

Chapter VI. Shrubs for Color and Winter Effects   87

    1. Shrubs that lose their leaves in winter   87
    2. The broad-leaved evergreens   96
    3. Azaleas and rhododendrons   98

Chapter VII. Planting and Moving Shrubs and Trees   102

Book Two: THE EVERBLOOMING GARDEN 107

Chapter I. Continuous Bloom in the Garden 109

Chapter II. Thanksgiving to Washington's Birthday 112

Chapter III. March 118

Chapter IV. April 127

Chapter V. May 136

Chapter VI. June 146

Chapter VII. July 154

Chapter VIII. August 161

Chapter IX. September 168

Chapter X. October 174

Book Three: COLOR IN THE GARDEN 179

Chapter I. Color and Its Management 181

Chapter II. The Red Garden 186

Chapter III. The Blue Garden 195

Chapter IV. The Yellow Garden 206

Chapter V. The Pink Garden 218

Chapter VI. The White Garden 229

Chapter VII. The Green Garden 240

Chapter VIII. The Gray and Lavender Garden 249

CONTENTS

Book Four: FRAGRANCE IN THE GARDEN   259

    Chapter I. The Nature of Fragrance and
        How to Identify Some Types of It   261

    Chapter II. A Garden of Fragrance from Trees,
        Shrubs, and Vines   266

    Chapter III. Fragrant Annuals and Perennials   286

    Chapter IV. Night Witchery   301

    Chapter V. Fragrance in the House   308

    Chapter VI. Perfume from Your Garden   315

    Chapter VII. Potpourri and How to Make It   323

Book Five: HERBS IN THE GARDEN   331

    Chapter I. Why We Need Them   333

    Chapter II. Annual and Biennial Herbs   343

    Chapter III. Perennial Herbs   360

    Chapter IV. How to Dry and Store Them   389

    Chapter V. Herbs in the Kitchen   392

Book Six: FRUIT IN THE GARDEN   397

    Chapter I. Why Grow Your Own?   399

        Fruit Districts   402
        Soils   404
        Fertile or Infertile?   406
        Planning the Fruit Garden   408
        Planting and After Care   409

Chapter II. Bush Fruits 418

Raspberry 418
Blackberry 422
Currant and Gooseberry 424

Chapter III. Strawberry 428

Chapter IV. Stone Fruits 435

Peach 435
Plum 440
Cherry 445

Chapter V. Pome Fruits 448

Apple 448
Pear 454
Quince 458

Chapter VI. Grapes for Eating and Wine 459

Chapter VII. Blueberry 465

Chapter VIII. Dwarf and Semi-Dwarf Fruit Trees 470

Chapter IX. Trained Fruit Trees 476

Espaliers, Cordons, Palmette Verrier, Fans, etc. 480

Chapter X. What to Do about Pests 485

BIBLIOGRAPHY 492

INDEX 497

The pictures in this book have been chosen to supplement the text, and to show some of the many ways in which plant materials can be used. Whether the home garden is to be large or small, there are ideas here which can be adapted to many situations and many parts of the country.

Book One

THE PERMANENT GARDEN

HOW TO LAY OUT A SMALL PLACE AND
THE PLANT MATERIALS TO USE

IF ONE is starting from scratch, a few things must be decided before anything can be done. For all except the smallest suburban properties, some sort of frame, a vista or two, and the location of buildings must be settled at the outset. It is impossible for any book to individualize all the problems that may arise, but the general principles leading to permanent satisfaction are outlined in some detail.

The most important is the frame of the site, and the necessity for this will be found in the first chapter, together with the details of accomplishing it, and some suggestions of various types of plant materials. The latter are treated in much more detail in Chapters IV, V and VI, because times of blooming, height of the tree or shrub, and climatic or soil preferences are so important to the final effect.

Once the boundaries of the property are suitably framed with shrubs or trees, depending upon its size, the next thing to study is the possibility of adding interest and variety to your future garden. Nothing will enhance it more than making a vista or capturing an existent one, and the judicious placing of one or more accents in the garden. For the details of this, and a selected list of shrubs and trees, see Chapter II.

If you have only a small suburban property where vistas are often impossible and accents rather uncertain, the plan of your permanent garden and the plant materials in it must be modified. These details are discussed in Chapter III.

A word as to the illustrations. Perhaps none of them will exactly fit your own problem, and they were not planned with this in mind. They are suggestions for the following:

Suburban Place, 30 x 100 feet, page 48
Somewhat Larger Place, 50 x 100 feet, page 26
One of 100 x 150 feet, page 28
An acre place, approximately 200 x 200 feet, page 30

In addition there is an illustration for three different types of vistas, a formal evergreen one, an informal one, and a small contrived vista for use on either large or small properties. There is also one illustration of correct and incorrect foundation planting, which makes or mars so many houses.

Not everyone will want to use the plant materials listed in the captions to these illustrations, nor those suggested in Chapters I, II or III. Conditions are so varied and climates so variable that many will want to select other shrubs and trees. All the most available and best of them, together with their culture and hardiness, will be found in Chapters IV, V and VI, with the details of moving or planting them given in the last chapter.

The Garden Frame

LIVE-FOREVER and many old-fashioned perennials seem as though they really lived forever, but they never can frame a vista, make a garden picture, or give accent to any garden, unless the garden is so small that one is forced to rely on the color of annual and perennial herbs for garden effects. Some very old and neglected places are still beautiful because of the trees and shrubs that have survived for years, but all that remains of herbs may be some pathetic patches of narcissus that generally fail to bloom, and a nostalgic clump or two of iris or tiger lily which no neglect can kill.

Without trees and shrubs it is impossible to create gardens, except on the smallest suburban properties, and most of these are vastly improved by the judicious placing of colorful trees or shrubs. So true is this that from the days of the Romans down through the elaborate gardens of Italy, France and England, the most skillful garden architects in the world have always relied on trees to frame these enchanting creations. To them no picture became a painting without a frame, and to us it is equally true that no garden becomes a real one without trees and shrubs.

Quite apart from their charm of bloom and branching, trees have several garden uses that in these days of high taxes and labor costs make them doubly desirable. There is first of all the welcome shade from summer sun. And the evergreens, with their somber verdure, go almost unnoticed while the garden is a summer riot of bloom. But what feature of any garden is so charming as a peep through a winter window over the white sheen of snow to a group of stately evergreens, perhaps splashed with a spot of red-berried shrubs.

The economic side is today one of the chief considerations in making any garden. It is certainly true that the first costs of shrubs and trees are much beyond annuals or perennials, unless you grow your own. However herbs need constant care, such as weeding and watering, but shrubs and trees, once they are really established, need very little upkeep expense. Many old gardens, once replete with borders, beds, arbors, nooks, statuary, and numberless timeful-and-expensive features, have abandoned all of them for the simplicity, dignity, beauty and low upkeep expense of tastefully grouped shrubs and trees.

YOUR GARDEN PLAN

Before digging a hole or planting a bush there are some things that must be settled. Owners of large properties no doubt will call in a professional landscape architect, but even such an expert will need to be told what you want your garden to look like in the years to come. If—as most of us must these days—you have only a small place, you can with the help of this book make your own scheme.

Not so long ago the mode was to make a show, impress the passer-by and forget that privacy in a garden is, to many, just as important as the seclusion that everyone demands for the interior of the house. Only on the smallest suburban lot is it impossible to secure that feeling of quiet retreat that should feature all gardens. To get it requires making a frame, especially at the front and sides of your property, and only trees and shrubs will do this. If you don't really want privacy, all you need to do is to omit the planting along the street front. If you want it immediately, as they do in England, only expensive, full-grown shrubs or a high brick wall will accomplish this.

If the property is large enough, and you want to provide ample play space for children, safe from the hazards of the street, your garden plan will be altered for the first few years. What will first be a play space can, after the children outgrow the need for it, become a beautifully screened off nook for tea or cocktails.

Although the general principle of framing your garden with trees or shrubs is sound enough, there are exceptions to it dictated by topography, the position of the house (and garage) and especially by distant views worth preserving, or unsightly ones that must be screened off as quickly as possible. In the latter case it might well pay to plant quick-growing but short-lived trees, alternating with better kinds that will be the permanent screen after the temporary trees have been cut down. Details of this will be found in Chapter IV.

Topography, unless the land is flat, will dictate not only the planting scheme, but the position of the house and garage. If you are building both it would pay well to visit the site many times before selecting the position of each. Access to the street and the slope of the land will often make it imperative to place both house and garage to conform to existing topography. Often, with no unwarranted grading expense, such a plan will be more pleasing than one derived from moving many cubic yards of soil in order to put a house in a place that shows far more expenditure of money than taste.

If topography is such that the house must be placed in the lowest part of the property (because of access to street), it is well to remember that both the house and whatever trees you plant will tend to obscure the depression and perhaps lose one of the most charming features of the site. Trees always tend to diminish a depression and accentuate an elevation. Topography thus plays a drastic role in your planting plan as well as in the position of your house. If the region is definitely hilly it is perhaps wiser to consult not only your architect but a landscape architect before making a decision. The position of the house, garage and your subsequent planting can well be a permanent mistake or, with good luck and taste, create that feeling of inevitability that comes only from good planning.

If your property is not too hilly and you decide not to employ a professional landscape architect, remember that many beautiful properties have been developed without one. It is, however, far better to make a plan of your ground to scale. This, for small plots, can be one inch to the foot, and for medium sized plots (say 100 x 200 feet), ½ inch to the foot. For larger places ¼ inch to the foot will be workable, because detailed planting plans will be in sections with the scale of one inch = one foot.

Your plan need not conform to engineering precision to be all that the average homeowner needs. Simply measure as accurately as convenient (preferably with a steel tape) the edges of your plot, from corner to corner. Then determine the number of square feet in it according to the following table:

> 1 acre = 209 x 209 feet (almost exactly) and contains 43,560 square feet
> 100 x 200 feet = ½ acre   Approximately
> 100 x 100 feet = ¼ acre   Approximately
> 50 x 100 feet = ⅛ acre   Approximately
> 25 x 100 feet = 1/16 acre   Approximately
> 33 x 66 feet = 1/20 acre   Exactly

Having the boundaries determined it is then wise to mark with a circle on the plan the existing trees or tree masses, if there are any, according to whatever scale you are using. Put in their names if you know them. Do the same with any buildings already on the property. Also see that the plan indicates north, south, east and west. You will then have a basic, skeleton plan of your grounds, with existing trees and buildings. Except for large and complicated properties, both the

measurements and the plan can be done in a few hours and may
save days of future work and some irrevocable mistakes. I know of
one Long Island millionaire who spent five thousand dollars to have
a large misplaced elm tree moved to reveal an otherwise hidden
vista. Make no mistake, however simple your property, a reasonably
accurate plan of it will always pay off.

Because we are dealing with permanent things like trees and
houses, not to speak for the moment of flowering shrubs, there is still
one more helpful thing to add to your plan before you begin to think
of planting anything. Along the margins (and leave at least a two-
or three-inch blank margin all around the plan), write in the direction of distant, off-property features that you want to preserve. A view
of a charming neighboring garden, the bay, sea, mountain, or whatever, should be indicated with reasonable accuracy using the location
of the house as the center from which such vistas are to be preserved.

At the same time mark on the margin, with approximate location,
all off-property views that you would rather hide, such as railway
embankments, gas stations, ugly houses or distant billboards, having
in mind particularly how high they are (according to distance), for
this will dictate the type of planting that will be needed to obscure
them.

Assuming that you can put the house and garage wherever you
like, as in all new properties that have no buildings on them, the
best method is the one followed by the experts. In determining the
exact location of the buildings of Peter Cooper Village and Stuy-
vesant Town, the Metropolitan Life Insurance Company spent
months with bits of paper cut to scale for each building. These were
moved about the plan in every conceivable way to insure each building receiving the utmost in view, air, light, privacy and still provide
play space, drives, walks and decorative planting.

Exactly this procedure is the best of all schemes to fix the final
location of house, garage, service yard, play space and any other
feature you want to include. If your plan is reasonably accurate, existing trees located and the margins tell you what to preserve in the
distance or hide forever, you are ready to play with your bits of paper. It is the most fascinating of games, but remember that the stakes
are permanence in the garden, that the results will no doubt outlive
you and that they will be perhaps the most permanent record of
your taste and skill. I know, for instance, of one old house in Maryland placed with such care that it is on the axis of a leafy vista out
to the bay, but is so off-center (as to southern sun) that it avoids
midsummer glare and heat in the main rooms.

If, on the other hand, the house and garage are already fixed, it is just as essential to fix them with reasonable accuracy on your plan. Whether for a new or old house, cut pieces of cardboard to the exact dimensions of your buildings. If the latter are already on the property paste the cardboard (or stiff paper) replica directly on the plan at its present location. If you are lucky enough to be building your own you still have a choice of location.

No one can fix the one most desirable site for house or garage, because it must depend on what type of house you are building, what its uses are (i.e., for an old couple, or a houseful of children) and what are among the *must* items you have included in your architect's plans. Also, in somewhat larger properties, space must be provided for a tennis court or badminton, or croquet, a vegetable garden, and perhaps a tool house.

The final location of house and garage must be your own responsibility, and no one can say, except yourself, where it will be. There are, however, a few Do's and Don'ts that are inserted here as reminders of what professionals have found after many years of study. They are framed with the idea that placing the house, or accommodating oneself to an existing one, is merely a beginning to be followed by your frame of permanent planting, your screening of unsightly views, and service yard, and a dozen other things that may come up in the years following.

THINGS TO TRY AND DO

1. If east of the Alleghenies, try to face the house, particularly living and sleeping rooms, toward the southwest, especially near the sea. The prevailing winds make it far cooler in summer and warmer in winter.
2. Place center of house on the axis of a pleasing vista if possible. If there is none it may be worth while to plant one, as explained in Chapter II.
3. If anywhere near a large city with the hazard of smoke, dust, fumes and drying wind, determine the average direction of it and place the house in the lee of a protective planting of smoke resistant trees. See Chapter IV.
4. If the house is in a region of intense cold, place it so as to be south of a protective planting (or existing forest) of evergreens. See Chapter V.
5. Visit the site at night. If there is constant glare of distant headlights, plan at once a screen to cut it off, preferably with evergreens. See Chapter V for the kinds.

6. Try to put the house so that service quarters and kitchen face the street, and are much closer to it than the living quarters which should face the more spacious part of the property and have a view of whatever planting scheme you adopt.

DON'TS

1. Try to avoid placing the house or planting trees too close together so that they will look crowded. Trees directly against a house may well dwarf it, and their litter stops up gutters, especially those that, in addition to leaves, drop copious lots of fruits—such as black walnut, linden, sweet gum, locust, honey locust, horse-chestnut, catalpa, *Paulownia* and others. See Chapter IV. Small trees should not be closer than 20 feet and large ones 30–40 feet from the house. They are a hazard any closer, especially in a storm.
2. If the property is flat and a rectangle, don't put the house too close to the street. It will look huddled, and leave no room for effective planting between it and the sidewalk or road. If the lot is deep enough allow at least 40–50 feet from it to the street.
3. Don't make the common mistake of letting some landscape contractor put in a lot of so-called "foundation planting." Examples are too common of windows and porches being smothered by shrubs and trees that have no place in such planting. See Chapter VI.
4. Don't place the house, or plan your planting, around some over-mature apple or other showy tree which may be rotten in the interior and either come down in a storm or cost far too much to preserve for a few more years. There are many examples of such misplaced affection for a potential wreck. You can easily make your own accent of color and beauty. See Chapter II.
5. Don't buy a place or plant valuable trees until you have dug a few test holes, preferably 3–4 feet deep. See what sort of topsoil you have, and how deep, and also the nature of the subsoil, whether sand, clay, pebbles, or rocks. See Chapter VII.
6. Don't expect valuable shrub and tree plantings to become established without adequate watering. Although all those mentioned in this book will survive with ordinary rainfall, when established, they need plenty of water the first summer after they have been transplanted.

No one of these Do's and Don'ts will apply to all sites, but some of them are applicable to almost any property. At least they are things to think about before you begin any real scheme of planting

for permanence in your garden. What that planting will be is now
before us—evergreen or deciduous, the latter comprising all those
trees that drop their leaves in the fall.

EVERGREEN OR DECIDUOUS?

There is no question but that evergreen plantings are far more
effective than plant material that is bare of leaves for six months of
the year, as are most deciduous shrubs and trees. Who does not remember the enchanting evergreen gardens one sees in northern New
England and eastern Canada. But evergreens, in spite of their
beauty, have climatic restrictions that limit their use to places having generally cool, moist nights, not too hot days, freedom from hot
drying winds and a rainfall of at least 35–40 inches per year. That
makes their successful culture too difficult to be safe for regions west
of Iowa, Nebraska, Kansas and Missouri, and many of them are impossible in the South.

Generally they have no obvious flowers, but all bear cones, some,
as in the balsam and pines, being quite handsome. One plants them
not for color, but as a background for showy shrubs or trees or, in
more elaborate gardens, for garden statuary. For such purpose they
have no rivals, and in any climate that will sustain them there is no
finer setting for a snow scene than an evergreen planting.

The objections to evergreens, however, are several:

(a) They are slow-growing and hence very expensive.
(b) They are more difficult to plant and keep alive than ordinary
shrubs and trees.
(c) They must not be planted in many regions perfectly suited to
deciduous shrubs and trees (see the preceding text).
(d) They, with a very few exceptions, will not stand the smoke, dust,
fumes and dry winds of city streets. They do far better in the
suburbs or country.
(e) Scarcely any of them under cultivation will ever attain the
stature, and never the grandeur of the same species in its natural home, such as Western China or our own Northwest.

People will continue to plant evergreens, in spite of the objections
cited, because of their beauty. While details of the different kinds
are given in Chapter V, it is well to repeat here the groups that are
most and least likely to be useful in gardens that are east of the Mississippi and north of the southern border of Virginia.

Most hardy: Cedars and junipers
Hardy: Pines, hemlocks, yew and arborvitae

Less hardy: Spruces and relatives

Least hardy: Firs and relatives

"Hardy" in this connection needs explanation. While it usually means ability to withstand winter cold, in the evergreens it means almost exactly the opposite—their tolerance of summer heat and deficient summer rainfall. Where heat is too prolonged and rainfall too meager, an evergreen may show its lack of hardiness by drying off, turning brownish or, in extreme cases, being killed outright. Those in the preceding list are arranged in the order of their ability to withstand conditions generally unfavorable for evergreens, leaving for Chapter V details of the different species in each group.

Because of their expense, their climatic restrictions, and the fact that many of them will never attain their true stature in cultivation, it is unwise for the average gardener to depend upon them for the major part of the garden frame. Although it is true that some of the pines become fine trees under cultivation, it is still more true that deciduous shrubs and trees will be the cheapest, safest and most satisfactory material for the average homeowner. They cost less, grow faster, and get to full stature far better than evergreens, with a few exceptions that are noted at the proper place.

The choice of trees and shrubs must depend upon the size of your property, its scale and the amount of your land occupied by buildings or to be devoted to open spaces (recreation, service, vegetable garden, pool, etc.). While the different sorts will be dealt with in detail in Chapter IV, there are some things that one should settle while still in the planning stage, such as mass, height and color. It is obvious, for instance, that placing a white oak on a small property will not only dwarf any moderate sized house, but make the planter of it somewhat ridiculous—say two hundred years hence when it may become a huge forest giant!

The list that follows will help to make a final selection, both for the owner of a small property and for those where space does not matter.

BORDER TREES FOR PLANTING
ALONG PROPERTY LINES

Properties 50 x 100 feet	Properties 100 x 200 feet and larger
Pin Oak	White Oak
Scarlet Oak	Red Oak
Elm	Linden
Sassafras	Beech
Sweet Gum	Horse-chestnut
Ginkgo	Sycamore
Hornbeam	Tulip-tree
Sugar Maple	Norway Maple
Sour Gum	Hackberry
Mountain Ash	*Paulownia*

These, and their relatives which are noted in detail in Chapter IV, may well form the basis for any garden frame. Those for smaller properties do not spread so far as the ones in the second column, and it should not be forgotten that the owners of the larger sites can use trees cited in both columns.

These lists comprise relatively large trees selected for shade, mass of foliage, stately habit and ability to make a convincing frame for any garden. Except for the horse-chestnut, tulip-tree and *Paulownia* they do not produce showy flowers and, more than any other plants in this book, they provide the finest mass of shade, the most interesting outlines, and such a profusion of foliage as to screen out any unwanted view.

But the trouble with all of them, except one or two, is that, like a lot of things in nature that are superlative, they are slow-growing. Which brings us to an economic problem in these days of mounting costs.

Any casual look at a nursery catalog reveals that young trees are relatively cheap and large ones fearfully expensive. If your purse matches your impatience, by all means start with specimens 10–15 feet high, or even higher. But most gardeners, especially if they are just recovering from the expenses of building or moving, will be glad of a less costly alternative. This does not mean growing your own from seed, for this is a slow process and often needs the knowledge and equipment of the expert.

A far better plan is to watch for sales at nurseries of excess stock, or, if such are not available, to bargain for lots of 5 or 10 of a kind which can always be bought for less per tree than single specimens. Also, and this is the basic rule, buy nothing over 5 feet high, which

will cut your costs down to a minimum. Of course this will mean
waiting but there is also a remedy for that—interplant with quick-
growing trees that will ultimately be cut out. By the time the temporary trees are removed, your permanent ones will be large enough
to make a convincing start on your garden frame.

The best of the quick-growing trees for temporary effect (8–15
years) are the following: catalpa (has showy flowers), white or gray
birch, poplars (especially the columnar types), weeping willow,
white willow, black willow.

These are discussed in detail in Chapter IV, together with their
heights, rate of growth, distance to plant apart and when to cut them
out because your more desirable trees will, by that time, be ready
to take over.

How we use these trees to make the frame of your garden depends
upon so many local conditions that it is impossible to give any one
standard plan that will fit all properties. To overcome this difficulty
a few basic plans that have proved successful are illustrated on pages
26–30. They are inserted not with the idea that you will follow any
one of them exactly, but to point the way to solving whatever type
of problem your own property suggests.

It should be understood that these aids deal only with the position
of future trees, for it is upon these you must depend for foliage
masses, the hiding of unsightly off-property scenes, for privacy if you
want it, and most of all for the architectural fitness of your garden
frame to the type of your house. It will ultimately reflect your mood,
your desire to use the garden as an outdoor room, your necessity to
provide for sports or play space for children, and all the things that
make your garden the expression of your hopes and aspirations.

SHRUBS

Having now settled the main frame of your garden you are ready
to embellish it. Bare tree trunks (except isolated specimens to be discussed in Chapter II) need the softening effect of flowering or evergreen shrubs. These make the most pleasing transition from the lawn
to the frame of trees, which will often, at first, have no branches near
the ground and hence make real privacy impossible unless they are
planted in such masses as few can afford for lack of space.

Just as much care must be used in choosing this underplanting of
your garden frame as in selecting the trees. While it is quite true
that shrubs cost less, and they can for the first few years be easily

moved if you make a mistake, it is desirable to find the right place
for them at the outset.

If you want a profusion of color in this underplanting you must
choose shrubs that will supply it and provide foliage masses to soften
the interval between trees as well. Then comes the question of
whether you want *evergreen* shrubs like holly, rhododendrons, and
scores of others. They will always be more expensive, but by getting
young plants and mixing them with a dash of patience you can get
garden effects obtainable in no other way. You will find in Chapter
VI a complete list of all the most desirable shrubs, separated into
those that lose their leaves each autumn (deciduous), the broad-
leaved evergreens (holly, evergreen barberry, firethorn, daphne, and
the like), and finally the most showy of all, the azaleas and rhododendrons, including the beautiful mountain laurel.

It is suggested that you thumb through Chapter VI before making any decision as to how you will plan this underplanting of shrubs.
From them will come practically all the color in your garden, for the
frame of trees, with one or two notable exceptions, will give you
privacy and foliage, but little color except the autumnal gorgeousness
of oaks, sassafras, maple, ginkgo, sweet gum and sour gum.

It is particularly important to plan your shrub planting so that the
flowering period comes when you are home and not on vacation.
Also color preferences should be decided now, for there is a wealth
of material to choose from and many gardeners, especially women,
have definite allergies to certain colors. Time spent in looking at the
details in Chapter VI may well prevent headaches a few years hence,

PROPERTY APPROXIMATELY 50 X 100 FEET

House near center. Vista possible. Street partially screened out. Unnumbered areas are lawn.

Key and Explanations

1. House
2. Garage
3. Service or play area
4. Drive to garage and turn around
5. Living porch
6. Walk to front door
7. Evergreen hedge (for plant materials see Chapter V). If a less expensive hedge is desired see the section on hedge plants at Chapter VI.
8. Vista from porch to distant view
9. Accent plants: Japanese flowering cherry
10. Vegetable garden

Trees	Shrubs
11. European linden	Numbers indicate massed plantings
12. Scarlet oak	18. Lilac
13. Dogwood	19. Chinese honeysuckle
14. Horse-chestnut	20. A specimen rhododendron
15. Cucumber tree	21. Weigela (Eva Rathke)
16. English hawthorn	22. Star magnolia
17. Snowdrop tree	23. Butterfly bush
	24. Rose-of-Sharon
	25. Mock-orange
	26. Cranberry tree
	27. *Deutzia gracilis*
	28. Garland-flower
	29. Blue spirea
	30. Flowering almond

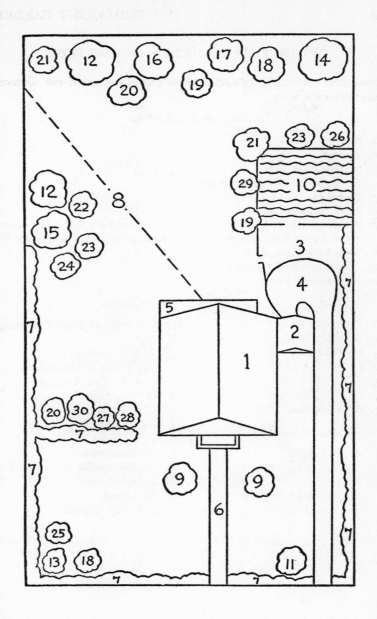

PROPERTY APPROXIMATELY 100 X 150 FEET

House in center. No vista possible. Street screened out. All unnumbered parts are lawn.

Key and Explanations

1. House
2. Garage
3. Accent plant: Flowering crab-apple
4. Accent plant: Snowdrop tree
5. Service or play area
6. Walk to front door
7. Drive and turn around
8. Formal evergreen planting, enclosing statuary, pool or outdoor living-room or fireplace. See Chapter V for plant materials.
9. Accent plant: Pagoda tree
10. Terrace or Porch

*Trees: no evergreens**

11. Pin oak
12. Sassafras
13. Mountain ash
14. Scarlet oak
15. Sweet gum
16. Horse-chestnut

17. Golden Chain
18. *Paulownia*
19. European linden
20. Catalpa
21. Dogwood
22. English hawthorn

*Shrubs: no broad-leaved evergreens, azaleas or rhododendrons**

23. Star magnolia
24. Double-flowered peach
25. Forsythia
26. Bridal wreath spirea
27. Japanese flowering cherry

28. *Deutzia lemoinei*
29. Chaste tree
30. *Tamarix pentandra*
31. Blue dogwood

* Expensive evergreens, broad-leaved evergreens, rhododendrons and azaleas are omitted from this plan, except for #8. The latter *can* be done much more cheaply with deciduous shrubs. See Chapter VI, Section a.

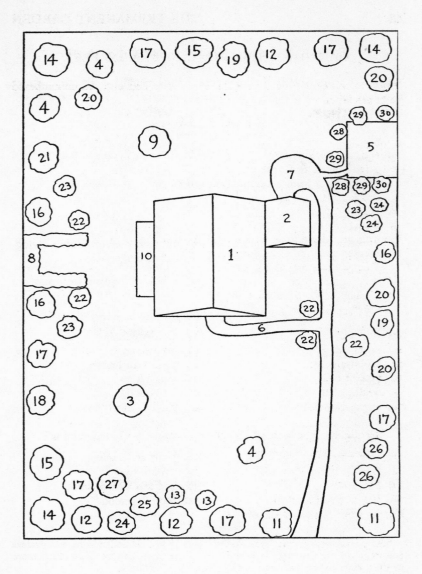

PROPERTY APPROXIMATELY 200 X 200 FEET

House off center. Hill in one corner. Vista almost obligatory. Street
screened out. Hill about 15–20 feet above general grade. Unnumbered
sections are lawn.

Key and Explanations

1. Hill, 15–20 feet above general grade. Tea house on summit, covered
   with vines. See page 31.
2. Axis of vista from tea house and end of porch to distant view
3. Porch
4. House
5. Garage
6. Entrance drive to front door and garage
7. Service area and turn around
8. Massed planting of azaleas, rhododendrons and broad-leaved evergreens at base and lower slopes of hill. For plant materials see
   Chapter VI, Sections 2 and 3.

Trees

9. Nordmann Fir
10. White spruce
11. Hemlock
12. White pine
13. Horse-chestnut
14. *Pinus mugo mughus*
15. Mountain ash
16. Japanese flowering cherry
17. Golden Chain
18. Yulan
19. Dogwood
20. *Paulownia*

*Shrubs: the numbers indicate
mass plantings*

21. Star magnolia
22. *Rosa hugonis*
23. Deutzia, Pride of Rochester
24. *Spiraea billiardi*
25. Snowberry
26. Mock-orange
27. Lilac
28. Cranberry tree
29. Mountain camellia
30. Chaste tree

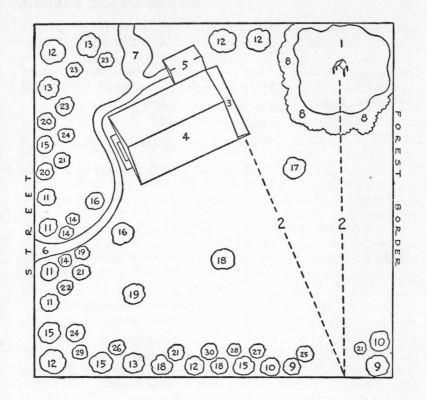

and unless you know all the shrubs it is almost imperative. Splashes of color of the wrong shade, at the wrong time or on a bush that may turn out to be a dud the year after next are hazards well worth avoiding.

Quite apart from their color, shrubs and small trees are the best of all materials for making embayments in your garden, little secluded nooks for play or peace or for borders of flowers if you mean to have such. A word of warning as to the latter is worth emphasizing here *before* you plan any shrub planting. Thirty years ago when labor was cheap, taxes negligible and leisure time more plentiful, nearly everyone had beautiful perennial borders, plentifully sprinkled with splashes of showy annuals and often with a profusion of bulbs some of which had to be planted each year. Conditions being what they are at the moment no modern landscape architect would knowingly let an owner in for such a display without warning him of the inevitable obligations of such a planting. He would tell the owner, and this book was written to tell you, to shun such a scheme unless money is plentiful to pay for its proper care, or you have the time and inclination to do it yourself. Few have either today.

The whole purpose of this book is to teach the prospective gardener how to achieve beauty, dignity and color in the garden without a bed or border. It is quite true that perennials and annuals provide color effects to be had in no other way. But it is also a depressing fact that many well-planned borders become a spotty, distressingly weedy spot if the care they demand is not lavished upon them. Only you can decide whether to avoid them, at least until your garden of shrubs and trees has a chance to show what it can do for you.

Shrubs and small trees are the best of all plant materials to soften the line or corners of otherwise stark buildings, to hide a service yard, frame a drive or garage, and to hide a tool shed if you have one, and if you don't to screen off a place for stored leaves or a compost heap.*

It is quite impossible to provide all owners with a planting scheme for shrubs that will fit all properties, for taste and gardens differ too much.

---

* Stored leaves are a necessity to cover the ground, about 8 inches deep, around all rhododendrons, azaleas and some other plants noted elsewhere. Known as a *mulch* such a dead leaf carpet is of the greatest value. A compost heap is simply alternate layers of garden loam and vegetable refuse (grass cuttings, leaves, weeds and even vegetable garbage). After a few months of decay and one or two mixings (by turning over with a shovel), the material will be ready for use in flower pots, window boxes, and as excellent material for seed beds, especially in the latter case if it is mixed about half and half with pure clean (not sea) sand.

In addition to the shrub embellishments shown on pages 26–31, the right and wrong uses of so-called "foundation planting" are shown on page 35. Foundation planting is legitimate and necessary, but its grotesque abuse is evident along almost any suburban street. How often does one see windows and porches, sometimes the very door-step, smothered by shrubs, trees or evergreens which cut off light, harbor insects and splash you with water any rainy day because they are too big for the site or too close to it.

The purpose of foundation planting is to soften the abrupt line between the wall of the house and the ground. No planting needs more care in its choice, to avoid cutting off subsequent light from windows, keep cellar windows from being covered, avoid certain essential pipes and perhaps meters, and most of all keep the porch and doorway light and airy instead of dank.

All the shrubs and low evergreens, as well as the broad-leaved evergreens that are described in Chapters V and VI, are especially designated there for their right use in foundation plantings. All are low enough or can be clipped to prevent the ills just noted, but they will give your home that indefinable touch of color and elegance that everyone desires.

FOUNDATION PLANTING

Upper Is Incorrect

1. Windows
2. Front door and steps
3. Base of clapboards
4. Ground level
5. Arborvitae or other evergreens (or any other bushes or trees) so planted that they ultimately cover windows and the door—a very common error.
6. Miscellaneous bulbs, annuals, etc., which have no place in the permanent garden.

Lower Is Correct

1. Windows
2. Front door and steps
3. Base of clapboards
4. Ground level

Planting Material

5. Columnar juniper, arborvitae, yew or other spire-like evergreens (see Chapter V)
6. Taller and more spreading evergreens such as red cedar, pines or hemlocks to soften corner of house
7. Garland-flower
8. Medium-sized shrubs: *Deutzia gracilis, Pieris japonica, Berberis sargentiana,* flowering almond, mountain laurel, Japanese holly, *Hypericum densiflorum,* Hortensia, *Viburnum carlesi,* Japanese flowering quince and *Spiraea arguta.* (See Chapter VI for colors of flowers and blooming periods. If planted 2–3 feet apart most of them will give a quick effect but will have to be thinned out in a few years.)
9. Use, as a ground cover beneath the shrubs and evergreens, the Japanese spurge (*Pachysandra terminalis*).

Accents and Vistas

CHAPTER II   𝓘F WE have followed step by step the main features dealt with in Chapter I, we have achieved the outer frame of your garden, which may be all that is possible if the property is as small as 50–100 feet. In fact local conditions may necessitate leaving out part of the marginal frame, especially if neighboring houses are too close, or there is no need for seclusion or privacy. Both depend upon your mood and temperament and these will ultimately dictate the density of your garden frame.

That leaves us with a theoretical or actual open space, except for the house and other buildings, and also with two major problems of garden design. For, after all, at this stage the garden owner is like a picture dealer who has spent all of his time in choosing a frame and little or none on the canvas within it.

Two of the main things, among several others, that will make something of beauty and fitness within that frame are accents and vistas. Such terms need to confuse no one, and to emphasize their true meaning to garden owners it is best to hunt for precise definitions.

Accent: In pictorial and decorative art, emphasis laid on a portion of a contour, a spot in a design, or the like, as by strengthening an outline or heightening a contrast of tone.—*Webster's New International Dictionary*, 2nd edition, 1947.

Accent Plant: An accent plant is a type with a well-defined decorative form.—*Taylor's Encyclopedia of Gardening*, 1948.

Vista: A view, or prospect, commonly more or less distant or through or along an avenue, as between rows of trees, . . . —*Webster's New International Dictionary*, 2nd edition, 1947.

Vista: A focalized view.—*Taylor's Encyclopedia of Gardening*, 1948.

Some of the finest gardens in the world and some of the simplest have utilized, often unconsciously, both vistas and accents to make a few of them world famous. No such gardening is possible today except for the very rich, but the principles upon which such gardens were designed are perfectly applicable for you and me, with a restricted garden budget and no rolling acres to play with.

Examples of the vista *par excellence* are some of the Italian palaces, and especially the incomparable vista down a pleached allée to the Schönbrunn Palace in Vienna. Nearer home is an old brick manor house in Maryland at the end of a mile-long tunnel of foliage, in this case cut from the native forest. At the end of both is a house, but to stand at the beginning inevitably urges one to go on, to see what lies beyond, what sort of a house it will be or what sort of people have chosen to live at the end of such a beauty-laden vista.

For most gardeners no such vistas are possible. What can be done is to reverse the process and capture some distant view, frame it in a tracery of foliage, and make it the one great feature of the garden. There are very few gardens, however small, where this cannot be done. Sometimes the view may not be distant at all, perhaps only a fine tree far enough off to suggest the mystery and grandeur that is inherent in any majestic tree. Or it may be a church spire, distant hills or mountains, a river, meadow, the sea, a cliff or the beautiful bays that indent our coastline. In the southwest it may be the distant, blazing desert with its grotesque cacti.

If none of these is available, and you cannot, even with much study, discern some off-property scene worth preserving, you can still create your own vista if the area is large enough, as outlined in the section of this chapter devoted to vistas.

If, on the other hand, you have no natural vista and have not enough room to create one, as will be true on many rectangular suburban properties, it is best to forget vistas and provide an alternative not only acceptable, but in perfect taste—accent plants.

ACCENTS

Who does not remember looking out of some friend's living-room window and being enthralled with the beauty of a lone weeping Japanese flowering cherry, a fine rhododendron, or a holly tree in full panoply of winter berries? All are specimen plants and their position and color are no accident, for they are accent plants chosen with care and put at some dramatic spot in the garden.

They differ altogether from the plant materials used to frame a vista, for accent plants are placed so that they may be seen, walked around, and sometimes smelled for their fragrance. Some accent plants are planted not for flowers at all but because their evergreen, almost architectural outlines are used to accentuate some feature of a garden, building or drive that needs to be emphasized both winter and summer. Some writers would restrict accent plants to the use of these formalized evergreens, but as here used the term applies to any plant used to make an accent of color, form or habit that enhances the beauty of a garden.

Accent plants should not be considered as a mere compromise, adopted by those for whom a vista is impossible, for they are used on great estates and in many cottage gardens with equal beauty and fitness. The choice of them and of their position requires taste, and your selection will naturally depend upon your personal preference.

Flowering Shrubs and Small Trees. These should never be more than 15–25 feet high, because taller trees would tend to destroy the intimacy and the special object of accent plants. Tall trees are meant for shade and should never be placed too near an accent plant, for they will dwarf it.

The material suitable for accent plants is quite extensive, and the details of those that follow should be sought in Chapter IV for small trees and Chapter VI for the shrubs.

A dozen extremely fine accent plants, among shrubs and trees, might include the following:

DOUBLE-FLOWERED WEEPING JAPANESE CHERRY. A tree 15–25 feet high with pink or white spring-blooming flowers in pendent clusters.

STAR MAGNOLIA. A shrub or small tree, not over 15 feet high, with star-like white fragrant flowers in late March or April.

FLOWERING CRAB-APPLE. Small trees in several varieties, not over 25 feet high, with a profusion of white or pink spring-flowering blooms.

WEEPING PAGODA TREE. Medium-sized tree with long, pendulous slender branches, covered in July with long, drooping clusters of yellowish pea-like flowers.

CHINESE HONEYSUCKLE (Nursery catalog name = *Lonicera fragrantissima*). A deliciously fragrant shrub, 8–10 feet high, nearly evergreen in the south and not hardy north of Boston. Flowers numerous, white, small and blooming from late February to mid-March, depending on location.

RHODODENDRON. Mature plants are among our finest broad-leaved, evergreen flowering shrubs. For the many varieties, their use as accent plants and special cultural requirements, see Chapter VI (Azaleas and Rhododendrons).

AZALEA. Among the showiest of flowering shrubs, related to rhododendron but generally not evergreen. See the special account of them in Chapter VI.

BUTTERFLY-BUSH. A shrub 4–10 feet high covered from July–August with a profusion of long, nodding, clusters of lilac flowers.

DOGWOOD. Medium-sized tree with a profusion of white bloom. Its pink-flowered form is equally fine and preferred by many.

HAWTHORN. There are many varieties, some double-flowered, and among the finest is the English hawthorn. Native American hawthorns have showy apple-like (inedible) fruit. All are spring-blooming.

HOLLY. Beautiful, broad-leaved evergreen trees (10–25 feet), with inconspicuous flowers but scarlet fruit. If climatically suited, use, by all means, the English holly; otherwise, the American holly. See broad-leaved evergreens in Chapter VI for important details of hardiness and culture.

GOLDEN CHAIN (Nursery catalog name = *Laburnum anagyroides*). A beautiful, low-branching small tree with long, hanging clusters of yellow, pea-like flowers in May or June.

It will not have escaped the inquiring gardener that this list includes none of the common flowering shrubs and trees. Such are very useful when planted in groups, for mass effects, but the accent plants just listed, and others that will be found in Chapters IV and VI, have a very different purpose. They *must* provide a focus, a compelling reason for being selected as a specimen plant, and that means some special distinction of form, habit, foliage, bloom, fruit or fragrance and especially the time that they are in flower. There are others which you may select from the longer lists in Chapters IV and V, and if you live in Washington, D.C., or south of it you may choose the incomparable crape myrtle, pomegranate and dozens of others.

Evergreen Shrubs and Trees. Where purely formal accent plants are needed nothing compares with the true evergreens or cone-bearing trees and shrubs. There is scarcely an architectural form that cannot be found among the many varieties stretching from the slender columnar forms of yew and the Italian cypress, to the perfect globe-shaped outline of some varieties of the arborvitae. Junipers and cedars also come in many forms, especially the slender, spire-like growth of the Irish juniper and the nearly flattish, radiating fronds of *Juniperus pfitzeriana* which is one of the most popular but so far has never had a common name.

All of these evergreens have quite different uses from the flowering shrubs and trees listed. The evergreens are mostly used to accent

something besides themselves. For instance, a pair of suitable evergreens at the foot or top of a flight of steps, or at an entrance to a path,
serves to accent such features better than an informal planting.

Because their form is chiefly architectural, these evergreen accent
plants find their greatest use at steps, paths, walls, summer houses,
in foundation planting, as background for statuary or fountains, and
most of all near the main house or other substantial buildings. There
is one necessary caution. Too many of them tend to make a garden
look spotty, especially in winter. Restraint in their use will overcome
the bargain-counter effect that one often sees where evergreen accent
plants have been overdone. Even though they are living plants, they
should be used with all the care you would expend on a bit of garden masonry. Never informal, they must be chosen, and clipped if
necessary, to conform to the needed architectural form.

All the evergreen accent plants in the following list, and many
others, will be described in detail in Chapter V, especially as to their
culture and hardiness. However, it will help the garden planner to
select the *type* of evergreen needed to outline a few of the main
possibilities.

Slender, columnar or cylindrical types, most suited to accentuate
    areas between windows, entrance to drives, or corners of
    buildings.

IRISH JUNIPER. Slender, with upturning branches; rarely over 10–15
    feet high.
IRISH YEW. Similar to the Irish Juniper, but with darker green foliage.
    There are also variegated and golden-foliaged forms.
ITALIAN CYPRESS. The finest, and often the tallest of all columnar
        evergreens, famous in Mediterranean gardens, but not safe to
plant north of Norfolk, Virginia.
ARBORVITAE (Nursery catalog name = *Thuja occidentalis fastigi-
        ata**). Of the many garden varieties of the arborvitae this one
is fine for evergreen accents; not usually over 8–10 feet high.

*Types with the crown almost perfectly candle-flame-shaped; nar-
    rowly conical*

RED CEDAR. A native tree, usually small, and in some of its varieties

---

* Fastigiate is a common horticultural term meaning that all branches turn up,
relatively close to the trunk making the tree appear slender, columnar or cylindrical. Common examples are the four trees listed above and the Lombardy poplar.
It is unknown in wild trees, being found only among cultivated varieties.

perfectly cone-shaped. In age and in the open it may become a large tree.

NORWAY SPRUCE. A huge tree in nature but the variety known as
    conica has a perfect cone-shaped outline and generally is not
more than 3 feet high.

WHITE SPRUCE. The variety known as *conica* is dwarf and perfectly
    conical.

SAWARA CYPRESS. The variety known as *plumosa* has beautiful feath-
    ery foliage and a somewhat broader conical outline. It may
ultimately reach 15–20 feet.

Types with ball-like shape, suitable only for special places.

You will find in any nursery catalog dozens of globular evergreens among arborvitae, spruces, firs and several other groups. They range from dwarf forms, scarcely a foot in diameter to some arborvitae varieties that will be 6–8 feet through. Nearly all will maintain the globe-shaped outline, and if they don't are easily sheared.

Types prostrate, more or less flat on the ground

JUNIPERUS PFITZERIANA. One of the best of all low evergreens. At
    first prostrate, it ultimately makes large bird's-nest-like
clumps, and is very handsome.

COMMON JUNIPER. A variety known as *depressa* hugs the ground and
    makes attractive flat patches of greenery.

ENGLISH YEW. Only the variety known as *repandens* is really pros-
    trate, and it is a fine evergreen with bluish-green foliage.

It will be noticed that the two kinds of accent plants are used very differently. The flowering shrubs and trees are themselves the accent and are put at some *distance* from the house. But the ever-greens serve chiefly to accent some aspect of the garden other than themselves, such as a wall, or any other garden structure, and are nearly always planted *close* to the object they emphasize. This fundamental distinction should be kept in mind as your garden grows, because failure to observe this simple rule will result in a spotty, scattered garden far removed from that sense of fitness and inevitability that characterizes all good gardens.

VISTAS

As one stands on the beach or on the edge of a prairie there is the immensity of the sea or grassland and the horizon, but nothing more. As a view it lacks variety, does not in the least pique the imagination, although it may make you wonder what lies beyond. But there is not one feature of landscape or seascape that suggests the emotional effect of viewing the same scene through a contrived or natural frame of trees—which is the essence of a vista.

No other feature of the garden, not even the marginal frame discussed in Chapter I, can be so important as a vista. By planting to form a vista, or cutting existing trees or forest to reveal one, the garden planner has laid the foundation of lasting interest and beauty. As explained earlier in this chapter, what that vista will be is dictated by so many local conditions that it is impossible to suggest what you will want the focal point to be. Generally, and in all natural vistas, the view is something in the distance, so that in planning a vista the foreground and middle ground need not be considered.

So true is this that some conditions demand an *aerial* vista—one that reveals only a distant hilltop or mountain summit or church spire, ignoring or deliberately obscuring the foreground or middle ground because they are uninteresting or must actually be hidden. Such a condition often happens in towns or villages where stores or gas stations may detract from an inherently fine prospect. Such unhappy intrusions are best solved by the aerial vista.

If one is fortunate enough to have existing trees, the making of a vista is relatively simple. During the winter when visibility is easier because of leaf-fall, pick out your focal point, from a doorway, porch or window, whichever will give you the best starting point for the axis, the other end of which will be your vista. Then plan to cut down one or possibly more trees from the exact center of the axis of your future vista. If this seems ruthless, remember that what you are trying to create is far more important than the complete continuity of your tree frame.

The cutting of a single tree may create enough of an opening to reveal at least a part of your vista. It may be that it will take the removal of two or three trees, and even more in dense plantings to open a passageway to your distant view. Great care must be used not to make the opening too wide. On larger properties the opening should not be more than 25–40 feet, and on smaller ones it is better to restrict it, at least initially, to 15–20 feet.

It is not always easy to pick out the exact center of your future vista. When, at the edge of your property, you are trying to decide which of one or two trees will reveal it, there is bound to be some uncertainty. A good practical suggestion, before you cut anything, is to go back to the porch, doorway or window and sight, with binoculars, if necessary, to what you *think* is the center. Then with good-sized pieces of old sheeting, tie one on what appears to be the tree, at stepladder height, or higher if possible. One or two trips from tree to house, adjusting the white cloth each time, will ultimately give you the exact center. Only then is it safe to cut the first tree.

Later, if your initial opening is correct, you may have to trim out enough branches from the remaining trees to keep the opening clear, especially after the first year or two when they will naturally attempt to occupy the open space, as all trees do when thinned out. In this case the technique of tying on pieces of cloth *before* doing any pruning is essential, for it is easy to ruin a good vista by the indiscriminate lopping of branches that may need only a mild trimming. Only sighting from the house will tell you this, and the tied-on pieces of cloth define the exact amount of pruning.

Not everyone will be fortunate enough to have a potential vista and hence need only to cut or trim a few trees to uncover it. Most of us will have to create one by careful planning, and usually wait until the trees are large enough to make a convincing frame for the vista. Which brings us directly to the decision of what kind of a vista —formal or informal?

The informal vista can be created by using any of the large trees that are in your garden frame. Generally they should be varieties that tend to be more upright than spreading. That is why elms, hickories, ash and many pines are better than the white oak, maples, lindens or sycamore, the dome-shaped crowns of which do not accentuate the idea of a narrow opening through which one peers. It is, of course fruitless to use small or medium-sized trees to create a vista, for you will never do more than look over them, rather than through them.

The selection of trees for making one's own informal vista can easily be done by consulting the list of trees in Chapter IV, but it is best to remember the distances or intervals upon which to plant them. For large properties, where the frame of the vista may be 100–200 feet from the house, tall trees will be needed and these should be spaced so that their ultimate branches will leave an opening of 25–40 feet wide.

Exactly the same care will have to be used to determine the center of your future vista as in cutting out the trees of a natural one. But in this case put a flag-topped pole in the center, and measure off from it, on both sides, the distance to the holes where the first pair of trees are to be planted. It is imperative not to plant the trees 25–40 feet apart, if that is ultimately to be the opening made by the

VISTAS

While only two trees are shown in the upper two plans, they can be repeated indefinitely, if the axis is kept open, which will greatly enhance the value of the vistas. See page 46 for distance apart to plant the trees.

FORMAL EVERGREEN VISTA

Trees should be spire-like evergreens such as red cedar, white spruce, blue spruce or Nordmann fir (see Chapter V). If evergreen trees are not available, a good formal vista can be made with pleached specimens of certain deciduous trees. See page 46.

1. Focal point from house or grounds. See page 46 for determining this.
2. Evergreen or flowering shrub planting.

INFORMAL VISTA

1. Focal point from house or grounds. See page 46 for determining this.
2. Massed planting of flowering shrubs.
3. A pair of deciduous trees: these should be fine, uninjured and naturally branched specimens of elm, ash, sweet gum, tulip-tree, sugar maple or hickory. Avoid round-headed trees.

SMALL, CONTRIVED VISTA

To be used mostly on small properties and is preferably made of sheared evergreens such as arborvitae or Japanese yew, kept 6–8 feet high and 4–5 feet thick. At the focal point there may be a bird bath, small pool, statue, outdoor fireplace or iron garden seat. For other evergreens suitable for a small contrived vista see Chapter V.

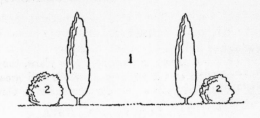

FORMAL EVERGREEN VISTA

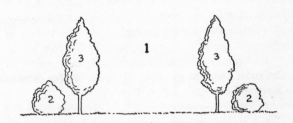

INFORMAL VISTA

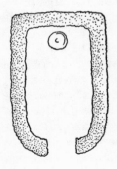

SMALL, CONTRIVED VISTA

branching of both trees. For a 25–40 feet opening, which depends upon the distance from the house to the frame of your vista, the trees should be planted as follows:

Ultimate Opening of Vista, in Feet	Distance Apart to Plant Trees, in Feet
25	55
30	68
35	75
40	90

Perhaps in no other part of the garden will it pay as well to get large trees as in this initial vista planting. You cannot very well substitute quick-growing trees to be cut out later, for most of them will not be high enough and they may distort the branching of the most important planted trees in your garden. If buying relatively large trees (15–20 feet high) is impossible, there is nothing to do but wait, choosing the most rapidly growing species. A list of these will be found in Chapter IV.

The *formal* vista requires quite different plant materials most of which will have to be evergreens, tall enough to make a convincing frame, and the branches must not spread as they will in many pine trees. For this spruces and firs are the best, although many beautiful effects can be obtained with cedars, Irish Junipers and most of all with the Italian Cypress, if you live south of Norfolk, Virginia.

Formal evergreen vistas are among the most architectural, stately and beautiful of all garden creations. They are expensive, however, fabulously so if really effective large plants are used, and are mentioned here merely to suggest what might be done if time and money are not limiting factors. All the evergreens suitable for use in formal vistas are noted in detail in Chapter V.

A substitute for evergreens in a formal vista is the use of pleached trees. The young trees are planted 6–8 feet apart, and all front and back branches are removed. The remaining lateral ones are more or less interwoven (pleached) and as the tree grows it is kept sheared to promote a narrow hedge-like effect. Such trees, instead of evergreens, make striking tree hedges often used to frame a vista. Species most suited for pleaching are the London plane, the small-leaved European linden, the beeches, and some birch trees. For their culture and hardiness see Chapter IV.

Not all gardeners can have either a formal or informal vista which captures a distant prospect because there is none to be captured. They might like to fall back upon the coziest, most intimate and, in small properties, the one fitting thing to do—make a secluded nook for a statue, fountain, small pool, or even for the exhibition of some particularly choice or favorite plant.

This is what might be called the contracted vista—a vista reduced in size and height and best made with formal evergreen materials. It should be almost architectural in its regularity, never more than 8–10 feet wide, often less than this, and its length scarcely more than 15–20 feet. At the closed end will be the focal point. Nothing is more charming than such a small vista, deliberately contrived, where the unexpected turns out to be a lithe piece of garden statuary, a fountain, a tiny pool with some choice aquatic, a bird bath, or whatever the owner thinks is worth secreting in such a verdant sanctuary. See Chapter V for plant materials suitable for these small vistas.

In the plans of vistas on page 45, will be found an illustration of the types of vistas that have been already noted, because after planning your garden frame there is nothing more conducive to permanent enjoyment of your garden. Perhaps none of the plans will be exactly applicable to your own property, but they will suggest, as have the illustrations of tree frames and shrubs, what to think about before making an actual planting plan for the garden to be.

All these schemes contribute to permanence in the garden, and most of them can be carried out, if not all at once, bit by bit. If one for financial reasons has to postpone any of several of the suggested features, it would be better to begin the vista first and let other things follow.

In Chapters IV, V and VI will be found the different plant materials that are easily available at any good nursery, as no plants are mentioned, however desirable, that are available only from specialists.

The Small Place

CHAPTER III   𝔗HE WHOLESALE migration from city apartments to suburban homes poses still another problem of permanence in the garden. Near New York, Philadelphia, Baltimore, Pittsburgh and Chicago, thousands of new homes have been built in the last few years, not to mention other thousands that have sprung up on the edges of smaller cities. Most of them lack sufficient space to make a frame of trees or to cut or make a vista. They may even have to forego accent plants, although this is less likely (see Chapter II).

Such places, whether selected from choice or necessity, need careful planning if one is not to achieve the commonplace which takes the form of a flower bed in the front lawn, a crystal ball on a pedestal, or even an old painted wash-boiler crammed with pathetic petunias. This is the kindergarten stage of garden design allied to the daubs of precocious children when asked to "show off."

Much more can be done with small places, even if they comprise only a limited area. If the houses are too close together and stretch in monotonous uniformity for blocks on end, that is unfortunate but it need discourage no one. Quite often, unless the developers of such tracts have much foresight, there may not be a single tree or shrub on the whole block. It will be a miracle if there are a few good-sized trees, and sometimes, lacking such good fortune, many management companies will not even have started young trees. If permanence in the garden were impossible for such places they would be doomed to mediocrity, or else to an annual garden expenditure of time or money beyond the interest of many and the pocketbook of most.

To achieve permanence in the small place means a careful selection of shrubs and trees, especially the sorts that will not dwarf the house. Real privacy will usually be impossible for there is not the room to plant marginal rows of trees or even have any between your house and your neighbor's. In such cases only a hedge will give you any sort of garden frame, and hedges, unless trimmed rigorously, will get too thick in a few years. Various hedge plants will be discussed in Chapter VI, and from these you can select the one most suited to your needs. They are better material for framing the small place than any fence.

One of the first things to do is to decide what type of foundation planting will be used. The need for this is obvious, especially in new houses, where bare walls hit the ground without benefit of anything to soften the stark line. But there are pitfalls worth avoiding, and these will be found toward the end of Chapter I in the section devoted to shrubs.

What then, does one do with the rest of the area between the house and sidewalk or with what most people call the "back yard." It need not be, for it is easy to make what might be merely a yard into a most attractive garden and a permanent one costing little or nothing after the initial expense of planting.

Let us consider the front of the property first. Assuming that it is covered with turf, a reasonable, effective and pleasing transition has been made from the sidewalk to your foundation planting. Nothing, except things that will give you permanence, should be put on such a lawn. Because it is small it is precious, and to dot it with horticultural knickknacks is just as distracting as having your living-room look like the counter in a bargain basement.

Trees must be the first consideration and their choice, especially if it means only one, is admittedly difficult. It should be a tree suited to suburban conditions (often windy, dusty, with paved streets and much summer heat), and hence most evergreens should be avoided in spite of their beauty and winter cheer. The only exceptions are possibly the Japanese black pine or the Austrian pine, both of which are better than any of our native species for this sort of planting. See Chapter V for cultural notes.

Among trees that drop their leaves (deciduous), we must select ones that remain relatively small in age, preferably have showy flowers, are dust and smoke-resistant, will have an interesting outline, and also provide shade. Among those with moderately showy or frankly spectacular flowers the choice will have to be rather limited, for most of them will not take kindly to the rigors of suburban environment. Those that might be considered are:

HORSE-CHESTNUT. Showy flowers in May. Casts very dense shade under which lawn grass will ultimately be impossible.

CATALPA. Showy flowers in June. Not very long-lived (30–50 years).

NORWAY MAPLE. Yellow flowers in early April. Casts extremely dense shade.

FLOWERING ASH. White flowers in dense clusters in early spring. Shade not dense.

SMALL PLACE APPROXIMATELY 30 X 100 FEET

House near center. Vista impossible. No garage. Street to be partly screened out. Dust, smoke and wind exclude all evergreens. No street trees. Unnumbered areas are lawn.

Key and Explanations

1. House
2. Sidewalk
3. Entrance path
4. Privet hedge
5. Foundation planting. Use any material shown on page 34, except evergreens.

Trees	*Shrubs*	*Vines*
6. Ginkgo	12. Mock-orange	20. Honeysuckle and
7. Pin oak	13. Flowering	*Clematis jack-*
8. Catalpa (may ul-	almond	*mani,* confined to
timately be shaded	14. Lilac	trellises on each
out by 7 and 6)	15. Bridal wreath	side of front
9. Norway maple	spirea	door.
10. Horse-chestnut	16. Hydrangea	
11. Flowering ash	17. *Rosa rugosa*	
(may ultimately	18. Snowberry	
be shaded out by	19. Japanese barberry	
9 and 10)		

Note: Some shrubs and parts of the hedge may ultimately be shaded out as trees reach maturity, but for many years you will have the advantage of trees, hedge and shrubs.

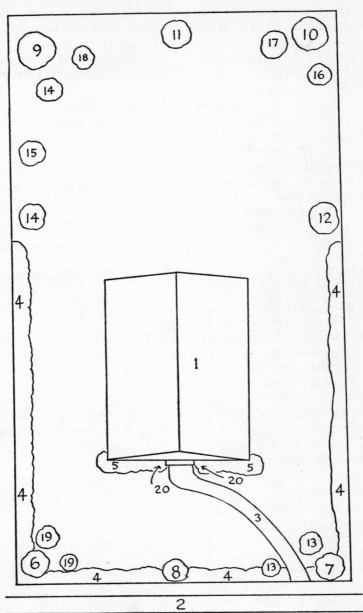

There are many others and further details should be sought in Chapter IV, where those suited to special conditions are noted particularly. Also in the same chapter will be found the trees in the list following which should be selected chiefly for their shade, autumnal color or showy fruits. All of them will stand the conditions usually found in suburban areas.

PIN OAK. Fine, permanent type of shade tree with spreading or drooping branches. Gorgeous red autumnal color.

GINKGO. Beautiful yellow autumnal leaf color, very well able to stand suburban conditions.

CHINESE ELM. Not as fine as our native elm but much more hardy if there is wind and dust.

LONDON PLANE. A sycamore, and the hardiest of all trees for city and suburban streets.

SCARLET OAK. Larger than the pin oak, and with a wider crown, hence to be used only if there is more room. It also has gorgeous red autumn color.

LINDEN (Nursery catalog name = *Tilia euchlora*). A medium-sized tree casting dense shade.

AILANTHUS. Will stand shade, dust, smoke or anything. It is essential to get a female tree. See Chapter IV.

Where to plant one or more of these shade trees, or the flowering trees just mentioned will be dictated by the size of your frontage, how far back from the sidewalk your house stands and whether or not there are any trees planted between the sidewalk and curb. While most of the trees in the foregoing lists are medium-sized (or likely to be so under suburban street conditions), they do demand some room for subsequent development of a crown of foliage.

If there are existing street trees and the house is less than 35 feet from the sidewalk, it is better to omit all large trees. Hedges, small trees and shrubs can be used instead, to give another kind of permanence and thus avoid the smothering effect of the street trees plus one or two of your own. This applies to places having 50 feet of frontage or less.

If there are no street trees it is then best to plant whichever one of those just listed, or others you may prefer (found in Chapter IV), as near the street boundary of your property as possible. Use only one if the place is small, but if you have a 50-foot frontage, by all means choose two different ones and put them as near the front corners of your property as possible. Some day they will make a pleasing frame for your house, cut off many street distractions, and provide welcome shade.

There is one caution about the use of trees on a small place. There is not room to space them properly, and when they get big, especially those casting the densest shade, they make hedges and lawns underneath them impossible. Some prefer to plant a marginal hedge in spite of this because they get the use of it for several years before the trees overshadow it. Also there are shade-enduring shrubs which can then be used, even if the lawn will ultimately be killed off some years hence.

Almost exactly the same tree-planting can be done at the rear corners of the property, unless the area is too restricted. Usually there is more space behind than in front of most rectangular suburban lots, and if so you may have room for three or more trees. The preferred position of these, and their spacing if there is more than one, will be found in the illustration on page 51.

If trees are impossible, or you prefer to have none, it is still possible to achieve permanence in the garden by the use of shrubs and woody vines. The latter are merely clambering shrubs that are unable to stand without support, but are just as permanent as true shrubs. The most useful sorts are found at the end of the shrub list in Chapter VI. They make attractive festoons over doorways, on trellises, and over a fence if you have one, taking very little space and often providing both color and foliage effects that are striking. Sometimes they can be trained over a simple wire arbor, or over an arched gateway to the garden in the rear.

As to the use of shrubs in masses or singly, there is scarcely any limit to your choice. Generally, true evergreens (see Chapter V) and broad-leaved evergreens, especially azaleas and rhododendrons (see Chapter VI), should not be attempted, however, unless you are relatively free from wind, dust and smoke, and are also prepared to give them the special attention they not only deserve but demand.

From all the shrubs listed in Chapter VI, with the foregoing exceptions, there is a wide choice as to color of bloom, height of the plant, and when they can be expected to be their showiest. Most shrubs will stand suburban conditions if properly planted and cared for the first year after setting them out. Planting and the subsequent care they need the first summer are described in detail in Chapter VII and need not be repeated here.

Such a program of planting trees, shrubs and vines can transform a stark and naked property into one of genuine charm and even distinction. It will achieve permanence in the small place and even point the way to other garden developments that lie beyond the scope of this book. All that is attempted here is to make it possible for the small homeowner to get shade, color, foliage masses and to relieve the monotony of endless vistas of often identical houses, which, without such planting, make pretty dreary scenery. And it can be done, once and for all, by the proper use of the plant material to be found in subsequent chapters.

Trees for Shade, Color and Fragrance

CHAPTER IV   *HE NUMBER* of trees in cultivation in America is numbered in the hundreds. Any attempt to list or describe half of them would confuse the gardener and fill a much bigger book than this one. The selection that follows has been made from those considered to be best, and their arrangement is very different from that found in books dealing mostly with their identification, which are rather technical.

Hence this chapter has only four main categories:

1. Flowering trees. Grown mostly for bloom.
2. Shade trees. Grown mostly for foliage.
3. Quick-growing trees. Temporary trees grown to be replaced by better ones.
4. Smoke-dust-and-wind-fighters. Grown on streets or in suburbs where others might perish.

Scarcely any evergreen trees are included here, as these are mostly grouped in Chapter V. Except for one or two, the trees that follow drop their leaves each fall and are hence *deciduous*. Some of them, like certain oaks, may hold their leaves late in autumn, or even all winter, but they all ultimately lose their leaves before the new crop comes out the following spring.

The foregoing arrangement, while simpler than that in more technical books, has the disadvantage of often separating, upon the basis of their uses, some trees that are closely related. Some, also, like the tulip-tree, might well be in more than one of the numbered categories previously mentioned. To avoid any confusion and for quick reference, the trees mentioned are included in a list at the end of this chapter, alphabetically arranged, and cross-referenced to the four main sections of this chapter. All, of course, will also be found in the general index.

Nearly everyone can tell a tree without any uncertainty, but there are many woody plants that are on the border-line between shrubs and trees. To avoid any possible confusion it is perhaps better to define them as the terms are generally understood by the experts, and used in this book:

Tree: A *woody* plant, usually large, although it may be small, with a single main stem—its trunk.
Shrub: A *woody* plant, usually lower than trees, but not always so, and with one or mostly several stems. They have no obvious trunks.

Common examples of shrubs that are sometimes trees in age, or in the south, are the witch-hazel, holly, magnolia, and one or two hawthorns. In other words, if you do not find the "tree" you are looking for here it may well be in Chapter VI which is devoted to shrubs.

Throughout this list and everywhere in the book the common or vernacular name of the plant will be used, if there is one. Where there is no common English name, the technical Latin name will be used, as this is the only way a nurseryman can tell what you want.

As to hardiness, all the trees are hardy in the region *north* of a line stretching from southern Virginia to Kansas and Oklahoma, up to the Canadian border, except where especially noted. Most of them can be grown in the foothills of the Rockies, but west of this deficient rainfall and summer heat make them precarious. On the Pacific Coast the conditions are quite different and other plants must be used which do not come within the scope of this book.

For directions on how to move or plant trees, see Chapter VII.

1. FLOWERING TREES
GROWN CHIEFLY FOR THEIR BLOOM

This is a somewhat misleading designation, because all trees bear flowers of some sort. But in many shade trees the flowers are greenish, inconspicuous or otherwise of no striking color, while all the trees in this section have extremely showy flowers. Some of them in addition have fine foliage, but they are included here so that, in one place, you may find all the trees that are cultivated for their bloom.

Flowers Red, Pink or Rose Color

FLOWERING CRAB-APPLE. Medium-sized tree (15–25 feet) with a profusion of pink bloom early in spring. There are several other sorts, some with double flowers. Extremely showy and a good accent plant. It is generally a round-headed tree, and there are also white varieties.

JAPANESE FLOWERING CHERRIES. For centuries the Japanese have cultivated these superb spring-flowering trees (some are shrubs), and they also developed hundreds of named forms. Some are weeping. Among the best are Kwanzan (double-flowered), Higan-sakura, Naden and Ruth Wohlert. No finer accent plants are to be found than these gorgeous, medium-sized trees.

LOCUST (Nursery catalog name = *Robinia viscosa*). It is safer to order this by its Latin name for there are several other locusts, and they are sometimes confused with the honey locust. *Robinia viscosa* is often called clammy locust and is a tree 30–40 feet high with sticky foliage and many-flowered clusters of pink, pea-like flowers. It is not quite hardy north of southern New York, Pennsylvania, Ohio, Indiana and Illinois. Its pea-like pods make a litter and may stop up gutters.

REDBUD. Of the several kinds in cultivation it is better to choose the American redbud, which is a small tree (not over 30 feet high) with heart-shaped leaves and a profusion of rose-pink flowers, the clusters of which bloom on the naked twigs before the leaves unfold in early spring.

Flowers Pure White, or Essentially So

MOUNTAIN ASH (Nursery catalog name = *Sorbus aucuparia*). It is safer to order this by its Latin name as there are others. The tree is 40–50 feet high and is covered in June with a profusion of tiny white flowers in flat-topped clusters, followed by nearly as showy clusters of bright red fruits. A good border tree for medium-sized properties.

MAGNOLIA. A magnificent group of shrubs and trees with immense, often very fragrant flowers. Of the dozen or more kinds in cultivation, the three selected here will add much beauty and distinction to any garden. The following are trees with white, waxy flowers (but there are many related shrubs, and a few trees have purplish or pinkish blooms). Those included here are: (1) The Yulan (catalog name = *Magnolia denudata*), which may reach 50 feet and has very fragrant flowers 5–6 inches wide that bloom in May. (2) *Evergreen magnolia*, a beautiful evergreen tree (50–70 feet) with large rhododendron-like leaves that are rusty beneath. Flowers 5–6 inches wide, fragrant. Not hardy north of Washington, D.C. (3) *Cucumber tree* (catalog name = *Magnolia macrophylla*). A round-headed tree not over 50 feet high, with leaves 1–3 feet long! Flowers 10–12 inches across, fragrant. Not quite hardy in extreme north.

Warning: All magnolias are difficult to transplant. Their roots are
fragile, will not stand exposure to sun and wind, and hence must
be moved with a large ball of earth. See Chapter VII for details.
Magnolias are not for city streets or windy, dusty suburbs.

SNOWDROP TREE (Nursery catalog name = *Halesia carolina*). Not
usually over 40 feet high and often less. Flowers less than 1
inch long, but borne in small hanging clusters. It is often called silver-
bell tree and is useful as a lawn specimen or accent plant for its May
bloom.

DOGWOOD. Beautiful white-flowered, medium-sized (20–30 feet)
tree, usually blooming in early May, before the leaves unfold,
or with their unfolding. It is one of the finest accent plants, especially favored by some in a pink-flowered horticultural variety. All
the native trees are white. It is the state tree of Virginia and much
planted by George Washington at Mount Vernon. It must be moved
with a ball of earth, as it is difficult to transplant. See Chapter VII.

HAWTHORN. An enormous group (over 1000 kinds!) of handsome,
thorny shrubs and trees of which only two are included here
for their showy flower clusters and almost as showy scarlet fruit like
miniature apples. All belong to the group known as *Crataegus* and
it is essential to order them by the Latin names for their identity
is in much confusion. Our two kinds are: (1) English hawthorn
(*Crataegus oxyacantha*). A small tree, covered in May with a profusion of white bloom. Fruit scarlet, in midsummer. There are pink-
flowered and weeping varieties. (2) Washington thorn (*Crataegus
phaenopyrum*), a native American, round-headed tree, the thorns
nearly 3 inches long. A profuse bloomer, followed by small, very
numerous red fruits.

CATALPA. Be sure to get the common or American catalpa which
may reach 30–40 feet in height. It is quick-growing, not very
long-lived, but quite suited to unfavorable sites like dusty or windy
suburbs. Flowers showy, in a dense cluster, white but yellow-striped
inside. Fruit a long slender pod which will easily clog gutters and
drains.

HORSE-CHESTNUT. A splendid tree for large or small properties, casting a very dense shade, and well suited to streets or suburbs,
except that the litter from its fruits needs clearing up, especially from
roof gutters. In May it produces large pyramidal clusters of white
flowers, sometimes tinged with rose (there is also a red-flowered
form). It is the "chestnut" of the streets of Paris and London but
has nothing to do with the true chestnuts. Besides its bloom it is one

of the best shade trees. Grass and most shrubs will not grow under it.

Flowers Greenish-white, Greenish-yellow, Yellowish-white or Yellow

FLOWERING ASH. The only ash tree with showy flowers (for others see
Shade Trees), and often 20–30 feet high, or higher in favorable places. It has medium-dense foliage and is fairly tolerant of poor soils and dusty windy places. Flowers greenish-white or whitish, fragrant, very small but in dense clusters at the ends of the twigs.

HONEY LOCUST. A very thorny, hard-wooded, slow-growing tree
which may reach 80–100 feet. Shade not dense as foliage is thin. Flowers greenish-white or greenish, in large, drooping clusters. Fruit a long, sickle-shaped, twisted pod which hangs on for months, and will easily clog gutters.

TULIP-TREE. A magnificent forest giant, usually with a trunk free of
branches for 30–40 feet, if in the forest, and in maturity often 100–150 feet high. Flowers tulip-shaped, solitary on the twigs, greenish-yellow and very handsome. Its broad leaves are prominently notched at the tip. A splendid tree for larger properties, and often called tulip-poplar.

PAGODA TREE. A Chinese and Korean ornamental tree, 30–50 feet
high, but often less in cultivation, with profuse, hanging, very showy clusters of yellowish-white, pea-like flowers. A variety with weeping branches makes an extremely handsome lawn specimen or accent plant. See Chapter II.

GOLDEN CHAIN (Nursery catalog name = *Laburnum anagyroides*).
Not over 15–20 feet high and sometimes shrubby, as it often branches close to the ground. Flowers showy, yellow, pea-like and in hanging clusters, not usually flowering until late May or June. Pod about 2 inches long, its seeds, if eaten, poisonous, as is the foliage, but not a contact poison like the poison ivy.

Flowers Pale Violet

PAULOWNIA. An extremely handsome but rather short-lived tree
much prone to interior rot, hence dangerous near a house, where its copious fruit will also clog gutters. In the open border or as a lawn specimen it is grown for its many, very large clusters of showy flowers that are pale violet, nearly 2 inches long, and suggest the snapdragon. It blooms in May before the leaves unfold and is not certainly hardy north of New York, because the flowerbuds are

formed in the fall and are hence exposed to frost. It is perfectly hardy
from Delaware, and Maryland, southward.

2. SHADE TREES

GROWN MOSTLY FOR FOLIAGE

Many of the flowering trees in Section 1 of this chapter are also
especially fine shade trees, notably the tulip-tree, horse-chestnut, cucumber tree and Paulownia, but there is no need to repeat the details of them here. Shade, beauty of outline or branching are the
features one looks to in planning a garden where the chief aim is
masses of foliage, the framing of a property, or the making of a vista.

For such purposes nothing else will take the place of the shade
trees that follow, and it should be emphasized again that only a
limited selection of the best can be included here. Even such a comparative minority may be confusing to the beginner, and perhaps
a summary of the different groups of them, as arranged here, will
help to find what you are looking for. The shade trees are here divided among: (a) oaks and beeches, (b) lindens, maples and ash,
(c) hickory and walnut, (d) elms, hackberry and hornbeam, (e)
gum trees and sassafras.

(a) *Oaks and Beeches.* No other trees are so permanent as the oaks,
specimens of white oak often reaching an age of 500–800 years. And
some of them are among our largest trees, especially the white oak,
old specimens of which may have a crown over 100 feet through.
Of the 25 kinds cultivated in the United States only five will be
necessary to include here:

Pin Oak. Not usually more than 50–70 feet high as cultivated, its
        spreading horizontal branches drooping at the tip. It is an ex-
cellent street or suburban tree and fine for border planting on moderate sized places. Rather quick-growing for an oak and with
gorgeous autumnal color.

Scarlet Oak. Larger than the pin oak but still suitable for border
        planting on moderate sized places. It is more or less upright
or cylindrical in outline, never spreading as in the white oak. It takes
its name from the scarlet foliage in the fall. It is fairly tolerant of
unfavorable places.

Red Oak. The quickest growing of most of the oaks, it may reach
        20–30 feet in 20 years, or sooner if conditions are favorable.
It needs space, and should hence be put in border plantings only on

places at least 100 x 200 feet. Autumnal color dull reddish brown. It frequently reaches a height of 70–90 feet.

WHITE OAK. The largest, most spreading, most slow-growing of all the oaks, and a magnificent tree on large properties. In age it is round headed, too spreading to frame a vista. Autumnal color negligible, and the withered leaves hang on most of the winter. It is hard to transplant and should always be moved with a large ball of earth. See Chapter VII.

LIVE OAK. A beautiful evergreen oak with unlobed, willow-like leaves, an immense crown of foliage, and in the south the favorite home of the hanging Spanish moss. Included here because it is the finest of the evergreen oaks for the eastern states, but it is not hardy north of Washington, D.C. In planting it should always be moved with a ball of earth. See Chapter VII.

BEECHES. These are related to the oaks, but usually not so large. Only the American and European beeches need be considered by the garden planner, and both have the fine, close, gray bark so characteristic of beeches and the long, pointed, silky leafbuds in early spring. From the garden standpoint the European beech is better than the native one, for it includes forms with purple foliage (the copper beech) and another with beautiful, drooping branches (the weeping beech). All beech trees must be moved with care, always with a ball of earth, unless very small.

(b) *Lindens, Maples and Ash Trees.* While quite unrelated this group of trees all differ from oaks and beeches in being smaller, quicker growing, and not so long-lived. They nevertheless contain some of our most valuable shade trees.

LINDENS. Of the many kinds only three need be considered here. In Europe they are known as lime trees, while our native one is the basswood. All belong to the group known as *Tilia,* and it is safer to order them by the Latin names. Lindens have extremely fragrant flowers beloved by bees, but the after-litter can clog drains and gutters. All are relatively quick growing, make wide, spreading crowns and hence not so good for framing a vista as some other, more upright trees. The best kinds are: (1) American Linden, *Tilia americana,* a tall tree, often 100 feet high, and a fairly quick grower, often called basswood. (2) Small-leaved European Linden, *Tilia cordata,* a beautiful lawn tree which if left alone will have its lower branches drooping at the tip so that they almost sweep the ground. Its twiggy growth makes it an admirable tree for pleaching. See Vistas in Chapter II. (3) *Tilia euchlora,* a hybrid tree with no common name, but one of our best lindens, well suited for planting in suburban properties. It may reach 70–80 feet.

MAPLE. Many kinds are grown in the United States but the four that follow will provide the beginner with enough choice, and this should certainly exclude the widely planted silver maple which is brittle and sheds its twigs and many small branches in only half a gale. The four preferred trees are: (1) *Norway Maple*. A round-headed tree, perhaps the most widely planted of any in the United States. It is relatively quick growing, will stand street and suburban conditions, and in early spring its bare branches are covered with tiny yellow flowers, followed by copious fruits that can clog drains and gutters. Its shade is so dense that nothing will grow under it. It has a variety, Schwedler's maple, that has red foliage in the spring, but the leaves turn green by midsummer. The tree spreads too much to make vistas, but is extremely useful in all gardens. Autumnal foliage yellow. (2) *Sugar Maple*. An American relative of the Norway maple, but differing in its more upright habit, and of course the ability of its sweet sap to provide maple sugar. It also has shaggy bark in age, very different from the close bark of the Norway maple. A splendid tree for larger properties and a fine street tree for northern villages, but not well suited to city streets. The autumnal foliage is a wonderful combination of yellow and scarlet. (3) *Red Maple*. A good, medium-sized, native maple, covered in early spring (February–March) with myriads of tiny red flowers that crowd the bare twigs. Grows naturally in moist places and thus thrives best in low sites. Autumnal color a brilliant scarlet. (4) *Japanese Maple*. From this Korean tree the Japanese have created a multitude of beautiful color forms (red, copper, yellow), and cut-leaved forms (feathery, lace-like, etc.) that make this the showiest of all temperate zone foliage plants. They are too small for shade, most of them scarcely exceeding 10–20 feet, but they are hardy up into Canada. A beautiful arrangement of them, very popular in Japan, is to plant one or two on a mound selected so that the setting sun shines through the colored foliage. Few garden groupings are so effective. The plants are slow-growing and inclined to be expensive.

ASH TREES. Most trees of this group bear inconspicuous green flowers, but one of them, the flowering ash, has showy enough bloom to be included in Section 1 of this chapter devoted to Flowering Trees. The ones below are generally tall, upright trees admirably suited to frame a vista or make part of a border planting. (1) *White Ash* is often 90–100 feet high, the young twigs lustrous green. It is hardy everywhere and appears to be indifferent as to site. (2) *Eu-*

ropean Ash is taller than the American Ash, and its twigs, while bright green, are not lustrous. It is not quite so hardy as the last, being precarious in southern Canada and northern New York.

(c) *Hickory and Walnut.* These nut-bearing trees are admirably suited for medium-sized and larger properties, both for shade, which is not too dense so that grass beneath is impossible and, when mature, for valuable nuts, especially the walnut. The latter often sheds many immature nuts which must be raked up to permit lawn mowing. Hickories and walnuts are of upright habit and hence useful to frame a vista.

HICKORY. It is better to buy one or two named forms of hickory rather than the wild species of which there are several. A variety called Hales yields nuts with thin shells, reasonably easy to crack, and the Kirtland has somewhat larger kernels, but it is not quite so easy to crack the nut. Both varieties will grow in most ordinary garden soils.

WALNUT. In the eastern states it is better to grow the native black walnut, as the more desirable English Walnut is best grown in California. The black walnut in the virgin forest was an immense tree, but most of these have long since been harvested for their beautiful wood. As cultivated, the tree has an open crown, rather brittle branches, and large leaves with many segments. It may reach 60–80 feet. If one is interested more in the nuts than in foliage, good varieties are the Stabler and Ten Eyck.

(d) *Elms, Hackberry and Hornbeam.* There is no finer street and lawn tree than the American elm in rural areas, but not for cities or smoky, dusty and windy suburbs. Unfortunately it is subject to the Dutch elm disease and should not be planted if your region is infested with this completely incurable and fatal disease. See your local nurseryman before choosing it. The disease is rampant within a radius of 200 miles of New York City.

ELMS. Only two of the 15 kinds of elms known to be cultivated in the United States are included here because of their special qualities. (1) American elm is one of the most widely planted trees in the country for its incomparable vase-like shape and the huge crown of lustrous green leaves. Many a village street is a cathedral-like aisle because of its branching habit. Beautiful as a lawn specimen, and as part of a border screen, or to frame a vista. (2) Chinese elm is a remarkable, fairly recent introduction, which will stand conditions of heat and drought that no American elm would tolerate. It has small leaves and never grows more than 40 feet high. It is admirably suited to city streets and thrives on bleak wind-swept prairies. It has, of course, nothing like the elegance of branching of the American elm.

HACKBERRY (Nursery catalog name = *Celtis occidentalis*). This relative of the elm is wider spreading and much more tolerant of unfavorable sites. It thrives in cities and a huge one on the author's farm in Maryland has its roots in brackish tidewater. Its shade is rather dense, and in age it produces a lot of wart-like protuberances on the trunk and larger branches.

HORNBEAM (Nursery catalog name = *Carpinus betulus*). This European tree is better than the native one for border planting as it reaches a height of 30–50 feet, is not too wide-spreading and hence useful on smaller properties. Like its American relative it is very slow growing, has curious smooth, close bark and is among the hardest wooded of any tree. If topped early enough it can then be sheared into a tree-like hedge.

(e) *Gum Trees and Sassafras*. These quite unrelated trees have been grouped together, partly because all of them are native in the eastern states, but chiefly because of their spectacular autumn coloration, of which there is nothing finer in our forest flora.

SWEET GUM. A beautiful high-branching tree with star-shaped leaves, and conspicuous, after these have fallen, for the persistent ball-like, weakly spiny fruits. Its chief glory is the fiery scarlet foliage in autumn. The litter of its copious fruit is deplored by tidy gardeners, but the tree is worth much raking.

SOUR GUM. The branching of this is unique among American forest trees. The horizontal branches at first stand straight out from the trunk, but ultimately sag at the ends, giving an almost funereal aspect to the tree. Unlike the sweet gum its leaves are without teeth or lobes, and turn a deep, burgundy red in the fall. It is generally a swamp tree and hence prefers low places. It should not be moved without a ball of earth. See Chapter VII.

SASSAFRAS. Often considered a mere shrub or weedy tree by those who have never seen a mature specimen. It may reach 100 feet and have a trunk diameter of more than 4 feet. It is highly aromatic, bears yellowish, very fragrant flowers and curious, diversely-lobed leaves that turn perhaps the most brilliant crimson of any native tree. It is indifferent as to soil, but is not for city streets or windy suburbs.

THE GARDEN FRAME

The frame may be simple, like that at top, outlining an area at the edge of the lawn, with perennials like iris and peonies, perhaps interspersed with annuals for summer bloom, and with flagstone paths and a few shrubs for balance and interest. (Photo: *Roche*) Or it may be more elaborate (below), using trees and fences, with shrubs and vines as part of the design. A wall or fence, like the one here, may be made decorative in itself, and can be developed along lines dictated by the taste and the purse of the gardener. (Photo: *Genereux*)

FOUNDATION PLANTING

Softening the abrupt line between housewalls and the ground is a matter
needing thought and care. Beauty and balance must be considered, but so
must more practical matters, such as windows that should not be shad-
owed, and pipes, drains or meters that must be avoided. These two
examples of sound planning show (above) the treatment of a modern,
glass-fronted home, and (below) borders for the more conventional type of
architecture. Both kinds of planting can be adapted to the requirements
of the average small home. (Photo: *Genereux*)

ACCENTS
Flowering trees are among the most useful of accent plants. The pink-flowering dogwoods, with azaleas in blending colors planted at their base, can turn a spring landscape into breath-taking beauty. (Photo: *Roche*)

ACCENTS

No element in garden design contributes more to the attractiveness of a property than a pool, and none lends itself better to variations in form and planting. On this and the following page are two ways in which pools can be adapted to special conditions. This one, surrounded by bog plants and evergreens, and set against a background of white birch and flowering shrubs, is a focal point in a broad lawn. (Photo: *Genereux*)

This pool, set as an accent point in a small garden, uses only potted plants and lawn to frame it, and is adaptable to many kinds of garden problems. The raised flower beds in the background, with low brick retaining walls and accent plantings of box, give another level to the garden — an idea useful in home landscaping and design. (Photo: *Roche*)

VISTAS

The contrived vista may be as small or large as the property permits. As its central point of interest, a garden statue, pool or bird bath may be used, flanked (left) with laurel and azaleas. (Photo: *Roche*)

The informal vista (right) is most often composed of massed flowering shrubs at the base of evergreens or deciduous trees. The line of planting is irregular, and by skillful planning, effects of great depth and distance can be secured. (Photo: *Genereux*)

Evergreens combine the virtues of year-round beauty, hardiness, and minimum requirements of care. With ground-cover of *Vinca minor* (used above),
a planting of taxus, ilex and juniper can take care not only of foundation
planting, but supply almost all the decorative elements needed to frame
a home. Note the careful use of a few deciduous trees to supply accent
points. (Photo: *Genereux*)

One well-placed tree, and a background of evergreens and flowering shrubs complete the permanent planting of a home. Flowers may be varied from year to year, but the permanent planting will always remain as a dependable background, setting off the lawn, and acting as a screen to ensure both beauty and privacy. The tree above is a flowering crab, and the border includes lilacs, arbor vitae and laurel. (Photo: *Genereux*)

3. QUICK-GROWING TREES

TEMPORARY TREES TO BE REPLACED BY BETTER ONES

In many planting schemes our more impatient gardeners fume against the experts for suggesting the perfect trees for permanence in the garden, when both of them well know that it may take years to get the desired effect. If one's pocketbook is greater than one's impatience the remedy, of course, is to plant really big trees, and dozens of nurserymen will be eager to further such an expensive solution of the dilemma.

But Nature seems in league with the impecunious and patient, in providing a few trees that grow far faster than more desirable ones, and some of these upstarts are beautiful enough in themselves to be worth keeping.

Among the many quick-growing sorts only three groups can be included here, the willows, poplars and birches. Some of the latter, especially the white-barked kinds, are worth keeping. But generally the trees that follow are chosen because they fill a temporary gap in a scheme. They are a little like the definition in Webster's Dictionary of a permanent wave—only semipermanent. Catalpa, noted in the section on flowering trees, is also a quick grower.

In choosing these semipermanent trees for quick effects it pays, because all of them are relatively cheap, to plant them more thickly than seems justified offhand. They will soon crowd each other and can be gradually cut down. They must be cut if they tend to smother young trees of the permanent planting of which the semipermanents are only the vanguard.

WILLOWS. Quick-growing, short-lived and brittle-twigged trees much subject to rot at the core and hence dangerous near a house in any real blow. The trees most useful are: (1) *Black Willow*, with strikingly dark bark, long slender leaves, and erect branches. Not over 35 feet high. (2) *White Willow*, a taller tree with silky-hairy leaves and erect branches. (3) *Weeping Willow*, the largest and most permanent of the three with long-drooping branchlets which sometimes almost touch the ground. Often cultivated for this beautiful effect, but not likely to be really permanent.

POPLARS. Faster growing than the willows and generally less permanent, but an exception comprises some of our western, wild cottonwoods, which are poplars that hug water courses and are little known in cultivation. Of the cultivated poplars the following seem worth including: (1) *White Poplar,* often 40–50 feet high, with showy, white-silvery quaking leaves. A very quick grower. (2) *Black Poplar,* a more widely spreading tree, with quaking, fluttery green leaves. A very common variety of it is (3) *Lombardy Poplar,* a tall columnar or cylindrical tree much used for avenue planting and to frame vistas, although it never will be really permanent and loses many of its branches in age long before it dies. Not to be used if you want effects 20–30 years hence, but quick-growing and quite striking for temporary effects.

BIRCHES. Two of the eight different birch trees in cultivation have use in the garden. Neither of them are long-lived, but both quick-growing. (1) *Gray Birch,* a tree with at first brilliant white bark, which becomes dirty gray in maturity. It will make a quick screen and is so indifferent to unfavorable conditions that it will stand the cindery wastes of factory yards. (2) *White Birch,* a beautifully and permanently white-barked tree, the trunks often in clusters. Unfortunately it is not long-lived but makes most effective contrast against the dark foliage of evergreens. Due to their twiggy growth these and related birches may be pleached to form a tree-like hedge. See, for an explanation of pleaching, the section on Vistas in Chapter II.

4. SMOKE-DUST-AND-WIND-FIGHTERS

GROWN ON CITY STREETS OR IN SUBURBS WHERE OTHERS MIGHT PERISH

Most trees prefer reasonably good soil, plenty of aeration for their root system, a decent water supply, freedom from hot drying winds, and from dust and smoke or the sooty deposit from oil burners. Yet it is in precisely these conditions that street trees must survive—with pavement stretching from curb to curb, and all rain water steered into the corner drains. Fortunately there are a few which not only survive these hazards but actually thrive in spite of them.

Besides the following ones there are others, already noted, which may be used, if not on city streets, at least in suburbs that are not quite so severe. Those already mentioned will be found in various other sections of this chapter as follows:

Horse-chestnut, Section 1
Catalpa, Section 1
Gray Birch, Section 3
Chinese Elm, Section 2

Any of these, except perhaps the horse-chestnut, can be tried in pretty unfavorable places, and all of them in suburban regions. But far exceeding them in capacity to put up with the intolerable are: AILANTHUS. A weedy Chinese tree, often running wild, and becoming a pest, especially in California. It is, however, *the* city tree which it is almost impossible to kill. Be sure to get female trees, which have handsome fruit, because the male tree, in bloom, has an offensive odor. Will grow in cindery factory yards and even in Brooklyn!

LONDON PLANE. A relative of our native sycamore or buttonball, but a much better tree for all garden uses. It is a hybrid developed in France and the most widely planted street tree on earth. But apart from its ability to stand dust and wind, the tree is often planted on lawns and will ultimately grow into a wide-spreading tree up to 100 feet high. It is too spreading for framing a vista, but if topped at the desired height its twiggy growth can easily be pleached. For an account of this see the section on Vistas in Chapter II.

SUMMARY

There are 56 different trees in this chapter divided as follows:

1. Flowering trees   20
2. Shade trees   26
3. Quick growing   8
4. Dust and wind resistant 2

From them you can easily make a choice to fit your needs. All, except the quick-growing kinds, contribute more to permanence in the garden than any other plant material in the book. To facilitate finding any particular tree, the names are listed alphabetically followed by a *Section* number. Under that section, in this chapter, will be found an account of each tree. In the case of the shade trees (Section 2) they have been further designated by letters (a), (b), etc. The key to this is found on pages 60 and 61.

INDEX TO CHAPTER FOUR

The numbers refer to Sections

Ailanthus 4
Ash 2(b)
Basswood. See Linden
Beech 2(a)
Birch 3
Buttonball. See London Plane
Catalpa 1
Copper Beech 2(a)
Crab-apple 1
Cucumber Tree. See Magnolia
Dogwood 1
Elm 2(d)
Flowering Ash 1
Flowering Cherry 1
Flowering Crab-apple 1
Golden Chain 1
Gum Trees 2(e)

Hackberry 2(d)
Hawthorn 1
Hickory 2(c)
Honey Locust 1
Hornbeam 2(d)
Horse-chestnut 1
Japanese Flowering Cherry 1
Japanese Maple 2(b)
Lime Tree. See Linden
Linden 2(b)
Locust 1
Lombardy Poplar 3
London Plane 4
Magnolia 1
Maple 2(b)
Mountain-ash 1
Oak 2(a)
Pagoda Tree 1
Paulownia 1

Pin Oak 2(a)
Plane Tree. See London Plane
Poplar 3
Redbud 1
Sassafras 2(e)
Silver-bell. See Snowdrop Tree
Snowdrop Tree 1
Sour Gum 2(e)
Sweet Gum 2(e)
Sycamore. See London Plane
Tulip-tree 1
Walnut 2(c)
Washington Thorn. See Hawthorn
Weeping Willow 3
Willow 3
Yulan. See Magnolia

Evergreens for Winter Effects

CHAPTER V   HE TERM *evergreen* needs definition, if one is not to become confused by trees
like the live oak and evergreen magnolia, the broad-leaved evergreens mentioned in the chapter on shrubs, and the truly evergreen
kinds discussed here. All the plants in this chapter bear cones (or
modifications of them) and they have needle-like leaves as in the
pines, spruces, firs, hemlocks and yews or scale-like leaves, sometimes
flattened against the twigs, as in cedars, junipers, arborvitae, cypress
and a few others.

All these plants are classed as true evergreens, partly because they
are cone-bearing and also because they are truly ever green—that
is, at no time are the plants bare of foliage. They constantly lose a
few leaves, as any one can see when they are scattered on snow, but
they just as constantly grow new ones, a few at a time, especially in
the spring, so that this stealthy loss and replacement of leaves are
pretty evenly balanced. Nature, however, appears to love deviations
from the overwhelming evergreen habit of this group and has hence
decreed some startling exceptions to it, in three trees that drop all
their leaves in the fall: the ginkgo, larch and our native American
cypress.

Another constant difference between true evergreens and all the
rest of the plants in this book is the fact that the evergreens, while
bearing extremely primitive flowers, have no colored petals, and
hence one grows such plants not for their showy bloom but in spite
of the fact that they have no flowers, in the usual sense, at all.

Evergreens are grown almost entirely for their dark, evergreen
foliage, their wide variety of almost architectural or formal outline,
and, when everything else is dormant, their wonderful capacity to
bring winter greenery into otherwise bleak landscapes. For formal
effects, for border planting, for vistas and as accent plants they are
unrivaled. Unfortunately most of them are slow-growing, very expensive, and they must all be moved with a large ball of earth. See
Chapter VII for the details.

Several hundred varieties of evergreens are known to be in cultivation in this country, and the differences between them are far too technical to be included here. For the beginner the best way to familiarize himself with the main groups is to visit a good nursery or a botanical garden where they are all labeled.

Without going into such technicalities it is perfectly possible for the amateur to make a selection of evergreens for every garden purpose. The main groups are listed subsequently, with some characteristic feature of each, and under each group will be found those most suited for adding permanence to the garden.

As discussed briefly in Chapter I, evergreens have cultural requirements that limit their use to areas having long cold winters, not too great heat in summer and adequate rainfall. They are peculiarly sensitive to sudden warm spells in February and March. All evergreens are active throughout the winter, taking in and giving off moisture. But they are not so active in winter as in the growing season, and a sudden warm spell or drying winds during these early months puts too great a strain on their water-gathering roots and the foliage dries up—"burned" the experts call it.

It is precisely this, far more than cold, that makes so many evergreens look forlorn in April, just when they should be ready for full spring growth. This is particularly noticeable in big cities where thousands of dollars' worth of evergreens are wasted annually, largely because they should never be planted in such places. Their one great fondness is coolness and moisture, and it is no accident that firs and spruces are found naturally almost up to the Arctic Circle, or that the greatest evergreen forests in the world are probably in our own northwest where it rains 60 inches a year and is constantly cool.

No one should, in the light of these facts, attempt to make evergreens part of a garden plan if the place is too exposed to hot drying winds, the fumes of cities or even of fairly small country towns, nor should they ever be tried in places of long-continued summer heat. Perhaps the most suitable, under such conditions, are cedars and junipers, while the Japanese yew survives longer in city parks and unfavorable suburban gardens than almost any other evergreen. But even this sturdy plant usually dies out after a few years.

Such discouragements and failures point the way to what to avoid and still more certainly what to do. Most evergreens do not need any winter protection, but in mid-February and all through March, many of the smaller ones, and all newly-planted ones, will profit by a screen of jute bagging, cornstalks, or cut-off branches of left-over or saved Christmas trees, to shield them from the sun and wind.

Such protective coverings should come off by April first in the latitude of New York, earlier south of this and later north of it. And they must not cut off all light and air. Build them therefore to permit filtered light and air to reach the plant. This can easily be done by a cage-like, open-topped structure, into which the protective material can be loosely spread. Or, for small plants, four corner posts can be driven and loosely woven jute bagging can be fastened to make a little, open-topped cage. Over the top of the plant spread a thin layer of loose straw or other litter. This must not pack down.

There is still one other feature for the care of evergreens in regions of heavy snowfall. All the trees will take care of themselves, for even if their branches are bent down with the weight of snow, this ultimately will melt or be blown off with little or no damage to the tree.

It is quite otherwise with certain lower evergreens with a different type of branching than the usually erect, unbranched, single trunk of most evergreen trees. In others, such as some yews, cedar varieties, and a few more, there are several main stems, all usually hidden by the outer mass of foliage. So dense is the latter that one is apt to ignore or forget that such plants, with a heavy blanket of snow, particularly if it is wet, are apt to be split apart or otherwise injured. The remedy is either to shake the snow off or else tie the whole plant together, near its top, with a belt-like strip of wide canvas (2–3 inches wide to prevent injuring leaves). This will prevent splitting; and ultimately melting or wind will remove the snow. In the early spring it is essential to remove such bands as they confine the plant too closely when growth becomes active.

The use of evergreens in gardens is perfectly simple if these precautions are observed, and failure is not only equally simple but certain if they are ignored. In the following notes special cautions will be enumerated where necessary, otherwise all the evergreens in the book can be grown if the general directions just outlined are followed.

WHAT KINDS TO PLANT

Evergreens have been so popular, particularly in England, that hundreds of horticultural forms have been developed for every conceivable garden purpose. Most of these are also grown here. The number of different *species* is not so great as in deciduous trees and shrubs, but the number of named *varieties* is legion. Still more confusing is the fact that some giant trees like the arborvitae, firs and spruces have small globe-shaped, columnar, cylindric or dwarf forms, not in the least resembling the parent type. But they carry the cultural preferences of these, and hence should be chosen with this in mind.

To simplify the undeniably complex problem of evergreen varieties and their garden uses, all those worth the attention of beginners have been sorted into nine major groups.

Evergreens That Lose Their Leaves in Autumn

    1. Ginkgo, larch and the cypress of our southeastern states.

Truly Evergreen Types, Continuously Covered with Foliage

    2. Yew
    3. Cedars and junipers
    4. Pines
    5. Hemlocks
    6. Spruces
    7. Firs
    8. Arborvitae
    9. Italian cypress. Sawara cypress.

So many of these plants, especially their horticultural forms, are known only by their technical Latin names, even although widely cultivated, that it is essential in ordering them to use these designations. But common English names are used wherever they are safely applicable. All others will be the Latin names used in nursery catalogs.

1. *Ginkgo, Larch and Cypress of our Southeastern States*

GINKGO. An extraordinary Chinese tree long thought to be extinct as a wild plant, and undoubtedly preserved only as cultivated for thousands of years around Chinese temples. It stretches back to fossil time, and brought with it, through millions of years, a type of reproduction known in no other modern tree. The male reproductive sperm cell has the power of motion, exactly as in human spermatazoa, a characteristic almost universal in fossil time, but long since replaced by other methods in all the trees in the world except ginkgo, which is its Chinese name.

The tree comes in two forms, male and female. The latter bear rather ill-smelling fruits and should not be planted if one objects to the odor. The male tree becomes in age a beautiful round-headed

tree (there are fine ones in Washington, D.C.), but in youth its
branching looks like a series of accidents, so gawky are the angles of
its young branches. It is covered by fan-shaped leaves that suggest
the maidenhair—hence its other name of maidenhair-tree. The foliage turns into a beautiful soft yellow, before it falls in autumn. The
tree is hardy up into Canada, is free of disease, will stand any sort
of abuse and hence is much planted in city streets. But it is also one
of our finest lawn trees, ultimately reaching more than 100 feet in
height.

LARCH. Beautiful, medium-sized trees, the needle-like leaves, which
are clustered in bunches, turning yellow before dropping in
the fall. Of the several kinds the most useful is the Japanese larch,
which is fairly quick-growing, and like all larches does better in the
north than in the south. It is wiser not to plant it along the coast
south of Delaware, although occasionally fine specimens are found
in Maryland and Virginia. A splendid specimen lawn tree, but not
for city streets or dusty, hot suburbs.

CYPRESS of our southeastern states. This has nothing to do with the
true cypress of Section 9 of this chapter, as our American one
drops all its leaves each autumn, and does not have the tall spire-like
or columnar habit of the Italian cypress. Our tree is mostly native
in the cypress swamps of the south, but will grow in low places in
the garden up to Massachusetts. It is a fine, upright-branching tree
with a mass of feathery, almost lace-like foliage. Even when bare in
the winter its reddish or cinnamon-colored, fibrous bark is attractive.
It almost never produces in cultivation the characteristic "knees"
found in real cypress swamps. Just before leaf-fall, the foliage turns
bright orange. Because of its deciduous habit it is often called bald
cypress.

2. *Yew.* The beautiful yews of English churchyards and their many
legends and stories, not to speak of the longbows of Robin Hood, all
make one want to grow these storied and beautiful evergreens. But
the plain fact is that the yew does not take kindly to our American
climate and, although hardy up to New York, it is better to plant the
much more adaptable Japanese yew.

This statement is quite literally true of the ordinary form of English yew, but there are horticultural varieties of it that require mention for their successful and most useful role in special places. One
is the Irish yew, a beautiful columnar form useful as an accent plant
(see Chapter II), or to frame a small contrived vista. It is most used
around pools, as part of foundation plantings, especially between

windows where its height (10–15 feet) does not matter. Another is a flat, prostrate form known only by the catalog name of *repandens*. It makes a splendid accent plant, at gateways, or at the bottom of steps and is one of the hardiest of the English yews. But none of these are really as hardy as the Japanese yew.

This is one of the best all-purpose evergreens, for it will stand more unfavorable conditions than most others. In its native country it is a magnificent tree, often 50 feet high, but cultivated trees rarely reach this. It has darker green, more lustrous foliage than most evergreens and is hence superb as a background for other plantings, especially red-berried shrubs. Such a combination against winter snow is most effective.

It is, however, in its horticultural varieties and hybrids that the Japanese yew finds its greatest usefulness. These must be ordered by their catalog names, and the following are noteworthy:

Taxus cuspidata nana. A fine shrubby form suitable for large-scale plantings to enclose a service yard, etc. One can also shear it into large cubes, oblongs and other architectural features.

Taxus cuspidata densa. A densely compact form, never over 3 feet tall, and a fine accent plant.

Taxus media hicksi. A columnar form best suited for making one of the finest evergreen hedges, as it is easily sheared.

There are several other kinds of yew, one of them native in our northeastern woods (nursery catalog name = *Taxus canadensis*). It is a not quite prostrate shrub, and will make large patches, but it must be grown in cool regions, preferably under the shade of trees. In such places it can be made into a delightful ground cover for a wild garden.

3. *Cedars and Junipers.* When the settlers landed in New England they first saw our common red cedar, and quite naturally called it that because it looked like the cedars they were used to. But these were mostly trees like the Atlas cedar and the Cedar of Lebanon, neither of which grows wild in the New World, nor are they related to our red cedar because they belong to a different group.

The mistake has persisted to this day and it would be foolish to try and correct it except for the fact that our red cedar and its true relatives are widely grown under their correct Latin name of *Juniperus*—hence juniper, a name universally applied to our semi-desert shrubs and trees from New Mexico and Arizona.

All of the plants here treated—and they are among the most grown of all evergreens—belong to this group known as *Juniperus*, no matter whether their common name be juniper or cedar. By whatever name, they are among the most drought-resistant and hardy of our evergreens, with one or two exceptions that will be noted.

Scarcely any group of evergreens have such a diversity of outline as the junipers. They come, as outlined briefly in Chapter II, in many forms and hence are suited for accents, border screens, framing a vista or as specimen plants on the lawn. Most of the more desirable varieties are derived from only three of the many species in cultivation. These have such attractive garden possibilities that it is worth becoming familiar with them. They are: (a) common juniper, (b) Chinese juniper, (c) red cedar.

All of these may have two kinds of leaves, sometimes on the same plant, or again on different plants of the same variety. Some leaves are needle-like, short, rather prickly and stand out from the twigs. Other twigs, or sometimes the whole plant, will have only very small, scale-like leaves pressed closely against the twigs. In choosing plants for purchase it is well to observe which type of leaf the plant bears, for the foliage aspect of the two is very different. The needle-like, divaricate leaves tend to create a bushier type of aspect, while the scale-like types depend for their beauty on the many, slender twigs which, at a distance, appear to have no leaves—only densely clothed twigs. The latter type is particularly common in some weeping forms.

COMMON JUNIPER. In its natural form this is a small tree, never over 40 feet high, spreading in habit and of such little distinction that it is not much cultivated. But its varieties are widely grown not only for their beauty but because they constitute one of the hardiest of junipers. The chief varieties, all of which had better be ordered by their catalog names, are:

Juniperus communis hibernica. The Irish juniper is a tall, slender, columnar form, admirable as an accent plant. In pairs they can be beautiful evergreen sentinels at gateways, path entrances, or as part of a foundation planting.

Juniperus communis depressa. A low-spreading form, never over 3–4 feet and useful to plant in masses as a ground cover. A form of it comes with the young growth yellow.

Juniperus communis pendula. An extremely graceful, upright form, the tips of all its branches and twigs drooping.

Of these three the Irish juniper is the most widely used for its almost architectural formality. As an accent plant it has few rivals, and even in small places it can be used to give a dash of elegance to winter scenes. Not for city planting.

CHINESE JUNIPER. In China, Japan and Mongolia this is a tree 40–60 feet high, but is little grown here in its original form. More than almost any other juniper it has given rise to many horticultural forms, in fact far too many to list here. The outstanding ones, all of which must be ordered by their catalog names, are:

Juniperus chinensis pfitzeriana. Although this is the correct Latin name of this superlative juniper, it is known to many nurserymen simply as *Juniperus pfitzeriana.* It is a prostrate form with obliquely ascending branches, which make mature plants look like a very large bird's nest. Full grown plants may be 10 feet across but not usually more than 3–5 feet high. It will stand abuse more than most evergreens.

Juniperus chinensis variegata. A bushy, shrub-like form, the tips of the branches white, or in a variant, golden yellow.

Juniperus chinensis pyramidalis. An upright, almost columnar form, the foliage greenish-gray.

Juniperus chinensis globosa. A dwarf, ball-like, compact plant, rather prickly because it bears only needle-like leaves.

RED CEDAR. This is one of the commonest of our wild evergreen trees of the eastern states, and the most hardy of all the junipers. It stretches from the cool provinces of Canada to the hot dry sands of Florida, and west to the Rocky Mountains. When mature its outline is almost exactly the shape of a candle flame; but very old trees, which may reach 50 feet, tend to spread, making them broadly pyramidal. They are excellent for border plantings, and individually they make superb lawn specimens.

The red cedar may be dug from the wild, but only very small specimens should be attempted—not over 2 feet high. Larger ones nearly always fail unless dug in winter with a large ball of earth. In attempting to dig plants from the wild see that no roots are exposed to the sun and wind. Wrap them in wet bagging as a protection and water frequently the first year after planting. Nursery-purchased plants will have been root-pruned and come with tight, canvas-packed balls of earth for successful planting. For details see Chapter VII.

While the red cedar has a few horticultural forms (golden-yellow, white-tipped, silvery-gray, etc.), the forms found in the common juniper and Chinese juniper, noted previously, are better for garden purposes.

4. *The Pines.* All the pines, more than 80 different kinds, have a single usually straight trunk, and the branches are arranged in tiers. They are among our most magnificent evergreen trees and all of

them have their long, needle-like slender leaves in clusters of 2–5, surrounded at the base by a parchment-like sheath. While they are of outstanding value as timber, their garden uses are equally as important. So popular are they in cultivation that over 40 different kinds are known in American gardens, but of these only a selection is possible here. Those interested in other kinds will find a much more extended account of them in *Taylor's Encyclopedia of Gardening* and in L. H. Bailey's *Cultivated Evergreens.*

Next to the junipers the pines are among the most hardy of our evergreens, some kinds growing in Canada and many others along the Gulf Coast, in the Rocky Mountains, and particularly along the Pacific Coast, especially in the Sierras and Cascades.

From there, and some foreign ones, it is possible but difficult, because of the many superb kinds, to make a selection for the average amateur gardener. They have been selected for hardiness, adaptability under cultivation and especially for their beauty of outline or foliage. Two of them, as noted subsequently, are even adapted to better sites in cities, and to most suburbs. Those selected are: (a) white pine, (b) Scotch pine, (c) Japanese black pine, (d) Austrian pine, (e) Swiss mountain pine, (f) Japanese red pine.

There are no finer evergreens for border planting, to screen out undesirable views, prevent off-property headlight glare, and to make a garden attractive in winter than the pines, especially those marked a, b, c and f in the list above. All of them become big trees and have dense foliage, especially the Japanese Black Pine. Few pines have the architectural symmetry of yews or junipers, but they have grandeur and scale, and they make the best kind of protective screen against bitter north winds.

WHITE PINE. Much of the wealth of colonial New England came from the exploitation of this, the most valuable timber tree of the eastern states. Nothing remains today but second or third-growth stands, and little did our timber barons care that they were destroying one of our finest evergreen treasures. It has, in the open, a flat, tier-like system of branching, a spire-like crown, and, as one writer has aptly put it, an outline not unlike a Chinese pagoda. The needles (5 in a sheath) are soft, bluish-green, and its candle-shaped cones 6–8 inches long. It is fairly quick-growing and may reach a height of 100 feet or more. It is tolerant of many kinds of soil, but not of smoke, dust, wind and city streets.

In rural gardens and in the real country, the white pine is perhaps our finest evergreen. In masses they make almost cathedral-like stillness and equally cathedral-like shadows. One reservation in northeastern Connecticut and another at Heart's Content, Pennsylvania, can still give the visitor some idea of the awesome grandeur of this incomparable evergreen. A cultural note worth remembering is that the carpet of dead needles under the tree makes the soil so acid that practically nothing will grow under the white pine.

SCOTCH PINE. A hardy, Eurasian evergreen useful in the north, especially in open windy places. Unlike most pines it tends to make branching trunks, the tips of the branches somewhat drooping. Ultimately the tree becomes broad and round-topped in outline, while in youth it is typically spire-like. Its cinnamon-reddish, stringy bark is attractive, and it has few rivals among evergreens in growing well and rapidly in poor soils. As a windbreak or border screen it is fine, but it is not primarily a tree for lawn specimens.

JAPANESE BLACK PINE. A densely foliaged evergreen, the stiff, sharp dark green needles crowded on the twigs. It becomes a tall (90–100 feet) tree with a broadly pyramidal crown forming an impenetrable screen. It grows rapidly and does well close to the sea, where winter winds and even occasional salt spray do not injure it. It is, together with the Austrian pine, the best of all pines for windy and dusty suburbs and has even done well in cities if they are not too full of smoke.

AUSTRIAN PINE. Resembles the one preceding, but the foliage is thinner, and hence it does not make such a dense screen. Its great virtue is that it is probably our best evergreen in thoroughly unfavorable sites.

SWISS MOUNTAIN PINE (Nursery catalog name = *Pinus mugo*). A variable European pine, often there a tree, but most cultivated here in the variety known as *mughus* which is a dense, almost prostrate shrub. It is splendid as a ground cover, especially on north-facing slopes, and as flat accent plants. Do not plant it on steep, south-facing slopes, as late winter sun and heat may be unfavorable. It may spread as much as 8–10 feet across, but will not usually be more than 3–4 feet high.

JAPANESE RED PINE. Of fairly recent introduction and hardy up into Canada, but not well suited to the warm regions of the southeast. It is a quick-growing pine, often reaching a height of 20 feet in 15 years. The needles are bluish-green, nearly 5 inches long and rather sharp-pointed. Ultimately the tree will form a picturesque open-headed crown. A variety of it, the Japanese Umbrella pine or Tanyosho, is a dwarf form having an umbrella-shaped crown. It is a very fine accent plant or lawn specimen.

5. *Hemlocks.* The evergreens casting the deepest shade are unquestionably the hemlocks, especially the two included here. Nothing will grow under mature trees, partly because of the shade but also because of the highly acid residue of the dead needles.

The leaves are small, needle-like and are arranged in such fashion that the twigs, with their leaves, are in flat fan-like clusters. These tend to droop at the tips, giving the foliage a feathery, soft texture that is most attractive. Both the kinds below stand shearing very well so that either of them, if sheared young enough, can be made into superb evergreen hedges. Their more common use, however, is as lawn specimens, if there is room for them; and either kind make wonderful evergreen borders or a frame for a vista.

Within the range of both kinds they are perfectly hardy, but throughout the middle west and in the prairie states they will either not survive at all or be miserable trees fighting against summer heat, deficient rainfall and drying winds. Neither sort should ever be planted near cities and only in smoke-free and dust-free suburbs.

The common hemlock of the northeastern states is naturally at home throughout that area and will thrive if planted in reasonably moist places, and in drier ones if they are protected from the wind, especially while young. Few evergreens make more attractive border planting, their pliable branches and feathery foliage swaying most gracefully in any light breeze.

Its close relative, the Carolina hemlock, is wild from the mountains of Virginia to Georgia, and, although hardy north to Boston, it is best planted from Philadelphia southward. Near Washington, D.C., there is a marvelous hedge of it, over half a mile long, about 10 feet high and nearly as thick. But even this southern sort does not like the hot sandy coastal plain of the southeast, preferring cool mountains.

6. *Spruces.* These are the spire-like evergreens that one sees in northern New England villages, along the cool Maine coast, and on the rocky islands off it, stretching finally far north into eastern Canada. If these were the only kinds grown in gardens, spruce culture would be much more restricted than it is. Actually more than thirty species and scores of varieties are grown in this country, many of the best of them from northern Europe or from China and Japan. Some of the horticultural forms, such as the blue spruce, are among our most widely planted evergreens. Others, as in the cedars and yews, already noted, have varieties that look nothing like the parent tree—some prostrate, ball-like, columnar or bushy, and still others with a

variety of colored foliage. Only five main sorts are included here, together with some of the best of their horticultural forms. Spruces do not like heat, dryness, smoke, dust and wind.

NORWAY SPRUCE. A tall, dark-foliaged evergreen, often reaching 80–100 feet in height, generally spire-like in outline, but the ends of the branches drooping. It is one of the most widely planted evergreens in the country, perhaps because it is the spruce most adaptable to unfavorable conditions. Splendid as part of a border screen and especially to frame a vista. More than any other evergreen it is so prolific in horticultural forms that over thirty are known here, and many more abroad. Of these the following are most likely to be interesting for special purposes. All of them must be ordered by their catalog names.

Picea abies argentea. Tree-like, with variegated foliage.

Picea abies aurea. Foliage golden yellow.

Picea abies compacta. Low, dense, almost globe-shaped.

Picea abies pendula. Medium-sized, shrub-like, and with drooping branches.

Picea abies conica. Almost perfectly cone-shaped, but dwarf. An excellent accent plant. See Chapter II.

Picea abies procumbens. Prostrate, and a good ground cover.

ENGELMANN'S SPRUCE. A densely foliaged, almost perfectly pyramidal evergreen, the lower branches practically touching the ground. Leaves not so prickly as in some spruces, pale bluish-green. An extremely fine tree, perfectly hardy up into Canada, but not well suited to the south. There are several garden forms with colored foliage, but they are not as fine as varieties found among the Norway or White spruces.

WHITE SPRUCE. An American spruce found everywhere in northern United States and Canada, but also enduring considerable heat and drought. It reaches heights of 60–70 feet, and is mostly grown for its beautiful, bluish-green foliage, and its habit of having ascending branches, the tips of which, however, nearly always droop. It is hence a fine evergreen for northern vistas. Two varieties are important, both of which must be ordered by their catalog names:

Picea glauca albertiana, the Black Hills spruce, is a geographical variety best suited to the northern plains states.

Picea glauca conica, a perfectly cone-shaped dwarf form, used widely as an accent plant, and so small it can be grown among the plants in a rock garden without dwarfing them.

TIGERTAIL SPRUCE. A remarkable Japanese evergreen tree, over 100 feet high in the wild, but considerably less as cultivated. It has stiff, very prickly, dark, glossy-green leaves, very densely crowded on the stiff twigs. So impenetrable and spiny is this habit that a well-planted border screen of tigertail spruce would be as effective a barrier as barbed wire entanglements. Not quite hardy north of southern Ontario.

BLUE SPRUCE. This native, Rocky Mountain evergreen, especially in the form known as Koster's Blue Spruce, is *the* evergreen if one wants perfectly pyramidal or spire-like outline, coupled with bluish-gray foliage. The needles are prickly, nearly 1½ inches long, and densely crowded on the branches, which, in mature plants, sweep the ground. Koster's Blue Spruce is thus one of the most popular lawn evergreens in America and it deserves it, both for beauty and the fact that it will stand fairly unfavorable conditions. In cultivation it may reach 60–80 feet, usually less. In Colorado it frequently reaches 100–125 feet and is a magnificent evergreen.

7. *Firs.* The last evergreen to give way to perpetual ice and snow, as one goes northward, is our native balsam fir, the best of all Christmas trees. This never has taken kindly to cultivation, but all the rest of the firs are either from northern Europe and Asia or from the Rockies or Sierras where they are among the noblest evergreens. No one should ever attempt to grow firs in the south or near any city, or on the Great Plains, and some don't like *any* lowland or sea-level locality.

Because of these climatic restrictions only three of the most satisfactory of those cultivated will be listed here, although there are over 20 species known to be in American gardens. Firs are by some mistaken for spruces, but in the latter the cones hang down, while in firs they are erect, almost candle-like.

Firs are the aristocrats of the evergreen world, not only for their distinction of habit, but because they are just as particular as to soil and site as a patrician is to his environment. The place must be well drained, the soil loose, never water-soaked, and yet there must be an adequate water supply, for they will not thrive in drought or heat. They, more than any other evergreens, are perfect for framing a vista, or for their beautiful outline as lawn specimens—like a candle-flame or church spire in outline. Not many horticultural forms have been developed, perhaps because the species themselves are so fine, but also because of the exacting demands of firs in general. The three most easily cultivated are:

WHITE FIR (Nursery catalog name = *Abies concolor*). This is one of the most satisfying of all cultivated firs, and while it comes from the mountains of Colorado and south of it, the tree thrives in the eastern states (with the restrictions noted previously). In its own home the tree may be 120 feet high, but usually half this in cultivation and often much less. It has bluish-green needles and showy, greenish-purple, erect cones often 5 inches long. There is one form, known as *globosa*, which is dwarf, nearly the outline of a ball, and a popular accent plant. See Chapter II.

NORDMANN FIR. An evergreen from the mountains of southeastern Europe and Asia Minor, but perfectly hardy (with restrictions noted previously) up to southern Ontario. It may reach 60–70 feet high in cultivation, but double that in its own home. It is perfectly spire-like in outline, densely branched and has dark green foliage. As in most cultivated firs, if let alone, without trimming, its lowest branches will sweep the ground—an extremely attractive feature of many other evergreen trees. There are no important horticultural forms.

VEITCH'S FIR. This Japanese evergreen is lower than the other two, and is hence recommended for gardens that may be too small for the larger kinds. It is broadly pyramidal in outline and, with its shining green foliage, is a handsome evergreen. Not the least part of its virtues, to the amateur, is that it can be grown in many gardens that would not be fit for any other firs. It is one of the most shapely of evergreens when young.

8. *Arborvitae.* The flat, fan-like sprays of this evergreen make it a favorite in all gardens. The tree (for it is a tree in its natural home in the hills and mountains of northeastern America) is commonly but incorrectly called white cedar, perhaps because of its reddish, stringy cedar-like bark. But it has nothing to do with our common red cedar, already noted in Section 3 of this chapter.

As a tree the arborvitae may reach 50–70 feet, but it is rarely grown in this form because it may have an open crown, or a narrow, compact head. From the garden standpoint the arborvitae is hence far more useful and attractive in its numerous horticultural forms than is the parent (tree) type. These garden forms, also, have the advantage of being comparatively indifferent of conditions that would interdict most evergreens. All those mentioned below are perfectly adaptable to gardens from Canada to Charleston, South Carolina and westward to the Alleghenies. In the central states they need more watering, and on the Great Plains they are impossible without irrigation. Do not plant them in any city garden.

The horticultural or garden forms are legion, over 35 varieties being known in American gardens, and still more in England. For accents, framing contrived vistas, screening a play space or service yard, and as hedges, there is no finer evergreen than arborvitae. The parent tree is properly known as *Thuja occidentalis*. To that is added a variety name which it is essential to use in ordering any of the following recommended garden varieties.

Alba. Tips of young foliage white.

Columbia. Foliage variegated with silver.

compacta. Dense low form, useful as ground cover.

fastigiata. A columnar shrub with densely clothed, erect branches. It makes superb hedges, and can be sheared into any architectural form. An extremely useful accent plant. See Chapter II.

hoveyi. A dwarf, perfectly globe-shaped shrub.

umbraculifera. A dwarf form with an umbrella-like outline. Useful as formal accent plant.

vervaeneana. A small shrub, compacted with dense, bronzy foliage. A beautiful plant, but as in all colored or variegated-leaved specimens to be used with restraint. Too many of them will give any garden that bargain-basement look.

9. *Italian Cypress: Sawara Cypress.* These quite different evergreens are both known as cypress, but the term rightly belongs only to the Italian cypress (and its relatives) which is certainly the tree of old Mediterranean gardens, the praises of which have been sung from Homer to yesterday.

There is no other evergreen in the world that is so straight, slender and columnar as the Italian cypress and nothing more impressive than a mile-long vista framed by these majestic trees, which may reach 70 feet. Unhappily, it is never safe to grow it north of Norfolk, Virginia, in the east; it is wholly unsuited to the middle west, Great Plains or Rocky Mountains; but there are beautiful specimens in California where it seems perfectly at home—perhaps like the subtropical orange, wine grape, fig and the apricot. It is rather important, if one wants to duplicate the effects seen so often in Italy (and California) to use the exact catalog name of this tree, which is *Cupressus sempervirens stricta,* the branches of which always turn up, and hence preserve the slender columnar habit. Sometimes the parent tree tends to have a more open type of branching, which would be fatal, perhaps years hence, to the very object that one expects from the Italian cypress. See the accounts of Vistas in Chapter II.

There are several relatives of the Italian cypress native in our own northwest, but most of them are unsuited to the Atlantic seaboard, the only exception being the Macnab or Shasta cypress from northern California and Oregon. It is a bushy tree, not over 35 feet high, and not in the least like the Italian cypress. Not certainly hardy north of New York.

The Sawara cypress is a very different plant to which Pliny applied the technical name of *Chamaecyparis*, or literally "ground cypress," perhaps because its foliage resembled the Italian cypress and the one he knew was prostrate. At any rate the name has stuck ever since and it is essential to use it for the Sawara cypress, which is a Japanese plant known here only since the Civil War, and for its close relatives that cannot be detailed here. Most unfortunately many nurserymen continue to call *Chamaecyparis* by the other and confusing name of *Retinospora*. Hence, you must look under both names in many nursery catalogs in order to find the Sawara cypress.

In Japan it becomes a not very distinguished evergreen, nearly 100 feet tall, rather open branching, and with the bad habit of losing its lower branches in age. No one would cultivate it in this parent form, for, as we have seen, there are far better evergreens. But it has given rise to many garden forms of outstanding importance. Of these the ones following are best suited for the purposes outlined at each, and they must be ordered by the technical name. All of them are hardy from Ontario southward. There are fine specimens at Miami and New Orleans, but it will not stand the deficient summer rainfall and bitter winter winds of the Great Plains. Nor should they be grown in cities. The varieties most worth growing, all derived from the Sawara cypress (*Chamaecyparis pisifera*), are known by the following varietal names:

aurea. With golden foliage.

sulphurea. With sulphur-yellow foliage.

filifera. The twigs and foliage thread-like and pendulous. A very handsome drooping evergreen.

plumosa. With a perfectly cone-shaped outline and with delicate, lace-like, plumy foliage. Sometimes the plant is almost the shape of a candle flame, and is fine for lawn specimens or as an accent plant. See Chapter II.

squarrosa. A small, bushy tree or shrub with spreading, almost feathery foliage, which is bluish-green above but silvery beneath.

SUMMARY

Although the evergreens are the outstanding shrubs and trees to give all-the-year permanence in the garden, it may have struck the reader that in spite of the restricted lists given the number of forms is great and that their identity is difficult. To simplify the material into the main uses of the evergreens, a good many of them have been rearranged below. It is understood that such a simplification cannot repeat the details of hardiness, culture, and so forth, already outlined, and you must turn to one of the nine sections to which all of them belong for these details. The figures after the names (in brackets) refer directly to the sections in this chapter.

1. For the garden frame; for screens and as windbreaks
    Japanese Yew (2)
    White Pine (4)
    Scotch Pine (4)
    Hemlock (5)
    Norway Spruce (6)
    White Spruce (6)
2. For framing natural vistas (see Chapter II)
    White Pine (4)
    Hemlock (5)
    Norway Spruce (6)
    White Spruce (6)
    White Fir (7)
    Veitch's Fir (7)
    Italian Cypress (9)
3. Prostrate or low ground covers
    English Yew, variety *repandens* (2)
    Taxus canadensis (2)
    Common Juniper, variety *depressa* (3)
    Chinese Juniper, variety *pfitzeriana* (3)
    Swiss Mountain Pine, variety *mughus* (4)
    Norway Spruce, variety *procumbens* (6)
    White Spruce, variety *conica* (6)
    Arborvitae, variety *compacta* (8)
4. For hedges, or other formal shapes. Plants can easily be sheared
    Taxus media hicksi (2)
    Carolina Hemlock (5)
    Arborvitae (8)
5. Columnar, slender and upright
    Irish Yew (2)
    Irish Juniper (3)
    Chinese Juniper, variety *pyramidalis* (3)
    Arborvitae, variety *fastigiata* (8)
    Italian Cypress (9)

6. With drooping twigs or branches, or both, hence nearly "weeping"
    Chinese Juniper, variety *pendula* (3)
    Norway Spruce, variety *pendula* (6)
    Sawara Cypress, variety *filifera* (9)
7. Cone-shaped or pyramidal evergreens
    Red Cedar (3)
    Norway Spruce, variety *conica* (6)
    White Spruce, variety *conica* (6)
    Sawara Cypress, variety *plumosa* (9)
8. Globe-shaped; naturally or by shearing
    Chinese Juniper, variety *globosa* (3)
    Norway Spruce, variety *compacta* (6)
    White Fir, variety *globosa* (7)
    Arborvitae, variety *hoveyi* (8)
9. For street and suburban planting
    Ginkgo (1)
    Japanese Black Pine (4)
    Austrian Pine (4)
10. Some accent plants
    Japanese Yew, variety *nana* (2)
    Irish Yew (2)
    Irish Juniper (3)
    Japanese Umbrella Pine (4)
    White Spruce, variety *conica* (6)
    Also most of those listed at cone-shaped and globe-shaped.

Shrubs for Color and Winter Effects

CHAPTER VI ℭHE OBJECTION that many people have to a green garden, which is what *The Permanent Garden* was written to advocate, is that there is no such riot of color as in pretty beds or borders crammed with beautiful annuals or perennials.

This is partly true, but not wholly so, because from wisely chosen shrubs it is possible to have permanence for good and color for practically all the growing season. While, as we have seen in the chapters on trees and evergreens, these must always be the most important contributors to permanence in the garden, they, with the exception of a few flowering trees, contribute practically no color but green.

It is precisely at this juncture of garden planning that the initiated turn to shrubs, in spite of the bewildering complexity of them, their great differences in height, color of flowers, period of bloom and cultural requirements. Also, some are grown chiefly for the winter color of their fruits. It will simplify matters at once to separate (1) those that lose their leaves in the fall, from (2) the broad-leaved evergreens, and finally (3) those rather specialized shrubs classed as rhododendrons and azaleas.

1. SHRUBS THAT LOSE THEIR LEAVES
IN WINTER (deciduous)

In Chapter I the necessity of making an underplanting of shrubs if you want privacy in the garden was emphasized, not to weary the reader with a commonplace, but because without shrubs your permanent garden will lack both color and a proper underplanting, no matter how well you have planned your tree locations. And, if you cannot use evergreens for screening service yards, play spaces, etc., shrubs will be essential for such purposes. Also, many of them are useful in foundation-planting, but their chief use is to give color, and sometimes fragrance, in the otherwise green garden.

Their functions are therefore threefold, (1) for screening and underplanting, (2) for foundation planting and (3) to provide color in the garden. Perhaps the most important feature of the latter is *when* the color will be obvious. Everyone admires the rush of bloom that comes in May and June, but what of March or September? And do any bloom in winter?

It is to answer these questions that the shrubs selected for inclusion here are arranged according to their usual period of bloom, taking the region approximately on the fortieth parallel as the center. This includes roughly New York-Philadelphia, Pittsburgh-Columbus, Indianapolis, St. Joseph, (Missouri) and Denver. In areas north of this, flowering will be later, and south of it, earlier. Also any considerable elevation or proximity to cool sea-water will retard the flowering of most shrubs.

There are hundreds of different kinds of shrubs cultivated in the United States and as many more horticultural forms and varieties. Only a selection of the better and most available kinds are included here. Wherever possible their common English names are used, and if, for accuracy in ordering, only the Latin name is safe, it is given. Sometimes both are necessary, in which case the Latin or catalog name will be in brackets. It is surprising that some very well known shrubs like *Deutzia* and *Rhododendron* have no valid English names.

All the shrubs below are hardy from Canada to the Gulf of Mexico unless there is a special warning to the contrary. To save space certain shrubs are marked thus:

* = Suitable for underplanting of garden frame of trees; and to screen service yard, play space, or other features.

† = Suitable for foundation-planting. See pages 33–35.

It will be noted that some plants appear in more than one place in the lists. This is necessary because some groups have either multiple uses or flower over a longer period than the time of their first opening of flowers. Remember, also, that a particularly "open" winter will bring some plants into flower earlier than indicated, and a correspondingly "late" winter will, of course, retard them. The times are thus the best average that is possible.

JANUARY–MARCH

* JAPANESE WITCH-HAZEL. 5–20 feet high. Its bright yellow flowers borne on naked branches.

* CHINESE HONEYSUCKLE (*Lonicera fragrantissima*). 8–10 feet high.
Flowers small, very numerous, and deliciously fragrant. A desirable accent plant. Not hardy north of Boston.

FEBRUARY–MARCH

† WINTER JASMINE. 2–4 feet high. Flowers yellow, on bare, greenish
    arching branches. Not hardy north of Boston.
* CORNELIAN CHERRY. 10–15 feet high and sometimes tree-like.
    Flowers small, profuse, yellow and covering the bare twigs.

MARCH–APRIL

STAR MAGNOLIA. 4–10 feet high, and sometimes more. Flowers
    white, showy, fragrant and nearly 3 inches wide, sometimes
blasted by late frosts. A fine accent plant but must be moved with
a ball of earth. See Chapter VII.
* FORSYTHIA. 6–10 feet high. Get the hybrid known as *intermedia* as
    it has far more and larger yellow flowers than the others. It
blooms before or with the unfolding of the leaves.
† JAPANESE FLOWERING QUINCE. 4–6 feet high. Flowers solitary or in
    small clusters, scarlet-red and very showy. White and pink-
flowered forms are also available.
DOUBLE-FLOWERED PEACH. 5–8 feet. Beautiful deep red double
    flowers borne on naked branches. A fine accent plant. See
Chapter II.

APRIL

BRIDAL WREATH SPIREA. 5–8 feet high. A round-headed bush com-
    pletely covered with clusters of small white flowers.
* JAPANESE FLOWERING CHERRIES. Shrubby forms, not over 8–12 feet
    high. Flowers pink, rose-pink or white. See also Flowering
Trees in Chapter IV.
† VIBURNUM CARLESI. 3–5 feet high. Fragrant white flowers in dense
    clusters.

MAY

* PEAR HAW (*Crataegus tomentosa*). 10–15 feet. Flowers white, re-
    sembling apple-blossoms but smaller.
* COCKSPUR THORN. 10–20 feet, sometimes a small tree, and very
    thorny. Flowers white. See also Flowering Trees in Chap-
ter IV.
BLUE DOGWOOD (*Cornus alternifolia*). 8–10 feet. Flowers small,
    white, very numerous in flat-topped clusters.
† JAPANESE BARBERRY. 3–5 feet. Flowers yellow, tinged with red,

small, not very showy, but autumnal color of foliage scarlet.

* LILAC. 8–15 feet. There are scores of named hybrids, single or double-flowered, and ranging in color from white, through lilac, pink, purple and violet.

† SPIRAEA ARGUTA. 4–5 feet. Tiny white flowers in profuse clusters that cover the bush.

† FLOWERING ALMOND. 3–5 feet. A beautiful shrub, its branches covered with a profusion of pink bloom.

DOUBLE-FLOWERED POMEGRANATE. 6–9 feet. A showy shrub with double, red flowers, and glossy green leaves. A beautiful accent plant but not hardy north of Washington, D.C.

MAY–JUNE

ROSA RUGOSA. 4–5 feet. Covered with single pink or white flowers. Does not need the care of finer cultivated roses and will live in sand along coastal dunes.

ROSA HUGONIS. 6–8 feet. Fine, Chinese, single rose, easily cultivated in any garden. Flowers yellow, about 2 inches wide. No tea, or other special classes of highly cultivated roses are included here, because they require culture in specially prepared beds.

* WEIGELA. 8–12 feet. A good variety is Eva Rathke, with deep red flowers, or *florida* with rose-pink or white flowers.

† DEUTZIA GRACILIS. 3–5 feet. Covered with a profusion of small white flowers.

DEUTZIA LEMOINEI. 5–7 feet. A variety of this profusely blooming shrub that is especially recommended is Boule de Neige, with white flowers.

JUNE

† JAPANESE SPIRAEA. 4–6 feet. An upright shrub, its small pink flowers in much-branched loose clusters.

* CRANBERRY TREE. 8–12 feet. In spite of its common name, a shrub with a profusion of white flowers. A double-flowered, sterile form with large globe-shaped flower clusters is the Snowball or Guelder rose.

GREEN OSIER. 3–8 feet. A small white-flowered shrub, grown mostly for its bluish fruit which are more handsome than the flowers.

MAGNOLIA VIRGINIANA. 5–10 feet, but a tree in the deep south. Flowers white, deliciously fragrant with a spicy odor. Prefers low moist places.

† SCOTCH ROSE. 2–4 feet. A densely spiny and bristly shrub with old-

fashioned pink, single flowers. There are also yellow and white-flowered forms.

* MOCK-ORANGE. 8–10 feet. A handsome, upright or arching shrub with many fragrant white, almost bell-shaped, flowers. There are several other varieties.

BEAUTY-BUSH. 4–6 feet. A profusely blooming Chinese shrub, its pink flowers in flattish clusters. The corolla is yellow inside.

* DEUTZIA, Pride of Rochester. 6–8 feet. An extremely handsome shrub with a profusion of shell-pink or pinkish-white, double flowers.

† SNOWBERRY. 2–4 feet. A pinkish-flowered shrub. Grown, however, for its persistent, white, berry-like fruit which hangs on most of the winter. Will stand city smoke.

JULY–AUGUST

INDIAN CURRANT. 5–8 feet. Resembling the last, but taller and with white flowers that bloom a little later. Fruit persistent, red and berry-like.

† HORTENSIA. 3–4 feet. A Japanese hydrangea with globe-shaped clusters of pink, white or pale blue flowers. A particularly fine form has deep blue flowers. Not certainly hardy north of New York.

† SPIRAEA BILLIARDI. 4–6 feet. A densely flowered shrub, the small, bright rose-red flowers in open, branching clusters.

† SPIRAEA ANTHONY WATERER. 2–4 feet. Flowers crimson in showy clusters. A fine accent of color on a lawn.

* MOUNTAIN CAMELLIA (*Stewartia pentagyna*). 10–15 feet. A hardy relative of the camellia with waxy, white flowers nearly 3 inches across. Prefers partial shade, as under a border screen.

CHASTE TREE. 6–10 feet. A wand-like shrub with slender spikes of lilac-blue flowers. In the north it sometimes dies down to the ground, but new shoots of the next summer ordinarily produce flowers. There is also a white-flowered form.

* HYDRANGEA PANICULATA GRANDIFLORA. 8–12 feet. This is the common, summer-blooming hydrangea, with very large, ball-like clusters of white flowers that turn bronzy in September.

WHITE JASMINE. A beautifully fragrant, weak-stemmed shrub, with almost vine-like branches. Flowers white, perhaps the most fragrant of all cultivated plants. Not certainly hardy north of Delaware.

† HYPERICUM AUREUM. 2–3 feet. A shrub with reddish, peeling bark, its flowers bright yellow, nearly 2 inches across.

* CRAPE MYRTLE. 10–25 feet. A magnificently floriferous shrub, with
    white, pink or red flowers in large, lilac-like clusters. A selec-
tion of varieties will extend the blooming period from mid-July to
early September. Not certainly hardy north of Washington, D.C.

BUTTERFLY BUSH (*Buddleia davidi*). 4–10 feet, or less if they are
    cut back for the winter, as is sometimes necessary in the north.
Flowers in nodding clusters, fragrant, lilac, but orange inside the
corolla. Leaves white and felty on the underside.

* TAMARIX GALLICA. 10–15 feet or more if it becomes tree-like as it
    may in the south. A slender branched shrub with myriads of
minute pink flowers, the whole shrub looking from a distance like a
pink haze.

ROSE-OF-SHARON. 5–15 feet. An open-branched shrub, in the typical
    form reddish-purple, a color that is anathema to some. There
are, however, very beautiful white forms, known as "Jeanne d'Arc,"
which is double-flowered, and "Snowstorm" with single flowers.

† BEAUTY-BERRY (*Callicarpa japonica*). 3–4 feet. Flowers white or
    pinkish, but not remarkable as the plant is chiefly grown for
its profusion of showy violet fruit.

AUGUST–SEPTEMBER

* AESCULUS PARVIFLORA. 8–15 feet. A kind of shrubby horse-chestnut
    with showy white flowers. Also a valuable lawn specimen.
Not certainly hardy north of Boston. See also Flowering Trees in
Chapter IV.

TAMARIX PENTANDRA. 10–15 feet. A slender-branched shrub, its
    thread-like, often drooping twigs with enormous numbers of
minute, pink flowers, in dense, finger-shaped clusters.

SEPTEMBER–OCTOBER

† BLUE SPIREA (*Caryopteris mastacanthus*). 2–5 feet. A half-tender
    shrub, with beautiful clusters of showy, blue flowers. It is not
certainly hardy north of Delaware, but is often grown north of this,
and if it winter-kills it is cut down to the base. Next year's shoots
will usually bloom if frost has not been too severe. A very handsome
late-flowering shrub.

HYPERICUM DENSIFLORUM. 4–6 feet. A partly evergreen native
    American shrub. Flowers yellow, in dense clusters.

ELSHOLTZIA STAUNTONI. 2–4 feet. A low, shrubby plant with beau-
    tiful lavender flowers in one-sided spikes that are nearly 12
inches long. Not certainly hardy north of Boston.

OCTOBER–NOVEMBER

* AMERICAN WITCH-HAZEL. 10–15 feet. A rather coarse-leaved shrub
    valuable because just as the leaves fall, or even when bare,
there are many bright yellow flowers about ¾ inch long. The latest
flowering of all native shrubs. For a January-March-blooming Asiatic
relative, see *January-March*, at the beginning of this list.

There are 53 different shrubs to choose from in the foregoing list
divided as to blooming period as follows:

January to March	4
March to April	4
April and May	11
May and June	14
July and August	14
August–October	5
October–November	1
	53

With all the horticultural varieties that are found among some
shrub groups, the number could easily be doubled. These are to be
looked for, if you want more than the 53, among the following groups,
of which most good nurseries carry a large stock.

Honeysuckles	Deutzias
Spireas	*Cornus*
Japanese Flowering Cherries	Magnolias
Lilacs	Jasmines
Roses	*Virburnum*

When flowers are past it is still possible to get color in the shrub
planting, and a list of those that have berries or other colored fruits
are arranged by color.

Red and Scarlet

Indian currant
Viburnum trilobum. 8–12 feet.
Japanese barberry
Cockspur thorn
Cotoneaster microphylla. 2–4 feet, in prostrate masses.
Black alder (*Ilex verticillata*). 4–5 feet.
Cranberry tree

Blue

Blue dogwood (*Cornus alternifolia*)
Green Osier (*Cornus rugosa*)
Symplocos paniculatus. 10–20 feet.

Orange

   Sea buckthorn (*Hippophae rhamnoides*)

Violet

   Beauty-berry (*Callicarpa japonica*)

White

   Snowberry

All of these are in the foregoing list except those that have the height stated, so that you can estimate whether they will fit into your scheme of planting. There are, also, very showy fruits on the mountain-ash. See Flowering Trees in Chapter IV.

For foundation planting there are 17 of the shrubs that, by stature, period of bloom, habit and color are quite suitable, and all of them are marked with a †. With these, and the evergreens noted in Chapter V, and the broad-leaved evergreens that follow later in this chapter, you will have ample material for the right kind of foundation planting. See Chapter I.

As mentioned in Chapter III on The Small Place there are gardens too small for many trees, and often the larger shrubs in the foregoing list will be out of place. Such gardens can be beautiful by picking out from the list those shrubs that are not too big. Lack of space will often make a border screen impossible, which means that hedges and vines will have to be relied upon. The former will separate your property from your neighbor's, or from the street, and the latter often give color and graceful furnishing for porches, arbors, etc.

HEDGE PLANTS

In the account of the evergreens in Chapter V there were a few outstanding hedge plants. But they are expensive, usually slow growing and unsuited to many localities. A universal substitute is the California privet, which holds its leaves nearly all winter and is hardy in all but the most severe climates. Its ease of clipping and rapid growth make it the best all-round hedge plant in America.

Many people, however, look for something less common than privet—some plant with more distinction and individuality. For those with a large enough purse and plenty of patience the only answer is boxwood. See Section 2 on The Broad-leaved Evergreens in this chapter.

There are, however, acceptable substitutes among shrubs far less expensive than box, and certainly not so excessively common as privet. For a low, somewhat informal hedge the Japanese barberry is fine, especially attractive all winter for its persistent red berries. Other, taller kinds include the following:

JAPANESE FLOWERING QUINCE. Makes a fine red-flowered hedge, 4–5 feet high. It must be clipped to make a hedge.

BEECH. A tree which must be headed back and clipped to make a hedge 8–10 feet high.

MOCK-ORANGE. Needs careful pruning when young to force out young twigs near the base. A good hedge, 5–8 feet high.

CARAGANA ARBORESCENS. Get a dwarf form of this tree which has yellow, pea-like flowers. It is spiny and the best of all hedge plants for regions of bitter winter winds that are too cold for privet.

VINES

Woody vines are just as permanent as shrubs of which they are merely climbing or scrambling prototypes. They do not have to be planted every year like annual vines such as morning-glory, the gourds or the cup-and-saucer vine. Once planted they are just as permanent as shrubs and trees, but garden pictures can be painted with vines that are impossible with erect plants.

Some of the most attractive uses of vines need to be considered in selecting the limited number that can be dealt with here. Some are ideal for covering walls, the tops of embankments or any other structure that one wants to hide or drape with greenery. Most of these are grown for their foliage. Four of the best are:

ENGLISH IVY. Will climb and stick to brick or stone walls, and is evergreen. It does not like exposure to southern sun and does better in half shade. Also it makes a wonderful ground cover under trees.

EUONYMUS RADICANS. This is probably the best and hardiest of all evergreen vines, but is slow-growing and relatively expensive. Beautiful on walls and fences.

BOSTON IVY. A high-climbing vine which clings firmly to tree trunks, masonry and woodwork. Used for quick effects, but in the north it nearly always drops its leaves in autumn. Easier to grow than the English ivy.

DUTCHMAN'S-PIPE, or sometimes called pipe-vine. A rampant vine with large leaves admirable for covering an arbor or trellis, or to frame, on posts, a doorway. In June it has quite a few, yellowish-brown flowers about 2 inches long, bent like a U.

If, instead of greenery, you want flower color from vines, there is a larger selection, because some of the groups below have many species and varieties. For the beginner, those most worth trying might well be:

Wistaria. Tall-climbing woody vine with beautiful, long, drooping clusters of pea-like flowers in early spring. It is better to choose the Japanese form rather than wild American sorts. In summer prune away most of the long new shoots to induce bloom next year.

Honeysuckle. Of the several twining honeysuckles the best is the Italian honeysuckle, which may scramble up 20 feet or more, or remain on the ground if there is no support. In midsummer it has many, yellowish-white very fragrant flowers followed by rather showy orange fruit. All honeysuckles, if allowed to run wild, may become one of the worst plant pests known to gardeners, completely smothering shrubs and even trees, and often covering the ground for acres!

Clematis. Beautiful woody vines of which over 30 are known in cultivation. Of these the following are most likely to prove useful—all of them with showy flowers:

jackmani superba, dark violet-purple.

Gipsy Queen, dark velvety-purple.

lanuginosa, grayish-white.

Ascotiensis, azure-blue.

Climbing hydrangea (*Hydrangea petiolaris*). A very large woody vine, often climbing 50 feet or more. In midsummer it has showy white-flowered clusters of bloom that may be 6–12 inches wide. Will cling to masonry or tree trunks.

2. THE BROAD-LEAVED EVERGREENS

This is a necessary garden term to distinguish the plants that follow from the true evergreens noted in Chapter V. The broad-leaved evergreens do not bear cones; they do not have needle-like or scale-like leaves; most of them hold their broad leaves all winter; and some of them have spectacularly beautiful flowers. All of them are fairly slow-growing and somewhat expensive, and many of them are among the handsomest of cultivated plants. Nearly all must be moved with a ball of earth, and watered carefully the first year after planting. For details see Chapter VII.

The uses of broad-leaved evergreens in garden design have quite naturally separated them into two general groups—those grown wholly for foliage effects, and those which in addition to evergreen foliage also bear either showy or interesting flowers and often

brightly colored fruits. Of the foliage plants by far the most important is the box, followed by the others listed.

Box. The finest, most slow-growing and expensive broad-leaved evergreen in cultivation. Single plants, 80–90 years old, 8 feet high
and as thick, may cost several hundred dollars. Its close, twiggy
growth and spicy-scented leaves make impenetrable thickets of
greenery, and it was planted at all Virginia manor houses. Dwarf
forms and young plants, however, can be purchased at not too great
cost and can be used for foundation planting or as accents, because
it can easily be sheared, even for hedges. Not hardy north of Boston
unless protected, and unsuited to the deep south. It grows only about
one inch per year.

HOLLY. A beautiful evergreen tree with the margins of the leaf
spiny-toothed. By far the best is the English holly with dark,
spiny leaves, but it is not hardy much north of Philadelphia and
does not like the extreme heat of the deep south. It is also important
to get a female tree, or one grafted for the purpose, to be sure of
getting a crop of its bright red berries at Christmas. If the English
holly is not hardy in your region (it will not thrive in the middle
west), you can substitute the American holly, which has dull green
foliage, bright red berries and is much hardier.

JAPANESE HOLLY (*Ilex crenata*). A beautiful shrub with box-like
foliage but more open branching than the box. Makes an extremely effective screen, and grows far faster than box. Not certainly
hardy north of Boston.

EVERGREEN BARBERRY. In the general list of deciduous shrubs the
Japanese barberry was noted for its scarlet foliage, just before leaf-fall, and its brilliant red berries that persist most of the
winter. But from China there has come since about 1907 many evergreen barberries that were expected to add a large number of broad-
leaved evergreens to American gardens. Experience has shown that
of the score or more species only three are suited to regions from
New York southward, most of the rest being not suited to regions
north of Washington, D.C. The three that have proved hardy are
valuable broad-leaved evergreens that are available at all good nurseries, but not likely to be found at small roadside stands. They make
excellent material for foundation planting. They must be ordered
by the Latin names that follow.

Berberis sargentiana. Not over 5 feet high, with spiny-margined
leaves, yellow flowers and bluish-black fruit.

Berberis julianae. 4–6 feet high, the leaves shiny-margined. Flowers and fruit similar to the one preceding.

Berberis verruculosa. Not over 3 feet high, the leaves only slightly
spiny. Flowers golden yellow followed by bluish-black fruit.

PACHYSANDRA. In many evergreen plantings, among foundation-
planting, and especially under the shade of trees where no
lawn is possible, an extremely valuable evergreen ground cover is
Pachysandra terminalis, sometimes called Japanese spurge. It is a
low, shrubby plant (8–9 inches high) with a crown of dark green
leaves which stay green all winter. Planted by the hundreds (they
are comparatively cheap), they make one of the finest ground covers
for shady places.

The broad-leaved evergreens grown both for foliage and flowers
are more limited, but much more showy. By far the most important
are the azaleas, rhododendrons, and their relatives, which are detailed in the final section of this chapter. Of the others, of which
there are several, only four are selected here, two of which are grown
mostly for their showy colored fruits and two mostly for their flowers.

COTONEASTER MICROPHYLLA, COTONEASTER HORIZONTALIS and COTO-
NEASTER DAMMERI all have bright red or scarlet fruit in abundance, all are relatively hardy from New York southward, and are
practically prostrate. Fine on embankments or spraying over the top
of retaining walls. They resent moving and hence should be planted
where permanently wanted.

FIRE-THORN (*Pyracantha coccinea lalandi*), related to the coto-
neasters, but a shrub 10–20 feet high. The fruit is orange-red,
profuse and very showy.

GARLAND-FLOWER (*Daphne cneorum*). A beautiful evergreen shrub,
almost prostrate and ultimately forming dense mats. Early in
April it produces its clusters of small, pink and very fragrant flowers.
A fine plant for low foundation-planting.

PIERIS JAPONICA. One of the most widely planted broad-leaved evergreens in America because of its hardiness, fine foliage and
profuse bloom. It is a shrub 3–8 feet high, with glossy green leaves
and hanging clusters of small, white, nearly bell-shaped flowers. It
has no valid common name.

3. AZALEAS AND RHODODENDRONS
(And the Mountain-Laurel)

These, the most gorgeous of the broad-leaved evergreens are so
well known that they scarcely need description. Everyone has seen
them as spectacular accent plants, as dramatic lawn specimens, and
in mass plantings in the gardens of the rich. Occasionally one sees

them in public places such as the incomparable "Vale of Cashmere" in Prospect Park, Brooklyn, or at Magnolia Gardens at Charleston, of which John Galsworthy, a very experienced gardener, once wrote: "I specialize in gardens and freely assert that none in the world is so beautiful as this."

Such spectacular beauty carries with it certain obligations that no gardener can ignore if he is to be successful with azaleas and rhododendrons. They are plants of special cultural requirements, the chief of which is that they must have naturally, or be provided with, adequate water when summer heat is worst and deficient rainfall threatens them. They do not like dry heat, and hence many of them do poorly in the middle west, except in the northern part of it, and they are impossible in the Great Plains. To conserve moisture and keep the roots cool the plants should have a mulch preferably of oak leaves, which is never taken off and added to if the leaves are blown away.

Their second requirement is that they prefer an acid soil, and hence will not thrive, or may even die, if planted in a limestone country. You should have your soil tested before planting them.

The third requirement, especially for rhododendrons, is that they prefer partial shade, or at least shade for part of the day. Rhododendrons, particularly, will not tolerate blazing sun all day or too much drying wind. The azaleas are considerably more tolerant of these unfavorable conditions. Both of them do not like to be moved. They will come from any good nursery with a ball of earth tightly wrapped in bagging or canvas—or small plants will come in flower pots.

All of them are expensive, particularly the rhododendrons, for they grow slowly and can be moved only with the greatest care. See Chapter VII for the details.

The experts insist that azaleas and rhododendrons are essentially the same and all of them properly belong to the technical group known as *Rhododendron.* But nearly all gardeners separate them upon the basis that most azaleas lose their leaves in winter while all rhododendrons are evergreen. They are so considered here.

AZALEAS

Shrubs or small trees from all over the north temperate zone, much hybridized, so that there are today hundreds of named forms in all colors from white, pink, salmon, red, yellow, but not usually blue or violet. The flowers are irregular, very showy, and, in the spring when most of them bloom, they provide such a riot of color as to be all but breath-taking.

It is impossible, in our limited space, to mention even a fraction of the different kinds of azaleas offered by any good nursery, but it is wise for the garden planner to keep in mind a few facts, as to hardiness, which may prevent future trouble.

In New England and northern New York azaleas derived from *Azalea calendulacea* and its many hybrids are perfectly hardy. Also, *Azalea kaempferi, japonica,* and *Schlippenbachi* will do well in the same region, as well as the many named forms derived from them.

To these, in the vicinity of New York City and southward, can be added the Ghent and Mollis azaleas, in huge variety as to form and color. From Delaware southward the beautiful, dwarf, Kurume azaleas from Japan are better suited. Further south are the gorgeous, and usually much larger, varieties derived from *Azalea mucronata* (half evergreen), *Azalea indica* and the native *Azalea canescens*.

RHODODENDRONS

These are the showiest of all broad-leaved evergreens. Their foliage is dark green, often shiny, and the underside of the leaf is rusty or scurfy in some kinds. Although their foliage value is striking, for they have generally large and conspicuous, almost leathery leaves, it is their giant flower clusters that make them the garden treasures they have been ever since they were first brought from our own Alleghenies and the Himalayas, where their kinds are legion. Their fondness for coolness, moisture and shade make them much more uncertain in the south than azaleas, and on the Great Plains they will not grow at all.

Rhododendron varieties are so numerous that their named forms run into the hundreds. Some are more hardy than others, depending upon the parent stock from which they have been derived. The technicalities of all this are beyond the scope of this book, but the following named forms have proved perfectly hardy at Stamford, Connecticut, not far from Long Island Sound. North and east of this rhododendrons may be precarious, although many varieties have been grown for years at Boston. Coolness and moisture they must have, but they do not like bitter, zero weather, and even less do they tolerate prolonged summer heat, especially if it is dry.

Ten of the rhododendron varieties that have proved hardy at Stamford, Connecticut, any one of which will give the beginner a good start, are *album elegans*, white; *atrosanguineum*, red; Boule de Neige, white and early blooming; Charles Dickens, red; *delicatis-simum,* rose pink; *everestianum,* lilac; Lady Armstrong, rose pink; Mrs. Charles Sargent, dark pink; *purpureum elegans,* rose pink; *purpureum grandiflorum,* purple-lilac.

MOUNTAIN LAUREL

A beautiful native broad-leaved evergreen, belonging to the same family as azaleas and rhododendrons, but much more tolerant of unfavorable sites. It is shrubby in the north but a tree in the Great Smoky National Park in the mountains of North Carolina. It has striking and most beautiful clusters of pinkish-white flowers in late May and June, borne in showy clusters. Planted in masses it makes extremely effective shrub borders. Although it grows naturally in partial or even deep shade, it will also grow, but not so well, in open sunlight. Like azaleas and rhododendrons, it prefers an acid soil, but survives better than either of the others where the soil is only slightly acid.

As to the uses of the broad-leaved evergreens, especially the azaleas and rhododendrons, it is well to remember that they are a little like champagne as compared to any other shrubs or trees. Because they are expensive, desirable, choice and showy, the ordinary gardener will use them as he does champagne—as an accent. Only the rich can use them in masses, which is the way they grow naturally, and should always be used. But for most of us a specimen plant or two, or a small group of them, will add that touch of distinction to a garden that nothing else will.

Planting and Moving
Shrubs and Trees

CHAPTER VII $\mathcal{A}LL$ *OF THE* plant material in this book comprises woody plants which do not die down to the ground as all herbs must each winter. The source of these shrubs and trees, for most gardeners, must be a nursery. All of them can be raised on your own place if you have the knowledge, time and patience necessary to raise them as the professionals do —which means familiarity with seedage, propagating from cuttings or grafts and the "hardening-off" of seedlings from propagating greenhouse or frame to the open ground.

Assuming that a package of shrubs and trees arrives from the nursery, what should be done? Unless you have all the holes dug and can plant them at once, put the bundle in the shade and out of the wind, and soak the bundle with water. They will keep this way for a day or two.

If it is obvious that you are not ready to plant for several days, open the bundle and "heel them in." This involves digging a trench deep and wide enough to hold the roots, and placing each shrub or tree in the trench tipped away from it at a 45° angle. Then cover *all* the roots with soil and wet it copiously. Ordinary, dormant nursery stock will keep, if heeled in, for a week or two. This does not apply to evergreens, broad-leaved evergreens and certain other plants noted subsequently, which should never be ordered unless you are prepared to plant them upon receipt.

Many amateurs make a great pother over the virtues of spring vs. fall planting. There is no real controversy, again excluding evergreens and broad-leaved evergreens, except for two trees. Neither *Paulownia* nor the LONDON PLANE should ever be planted in the fall. For all the rest of the deciduous shrubs and trees it is a matter to be decided only by convenience. It is axiomatic that no deciduous shrub or tree should be moved when its leaves are expanded. In spring, plants are hastening into growth, while in fall they are gradually becoming dormant. That is why many professionals prefer fall planting, for there is no danger of the planting rush that may be forced upon one by a sudden heat spell in early spring. All nursery-men will deliver deciduous shrubs and trees when they are dormant (leaves all off) and any time before the leaves open is good planting time.

The mechanics of planting are simple enough. Dig a hole deep and wide enough to take care of all roots—do not crowd them. It is better to make it considerably larger than the spread of the roots rather than to force the roots into a well-like prison.

Put back in the hole some of your best soil, tramp it down firmly (but do not pack it), then put your shrub or tree on this tramped soil, see that it is erect, and then begin to fill in the soil. When the hole is half full, shake the stem gently to allow the soil to sift in among the roots, fill in 4–6 inches more soil and with the feet or a heavy stick, pack the soil firmly. Finally fill up the rest of the hole to within 2 inches of the ground level. This will, for the first year, make a shallow well around each plant which will hold water—an admirable plan if you must water your plants the first summer, which you may have to do, especially if it is hot and dry.

When you have finished planting, cut, with pruning shears or a sharp knife, about ⅓ off the end of all larger branches and twigs. This may seem drastic, but actually it is the kindest thing you can do, for by it you reduce by ⅓ the amount of foliage which the roots will have to supply with water. In other words such pruning reduces the shock of transplanting, especially for the plant's first and most critical year in its new home.

EVERGREENS: BROAD-LEAVED EVERGREENS AND OTHER PLANTS THAT RESENT MOVING

All the plants mentioned in Chapter V, and the broad-leaved ever-greens in Chapter VI, as well as a few other shrubs and trees in the rest of the book, must be moved only with a tightly wrapped ball of earth around the roots. Such plants will come from all good nurs-eries so wrapped, and their catalogs usually mark such items B&B (balled and burlapped).

This is done because some plants, like magnolia, have very fragile roots. Others, like the white oak and the dogwood, are just plain hard to transplant. Still others, like azalea and rhododendron, have micro-organisms attached to their roots and the only safe way to transfer these precious and essential organisms is to preserve them

in the ball of earth. Many others have very fine roots that will perish
in the sun and wind.

Whatever the reason for ball and burlapped nursery stock it must
be handled with the greatest care. Follow the directions for ordinary
planting just given, but on no account allow the ball of earth to break
apart or dry out. If it looks as if it would crumble, water the bundle
which will ordinarily make the ball stick together. If the ball is covered with loosely woven jute bagging, slit it once or twice and plant
it with the ball of earth, for it will soon rot away, does no harm and
helps to keep the ball from crumbling to pieces.

Large evergreens, box, etc., may come with the ball tightly sewn
up in canvas. This must be carefully removed before the hole is filled
up, as it is too tough and impervious to allow roots to pass through
it, and it may last several years.

All ball and burlapped plants must be thoroughly watered the first
year, after planting, especially if it is hot and dry. Also, they should
not be pruned when planted. Many of them would appreciate an
occasional soaking during the second summer. After that they should
be able to take care of themselves if you have followed the climatic
restrictions advised for most evergreens and broad-leaved evergreens.

The planting time for evergreens and broad-leaved evergreens
differs somewhat from deciduous plants. The former can be planted
in the spring, which most experienced gardeners prefer for this ball
and burlapped stock. If, however, you cannot plant them then, they
can also be planted between August 15 and September 15, in the
latitude of New York. It should be a few days later than this for
places south of New York, and a few days earlier for places north
of it. Such plantings should be watered thoroughly, because the
theory of planting at this time is to permit them to make fresh roots
in their new home before winter finally comes. Such plants, if properly watered will generally survive, but spring planting is preferred
by many for most evergreens and broad-leaved evergreens.

In the general account of the trees and shrubs a few were noted
that must be moved with a ball of earth. They should be treated
exactly as all ball and burlapped stock, and preferably planted in
the spring. Being deciduous plants they cannot, or should not be
moved in late August or early September, for they would then be
in full leaf. All such trees, especially magnolias, dogwood and white
oak, are hard to get established, and special warnings are given,
wherever necessary in Chapters IV and VI, for those deciduous
shrubs and trees that must be handled with this extra care.

If all of these suggestions are followed, the loss from planting should not be more than a small fraction of your shrubs and trees —scarcely 3 per cent. It may well be less, but remember that Nature appears to resent the shock of transplanting anything, and it is our obligation to make that shock as little damaging as possible. You can, by taking these precautions, translate your hopes and dreams into that kind of permanence in the garden which will give lasting satisfaction.

Book Two

THE EVERBLOOMING GARDEN

THE EVERBLOOMING GARDEN

Arranged month by month are the plants that will give continuous bloom in the garden.

Continuous
Bloom
in
the
Garden

WHO WOULD not like flowers all the year and how many think it is impossible? No one in the general latitude of New York, Pittsburgh, Columbus, St. Louis, and points west can hope to get the riot of color throughout most of the year that is possible in New Orleans or Miami. But it is equally true that, with a little forethought, one can have continuous bloom in the garden—it is a mistake to think that winter drabness needs to afflict us from Thanksgiving to the end of February even in the North. Nature provides many splashes of color, besides the red-berried shrubs, the cool evergreens, or the dramatic combination of them with the glistening white bark of the paper birch, set in a sheen of snow.

Under that snow, and peeping through holes in it, especially in favored places, you may grow quite a few real winter-blooming herbs and bulbs, and several shrubs will flower both before and after Christmas. They often act as though they could not quite decide whether they are late-blooming autumn flowers or early-blooming spring ones. Hence, the first few winter-flowering plants are noted in the chapter headed *Thanksgiving to Washington's Birthday.* Some of them will be a surprise to those who think that a few straggling annuals (*Cosmos* often flowers up to Christmas in open seasons) and the last of the chrysanthemums are all that anyone has the right to expect. Great expectations are as foolish as Pollyanna optimism, but this little book was written for those who have a dash of both. There are risks and there will be triumphs. There must be care and some skepticism, for the seasons vary and everyone has what the meteorologists call a micro-climate.

Two factors will always affect our floral timetable—site and the weather. The south side of a building or a south-facing hillside will be much more likely to provide winter bloom than any north or north-west exposure; and protection from bitter winter winds also helps—by lath screens, evergreen hedges, or even a "fence" of cornstalks or cut-off branches of discarded Christmas trees. Only two of the winter-blooming plants in the next chapter are native. So, to assure success, we must do whatever is possible to make the foreign plants feel at home both climatically, which we can only partially control by pro-tection, and as to soil, which we can regulate much more effectively. The plants in the next chapter are thus the most critical, the most likely to fail and, if the gods are with us, most likely to give us that most thrilling garden climax, bloom in winter. From March to Octo-ber, however, there is so much material that a drastic selection is all that is possible here. Under each of these months are grouped only those plants most easily grown, most readily available from ordinary nurserymen or seedsmen, or that you can raise yourself from seed or cuttings. Under each month there are alternatives to those selected, for gardener's tastes are as fickle as the weather—particularly as to color.

Nothing, however, is so really fickle as the weather, even during the growing season. Blooming time will therefore be altered by vio-lent fluctuations from the usual. Generally, the plants selected will be flowering in the month indicated, but they may bloom before or after that month if conditions are out of line, particularly if there is a protracted drought.

It should be also mentioned that the blooming dates are fixed for the latitudes of approximately the 39th to 41st parallels, hence on a line including the vicinity of New York, Philadelphia, Pittsburgh, Columbus, Indianapolis, St. Louis, and Lincoln (Nebraska). If you live much north or south of this line, flowering periods will be later or earlier; a fair estimate would be about one week for each degree of latitude. Also, proximity to cool sea water will locally retard the onset of spring, and elevation will also upset the reckoning, especially on high mountains.

No annuals are included, so that the everblooming garden will be a permanent one, except for the bulbous plants which are every-where noted—the spring, summer, autumn, and winter-blooming kinds, with dates for planting. All the trees, shrubs, or perennial herbs mentioned can be purchased from nurseries. Those derived from tubers or bulbs are available from any good seed store. All rare or unusual plants have been omitted because of the difficulty of finding them.

The selection of plants will be a surprise to the knowing, because they will be expecting far more species and varieties, especially for the months of the growing season—the period from the last killing frost of spring until the first nip of winter in the fall. This season varies from 176 to about 186 days in New York and, of course, coincides with the greatest profusion of bloom—especially in May and June. Soon after July first there is a perceptible waning in the length of the day, and this gradually diminishing amount of sunshine is reflected in the smaller number of plants that come into bloom from about August 15th to the first frost.

If the book were written for those who know everything about gardening it would have to include so many plants that it would be many times its present size. That would defeat its purpose, which is, as simply as possible, to help the home gardener to have continuous bloom in the garden. That can be accomplished with far fewer plants than are contained in more comprehensive books, and the aim here is to select only those that are necessary to insure success.

Most of the plants can be grown anywhere in your garden and can be mingled with existing plantings; or, if you are immune to garden history, you can devote a single border to a kind of floral calendar.

The latter scheme, however, would be like the "Floral Clocks," once popular but now abandoned because they were a maintenance headache and artistically foolish, notwithstanding the skilled attention they demanded.

The Latin names of plants have been omitted wherever this is safe, or, in other words, they are included where there are many related plants, some of which have no valid common name. In such cases the Latin names of science and the better catalogs are the only names to use, if you want to be certain that you will get the desired plant. This is especially important where many related plants have widely varying blooming periods. Latin names are often inserted after the common one, because they are, after all, the only precise ones, and really no harder to remember and spell than rhododendron, chrysanthemum, fuchsia, or nasturtium, all of which are the Latin as well as the common names of those plants. There are scores of others.

CHAPTER II

Thanksgiving to Washington's Birthday

*"Leafless all the winter time
and pining for the Spring"*

F<small>ROM</small> Thanksgiving to almost Christmas there will likely be a few stragglers from the October-blooming flowers that can be counted on to continue flowering unless cut off by very severe cold, which is unusual, particularly near the coast. Even some roses have been known to bloom in a mild November, and from Wilmington southward flowers, especially those that flourish in late October, are almost sure to have scattered blossoms.

But it is obligatory for most northern gardeners to plan rather carefully if bloom is expected in December, January, and February, and there are only a handful of plants that can be relied upon. Of these the most certain are a group of shrubs from North America and their relatives in China and Japan, all belonging to the witch-hazel family and all of them blooming on bare twigs long after last year's crop of leaves has fallen and long before next season's leaves unfold. There are also two very fragrant shrubs to be noted separately.

The witch-hazel family, besides the familiar sweet gum tree, contains two genera which have the habit of blooming in late fall, early winter, or very early in the spring, depending partly upon the age of the shrubs (they may be tree-like in the South), partly upon the severity of the season, and a good deal on the site chosen to grow them. These groups are *Hamamelis*, the true witch-hazels, and *Corylopsis*, which appears to have no common name and is wholly Asiatic.

WITCH-HAZELS

About the time our ancestors were celebrating the first Thanksgiving there was blooming in the New England forests the common witch-hazel which was entirely new to them. None of its Asiatic relatives were then in English gardens because they had not yet been discovered, and the colonists were intrigued by Indian tales that its leaves and bark, in an infusion, were good for sprains. This was the origin of witch-hazel which is a household remedy to this day.

The peculiar habit of flowering when all other woody plants were bare naturally attracted their attention, and the shrub was soon in cultivation because it provided, almost by stealth, a mass of yellow bloom. It was the common witch-hazel (*Hamamelis virginiana*), since found wild from Canada to Georgia, particularly along streams, although it will grow perfectly well in ordinary garden soil.

The common witch-hazel has four strap-shaped petals, about 1 inch long; and, because they are borne rather sparsely, it pays to plant the shrubs in masses to get the full effect. The plant is particularly charming if it can be placed so that the afternoon sun shines through the blossom-laden twigs. It is perfectly hardy everywhere, blooms from late October to mid-December, depending on the site and season. It grows 6-10 feet high but may be tree-like in the South.

A much less showy American witch-hazel (*Hamamelis vernalis*) was afterward discovered in the drainage of the Mississippi from Missouri to Louisiana. It is now cultivated because its yellow flowers are fragrant, which the common sort is not, and it blooms from about December 15 to mid-February, depending on the season. It is a smaller shrub than the common sort, rarely growing much taller than 5 feet.

Two Asiatic witch-hazels are most worthy of attention by the winter gardener. One is Japanese (*Hamamelis japonica*), which is almost tree-like, has yellow flowers like our native species, and blooms from January to March. The late Alfred Rehder was so impressed by it that he wrote, after years of observing it at the Arnold Arboretum, the "delicate petals withstand zero weather without injury." The other is a Chinese witch-hazel (*Hamamelis mollis*), which is usually a medium-sized shrub but may become a small tree. Its flowers are golden yellow, tinged with red at the base, blooming from January to March, and considered by the experts as the handsomest of all the witch-hazels.

Among the witch-hazels, then, is to be found yellow flowers from mid-November to March as follows:

Two American species (*Hamamelis virginiana* and *Hamamelis vernalis*), blooming from mid-November to mid-February. Two Asiatic species (*Hamamelis japonica* and *Hamamelis mollis*) blooming from January to March.

CORYLOPSIS

Related to the witch-hazels and differing only in technical characters is the genus *Corylopsis,* of which several species are found in American gardens, but none of them seems to have acquired a common name. The chief difference between *Corylopsis* and the true witch-hazels is that the former bear their flowers in small, finger-shaped, nodding clusters and hence are showier than in *Hamamelis*. The best of them is *Corylopsis spicata*, whose flowers are yellow, fragrant, and bloom in February and March. Unlike the true witch-hazels, which can be grown anywhere, *Corylopsis spicata* prefers a somewhat peaty and sandy soil, definitely on the acid side.*

WINTER FRAGRANCE

The odor of the witch-hazel that grows wild from Missouri to Louisiana (*Hamamelis vernalis*) is rather mild, faintly spicy and most welcome, but it has nothing like the fragrance of a Chinese honeysuckle or of *Chimonanthus praecox,* both of which flower in February, and the latter will often be in bloom most of the winter in the South. Both of them are among our most fragrant garden plants.

CHINESE HONEYSUCKLE (*Lonicera fragrantissima*). A beautiful, round-headed shrub, 8-10 feet high, covered in February with a profusion of small, white flowers, which have the typical odor of honeysuckle, but tinged with the spicy fragrance of orange peel. It is perfectly hardy in the North, but severe frosts will often blast its flowers, although this rarely happens south of Wilmington; and further south it often blooms in January. It is of easy culture in any garden soil.

CHIMONANTHUS PRAECOX. A Chinese shrub, 8-10 feet high, christened *praecox* (meaning "very early") by its sponsor because it blooms from December to February in the South. Unfortunately it is not certainly hardy north of Wilmington, Delaware, but perfectly so on the eastern shore of Maryland and Virginia, and from Washington southward on the mainland. In the northern part of its range the

* If you are unfamiliar with the measurement and regulation of acid and alkali soils, a full account of it will be found at "Acid and Alkali Soils" in Taylor's *Encyclopedia of Gardening.*

flowers appear before the leaves unfold, but it may be nearly evergreen in the South. Flowers yellow, the inner segments striped
purplish-brown, so fragrant as to be hyacinth-scented. In some nursery catalogs it may be listed as *Meratia fragrans,* but its correct name
is *Chimonanthus praecox, Chimonanthus,* appropriately enough, being Greek for winter-flowering!

CHRISTMAS AND NEW YEAR'S

Not all gardeners want winter bloom only from the seven shrubs
already noted and may well be asking, "What about perennials or
bulbs?" In other words, are there no winter-blooming herbs to carpet
the bare ground or peep out of pockets in the snow? There are at least
two for northern gardeners, both showy relatives of our common
buttercup, both Eurasian, one of them grown from small wizened
tubers, the other a perennial with rather brittle roots. They are:

CHRISTMAS ROSE. Often called Winter Rose. The root of this small,
          evergreen perennial herb is very poisonous (only if eaten)
and the source of the drug hellebore. Grown for its beautiful, waxy,
white or pinkish-green showy flowers that are almost 2½ inches wide.
It prefers some summer shade and a moist place, but will grow in
most ordinary garden soil. Roots are brittle and must be handled with
care when transplanting, which should be done in August or September. Leave it alone when once established, because it does not
like to be moved. Althought it is commonly called Christmas rose, it
sends up its showy flowers any time between late November and
early February, often blooming under the snow. There are also one or
two color forms offered by dealers. All make delightful cut flowers
that suggest the large-flowered anemones.

NEW YEAR'S GIFT. Often called Winter Aconite. Yellow-flowered,
          and like the Christmas rose, a relative of the common butter-
cup. It has finely dissected leaves, and a solitary flower about 1½
inches wide, borne on a stalk 3-6 inches high. Grows easily on shaded
banks, but will flourish in good, well-drained garden loam. It springs
from a tuber which rests during the summer, but sends up new leaves
in September. Tubers should be planted 3 inches deep and 3 inches
apart, preferably in late August or early September, after which
the plant will spread rapidly because it seeds very freely. Early in
January it will produce its handsome flowers which are surrounded
by frilly, thread-like leaves. It may, in some situations, flower as late
as mid-February.

SNOWDROPS AND CROCUSES

The common garden crocus is never winter-blooming, as it usually does not flower until late March and hence should be sought in the next chapter. But there are species of crocus that bloom in late fall and in winter. These are not the autumn crocus (*Colchicum*), an account of which will be found in the chapter on September, but real species of the genus *Crocus* and closely related to the common kind, but with a different blooming period.

Also winter-blooming bulbous plants are two kinds of snowdrop, not to be confused with the snowflake which blooms mostly in March and will be found in the chapter devoted to that month. The combination of snowdrops, crocuses (as outlined below), the Christmas rose, and the New Year's Gift, means that, for those who do not have room for shrubs, it is still possible to get winter color with these perennials and bulbous plants.

SNOWDROPS. Low, white-flowered bulbs, among the earliest of bloomers. Plant in scores or hundreds, about 3 inches deep and 3 inches apart, preferably in late August, never later than September. They may be left alone and will provide sheets of bloom in a few years. Besides the common snowdrop (*Galanthus nivalis*), there is a taller sort from Asia Minor (*Galanthus elwesi*), the giant snowdrop, which is all of 12 inches high. It often flowers before Christmas, while the common snowdrop will not usually bloom until early February, and only then in favorable places. Both the snowdrops will grow in any good garden soil, but *Galanthus elwesi* prefers a somewhat sandier soil. It will also respond to a mulch of well-decayed manure spread every other autumn.

CROCUSES. Of the many species of crocus (over 30 are known in American gardens, besides the common sort), only a few will be included here, some predominately fall flowering and others blooming long before the common garden crocus. The fall blooming sorts should be planted in late August or early September, and those that bloom in late winter or early spring should be planted from about mid-October through November. Plant both kinds about 3 inches deep and the same distance apart. It is useless to start with less than a dozen corms, and it is better to plant them by the hundreds to get sheets of bloom. Some prefer to "naturalize" crocuses in the lawn, but the idea is not so good because, if the grass is cut while the crocus leaves are maturing, the crocus will not accumulate in its corm the nourishment for next year's bloom that the normally withering leaf will send down for storage in the corm.

Crocuses should generally be left alone once they are planted, because they are inclined to increase naturally, some plantations surviving for years. If they stop flowering it means that the corms are crowding each other and there is nothing to do but dig them up and re-space them 3 inches apart. All of these species of crocus are smaller than the common garden kind, none of them being more than 6 inches high and usually less. None have common names and should be ordered by those used below.

LATE AUTUMN-BLOOMING

CROCUS PULCHELLUS. Lilac or lavender flowers but faintly striped with blue, the throat of the flower yellow. It is native in the eastern Mediterranean region.

CROCUS SPECIOSUS. A Eurasian plant, considered by many as the finest of the autumn-blooming crocuses. The lilac or bluish-lilac flowers are nearly 2 inches high.

LATE WINTER-BLOOMING

CROCUS IMPERATI. An Italian crocus and one of the first to bloom, often peeping out from pockets in the snow. Flowers pale lilac or white, the outer segments purple-striped.

CROCUS TOMASSINIANUS. A little later blooming than *Crocus imperati*, its flowers nearly 1½ inches long, pale reddish-blue, often dark-spotted at the tip.

CHAPTER III

March

"Now fades the last long streak of snow"

WHEN time does finally dissolve the snows of winter, the ides of March often give little hint of it. The tempests of February too frequently stretch their frigid fingers into March, and the icy air of night reveals in the glistening morning that worst of the gardener's worries—an ice storm. Nothing can be so destructive, and there is nothing that one can do about it but pray for warm melting sunshine.

March may come in like a lion, even if it does not always go out like a lamb, but something besides an ice storm is happening in this month that is of profound interest to the gardener. There is, of course, a gradual thawing out and warming up, but perhaps, because it is so gradual, we never notice the increase in the length of the day. Not only is it generally warmer, although this varies from year to year, but there is the much more important and quite invariable increase in the hours of sunshine. In New York, for instance, the difference in the possible amount of sunshine, between March 1st and 31st is 154 minutes, regardless of the weather. This has such an effect upon plants that March is truly the harbinger of spring, even though it may not be very spring-like.

Perennials begin to stir, early bulbs peak into bloom, the red maple first shows its color, early-flowering shrubs and even trees burst into bloom, peepers begin to peep, and, as Thackeray once wrote, we are all "pining for the spring." It really will not come for some weeks, but there are many reminders that winter is over and spring definitely on the horizon. The gardener can help that illusion of spring and make March a month of hope and promise.

The plant materials to tide over this illusion of spring are not too numerous, because we must exclude all those that are fit only for fanciers, those that are hard to come by, and those too difficult to grow. Depending on the size of your garden you can choose some of the shrubs and trees, and anyone, with a pocket-sized garden, can grow the perennials or bulbs in the lists below.

SHRUBS AND TREES

It is axiomatic that March bloom is most permanently secured by the planting of one or all of the six shrubs and trees below. Once established they need little further attention and do not have to be weeded, as borders of perennials or bulbs must be. Their only disadvantage, which they share with later blooming woody plants, is that the period of bloom varies from one or two weeks—and the rest of the year they are just colorless shrubs and trees. That is why, if you have room, you should scatter them among later-blooming shrubs and trees, so that your planting may be not only exciting in March but interesting throughout the year. This can be done by culling the shrubs and trees in the chapters devoted to other months, because from them, and those given below, you can have continuous color in the garden without planting a single perennial or bulb.

The six shrubs and trees, arranged approximately in the order of their blooming are:

WINTER JASMINE (*Jasminum nudiflorum*). A Chinese, rather sprawling shrub with greenish, arching branches which are bare of foliage in the winter, but have scattered on these twigs a pretty yellow flower that is erratic in its blooming period, depending on the site and season. In mild winters it may bloom in mid-February (or even in January on the eastern shore of Maryland), but these early flowers are often blasted by frost. It is sure to be in bloom early in March and is perfectly hardy from the coastal region of southern New England southward, where it may reach a height of 8-10 feet. At New York it is usually not over 3-4 feet. It almost suggests a forsythia, but the yellow flowers are smaller and not so plentiful. It is easily the earliest of March-blooming shrubs.

CORNELIAN CHERRY (*Cornus mas*). A useful shrub or small tree, usually 8-12 feet high. It will stand the smoke and dust of suburbia better than any early-blooming woody plant. It is hardy everywhere, needing space in age, particularly southward where it may form a round-headed tree up to 20 feet. On the bare twigs in mid-March (or later northward) it bears scores of tiny yellow flowers crowded into globular clusters. These are so numerous that the whole plant seems covered with yellow bloom. Its red fruits are edible and gave the plant its name, i.e., *cornel* being the old name for the genus *Cornus*, and "cherry," with which it really has nothing to do, being suggested by its red fruit. It is related to our flowering dogwood, but comes from central and southern Europe and western Asia. It has been cultivated since the days of the Romans.

FLOWERING QUINCE, often called Japanese flowering quince, although it is native in Central China. In ordering, it is better to use its scientific name of *Chaenomeles lagenaria*, because there is a smaller and less desirable form known as Japan quince (or often merely japonica). Our plant is a shrub, a little bit prickly, the bare twigs of which in March have showy red or scarlet flowers in the typical form. But there are many horticultural forms with pink, pale rose, and even white flowers, some of them double. The shrub normally grows 4-6 feet high, is very twiggy, and can easily be shorn into a hedge-like growth. It is perfectly hardy everywhere, will grow in a variety of soils, and is one of the handsomest of the early-flowering shrubs. In the South it may bloom in February.

MEZEREON (*Daphne mezereum*). A low, Eurasian shrub, not over 3 feet high and usually less, the foliage not evergreen as it is in some more desirable, but tender relatives. Flowers small, but in close clusters, rosy-purple, and blooming before the leaves unfold. They are by far the most fragrant of any of the early-blooming shrubs, even suggesting the jasmine. The leaves, which follow the flowers in a fortnight, are inclined to be grayish, especially on the underside. Hardy from Boston southward, and along the coast perhaps safe up to southern Maine. If you live south of Washington the evergreen *Daphne odora* is equally fragrant and a more showy plant than the mezereon. Both of them thrive best in a sandy loam, mixed with peat or a slightly acid leaf mold. A still lower plant, *Daphne cneorum*, is also evergreen, has pink, fragrant flowers and is fine for a ground cover, but it blooms later than the other two, and should perhaps be in the chapter devoted to April. All the daphnes are slow-growing and inclined to be expensive, but they are worth it.

STAR MAGNOLIA (*Magnolia stellata*). The earliest flowering of all the magnolias, the blossoms appearing on the naked twigs from March 15 to early in April, depending on site and season. It is a Japanese spreading shrub, rarely in cultivation becoming tree-like, usually 4-8 feet high, and shrubby. The twigs and unopened flower buds are covered with dense, downy hairs, as if the plant needed this felt-like sheath to protect it against the often inclement weather. Its flowers are white, star-like, and the segments are strap-shaped, the expanded flower being about 2½ inches wide, very showy, and fragrant. It is a splendid accent plant for the lawn, and its only drawback is that its flowers are sometimes blasted by late frosts and are also injured by pelting rain. If you are fortunate enough to avoid both it is an extremely handsome harbinger of spring. Like all the magnolias it is difficult to transplant, and it is rather expensive. But as it will come with a ball of earth (do not accept it without) well tied up in bagging, it should be planted without injury to its decidedly brittle roots. With this precaution, and plenty of water the first season, there is no reason why it cannot be a permanent and very desirable feature of the early spring garden. The star magnolia may be planted from August 15 to September 15, or in early spring just before the leaves unfold, i.e., about a week after flowering.

FORSYTHIA, often called Golden bell. It is hard to think what American and English gardens must have been like before William Forsyth, an English horticulturist, brought the first living shrub that has since borne his name from Japan to England. That was only a century and a half ago, but the group, as garden shrubs, never became popular until Robert Fortune, in 1833, brought from China the plant often called *Forsythia fortunei*. This is one of the parents of our best forsythia today, which it is safer to order as *Forsythia intermedia spectabilis*. This is a hybrid shrub 5-9 feet high, its arching branches completely covered by its golden-yellow flowers, usually blooming about the third week in March in New York, but often by March first in Washington. There is no other forsythia to compare with it, although there are many varieties and some species—mostly with sparser and smaller flowers. If you want a still earlier blooming kind it is better to get the Korean *Forsythia ovata*, which is two weeks earlier, but not so floriferous as the hybrid plant. All the forsythias are of the easiest cultivation in any ordinarily good soil and they transplant readily.

PERENNIAL PLANTS

Shrubs and trees will give you permanent March color in the garden, but many people have no room for them and nearly everyone would like a few flowers for cutting. These, of necessity, must come from perennials and from bulbs. No matter how small the garden, there is always room for a few perennials, and bulbs by the score or hundreds do not take up much space. Many of them can be scattered among shrubbery or put into beds or borders.

Unfortunately there are few perennials that bloom as early as March, and our choice must be limited to three:

COLTSFOOT (*Tussilago farfara*). At least one reputable garden book says that coltsfoot is of no garden interest, and it would not be if there were a wealth of March-blooming perennials. Its leaves were once esteemed as a medicine, and its long cultivation in Europe finally led to its introduction into America. It is closely related to the common dandelion and like that "tramp with the golden crown" it has golden-yellow flower heads at the end of a naked flower stalk which pushes up before the heart-shaped leaves appear. Unlike the dandelion it is no pest in lawns and its golden-yellow flower heads are often a welcome sign that spring is not too far away. It will grow in any soil, but most luxuriantly in dampish places.

SIBERIAN TEA. From the cool regions of Siberia and the Himalayas come two thick-leaved, almost fleshy, stout herbs that can be counted on for March bloom. Although they are called Siberian tea, the only safe way to order them is by their Latin names of *Bergenia crassifolia* and *Bergenia ligulata*. Both of them are closely related to saxifrages, and some catalogs may list them under *Saxifraga*. By whatever name, they are fine sturdy plants, differing however in certain features that matter in making a choice. *Bergenia crassifolia* from Siberia is perfectly hardy, has rose-pink flowers in clusters that stand above the large, roundish leaves which may be 4-6 inches wide. In *Bergenia ligulata* the thick fleshy leaves are scalloped on the edges which are also fringed with red hairs. The very handsome flower clusters are nodding, white or rose-purple. So popular is this Himalayan herb that there are several varieties of it, one of the best being variety *leichtlini* with crimson leaves and rose-colored flowers. Both the bergenias will grow in ordinary garden soil, but *Bergenia ligulata* will need a winter mulch of straw or strawy manure if you live north of Philadelphia.

NETTED IRIS (*Iris reticulata*). A tiny iris from the Caucasus which persists for years in gardens as far north as Massachusetts, but best started from a bulb, which should be planted in October or early November. The plant is so small that care must be taken not to root it out in weeding or mistake its narrow leaves for those of garlic or some wild onion. Many prefer to grow it in the rock garden, but this is not necessary. Its beautiful reddish-purple veined and spotted flowers are more fragrant than any of the later-blooming irises and often bloom amid snow, which does not appear to hurt it in the least.

This violet-scented iris is scarcely 5 inches high. It is essential to get bulbs of true *Iris reticulata*, because there are varieties of, and substitutes for, it on the market.

BULBS

All of the March-flowering bulbous plants depend for their bloom upon the nourishment stored in their bulbs. This is renewed annually by the food, manufactured in the leaves, which drains down to the bulb as the leaves wither—usually soon after the blooming period. For this reason none of the plants below should be disturbed, nor should the leaves be mown if you have naturalized them by the scores or hundreds in the lawn. After the leaves have withered (they disappear by midsummer) such plantations can be mown. But it is important, so far as next year's bloom is concerned, to let nature take its course, even if the withered leaves are a little unsightly.

All of these early-flowering bulbs should be planted from about mid-October to the end of November for next year's flowering, and all of them can stay where they are planted because they do not need lifting and they resent it. If, after a few years, they show signs of failing to bloom, they must then be dug up (in October) and respaced, in accordance with the planting depths and distances apart specified below.

Far more than the meager list of perennials, these March-blooming bulbs can bring sheets of color to the early spring garden, especially if they are planted in drifts or masses. All, except perhaps one tulip, are low-growing plants and hence not much use as cut flowers except in shallow vases. The groups are arranged in approximately the order of their blooming, but this may vary with the season, especially if the site is on a north- or south-facing slope, or if they are protected from north and northwest winds. All of these are ordinarily raised from "bulbs," but some are actually grown from corms, such as the crocus and spring meadow saffron. Corms are rarely differentiated by the average gardener from bulbs, and they are here called bulbs to avoid confusion.

EARLY MARCH

(Any of these three may bloom early enough to overlap the bulbous plants which flower in later February. See Chapter II. Likewise, they may stay in flower until mid-March.)

GLORY-OF-THE-SNOW. A group of early-blooming bulbous plants from Asia Minor, best planted 3 inches deep and 3 inches apart in any ordinary garden soil. The best species, which better be ordered by its technical name, is *Chionodoxa luciliae*. It grows only 3 inches high and has deep blue, rather small, nodding flowers, with a white eye. They may not bloom so well the first year after planting, but if left alone will provide sheets of bloom in a few years. A related plant, *Chionodoxa sardensis*, which may be only a variety, has deeper blue and smaller flowers, without the white eye.

SIBERIAN SQUILL (*Scilla sibirica*). An Asiatic bulbous herb, 4-6 inches high, its small nodding, chalice-like flowers brilliantly blue, and borne in small clusters of 3-5. It should be planted 3-4 inches deep and about the same distance apart, and will thrive in any good soil. Unlike most other bulbous plants, which demand full sun, the Siberian squill does well under shade, even that of evergreens. An especially fine variety is Spring Beauty. Later-blooming squills will be found at the end of this chapter.

SNOWFLAKE. As there are several forms of these attractive early-blooming bulbous plants, it will be safer to order this one by its Latin name of *Leucojum vernum*, because it is the best of all the snowflakes. The white flowers are solitary, borne at the end of a stalk 9-12 inches high, and are quite fragrant. The snowflake is perfectly hardy, and the blossom is not injured by an occasional snow. Plant the bulbs 4-5 inches apart and as deep.

MID-MARCH

SPRING MEADOW SAFFRON (*Bulbocodium vernum*). A crocus-like plant, its leaves not over 4-6 inches high, while the purplish-rose crocus-like flower is all but stemless and thus grows directly on the ground. It comes from the mountains of eastern Europe and western Asia, and the corolla is white-spotted on the inside. It generally flowers a week or two before the garden crocuses and should be planted about 3 inches deep and the same distance apart. It is not superior to the crocus, but has the advantage of blooming a little earlier.

WATER LILY TULIP (*Tulipa kauffmaniana*). This is a wild species of tulip, one of the so-called "species" tulips or "botanical" tulips to distinguish them from the common garden kinds that will not be blooming for a month or six weeks. It should be planted at least 6-8 inches deep in good rich soil, and it will bloom about the middle of March, or a little earlier in favorable sites. The whole plant may not be any higher than 10-12 inches, and its very slender, long-pointed flower, which is generally whitish-yellow, but with a pinkish blotch, also has a reddish center. It has become so popular that there are now garden varieties of it, notably Brilliant, Gaiety, and Scarlet and Gold. The water lily tulip usually bears only one flower, but old and vigorous plants will sometimes bear two or even three. Unlike most of the garden tulips it can be left in the ground so long as it continues to flower, failing which it should be dug up and replanted in October.

LATE MARCH

CROCUS. Garden crocuses, while legion in named and unnamed varieties, are all derived from *Crocus vernus* which is a native of Europe and was named *vernus* because that is the Latin name for spring. And scarcely any spring-flowering bulbs are so popular as crocuses. They should be planted 3 inches deep and as far apart, in a good sunny place, preferably in rich sandy loam, although they grow pretty well in almost any average garden soil.

They usually flower before the leaves appear, and the latter are narrow, grass-like and with a whitish midrib. The leaves must be allowed to mature and wither if bloom is wanted next year. A plantation of crocus will last for years if left alone, or a light mulch of well-rotted manure can be put on every other autumn. Do not make the mulch too thick, because the flowers are practically stemless and may be half hidden by a thick mulch.

Most people will buy the collections of mixed colors offered by all dealers, and the informality of most crocus planting is enhanced by the sheets of white, purple, blue, striped, lavender, and lilac colors. If special or exclusive varieties are wanted they will be found in King of the Whites and Kathleen Parlow (white); Pallas (violet-striped purple); Maximilian (soft lavender); Gladstone (reddish purple); and there are some varieties that are porcelain blue, but they had better be ordered by color for many of the horticultural names are confusing or unreliable.

It will be noted that there are no yellows among these, as this is a color not found in the derivatives of *Crocus vernus*. For yellow kinds one must order either *Crocus aureus*, often called Dutch Yellow, or *Crocus susianus*, which is often called Cloth of Gold.

All of these horticultural varieties of the garden crocus are quite separate from the *species of Crocus*, some fall-blooming and some flowering much earlier in the late winter (see Chapter II). Also they have nothing to do with the autumn crocus, which is really a *Colchicum* and will be found in Chapter IX.

Many of the garden crocuses will last well into April, and in cold, wet years they may fail to bloom in March at all. They are quite sensitive to changes in the weather and the writer remembers that in the spring of 1950 they were in full flower, on the eastern shore of Maryland on February 17th!

BLUEBELLS OF ENGLAND (*Scilla nonscripta*). A fairly stout bulbous plant from northern Europe, the typical form making sheets of blue at the Kew Gardens in London. They should be used by the scores or hundreds, planted 4 inches deep and the same distance apart. The plant is 6-10 inches high and bears terminal clusters of small, bell-shaped flowers. The common form is always blue, but Blush Queen is pink, and white varieties are also offered. It is better to leave the plants alone once they are established, and of course the leaves must be allowed to wither.

SPANISH BLUEBELL (*Scilla hispanica*). A little taller than the above, grown like it, and coming in several named and superior varieties. Blue King and Blue Queen are blue; Rosalind is pink; Rose Queen is rose colored and white varieties are also offered. It is sometimes known as Spanish jacinth which is an old name for hyacinth, perhaps because the plant bears miniature, hyacinth-like clusters of flowers. It is a fine garden plant and often blooms well into April.

CHAPTER IV

April

> *"Come, gentle Spring,*
> *ethereal mildness, come."*

IT IS the season of showers, of sun, of leafing and flowering, and hope, but how often it is merely the "uncertain glory of an April day." Uncertain it surely is, but it's Spring and time for rusty joints to limber up, for lovers to seek April's madness, and for gardeners to gather the spoils of winter dreams and autumn planting.

Fit for All Fools Day is the gardener who has put off until restless April what should have been done last month or last year. To him April brings frustration. He sees April painting the garden with color and wonders, a little wistfully, if he can some day have it all for his very own. If April's foolishness has not bewitched him he can. But an April garden, like any other, needs to be planned for—preferably a year ahead.

And planning means just that. First comes the weather, for April is the month of erratic and disastrous frosts, especially away from the coast and in valleys among the hills. Here cold air drainage often ruins the peach crop in low places, just as it can blast some of the flowers to be mentioned presently. The plants from foreign countries never seem to understand our Aprils, for they retain their ancestral flowering period, forgetting that the United States is not southern China, the Mediterranean, or Persia. The peach, originally from a part of China that was frost-free at flowering time, is a good illustration of this. Here, in many places, peach blossoms get caught by erratic frosts, ruining the crop for that year, but doing no permanent harm to the tree.

Such erratic frosts can, and often do, ruin the flowers of some shrubs and trees in the lists below, and one has to make up his mind whether a particular sort is worth growing for April bloom if, in one out of three seasons, it may be blasted. This is particularly true of those that bloom in the first third of the month. In deciding whether or not to risk it, remember that distance from the sea, or a river or lake, and a local depression in the topography are both unfavorable.

Generally speaking the perennials and bulbous plants are much less damaged by erratic April frosts than the woody plants, so that one can choose any of those below with a relatively free mind. And from April until October the average temperate zone gardener can forget the weather, because except droughts which are easily overcome by watering there is nothing to think of between the last April frost and the first killing frost of autumn.

In 1912 the city of Tokyo presented to the city of Washington what is probably the finest collection of Japanese flowering cherries in the New World. Millions have walked around that magical Tidal Basin ever since, and Washington, during the first two weeks in April when the trees are usually in full flower, is an enchanted city. Less notable, but fine collections of these superb trees are also at the Brooklyn Botanic Garden; at Rochester, New York; and at the Arnold Arboretum, Jamaica Plain, Massachusetts. Everyone who has seen these striking examples of Oriental garden skill wants one or two of them in his garden, which reminds us that April is the month when other and almost as striking trees and shrubs will be in flower.

SHRUBS AND TREES

Because the average suburban garden has limited space for trees and shrubs, only five different groups are discussed, for there are, after all, other months to plan for. From them, without the use of any bulbs or perennials, the home gardener can get continuous color throughout April. Local conditions, particularly erratic frosts, may upset the floral timetable, but in reasonably average years the gardener can count on them.

DOUBLE-FLOWERED PEACH. A superb derivative of the common peach tree, but usually lower and often shrub-like. Its flowers are double or semi-double, and come in several varieties—white, pink, and deep red. The latter is an especially fine form with waxy almost camellia-like flowers. All the varieties are very early flowering (often

WINTER

This sequence of four photographs was taken in one garden in the course of a single year. It begins with winter, with the garden dormant, the planting covered with snow. But the Christmas Rose will soon be blooming, and New Year's Gift, the Winter Aconite, may push through the drifts in January and February. Winter is a time for dreaming and planning for the garden to come, but even winter need not be without the color of evergreens and some patches of bloom. (Photo: *Gottscho-Schleisner*)

SPRING

The first great show of the gardening year comes now. Against the new green of trees and lawn early azaleas and the flowering shrubs have appeared, with tulips, daffodils and other spring bulbs in full flower. This is the season when ornamental crabs, peaches and cherries reach their prime, and a well-planted garden is at its most spectacular. (Photo: *Gottscho-Schleisner*)

SUMMER

Annuals and perennials come into full flower from June until frost. Poppies,
iris, foxglove, dahlias and the other summer and fall blooming plants make
the garden a mass of color through summer to fall. In the borders, box
gives an evergreen background, and the many varieties of shrubs, chosen
for habit of growth and succession of bloom, form an ever-changing frame
for lawn and garden. (Photo: *Gottscho-Schleisner*)

FALL

The beds have been cleaned, the old vegetation cut to the ground, and a mulch of salt hay applied to protect the tenderer plants and to prevent the heaving of others. Color remains in the evergreens and in the bright branches of some of the shrubs, and the witch-hazels and corylopsis will supply yellow flowers from November and into the winter months. (Photo: *Gottscho-Schleisner*)

Broken by the lines of an informal pool edged with native stone, this flower border, designed by Dorothy Nichols, edges both sides of a low wall. Rock plants grow over the top of the wall, and perennials of varying heights give a long season of bloom. Flowering now are the iris and peonies, foxgloves, pinks and bellflowers. (Photo: *Gottscho-Schleisner*)

For great areas of solid color in May and June, the azalea is unsurpassed. Happiest with a little shade, it can be grown in most soils and situations, and the colors, in every shade except blues, complement the spring bulbs and the dogwoods which grow easily with them. Hybrids like the Glenn Dale, Gable and U.S.D.A. types, are bringing new forms and colors constantly into the home garden. (Photo: *Genereux*)

The flower border need not be large. It can fill an odd corner by a fence, or the bend of a path, as well as a long bed or wall. In the early fall, the chrysanthemums supply color in whites, reds, yellows and all their combinations. Dwarf box edging gives beds neatness and form, but weeding between the box and the line of the lawn takes time, and while it is used at lower right, the bed at left omits it. (Photo: *Genereux*)

In the garden picture small areas can be given special treatment. Above
is a flower-bordered small lawn, with brick-edged beds of annuals and
perennials surrounded with brick walls, high at the end, low at the sides,
and tied to the house by flag-stones laid in sand. The basic design of such
a garden is adaptable to the city backyard or a dooryard garden in the
country. (Photo: *Roche*) Below is a simple terraced pool, planted with
materials that ensure year-round color: azaleas and rhododendrons in the
background, spring bulbs, lilies and iris around the pool, with summer
flowering petunias and pansies, and a single dwarf evergreen for contrast.
(Photo: *Genereux*)

the last week in March at Washington), and stay in flower about a fortnight. The true double-flowered forms, in contrast to the semi-doubles, are almost immune to frost injury or pelting rain. The deep red form makes a striking and lovely foil for forsythia, when the two happen to bloom together. The double-flowered peach is perfectly hardy everywhere, and will grow in almost any good soil, as will peach trees. Unlike the latter the double-flowered peach bears either no fruit or a withered and futile imitation of it. But it is one of the most welcome of April's signs that Spring is here. It blooms before or with the unfolding of the leaves; and, as it is quite floriferous, a group of these plants is a memorable sight.

VIBURNUM CARLESI. This little Korean shrub, although introduced as recently as 1902, still has no common name. But everyone can recognize that it is first cousin to the wayfaring tree, and there the resemblance ends. *Viburnum carlesi* is one of the most fragrant of garden shrubs, and to have that rich spicy odor early in April has made the plant such a general favorite that it is a must in every garden. Fortunately it is small, usually 3-5 feet high, compact, round-headed, and before the leaves unfold it bears its flat-topped clusters of white or pinkish-white flowers. It is not a "showy" shrub, but one of the best for foundation planting, and will thrive almost anywhere.

SPIREAS. So popular is the name Bridal Wreath that it has been applied to at least two and perhaps incorrectly to three species of small-flowered spireas all belonging to the genus *Spiraea*. They bear minute white flowers in very floriferous clusters in April, early May, and even June, so that they are quite confusing to the amateur. If you go to a nursery and ask just for Bridal Wreath, you'll probably get the second of those below, as it is the commonest *Spiraea* in cultivation. These spring-flowering spireas all provide a mass of bloom, no odor, and, especially the second species, will stand a good deal of city smoke, dust, and wind. Arranged approximately in the order of their flowering the spireas of interest in April, which should be ordered by their scientific names are:

Spiraea thunbergi. A low shrub 3-5 feet high, very twiggy, moderately floriferous, and a native of China. It is the earliest of all the spireas to bloom, followed by its near relative, *Spiraea arguta,* which is a hybrid, a little taller, and much more floriferous.

Spiraea prunifolia plena. This is the plant to which the name Bridal Wreath should perhaps be confined. It is widely cultivated, because it is covered by its myriad clusters of tiny white, double flowers. The bush came originally from

China, Korea, and Formosa and has since gone around the
temperate world. It grows into a compact shrub 5-7 feet
high, the outer branches arching. In the spring it is almost
impossible to see the twigs or branches for the mass of flowers.

Spiraea vanhouttei. A hybrid shrub, 5-9 feet high, and the name
Bridal Wreath is often attached to it. Branches more or less
erect, and the flower clusters, which are very numerous are
not so compact as in the preceding. It is one of the most
planted of spireas, and it blooms late in April and usually
until mid-May.

Perhaps it is unnecessary to add that all these spireas are perfectly
hardy everywhere, will grow in a variety of soils, but all of them
thrive best in full sunshine.

REDBUD. About peach-blossom time there are two attractive shrubs
or small trees that have small, pea-like flowers on perfectly
naked twigs. Both belong to the genus *Cercis,* and one of them, the
Chinese redbud (*Cercis chinensis*), is a fine garden plant. It is a
tree in its native home, but rarely reaches 10-15 feet here and is
inclined to be shrubby. Flowers very numerous, reddish-purple, almost magenta and not liked by some on this account, but in masses,
the color is very handsome against bare twigs. The Chinese redbud
is not certainly hardy north of New York, but there is the American
redbud (*Cercis canadensis*) to substitute for it, which is perfectly
hardy everywhere. It is not quite such a desirable shrub as the Chinese kind, but the horticulturists have developed a white-flowered
variety which is much preferred by those allergic to magenta, and
for those who do not mind magenta there is a double-flowered form
of the American species. Both of them grow well in sandy loams, but
neither of them do so well in moist places. While they will grow
well in open sunshine they do not mind partial shade, perhaps because they are naturally at home in the under-canopy of the forest.

YULAN (*Magnolia denudata*). For anyone with lawn space this is the
finest magnolia tree ever to come out of China and it has been
deservedly popular ever since it was first brought to Europe just
eight years after the American Revolution. It is a magnificent flowering tree with handsome light green ovalish leaves, which do not come
out until the flowers are through blooming. The flowers are large,
cup-shaped, 4-6 inches wide, pure white and fragrant. There is a
variety of it with the flowers rose-red outside and pink inside.

For those who do not have space for this most majestic of flowering
trees (it may reach a height of 40 feet) a shrubby substitute is the

hybrid *Magnolia soulangeana,* which rarely exceeds 20 feet and has
even larger white flowers, while a variety of it (known as var. *lennei*)
has flowers rose-purple on the outside.

Both these magnolias require full sun and are hard to transplant,
because like all the tribe they have brittle and fragile roots. They
will come from any good nursery with a ball of earth tightly wrapped
in bagging or canvas, which should never be taken off until planting
time. Both kinds are relatively expensive, and the Yulan should
flower about mid-April, the other a week or two later.

JAPANESE FLOWERING CHERRIES. For centuries the Japanese, among
        the most skillful gardeners in the world, have been working
to improve a trio of Asiatic species of *Prunus* (a huge genus that also
includes the edible cherry, the plum, and dozens of ornamental
shrubs and trees). There has been so much hybridizing that the
parentage of the named and unnamed forms (of which there are
scores) is so confused that there is little need to untangle it here.
From among them it is possible to make a selection that will include
some of the finest flowering shrubs and trees in existence, most of
them flowering in April, especially toward the latter half of it. Most
of them require full sunshine, and they are not quite hardy from
Boston northward. All those below are perfectly hardy from Connecticut (especially near the coast) southward. Some of the varieties
still have their Japanese names, but these are often in doubt, so
that the safest course, before planting, is to visit a good labeled collection at a nursery and pick out your choice for future delivery.
The best varieties for a small collection should include:

> *Rosebud cherry.* This is the most popular of the weeping Japanese
>   cherries. It is grafted on a standard and the fountain-like,
>   weeping branches, covered with pink bloom reach almost
>   to the ground.
> *Kwanzan.* A tree (10-20 feet) with double, rose-pink flowers in
>   immense profusion.
> *Yoshino.* A tree up to 40 feet, with a great profusion of single pink
>   flowers.
> *Pink Wohlert.* A semi-dwarf variety with deep pink, double flow-
>   ers.
> *Fujisan-sakura.* A tree 15-25 feet with white flowers.
> *Kofugen.* A tree up to 40 feet, with deep pink double flowers.

If this seems a meager list, from the scores that are available,
it should be remembered that most of them take considerable space
(the trees should be 20-30 feet apart). Most readers will not have

room for the half dozen suggested above, but from them even one or two will make a memorable garden feature.

BULBS

From bulbous plants, using only the three groups below, the garden can have continuous April bloom, and the various kinds of narcissus will provide plenty of cut flowers. None of these bulbs need annual planting. They can be left alone, once they are established, until they show signs of failure to bloom, at which time they must be dug up, the small bulblets separated from the old one, and replanted. This is particularly true of narcissus, where, in old gardens it is common to see a good growth of leaves each spring, but no flowers. Such plantations are over-crowded and must be replanted after the leaves normally wither.

GRAPE-HYACINTH (*Muscari botryoides*). The grape-hyacinths look not unlike tiny replicas of the hyacinth, and because they are so small, should be planted by the scores or, better yet, by the hundreds. They do well under the shade of shrubs and, if planted 3 inches apart, will in a few years provide sheets of color. The typical form is blue, and an especially good variety of it is Heavenly Blue. Other color forms are available, especially fine being a white variety, also pink. They should be planted about 3 inches deep, preferably in early October, and will ordinarily spread and continue blooming for years.

STRIPED SQUILL (*Puschkinia scilloides*). Related to the true squills (*Scilla*) which will be found in the chapter devoted to March. The striped squill, often called Lebanon squill, is a pretty little bulbous plant from the eastern Mediterranean with basal, narrow leaves and a cluster of striped, bluish bell-shaped flowers that are scarcely one-half inch long, but the terminal flower cluster is handsome. Plant, about 3 inches deep, preferably in masses, in any good garden soil in October. They flower early in April and will usually last a fortnight if there is no pelting rain.

NARCISSUS. Old garden favorites scarcely needing description except to note the groups that will keep almost continuous April bloom in the garden. Arranged approximately in the order of their flowering, these are:

Jonquil (*Narcissus jonquilla*). Flowers in clusters of 2-6, decidedly fragrant, generally yellow or pale yellow, each flower with a short, central "trumpet." There are double-flowered forms, but they are not especially desirable.

Poet's narcissus (*Narcissus poeticus*). A beautiful white-flowered, very fragrant bulbous plant from southern Europe. It, too, has a very short central trumpet or crown at the center of each flower and the crown is both wavy-margined and red-edged, so that the flower is very showy.

Trumpet narcissus (*Narcissus pseudo-narcissus*). This is the common daffodil, forced by the florist for winter bloom and found, or should be, in every garden. It has a great, central, wavy-edged "trumpet," and although most varieties are yellow, there are also forms with golden-yellow, or white flowers, and others where the trumpet is white and the petals yellow or vice versa. Some of the recently introduced, named forms, which are little better than older varieties, are relatively expensive.

The paper white and the Chinese Sacred Lily, both of which are forms of a related species of *Narcissus*, are, unfortunately, not hardy in our area.

All forms of the above groups of narcissus should be planted in the fall, in open sunshine, and are likely, within three years, to become so crowded that they cease to flower. Lifting and replanting will then be necessary. This, and the initial planting, should leave the bottom of the bulb at least 5 inches below the surface. They need good average soil, but no manure must touch the bulbs.

PERENNIALS

While April bloom can be pretty well provided for with the shrubs, trees, and bulbs, there are a few perennial herbs which most gardeners will always want, to supply variety and also provide cut flowers. The following, arranged approximately in the order of their flowering, are:

ADONIS VERNALIS. Related to the annual pheasant's-eye, this perennial from Europe is only about 9 inches high, has finely dissected leaves and a solitary, waxy, yellow, rather showy flower. It may, in favorable places, bloom late in March, and there are both white and double-flowered varieties of it.

PASQUE-FLOWER. There are two species of these attractive, anemone-like perennials, one American, the other European. They are closely related to *Anemone* but have silky plume-like fruit almost as handsome as the flowers. The first to bloom is the European pasque-flower (*Pulsatilla vulgaris*), which has blue, reddish-purple or lilac flowers, bell-shaped and about 2 inches wide. The American species (*Pulsatilla patens*) has predominately bluish-purple flowers which bloom a little later. Both of them are still sometimes listed in the catalogs as *Anemone*, but if the above names are used, you will get the pasque-flowers and not garden anemones. As border plants (they vary from 10-18 inches high) the pasque-flowers are handsome, April-flowering perennials, suitable to any site.

PRIMROSE. Of all the primroses grown in American gardens (more than two dozen different kinds), only two will be included here, and they should not be tried unless you can give them the right conditions. Wordsworth knew this when he wrote: "A primrose by a river's brim," for the plants need shade and a moist site. If you have such a place, few plants are more attractive than the English primrose (*Primula vulgaris*) which grows 4-6 inches high, has a basal rosette of leaves and, in the typical form, a yellow flower. So popular is this plant that blue, white, and double-flowered forms have been developed. Related to it is the oxlip (*Primula elatior*), which is a little taller, and flowers as Shakespeare said it would on a bank "where oxlip and the nodding violet grows." The oxlip is very showy, its yellow flowers being crowded in a close cluster. If you have a moist place under the shade of deciduous trees, both of the primroses are splendid for naturalizing in masses or drifts.

IRIS. Nearly a month before German iris, and practically two months before the Japanese iris are in bloom, there are a couple of low stemless irises that are especially welcome in mid-April and a little later. The first to bloom is the crested iris (*Iris cristata*), native in the southeastern states, but perfectly hardy up to Boston. It has stemless lilac flowers and is fine for edging a border. Flowering a little later is a Eurasian species (*Iris pumila*), which has also practically stemless flowers, that now come in a variety of colors. Unlike the American plant, *Iris pumila* has rather shallow roots and needs frequent transplanting.

LUNGWORT (*Pulmonaria angustifolia*). While this rough-hairy perennial will first bloom in April, its blue flowers will still be found up into June or even July. It is a somewhat sprawling plant, 6-12 inches high, perfectly hardy everywhere, and of easy culture. Its irregular flowers are in a coiled cluster which unwinds as the flowers open. There is also a pale-blue form listed in the catalogs as var. *azurea*.

VIOLET. Any of the native violets can be dug from the wild, and most of them require partial shade and a reasonably moist site. One of the best is the Confederate violet (*Viola priceana*), native from Maryland southward and perhaps the most adaptable and the showiest of all our native violets. It grows 5-8 inches high, has large flowers, partly blue, but partly white with dark blue stripes. It is hardy at least as far north as New York and will grow well in open places.

GROUND PINK. Low, ground-hugging, almost moss-like plants, admirably suited to covering rocky banks and growing easily in any open place. The typical, and many think the most objectionable form, has magenta flowers. But there is a fine pink variety known as Alexander's Pink, and one of the most attractive is pure white. It is quite prostrate, a good ground cover and in a few years will provide sheets of color from late April into May.

CHAPTER V

May

*"Fair laughs the morn,
and soft the zephyr blows"*

A REASONABLY complete floral calendar of May-blooming plants might easily comprise over 500 kinds, even if we limited it to fairly well-known garden species. But have no fear—this is not to be a staggering list of what might be. It is rather a selected list, not over fifteen groups in all, of what every gardener can easily do to make this enchanted month what Milton called "The flowery May."

May-day and the Maypole were no accident in the history of England, even if our New England ancestors frowned on such frivolities. Not for them that wild rustic gaiety—no Queen-of-the-May, no ale and games—it was for them merely the first day of the fifth month. We have come a long way from those dour, bleak days with our modern apple-festivals, the tulip festival at Holland, Michigan, and lilac time at Rochester, New York, where special trains are needed to take happy throngs. We know in our hearts that it is the season of flowers, that Spring is really here, and the last fling of winter is safely behind us. It is the season of countless outdoor flower shows, not the indoor and premature pageants of March, but the outpouring of garden lovers who bring their blooms to be seen, and look themselves at the glories of tulip, hyacinth, wisteria, dogwood, peony, iris, and a score more.

At such shows, especially if they are near big cities, novelties will often be shown. Some of them may be better than existing varieties, but many will not, and even some that have been patented will ultimately disappear. All of them, while still in the magical category of being a "novelty," will be expensive—often three or four times as much as an equally good and much more reliable older variety. Flashy descriptions and extravagant advertising are no guarantee of perfection, and in purchasing plant novelties the wise buyer will keep constantly in mind that old Roman caution *caveat emptor*.

Which brings us to the selection of plants for this chapter. It is purposely restricted, and those wanting data about other plants had better go to a bigger book than this one. It is of no use to crowd these pages with more plants than the average home gardener can grow. What are listed below will provide continuous bloom throughout May, and some of them will still be flowering into early June.

Notwithstanding, it is with some temerity that the list is so restricted and yet so common. But many years of watching flower shows and gardens brings a measure of caution and a skepticism of blatant claims. Horticultural magazines are full of "rare" finds, new and misleading names for old favorites, and a come-on attitude that, translated into purchases by the unwary or the puzzled, often leads to disillusionment. There will be none with the plants below. You may not be able to indulge in the questionable pastime of implying, ever so politely, that you are an incipient fancier or expert. But the knowing will recognize that your garden has a well-planned scheme of May bloom, in many colors, with a judicious mixture of shrubs, trees, perennials, and bulbs.

TREES

In the average suburban garden the owner is lucky if he has room for more than three or four trees, and at least one of these must be a shade tree, grown for foliage and never mind the flowers. But by a little planning, he can get in one or two flowering trees, and if possible they should be accent plants, so placed on the lawn that they invite attention, excite wonder, and in bloom are a yearly thrill. Scarcely any May-flowering trees are better for this purpose than the two below.

CRABAPPLE, or simply *Crab*. The bitter, small apples used by our grandmothers to make jelly have a prolific progeny, among them some of the most showy of flowering trees. They are often mistaken for the Japanese flowering cherries (see *April*), but the crabapples flower generally in May, and in the single varieties have apple-like blossoms. All belong to the group known as *Malus*, and they should be carefully specified as there are many species and hybrids. The one selected here is *Malus spectabilis,* a Chinese tree not usually over 25 feet high, and one of the most showy trees in cultivation. In the typical form the buds are rose-red, opening into a blush flower that is either single or semi-double. This sort bears a sour and bitter miniature apple. There is a stunning double, white-flowered variety which should be ordered as var. *albiplena,* and perhaps the finest of all is var. *riversi,* which has larger and double, pink flowers. The latter two varieties bear no fruit. All of them are perfectly hardy and will grow in any garden. As specimen trees, when in full bloom they are breathtaking.

DOGWOOD. When dogwood is in flower, its greenish inconspicuous petals pass unnoticed. These are the real flowers, however, that produce the handsome red berries of autumn, but no one would grow dogwood if it were not for the showy, notched, white bracts that are just under the true flower and ten times the size. This is what splashes great patches of white in our forests, during most of May, and it is for these that we grow it in the garden. The tree is naturally one of the under-canopy of the forest, and hence should prefer partial shade. But it is sufficiently adaptable so that it will grow also in the open. However, it does not like wind, and if you can give it a site that has shade for part of the day it will be likely to thrive better. The tree is slow-growing, scarcely ever exceeds 25 feet, and in cultivation it is usually less. While the dogwood is normally pure white, a red or pink variety is even more showy. Many who have the room plant both of them in proximity, and the effect is enchanting.

Dogwood is not an easy tree to move. It is thus better to start with a young specimen (3-4 feet), and it should come from the nursery with a ball of earth tightly wrapped in bagging. Do not take this off until actual planting time, and see that the ball of earth is kept moist if planting is to be delayed. The plants are relatively expensive, and you can often dig your own from the woods, but this generally will fail unless you select a young plant (1-2 feet), dig it very carefully, and prevent the roots from drying out. Once established, the dogwood is a thing of beauty as George Washington knew, when on his birthday in 1785 he planted a "circle dogwood with a redbud in the middle." They are still at Mount Vernon.

SHRUBS AND VINES

For those with no room for trees, it is still possible to have continuous May bloom from only three groups of shrubs and our most handsome of woody vines. They are:

WISTERIA. Of the several kinds of these showy, woody vines, it is best to order by its name *Wistaria floribunda* which is a native of Japan, but will, from any good nursery, come as a grafted plant on the roots of another species. Insist on this to be sure that the vine will bear its magnificent trusses of violet-blue, pea-like flowers. Many complain that wisteria is erratic about blooming, or that it fails to bloom for years. It is often because they do not have the right variety, and it may not be a grafted plant. Also, as it will climb 30-50 feet, it is better to snip off the straggling lateral growth, which will help flowering, and promote its growth up a tree or building, to which it must be tied at first. Later it will cling to its support unless this is merely a bare wall. For such it is better to grow it on a trellis. Wisterias are slow to get started but rampant once they are established. A fine variety has white flowers, and the variety *macrobotrys* has huge flower clusters nearly 3 feet long. Wisterias are hardy everywhere.

DEUTZIA. Very popular shrubs of many kinds, but the two here suggested are May-blooming, very floriferous, and have no common name. They are perfectly hardy, of the easiest culture in open sunshine, and tolerate a variety of soils. *Deutzia gracilis* is one of the most widely cultivated shrubs in America, because of the profusion of its small, white flowers (there is a pink variety known as *rosea*), and its compact habit which rarely exceeds 2½ feet in height. A related plant is *Deutzia lemoinei*, which is more open in its branching and may be 4-7 feet high. Its white flowers are produced in profusion, each blossom being about ½ inch wide. A variety of it, Boule de Neige, is far handsomer than the typical form, as its flowers are nearly twice the size. Another good deutzia will be found in the chapter devoted to June.

LILAC. It is now nearly 400 years since the common lilac was brought into cultivation from wild bushes in southeastern Europe. No one then would have dreamed that French hybridists would, from that old favorite and other species, have produced hundreds of horticultural varieties, both single and double-flowered, and in many colors, except yellow and orange. Some of this prolific production of varieties has been at the expense of the wonderful fragrance of the parent type. But some of the hybrids are very sweet smelling. The lilac will grow from 8-15 feet high and demands full sunshine for the production of its great trusses of flowers. Of the scores of varieties offered by the expert lilac growers, the amateur can obviously grow only a few, if for nothing else because they demand plenty of space. Those listed below will provide almost continuous bloom in May and are the varietal names under which they will be found in the catalogs:

White, single-flowered: Vestal, Mont Blanc, Marie Legraye.
White, double-flowered: Ellen Willmott, Edith Cavell.
Red, single-flowered: Congo, Monge.
Red, double-flowered: Charles Joly.
Purple or lilac-purple, single-flowered: Descaine.
Purple or lilac-purple, double-flowered: Colbert, Waldeck Rousseau, Charles Sargent.
Bluish-lavender, single-flowered: Crampel, President Lincoln.
Bluish-lavender, double-flowered: President Grevy.
Rosy-pink, single-flowered: Marechal Foch.
Rosy-pink, double-flowered: Leon Gambetta.

There are, in addition to these hybrid lilacs, a number of wild species, that extend lilac bloom beyond May or anticipate it in late April. Among them are the Hungarian lilac and Persian lilac, both of which are available at the better nurseries.

AZALEA. When Linnaeus coined the name *Azalea* he took it from a Greek word for *dry*, upon the assumption that these most beautiful of flowering shrubs need dry sites. Nothing could be further from the truth; although they do not want their roots in water, they must be protected from summer droughts by a mulch of leaves. Also it is useless to attempt growing them unless you have a soil with considerable sand and humus, free of lime, and a site that is preferably in shade for part of the day.

May is *the* month for Azalea bloom although the rhododendrons, which are first cousins, or almost brothers, are mostly in bloom in June and are evergreen, the azaleas, at least those below, generally drop their leaves in winter, especially in the North. So popular are these shrubs that hybridizers, mostly in Europe have developed hundreds of named forms, the parentage of which, while it dictates their hardiness, is in such confusion that even the experts are uncertain. From this mass of material, all that can be done here is to list a few groups that will give continuous May bloom. All are hardy at New York and south of it, and many of them will grow north of it if along the coast or in protected places. The dates given are for the time when the plant should be in full bloom at New York in an average season. South or north of this the expected period of full bloom will be earlier or later. Arranged in the approximate order of their blooming, those selected are:

Azalea vaseyi. May 5-10th. A beautiful native species from North Carolina, 6-10 feet high, its flowers light rose, but spotted with brownish-orange dots.

Kurume azaleas. May 9-15. A low (1-1½ feet) compact race of azaleas, developed years ago near Kurume, Japan, and so covered with bloom that it is almost impossible to see the twigs. They come in almost every color except yellow, and more than 50 varieties are offered. Not hardy much north of Delaware.

Mollis azaleas. May 15-20, and often beyond. A race of hybrid azaleas derived from crossing *Azalea mollis* of China with *Azalea japonica* of Japan. The mollis azaleas, of which there are scores in the trade, are medium-sized shrubs (2-5 feet), and their colors vary from yellow, orange, and orange-red to copper, flame, and salmon-pink.

Ghent azaleas. May 20-25, and often beyond. A highly complicated race of hybrid azaleas, all developed in Europe, especially in Belgium, from crossing and inter-crossing American and other species. They are somewhat taller shrubs (6-9 feet), and among the most popular of all cultivated azaleas, of every color, some double-flowered, and are offered in scores of varieties. Not quite hardy in exposed places north of New York.

Azalea mucronata. May 25-31, and beyond. A Chinese, usually evergreen shrub 4-6 feet high, with brilliantly white, fragrant flowers. It needs a sheltered place from New York northward, and is uncertainly hardy north of Boston.

Flame azalea (*Azalea calendulacea*). May 28 into June. A magnificent native shrub, 6-15 feet high, and one of the parents of the Ghent azaleas. It is, however, more hardy than the hybrids and can be safely grown from northern New England southward. Flowers very showy, yellow, orange or scarlet. One of the most hardy and gorgeous of all cultivated azaleas.

It is obvious that the average amateur will have room for only one or two in each group of the above, but in case you have a woodland path or a partially shaded border, massed plantings of these shrubs will give an effect second only to the evergreen rhododendrons.

PERENNIALS AND BULBS

If the trees and shrubs of May seem somewhat formidable, and you have room for only a handful, it is still possible to have continuous May bloom by using one or more of the perennial herbs and bulbous plants mentioned below. They can be grown in limited space, and some of them provide the best cut flowers you are likely to grow.

PINKS. The genus *Dianthus,* which includes the carnation of the florists, contains also many hardy plants easily grown in any ordinary garden, which the carnation is not. Of the readily grown sorts, the best are:

Maiden Pink (*Dianthus deltoides*). A prostrate, mat-forming plant with greenish foliage, from which spring flowering stalks 8-12 inches high crowned by red or pink, fringed flowers, one variety of which is white with a crimson eye.

Cheddar Pink (*Dianthus cruentus*). A small plant, growing in tufts with dense, head-like clusters of deep red flowers, which stand well above the grayish foliage.

Grass Pink (*Dianthus plumarius*). Many of the garden pinks are included here. Foliage bluish-gray, the plant mat-forming. From this bed spring forked flowering stalks crowned by two or three fragrant flowers with beautifully fringed petals. It comes in many colors, except yellow and blue, and some varieties are double-flowered. It is an old garden favorite and will bloom also long after May.

WALLFLOWER (*Cheiranthus cheiri*). One of the most sweet-smelling of early-blooming perennials, the wallflower, in spite of its name can be grown in ordinary garden soil, so long as the site is not too wet. The plant is about a foot high, and has terminal clusters of yellow or orange-brown flowers (red in a horticultural variety), and is good for window boxes, as its perfume will scent a room through an open window.

LILY-OF-THE-VALLEY. Not over 6-8 inches high, its nearly evergreen leaves handsome, especially when the plants are in masses, and partly or wholly under the shade of trees. It does not like the open sunshine. Flowers, small, bell-shaped, nodding, cream-white and delicately fragrant. Planted from "pips," which are erect growths from the rootstock, preferably in March. They may not flower the first year, and when the clumps get too crowded they must be re-spaced, or flowering will become erratic.

PEONY. Strikingly bold perennials with large leaves that are reddish early in the spring, but green later. The plant may be 18-30 inches high and needs space (at least 2 feet apart). It is grown, however, for its magnificent, globe-shaped flowers which may be

4-5 inches in diameter, and are among our most handsome of cut flowers. Peonies do not like to be disturbed, so they should be planted where wanted, and may not flower the first year after planting. There are many varieties (over 200) and of these a selection might be:

White: LeCygne, Alice Harding, La Perle, Kelway's Glorious.

Light Pink: Lady Alexandra, Milton Hill, Cornelia Shaylor.

Pink: Walter Faxon, Venus, President Wilson.

Red: Longfellow, Augusta Dessert, Cherry Hill.

For yellow colors in peonies one must turn to the so-called tree peonies, which are a little shrubby and are hybrids based on a different species from the above varieties. Good yellows, all derived from *Paeonia lutea* are: La Lorraine, Chromatella, and Argosy.

Peonies should be planted in rich soil, for they are robust plants and heavy feeders. Do not plant them deeper than 2-3 inches below the soil level, and see that the hole is wide enough so that the roots can be spread without crowding. Plant the roots in late September or in October; avoid planting in the spring if possible. They will grow in full sunshine, but cut peony flowers will last longer if from plants that have shade part of the day, which they tolerate very well. Peony bloom will generally begin about mid-May and often last through June.

IRIS. May is *the* month for German iris, so known before World War I, but now quite often known as tall bearded iris. Although more of the 1500 varieties bloom in May than in any other month, they are scattered throughout the growing season, some having another blooming period in the fall. No garden plant is so easy to grow as the German iris, and short of absolute abuse it is difficult to kill. Hence their enormous popularity with amateurs from Maine to California, not to speak of their most beautiful, bearded flowers of almost every color. The taller Japanese iris mostly flowers in June and will be found in that chapter.

Tall bearded irises have a stout rootstock which may be chopped up and planted almost anywhere. Each piece will make a new plant which varies from 15-30 inches in height. Of course, like any other garden plant they will do better in reasonably good soil, but German iris resents neglect less than most garden favorites. Do not, however, expect it to do well in dense shade.

When it comes to selecting from among the 1500 varieties, the task is almost hopeless. There is a constant crop of novelties, at high prices, which the amateur will do well to avoid. From among the well known and dependable varieties, all of which are cheap, a reasonable selection might include:

White (but often marked with other colors): White Knight, Rhein Nixe, Alba superba, Arctic, Snow Flurry.
Blue and bluish-purple: West Point, Baldwin, Storm King, Princess Beatrice.
Pink to Red-Purple: California Peach, Mary Senn, Pink Satin, Lighthouse.
Blending colors: Afterglow, Dolly Madison, China Maid, Copper Rose.
Yellow: Gold Imperial, Jasmine, Ming Yellow, Treasure Island.

PURPLE ROCK CRESS (*Aubrietia deltoides*). A delightful little perennial, never more than 6 inches high, usually half that, its grayish-green foliage forming a ground-hugging mat. Flowers small, pinkish-purple in the typical form, but found in many color forms in some of its varieties. It is fine for edgings, for a rocky bank, or any other open place. Purdy's Blush and Lavender Queen are two good varieties.

TULIPS. For the average small garden, the tulip is best restricted, so far as May bloom is concerned, to Cottage tulips and Darwin tulips, because of the availability of the bulbs, ease of culture, and range of color. From the varieties below, there will be some tulips in bloom throughout May, without resorting to various tulip species or classes such as Bizarres, Parrots, etc.

Cottage and Darwin tulips should be planted in October or November for bloom the following spring, about 4 inches deep for the Cottage and 6 inches deep for the Darwins from the top of the bulb to soil level. Both are May-flowering, but the Darwins are generally taller, and their large squarish blossoms have bluntish, in-turned petals. The Cottage tulips have pointed petals, which may or may not be in-turned at the tip, and the flower is generally smaller than with the Darwins. The latter are the finer and consequently most expensive. Cottage tulips may, in some catalogs, be classed as May-flowering tulips.

There are hundreds of varieties, and the craze for novelties became so great in Holland, even as far back as 1630, that the Dutch government finally put a stop to tulipomania when a single bulb fetched $10,000 at auction. Novelties are still expensive, and the varieties selected below are older, well-tried ones that will give splendid color, particularly in masses where tulips are always the most effective. And they are relatively cheap.

Cottage Tulips, generally 15-20 inches high when in flower:

Red: Fulgens, Glare of the Garden.
Pink: Siren, Barbara Pratt.
Yellow: Ellen Willmott, Moonlight, Avis Kennicott.
White: Albino.
Darwin Tulips, generally 18-30 inches high when in flower:
Red and Scarlet: William Pitt, City of Haarlem, Farncombe
Sanders.
Pink: Gretchen, Baronne de la Tonnaye, Matchless.
Yellow: Mrs. John Scheepers, Niphetos (sulfur yellow), Yellow
Giant.
White: White Giant, White Queen, Zwanenburg.
Almost Black: Le Noire.
Salmon-Pink: Clara Butt, Afterglow, Venus.
Purple-maroon: Faust.
Lilac: Dream, Duchess of Hohenburg.
HYACINTHS. Unlike the tulips, which have little or no odor, hyacinths
are among the sweetest-smelling of all spring-blooming bulbs.
They are of easy culture if the bulbs are planted in any good garden
soil, in October or November, and at least 5 inches below soil level
(to the top of the bulb). They grow 8-12 inches high and have a
showy, tight cluster of small, bell-shaped flowers of infinite colors in
the many varieties, mostly produced by Dutch bulb growers. The following varieties, without using expensive novelties, will provide a
range of color that may well be more extensive than your space for
them. They should be planted 7-9 inches apart.
White: L'Innocence, Purity, Queen of the North, Queen of the
Whites.
Pink: Lady Derby, Pink Pearl, Queen of Pinks, Gertrude (deep
pink).
Red: Roi des Belges, La Victoire.
Blue: King of the Blues, Oxford Blue, Queen of the Blues.
Yellow: Yellow Hammer.
Violet-mauve: King of the Violets.

CHAPTER VI

June

"Then, if ever, come perfect days."

No POET need remind us that June is the month of roses, that toward its end comes the beginning of summer, that on the twenty-first sunshine is at its highest and will soon be waning toward the long-distant dread of winter. But no dry meteorological or astronomical data, not even the lavish horticultural display, can explain what Lowell meant when he wrote: "What is so rare as a day in June?"

Poets understand it, so do the young, and those fortunate few of the oldsters who never grow old. One can always remember June days, and as for the nights, Charles Hamilton Aide well knew that "Never can I forget that night in June." Nor can any gardener; for crowded into this thirty days of warm sunshine and cool nights, with ample rainfall and sparkling dews of a morning, are some of our most ravishing flowers. No trouble here to get continuous bloom. The wonder is what to choose amid the hundreds of June-flowering plants? What can the average amateur, with small space and perhaps as lean a purse, select from the opulence of June?

Any tyro could suggest scores of trees, shrubs, vines, and perennials, and the experts would add several hundred more. This little book shuns such encyclopedic complexities, for what the average gardener seeks is an everblooming garden that will be a reflection of his own taste with no tinge of competition with those who know it all or with the lavish displays of the rich.

This can be done with a comparatively small group of plants, and those selected here will give continuous bloom through June and, except for rhododendrons, do it comparatively cheaply. Rhododendrons are never cheap, but almost everyone will scrimp to have one or two, and the fortunate will indulge in mass plantings.

June is as prolific with shrub and tree bloom as May, but toward the end of the month there is a notable slackening which is accentuated in July and, of course, reaches a climax of paucity from August to frost. There is excellent scientific evidence that this waning of shrub and tree bloom is due to the constantly decreasing amount of sunshine as the summer progresses. When we begin to say that the "days are getting shorter," which happens about the end of June, most of us never realize that garden shrubs and trees appear to know it too. At any rate they act that way and seem to anticipate July, when only about half as many shrubs and trees will bloom as in June.

If you have the space, by all means put in one or more of the shrubs and trees noted below, for they are permanent and need, except for rhododendrons, little subsequent care. Without any perennials you can have continuous June bloom from the five groups here selected.

SHRUBS AND TREES

Not many trees start their bloom in June, but a showy exception is the Golden Chain (*Laburnum anagyroides*), a tree 10-20 feet high with feathery compound foliage and handsome clusters of pea-like, yellow or golden-yellow flowers that stay in bloom for a fortnight. It is an admirable tree for a lawn specimen, and takes far less space than some of the June-flowering magnolias, which clamor for inclusion, but are generally too large for the small garden.

Among June-flowering shrubs are:

PRIDE OF ROCHESTER (A form of *Deutzia scabra*). A dense shrub, often 5-9 feet high, covered with a mass of small, almost bell-shaped flowers that are double, white with a blush of pink, and very showy. As an informal border and unclipped "hedge" it makes a fine screen. Hardy everywhere and of easy culture in any garden.

ROSES. The tribe is legion and one must decide whether to have only the popular hybrid tea roses, some species roses, or some climbers, or all three. From them you can have roses all through June, and with some varieties, for the rest of the summer. There are many other classes of roses, but these three groups will be all that the average garden can accommodate.

Hybrid Tea Roses. An immense group of hybrid roses, generally less than 5-6 feet high, and as usually grown, often half this. They need, for proper blooming, a bed of rich soil, at least 1 foot deep, and 2 feet is even better. They also need full sunshine. In the north, they should be pruned back almost to the level of the ground at the approach of spring, taking out all dead canes and the dead part of all live ones. More than 500 hybrid tea roses are offered by dealers. Most amateurs will be happy to make a selection, according to his color preference from the following:

White: Mme. Jules Bouche, Snowbird, White Briarcliff (also called Mme. Louis Lens).

Red: Christopher Stone, Crimson Glory, Red Radiance.

Yellow: Eclipse, Golden Dawn, Mrs. Pierre S. du Pont.

Pink: Radiance, Editor McFarland, Mary Margaret McBride.

Salmon: Mme. Butterfly, President Herbert Hoover, Comtesse Vandal, Autumn.

Climbing Roses. Nothing is finer for covering arbors, trellises, or walls than the climbing roses, which are just as showy as the hybrid teas, but have climbing stems that are 10-20 feet long. The only pruning they need is to cut out dead shoots, or those that have been winter-killed, which in the North may, in a very cold winter, be considerable. Cut out only that part of the shoot that has been killed. Among good climbing roses are:

White: Silver Moon, Purity.

Red: Crimson Rambler, Chevy Chase, Paul's Scarlet Climber.

Yellow: King Midas, Elegance, Jacotte, La Reve.

Pink: American Pillar, Isle de France, Mary Wallace.

Species Roses. Whenever these Hybrid Tea and Climbing roses have any fragrance, and most of them have some, it is derived from old species of roses cultivated for more than two thousand years by the Persians for perfume, and in modern times in France and Bulgaria for the extraction of attar of roses. These and other species of rose were used by breeders to produce by hybridization the enormous number of hybrid roses we know today. The flowers are not so showy as any of those above, but some may like to tuck a plant or two of these old-fashioned species among their more spectacular descendants:

Damask Rose (*Rose damascena*). A shrub 5-7 feet high, its flowers

somewhat double, or single, pink or red, and so fragrant
that it is, in Europe, a source of attar of roses.

Provence Rose (*Rosa gallica*). A shrub 3-4 feet high, its single,
very fragrant, pink or red flowers, used in France for perfumery.

Father Hugo's Rose (*Rosa hugonis*). Not fragrant, but a striking
Chinese shrub, 6-8 feet high with a profusion of yellow,
single flowers.

RHODODENDRONS. These aristocrats of the garden, the finest broad-
leaved evergreen flowering shrubs in the world, should not be
grown unless you can give them the conditions they demand and
deserve. They do not like heat, wind, dust, or smoke; they should be
grown only in soils especially prepared for them; and the site should
preferably be in partial shade, or at least shaded for part of each
day. Dig out all existing soil for 1-2 feet and fill the hole with a
mixture of one part loam, one part sand, and one part acid peat,
thoroughly mixed. All rhododendrons are impatient of drought; and
to conserve moisture and protect the shallow roots (in the North)
from cold, there should always be a mulch 6-8 inches thick of oak
leaves. Never take this off, and add to it if decay or the wind has
reduced the depth of the mulch.

Although there are many species of rhododendrons, some American, but mostly Chinese or Himalayan, the most satisfactory for their
beautiful evergreen foilage and the huge flowers are hybrids, a few
of which are listed. All are shrubs that may be 6-9 feet high, or more
in favorable places, and some of them are in age tree-like.

White: Boule de Neige, Album elegans, Album grandiflorum.

Pink: Delicatissimum, Abraham Lincoln, Lady Armstrong, Hen-
rietta Sargent.

Purple: Purpureum elegans, Purpureum grandiflorum, Everestianum.

Red or Scarlet: Charles Dickens, Kettledrum, Atrosanguineum,
H. W. Sargent, Caractacus.

MOUNTAIN LAUREL. A native American shrub 4-8 feet high (tree-like
in the mountains of North Carolina) with fine evergreen
leaves and a handsome truss of white or pale pink flowers. It prefers
the same conditions as to soil and site as the rhododendrons, but will
survive and bloom in more unfavorable sites, that is, in full sun and
in most light (not clay) garden soils. It blooms about the first week
in June and will stay in flower for a fortnight.

PERENNIALS

For those without space for shrubs or trees, the ten groups of herbaceous perennials listed below will give continuous June bloom. Among them are some of the showiest garden plants, and all, except perhaps the lilies, are of the easiest culture. Either they can be planted from roots purchased from a nursery (often from a roadside stand) or you can grow your own from seed, except in the case of the lilies. Starting from seeds is far cheaper, but takes more time. Seeds of perennials can be sown in pots or boxes in August, and two or three weeks after germination the young seedlings should be pricked out, replanted with more space between each seedling, either in boxes or in a prepared bed, and permitted to grow along until frost. Late in November or December they should have a light mulch of straw or strawy manure. In the spring the young plants can be put where wanted, and most of them will flower during this second growing season and thereafter.

DELPHINIUM. Often called larkspur, very showy, erect perennials 4-6 feet high, their immense terminal, spire-like clusters among the handsomest of garden flowers. They prefer coolness to heat, and do particularly well in New England, especially near the sea, and in interior locations where elevation brings cool nights. Originally the larkspurs were blue, and the hybrids are still prevailingly blue, but very handsome varieties are found in pink, lavender, white, red, scarlet, and one particularly fine blue sort known as Blue Bird. The number of named forms is bewildering, and often inaccurate, so it is safest to order by color. Many of the delphiniums will stay in bloom for most of the summer, especially if the spikes are picked for cut flowers.

DAYLILIES. Stout, perennial, lily-like herbs, 2-3 feet high, of easier culture than real lilies, and providing continuous bloom through June, and in other varieties for most of the summer. They will grow in any ordinary garden soil and need scarcely any attention once they become established. There are scores of varieties, and there well may be hundreds in a year or two, for daylilies are popular with the plant breeders. Among the June-flowering varieties, some of which will stretch through July, are:

Mikado: Orange, with mahogany blotch.
Tangerine: Dark orange, lower than most varieties.
Hemerocallis flava: Yellow.
Gold Dust: Golden-yellow.

Queen of May: Yellowish-orange, early June and late May.
Cinnabar: Vermilion.
Luteola: Yellow.

For those who wish continuous daylily bloom, from mid-May until September, it is well to visit a nursery and select your plants by color and blooming period, as some of the newer hybrids are confusing as to name.

LILIES. Perhaps the aristocrats of all perennial plants. They have a wide range of colors, all of them must be started from purchased bulbs, planted at different depths below the surface, and they will repay adequate preparation of the soil. As they should not be disturbed once they are planted, it is well to dig out existing soil, if it is poor, and put in a mixture of equal parts of rich loam, clean sand, and rotted leaves, thoroughly mixed. This should be at least 18 inches deep and 2 feet will not be resented by these rich-feeding perennials. While they are so classed, they have a tendency to die out in a few years, and the simplest method of renewal is to replant with new bulbs.

The number of lily species is legion, and there are still more varieties.* Because of this it is safest to order these plants only by the technical or varietal names below. June-flowering sorts, which often stretch into the summer, might include the following, planted in full sunshine, unless otherwise noted:

Brocade: Orange-yellow, with brownish red spots; 5-6 feet high. Plant 8 inches deep, in partial shade.

Golden Orb: Yellowish-green, crimson-spotted, 5-6 feet high. Plant 8 inches deep, in partial shade.

Lilium browni: Outside brown-purple, inside cream-white, 3-4 feet high. Plant 8 inches deep.

Lilium candidum: White, 3-5 feet high. Plant 2 inches deep.

Lilium canadense: Reddish-yellow, spotted with dark spots, 2-5 feet high. Plant 10 inches deep.

Lilium concolor: Scarlet, 1½-2½ feet high. Plant 3 inches deep.

Lilium elegans: Crimson or yellow, 1-2 feet high. Plant 5 inches deep. There are several varieties of this, in shades of mahogany, dark yellow, dark red, and apricot.

Lilium martagon: Purplish, 4-5 feet high. Plant 4 inches deep in partial shade.

---

* A variety is a variant of a species, usually differing from the parent in color, form, height or other character, but not sufficiently so that it obviously belongs to a different species.

Lilium monadelphum: Yellow, 5-6 feet high. Plant 5 inches deep in partial shade.

FOXGLOVE. A showy biennial, 2-4 feet high, the source of digitalis and hence poisonous if eaten. Flowers somewhat bell-shaped, slightly irregular, nodding, typically purple-spotted, but coming also in white and pinkish forms. Of easy culture, but because it tends to die out in a year or two it has to be replanted every second year. Its discovery as a drug in an English stableyard by an observant widow and a country doctor is one of the most fascinating bits of medical history.

BELLFLOWER. Although most of the tall bellflowers, such as Canterbury Bells, flower in July or later, and will be found in the chapter on July, there is one beautiful June-flowering kind that is much lower and will grow in any garden soil. It is *Campanula portenschlagiana* and must be ordered by its horrendous name. It grows only 6-8 inches high and has bluish-purple flowers.

CORAL BELLS. Beautiful low-growing perennials, usually not more than 18 inches high, the typical form with coral-pink flowers, but a showy white variant is known as Perry's White. They prefer partial shade but will grow in the open if shade is not available.

BLUE SUCCORY. A handsome perennial from southern Europe, demanding full sun, but indifferent as to soil, growing 12-15 inches high, and crowned with showy heads of blue flowers nearly 2 inches wide. The head is dandelion-like, with the rays notched.

JAPANESE IRIS. (For German iris, see May.) These taller-growing irises, which have been hybridized by the Japanese for centuries, are among the most showy of June-blooming flowers. The plants vary from 18-30 inches, and the flowers may be 6-8 inches in diameter or even more! They come in nearly every color and had better be ordered by your preferred color, because the Japanese varietal names are in nearly hopeless confusion. Some American named varieties appear to be reliable, such as Cassandra and Morning Mists (white); Blue Danube and Blue Jay (blue); Pink Progress (pink); Mahogany and Orion (reddish-purple). They much prefer moist sites to dry ones and do well in partial shade. Most of them bloom late in June and stretch into mid-July, when most iris bloom is over.

LUPINES. Of all the many garden lupines on the market, the finest are the Russell hybrids, developed by George Russell of Yorkshire and now available by all good American dealers. They grow from 2½-3½ feet high, and the clusters of pea-like flowers, in reds, yellows, pinks and whites, give far greater color range than the original parent which was blue. Lupines are rich feeders and hence need good garden soil, but their culture, always in the open sun, is otherwise not difficult. Most of them will bloom well into July, and in some varieties, beyond.

POPPIES. Fragile, ephemeral, showy and most beautiful flowers of scarcely any use for cutting, because they wilt so soon. The group includes many species (an annual one is the source of opium), usually 15-36 inches high, and with quite gorgeous, solitary flowers. Of the several types only one needs to be considered here:

Oriental Poppy, 2-3 feet, with divided, hairy, large leaves, the brilliant scarlet flowers often 5-6 inches wide. There are also named varieties: Perry's White, Mrs. Perry (pink); Beauty of Livermore and Olympia (red).

These perennials need an open site, a reasonably open soil (little clay), and once planted they should be left alone for several years, as they flower better after becoming well established. Most Oriental poppies will continue to bloom throughout the summer.

CHAPTER VII

July

"No price is set on the lavish summer."

LAVISH summer may be, but not in flowering trees and shrubs, and many gardeners begin to wonder what they can plant to provide July bloom in shrub borders or whether Nature means us to have even one striking flowering tree as a lawn specimen. The truth is that the great rush of flowering trees and shrubs is pretty well over by the end of June. It is thus no longer a question of picking a few favorites from among scores, but quite definitely selecting from among the few those that seem most suitable.

Of course anyone can have masses of shrub and tree bloom in July by planting in quantity, but not everyone has space, and some prefer variety. And it is equally obvious that among perennials there is a lavish display throughout the month and well into August. When planning for the future, all that the gardener should remember is, that July is a comparatively lean month when it comes to showy bloom among shrubs and trees.

All the more welcome, then, is the quite spectacular bloom of the yellow-wood (*Cladrastis lutea*), which is native in the moonshine country of Kentucky, North Carolina, and Tennessee, and picked up its name of yellow-wood because pioneer women found that the inner bark of its roots was useful to dye homespuns a lasting yellow. That is why you will also find yellow-wood, in some nursery catalogs, listed as *Cladrastis tinctoria,* the latter name meaning "used by dyers."

For us, today, synthetic dyes have supplanted yellow-wood, but the tree, which grows 30-50 feet high, is almost our only showy flowering tree with July bloom. The flowers are white, pea-like, fragrant and hang in wisteria-like clusters that are from 12 to 20 inches long. It also has large compound leaves made up of 7-9 leaflets, each of which may be 3-4 inches long. The tree needs space, is perfectly hardy as far north as northern Massachusetts, and will thrive in any ordinarily good garden soil.

SHRUBS

SPIREAS. Long after the early spireas (see April) have finished blooming, there is a handsome group of summer-flowering kinds, which begin flowering about mid-July and may last well into August. These are best ordered by their technical names.

Spiraea alba, 4-6 feet high, its white flowers in spire-like clusters.

Spiraea bumalda, 1-2 feet high, its rose-red flowers in close, finger-shaped clusters. A particularly fine variety is known as Anthony Waterer.

Spiraea billiardi, 4-6 feet, its showy, red flowers in narrow, finger-shaped clusters.

All of these late-flowering spireas are perfectly hardy, will grow in any soils, and if given open sunshine will stand more neglect than most shrubs.

CHASTE TREE (*Vitex agnus-castus*). A very handsome shrub, 5-8 feet high, its compound leaves with 5-7 narrow, willow-like leaflets arranged finger-fashion. In mid-July it has showy, spire-like clusters of pale, lilac-blue flowers. An especially good variety, with deeper blue flowers is known as var. *macrophylla.* The chaste tree needs good soil, open sunshine, and in the region north of New York often winter-kills. However, even if some of the branches are winter-killed it will send up new flowering shoots next spring. There is also a white-flowered form.

BUTTERFLY-BUSH (*Buddleia davidi*). This quite fragrant shrub, 4-10 feet high, is often called summer lilac. It has beautiful green leaves that are nearly 8 inches long and prominently white-felty on the lower side. Flowers small, lilac, but with an orange spot in the throat, arranged in showy nodding clusters that are 6-12 inches long. Like the chaste tree, it is likely to winter-kill, but it responds to the same treatment. Besides the lilac-flowered common sort, there are a couple of varieties: var. *magnifica* with rose-purple flowers, and var. *veitchiana* with mauve flowers. The butterfly-bushes are among the

most attractive of summer-flowering shrubs and will continue blooming into August.

GENISTA TINCTORIA, sometimes called woadwaxen, is a Eurasian
shrub 2-3 feet high, with yellow, pea-like flowers in profuse
clusters. It is perfectly hardy and will stand rather dry places, such
as a south-facing bank.

BUTTON-BUSH (*Cephalanthus occidentalis*). A native shrub, 5-12 feet
high, which prefers moist rather than dry sites but will thrive
in most garden soils. In July it is lavishly covered with ball-like clusters of white, fragrant flowers. It is somewhat coarse-growing and
hence more suitable to a shrub border than as a specimen plant on
the lawn. Hardy everywhere.

PERENNIALS

The comparatively sparse shrub and tree bloom in July is amply
compensated by the profusion of perennials. From more than one
hundred groups that begin to bloom this month the following ten,
and their varieties, will provide a riot of color throughout July, while
many of them will stay in bloom for the rest of the summer. Two of
them, gladiolus and dahlia, should not properly be included among
perennials, as they are tender and need special attention, but they
are so much a part of the July garden that they are included here,
with directions for their culture. All the rest are true perennials and,
when once planted, are better left alone.

If, in a few years, they become too crowded, they can be dug out
in April, divided, and thus be made into three or four new plants,
which should immediately be replanted or given away if you have
no room for the increased stock. This division of the roots can just
as well be done in the autumn, unless the plants happen to be late-
blooming, when division should always be done early in the spring.

Some gardeners, especially beginners, are in doubt as to how far
apart plants should be set. If you want immediate effect you can
crowd them—all but the tallest going in about 8-10 inches apart. That,
of course, will mean lifting them a year or two hence to prevent overcrowding. If you are willing to wait a reasonable time for your effects,
most perennials, except the very tallest, are best planted 14-18 inches
apart. Some of the tallest kinds need 2-3 feet of space to mature
properly. It is for this reason that the approximate height of all the
perennials is stated so that you can tell how far apart you should
plant them and also how many plants you have room for.

GLADIOLUS. To judge by the florist's windows this is the most popular of all cut flowers that can be raised by both amateurs and professionals. It is certainly the most striking and satisfactory of cut flowers from the garden and will provide bloom throughout the summer, depending on how much space you can give to the innumerable varieties. Only a few can be listed here, by color, and from these you can make your choice.

Gladiolus (the preferred pronunciation is gla-dyé-o-lus) are all tender plants, originating in Africa, and must not be planted until all danger of frost is over. Their corms must be dug up in the fall and stored in a frost-free, cool cellar (no furnace fumes) until ready for planting next season. Most varieties have flowering spikes 18-36 inches high. The plants are best planted 8-10 inches apart, and at least 4 inches deep; if the corm is large, 5-6 inches deep. Many prefer to plant them in rows in the vegetable garden in order to have sufficient cut flowers. Often, in the tallest varieties, it is necessary to stake the plants or the wind may blow down their huge flowering spikes.

Most of the hybrid gladioli given below have either no odor or only a faint one. It is fortunate that a species from South Africa, *Gladiolus tristis,* is most beautifully fragrant, but only in the evening. It is not as robust or as tall as the hybrids below, and has yellowish-white, purple-streaked, night-blooming flowers that suggest the tuberose in sweetness.

The gladiolus hybrids for July bloom, and later, are:

White: Albatross, Mammoth White, Maid of Orleans.
Pink: Picardy (salmon-pink), Betty Nuthall (salmon-pink), Mrs. P. W. Sisson, Giant Nymph.
Red: Dr. E. F. Bennett, Aflame, Commander Koehl, Red Glory.
Lavender: Minuet, Pelegrina.
Yellow: Golden State, Oregon Gold, Golden Dream.
Smoky: Marmora, Mother Machree, Emile Auburn.

DAHLIA. Like the gladiolus, the dahlia is tender, its origin being in the uplands of Mexico and Guatemala, where its progenitors are still to be found as roadside flowers. It, also, must be planted each spring when warm weather is assured, dug up in the autumn before serious frost, and stored for the winter.

Most dahlias make bushy, robust plants 3-6 feet high and need plenty of space to mature properly—at least 4 x 4 feet apart. They should be planted (from purchased roots) about 6 inches deep, and all but the smallest plants will need staking.

There are at least 2000 named varieties on the market, divided by the experts into more than a dozen classes. Those below fall into only three of these, and one needs to know what they are like before ordering.

1. Decorative—much doubled, often immense, and sometimes cabbage-like flower heads.

2. Cactus—much doubled, but the tips of the rays curving toward the center of the head, hence not so "formal" as No. 1.

3. Pompon and Minatures—flower heads smaller than in the other two classes.

The varieties listed below, by color, are all in the above classes, which are indicated by the numbers in parentheses:

White: Jersey's Dainty (1), World's Best White (1), Snowsprite (3), Joe Fette (3), Mrs. D. B. Crane (2).

Yellow: Lord of Autumn (1), Frau O. Bracht (2), Little Edith (3), Golden Standard (2), Crescent (2).

Red: Murphy's Masterpiece (1), Scarlet Satan (1), Fort Monmouth (1), Atom (3), Tom Thumb (3), Royal Sussex (2).

Pink: Baby Royal (3), Jersey Beauty (1), Marion Walton (2).

There are, in addition, a few old-fashioned single dahlias, the starlike flowers of which are not doubled. Good varieties of these are Newport Wonder (raspberry), Crawley Beauty (maroon), Scarlet Century (scarlet), Purity (white), and James Weller (yellow).

SHASTA DAISY. A beautiful daisy-like perennial from the Pyrenees, "developed" by Luther Burbank and christened Shasta Daisy. It was one of his most successful importations. It grows 1-2 feet high and has beautiful white, single flower heads often 2½-3 inches wide. Of easy culture anywhere.

SPEEDWELL (*Veronica spicata*). 15-24 inches high and one of the best of blue-flowered plants to bloom in July. Flowers small, but in dense spikes. If you prefer another color it also comes in the variety *rosea,* with pink flowers. There is another speedwell, *Veronica incana,* only 6-8 inches high, with blue flowers, and suitable for edging a border.

STONECROP. More or less fleshy-leaved perennials, neither of those below growing more than 4-7 inches high, and thus good for a ground cover. *Sedum spurium* is nearly evergreen and has pink flowers in a branching cluster, whereas *Sedum album* is not evergreen and has small white flowers in a terminal, branching cluster. Both demand full sunshine.

MONKSHOOD. Showy perennials, poisonous if eaten, and one of the species is the source of the drug aconite from which the plants derive the name *Aconitum.* All have terminal spikes of somewhat irregular flowers and will grow in any reasonably good soil. *Aconitum*

anthora is 1-2 feet high, with pale yellow flowers; *Aconitum fischeri,*
3-4 feet high, is extremely handsome with deep blue flowers; and
Aconitum napellus, 4-5 feet high, has purplish-blue flowers and is,
as commercially grown, the source of the drug.

HOLLYHOCK. These old-fashioned favorites in all cottage gardens,
    and now much improved, are scarcely ever perennials in the
North, although they persist for years in the South. They grow 4-6
feet high and have handsome pink, yellow, smoky white, and even
red flowers in stiff, tall spikes. Here they must be started from seed,
planted ½ inch deep about mid-April, and will re-seed themselves
when once established. The names are in much confusion, and they
are best ordered by color.

LILIES. These superb perennials bloom later than those mentioned in
    the chapter entitled June, but cultural directions need not be
repeated here as they will be found in that chapter. The July-flowering species, which may bloom for the rest of the summer, are:

   Lilium auratum, 3½-5 feet high, the flowers white, but gold-
      banded. Plant 10 inches deep, in full sun.
   Lilium chalcedonicum, 3-4 feet high, the flowers scarlet. Plant 4
      inches deep, in full sun.
   Lilium pardalinum, 5-7 feet high, the flowers orange, but purple-
      spotted. Plant 5 inches deep, in full sun or partial shade.
   Lilium parryi, 4-6 feet high, the flowers lemon-yellow. Plant 5
      inches deep, in partial shade.
   Lilium regale, 3-5 feet high, the flowers white, but rose-striped,
      the throat gold. Plant 8 inches deep, in full sun.
   Lilium sargentiae, 4-6 feet high, the flowers white, with a yellow
      throat. Plant 8 inches deep, in full sun.

BELLFLOWERS. Rather tall perennials, with usually the most com-
    pletely blue flowers, except gentians, found in the garden.
They like rich garden soil, open sunlight, and are of easy culture.
They are striking plants for the border, and of the many kinds three
are especially chosen for the beginner.

   Chimney Bellflower (*Campanula pyramidalis*), 3-5 feet high, its
      bell-shaped flowers about 1 inch long, but the clusters of
      them showy.
   Canterbury Bells (*Campanula medium*), 2-4 feet high, the flowers
      in open clusters or solitary on the stems.
   Coventry Bells (*Campanula trachelium*), 2-3 feet high, the flow-
      ers purplish-blue.

All of these, if you prefer other colors, come also in white and
even pink-flowered varieties.

SNEEZEWORT (*Achillea ptarmica*). An old and very popular garden perennial, 12-20 inches high, its foliage scented like the common yarrow, to which it is closely related. It is scarcely ever planted in its original form but in double-flowered varieties, of which the best are Boule de Neige, Perry's White and The Pearl. All require full sun, but will do well otherwise in a variety of soils. They will stay in bloom all summer, particularly if cut for house decoration.

CHAPTER VIII

August

"From that full meridian of my glory
I haste now to my setting."

THERE ought to be a word for it—something like summer-fall. Who has not stolen down some August morning, early enough to catch the magic of fairy cobwebs on dew-drenched grass, and a nip in the air that's neither summer nor autumn, but a little of both. One has the feeling that somehow the full meridian of summer glory is stealing quietly into unmistakable autumn.

Not all the days, of course, for we can still swelter, but some August mornings tell us in language unknown to the scientist that Summer, if it were a poet, would be whispering to the quiet dawns, "I haste now to my setting."

So far as the garden is concerned, August is still lavish of bloom, a good deal of it held over from opulent July. Some of it also heralds the autumn by the flowering of plants that never bloom until the days grow shorter, and the scientist, who never speaks of August as the "full meridian" of summer glory, tells us why it is precisely that. No more significant studies have ever been made than the effect of the length of the day on plant growth. That explains why corn from Virginia, with its "long day," will not grow in Bolivia which has a "short day." In June, for instance, Virginia will average more than fifteen hours of possible sunshine, but Bolivia during its "June" (which is our December) will have no more than twelve.

Such figures are astounding when they are rightly understood and, in our own North, August reflects the fundamental effect of the

length of the day upon the garden and all other vegetation. Taking
New York as an example, August first will have just over 14 hours of
possible sunshine, while the last day of that month never has more
than thirteen. In some mysterious way, as yet little understood, it is
these waning daylight hours that tell the garden, and us, how
Shakespeare, thinking more of Henry VIII than August, wrote with
prescient genius "From that full meridian of my glory, I haste now
to my setting."

August, too, is the month for the ripening of fruits, perhaps as
some scientists surmise because it is, of all the summer months, the
most likely to be dry. Summer heat, waning daylight, dew-drenched
dawns, and somewhat deficient rainfall—they all add up to August.
If it is not quite farewell to summer at its opening, it certainly is
at the end, and the gardener, who keeps his eyes open, sees everywhere those sad signs that tell us to plan now for April, while en-
joying the lavish August bloom which nature, in spite of these
handicaps, never fails to provide.

So far as August-blooming shrubs and trees are concerned our lists
are, however, narrowly restricted. Gone is the rush of May-and-June-
flowering dogwoods, lilacs, azaleas and deutzias, the gorgeous rhododendrons, and all but a few of late-flowering roses. Finished
for another year is the marvellous bloom of the Japanese flowering
cherries and the flowering crabapples. If one walks about the garden
of an August morning, his memory goes wistfully back to the breath-
taking thrills of May and June and wonders whether August can possibly be so kind.

So far as flowering trees are concerned, it never can. Fortunately
Japan has supplied us with perhaps the latest blooming of all flowering trees, which it always does about mid-August (later or earlier
if you are much north or south of New York). This precious import
is the Japanese Pagoda Tree (*Sophora japonica*), a medium-sized
tree in cultivation, but reaching 60-70 feet in its native home. It has
compound leaves, comprised of 7-15 leaflets, and terminal, loose clusters of showy, pea-like yellowish-white flowers. It is perfectly hardy
up to Boston and perhaps beyond along the coast, and somewhat
indifferent as to soils. There are, for those who prefer them, a beautiful variety with weeping branches, and another with violet-tinged
flowers.

While the pagoda tree is a real one, some of the shrubs below
may reach tree-like proportions if they are grown in the south, and
are hence perhaps better classed as trees. But in cultivation they usually act like shrubs, and if tree-like are only small ones. The list

below is not one culled from among many, but almost the end of
shrub bloom, except for the still more meager list in September.

SHRUBS

August-flowering shrubs are so limited that the few below are beyond price. It is unfortunate for most gardeners that we cannot include (unless they live south of Delaware) the finest of all August-
flowering shrubs, the Crape Myrtle (*Lagerstroemia indica*). As I
write, in southern Maryland, this is a shrubby tree outside my window, 25 feet high and nearly as wide, completely covered with lilac-
like clusters of pink bloom on August 20. Other varieties bloom later,
and some in the last weeks of July, and there are also white and
deep red forms. It is perhaps the most floriferous of all deciduous
shrubs, but is hopeless anywhere north of Dover, Delaware.

Sweet Pepperbush (*Clethra alnifolia*). A native shrub, 3-7 feet high
        and one of our most fragrant native shrubs. The small white
flowers are numerous in many spire-like terminal clusters. Although
it grows naturally in swamps and bogs, it seems perfectly at home
in the garden, but, of course it will do better in a moist place than
in a dry one.

Heather (*Calluna vulgaris*). The bonny, bonny heather is not to be
        grown unless you can give it the conditions it needs. The soil
must be sandy, somewhat acid, and the plants, once established,
should be left alone. Plant in full sun. The heather is a prostrate
shrub, best planted in masses, with tiny evergreen leaves and small,
bell-shaped pink flowers in dense terminal clusters. There are many
varieties, some dwarf, some white, and one purplish. While it grows
in Scotland, and over a good deal of Northern Europe and Asia, it has
become naturalized on Nantucket, and is perfectly hardy. But it will
not stand wet or heavy clay soils.

Mountain Camellia (*Stewartia ovata*). A native shrub, 10-15 feet
        high, mostly from the mountains of North Carolina and Ten-
nessee, and apt to flower in early rather than late August. It has
solitary white, showy and rather waxy flowers, more or less cup-
shaped, and nearly 3 inches wide. It should be planted in partial
shade in good rich loam, preferably somewhat acid.

Tamarisk (*Tamarix pentandra*). A peculiar Eurasian shrub, 10-15
        feet high, its swaying, thin twigs covered so closely with myr-
iads of tiny leaves that the plant seems almost leafless and the
twigs greenish. Flowers very small, pink, crowded in dense clusters.
The smaller twigs are shed in the autumn when leaf-fall occurs.

The plant is a semi-desert inhabitant, and, while it will grow in any light soil, it prefers sand and does well along the dunes. It is a valuable shrub for such sites, its slender branches and twigs swaying with the wind and hence not harmed by seaside gales. Another species (*Tamarix gallica*) is taller and apt to flower in late July or early August.

ROSE-OF-SHARON. The common magenta form of this is so unpopular that no one would grow rose-of-Sharon if there were not much finer varieties. Originally a Chinese shrub it was imported in the magenta form because of the scarcity of August-blooming shrubs. It grows 5-15 feet high, will thrive in any sort of soil, and the varieties below make it a valuable addition to August-flowering shrubs. The best varieties are:

Jeanne d'Arc: Double white flowers.
Snowstorm: Single white flowers.
Coelestis: Purplish-blue, single flowers.
Rosea: Single white flowers with a crimson eye.
Speciosa plena: Double, pink flowers.
Rubis: Single red flowers.

BUSH BROOM (*Hypericum prolificum*). A shrub, 4-5 feet high, native from New Jersey southward, with bark that peels off in long strips. It is a bushy plant, covered in early and mid-August with yellow flowers about ¾ inch in diameter. Not a very striking shrub, but providing yellow color when few other shrubs are in bloom. It does well in ordinary garden soils and is hardy everywhere.

PERENNIALS

If shrubs and trees are scarce so far as August bloom is concerned, there are many perennials, and using only those selected below will give continuous bloom throughout August, not to speak of those July-flowering perennials whose bloom continues into August. Also many plants that start flowering this month will continue to bloom throughout September, and some of them well into October.

August is the precursor of all the autumn-blooming plants of the huge daisy family, so that we find in the lists below early-flowering representatives of a family of plants that are at their height in September and October, notably some asters, chrysanthemums, etc. These are included here because they make an important element of August bloom even if their relatives flower later and will be found in the chapters devoted to September and October.

Most of these perennials are best ordered from nurseries in March or April, and will usually provide bloom, if they are planted at once, by August, except the lilies which may not flower for another year. If one wants to save expense, seeds of some of the species may be started in boxes or pots early in the spring, and not a few will flower the first year, and all of them by the second. It is generally unwise, and often impossible, to attempt to raise the named horticultural varieties from seed, for many of them are hybrids and either set no seed or, if they do, it may not come true. The perennials selected for August bloom might include:

STOKE'S ASTER (*Stokesia laevis*). A native, aster-like perennial found wild from South Carolina to Louisiana, but perfectly hardy and suitable to most garden soils. It is 12-30 inches high and has star-like, lavender-blue flower heads about 3 inches across. A particularly fine blue form should be specified as Blue Boy.

YELLOW STAR (*Helenium autumnale*). 4-6 feet and a bushy perennial from eastern North America, somewhat resembling a sunflower, and with yellow flower heads about 2 inches wide. It is somewhat rampant and coarse, but there is a variety *pumilum,* which is not over 2 feet high, and is more suitable for small gardens. There is also, of the tall sort, a variety with red flowers which should be ordered as var. *rubrum.*

CHRYSANTHEMUM. Of these predominantly fall-flowering favorites there are a few that bloom in August. They are listed below, but notes on their culture will be found in the chapter headed October. The flowering time is that of New York, and chrysanthemums are particularly responsive to local conditions of exposure, climate, and soils, all of which may affect their blooming period. All those below are the ordinary hardy chrysanthemums, unless specified as pompons, which have much smaller flower heads than the usual types. August-blooming forms are:

Barbara Cumming: Yellow.

Early Bronze: Bronzy-yellow and a pompon.

Mercury: Bronzy-red and single-flowered.

There are a few listed in the chapter on September that may flower in August, but the great profusion of chrysanthemums is from October to frost and sometimes later. See chapters on September and October.

RED-HOT POKER (*Kniphofia uvaria grandiflora*). By all means order this striking perennial by its technical name or you will likely get an inferior sort. It is an erect plant, 2-4 feet high, the long, sword-shaped leaves nearly 3 feet long. From the center arises a stiff flowering stalk, covered toward the summit by a compact mass of small flowers that are fiery red at the top of the spike, but yellow toward the base of it, hence its name of red-hot poker. It has fleshy roots that must be planted carefully, and from New York northward it needs a light winter mulch of straw or strawy manure.

TURTLEHEAD. These comprise a small group of American perennials of which the red turtlehead (*Chelone lyoni*) is by far the best. While it is native in the mountains of North and South Carolina and adjacent Tennessee, it is perfectly hardy as far north as Boston. The plant is 10-20 inches high and has a compact, stalkless cluster of irregular, rose-purple flowers that are very handsome. It will grow in most garden soils, but much better if the site is moist and there is partial shade.

SAGE. Besides the flavoring herb, there are at least two species of perennial sages that are well worth inclusion for August bloom. One is the blue sage (*Salvia patens*) from the mountains of Mexico, which has the purest gentian-blue flowers of almost any garden plant. It grows 18-30 inches high, and it is not quite hardy north of New York without the protection of a mulch.

Much more hardy is the paler blue sage (*Salvia azurea*) from the southeastern states, which grows 4-5 feet high and has pale blue, or sometimes white, flowers in attractive, interrupted clusters. Its culture is perfectly easy in any garden.

MICHAELMAS DAISIES. Most of these tall, aster-like perennials were derived by hybridization and selection of two or three native American asters, mostly in England. They bloom in September and should be looked for in the chapter on that month. But some Michaelmas Daisies were derived in part from the Italian aster (*Aster amellus*), and are lower plants that bloom generally in mid- or late-August. They are 2-3 feet high and have showy star-like heads of flowers in branching clusters. Among the Michaelmas daisies derived mostly from *Aster amellus,* and hence August-blooming, are:

Elegans: Lavender heads in long sprays.

King George: Flower heads nearly 3 inches wide, bluish-violet.

Arethusa: Flower heads deep rose.

Mrs. Perry: Violet-purple flower heads.

Nancy Perry: Light blue flower heads; the plant not over 12 inches high.

SCARLET CLEMATIS (*Clematis texensis*). This is a sprawling, slightly woody vine, 4-5 feet high, and needing to be staked for best development. It is a native of Texas, and a relative of the great climbing vines that are sometimes too rampant for the small garden. The scarlet clematis has brilliant scarlet, urn-shaped flowers about

1½ inches high, and will grow best in a limestone region, although it does well in ordinary garden soil if it is reasonably rich and the site is not too dry. A very striking and handsome plant that may bloom from the last of July to mid-September depending on the site and season.

LILIES. The procession of these gorgeous perennials from June to August is certainly one of the glories of any garden. They demand special attention and these details are mentioned in the chapter on June and need not be repeated here. Those whose bloom starts in August might include the following:

    Lilium speciosum, 3-5 feet high, the flowers white, with a green-ish-gold stripe. Plant 10 inches deep in full sun. There are also magnificent carmine forms with crimson spots, and a white form which is rose-spotted.

    Lilium superbum, 3-7 feet high, the orange-red, nodding flowers dark-spotted. Plant 5 inches deep in partial shade.

    Lilium tigrinum, 4-5 feet high, the flowers orange-red but purple-spotted. Plant 9 inches deep, in full sun.

MONTBRETIAS. Beautiful but tender, August-blooming relatives of the gladiolus, and to be grown as are the latter. See *July* for the details. They resemble gladiolus in habit, but the flowers are more regular and nearly bell-shaped. There are scores of named varieties on the market, but the following will give a fine range of color. All require full sun, and are 2½-4 feet high.

    Yellow: Golden Yellow, His Majesty, Lady Hamilton.

    Red: James Coey, Lord Nelson, Princess.

    Orange: Croesus, Queen Mary, George Davidson, Prometheus.

    Pink: Rosea.

    Orange-scarlet: Queen Elizabeth.

STONECROP (*Sedum spectabile*). A splendid Asiatic perennial, 1-2 feet high, its grayish-green fleshy leaves in clusters of three. It bears a flat-topped cluster of many, small pink flowers, which bloom from mid-August through September. It will grow in the open, or in partial shade, and is a strong-growing plant most welcome for its pink bloom at the end of waning summer.

CHAPTER IX

September

"*And this same flower that smiles today,*
Tomorrow will be dying."

A PREMONITION of the equinox creeps over the garden and over us in the first days of September. We sense, perhaps a little wistfully, that the flower of today will be gone tomorrow, and worse, still, that waning daylight does but herald inevitable winter. And plants react as if they knew it, for we see in September the first hint of autumn color, as some precocious maple or sumac along a stream flaunts the scarlet insignia of fall.

Two thirds of the month are all that's left of summer, and on the twenty-first the sun will be briefly hovering over the equator on its southward trek. That means gardens will be getting darker and cooler each day, and the full significance of autumn soon becomes apparent.

What does that mean to gardeners in the North Temperate Zone? If the earth were but an orange and one had an electric light to play with, it would be easy to show that as the sun goes below the equator, not only do we daily get less light, but the angle of the sun's rays becomes daily more unfavorable.

The effects upon vegetation are profound. There is, for instance, scarcely a single flowering tree and only a handful of shrubs that start their bloom in September, and only two in October, one of these being a "freak" (see October).

SHRUBS AND TREES

The garden value of the meager list below is thus obvious, for there are practically no others. Only one of them, the legendary franklinia, even pretends to be a tree, and only then in the South. But in spite of the paucity of the list, it is still possible to get continuous bloom in September from woody plants, although nothing like so lavishly as from the perennials.

All of these shrubs, being late-flowering, should be planted in early spring, or else well after they have finished blooming, if spring planting is impossible. One or two of them require special conditions for successful culture and, if you cannot provide these, it still further reduces the number of woody plants with September bloom.

FRANKLINIA (*Gordonia alatamaha*). Somewhere along the Alatamaha River, in Georgia, there grew in 1770 the fabulous tree or shrub commonly known as franklinia but christened *Gordonia* by John Ellis, in recognition of James Gordon, a British nurseryman. It grew there as late as 1790, but has never been found wild since! It is thus as unique as the ginkgo, which is all but unknown as a wild tree. For many years there grew in Bartam's Garden in Philadelphia what was thought to be the only living speciman of *Gordonia,* from which all present specimens are assumed to be derived.

While search for the tree in the wild has gone on ever since, it is fortunate that the plant is now available from any good nursery and it is perfectly hardy as far north as Boston. It is, as cultivated in the South, a tree up to 25 feet high, but most likely to be shrubby and half that height in the North. It has handsome leaves that turn brilliant crimson in October but in September it bears beautiful white, cup-shaped, waxy flowers that are about 3½ inches wide, faintly spicy as befits a plant closely related to tea.

Gordonia, while it will grow in reasonably moist garden soil, thrives best in low, moist, and somewhat acid, peaty soils. It is by all odds the most showy of all late-blooming woody plants, and worth any effort to get it established.

BLUE SPIREA (*Caryopteris incana*). An attractive, Asiatic shrub, 2-5 feet high with grayish-hairy foliage, and showy clusters of small bluish-purple flowers, which in some strains are pure blue. It does not begin to bloom before early September and may continue to do so into October. It will grow in ordinary garden soils, but north of Philadelphia it may winter-kill, particularly away from the coast. If it does, cut it back to the ground and the new shoots will bloom in September.

ABELIA CHINENSIS. A shrub, 3-4 feet high, with small leaves and a
profusion of small, funnel-shaped white flowers in dense clusters. It is of the easiest culture, but not certainly hardy north of Philadelphia, except in protected places. Its close relative, *Abelia grandiflora,* is half-evergreen, much more hardy, and its pinkish flowers are
in bloom from June to nearly frost. They have no common names.
ELSHOLTZIA STAUNTONI. A Chinese undershrub, 2-4 feet high, its foliage aromatic. It is one of the few woody plants of the mint
family that is hardy in the North, and this one often winter-kills north
of New York. This, however, does not prevent its producing its long,
spire-like clusters of pinkish-purple, very fragrant flowers in September and October. It may, in the North, be only slightly woody, hence
herb-like, but from Philadelphia southward it is a true shrub, and a
valuable one for its late bloom.
GROUNDSEL BUSH (*Baccharis halimifolia*). A rampant shrub of our
salt marshes, 6-10 feet high, which will grow in ordinary garden soil if it is in full sunlight. The flowers are rather small, yellowish
or dirty-white, followed in September by showy, misty-white clusters
of fruit which make snowy white masses, for which the plant is grown
as the flowers are inconspicuous. It is interesting as the only hardy
shrub of the huge daisy family, which has many tropical shrubs and
trees, but only the groundsel bush in the North to keep company with
the hosts of its close relatives like the asters, goldenrods, chrysanthemums, and Michaelmas daisies.

PERENNIALS

Nature is a little more kind to us in September by conferring upon
us a relative wealth of perennials. Compared to the meager list of
shrubs and trees, she might almost be said to be lavish, for this is the
season when the daisy family is at its height, and it is the time of
autumn crocus and a few other bulbs. These will be found grouped
together at the end of this chapter.

There will, of course, be many August-blooming perennials whose
flowering period trails over into September, depending on the site
and whether you live near Boston or Norfolk. But in addition to these
there are at least six groups of perennials that will start their bloom
in September, and many of them will flower right through October
up until frost.
JAPANESE ANEMONE (*Anemone japonica*). A stout, branching Asiatic
herb, 2-2½ feet high, of easy culture in any garden, and with
divided foliage. It has showy buttercup-like flowers, which are, how-

ever, nearly 3 inches wide, and of many colors, except yellow and blue. Of the horticultural varieties a choice might include:

September Queen: rosy-red and semi-double.

September Charm: silvery-pink.

Prince Henry: rosy-red.

Queen Charlotte: white and semi-double.

Alice: rose-pink.

Prince Heinrich: crimson and semi-double.

GAY-FEATHER (*Liatris spicata*). A native perennial, admirably suited to dry sites and indifferent as to soil, but it does best in full sunshine. It grows 4-5 feet high, the flowering stalk crowded with button-like heads of rose-purple flowers. It is showy, and often listed as *Lacinaria spicata*.

IRONWEED (*Vernonia noveboracensis*). A showy perennial, 3-7 feet high, found wild from Massachusetts southward, and cultivated for its heads of dark purple flowers in terminal clusters. Of the easiest culture and, although flowering in early September in some localities, it may bloom in late August. Rather coarse for a fine border, but useful in the wild garden.

CERATOSTIGMA PLUMBAGINOIDES. A very popular prostrate garden perennial, often a little woody, a native of China and not over 12 inches high. It makes a good ground-cover, and early in September (or late August) it is covered with deep blue flowers that are about one-half inch wide. It has no special soil preferences, and in spite of its popularity has no valid common name. Some dealers list it as *Plumbago larpentae*.

ASTERS. What most people call asters are annuals and hence not in this book. They are, in any case, not true asters at all, but belong to the genus *Callistephus*. The word *aster* requires a bit more of definition to straighten out the muddle that surrounds it, and make what follows easier. The true genus *Aster* contains many species of which perhaps three are worth mentioning here, although there are dozens of wild ones along any roadside.

But in addition the genus *Aster* contains also the Michaelmas daisies, all of which are hybrids and are considered in the next main entry.

Of the species asters (one is also a hybrid), the following might be included for September bloom.

Aster acris, 2-3 feet high, with mauve-blue flowers, the heads about 1 inch wide, often lasting into October.

Aster ericoides, 3-5 feet, with hundreds of tiny white flower heads.

Aster frikarti, 2-3 feet high, its lavender flower heads 2-3 inches

wide and fragrant. A very showy hybrid plant, of which
Wonder of Stafa is a fine form.

MICHAELMAS DAISIES. Some of these showy hybrid asters are August-
blooming, and shorter plants than those below. Also they are
derived mostly from the Italian aster (*Aster amellus*), and are noted
in the chapter on August.

The taller, and chiefly September-blooming Michaelmas daisies
were mostly developed by hybridizing several tall-growing American
wild species of *Aster*, and most of this was done in England, where
scores of named varieties are available. A selection of those found in
American nurseries, which comprise tall, showy perennials, might
include:

Sam Banham, 4-6 feet high, the heads white.

Barr's Pink, 4-5 feet high, the heads pink.

Climax, 4-6 feet high, the heads lavender-blue.

Queen Mary, 3-4 feet high, the heads a rich blue.

Blue Gem, 4-5 feet high, the heads blue.

CHRYSANTHEMUMS. October is the month when most of these fall-
flowering favorites are at their height, and cultural notes on
them should be sought in the chapter devoted to that month. Some,
however, start blooming in September, and a few of the August-
flowering sorts will be still blooming well into September.

Among those that start their bloom in September the following
varieties should certainly be in any garden that wants plenty of color.
All those below have ordinary double-flowered heads, 2-3 inches
wide, unless they are marked *pompons* in which case the flower
heads are much smaller and button-like.

Ruth Hatton, pompon, white.

Jean Cumming, white.

Apollo, rose-salmon, and single.

Louise Schling, crimson and old rose, and single.

Mars, red and single.

R. Marion Hatton, pompon, yellow.

BULBS

AUTUMN SNOWFLAKE (*Leucojum autumnale*). A low bulbous plant,
7-8 inches high, the nodding white flowers tinged with red. It
will bloom on naked flower stalks, and the narrow thread-like leaves
will develop later. Plant in masses, from bulbs that should be set out
early in the spring, 4 inches apart and as deep. Do not disturb the

bulbs and they will provide sheets of bloom in September and October.

CROCUS. Most gardeners think of crocus as spring-blooming, but there are a few species of the genus *Crocus* that bloom in the fall, of which two might be included here. These are not to be confused with the autumn crocus (*Colchicum*) which are included in the paragraph below.

The autumn-flowering species of true *Crocus* should be planted in spring, from bulbs set 3 inches deep and are best grown in masses.

Crocus longiflorus, 3-8 inches high, the flowers lilac, about 1 inch high.

Crocus nudiflorus, 3-8 inches high, the flowers lilac, but nearly 2 inches high.

Crocus speciosus, 3-8 inches high, the flowers purple-tinged or lilac, about 2 inches high.

AUTUMN CROCUS. Much more showy than the species of *Crocus* above, and belonging to the genus *Colchicum* which is in the lily family and not a relative of iris as is *Crocus*. The autumn crocuses are raised from bulbs which should be planted as soon as they are available, which ought to be mid-August, or even August first. Plant them 3-4 inches deep (to the top of the bulb), and 5-6 inches apart. They should flower in about 5-6 weeks after planting, and their narrow, grass-like leaves may not appear until next spring. Once established they can be let alone for several years and will bloom in September and into October or later. The best species are:

Colchicum autumnale, the commonest sort in cultivation, the flowers 3-4 inches wide, pink.

Colchicum bornmuelleri, flowers nearly 5 inches wide, mauve. One of the best, but not carried by all dealers.

CHAPTER X

October

"Nor wanting is the brown October."

No POET can overcome the deficiencies of October, not even James Thomson and *The Seasons*, for it is the month just ahead of crippling winter. And in spite of Indian Summer it sinks inexorably into the chill winds and the icy fingers of frost. Nowhere is that better reflected than in the meager quota of woody plants that come into flower this month.

Of these one is a medium-sized tree, hardy only from southern Delaware southward, and the other is a "freak," which blooms either early in spring or in October, or both, but not between. October may have its compensations, such as the gorgeous autumnal color of sumac, sugar maple, the oaks, sassafras and the sweet-gum, but these are, after all, only the reflection of the very factors that make this month nearly wanting in woody plants that come into bloom. The two are:

STRAWBERRY-TREE (*Arbutus unedo*). A medium-sized tree from southern Europe and southwest Ireland, the foliage evergreen. Flowers very small, often less than ¼ inch long, in a drooping cluster about 2 inches long, which is not showy. Much more conspicuous is the edible but flavorless, strawberry-like fruit, which may be ¾ inch in diameter and orange-red. The plant prefers a wind-sheltered site and is not safe north of southern Delaware, except in protected places.

PRUNUS SUBHIRTELLA AUTUMNALIS. A shrub 6-12 feet high, related to the rosebud cherry (see April), and like it, with semi-double pink flowers. It was developed in Japan and has the curious habit of flowering in spring or in October, sometimes in both seasons, but not in the months between. It is perfectly hardy up to Boston, and will grow in any good garden soil, but it must have full sun. It generally does not flower as freely in October as in the spring.

PERENNIALS

Except for chrysanthemums, which are at their peak in October, there are not many perennial plants that come into bloom this month. There are, in addition, a couple of bulbs that bloom in October and they are noted at the end of this chapter.

While few plants come into flower now, there are many hold-overs from September, and some from August, so that the garden need not depend on the meager list below:

WINTER DAFFODIL (*Sternbergia lutea*). An attractive bulbous plant, which, however, persists for years when once established. Plant the bulbs in August, 3-4 inches deep and as far apart. They should flower in 7 or 8 weeks and may stay in bloom when the last chrysanthemum has gone. The plant is 8-12 inches high and the yellow flowers are about 1½ inches high. Its leaves, which follow the flowers, may persist all winter. It wants a gritty soil, in full sun.

SNEEZEWEED (*Helenium hoopesi*). A sunflower-like perennial from the Rocky Mountain region, but rarely over 3 feet tall. Flower heads yellow, nearly 3 inches wide, and blooming early in October or even the latter part of September. It is indifferent as to soils.

BUSH CLOVER (*Lespedeza thunbergi*). A shrub-like herb, or an herb-like shrub, 3-6 feet high, and usually dying down to the ground each winter. Flowers small, pea-like, in long drooping clusters. It is of easy culture nearly anywhere in open sunlight, and will flower either late in September or early in October, depending on site and location. North of New York it will benefit from a winter mulch of straw or strawy manure.

CHRYSANTHEMUMS. Hardy, perennial herbs, the national flower of the Japanese who have developed hundreds of varieties, of which we have in America scores to provide continuous chrysanthemum bloom from the first of August to killing frosts. The greatest concentration of varieties bloom in October, and most of them will be flowering into November or December in mild seasons.

All those below are true perennials and easily divided once they are established, so that in a few years any gardener can increase his stock tenfold. Except in the North they need no protection except their own withered leaves, but from Boston northward they appreciate a light mulch.

Those who want bloom chiefly for cutting should dis-bud or pinch back the plants to increase the size of the remaining flower heads. Those who grow them for outdoor display—and there is scarcely any finer autumnal spectacle—can simply let them bloom without doing anything.

Most chrysanthemum hybrids are double-flowered, and all those below are unless specified as singles. These will have flower heads 2-4 inches wide. A group of much smaller button-like flower heads comprise the pompons, and these are so specified below. The dozen varieties below will give continuous bloom in October.

Amelia, pink.

Jean Treadway, pink.

Ruth Cumming, bronze-terra-cotta.

Alice Howell, orange-yellow and single.

October Girl, pink.

Cavalier, vermilion and single.

Irene, white and a pompon.

Yellow Gem, yellow and a pompon.

Grenadier, red and bronze and single.

Granny Scovill, reddish-orange.

Sunbright, yellow and single.

Red Flare, red.

BULBS

To finish the October Garden there are two bulbous plants, both tender, so that their bulbs must be lifted each year just after their flowering period, which can be controlled a little by the time of planting them. One of them is one of the most fragrant plants in cultivation while the other is chiefly grown for its star-like spotted flowers which have little or no odor.

TUBEROSE (*Polianthes tuberosa*), 12-30 inches high, with weak, sword-shaped leaves, and an extraordinarily fragrant, white, waxy flower in short clusters. These are even more fragrant at night. Plant the bulbs 4 inches deep in June or July (especially for October bloom), and these must be lifted and stored over the winter. Plants may not always flower from purchased bulbs the first season, in which case they should be replanted, with the same bulbs, the second year.

TOAD LILY (*Tricyrtis hirta*). A tender bulbous plant from Japan, 2-3 feet high, its star-like flowers 1 inch wide, white and purple-spotted on the outside but blackish inside. They are late-bloomers, and the rootstock (it has no real bulb) should be planted each spring when all danger of frost is over, and lifted in the fall, after the flowers wither. They should be stored in a frost-free, cool place, preferably in sand. Further south they can be left in the ground all winter.

These do not end the progression of bloom from March to October, for many stragglers, particularly in mild seasons or in specially protected sites, will keep on blooming until Thanksgiving or even beyond. They will then catch up with those plants mentioned in the second chapter who brave the elements from Thanksgiving to Washington's Birthday, and so make the everblooming garden a reality.

Book Three

COLOR IN
THE GARDEN

COLOR IN THE GARDEN

WHILE few will want to make a garden all of one color, many will like to have sections of a border, or some special accent in an existing one with a single color predominating. Unfortunately flowers are not permanent, like fabrics and clothes, so that the selection of plant materials for particular color effects needs precise definition as to the color, height and blooming period of all the plant materials.

It is these details that are outlined in chapters two to eight, together with the necessary notes on hardiness. From them one can select any plant material for his preferred color scheme, and even make diverse color schemes for different parts of the garden.

To illustrate the details of this would be endless, but six simple plans are included for borders where white, pink, yellow, blue, red, or gray and lavender flowers are the dominant colors. Each of the plans has a key to the plant materials in them, and reference to the text gives pertinent data as to height, period of bloom, hardiness and cultural directions if the plant requires special care.

It is hoped that such a scheme will permit any amateur to plan for color in the garden with reasonable assurance that the color of his choice will be in bloom when he wants it. And the book tells whether it ought to be a bulb, annual, perennial, a shrub or a tree to accomplish that purpose.

Chapter One

Color and
Its Management

*T*HE EMOTIONAL VALUE of color has stirred poets and musicians to flights of rhetoric. Charts of color have been made by the physicists; and the gardener, too, must sometimes wonder what nature is up to when she splashes the red passion of a peony against the white purity of dogwood. Why colors have these emotional overtones no one really knows, in spite of endless "explanations." All we know is that plants provide us with a veritable kaleidoscope limited only by our taste and knowledge.

While the rest of this book is divided into red, yellow, blue, and other color gardens, scarcely anyone wants to make a garden devoted exclusively to one color. It would be monotonous for one thing and, although perfectly feasible, would show considerable lack of imagination. If color gardening is a reflection of one's sense of harmony— and good ones always are—the plant world provides a palette such as no artist could ever imitate.

The chief difficulty is that flowers do not bloom continuously and forever; hence the gardener must use his favorites only after answering several rather important questions:

1. When will the plant be in bloom and for how long?
2. Is it a tender or hardy annual?
3. Is it a perennial?
4. What will be the probable height of the plant?
5. Is the plant derived from a bulb, corm or tuber and when must these be planted?
6. If the plant is woody, is it a shrub, vine or tree?

There are several hundred plants mentioned in subsequent chapters, and in the brief space available it would be endlessly repetitious to answer all six questions at every mention of each one of them. Hence familiarity with the notes below will save much space, the reader's time and many future errors of timing, uncertainty as to heights, and other details.

1. *When will the plant be in bloom?* This is specified at the mention of each plant, using the latitude of New York City as average. Places decidedly north of this will be a few days or even a week or two later, while places south of it will be correspondingly earlier. Also, proximity to cool sea water and any elevation above 1500 feet will retard the onset of spring and, in the case of mountainous places, reduce the length of the growing season. In such places some late-blooming flowers may be cut off by early fall frosts. The seaside places, on the other hand, will generally have milder autumns, and hence prolong the blooming of many fall-flowering plants.

2. *Is it a tender or hardy annual?* All such plants are specified throughout the remainder of the book. If they are hardy annuals, as most of them are, they are designated as ANNUAL. If they are tender annuals they will be specified as TENDER ANNUAL. The gardener will find it helpful to follow the directions below for the planting of the seeds of both annuals and tender annuals.

a. *Annuals.* These hardy plants live but a single growing season, bloom and then die after setting (and sometimes self-sowing) their seed. The seeds of all such should be planted where wanted, usually in masses, and thinned out later to prevent crowding, unless specific suggestions are attached to certain of them that actually bloom better when crowded.

b. *Tender Annuals.* These are also true annuals, but are called tender because they are often of tropical origin and need a longer growing season to come into bloom. To overcome this difficulty they are started in the hotbed, or on a shelf at the kitchen window. Seeds should be sown from four to six weeks before the plants are needed outdoors, which should be after settled warm weather has arrived. Many amateurs will prefer to buy plants of tender annuals, which are offered by most growers about the end of May, and sometimes earlier if the season has been "open." Do not be misled by the term *tender;* it is simply horticultural jargon for an annual plant that needs a longer growing season than an ordinary annual, and remember that a tender annual, if planted when warm weather is assured, is perfectly hardy. Common examples of tender annuals are China aster, ageratum, marigold, petunia, etc.

3. *Is it a perennial?* Most garden flowers are produced by plants that have permanent underground roots, rootstocks or stems that send up each year a stalk with leaves and flowers, die down to

the ground each fall, and the following spring repeat the cycle. All such plants are specified as perennial and, because they come up year after year, should be planted where they are to stay. Amateurs usually will prefer to purchase perennials from a dealer, although they can be raised from seed if one has patience and sufficient knowledge. Details will be found in *Taylor's Encyclopedia of Gardening*. Perennials can be planted when dormant, either in spring or fall.

4. *What will be the probable height of the plant?* Scarcely any other detail is so important as this if one is planning a border, screening an ash can, or hiding some service feature of your garden. The ultimate heights of all plants are hence specified. They may be lower on poor soils and considerably higher on rich ones. But the average height will tell the gardener of the range from prostrate, ground-hugging plants like the ground pink to the giant foxtail lilies which may tower 10-12 feet above the ground.

5. *Is the plant derived from bulb, corm or tuber?* All of these are really underground and have modified stems from which spring the flower stalk, such as in the familiar tulip, gladiolus or dahlia. The latter is commonly called a tuber by the horticulturist, but actually it is a tuberous root. Such hair-splitting, inserted here for accuracy, does not really matter, because from the amateur's standpoint the chief question is how such plants are grown and, particularly, when they should be planted. The complete details of this are somewhat formidable and should be sought in *Taylor's Encyclopedia of Gardening*, but a simplification of the essentials is given below as a guide.

a. *Bulbs.* Some are spring-blooming like squill, hyacinth and tulip. These need a winter chilling in the ground and hence should be planted in October or November for next season's bloom. Others, like the autumn crocus, are fall-blooming, and should be planted in July or early August for bloom six or eight weeks hence. Most bulbs are better purchased direct from dealers as growing them from seeds is a slow business. Some, like grape hyacinth and daffodils, can stay in the same place more or less indefinitely, but most bulbs, to be sure of perfect blooming, must be planted yearly.

b. *Corms.* These are bulb-like, but lack the outer fleshy scales of true bulbs. Common examples are crocus, gladiolus and montbretia. Some like gladiolus and montbretia are tender and hence planted when settled warm weather has arrived. They will bloom the same summer, after which they must be stored over winter in a frost-free but cool place. The true crocus (not the autumn cro-

cus) of which there are spring and fall blooming sorts, are treated
and planted as if they were true bulbs. (See Bulbs.)

 c. *Tuber and tuberous roots.* The best example is found in the
dahlia, which, being of tropical American origin, will not
stand cold. Hence the tubers must be planted after all danger of
frost is well past, after which they will bloom the same season. In
the fall, before the first hard frost the tubers must be dug up and
stored in a frost-free, cool, dark place. Do not put near the furnace or
they will shrivel and be useless next year.

 Where necessary for cultural reasons, all plants in the book will
be specified as to being bulbs, corms or tubers, together with their
flowering period. Reference to the details above will guide the reader
as to how such plants must be handled to ensure success.

 6. *If the plant is woody, is it a shrub, vine or tree?* All of these
woody plants have stems above ground all winter, and
hence do not die down to the ground, as do all perennials. Shrubs
usually have several main stems and are generally lower than trees,
most of which have a single stem (the trunk). Vines, at least the
sorts mentioned here, are merely scrambling or twining shrubs.

 There are not many of these woody plants in the book, for color
comes mostly from annuals, perennials, bulbs, corms and tubers. But
a few shrubs and trees, and in small places, a few vines, add accent
to the design as well as color. The height and blooming period of all
of them are specified.

 As for the materials to make color gardens, the amateur can be
guided by the following:

Trees, Shrubs and Vines. Best purchased from a reliable nurseryman. If expense matters, young plants are far cheaper than
older ones—often one-fifth the price.

Seeds, Bulbs, Corms and Tubers. Purchase from any good seedsman.

Tender Annuals and Perennials. There are usually neighborhood
growers, roadside stands or florists' greenhouses where tender
annuals are for sale at the proper time. Perennial plants, especially
when a particular color form is desired, had better be purchased
from a nurseryman who specializes in perennials.

 There are about 65 different plants mentioned under each of the
color schemes in the chapters that follow—in all nearly five hundred.
Every variety has been rigorously checked against current catalogs,
so that all the plants are readily available. Not all of them, however,
are to be picked up at every roadside stand, so it is well, in planning
your color garden, to get a few catalogs of first-class dealers before

doing any ordering. Over five-hundred varieties have been rejected because they were too common, too rare, or too difficult to grow.

The cost of a color garden need not be excessive. Seeds are still relatively inexpensive and all annuals must be grown from seed. Bulbs, corms and tubers are somewhat more costly, but in most color gardens only a few plants are wanted. Perennials do cost more, but in a year or two you can divide your clumps and hence the initial purchase can be small. Trees, shrubs and vines cost the most, but this expense can be reduced by ordering small specimens. Your greatest cost will be the time you give to it, and if you have the urge you will find that time.

Wherever possible, and where there will be no uncertainty as to identity, only the common names of plants will be used, such as Shasta daisy, rhododendron, lilac, gladiolus, iris, etc. Often, in order to be precise, especially where particular color forms are selected, certain horticultural names, like "Louise Schling" for a chrysanthemum, "Goliath" for a phlox, "Glare of the Garden" for a tulip, etc., must be used. In the latter case it is essential to order the seed or plant by this name, or you may get some entirely different color. There are thousands of such named horticultural forms, but only those that are readily available have been included here.

For those plants that have no common English name we must fall back upon the Latin names of science, which fortunately are also listed in most good catalogs. There are not very many of these in this book, and only those are included that are readily available and where there is no other exact name. They will always have two names; first a generic one such as *Clarkia,* followed by a specific one like *elegans*—the name thus appearing as *Clarkia elegans,* or, in different genera, as *Dianthus cruentus,* and *Pentstemon torreyi.* It is just as important to order such items exactly as they are written for in many groups there are dozens of species, while only the one specified here can be chosen to give the desired effect. As in the examples above all such Latin names used in the text will be printed in *italics.*

There is sometimes confusion in the common names of plants that have many species in the group, such as stonecrop, speedwell, iris, etc. In all such cases, again for certainty, such names will appear as: Stonecrop (*Sedum spurium*) which indicates that only *Sedum spurium* is referred to at this entry, all the dozen or so other stonecrops being for the moment ignored.

Chapter Two

The Red* Garden

*R*ED IS so much the color of passion, violence and revolution that few gardeners would have the temerity to inflict on themselves, or their friends, an all-red garden. The plants discussed below range from vermilion, through scarlet, carmine, cardinal, crimson and claret to so-called spectrum-red and the fiery scarlet-vermilion. Most of them are too intense to be used exclusively, but they give a dash of brilliance, add striking accents to any grouping, and, in larger gardens, may well be the motif of considerable areas. In small ones there are often nooks or embayments in borders where red can be an extremely effective accent.

For most of us a judicious mixture of red and other colors will be the best solution, and a few hints of what the experts have used may be helpful to anyone planning a predominately red garden. If there are buildings, fences or arbors, near the red garden some of the garish and crude violence of the flower color can be softened by painting such structures pure white.

Any of the plants mentioned in the chapter on the White Garden can also be used, and should be in appreciable amounts, remembering that no color is wrong mixed with white. It is the great ameliorator of red, as it is of any other color, perhaps because it is itself not a color at all and hence neutralizes what might otherwise be garish, startling or just plain gauche.

When it comes to choosing plants that harmonize or pleasantly contrast with red, there are several interesting possibilities. Among them are the following:

Red, with gray foliaged plants, some blue flowers and several yellows. See the chapters on blue, yellow and gray gardens.

---

* The nomenclature of flower colors is in so much confusion, that it seems best to conform to some accepted standard. That adopted here is from the writer's *Encyclopedia of Gardening*, where at the entry at *color* there is a colored plate of the 63 most usual flower colors, black and white excepted. The names used there are those adopted for this book.

Red, with white and yellow flowers, excluding blue and gray. See
the White Garden and the Yellow Garden.

Red, with only green background, such as evergreen shrubs and
trees. See the Green Garden.

Red, with only variegated leaved plants of which the nurseries
carry many, notably privet, scores of evergreens and horticultural forms of holly, and some variegated foliage-plants used for
bedding.

PLANT MATERIALS FOR A RED GARDEN

If permanent effects are desired, and there is space for them, one
should consider perhaps a dozen shrubs, trees and vines that have
the requisite color and will bloom year after year without too much
attention after they are once established. A list of such material, arranged according to their approximate time of blooming follows.

MARCH–APRIL

FLOWERING QUINCE, a shrub 4-6 feet high, blooming about the time
the leaves unfold. Makes a good hedge if sheared.

DOUBLE-FLOWERED PEACH, a shrub or small tree 5-8 feet high, blooming before the leaves unfold. A very striking deep cardinal
red; fruit inedible.

MAY

LILAC, a shrub 8-15 feet high, needing open sunlight. The variety
Congo is single-flowered; Charles Joly is double-flowered.

AZALEA, a shrub 4-6 feet high. Of the hundreds of named forms one
of the best reds is Cocanea major.

RED-FLOWERING DOGWOOD, a tree 10-20 feet high, and a beautiful
color form of the common white dogwood. It prefers shade for
at least part of each day.

FLOWERING CURRANT (*Ribes sanguineum*), a shrub 4-8 feet high. One
of the showiest shrubs in cultivation, with flowers in hanging
clusters.

JUNE

CLEMATIS, a woody vine 8-12 feet high; be sure to get the hybrid
known as Duchess of Albany. A lower sort, *Clematis texensis*,
is less woody, only 4-6 feet high, and blooms earlier than Duchess
of Albany.

RHODODENDRON, Charles Dickens, a shrub 4-10 feet high, evergreen
        and with brilliant deep red flowers in large, showy clusters.
ROSES. Of the hybrid tea roses, 3-5 feet high, the best are Christopher
        Stone, Crimson Glory and Red Radiance. Among the species
of roses might be included *Rosa moysei,* 7-10 feet high, with dark
red, single flowers nearly 2 inches wide, and *Rosa rugosa,* 5-7 feet
high also with single flowers that are pale rose colored and bloom
toward the end of June.
WEIGELA EVA RATHKE, a shrub 5-8 feet high, with deep maroon
        flowers. There are pink and white-flowered relatives of this.
See the Pink Garden and the White Garden.

JULY–AUGUST

ROSES. Two good climbing roses, blooming later than some sorts are
        Crimson Rambler and Chevy Chase. Among the hybrid per-
petual roses a good choice would be J. B. Clark or Ulrich Brunner,
both of which are 3-5 feet high.

LATE SUMMER

SPIRAEA ANTHONY WATERER, 4-6 feet high. This is the best of all late-
        flowering spireas, and with its crimson flowers one of the most
showy shrubs in cultivation. Some strains of it may flower by
July 1st.
TRUMPET-CREEPER, a sprawling vine, climbing 8-20 feet high, or even
        higher. Flowers orange-red, blooming from August 1st, spo-
radically to mid-September. Flowers showy, nearly 3 inches long.

All of these shrubs, vines and trees should be planted only when
you are sure of your general garden plan, because, unlike the plants
that are to follow, they are difficult to move if you initially pick the
wrong site. All of them *can* be moved, but it is relatively more expensive and time-consuming than the comparatively easy shifting of
annuals, perennials, bulbs, etc.

The remainder of the plant materials for a red garden comprise
annuals, perennials and those herbaceous plants grown from bulbs,
corms and tubers.

HERBACEOUS PLANTS FOR THE RED GARDEN

Most of the show in any color garden must come from herbaceous
plants, which are distinguished from those just treated by the fact

that they either die down to the ground each winter but come up the following season (herbaceous perennials); live but a single season and hence are planted from seed each year (annuals and tender annuals); or are derived from bulbs, corms or tuberous roots. If these categories seem confusing look at the explanation of them in Chapter One.

The arrangement of this herbaceous material is most conveniently accomplished by the *time at which the plants bloom,* and this plan has been followed here. Although flowers have fairly definite periods of bloom, they do vary somewhat, especially in very cool or hot seasons, in cloudy or wet spells, and the period of bloom of some annuals may be prolonged far beyond the time of their first coming into flower. With these facts in mind, and especially remembering your particular locality as to elevation, proximity to the sea and how much of your garden is shaded (a notably restraining influence), the herbaceous plants are here divided into:

1. Early Spring: approximately April 20-May 30.
2. Later Spring: approximately May 20-June 15.
3. Early Summer: approximately June 15-July 15.
4. Summer: generally July 15-August 31.
5. Late Summer or Fall: beginning about August 15, ending at frost.

1. EARLY SPRING. APRIL 20–MAY 30

CROWN IMPERIAL, 1-2 feet. A lily-like plant; to get the red color it is important to order Maxima Red. A bulb, which must be planted the autumn before flowers are wanted.

BARRENWORT, 6-10 inches. A rather woody perennial, with red-margined leaves. To secure red flowers order *Epimedium alpinum rubrum.*

DIANTHUS CRUENTUS, 6-9 inches high, and a perennial. One of the numerous pinks, all related to the carnation; this one has grayish foliage and grows in dense tufts or clumps.

TULIPS, 1-2 feet. Of the Cottage tulips, Fulgens and Glare of the Garden; of the Darwin tulips, William Pitt. Bulbs, fall-planted.

HYACINTHS, 8-12 inches. Bulbs, fall planted. The best reds are Roi des Belges and La Victoire.

2. LATER SPRING. MAY 20–JUNE 15

FIRE-PINK, 6-10 inches. Safest to order *Silene virginica,* a perennial doing well in ordinary garden soil, but also in sandy places.

SWEET PEA, 4-6 feet. An annual, the seeds of which should be sown
in late February or early March, as the plants do not like summer heat. The best reds are Red Boy, Leviathan and Welcome.

LUNGWORT (*Pulmonaria officinalis*), 6-12 inches, and a perennial.
Flower purplish-red, in terminal, branching clusters.

PEONIES, 2-3 feet. Stout, bushy perennials which do not like to be
moved and hence should be planted where wanted. Flowers
globe-like, 3-4 inches wide, very showy, of which the best reds will
be found in Longfellow, Auguste Dessert and Cherry Hill.

3. EARLY SUMMER. JUNE 15–JULY 15

ORIENTAL POPPY, 1-3 feet. A perennial with very showy but usually
ephemeral flowers that do not stand picking. Beauty of Livermore and Olympia are good fiery reds.

MALTESE CROSS (*Lychnis chalcedonica*), 2-3 feet. A perennial with
scarlet flowers about 1 inch wide in dense, terminal clusters.

LYCHNIS HAAGEANA, 6-12 inches. A perennial with flowers twice as
large as the Maltese Cross, but in fewer-flowered clusters.

TREE CYPRESS, 3-5 feet. A misleading name for *Gilia rubra*, which is
a perennial that tends to die out after a year or two. Its handsome, feathery foliage and scarlet flowers that are yellow and red-
dotted inside make it an old garden favorite.

RED VALERIAN, 1-3 feet. A perennial with tubular, fragrant red or
crimson flowers in dense clusters.

YARROW, 1-2 feet. A variety, Crimson Beauty, of the common white
yarrow, which is usually considered as a perennial weed.
Crimson Beauty is, however, an attractive garden plant.

NASTURTIUM, 1-2 feet. Free-flowering annuals of which only the
variety *coccineum* or Scarlet Gleam are certainly red, most
other varieties being yellowish or orange.

4. SUMMER. JULY 15–AUGUST 31

Midsummer is emphatically the time when the red garden is at
its height of bloom, and in planning for this riot of color there is a
variety of material to choose from. Because the height of the plant
means so much in garden planning it seems best to divide these summer-blooming, red-flowered plants into the following:

Plants not over 14 inches high, usually less.

Plants generally 16-24 inches high.

Plants 3-5 feet high, often considerably more.

NOT OVER 14 INCHES HIGH

HOUSELEEK, 3-8 inches. A perennial best ordered as *Sempervivum triste,* but carried by many dealers as *Sempervivum tectorum triste.* It is a form of the common houseleek with reddish foliage.

GODETIA GRANDIFLORA, 8-14 inches. An annual from California which will bloom better if crowded; hence do not thin out. Flowers very showy, 2-4 inches wide.

PETUNIA, 8-15 inches. A tender annual, and of its innumerable varieties Glow is a good deep red.

PLANTS 16–24 INCHES HIGH

Annuals and Tender Annuals

SNAPDRAGON. Tender annuals of which Gloria is rose red and Empress is scarlet.

CHINA ASTER. Tender annuals, splendid for picking. Heart of France is red, while Semple's Crimson is one of the showiest of all the China asters.

ZINNIA. Tender annuals, commonly used as bedding plants and for window boxes. Scarlet Queen and Crimson Queen are the two most popular in the red series.

TEN-WEEK STOCK. A tender annual, or usually best treated as such with terminal clusters of cruciform flowers, crimson in the variety Crimson King.

CLARKIA ELEGANS. A usually purplish-flowered Californian annual, but the variety Vesuvius is red. It blooms better when crowded so do not thin out.

ANNUAL BLANKET-FLOWER (*Gaillardia pulchella*). A predominately orange-flowered, very profuse annual, but the variety Burgundy suggests wine of that color.

FLOWERING FLAX. A somewhat sprawling annual grown chiefly in the variety *rubrum* for red and *coccineum* for scarlet flowers, which fade quickly after picking.

Perennials

RED LARKSPUR (*Delphinium nudicaule*). A relative of the tall larkspur, but a native of our Pacific Coast and much shorter. Its red spurs are contrasted with the small yellow petals.

GEUM CHILOENSE. One of the avens, but its flowers, which are nearly 1½ inches wide, are pure scarlet only if the variety Mrs. Bradshaw is chosen.

BEE BALM (*Monarda didyma*). A native perennial, much loved by
    bees, and suitable for dry, open places. Flowers scarlet.
PHLOX. Among the most showy and easily grown perennials, often
    blooming for weeks. Africa and Goliath are red, and Firebrand
is scarlet.
POTENTILLA. Of the many varieties and forms Gibson's Scarlet is the
    best in the red series. Its flowers are in loose, long-stalked
clusters and keep well after cutting.

PLANTS 3–5 FEET HIGH, OR MORE

Most of these are bold or striking plants, of such stature that they
can be used only toward the back of a border or bed. Some of them,
if grown in rows like vegetables, yield, in quantity, our finest cut
flowers—notably gladiolus, dahlia and canna.

Perennials

CARDINAL-FLOWER, 3-4 feet. A showy, native *Lobelia*, preferring par-
    tial shade and a moist place. Flowers useless for picking.
RED-HOT POKER (*Kniphofia uvaria grandiflora*), 3-4 feet. A showy
    herb, so called because of its close, pointed spike of tubular
flowers. It is not quite hardy north of New York City.
PENTSTEMON TORREYI, 3-4 feet. A native, western beardtongue, with
    scarlet, 2-lipped showy flowers.

Annuals and Tender Annuals

HOLLYHOCK, 4-6 feet. Really a biennial, but treated as an annual and
    often self-sown. Of the great number of varieties, many of
them unnamed, choose seed of a red or scarlet form. The seedsmen
usually specify them only by color.
SCARLET SAGE, 3-4 feet, often less if poorly grown. A popular, tender
    annual, widely used for bedding and often remaining in
flower for weeks.

Grown from Corms or Tuberous Roots
(See Chapter One for details of Planting)

GLADIOLUS, 3-4 feet. Grown from corms and one of the finest of sum-
    mer cut flowers. There are hundreds of varieties, but Dr. F. E.
Bennett and Aflame are among the best of the reds.
MONTBRETIA, 3-4 feet. Related to gladiolus and treated as such.
    Flowers 2 inches wide, curved and in shades of red in James
Coey, Lord Nelson and Princess.

For permanent effects the azalea, whether grown in the kind of mixed planting shown here, or in groups of a single color, has no equal. It can be naturalized among woods and rocks, grown in borders, or used in foundation plantings. Available in countless shades of red, pink, yellow, orange, lavender and white, in deciduous or evergreen forms, and in kinds hardy over most of the United States, it should be a part of every permanent planting. (Photo: *Genereux*)

A single type of flower, used as a bright accent color in home landscaping, can lend an unusual effect. Here, in a shady spot otherwise difficult to plant, tuberous begonias of several types flourish beside a stone walk. Averse to bright sun, the tuberous begonia has many uses in areas where shade is unavoidable. (Photo: *Roche*)

The uses of massed color are well illustrated in this garden at Williamsburg, where plantings of zinnias, asters, scarlet sage and other flowers in tones of red are framed in unbroken outer borders of purple. The resulting effect can be easily duplicated on a smaller scale in the home garden.

The perennial border, available in almost all the colors of the rainbow, is the standby of the gardener. Requiring little care, flexible as to height, color and time of bloom, its design can vary with any taste and any requirements. This one, growing in a northern state, uses commonly available materials and could be duplicated almost anywhere except in areas of great heat or extreme dryness. (Photo: *Genereux*)

CANNA. Tuberous rooted, chiefly tropical, very showy herbs, used
    mostly for bedding, but superb as cut flowers. The President,
3-4 feet, and Wintzer's Colossal, 5-6 feet, are two good red or scarlet
varieties.

DAHLIA, 3-5 feet. Of the hundreds of named forms few are in the
    red or scarlet series, hence Murphy's Masterpiece (red), Sa-
tan (scarlet) and Fort Monmouth (dark claret) are welcome in any
red garden.

5. LATE SUMMER OR FALL

Many of the plants mentioned in Section 4 of this chapter will
continue to bloom well into September, or even later. But beyond
that the red garden might well be without bloom if it were not for
the numerous varieties of the daisy family, of which only two call
for special mention here.

YELLOW STAR (*Helenium autumnale*), 3-5 feet. This normally yel-
    low, sunflower-like plant has in its variety *rubrum*, a good
dark red, fall-blooming perennial.

CHRYSANTHEMUM. Hardy perennials, with hundreds of varieties, and
    of easy culture in the border as they multiply readily. Some
are summer flowering, but among fall-blooming sorts that are red are
Louise Schling, 1-2 feet, which flowers from September 15 to frost,
and Vivid which flowers from about October 8 to frost.

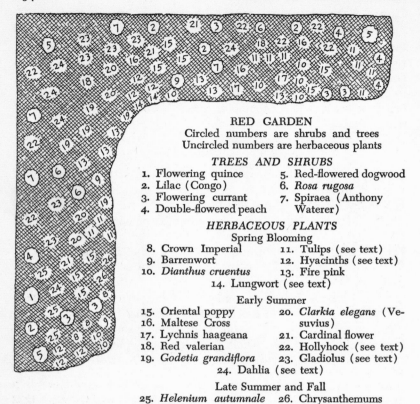

RED GARDEN

Circled numbers are shrubs and trees
Uncircled numbers are herbaceous plants

TREES AND SHRUBS

1. Flowering quince
2. Lilac (Congo)
3. Flowering currant
4. Double-flowered peach
5. Red-flowered dogwood
6. *Rosa rugosa*
7. Spiraea (Anthony Waterer)

HERBACEOUS PLANTS

Spring Blooming

8. Crown Imperial
9. Barrenwort
10. *Dianthus cruentus*
11. Tulips (see text)
12. Hyacinths (see text)
13. Fire pink
14. Lungwort (see text)

Early Summer

15. Oriental poppy
16. Maltese Cross
17. Lychnis haageana
18. Red valerian
19. *Godetia grandiflora*
20. *Clarkia elegans* (Vesuvius)
21. Cardinal flower
22. Hollyhock (see text)
23. Gladiolus (see text)
24. Dahlia (see text)

Late Summer and Fall

25. *Helenium autumnale rubrum*
26. Chrysanthemums (see text)

Note: The border is approximately 20 feet long on each angle and averages about 5 feet in width. Some of the shrubs may have to be thinned out later on. Consult the text for heights of the different plants, and for contrasting colors to mix with red, notably the plants at White Garden, Yellow Garden and Green Garden.

Chapter Three

The Blue Garden

$\mathscr{N}$OT MANY flowers are true blue, at least not as blue as the bluing one puts in the wash or blue vitriol. Perhaps only a few gentians and bellflowers can claim this distinction, all the others varying from pale or sky blue, through hyacinth, cobalt and royal blue to the darkest of them all, Antwerp blue. Fortunately for gardeners, interior decorators and shirtmakers this family of blues is easier to blend with other colors than most of those chosen for the chief color gardens in this book.

Blue is the color of peace and reflection, of magnificence in royal fabrics, and in the heavens the sign of fair weather. No wonder it has so many uses in decoration, especially in combination with blue and gold as in so many sumptuous mansions. However, few want an all-blue garden, although there is more justification for it than almost any other one-color garden.

If one is to make a predominately blue garden—and there is a striking one at Newport, Rhode Island—it is well to remember that natural stone makes a fine background for it. If there is no stone, then fences, woodwork, garden furniture and even buildings will make a pleasant contrast if painted yellow. Other colors for such painted features of the garden might be white, pale gray or even grayish-green.

When it comes to adding attractive contrasts to the predominately blue flowers, yellow is by far the most striking and effective (see the Yellow Garden). Of course white is satisfactory but should be used more sparingly than in a red garden, for instance. A blue garden does not overpower one as the red garden is apt to do. It needs less ameliorating influences to make it one of the loveliest of all color gardens. Even a bit of red can be mixed with it, as the designers of our national standard were smart enough to see years ago.

Also, many of the plants mentioned in the chapter on the Gray and Lavender Garden can be introduced into the blue garden with charming effects. This is particularly true of those with grayish or ashy foliage, most of which are grouped in the latter chapter, although some are mentioned here. The ordinary green of shrubs or evergreens does not seem to be as necessary for blue gardens as it is for so many others. Perhaps blue needs it less, and if any greens are to be used they should be yellowish-green—not the deep greens of evergreens or rhododendrons. If there is any chance for the reflection of a blue garden in a pool, the effect is enchanting.

PLANT MATERIALS FOR A BLUE GARDEN

Among shrubs, trees and woody vines there are only a few that have blue flowers, and most of them are showy only during the summer or early autumn, none appearing to be available for spring bloom. The few that may give permanence or accents to the blue garden are arranged below in approximately their sequence of flowering.

BLUE MYRTLE (*Ceanothus thyrsiflorus*), a magnificent evergreen shrub, often growing up to 25 feet high. Unfortunately it is hardy only from Washington, D.C., southward, but its copious sprays of showy flowers make it a striking plant for southern blue gardens where it blooms in midsummer.

CLEMATIS CRISPA, a woody vine, 6-9 feet high, summer-blooming and often called blue jasmine, although the bell-shaped flowers are really purplish-blue.

CLEMATIS, woody vines, 8-15 feet high. Among the named hybrids, with immense showy flowers, in summer, are Ascotiensis (azure blue) and Mrs. Cholmondeley (light blue).

ROSE-OF-SHARON, a shrub 8-10 feet high. Only the variety *coelestis* has purplish-blue flowers, the rest of the varieties being pink, magenta or white. A stout shrub easily grown anywhere.

CHASTE TREE, a shrub 5-7 feet high, with beautiful spire-like clusters of blue flowers in late summer. The underside of the leaves is ashy-gray.

LEAD PLANT, a shrub not over 4 feet high, the foliage white-hoary. Flowers small, pea-like, in clusters nearly 4 inches long, not very showy, and blooming in late August and September.

BLUE SPIREA, a very handsome shrub, 3-5 feet high, with showy clusters of fringed flowers that do not bloom until mid-September. Foliage grayish and hairy.

This seems a meager selection of blue-flowered shrubs, trees and woody vines, but their very rarity makes them particularly valuable in planning for a garden predominately blue. Both blue spirea and the chaste tree may winter-kill from New York northward, but many cut them to the ground in this area, as next season's growth will produce an abundance of flowers. From Philadelphia southward they do not need this winter pruning.

HERBACEOUS PLANTS FOR THE BLUE GARDEN

As in any other color garden by far the greatest concentration of blue flowers is found among herbaceous plants. Some are annuals, others tender annuals, many of them are perennials and quite a lot are derived from bulbs. For the significance of these simple categories and how to go about growing the different kinds, see the general directions in Chapter One.

Perhaps the most important feature of any garden is when the plants will be in bloom. Everyone wants a succession of bloom from spring to frost, and this provides us with the following division of the blue-flowered herbaceous plants. It should be remembered that there never can be hard and fast rules in nature, and the dates that follow are therefore guides rather than absolute statements of fact. Also, many plants, especially annuals and tender annuals, will begin to bloom at about the indicated time, but go on blooming the rest of the summer, and some of them flower right up to the first killing frost. This is also true of some perennials which may start flowering by June first and continue, sporadically, to bloom all summer and sometimes until overtaken by cold weather.

In other words, it will pay to look up *both* categories, as listed below, especially if the dates overlap, as they must do, for the five blooming periods are not so much a floral timetable as a guide to when, generally speaking, it is expected that the flowers will be first in bloom. Local conditions, especially elevation, a northern exposure, proximity to the sea and shade will affect the blooming period of any plant. In those that bloom early the flowering period may be retarded by a long, late and cold spring, and hastened if the reverse is true.

With these limitations the remainder of the plants in this chapter are divided into the following periods:

1. Early Spring. April 20-May 30
2. Later Spring. May 20-June 15
3. Early Summer. June 15-July 15
4. Summer. July 15-August 31
5. Late Summer and Fall. About August 15 to frost.

1. EARLY SPRING. APRIL 20—MAY 30

This, of course, is *the* period for the early, spring-flowering bulbs,

all of which must be planted the autumn before. Some, like the bluebells, squills, glory-of-the-snow and grape hyacinth, are best planted
by the hundreds, when they will make sheets of delightful blue color.
The bulbs are arranged approximately in the order in which bloom is
expected.

GLORY-OF-THE-SNOW, not over 3-4 inches. Often blooming in late
        March in favorable places and seasons. The two best kinds are
Chionodoxa luciliae, blue with a white eye and *Chionodoxa sardensis,*
pure deep blue.

CROCUS, 4-6 inches. Often blooming by April 1st in favorable places.
        The named sorts are in much confusion as to identity, and it
is safer to order by *color.* Several dealers carry plants advertised as
being porcelain blue.

BLUEBELLS OF ENGLAND, 6-10 inches. These are the bulbs that cover
        acres of meadow in the Kew Gardens, London. They are
listed as *Scilla nonscripta.* Other squills are the Spanish bluebell
(*Scilla hispanica*), 6-10 inches; but order the variety Blue King or
Blue Queen to be sure of color. A smaller plant, the Siberian squill
(*Scilla siberica*), 4-6 inches, is best used in the variety Spring
Beauty. All of them bloom in early April.

GRAPE-HYACINTH, 5-9 inches. A fine bulb for naturalizing, but order
        the variety Heavenly Blue for the desired color. It has tiny
bell-shaped flowers in a short, spiky cluster, resembling a miniature
hyacinth.

HYACINTH, 8-12 inches. King of the Blue's is porcelain blue; Oxford
        Blue is nearly true blue; and Queen of the Blues is a dark
blue. The showiest of blue, spring-flowering bulbs.

    The balance of early spring-flowering plants are not derived from
bulbs or corms and a fair selection might include the following.

FORGET-ME-NOT (*Myosotis sylvatica*). An annual, 3-8 inches high,
        often sprawling. There is also a taller variety, often erect,
known as Blue Eyes. Both are pale blue.

PRIMROSE (*Primula vulgaris caerulea*). A blue-flowered form of the
        English primrose and a perennial 4-6 inches high. The blue
may fade into purplish-blue.

FLAX. There are two good sorts for the blue garden: *Linum perenne,*
        the blue flax, a perennial 1-2 feet, and *Linum narbonnense,*
also perennial, 18-24 inches.

VIOLETS. Any of the wild blue violets can be easily dug from the
        woods and naturalized in the garden. From Maryland south-
ward a particularly fine one is the Confederate violet, pale blue.

LUNGWORT (*Pulmonaria angustifolia*). A perennial, 6-12 inches, with a terminal, coiled cluster of small blue flowers, the cluster straightening when mature.

VIRGINIA COWSLIP, 1-2 feet. A beautiful, native wild flower with
    funnel-shaped flowers that are purplish at first but turn blue
as the corolla expands.

2. LATER SPRING. MAY 20—JUNE 15

Among these precursors of summer, a few are best suited to the front of a border or other planting; because they never grow much higher than 12 inches, and some are prostrate.

PLANTS LOW, SCARCELY OVER 12 INCHES HIGH, OR PROSTRATE

BELLFLOWER (*Campanula garganica*). A sprawling and prostrate an-
    nual. Flowers scarcely ½ inch wide and not so showy as the
taller, later-blooming sorts.

GLOBULARIA CORDIFOLIA. A prostrate perennial with small flowers in
    dense blue heads—May-flowering. A related plant, *Globularia
trichosantha*, 4-6 inches high, blooms in early June.

NAVELWORT. A perennial, 6-10 inches high, with bright blue flowers
    in one-sided clusters. Does well in partial shade.

PERIWINKLE. A prostrate and beautiful evergreen ground cover. Its
    deep blue flowers are not profuse, but it is a fine carpet under
shrubs and trees.

PLANTS TALLER, MOSTLY 1–2 FEET HIGH OR MORE

TUFTED PANSIES. Perennials, 12-20 inches high. The variety Blue
    Butterfly will usually flower in mid-June and continue all
summer.

JACOB'S LADDER. Perennial, 18-30 inches. Flowers nearly an inch
    wide, drooping, in showy clusters. Will stand shaded places,
and fine for the wild garden. It will also grow in full sun.

BRUNNERA MACROPHYLLA. Perennial, 18-24 inches. Flowers small, but
    in handsome, showy clusters. It is often, but incorrectly, listed
in the catalogs as *Anchusa myosotidiflora*.

COLUMBINE (*Aquilegia coerulea*). A Rocky Mountain perennial, 2-3
    feet high. Flowers bluish-purple and very handsome, the long
spurs with a knob at the end.

IRIS. There are a few wild species of iris worth cultivating in the blue
    garden, notably the blue flag (*Iris versicolor*), 1-2 feet, with a
dash of yellow against its blue petals, and *Iris missouriensis*, 1-2 feet
with pale blue flowers. Among the tall bearded (German) irises the

named forms are West Point, Baldwin and Storm King, all 18-30 inches. All the irises are perennial.

3. EARLY SUMMER. JUNE 15–JULY 15

Among the blues of early summer three groups of plants stand out for their intense blueness, and some of them because they are tall, striking border plants. These comprise the speedwell, bellflowers and delphiniums. Because of their importance in any blue garden it seems best to separate them from the other early summer plants.

SPEEDWELLS. A large group of prevailingly blue-flowered perennials, of which the following are worth trying.

Veronica spuria, 1-2 feet, and often called bastard speedwell, with feathery foliage, and flowers in branched clusters.

Veronica incana, 6-8 inches, with white-hoary foliage, the flower clusters nearly 6 inches tall. Good for edging a bed or border.

Veronica gentianoides, 1-2 feet, with blue flowers veined with darker blue, in loose showy clusters. Other kinds are later blooming. See Section 4 (summer).

BELLFLOWERS. Very showy perennials and a standby for all who garden in blue. Of the many species perhaps the best of those blooming in early summer are:

Canterbury bells (*Campanula medium*), 2-4 feet, and really a biennial, but as it frequently is self-sown it can be treated as a perennial. Flowers violet-blue. Much cultivated and coming in several forms such as cup-and-saucer flower, etc.

Coventry bells (*Campanula trachelium*), 2-3 feet, and a vigorous plant with nodding, purplish-blue flowers in a loose cluster.

Chimney bellflower (*Campanula pyramidalis*), 3-5 feet, and blooming a little later than the other two. Flowers pale blue, bell-shaped, and nearly 1 inch long. A bushy, handsome perennial.

DELPHINIUM. Extremely showy perennials, the long, floriferous spikes of closely packed flowers often 4-6 feet high. They much prefer coolness to heat and do exceptionally well along the cool, northeastern New England coast and in maritime Washington, and Oregon. The group has been extensively hybridized and named forms are in much confusion. Blue Bird is a reliable blue, but it is safer to order others by *color.*

Speedwells, bellflowers and delphiniums are the most important of the early summer-blooming blue flowers, but there are a few more that find a place, three of them annuals, which are always useful to fill up bare places left by spring-blooming bulbs. The rest of this group are all perennials.

THE BLUE GARDEN 201

ANNUALS

CALIFORNIA BLUEBELL, 4-8 inches. Grow it in masses, and it blooms
better if kept crowded. Flowers deep blue, in one-sided
clusters.

BLUEBOTTLE, 12-18 inches. The national flower of Germany and often
called cornflower or ragged sailor, perhaps because its marginal rays are cut to pieces. Flowers deep blue.

BORAGE, 1-2 feet. Flowers much liked by bees, and it continues
flowering all summer.

PERENNIALS

SHEPHERD'S SCABIOUS (*Jasione perennis*), 8-12 inches. Flowers in
dense, globular heads nearly 2 inches in diameter. Of very
easy culture either in sun or partial shade.

LUPINE, 12-20 inches. Most of the varieties are yellow, white or pink,
but the Wayside Gardens carry a blue, but unnamed variety.
There are also some annual varieties listed by seedsmen, but it is
safer to order them by color, as the names are often inaccurate.

GERANIUM PLATYPETALUM, 12-20 inches. This is not the common
geranium (*Pelargonium*), but is a Chinese perennial well
suited to the border or bed.

LADYBELL (*Adenophora potanini*), 2-3 feet. A Chinese herb, closely
related to the bellflowers and just as blue, the flowers in
showy clusters.

ALKANET (*Anchusa azurea*), 2-4 feet. The ordinary species is less
desirable than Dropmore (bright blue), Opal (sky blue) and
Perry's (dark blue). All of these may bloom again in September.

4. SUMMER. JULY 15–AUGUST 31

There are more midsummer flowers for the blue garden than for
any other season. In fact there are so many that to come within
the compass of a small guide it has been necessary to limit our list
to those that will best fit the needs of the average reader, leaving for
the experts a variety of items that would be included if there were
space for them.

Even with such a reduction there are enough blue-flowering plants
that bloom in midsummer to confuse the amateur, and as it is the
time when the annuals are in perfection it seems helpful to divide
our midsummer bloomers into annuals and perennials.

ANNUALS

Love-in-a-mist, 8-12 inches. Foliage lace-like, the flowers set in a
    basket-like nest of thread-like bracts; good for cutting. The
variety Miss Jekyll is blue, but other forms are often white.

Baby Blue-eyes, 4-6 inches. Foliage cut into fine segments. Flowers
    bell-shaped, about 1 inch wide. It is safer to order by *color* as
there are white forms.

Chinese Forget-me-not (*Cynoglossum amabile*), 18-24 inches. A
    biennial, but treated as an annual as it will usually flower
the first season from planting the seed. Flowers small, but in showy
clusters. Order by color, for there is a pink form.

Gilia capitata, 18-24 inches. A Pacific Coast annual, its light blue
    flowers bloom in head-like clusters and are good for cutting.
Order by color, as there are also white forms.

Morning-glory. Of all the forms of this annual vine, which can
    easily climb 8-12 feet in a single season, by far the best for the
blue garden is the Mexican variety known as Heavenly Blue, which
is a pale, heavenly blue.

TENDER ANNUALS

(See Chapter One regarding how to grow these)

Ageratum, 4-8 inches high. A widely grown bedding plant, with
    blue, misty flowers in small heads. As there are many color
forms it is safer to order by *color*.

Nemesia, 6-8 inches. A tender, African annual, the two-lipped flow-
    ers fine for cutting. As there are many color forms, it is neces-
sary to order Blue Gem for the blue garden.

Petunia, 8-15 inches. Of the scores of varieties of this ever-popular
    plant for window boxes and bedding, the best for the blue gar-
den is Heavenly Blue, which is a pale blue.

Blue Wing Flower (*Torenia fournieri compacta*) nearly prostrate,
    and a fine plant for edging a bed or border. It has 2-lipped
flowers not unlike small snapdragons.

PERENNIALS

Here lie most of the summer-flowering blue plants of which scores
could have been included, but only sixteen have been selected for
their availability and ease of growing. Anyone planning a midsummer blue garden, as relatively permanent as a perennial border
should be, must first of all ask himself what are the heights of the
plants. To answer this question the plants below are grouped in three

sections, those 3-5 feet high; a lower group averaging 12-30 inches, and a couple of still lower plants that do not usually exceed 12 inches in height.

Tall perennials, 3–5 feet high and often more

MONKSHOOD (*Aconitum fischeri*), at least 4 feet high and sometimes more. A related plant, *Aconitum napellus,* in the variety known as Sparks is even taller; both are poisonous (aconite) if eaten, but not by skin contact.

BLUE FALSE INDIGO, 3-4 feet. A native American perennial, with showy, pea-like flowers in clusters 3-5 inches long. Prefers open, almost sandy places.

GLOBE THISTLE (*Echinops exaltatus*) 3-4 feet. A bold, showy thistle-like herb with white-woolly foliage and large heads of blue flowers. A related and somewhat lower plant is *Echinops ritro,* 12-30 inches, which has its white-felty leaves cut into fine segments.

SATIN POPPY (*Meconopsis wallichi*), 3-6 feet. A stout plant making a mound of foliage which is covered with a bloom. Flowers pale blue, not particularly showy.

PHLOX. The variety Blue Boy is 3-4 feet high, and a favorite in some blue gardens.

BLUE SAGE (*Salvia azurea*) 4-5 feet. A native perennial from the southeastern states. Flowers in interrupted clusters. It is better to order by *color* as there is a white-flowered strain.

Medium-sized perennials, 12–30 inches high

SEA HOLLY (*Eryngium planum*), 12-30 inches. A stout herb, with spiny-margined leaves and blue flowers in a dense head. A related, but lower plant is *Eryngium amethystinum,* 1-2 feet, with bluish-purple flower heads.

BALLOON-FLOWER (*Platycodon grandiflorum*), 18-30 inches, and a relative of the bellflowers. It has showy flowers, 2-3 inches long and a variety of it, *mariesi,* is dwarf. It is essential to order both by *color* as there are also white forms.

SAGE (*Salvia patens*), 18-30 inches. Unfortunately this is not generally hardy north of Philadelphia, as it has flowers that are "one of the purest, most intense blues in cultivation"; related, and perfectly hardy, are *Salvia pratensis* (purple-blue) and *Salvia farinacea* (purple-blue) which has white-hairy foliage.

SCABIOUS (*Scabiosa caucasica*), 1-2 feet. A sturdy perennial, the blue flowers in dense flattish heads 2-3 inches wide. A taller variety of it will be found in the Gray and Lavender Garden.

STOKE's ASTER (*Stokesia laevis*), 12-30 inches. A native plant from
the southeastern states with white-woolly foliage and lavender-blue flower heads, 2-4 inches wide.

SPEEDWELL (*Veronica spicata*) 1-2 feet and often called cat's tail. It
has a terminal spike of bright blue flowers. A related plant
(*Veronica maritima subsessilis*), 12-20 inches, has very deep blue
flowers.

Lower perennials, 6–15 inches high

GENTIAN (*Gentiana cruciata*), 6-8 inches. Of all the intensely blue-
flowered gentians, mostly for expert, rock-garden culture, this
is the only one relatively easy to grow, and even this will not thrive
in regions of great summer heat. Fine for mountainous areas in the
North.

BLUE SUCCORY, 12-15 inches, and an easily cultivated perennial from
Southern Europe. Flowers in dense heads, followed by
dandelion-like heads of puffy fruit.

5. LATE SUMMER OR FALL, BEGINNING ABOUT AUGUST 15 AND ENDING AT FROST

Most of the late-flowering blue herbs are tall and rather striking,
so that a couple of low, sprawling or prostrate plants are doubly welcome for the front of a bed or border, for edging and for pavement
planting. These low, nearly prostrate late-bloomers are:

EDGING LOBELIA, 3-7 inches high, and a tender annual, with very
deep blue flowers. The variety known as *compacta* is even
lower than the typical form and much used as edging.

CERATOSTIGMA PLUMBAGINOIDES, prostrate and sprawling and a perennial. Although rather widely grown for its deep blue flowers this Chinese herb appears to have no common English name.

Tall, striking perennials, 1½–5 feet high or more

MONKSHOOD (*Aconitum autumnale*) 3-4 feet, and a poisonous plant
if eaten, but harmless to touch. Closely related to the summer-
blooming *Aconitum fischeri,* and perhaps only a late-flowering variety of it.

HARDY AGERATUM (*Eupatorium coelestinum*), 18-24 inches, and a
spreading, attractive native plant often called mist flower,
from its numerous small heads of light blue or violet-blue flowers.

BLUE VERVAIN, 4-6 feet, and another native perennial that produces
slender, spire-like or wand-like, pointed clusters of almost
pure blue flowers.

BLUE LOBELIA, 2-3 feet. Related to the cardinal-flower, but lower, and later flowering, the irregular blooms pale blue.

MICHAELMAS DAISIES. These English creations, based mostly upon native American asters are much finer than their wild ancestors. They are perhaps the finest of our late-flowering perennials, often staying in bloom until frost. Of the scores of named varieties the best among the blues are Climax, 5-6 feet; Queen Mary, 3-4 feet; Blue Gem, 4-5 feet.

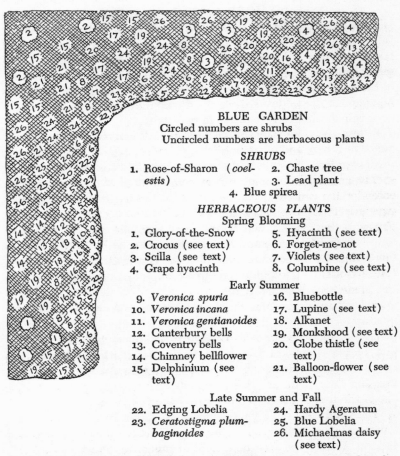

BLUE GARDEN
Circled numbers are shrubs
Uncircled numbers are herbaceous plants

SHRUBS

1. Rose-of-Sharon (*coelestis*)
2. Chaste tree
3. Lead plant
4. Blue spirea

HERBACEOUS PLANTS
Spring Blooming

1. Glory-of-the-Snow
2. Crocus (see text)
3. Scilla (see text)
4. Grape hyacinth
5. Hyacinth (see text)
6. Forget-me-not
7. Violets (see text)
8. Columbine (see text)

Early Summer

9. *Veronica spuria*
10. *Veronica incana*
11. *Veronica gentianoides*
12. Canterbury bells
13. Coventry bells
14. Chimney bellflower
15. Delphinium (see text)
16. Bluebottle
17. Lupine (see text)
18. Alkanet
19. Monkshood (see text)
20. Globe thistle (see text)
21. Balloon-flower (see text)

Late Summer and Fall

22. Edging Lobelia
23. *Ceratostigma plumbaginoides*
24. Hardy Ageratum
25. Blue Lobelia
26. Michaelmas daisy (see text)

Note: The border is about 20 feet long on each edge and approximately 5 feet wide. Consult the text for heights of the plants. See, also, contrasting plants that can be mixed in a blue border from among those listed at the Yellow Garden, the Gray and Lavender Garden, and the White Garden.

Chapter Four

The Yellow Garden

*P*OPE, in his Essay on Criticism, appears to anticipate what most of us would think of an all-yellow garden for "all looks yellow to the jaundiced eye." It is one of the most risky colors to work with because in the back of ones mind there seems always to lurk some unhealthy connotation. It may be the memory of the fight against yellow fever, the pest ship with its ominous yellow jack, or, if one loves fruit, the devastating peach yellows which once ruined the peach industry in two states.

Yellow, however, is one of the best of garden colors, both for blending with others and as a contrast with red or blue. Perhaps the old royal standard of Spain had the most dramatic contrast of red and yellow, and there are many garden combinations of these contrasting colors which can easily be contrived by the ingenious gardener. A comparison of the plants mentioned in the chapter on the Red Garden with those below will reveal many that bloom about the same time, are nearly the same height, and can hence be combined into delightful and somewhat forceful color contrasts. Sometimes such contrasts are to be found in the same group of plants, notably among iris, gladiolus, phlox and dahlia.

Perhaps no other contrast in the garden is so pleasing as a judicious mixture of yellow and blue. In a predominately yellow garden, patches of blue stand out because of their fitness, and the combination pleases the most fastidious. Such combinations are plentiful among the spring-flowering bulbs, especially narcissus, tulip and crocus, and later there are many annuals and perennials that provide one of the best of all garden contrasts—the yellow and blue.

White adds little to a yellow garden, unless it be the mixture of a few white perennials in a striking or even violent mixing of reds and yellows. White can then be a neutral influence, and there are any number of white-flowered plants to choose from in all the five seasons of bloom adopted for this book.

No background material for the yellow garden is so fine as the deep green of evergreens, or, as second choice the yellowish green of ordinary shrubs and trees. But one must think ahead. Will the shrub or tree have autumnal color that blends well with late-flowering yellow plants, such as the gorgeous scarlets of certain oaks, the sweet gum and the sassafras. Consult the chapter on green gardens as to autumnal foliage, which, with late-blooming chrysanthemums can prolong color in the garden to leaf-fall.

For the reasons just outlined, the best color to paint accessories of the yellow garden, as well as fences and buildings, is green; if there is objection to this, then blue would be next choice, and by many it would be considered *the* background for a predominately yellow garden. A particularly striking example of this is a blue-tiled pool with yellow aquatics. Also a grayish-blue slate, broken up for random walks, is delightful if the crevice planting is of prostrate or tiny yellow-flowered herbs.

Scarcely any color in nature has so many shades as yellow. On one end of the scale are the imperceptible blends that shade off into green, and from these greenish-yellows one can easily choose half a dozen yellows, finally leading up through chrome yellow and lemon yellow to those that have a touch of pink or red in them, such as marigold yellow, and ending up with orange. Most of the plants that follow are "just yellow," and only special yellows will be noted.

PLANT MATERIAL FOR A YELLOW GARDEN

There is a surprising amount of shrub and tree material to help provide permanence in the yellow garden. In fact almost continuous yellow bloom can be secured with shrubs and trees alone, from February and March right through to October and November. These shrubs and trees should make the frame or provide permanent accents in the yellow garden, and they are arranged below approximately in the order of their blooming.

WITCH-HAZEL. Two Asiatic shrubs and small trees, known as *Hamamelis mollis,* 10-20 feet and *Hamamelis vernalis,* 3-6 feet; bloom in February and early March on leafless twigs. A more showy relative, *Corylopsis pauciflora,* 4-6 feet, blooms about the same time.

WINTER JASMINE, 3-4 feet. A beautiful, wand-like shrub, nearly leafless during the winter but with green-twigged, arching branches. Flowers solitary, about 1 inch wide, blooming before the leaves unfold, in early March or even late February.

CORNELIAN CHERRY, a tree 8-12 feet high. During March and early

April the bare twigs are covered with close-clustered, tiny yellow flowers. Not particularly showy.

FORSYTHIA INTERMEDIA, a shrub 6-10 feet, and the best of these popularly planted bushes. Flowers about March 20-April 15.

FLAME AZALEA, a shrub 6-12 feet high. In its typical form the flowers are orange yellow, and bloom in late April or early May. Many hybrids, developed from or related to the Flame Azalea, provide good yellows, notably Miss Louisa Hunnewell, Anthony Koster and Brilliant.

WINTERGREEN BARBERRY (*Berberis julianae*) an evergreen shrub, 4-6 feet high, with spiny-toothed leaves and close clusters of handsome yellow flowers in May. Not quite hardy north of New York.

KERRIA JAPONICA, a shrub 5-8 feet high, its deep yellow flowers appearing in late May or early June. A variety, the Japanese rose (variety *pleniflora*), has double flowers.

ROSES. Among the single-flowered species, scarcely any can compare with the Chinese shrub, Father Hugo's rose, 5-6 feet. Among the hybrid tea roses, which are 3-5 feet, good yellow varieties are Eclipse, Golden Dawn and Mrs. Pierre S. du Pont. King Midas and Elegance are favorite climbing roses. All of the roses bloom in June, and sometimes later.

BLADDER SENNA, a shrub 3-4 feet high. Flowers pea-like, bright yellow and in long stalked clusters. Fruit papery and inflated.

GOLDEN CHAIN, a tree 10-20 feet high, with extremely handsome, pendulous clusters of pea-like flowers in late June.

SCOTCH BROOM, a shrub 4-9 feet high, safer ordered as *Cytisus scoparius*. It has green twigs and a profusion of yellow pea-like flowers. A relative, *Cytisus nigricans*, 4-6 feet, blooms about a month later.

SCORPION SENNA (*Coronilla emerus*), a shrub 3-7 feet with green-striped twigs. Flowers pea-like, in long-stalked clusters. It blooms from midsummer to September.

WITCH-HAZEL (*Hamamelis virginiana*), a shrub 5-10 feet high, and a native of eastern North America. Blooming at the time of, and after, leaf-fall, during October and November.

HERBACEOUS PLANTS FOR THE YELLOW GARDEN

There are so many yellow-flowered annuals and perennials that only by drastic cutting is it possible to select a group easy to grow, providing continuous bloom and readily available from seedsmen or nurserymen. The number discarded from this chapter exceeds the number of those retained, and the recommended plants have been arranged in the order of their blooming.

Most of the early-flowering kinds are derived from corms or bulbs, all of which must be planted the autumn before. Nearly all the rest are perennials or annuals; and the management of all of these, as well as the bulbous plants, is treated in Chapter One. In planning a yellow garden it is well to look over the shrubs and trees listed in the previous section, then determine how many of the perennials you would like to use, leaving space for annuals, tender annuals, bulbs and, of course, tuberous-rooted plants such as dahlia.

Without drawing a plan, it is perfectly simple to arrange the main accents of such a mixture of plants, leaving until later the filling in of gaps, the planting of bulbs, corms, annuals and tender annuals as the scheme develops. Finally the bed or border will take definite outlines of color, height and period of bloom, after which, or from the beginning if you prefer, a simple plan should be drawn with a key to the plants in it. Only so can you keep track of the named forms that are in the lists that follow, which are again divided as to their flowering periods:

1. Early Spring. April 20-May 30
2. Later Spring. May 20-June 15
3. Early Summer. June 15-July 15
4. Summer. July 15-August 31
5. Late Summer and Fall. Beginning about August 15 and ending at frost.

Before the early spring flowering plants there is the unique winter aconite (*Eranthis hyemalis*), which blooms in February or even in December-January if the winter has not been too severe. It is best grown from September-planted tubers, from which spring the solitary, yellow flower on stalks 3-8 inches high. The plant dies down during the summer, but increases rapidly and will soon cover considerable areas. It is a very welcome precursor of spring.

1. EARLY SPRING. APRIL 20—MAY 30

The following, nearly all derived from bulbs or corms, should be planted the autumn before bloom is expected. They are arranged in the approximate order of their flowering.

CROCUS. Early flowering plants, frequently blooming in late March if the weather is mild, but more generally in April. Of the many kinds the Dutch crocus (*Crocus aureus*) and the Cloth of Gold (*Crocus susianus*) are yellow. Neither is over 6 inches high.

Can be left in the ground and will cover considerable areas in a few years.

ADONIS VERNALIS, 6-8 inches high and a perennial. It has finely dissected leaves and a solitary, buttercup-like flower that is nearly 3 inches wide.

NARCISSUS, 6-9 inches. Any of the varieties known as trumpet narcissus will flower freely in mid-April, and earlier if the season is mild or the region south of Washington, D.C. Can be left in the ground for years; however, as they crowd each other the bloom disappears, and every three years they should be dug up and replanted about 5 inches apart.

OXLIP (*Primula elatior*), 4-8 inches high. Related to the next and a showy, yellow-flowered perennial with basal leaves. It prefers coolness, moisture and shade.

ENGLISH PRIMROSE (*Primula vulgaris*), 4-6 inches high. Leaves crinkled, basal, and from them springs the single stalk crowned with a cluster of yellow flowers. Must be grown in shade where it is cool and moist.

TULIP. Only the Cottage and Darwin tulips are here included, as they provide a wealth of color from about May first to the end of the month and even later in some of the Darwin varieties. Cottage Tulips (with pointed, slightly incurved petals), 10-15 inches: Alaska, yellow; Avis Kennicott, deep yellow; Moonlight, pale yellow. Darwin Tulips (with blunt, slightly incurved petals), 15-24 inches: Heroine, lemon yellow; Mrs. John Scheepers, pure yellow; Niphetos, sulphur yellow.

HYACINTH, 8-12 inches. Of the scores of varieties of this most showy of spring-blooming bulbous plants one of the only yellows is Yellow Hammer. It is not carried by many small dealers but is worth hunting for.

2. LATER SPRING. MAY 20–JUNE 15

All of this group are perennials, and should hence be put in places where permanently wanted, especially the peonies which resent moving and are quite apt to reflect that resentment by not flowering at all for a year or two after planting. The selected plants, for convenience in planning a border, are grouped by height as follows:

PLANTS USUALLY ONE FOOT HIGH OR LESS

GOLD-DUST. A compact, very free-flowering plant good for the border, for planting in dry walls and especially for pavement planting.

VIOLETS. The common, native *Viola pubescens,* can be collected from
the woods and prefers shade. It is our showiest native yellow
violet. Of the tufted violet varieties, good for the open border, Yellow
Gem is about 1 foot high.

HOUSELEEK (*Sempervivum arenarium*). A curious fleshy-leaved
plant, the leaves packed in a globe-shaped basal rosette, from
which springs a yellow, also globe-shaped flower cluster.

DOUBLE ORANGE DAISY (*Erigeron aurantiacus*). A Turkestan perennial with narrow leaves, the flower heads orange-yellow and
nearly 1 inch wide.

ADONIS AMURENSIS, a perennial with finely dissected almost fern-like
foliage and a golden-yellow, solitary flower about 2 inches
wide. Needs a good rich soil.

PLANTS 2–4 FEET HIGH

PEONIES. Almost none of the Chinese or ordinary peonies of the garden are yellow, but this color may be had from some hybrids
derived from the species *Paeonia lutea.* Of these the predominately
yellow sorts are La Lorraine, Chromatella and Argosy. All are 2-3
feet high.

IRIS. While there are several wild irises with yellow flowers, that
color is better found among the tall bearded (German) iris
varieties known as Gold Imperial, Jasmine, Ming Yellow and Treasure Island. They vary from 2-3 feet, and all are perennials.

DAYLILY. Stout, perennial herb, 2-4 feet high, comprising many, prevailingly yellow-flowered types of which a selection should
include Flava, May, pure yellow; Gold-Dust, June, golden-yellow;
Luteola major, June, pure yellow; August Orange, June-July, orange,
yellow.

3. EARLY SUMMER. JUNE 15–JULY 15

Most of the plants in this small group may flower before the dates
given, and a good many of them continue to flower well into the next
group of midsummer flowers. Generally speaking, however, all the
half dozen may be expected to flower about June 15-July 15. All are
perennials except the first.

NASTURTIUM. An annual of the easiest culture, and with a variety
of colors. Golden Gleam, growing to 12-20 inches, will produce clear golden-yellow flowers. Golden King, also golden-yellow,
is half climbing and will sprawl without a support.

ACHILLEA TOMENTOSA, 3-8 inches. A yarrow, with finely dissected, hairy leaves and, in the variety Moonlight, with small button-like heads of yellow flowers. It frequently stays in flower until the end of September.

STONECROPS. Two creeping or prostrate species of *Sedum* make excellent yellow-flowered ground covers. One of them, the golden moss (*Sedum acre*), is nearly moss-like and carpets the ground with tiny yellow flowers. The yellow stonecrop (*Sedum reflexum*) has creeping stems, evergreen leaves and flower stalks nearly a foot high, the flower about ½ inch wide.

YELLOW TUFT (*Alyssum argenteum*), 9-15 inches. Foliage silvery on the under side. Flowers in close, small, head-like clusters, deep yellow, and staying in bloom all summer. It is closely related to Gold-Dust (See 2. Later Spring, in this chapter).

POTENTILLA PYRENAICA, 1-2 feet. A stout-growing perennial from the Pyrenees with golden-yellow flowers in loose clusters. It thrives in almost any ordinary garden soil.

COLUMBINE (*Aquilegia chrysantha*). A showy garden perennial from the Rocky Mountains, 2-4 feet high, its irregular, spurred flowers very handsome, and nearly 3 inches wide. It continues to bloom until mid-August.

4. SUMMER. JULY 15–AUGUST 31

Midsummer is the time of annuals and tender annuals, the burgeoning of montbretias, dahlias and gladiolus, as well as a lot of yellow-flowered perennials. As in other color gardens, July and August is so packed with color that it is not easy for the amateur to make a wise selection. But the decision must be made, for upon it depends a lot of garden operations which have to be started weeks or months before the desired effects can be certain. Tender annuals must be started in time to be hardened off so that they are fit for the open border, the roots of dahlia, and the corms of gladiolus and montbretia should be planted after settled warm weather has arrived (about May 20-30 near New York), and all perennials should be in the ground before they start growth in the spring (March 15-April 15). The details of growing these different groups will be found in Chapter One, so there is no need to repeat them here.

Perhaps the simplest method of separating these midsummer bloomers is upon the basis of how they must be planted. Using such a division the plants might well be separated thus:

A. Grown from tuberous roots or corms—dahlia, gladiolus, montbretia.

B. Annuals
C. Tender Annuals
D. Perennials

A. GROWN FROM TUBEROUS ROOTS OR CORMS

DAHLIA. There are scores of varieties to choose from in this protean
family of Dahlia, all of them stout plants 3-5 feet high or even
higher. Among the large flowered types Lord of Autumn is canary
yellow; Frau O. Bracht is primrose yellow; and Lady Moyra Pon-
sonby, pure yellow. Among the smaller-flowered pompon dahlias,
Honey is primrose yellow; Yellow Gem is canary yellow; and Sunny
Daybreak, lemon yellow tipped with scarlet. In the old-fashioned
single dahlias, James Weller is yellow but likely to be tinged with
red.

GLADIOLUS. Perhaps the showiest of summer-blooming plants and so
popular for cutting that there is a large industry in growing
them for the florist trade, where, by forcing there is scarcely a month
in the year without gladiolus bloom. For the average home grower
they are *the* midsummer flower, the tall spikes frequently reaching
2-3 feet high. Of the hundreds of varieties not many are yellow, but
that color is found in Golden State, whereas Oregon Gold is light,
almost pale yellow. Golden Dream is golden-yellow. All of these
varieties are so well liked that they were among the few chosen
by gladiolus experts from hundreds of candidates.

MONTBRETIA. Related to gladiolus, but somewhat taller, frequently
reaching 4 feet in height. Flowers smaller than in gladiolus,
generally not over 2 inches wide, the cluster branched. The variety
Golden West is golden yellow. The corms should be planted after
warm weather has arrived.

B. ANNUALS

YELLOW BELLS (*Emmenanthe penduliflora*). This showy annual
from California and Mexico is 12-18 inches high, its bell-
shaped, rather lasting flowers in hanging clusters. Usually grown as
an annual, but if early bloom is desired it can be started as a tender
annual.

CALIFORNIA POPPY, 8-12 inches. One of the most showy of our Western annuals, coming in a variety of colors, so that it is safer
to order seed by color. The flowers are particularly good for cutting.

GAILLARDIA, 18-24 inches. Most of the annual blanket-flowers, which
is the name for the annual species of Gaillardia, are in shades

of red, orange or combinations of them. But the variety Golden Yellow is that color, and keeps well after cutting.

C. TENDER ANNUALS

All of these should be started from seed sown in the hotbed or on a shelf at the kitchen window from 4-6 weeks before they can be transplanted to the bed or border, and from 9-12 weeks before you expect bloom. Many of the plants will go on flowering until frost.

SNAPDRAGON, 12-18 inches. Four excellent varieties are available. Amber Queen (yellow), Navajo (canary yellow), Golden West (deep yellow) and Newport Yellow (a deep rich yellow). All of them are good for cut flowers.

CAPE MARIGOLD (*Dimorphotheca aurantiaca*), 1-2 feet. This is really a perennial, but blooms from seed in one season if treated as a tender annual. Flower heads solitary, long-stalked, a rich, orange-yellow. A very popular garden plant.

POT MARIGOLD, 12-20 inches. A popular tender annual, its foliage undivided and scentless. Flower heads solitary, orange-yellow and one of the best for cutting because the flowers keep well.

AFRICAN MARIGOLD, 18-24 inches. A tender annual, with finely dissected, strong-smelling foliage, and so popular that there are many varieties. Pride of the Garden and Yellow Supreme are both yellow-flowered. The related French marigold has some yellow varieties, but they are of uncertain naming.

ZINNIA, 2-3 feet. Perhaps the most widely grown of all tender annuals, as the improved types come in many colors, and in some varieties with large, rather stiff flower heads. Not many are yellow but Buttercup is that color, and Golden Queen is a golden-yellow.

GOLDEN COREOPSIS (*Coreopsis tinctoria*), 20-36 inches. A wild plant from the central United States, now widely grown as a tender annual for its profusion of yellow flower heads, which keep well after cutting. The plants will produce more flowers if kept crowded, so do not thin them out too much.

D. PERENNIALS

Not over 2 feet high

BUTTERFLY-WEED. A native perennial milkweed, apt to sprawl, growing naturally in sandy places and producing showy, orange-yellow flower clusters. It is deep rooted and hard to dig from the wild.

WELSH POPPY (*Meconopsis cambrica*). A striking European perennial, with pale green, finely divided leaves, and a distinct bloom on the underside. Flowers pale yellow, solitary, nearly 2 inches wide and standing well above the mass of dissected foliage.

LUPINE. Most of these showy perennials, with pea-like flowers, are in shades of blue, pink or white, but Gold Crest is a deep, golden-yellow, on stalks 12-20 inches high.

GOLDEN FLAX (*Linum flavum*). A weak-stemmed perennial, hence likely to sprawl. Flowers golden-yellow, in loose clusters, the individual flowers about ¾ inch wide. It is closely related to the true flax, which is blue, and as they flower together they make an attractive color contrast.

COREOPSIS GRANDIFLORA. A perennial relative of the annual golden coreopsis (see Tender Annuals) but a native of the southeastern states. It is 1-2 feet high, and a profuse bloomer, its heads, which are pure yellow, often 2½ inches wide. Of the easiest culture and apt to run wild.

At least 4 feet high or more

FOXTAIL LILY (*Eremurus bungei*). An extraordinary Persian perennial with a basal rosette of narrow leaves from which springs a tall wand-like flower stalk at least 4-5 feet high, crowded with hundreds of tiny bell-shaped flowers. For a related, and still taller flower, see the Pink Garden. As their brittle roots are easily injured, they must be planted with care.

BUSH BROOM (*Hypericum prolificum*). A bushy, native perennial, 4-5 feet high, almost shrubby, with evergreen leaves and yellow flowers in showy terminal clusters. It is not certainly hardy north of Boston.

5. LATE SUMMER AND FALL. BEGINNING ABOUT AUGUST 15, AND ENDING AT FROST

As one approaches the end of summer, knowing that frost is not far distant, the number of yellow-flowered plants is quite naturally reduced to a minimum. Nevertheless, it is possible to have bloom in the yellow garden up to, and sometimes beyond, the first killing frost. Some of that color comes from tall, sunflower-like perennials, from the ever-popular chrysanthemums and cosmos and finally from a little known fall-flowering bulbous plant called, for some unknown reason, autumn or winter daffodil (*Sternbergia lutea*). It has, however, crocus-like flowers that bloom in autumn, and it is never more than 7 inches tall. This attractive, fall-blooming bulb should be planted in August, about 4 inches deep for bloom about two months hence.

Among taller plants, yellow may be found among the following:

GOLDEN GLOW. A somewhat coarse perennial, 5-8 feet high, with a profusion of double-flowered heads. Some consider it too common to be worth cultivating, but it is dependable and showy.

YELLOW STAR (*Helenium autumnale*), 4-6 feet. A sturdy, sunflower-like perennial, the flower heads about 2 inches wide. If a lower plant is needed, the variety *pumilum* is not over 2 feet high.

CHRYSANTHEMUM, 1-3 feet. It is quite possible to have yellow bloom from August 15 to frost and sometimes beyond by choosing the following varieties. The dates given are when they first come into bloom.

August 14. Barbara Cumming. Yellow.

August 30-September 30. Early Bronze, a bronzy-yellow pompon variety.

September 30. R. Marion Hatton. A pompon variety.

October 6. Alice Howell. A single variety.

October 10. Yellow Gem. A pompon variety.

COSMOS. Weak-stemmed, tender annuals, 5-8 feet high, with feathery foliage, and a profusion of daisy-like flower heads in all colors, unless one chooses the varieties Yellow Flare and Orange Flare. Cosmos is excellent for cutting, will begin blooming in late summer, and in mild seasons stays in flower until Thanksgiving.

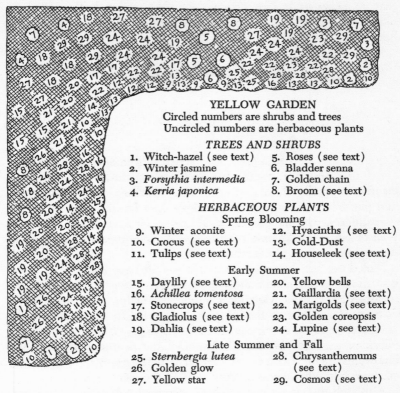

YELLOW GARDEN
Circled numbers are shrubs and trees
Uncircled numbers are herbaceous plants

TREES AND SHRUBS

1. Witch-hazel (see text)
2. Winter jasmine
3. *Forsythia intermedia*
4. *Kerria japonica*
5. Roses (see text)
6. Bladder senna
7. Golden chain
8. Broom (see text)

HERBACEOUS PLANTS

Spring Blooming

9. Winter aconite
10. Crocus (see text)
11. Tulips (see text)
12. Hyacinths (see text)
13. Gold-Dust
14. Houseleek (see text)

Early Summer

15. Daylily (see text)
16. *Achillea tomentosa*
17. Stonecrops (see text)
18. Gladiolus (see text)
19. Dahlia (see text)
20. Yellow bells
21. Gaillardia (see text)
22. Marigolds (see text)
23. Golden coreopsis
24. Lupine (see text)

Late Summer and Fall

25. *Sternbergia lutea*
26. Golden glow
27. Yellow star
28. Chrysanthemums (see text)
29. Cosmos (see text)

Note: The border is approximately 20 feet long on each edge and about 5 feet wide. Consult the text for heights of plants. For plants of contrasting colors, see especially the lists at the Red Garden and the White Garden and some of the striking contrasts in the chapter on the Blue Garden.

Chapter Five

The Pink Garden

HE VERY flavor of romance and perfection clings to a pink garden. It is no accident that in *Romeo and Juliet* occurs the phrase, "I am the very *pink* of courtesy." There is romance and perfection in that phrase, as there may be in a garden. In the very different *She Stoops to Conquer* also occurs the phrase, "the very *pink* of perfection," while the prosaic Mr. Webster cites a dandy as dressed in the *pink* of elegance.

Pink long ago became synonymous with superlative, and many gardeners, both ancient and modern, have lavished care beyond measure in creating what most authorities claim is the finest of all color gardens. It is as though they have tried to translate into the language of flowers, the courtesy of Shakespeare, the perfection of Sheridan, the elegance of Beau Brummel, the aspiration of youth and finally just plain love of a color that is neither red nor yellow nor blue nor white but some mixture of all of them—namely pink.

Although the young and romantic may insist that an all-pink garden is the only one to consider, wiser and older gardeners will suggest that there can easily be too much of pink perfection, unless, of course, one is hopelessly and forever in the pink haze of love—or the love of beauty.

For those who like to mix their pinks, the following combinations have been found useful.

Pink with pale, ashy-gray foliaged plants, which are grouped together in the chapter on the Gray and Lavender Garden.

Pink, especially the pale sunset varieties of it with pale blue flowers that also suggest sunset colors. See the Blue Garden.

Pink with only the greens of lawn, shrubs and trees. See the Green Garden.

Pink, with a few pale yellows, a combination, however, anathema to some. See the Yellow Garden.

Gray stone or slate make admirable background material for the pink garden, and if there are wooden steps, furniture, arbors or buildings, they are best painted silvery-gray, white or some shade of sky blue.

Although it is possible and in fact desirable to be romantic in a pink garden, there is a quite prosaic side to the creating of one. Plant materials do not just grow and stay that way. They are of different heights, shades and foliage, and especially trying is the time when they *are* pink. Some of the shrubs and trees may be pink only for a fortnight or less, while some of the annuals will bloom all summer. To reduce the plant material for a pink garden to some sort of order is the first requisite for the ultimate possession of one that "is in the pink."

PLANT MATERIAL FOR THE PINK GARDEN

Nature and the plant breeders have been particularly kind in furnishing us with a variety of shrubs, woody vines and trees, so that from these materials alone it is possible to have pink in the garden from early April to September and in some localities into October. As the succession of bloom among these shrubs and trees is their most important character, in planning the permanent fixtures of a pink garden it will be most helpful to group them by seasons:

APRIL

REDBUD (*Cercis canadensis*). A small tree or shrub, 8-20 feet high.
    In early spring, before the leaves unfold, its bare twigs are covered with a profusion of pea-like flowers.
DAPHNE CNEORUM, a prostrate, evergreen shrub, not quite hardy
    north of New York. It has fragrant, small flowers in close, terminal clusters. Fine for foundation planting or as ground cover.

MAY

FLOWERING ALMOND. Two different plants are so called: *Prunus glandulosa rosea*, 3-5 feet, and *Prunus triloba*, 4-10 feet. Both are covered with single or double flowers, often profusely so.
JAPANESE FLOWERING CHERRY. These are in such confusion as to Japanese and American names that it is safer to order them by color. They ultimately become trees 10-30 feet high. Magnificent weeping forms are available.
ROSEBUD CHERRY (*Prunus subhirtella*). A fine Japanese tree, 20-30 feet high, most popular in a weeping variety, the long pendulous branches of which nearly reach the ground. Very floriferous.

CRABAPPLE. Several species are available, and among the finest is
    Malus floribunda, 10-15 feet. Bechtel's Crabapple, 10-15 feet,
is a fine double-flowered form. Both these are small trees, but a lower,
shrub-like crabapple is the Japanese Toringo, with single apple-like
blossoms.

ENGLISH HAWTHORN, a tree 10-20 feet. While the typical form is
    white or blush, there is a particularly fine double-flowered
variety that is pink.

CLEMATIS MONTANA RUBENS. A woody vine, 10-20 feet high, with
    the young foliage purplish and pink flowers about 2 inches
wide.

AZALEA. Among the best of the pinks is the native pinkster flower
    (*Azalea nudiflora*) 5-8 feet; also *Azalea schlippenbachi,* 9-
15 feet, from Japan, with large flowers in close clusters. More nearly
rose-pink is the very fine *Azalea vaseyi,* 5-12 feet, from the mountains of North Carolina whose flowers are spotted with brownish-
orange. As to the many hybrid azaleas they are best ordered by *color*.

JUNE

RHODODENDRON. Magnificent evergreen shrubs, of which the two fin-
    est native kinds, with pink flowers are *Rhododendron carolin-
ianum,* 3-6 feet and *Rhododendron maximum,* 5-12 feet, and often
called the great laurel. Finer than either are the hybrids, of which
Pink Pearl (from Philadelphia southward), and Delicatissimum are
noteworthy. The hybrid, Mrs. R. S. Holford, is 6-8 feet.

MOUNTAIN LAUREL, 4-8 feet, but higher in the mountains of North
    Carolina. A beautiful evergreen shrub, covered in early June
with a profusion of pale pink, or pinkish-white flowers.

DEUTZIA ROSEA, 1-3 feet. A delightful, small, very floriferous shrub,
    covered with small, bell-like flowers. Of the easiest culture.

DEUTZIA, PRIDE OF ROCHESTER, 5-8 feet. A striking, handsome shrub,
    with very numerous flowers. Will form a thick, informal
hedge.

WEIGELA FLORIDA, 5-8 feet. A popular, and some think, a too much
    planted shrub. It has, however, a profusion of chalice-shaped,
pink flowers and is of the easiest culture. A deep red variety is noted
in the Red Garden.

BEAUTY-BUSH, 4-6 feet. A showy shrub, related to the honeysuckle,
    completely covered with bell-shaped flowers in flattish clus-
ters that are nearly 3 inches wide.

JUNE–JULY

ROSES. Of the wild single roses, *Rosa blanda,* 4-6 feet, and *Rosa nitida,* 1-2 feet, are both pink. Among the hybrid climbing roses, good varieties are American Pillar and Mary Wallace. The varieties Mary Margaret McBride, Radiance and Editor McFarland are all hybrid tea roses and fine for any pink garden.

CRAPE MYRTLE, 8-20 feet. A magnificent shrub or small tree covered with immense trusses of lilac-like clusters of showy flowers. The typical form appears to be pink, but white and deep maroon forms are available. By choosing early- and late-flowering strains it is possible to have continuous bloom in the garden from mid-July to September 15. Unfortunately the plant is hardy only from Delaware southward.

AUGUST–SEPTEMBER

ABELIA GRANDIFLORA, 3-5 feet. A half-evergreen shrub with bell-shaped flowers about 1½ inches long, in loose clusters.

TAMARISK (*Tamarix pentandra*). A shrub 10-15 feet high or tree-like in the South and California. Its long, greenish-pink twigs are covered with hundreds of tiny, pinkish flowers. Fine for seaside planting and hardy as far north as Boston.

BUSH CLOVER (*Lespedeza thunbergi*). A shrub 3-7 feet high, but often dying to the ground and hence herb-like. Flowers rose-pink or purplish, pea-like and blooming through most of September and October. Not certainly hardy north of New York.

HERBACEOUS PLANTS FOR THE PINK GARDEN

The herbaceous material for the pink garden is best divided according to its period of bloom. As in the other lists in this book it should be understood that these dates are relative rather than accurate, and hence are a guide to the procession of bloom rather than a strict floral timetable.

1. EARLY SPRING. APRIL 20–MAY 30

BLUEBELLS OF ENGLAND (*Scilla nonscripta*), 6-10 inches. A bulbous plant, prevailingly blue, but the variety Blush Queen will provide sheets of pink if planted in quantities.

SPANISH BLUEBELL (*Scilla hispanica*), 6-10 inches. The variety Rose Queen is deep pink. The typical form is blue.

TULIP. Among the Darwin Tulips, 12-24 inches, Gretchen, Baronne
de la Tonnaye and Camellia are all pink, while Clara Butt
is salmon-pink. In the Triumph class is Lord Carnavon, and among
the Cottage Tulips will be found Dido (deep pink).

HYACINTH. Of the scores of varieties, in many shades, there are several that are pink. Among the best is Lady Derby, General
de Wet, Mont Rose, Pink Pearl and Queen of the Pinks.

GROUND PINK (*Phlox subulata*), a prostrate perennial, and almost
moss-like in its capacity to cover the ground. Use the variety
Alexander's Pink.

2. LATER SPRING. MAY 20–JUNE 15

SAXIFRAGE PINK (*Tunica saxifraga*), 5-9 inches. A delicate sprawling
perennial with fine foliage and small, pink, rather ephemeral
flowers, useless for cutting.

THRIFT (*Armeria maritima*) 8-12 inches. By getting the variety
called Six Hills Hybrid, there will be delicate pink bloom,
in dense globe-shaped heads of chaffy flowers suggesting an ever-
lasting.

ROCK ASTER (*Aster alpinus ruber*) 4-10 inches, and a perennial. The
variety *ruber* is pink and unusual in being a spring-flowering
representative of a generally fall-flowering group.

MAIDEN PINK, a prostrate perennial forming dense mats or cushions
of foliage from which spring branched flower stalks, 4-12
inches high, crowned by pink flowers. (The color should be specified, because there are white and red strains.)

BABY'S-BREATH, 4-6 inches and a weak-stemmed perennial. Generally white, but the variety Rosey will provide the pink, tiny
flowers so popular in flower arrangements.

BLEEDING-HEART (*Dicentra spectabilis*), a perennial, 12-24 inches,
with beautiful pink, spurred flowers in a one-sided cluster.
It often flowers well into summer.

3. EARLY SUMMER. JUNE 15–JULY 15

Pink flowers become more numerous as one reaches the early summer, and still more so as midsummer arrives. For the flowers of early
summer it will save the gardener much effort if they are separated
upon the basis of how they are grown, viz., as annuals, tender annuals
or perennials.

ANNUALS

All are raised from seed sown where wanted. See Chapter One for details.

ANNUAL SWEET WILLIAM, 12-24 inches. Use the variety Pink Beauty of these old garden favorites.

SWEET PEA, 4-6 feet. Plant in mid-March as the plants do not like summer heat. Pinkie is deep pink and Floradale cream-pink.

ICELAND POPPY, 8-12 inches. While this is really a perennial, it is treated as an annual because it blooms from seed the first year and is apt to die out in the second or third year. The variety Coonara is one of the few pink-flowered forms of this ephemeral flower, which is thus useless for cutting.

CATCHFLY. Resembling pinks, and one of them called the Sweet William catchfly. It is 1-2 feet high. A little lower is a close relative, *Silene pendula rosea*, 6-10 inches high, and sprawling. It has flesh-pink flowers about ½ inch wide.

TENDER ANNUALS

Start from seeds planted weeks before the plants are set out in the bed or border. See Chapter One for details.

STOCKS, 1-2 feet. These old favorites, which keep well and are good for cutting, provide a good pink in the variety Rosy Morn.

ENGLISH DAISY, 4-6 inches. A popular bedding plant, generally blue or white, but the variety Rose Monstrosa provides pink heads larger than in the typical form.

PERENNIALS

Low Plants, Not Over 9 Inches

PURPLE ROCK CRESS (*Aubrietia deltoidea*), 3-6 inches, and a fine mat-forming plant for edging, pavement planting, the dry wall or the open border. Purdy's Blush is pink and should be specified as there are many other color forms.

SAPONARIA OCYMOIDES, 6-9 inches, and usually sprawling. The bright pink small flowers are in loose, branching clusters.

Plants of Medium Height, Mostly 12–20 Inches

SWEET WILLIAM, a perennial relative of the annual Sweet William, generally white, red or purple, but pink in the variety Newport Pink.

CAT'S-TAIL SPEEDWELL (*Veronica spicata rosea*). Blue in the typical form but pink in the variety *rosea,* and attractive with its pointed flower clusters.

GARDEN PHLOX. Of the scores of varieties of this most popular perennial, the varieties Annie Cook, Enchantress and Painted Lady all provide pink bloom.

ORIENTAL POPPY. Perhaps the most showy of all garden plants, the prevailingly scarlet flowers nearly 6 inches across. Only the variety Mrs. Perry is pink and its flowers, unfortunately, do not keep after cutting.

CORAL BELLS (*Heuchera sanguinea*). A widely grown perennial, often forced by florists, for its graceful bell-shaped flowers. The variety known as Coral is pink.

Taller Plants, Usually 18–40 Inches

IRIS. Among the tall bearded (German) irises, which vary from 18-30 inches, pink varieties are California Peach, Mary Senn, and Pink Satin. The names of these are in some confusion, and if there is doubt it is better to order by *color.*

PEONY. These showy, June-flowering perennials, have several pink varieties, those that are light pink being Lady Alexander Duff and Milton Hill. Among darker pinks are Walter Faxon and Venus.

4. SUMMER. JULY 15–AUGUST 31

As in the other color gardens, summer is the time for the flowering of dahlias, gladioli and lilies, and it is in the warm season that most pink-flowered annuals and tender annuals rush into bloom, some of them lasting until cut off by frost. Many perennials also flower in midsummer and it will be most helpful to consider this fairly large group of pink-flowered, summer-blooming plants in several sections, depending on how they are grown. First will come those raised from tuberous roots, corms, or bulbs—comprising dahlia, gladiolus and lily.

DAHLIA. Tuberous-rooted plants (see Chapter One for proper handling) 3-6 feet high, mostly in colors other than pink. But Jersey's Beauty and Kathleen Norris (rose-pink) are found among the large-flowered types, while among the smaller-flowered kinds are Baby Royal (salmon pink), Pink Pearl (rose pink) and Little Jewel (peach blossom pink).

GLADIOLUS. Raised from corms (see Chapter One for details). Of the hundreds of rather confusing varieties, pink-flowered forms are not common. Doubly welcome consequently are Picardy and Betty Nuthall, both salmon pink; Giant Nymph (pink) and Mrs. P. W. Sisson (light pink).

JAPANESE LILY (*Lilium speciosum rubrum*), 3-4 feet. Derived from
a bulb which should be planted 10 inches deep, in August,
for bloom the following year. Pink is a rare color among lilies, so
that this pink-flowered form of the Japanese Lily is a boon to gardeners in pink.

ANNUALS

(See Chapter One for Details of Planting)

HOLLYHOCK, 5-9 feet. Of this biennial, which is best treated as an
annual and is often self-sown, the best pink is Newport Pink.
CLARKIA ELEGANS, 18-36 inches. Flowers normally purplish, but pink
in the variety Salmon King. The showy flowers are good for
cutting and bloom better if the plants are a bit crowded.
GLOBE CANDYTUFT (*Iberis umbellata*), 8-15 inches. An annual
candytuft good for cutting, and, in spite of the name, pink in
the variety called Cardinal.
TREE MALLOW (*Lavatera trimestris splendens*), 3-6 feet. A stout
herb, the flowers nearly 4 inches wide, not always pink, so
that it is safer to order by *color*.
PHLOX, 12-20 inches. These popular garden annuals, especially good
for cutting, have pink varieties in Lillian and Rynstrom.

TENDER ANNUALS

(See Chapter One for Details of Planting)

CHINA ASTER, 12-20 inches. Perhaps the most widely grown of tender
annuals because of ease of culture. They come in all colors
but yellow, and pink flowers are found in Pink Pearl and American
Beauty.
SNAPDRAGON, 12-18 inches. These tender annuals can as easily be
grown by the amateur as by the professional, who force them
by the millions for the florist trade. They come in a wide variety of
colors, among which Geneva Pink and Philadelphia Pink are pink,
while Jennie Schneider is a lighter pink.
PETUNIA, 8-15 inches. This favorite window box tender annual does
perfectly along both the Atlantic and Pacific seaside. Some
of the newer, frilled varieties are expensive novelties, but good pink
flowered sorts among the older varieties are Exquisite, Pink Beauty
and Pride of Portland.

PERENNIALS

Perhaps only in large borders is there room for the tallest of pink-flowered perennials, the foxtail lily (*Eremurus elwesi*) the flower stalk of which towers 10-12 feet high. Foxtail lilies are certainly the aristocrats among perennials for their flowering spike carries hundreds of small bell-shaped flowers. Besides the one mentioned, there is *Eremurus robustus*, 8-10 feet high, also pink, and another noted at the Yellow Garden. All have peculiar starfish-like, brittle roots which must be planted with great care, 6-9 inches deep, in good rich soil.

Among pink-flowered perennials not so tall as the foxtail lilies, there are a few midsummer bloomers that are worth including in any pink garden. They can be conveniently divided by height:

Plants 4–6 inches high

STONECROP (*Sedum spurium*), a low creeping evergreen with pale
       pink flowers about ½ inch wide. Good for a ground cover, or
in the rock garden.

Plants 4–6 feet high

ASTILBE DAVIDI, a showy perennial, resembling a spirea and often
       forced by florists and sold as spirea. Normally it has showy
clusters of small white or cream-colored flowers, but America and
Rose Pearl are both pink. Both are perfectly hardy outdoors.

Plants of moderate height, 1–2 feet

PYRETHRUM. A summer-blooming Chrysanthemum-like plant, with
       many, showy flower heads. Among the many varieties, Rosy
Morn and Agnes Mary Kelway are single-flowered, while Queen
Mary is double-flowered.

RED TURTLEHEAD (*Chelone lyoni*). A native perennial, with irregular,
       interesting, but not particularly showy flowers that are pink
or sometimes rose-purple.

RESTHARROW (*Ononis rotundifolia*). A bushy perennial, with pea-
       like flowers often likened to a pink butterfly. A handsome
flower-garden perennial from Southern Europe.

BEARDTONGUE (*Pentstemon barbatus*). While the typical form has
       red flowers and is 4-6 feet high, the variety Pink Beauty is
pink and usually 18-24 inches high.

MUSK MALLOW. A rather showy mallow, the flowers nearly 2 inches
    wide; not very lasting.
WILD HOLLYHOCK (*Sidalcea malvaeflora*). A Californian perennial,
    1-2 feet high, its flowers not over 1½ inch wide, but crowded
in many-flowered spikes. The variety Rosy Gem is pink.

5. LATE SUMMER AND FALL. BEGINNING ABOUT AUGUST 15, AND ENDING AT FROST

While most of the late-blooming plants for the pink garden are
perennials, one of them, the cosmos, is a tender annual, 5-8 feet
high and available in a profusion of colors. Pink Beauty is the best
for our color scheme. Among late-flowering perennials with pink flowers the following will provide bloom almost until frost, and beyond
it in some chrysanthemums.
CHRYSANTHEMUM. Of the many varieties, the pink sorts will bloom
    in about this order: Amelia (a dwarf and the parent of the
so-called azaleamum), Jean Treadway and October Pink, which
may not come into flower before early October.
FALSE CAMOMILE (*Boltonia latisquama nana*). The typical form is
    noted at Blue Garden, and is taller than the pink-flowered
variety *nana* which is usually 2-3 feet high.
MICHAELMAS DAISY. Of these popular perennials developed in Eng-
    land from wild American asters, a good pink variety, 4-5 feet
high, is Barr's Pink, which is also good for cutting.
STONECROP (*Sedum spectabile*), 12-20 inches, the grayish-green
    leaves in groups of three. Flowers not over ½ inch wide, but
showy as they are crowded in terminal clusters.

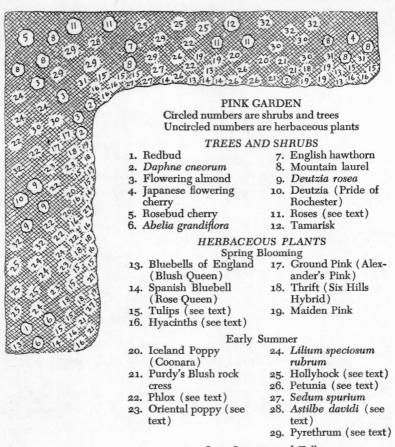

PINK GARDEN
Circled numbers are shrubs and trees
Uncircled numbers are herbaceous plants

TREES AND SHRUBS

1. Redbud
2. *Daphne cneorum*
3. Flowering almond
4. Japanese flowering cherry
5. Rosebud cherry
6. *Abelia grandiflora*
7. English hawthorn
8. Mountain laurel
9. *Deutzia rosea*
10. Deutzia (Pride of Rochester)
11. Roses (see text)
12. Tamarisk

HERBACEOUS PLANTS
Spring Blooming

13. Bluebells of England (Blush Queen)
14. Spanish Bluebell (Rose Queen)
15. Tulips (see text)
16. Hyacinths (see text)
17. Ground Pink (Alexander's Pink)
18. Thrift (Six Hills Hybrid)
19. Maiden Pink

Early Summer

20. Iceland Poppy (Coonara)
21. Purdy's Blush rock cress
22. Phlox (see text)
23. Oriental poppy (see text)
24. *Lilium speciosum rubrum*
25. Hollyhock (see text)
26. Petunia (see text)
27. *Sedum spurium*
28. *Astilbe davidi* (see text)
29. Pyrethrum (see text)

Late Summer and Fall

30. Chrysanthemum (see text)
31. False camomile (variety *nana*)
32. Michaelmas daisy (Barr's Pink)

Note: The border is about 20 feet long on each edge and approximately 5 feet wide. Consult the text for the heights of plants. Suitable contrasting flower colors will be found in the lists at the White Garden, the Gray and Lavender Garden and, if only a green background seems appropriate, see the lists at the Green Garden.

Chapter Six

The White Garden

WHITE is such a necessity in the garden that some people think that you can never have too much of a good thing and hence advocate an all-white garden. This book does not encourage such enthusiasts, because nothing but white would be monotonous and indicates a too-pale and tranquil approach.

White is the great ameliorator among clashing colors; it provides a foil for reds, blues, pinks and lavender, and by itself, in sections of a bed or border, can be used with great effectiveness.

When sunset is overtaken by dusk and dusk by darkness, white flowers are the last to be swallowed by the blackness of night. On this score a plentiful mixture of white is very nearly dramatic, for it persists after all other colors have given way to the obscurity of darkness. For those that illuminate their gardens, white flowers are by far the best, for they stand out under diffused or direct electric lighting more than any colors.

Symbol of purity, beloved by brides, white has stirred the imagination of poets especially, and it suggests to the gardener, who seeks the evening perfumes of some white flowers, the ideas that white has accumulated during the centuries. Tennyson sang in *Idylls of the King* of "wearing the white flower of a blameless life" and the immortal Shakespeare knew its purity—". . . as chaste as ice, as pure as snow . . ."

In the rest of this chapter will be suggested plants that will fill every need of those seeking contrasts. White is wrong nowhere, is often a necessity to soften the stark reds, cool blues or romantic pinks, and is itself best set off against the dark foliage of evergreens.

PLANT MATERIALS FOR A WHITE GARDEN

There is no dearth of white-flowered herbs, shrubs, vines and trees, and, in fact, to keep this section within bounds many have been discarded—perhaps three times the number included here. That may account for the omission of some that the initiated would expect to find. But those that are included, arranged generally as to their time of bloom, will be found useful to those seeking foils or contrasts for other color schemes.

TREES

It is practically impossible to secure continuous bloom from white-flowered trees as most of them are in flower in May or June. Those included here are:

DOGWOOD, 10-20 feet, and a tree that grows naturally under the shade of taller ones. Flowers greenish-white, small, but showy from the great white, petal-like bracts beneath the true flower. It is difficult to transplant, especially when old, and should be dug with a large ball of earth.

FRINGE-TREE, 10-25 feet, and sometimes shrub-like. It bears numerous bell-like flowers in showy hanging clusters that may be as long as 7 inches. The flowers have 4 separate petals.

SILVER-BELL TREE, 10-20 feet; superficially resembling the last, but the bell-shaped flowers bloom earlier than the fringe-tree and the corolla does not have separate petals. It prefers sheltered to windy sites.

EVERGREEN MAGNOLIA, 20-60 feet, a magnificent, broad-leaved evergreen tree, with fragrant white flowers frequently 5 inches wide. Not hardy north of Maryland.

WHITEBEAM (*Sorbus aria*), 20-40 feet, but shrub-like in poor sites. Flowers tiny, but in broad, flat-topped clusters and hence showy, followed by an abundance of orange-red or scarlet, very handsome fruit.

To these, of course, can be added any of the profusely flowering white-flowered fruit trees, notably plum, cherry, pear and some varieties of apple. More showy than any of these are white Japanese flowering cherries, but white must be specified as the Japanese and American varietal names are in much confusion.

SHRUBS

Three of the earliest white-flowered shrubs are the very fragrant Chinese honeysuckle, the star magnolia, and a viburnum. The rest of the shrubs included here flower in May, June and a few later.

CHINESE HONEYSUCKLE (*Lonicera fragrantissima*), 8-10 feet, its numerous small white flowers extremely fragrant, and blooming in February or March, according to location.

STAR MAGNOLIA (*Magnolia stellata*), 5-8 feet. One of the most beau-
     tiful shrubs in cultivation, its white bloom opening on bare
twigs in April. Sometimes, a late frost will blast the blossoms, especially north of New York, but this does no permanent damage to the
shrub.

VIBURNUM CARLESI, 3-5 feet. A beautiful Korean shrub, its fragrant
     flowers in April or early May, grouped in dense clusters.

LATER FLOWERING SHRUBS
APRIL–MAY

BRIDAL WREATH, 4-8 feet. Three different species of Spiraea have
     been so called, one of the best being *Spiraea prunifolia plena*.
All of them are completely covered by the clusters of small white
flowers.

MALUS SARGENTI, 3-5 feet, and a spiny shrub, covered in late April
     or early May with a profusion of white flowers that are about
1 inch across.

PRUNUS TOMENTOSA, 6-10 feet, and a cherry-like shrub or small tree,
     covered by white or pinkish-white bloom in late April or early
May.

PIERIS JAPONICA, 3-8 feet. A broad-leaved evergreen Japanese shrub,
     its small urn-shaped flowers in showy, narrow clusters. It
needs an acid soil, somewhat peaty.

MAY–JUNE

CRANBERRY BUSH, 8-12 feet. Flowers small, white, crowded in dense
     clusters which are so numerous that the shrub is very showy.

JAPANESE SNOWBALL, 7-10 feet. Flowers in large globe-shaped, gen-
     erally sterile clusters, which are profuse.

SWEETBELLS, 4-6 feet, and a useful shrub for foundation planting.
     Its small, bell-shaped flowers are borne in terminal clusters.

DEUTZIA GRACILIS, 1-3 feet, and an extremely popular bush for its
     profusion of small bell-like flowers. A taller relative, *Deutzia
lemoinei*, is 4-7 feet high.

LILAC, 8-15 feet. Hundreds of varieties of this old garden favorite
     have been produced. Among the single-flowered white sorts
are Vestale, Mont Blanc and Marie Legraye. Double-flowered whites
are Ellen Willmott and Edith Cavell.

AZALEA, 4-10 feet. Of the scores of varieties it is safer to order the
     white varieties by specifying *white*.

JUNE

SWEET BAY (*Magnolia virginiana*), 5-10 feet, and perhaps the most
    fragrant of all native shrubs. It prefers a moist, partly shady
place.

MOCK-ORANGE, 6-10 feet and often called syringa. Flowers wax-like,
    very fragrant. The plant is indifferent as to soils and will stand
city conditions.

RHODODENDRON. There is a beautiful white-flowered form of the na-
    tive *Rhododendron carolinianum,* but the variety *album* must
be specified. Among the hybrid rhododendrons, which have far finer
flowers, white varieties are *catawbiense album,* 12-18 feet, and Boule
de Neige, 6-12 feet.

JETBEAD (*Rhodotypos tetrapetala*), 5-6 feet, a handsome shrub, its
    four-petaled flowers, nearly 2 inches wide, spreading and sug-
gesting a single rose.

WEIGELA FLORIDA ALBA, 5-8 feet. A white-flowered form of the ever-
    popular Weigela, which also has pink and red relatives. Flow-
ers funnel-shaped, nearly 2 inches long.

JUNE–JULY

WAYFARING TREE (*Viburnum lantana*), 10-15 feet, and a tree-like
    shrub. Flowers small, but in large, flat-topped clusters that
are nearly 4 inches wide, the plant showy. Fruit bright red, fading
to black.

ROSES. Of the beautiful climbing varieties two of the best are Silver
    Moon and Mermaid. Among hybrid tea roses, 3-5 feet, white
flowering varieties are Mme. Jules Bouché, Snowbird, White Briarcliff and Caledonia.

AUGUST AND LATER

CRAPE MYRTLE, 8-20 feet. White-flowered varieties are available of
    this magnificent shrub, but they must be ordered by *color.*
Not hardy north of Delaware. See the Pink Garden for a more extensive account of this plant.

ROSE-OF-SHARON, 8-10 feet. To avoid the purplish-magenta, and some
    think objectionable color of the typical form, order Jeanne
d'Arc (double-flowered white) or Snowstorm (single white).

VINES

CLEMATIS. There are three of these that merit inclusion, the first
   Clematis recta, is more or less erect, and never more than 5
feet high and blooms in midsummer. *Clematis montana*, however, is
a woody vine, reaching up to 20 feet, blooming in May. Much more
showy than either is the hybrid Henryi which may reach 8-12 feet,
has white flowers nearly 4 inches wide, blooming from July to October.

CLIMBING HYDRANGEA, a woody vine, often reaching 40-50 feet, with
   large, showy flower clusters that may be 6-12 inches wide. It
easily clings to brick or masonry walls. Midsummer bloom.

HERBACEOUS PLANTS FOR THE WHITE GARDEN

Among the white-flowered plants there are two that bloom before
any other herbaceous plants in the various color gardens except the
winter aconite (see the Yellow Garden). One is a perennial, the
Christmas rose, 6-12 inches high, with generally white but occasionally pinkish-green flowers that may be in bloom at Christmas, before
this in some mild seasons, and often in January-March. The other is
the Snowdrop, 7-12 inches, which must be raised from fall-planted
bulbs, and whose white flowers may peep out of the snow at any
time from January to April, depending on the season and locality.
   The rest of the white-flowered herbs can be most conveniently
grouped, according to their approximate time of bloom as follows:
   1. Early Spring. April 20-May 30.
   2. Later Spring. May 20-June 15.
   3. Early Summer. June 15-July 15.
   4. Summer. July 15-August 31.
   5. Late Summer and Fall. Beginning about August 15, and ending
      with frost.

1. EARLY SPRING. APRIL 20—MAY 30

As in all color gardens this is the season for spring-blooming bulbs,
all of which must be planted the autumn before flowers are expected
(see Chapter One for details). Arranged about in the order of their
flowering, there are six groups that would have to be included in any
white garden.

GLORY-OF-THE-SNOW, not over 3 inches high. Frequently in bloom
   by late March or early April in favorable sites, later otherwise.

It is necessary to specify white bulbs as the typical form is blue.

GRAPE HYACINTH, 5-9 inches. Like a miniature hyacinth but with a
pointed flower cluster, which generally blooms in early April,
and in the typical form is blue. It is important therefore to specify
white bulbs. Plant in quantity for full effect.

CROCUS, 3-6 inches. Best planted by the hundreds when, if the varieties Kathleen Parlow and King of the Whites are specified,
they will provide sheets of whiteness.

NARCISSUS. Of these prevailingly yellow bulbous plants there are two
white forms, the white trumpet narcissus, 12-18 inches, and
blooming a little earlier than the fragrant poet's narcissus, 8-12
inches.

TULIP. Among the Darwin tulips, 12-30 inches, three white varieties
are White Giant, White Queen and Swanenburg. In the Cottage tulips, 12-24 inches, is Albino.

HYACINTH. There are many white varieties of this deservedly popular plant, among the best being Purity, L'Innocence, Queen
of the North and Queen of the Whites.

In addition to this group of early spring-flowering bulbs, there
are a few perennials that bloom late in April or early May, of which
three are worth noting.

GROUND PINK, a prostrate ground cover that will carpet the ground
with white bloom, but only if the variety *alba* is specified,
as the typical form is magenta.

LILY-OF-THE-VALLEY, 6-8 inches. Prefers a wholly or partially
shaded place. Flowers fragrant, nodding, bell-shaped and in
a partially one-sided cluster.

SWEET WILLIAM, 12-24 inches. An old garden favorite, and always
white in the variety White Beauty.

2. LATER SPRING. MAY 20–JUNE 15

SNOWDROP WINDFLOWER (*Anemone sylvestris*) 5-9 inches. A fine European perennial relative of our common wild windflower, but
with larger flowers, often nearly 2 inches wide. Prefers partial shade.

IRIS. Among the tall bearded (German) irises the best whites will
be found in White Knight, Rhein Nixe, and Alba Superba.
All are about 12-30 inches high, and sturdy perennials.

PEONY, 2-3 feet. These showy perennials, which do not like to be
moved and may fail to bloom for a year or two after moving,
have three splendid white varieties: Le Cygne, Alice Harding and
La Perle.

SWEET PEA, 4-6 feet. Annual, and the seed should be planted mid-
March, as they will flower better before than after summer
heat. Avalanche is a good white form, but there are others that
should be ordered by *color*.

3. EARLY SUMMER. JUNE 15–JULY 15

One of the nicest tender annuals, if started soon enough, is apt to
be available for bedding out, pavement planting, and window boxes.
It is the pert little English Daisy, 4-6 inches, which can be had in
white if that is specified. All the rest of the early summer plants are
perennials, best classified by their height.

NOT OVER 10 INCHES HIGH, USUALLY LESS

WORM-GRASS (*Sedum album*), a creeping, prostrate evergreen, good
as a ground cover in the border or rock garden, the small
white flowers in terminal, erect clusters, 3-7 inches high.
ALPINE CATCHFLY (*Silene alpestris*), 3-6 inches, the sprawling stems
sticky. Flowers satiny, nearly ½ inch across and in terminal
clusters. The plant prefers good drainage and is preferably grown
in the rock garden.
CANDYTUFT. A fine, almost evergreen perennial, 8-10 inches high,
useful in the border where its masses of white flowers make
attractive accents. Little Gem is a good form.

PLANTS 18–24 INCHES HIGH

BABY'S-BREATH. An ever popular perennial, widely forced for its
feathery, sprawling foliage and the profusion of small white
flowers that make up part of many florists' and home bouquets. There
are many varieties, but the typical one is a perfectly satisfactory
form.

PLANTS 4–6 FEET HIGH OR MORE

GOATSBEARD (*Aruncus sylvester*), 4-6 feet, often mistaken for a
spirea and sold for one. It has tiny white flowers in a spire-like
branching cluster that may be 6-10 inches long.
PLUME POPPY (*Macleaya cordata*), 4-6 feet, its handsome, 7-lobed
leaves white on the underside. Flower cluster branched,
nearly 1 foot long, very showy. The plant needs plenty of space.
ADAM'S-NEEDLE (*Yucca filamentosa*), and often called Spanish bay-
onet. It has a basal rosette of sword-shaped leaves and a flower

stalk 8-12 feet tall, the flowers waxy, cream-white and about 2 inches
high.

4. SUMMER. JULY 15–AUGUST 31

Midsummer brings, among white flowers, the same wealth of annuals and tender annuals, as well as those plants that must be started
from bulbs, tuberous roots or corms, such as lilies, dahlia and gladiolus, and a good many perennials. Among the annuals there is the
annual phlox, 12-20 inches and excellent for cutting, but the varieties
Mrs. Jenkins and Mary Louise had better be specified if whites are
desired.

Among the tender annuals, which yield some of our best cut flowers the following provide good white varieties (see Chapter One
for the proper handling of these tender annuals).

SNAPDRAGON, 12-18 inches. Use the variety White Rock.

CHINA ASTER, 12-20 inches. The varieties of this extremely popular
tender annual are legion and not always accurate as to naming. It is safer, in ordering seed, to specify *white*. Fine for cutting.

STOCKS, 1-2 feet. Of the many varieties, Madame Rivoire and Mont
Blanc are two white favorites. Fine for cutting.

PETUNIA, 8-12 inches. Useless for cutting as the flowers are rather
ephemeral, except on the plant. Cream Star and Snowstorm
are good whites. Petunias are fine for window boxes or for bedding,
particularly along the seacoast.

There are a few summer-blooming plants raised from tuberous
roots (dahlias), corms (gladiolus) and bulbs (lilies). All of them
must be planted in accordance with the directions in Chapter One,
except the lilies.

DAHLIA, 4-6 feet. Tuberous-rooted, showy, summer-blooming, and
among the most lasting as cut flowers, while prevailingly red,
pink, yellow, and other colors, the white varieties are as follows:

Large-flowered types: Jersey Dainty, World's Best White.

Pompon or small flowered: Joe Fette, Snow Sprite.

Single dahlias: Purity.

GLADIOLUS, 2-4 feet, and derived from corms. Perhaps the most
widely grown and popular of all cut flowers. White varieties,
which are not always the same among different dealers, are Albatross, Mammoth White and Maid of Orleans. Directions for growing
dahlia and gladiolus will be found in Chapter One.

LILIES. Bulbous plants and among the most showy in the garden.
Of the scores of species and far greater number of named va-

rieties, the following are worth a trial in the white garden. Follow
the directions as to the summer planting of the bulbs for next year's
bloom.

Lilium auratum, 4-6 feet. Plant 10 inches deep.

Lilium candidum, 3-5 feet. Plant 2 inches deep.

Lilium martagon album, 4-5 feet. Plant 4 inches deep.

PERENNIALS FOR THE WHITE GARDEN

With such a wealth of annuals, tender annuals and the plants just
noted, many gardeners will decide to forego any more midsummer
flowers, but this would be as great a mistake as in any other color
garden. At the end of the season there would be only the bare places
left as the annuals and tender annuals died out, and the gladiolus
and dahlias were lifted for winter storage. No flower garden worth
the name can exist without perennials. They are the fixed points in
any border, and consequently a few midsummer-blooming perennials are inserted here to fill the need for some sort of permanence
in the white garden. They can be sorted into two helpful categories.

Plants Less than 20 Inches high, Often Considerably Less

SHASTA DAISY, 12-20 inches. The most showy of the white, daisy-like
     perennials, and splendid for cutting.

GARDEN VERBENA, 6-12 inches. The typical plant comes in various
     colors, but White Beauty is a fine white.

ORIENTAL POPPY, 10-20 inches. Perry's White is a splendid plant,
     but useless for cutting as like the typical scarlet original, its
flowers are fleeting.

LUPINE, 12-20 inches. Among the perennial lupines, white varieties
     are available, but they must be specified, as there is consid-
erable confusion in the naming of varieties.

SNEEZEWORT (*Achillea ptarmica*), 12-20 inches. An old garden favor-
     ite, particularly in the varieties Boule de Neige, Perry's White
and The Pearl—all white.

Plants 2–3 feet high or more

QUEEN-OF-THE-MEADOW, 3-5 feet. A spirea-like herb and frequently
     sold for it. Flowers small, but in large, terminal branched
clusters, very numerous and hence showy.

DROPWORT, 2-3 feet. A close relative of the last, but lower and with
     finely cut, almost fern-like foliage. Commonly sold as a spirea.

NICOTIANA SYLVESTRIS, 2-5 feet. A beautiful relative of the plant yielding tobacco, but with long, tubular, very fragrant flowers, particularly odorous at night.

The waning summer and oncoming autumn makes all gardeners turn to the old favorites that thrive as the days get shorter and bloom when most other plants are ready to go into dormancy as though sensing the approach of winter. The few that flourish are hence twice welcome, for they brighten the sere fall landscape and make the garden an autumnal joy.

A few of these white-flowered, late-blooming plants follow.

TUBEROSE, 12-30 inches. A tender, tuberous plant, the tubers of which should be planted after warm weather is assured, for bloom in late September and October. Flowers waxy white, fragrant. The tubers must be stored in a cool, frost-free place over the winter.

COSMOS, 5-8 feet. A tender annual, coming in many colors, all good for cutting, up until frost and often beyond. The only way to get white varieties is to specify them to the seedsman.

ASTER. Of the perennial native sorts *Aster ericoides* 3-5 feet, and *Aster ptarmicoides,* 18-20 inches, are both suitable for the informal border, their numerous flowers in branching clusters. Much finer are the Michaelmas Daisies, which were derived mostly from American wild asters. Two good whites are Sam Barnham, 4-6 feet, and Snow Sprite, 1-2 feet.

CHRYSANTHEMUM, 8-20 inches. The most popular of the fall-flowering perennials and splendid for cutting. Of hundreds of varieties the following white sorts will bloom about at the indicated time and continue up to frost or beyond:

Jean Cumming, September 15
Ruth Hatton, September 27
Irene, October 8

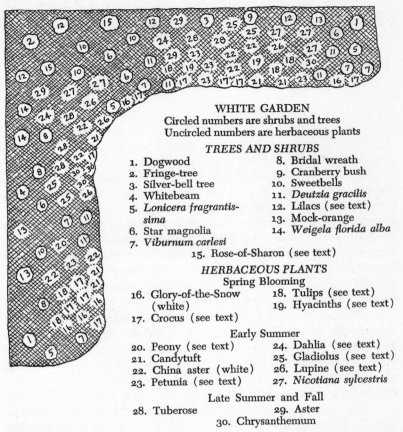

WHITE GARDEN
Circled numbers are shrubs and trees
Uncircled numbers are herbaceous plants

TREES AND SHRUBS

1. Dogwood
2. Fringe-tree
3. Silver-bell tree
4. Whitebeam
5. *Lonicera fragrantissima*
6. Star magnolia
7. *Viburnum carlesi*
8. Bridal wreath
9. Cranberry bush
10. Sweetbells
11. *Deutzia gracilis*
12. Lilacs (see text)
13. Mock-orange
14. *Weigela florida alba*
15. Rose-of-Sharon (see text)

HERBACEOUS PLANTS
Spring Blooming

16. Glory-of-the-Snow (white)
17. Crocus (see text)
18. Tulips (see text)
19. Hyacinths (see text)

Early Summer

20. Peony (see text)
21. Candytuft
22. China aster (white)
23. Petunia (see text)
24. Dahlia (see text)
25. Gladiolus (see text)
26. Lupine (see text)
27. *Nicotiana sylvestris*

Late Summer and Fall

28. Tuberose
29. Aster
30. Chrysanthemum

Note: The border is about 20 feet long on each edge and 5 feet wide. Consult text for heights of plants. White needs other colors for contrast, and according to your preference you may select from the other lists the contrasting colors, especially from among the reds, blues and pinks.

Chapter Seven

The Green Garden

REEN is the very child of nature. Without it man would soon cease to exist. Proletarian revolutions and kingly thrones, the industrial monolith and the song of poets—all would perish but for the greenness of grass and leaf. For that greenness is incomparably the most important product in the world. Without it there would be no food for animals, or for us, no timber, coal, gasoline, rubber, oils, fats, waxes, resins—not the very pencil with which this is written nor the paper upon which it is printed. It is easy to say that synthetic substitutes are crowding wool, cotton and many other fibers, as well as natural rubber, out of our modern world. But chemistry, with its magical formulas, has never yet been able to make chlorophyll, which is, quite simply, the green coloring matter of plants.

Every gardener takes it for granted, perhaps not knowing, and often not caring, that chlorophyll is the substance that makes sugar, starches, the woody stems of shrubs and trees, and ultimately the very colors upon which we rely to make our color gardens. Without the miraculous welding of sunlight, various gases, nutrients from the soil and water, there would be no color in the garden, and no food or clothing for us, for even some of the synthetic fibers come from cellulose, another product of the greenness that is in every blade of grass, on every tree, and in the scum that floats on ponds. Volumes have been written about chlorophyll and a foundation set up to study it, for the industrialists never tire of probing the infinite and endless energy generated by the green cells of plants.

We can leave such researches to the erudite, and look for a moment at what greenness means to color gardening. While white is the great ameliorator of clashing colors, try to think what any color garden would be without a lawn or the cool shadows of evergreens, or the restful and completely satisfying greenery of shrubs or trees.

A companion book in this volume called "The Permanent Garden" is wholly devoted to the plants that will be as permanent as most of the buildings, provide accents and vistas all without the labor and care which any color garden demands for its success. This is based upon the study of many beautiful places where the magic of greenery has been utilized to make pictures of lasting perfection, without a flower bed or border and where taxes and labor costs have forced owners to forego the raising of tender annuals, the yearly planting of bulbs, tubers, corms or the weeding and cultivation that are essential for beds and borders.

The color gardener has solved that problem, or he would not be a color gardener. One likes to think of him or her as a person to whom no other use of leisure time is so satisfying as growing the different plants of his choice. They provide color, and incidentally cut flowers for the house, as no scheme of mere greenery will ever do.

But in any garden, no matter what the color, we must rely upon greenery to set off our color schemes, and it is necessary for the amateur to be as assured of that greenery as of any color scheme that takes the fancy. To the question of why bother to devote even such a short chapter as this one to greenery, when it is one of the inherent attributes of nature and hence all about us, the obvious answer is that trees and lawns don't just grow Topsy-like, but must be planned for.

There have been a few trees and shrubs noted in other chapters, all selected because they, too, add color by their bloom. They were not selected for shade, for the framing of a vista, the cutting off of an unwanted view of buildings, streets, advertising signs or any of the off-property things that can ruin the peace of mind of the sensitive. Nor has anything been noted about a lawn, its making, care, mowing and feeding. While the details of trees to use for such a scheme should be sought in the companion book to this one, it seems that to omit some reference to them here is to ignore the basic need of any color gardener to have a green garden—to supply the materials that will ensure greenery, even in winter when grass is sere and most trees drop their leaves. For convenience these are best grouped into (1) trees, (2) evergreens and (3) the making and care of a lawn.

TREES

Some years ago a census of garden opinion tried to decide what were the best trees for the average homeowner, taking into consideration the shade they cast, their hardiness, ease of cultivation and cost. From that list, and from years of study of other trees it is possible to make a list from which the color gardener can make his own selection, based not only on knowledge, but his personal preferences.

The ten best all-round shade trees, arranged not in the order of the writer's preference, but alphabetically, so you can impartially choose your own, follow with some brief notes. All of them are long-lived, some are slow growing, and every one of them is perfectly hardy from Canada southward. They are:

BEECH. The common native American beech, with its grayish bark, golden buds and handsome foliage frequently reaches 90 or 100 feet. It is slow growing and only young specimens should be planted, as old ones are hard to transplant. A close relative, which many prefer, is the European Copper Beech, with bronzy or coppery foliage. Autumnal color yellow.

ELM. Our American elm has no rival for street planting in country towns (never in cities) and its beautiful vase-like outline makes it one of the loveliest of all lawn trees. The only objection to it is that it cannot be planted in the area infested with the Dutch elm disease. You must inquire of your local nurseryman or county agent before planting the American elm. Autumnal color negligible.

HORSE-CHESTNUT. A Eurasian tree often reaching 100 feet, and casting a shade so dense that almost nothing (including a lawn) can be grown under it. In May it has very showy clusters of white (or red in a variety) flowers followed by rather large fruits, the litter of which is disliked by some. A very desirable shade tree, its lower branches, if not trimmed off, sweeping the ground. Autumnal color yellowish-brown.

LINDEN. Do not plant the native American linden, because the small-leaved European linden is far better as a lawn tree or part of a marginal planting. It reaches 80-100 feet, is round headed, casts a deep shade, and untrimmed trees have their lowest branches arching down at the ends to touch the ground. Autumnal color negligible.

NORWAY MAPLE. Probably the most widely planted shade tree in America because of its very dense shade, freedom from pests and relatively rapid growth. In the open it will have almost a completely round-headed canopy. Autumnal color a beautiful soft yellow.

PLANE TREE. Do not plant the American plane tree, which is usually called sycamore. Far better is the London plane, which is a hybrid. It will stand city smoke, dust and wind better than almost any other tree; autumnal color negligible.

RED OAK. Rather quick growing for an oak, and a fine tree for marginal planting or a lawn specimen, reaching a height of 75-90 feet. Its large, rather leathery leaves turn a dull red in autumn.

SCARLET OAK. A close relative of the last but with smaller, more glossy leaves which turn brilliant scarlet in the fall. Shade only moderately dense.

SWEET GUM. A magnificent native tree, 90-120 feet high, with large star-like leaves resembling a maple. About midsummer it sheds ball-like spiny fruit, the litter of which deters some from planting it. However, its autumnal foliage (brilliant scarlet or crimson) is more colorful than almost any other tree.

TULIP-TREE. A tall, straight-trunked tree, frequently without a branch for the first 40-50 feet, with a wonderful columnar crown of large leaves each of which looks as though a cow had chewed the end of it. It has tulip-like flowers in June. Autumnal color golden yellow.

If this seems a meager list the reader is referred to Book One, or to still more inclusive reference works.* From the ten above, however, one can make a very creditable start on the most essential features of the green garden. Some may complain that only their grandchildren will live to see these in maturity, which is quite true, especially if only young specimens are set out.

For the impatient, quicker growing trees can be found among poplars, birches, willows, ash-trees and that friend of all city dwellers, the ailanthus. Not one of them is recommended here for permanent effects, but all of them are good temporary substitutes for the far better trees listed. A practical solution is to plant both, with the idea of getting an almost immediate effect from the quick growing sorts, which will be cut down when the more permanent kinds take over.

EVERGREENS

All of the trees mentioned above lose their leaves in the fall, and some color gardeners want a substitute for the bare branches of winter. Evergreen trees and shrubs are the answer, but an expensive one, for most evergreens will cost from three to seven times as much as those that shed their foliage each autumn.

A solution of course is to buy only young evergreens, and these can be had for about one-fifth the cost of larger specimens but you have then to wait several years for some kinds, and half a century

* In the writer's *Encyclopedia of Gardening*, for instance, 25 different oaks, 7 lindens, 16 maples, 9 elms and over 50 other shade trees are discussed which cannot be considered here.

for others to become really effective. One must, too, be much more careful about choosing evergreens than the others, which, with reasonable care will live in a variety of soils, climates, elevations, etc.

Evergreens are not so tolerant of unfavorable conditions. It is, for instance, foolish to plant any evergreens in a dusty, windy, smoky or dirty city, except possibly the Japanese black pine and the Japanese yew. Even in suburban or country places evergreens demand as much coolness and moisture, and as little dry heat as possible. Most of them will stand any reasonable amount of cold, but will shrink and perhaps die without adequate summer rainfall and with too much heat. That is why they are unsuited to the prairie states and diminish in usefulness as one goes south in the southeastern states. They are ideally at home along the Pacific Coast from northern California to Vancouver, and the Atlantic Coast in New England and New York.

With these simple restrictions in mind, it is possible for the maker of a green garden to get effects from evergreens, obtainable in no other way. Their dark foliage masses make marvelous backgrounds for the white garden, which is perhaps why they are so lovely where there is winter snow. And what snow-covered evergreen garden is not enhanced by the white bark of birches, the cherry red berries of holly and many other shrubs and trees that hold their fruit for half and sometimes all winter?

If evergreens are going to be part of your green garden it is well to remember that they are not all alike in their tolerance of the unfavorable conditions just mentioned. Ignoring cold, which most of them stand with impunity, the various groups of evergreens can be separated on their ability to stand summer heat, deficient summer rainfall and drying winds as follows:

Most tolerant of unfavorable conditions: Junipers and cedars.

Somewhat less tolerant: Pines and hemlocks.

Still less tolerant: Spruces, Douglas Fir, nearly all Pacific Coast evergreens and *Cryptomeria.*

Least tolerant: Firs and many miscellaneous evergreens from the Himalayas and western China.

By following such a guide you should have fewer failures than with indiscriminate planting of evergreens. One often sees city and suburban gardens with browned or unthrifty evergreens because of not following the simple rules that nature has laid down for these most majestic and beautiful trees for the green garden.

As to the details of selecting individual varieties among these different groups, reference should be made to Book One called *The*

Permanent Garden. There, also, will be found the details of how to plant evergreen shrubs and trees, and how to care for them until they can take care of themselves.

LAWNS

It is related of a fanatical Englishman that he prized his lawn so much that he lifted it each autumn, grew the sods in the greenhouse all winter and relaid the turf each spring. No country in the world has better lawns than England, partly because the rainfall and coolness is ideal for lawn grasses and also because some of them have had continuous care for a century or two.

No one here needs to be discouraged by such English perfection, for anywhere in the United States with an annual rainfall above 20-25 inches, and not too much heat, can have a good lawn, and most places north of southern Virginia and east of the Alleghenies are cool and moist enough to have excellent lawns without expensive irrigation and more or less constant sprinkling. In the following notes we must exclude the kind of turf that is found on well-kept golf greens, for the initial outlay and constant attention are far too great for the average home gardener.

Making a beautiful lawn, however, involves something more than scattering grass seed and haphazard mowing. Soil conditions are important, as few grasses will thrive in sandy soil so porous that it has little moisture-holding capacity. It is essential therefore to correct such a condition before attempting to sow grass seed. On small areas this is best accomplished by application of commercial humus (it must not be acid). Cover the spaded up or plowed land with a layer of the humus about 3-4 inches deep, and thoroughly mix it with the soil by raking in, or on larger areas by disc harrowing. This will make a perfect seed bed for the grass, if the conditions that follow have been attended to.

To prepare the soil for a lawn the topsoil should be kept *at the top.* Do not by spading or plowing turn up the subsoil so that it is at the top, hence burying the topsoil. The land must, however, be spaded, all lumps broken up, and finally hand raked. Grass seed will not germinate in lumpy soil or among stones and pebbles. All such must be raked out. Assuming that it is not too sandy—or, if it is, you have corrected this by the addition of humus—the kind of soil does not seem to matter. Tests of 200 soil types have proved that all of them will maintain good lawns. The only exception is soil that is too acid. If you cannot make the test for acidity yourself your county agent or a nurseryman will do it for you. If the test shows a pH of 5.5 or below, the soil must be limed until it tests at least a pH of 6.5 or 7.0, which is neutral and ideal for the kind of grasses that make good lawns. Good lawns do not need to be limed every year or two as some amateurs insist, unless you live in a notably acid-soil region.

As to the kind of seed, it is better for the amateur to buy the ready mixed kind, but be sure it comes from a highly reputable seedsman. Many cheap lawn mixtures contain poor types of grasses, chaff and worst of all the seeds of noxious weeds. In other words, buy the most expensive (because it is the cleanest) grass mixture you can get. The cost is trifling, compared to the final result. The mixture, which should show its composition on the container, ought to consist of approximately 80 per cent Kentucky bluegrass, 10 per cent redtop and 10 per cent Rhode Island bent. It will ordinarily not contain any clover, and you must buy and sow this separately if you want clover in your lawn. It is of considerable value to the soil but many people object to it because it stains children's clothes far more than grasses. It will take at least 5 pounds of grass seed for each 1000 square feet, and it is better to use 7-8 pounds on the theory that the thicker the turf the fewer the weeds. If you sow clover, which must be done separately, just after you have sown the grass seed, use it at the rate of 6 ounces for each 1000 square feet.

In sowing grass seed, which must only be done on freshly raked, perfectly smooth ground, see that it is scattered evenly and generously. Rake it in very lightly but do not attempt to cover all the seed. If you have a roller, roll the area *once*. If you do not have a roller, use a plank. Lay it over the seeded area and walk its length, moving it and repeating the process until the whole seeded plot has been thus lightly tamped. Remember also that grass seed is very light, cannot be properly sown on a windy day and that many experts choose the usually windless dawn as the best time to plant.

As to the time to plant a lawn the best is undoubtedly September 1-October 15, largely because in preparing the ground you have destroyed the summer crop of weeds. If this time is inconvenient, it can be done in the spring, the earlier the better—in other words just as soon as the soil is friable, or, as the gardeners say, "in good tilth."

In a few days, and not later than a week, the seed should sprout, especially if you are lucky enough to have a gentle rain after seed sowing. Pray fervently that you do not have a tremendous downpour during this critical week for on all except absolutely flat areas a lot of seed will be washed out and reseeding is the only remedy. This is difficult, because the grass that has sprouted should not be walked over for at least three weeks, which brings us to the proper time for the first mowing.

Do not mow the new grass until it is 3-4 inches high, leaving the mowings on the area. After this the lawn should be mown whenever you can clip ½-¾ inch from the top of the grass. This will be every 5-6 days in early spring, but often 9-15 days in a dry August or early September. By such continuous mowing you ought never need to rake off the mowings, because it is better to let them filter down to the base of the grass. If you have neglected to mow and must hence cut 3-4 inches off the top, it is better not to leave such a mat of grass mowings on the lawn—in other words rake it off.

There will always be the problem of weeds. All annual weeds are taken care of by mowing, because no annual will survive constant mowing. But deep-rooted perennials like dandelion, dock, burdock, etc., will persist despite mowing. For them digging out with an old knife, or better yet with an asparagus knife, will get rid of them, being careful to fill in the hole with a mixture of soil and grass seed, and constantly remembering that bare spots in the lawn invite weeds, but close turf repels them. The cure for weeds is more grass. Some will prefer to kill perennial weeds with one of the chemical weed-killers which come with directions for use.

The subsequent care and feeding of a lawn is pretty simple. It should need no sprinkling if your soil is good and there is a reasonable distribution of summer rainfall. If you have plenty of water and time to move sprinklers, it will certainly help to improve any lawn to see that it avoids long spells of dryness and summer heat. But in ordinary seasons, assuming you are in an area with at least 20-25 inches of annual rainfall (New York has 44 inches), you ought not to need sprinklers. Elsewhere they are essential.

It is a good plan, at least once a year, to top-dress the lawn, about 1 inch deep, with a non-acid, absolutely weed-free (because it is baked) humus, to which has been added a good commercial fertilizer (a 4-8-4 ratio is a fine mixture) at the rate of 30 pounds for each 1000 square feet of area. Gently rake among the grass the mixture of humus and fertilizer, which adds both humus and plant food to the lawn. Do not top-dress the lawn or fertilize the land upon which a lawn is to be made, with even well-rotted horse or cow manure, because either will inevitably infest the ground with weed seeds.

All of these notes apply only to places where the soil is not too sandy and not too acid, where rainfall is adequate and where the lawn will be in open sunlight. Under trees or where shadows cover the lawn for most of the day you must plant special shade mixtures of grass seed. These are stocked by all good seedsmen. Also, in the extreme heat and the generally sandy soils of the southeastern states quite different grasses must be used. In the desert areas, and in most of our western prairies no lawn is possible without expensive and daily sprinkling. If this can be done, beautiful lawns can be maintained even in Arizona and southern California.

The life-giving chlorophyll, which paints nature with a green mantle and gives us food and ultimately color in the garden, is thus quite truly the most important substance in the world. What, to the color gardener, is finer than the green carpet of lawn, upon which he paints his pictures? What would our gardens be like but for the light and shade of shrubs and trees? And in winter think what the cool, coniferous evergreens add to any landscape. All are possible because, as Donald Culross Peattie has so well put it, chlorophyll is not just a synthesis of energy and chemicals. "It is the same unchanging green stuff from age to age, passed without perceptible improvement from evolving plant to plant. What it is and does, so complex upon examination, lies about us tranquil and simple, with the simplicity of a miracle."

Chapter Eight

The Gray and
Lavender Garden

*T*HE NEUTRALITY of gray, the fact that it is a mixture of black and white, neither of them true colors, makes it of outstanding use in the garden. While it is scarcely a color itself, there is hardly any color with which it does not blend, except possibly the yellow series. It is a perfect foil for red, sufficiently close to blue and pink to make ideal backgrounds for them; and for mauve, lavender, lilac, purple and violet, it is the perfect mixture. No wonder that the garden experts have linked gray and lavender as though their fitness was unquestioned.

Someone has said that he who has no penchant for gray cannot appreciate the plays of Maeterlinck or the music of Debussy, and it may be that he who does not like a gray garden is lacking in some of the finer nuances. The gray and lavender garden is popular with the experts, and most of us like its suggestion of peace, reserve, age (for it always seems old and tried), its indefinable atmosphere of distinction as though it scorned the gaucheries of red, and would have nothing to do with the clashing of any violent color. As for its being a symbol of sorrow or sadness, that it might well be, if one went in for an all-gray garden. Some old monastery gardens were and consequently ideally suited to keep the mind on the sins of this world and the transitory nature of our flight to a better one—if at all likely or possible!

All-gray gardens are no better or worse than ones devoted exclusively to any other color. They need accents of other colors, and among these the reds, blues and pinks, are especially fine. It is therefore wise to consult the chapters devoted to these colors in planning a gray and lavender garden. This is especially true of pale-blue flowers and a few of these are to be found in both this chapter and the one devoted to blue, for they will fit in either plan.

A scheme, widely adopted by interior decorators, carpet manu-

facturers and shirtmakers is just as applicable to garden design, when
it comes to mixing gray and other colors. There will be found below
a list of plants, needed also in almost every other color garden, because their foliage ranges from gray to pale blue, bluish-gray, ashy-
white, and what the botanists call glaucous or pale bluish-green.
Such plant material is found chiefly among herbaceous plants, but
also in a few shrubs, scarcely ever among garden trees. These, for
short, will be called gray-foliaged plants, and it is these that give the
main color motif to the gray garden. And it is against this predominately gray background that the following combinations are suggested:

Gray and lavender (the subject of this chapter).

Gray and all the greens, except possibly the most yellow of
them. This will be supplied by ordinary green foliage and
the lawn.

Gray and all the reds, including scarlet, carmine, claret and
crimson.

Gray and pink.

Gray and orange, but not pure yellow. Orange-yellow flowers
will be found in the chapter on the Yellow Garden.

Gray and all the blues, especially the pale, and sky-blues.
This is perhaps the finest of the combinations and many of
the plants listed at the Blue Garden are equally at home in
the predominately gray one.

Foliage color is so important to the gray garden, and so necessary
in many others, that the following list has been kept apart from those
plants where such colors as lavender, mauve, and violet are provided
by their flowers. In the list that follows the colors of the flowers are
incidental, for they will be grown only or chiefly for their foliage
effects, unless, of course, they have also outstanding color in their
flowers. Flower color is mentioned for each of them, for convenience,
but unless it is a violent contrast to the desired effect, or a positive
detriment to it, flower color can generally be ignored in choosing
these gray-foliaged plants.

PLANTS WITH GRAY FOLIAGE

While this is a useful generic term it includes too many other
colors to be wholly safe in making a selection. Some plants have grayish foliage, some dirty white, pale gray-green, ashy-gray, bluish-
green (glaucous) and other shades. While these are conveniently
grouped as "gray," and *en masse* can be so used, it is often desirable

for the color gardener to know just what his "gray" plant is likely to turn out to be. Foliage color is thus specified as closely as possible in the following list, but the reader is cautioned that foliage looks different in changing light, when wet or dry, in the young growth of spring and the waning colors of autumn. The list, therefore, is to be used as a guide rather than a statement of hard and fast truth. All but two are perennials.

NOT USUALLY OVER 12–15 INCHES HIGH, OFTEN PROSTRATE

WOOLLY THYME (*Thymus serpyllum lanuginosus*), prostrate, and mat-forming, the foliage grayish-hairy. Flowers small, purplish, in summer.

GRASS PINK (*Dianthus plumarius*), forming dense, ground-hugging mats, the foliage bluish-gray. Flowers small, rose-pink, in early summer.

SNOW-IN-SUMMER (*Cerastium tomentosum*), prostrate and a good ground cover, the foliage ashy-white. Flowers small, white, chickweed-like, in spring.

WALL CRESS (*Arabis albida*), erect but not over 12 inches high. The foliage ashy-white. Flowers small, white, fragrant, in May-June.

ALPINE WALLFLOWER (*Erysimum linifolium*), erect and 6-12 inches high, the foliage grayish or gray-white. Flowers lilac or mauve, in showy clusters, in spring.

BLUE FESCUE (*Festuca ovina glauca*), a tufted grass, the silvery-blue leaves providing a most unusual foliage effect. Flowers negligible.

PLANTS TALLER, 1½ TO 6 FEET HIGH

PURPLE MULLEIN (*Verbascum phoeniceum*), 2-5 feet, the foliage purplish-woolly. Flowers reddish-purple, in summer. A related mullein (*Verbascum olympicum*), 3-6 feet, has white-woolly, or grayish foliage, and yellow flowers in summer. Both these mulleins are biennials and will die out unless fresh seed is sown every other year.

LAMB'S-EARS (*Stachys lanata*), about 18 inches high, the foliage white-woolly or ashy. Flowers small, purple, in summer.

NEPETA MUSSINI, 1-2 feet high and an old garden favorite. Foliage whitish-gray or silvery. Flowers blue, with darker spots, in showy clusters, in summer.

ERYNGIUM AMETHYSTINUM, 1-2 feet. Foliage pale, grayish-green. Flowers bluish-purple, in summer.

ELYMUS GLAUCUS, 3-5 feet. A showy grass, its pale, bluish-green foliage very striking. Flowers negligible.

DUSTY MILLER (*Centaurea cineraria*), about 1½ feet high, the foliage dirty-white and felty, the whole aspect grayish. Flowers yellow or purplish. It has nothing to do with the florists' cineraria, but is one of several plants known as Dusty Miller.

DUSTY MILLER. The name is usually restricted to ashy-foliaged or white-woolly species of *Artemisia*. Two of the best are *Artemisia vulgaris*, 2-3 feet, and *Artemisia stelleriana*, 18-24 inches. Flowers of both can be ignored. Still other plants to which the name dusty miller is applied, all with ashy-gray foliage, are:

Senecio cineraria, 18-30 inches. Flowers pale yellow.

Lychnis coronaria, 18-30 inches. Flowers red.

LAVENDER COTTON (*Santolina chamaecyparissus*), 18-24 inches, a shrubby plant with silvery-gray foliage. Flowers inconspicuous, yellow. Not certainly hardy north of Maryland.

There are, in addition to these herbaceous plants, three shrubs which contribute to grayness in the garden, and also have lilac, lavender, mauve or pale blue flowers. They are:

BUTTERFLY-BUSH (*Buddleia davidi*), a shrub, 4-10 feet high, the long handsome leaves, green above, but white-felty beneath. Flowers lilac, fragrant, in a long, nodding, spire-like cluster, in late summer. A variety known as *veitchiana* has mauve flowers.

CHASTE TREE (*Vitex agnus-castus*), a shrub 5-7 feet, the compound leaves gray beneath. Flowers lilac-blue, in showy spire-like clusters in midsummer.

LAVENDER, 1-3 feet high, and a woody herb or low shrub, with beautiful grayish-white, felty aromatic foliage, for which it has been cultivated for centuries. Flowers lavender, not showy, crowded in small clusters around the stem, highly aromatic.

PLANTS FOR THE LAVENDER GARDEN

Except for the butterfly-bush and chaste tree, all of the above plants are cultivated chiefly for their foliage, and it is from them that gray gardens, or gray nooks in a border, must be made. The colors that are the most attractive in the gray garden are lavender, lilac, pale blue, violet-blue, mauve and purple. All of these are found among the following plants, some of which have very showy flowers, particularly among some of the shrubs and woody vines.

CHINESE WISTERIA (*Wistaria sinensis*), a sturdy vine, 20-30 feet high, the beautiful, pea-like flowers, lilac or bluish-violet, and in showy hanging clusters, blooming in May.

CLEMATIS CRISPA, 6-9 feet high. Flowers about 1 inch long, bluish-purple, in summer. The plant is sometimes called the blue jasmine. Among hybrid clematis is the much larger-flowered William Kennett, 10-15 feet high, with deep lavender flowers.

While most of the shrubs reach a height of 3-10 feet, or more, a couple of low or prostrate ones are particularly fine for covering banks, as part of a foundation planting, or to use as ground covers in the border. They are:

BROOM (*Cytisus purpureus*), a prostrate or sprawling shrub, the flowers pea-like, purple or pink (also white in another form), in May-June.

MEZEREON (*Daphne mezereum*), a compact shrub, 18-30 inches high, with a profusion of small, lilac or rosy-lilac flowers in March-April, which are very fragrant.

The rest of the shrubs with the desired colors are taller, and the first one is grown chiefly for its showy fruits.

BEAUTY-BERRY (*Callicarpa dichotoma*), a shrub 2-3 feet high, with inconspicuous, small pink flowers, followed by showy, violet or lilac, egg-shaped fruit, in handsome clusters which hang on all the fall.

LILAC, 8-15 feet. In this, one of the finest of oldtime shrubs there are several choices. Among the single-flowered varieties are Crampel (bluish-lilac) and Decaisne (purplish-lilac). Double-flowered varieties are Waldeck Rousseau (rosy-lilac) and President Grevy (bluish-lavender).

BUSH HONEYSUCKLE. There are two species, both fragrant: (*Lonicera syringantha*), 5-8 feet, with rosy-lilac flowers in May-June, and *Lonicera thibetica*, a low, rounded shrub 3-5 feet, with the young shoots purplish-downy and rosy-purple flowers in May-June.

ROSE-OF-SHARON (*Hibiscus syriacus coelestis*), 8-10 feet. It is essential to get the variety *coelestis* to be sure of having the purplish-blue bloom in late summer. The regular form is magenta.

ROSEMARY, 4-6 feet. An old garden favorite and in England there is an ancient saying "where rosemary grows best the mistress is master." Flowers pale lilac-blue. The plant is not certainly hardy north of Philadelphia, and if attempted north of this it is to be grown in a sheltered place.

RHODODENDRON. Among native species are the magnificent *Rhododendron catawbiense,* 12-18 feet, with evergreen foliage and huge clusters of lilac flowers in late May or June: often called Mountain rose bay. Also evergreen is *Rhododendron minus,* 4-5 feet, with funnel-shaped, lilac-purple flowers in June-July. Finer than either of these are the hybrid varieties Purpureum grandiflorum (purple-lilac), Elegans (also purple-lilac) and Everestianum which has lilac flowers with frilled edges.

HERBACEOUS PLANTS FOR THE GRAY AND LAVENDER GARDEN

Perhaps because the colors are more delicate and difficult to find in nature, garden varieties for this particular color garden are far more scarce. Only about three dozen are in the lists of herbs, many of them perennials, a few annuals or tender annuals, and with only a few of them derived from bulbs or corms. For the convenience of the reader these herbs will be arranged according to these categories, and if you are uncertain as to how each group is grown, see the directions in Chapter One.

ANNUALS

ANNUAL PHLOX, 12-20 inches. It will be necessary to specify lilac-colored varieties to the seedsman as the named forms are uncertain.

SWEET PEA, 4-6 feet. Start seed as early as possible, as the plant does not like summer heat. Among the hosts of named forms, Ambition is lavender and International is mauve.

GILIA CAPITATA, 18-24 inches. Also in the list at Blue Gardens, as its pale blue flowers are equally attractive in either of the color schemes. Blooms in summer.

CHINESE HOUSES (*Collinsia bicolor*), 12-24 inches. A curious Californian annual, the irregular flowers about 1 inch long, composed of an upper white lip and a lower, rose-purple or violet lip. Blooms in summer.

TENDER ANNUALS

BLUE LACE-FLOWER, 18-30 inches. A beautiful Australian annual, resembling the weedy Queen Anne's lace (wild carrot) but with

showy lavender-blue flowers. Enormously popular but only recently
introduced into American gardens. Summer.

PAINTED-TONGUE (*Salpiglossis sinuata*), 1-3 feet. Actually an annual,
    but better grown as a tender annual. Flowers in loose, termi-
nal clusters, and of many colors, so it is safer to order a lavender,
mauve, or purplish-violet variety.

PETUNIA. A good, but rather short (8-15 inches) variety is Violet
    Queen. Good for window boxes, beds, and especially for sea-
side planting. Summer.

CHINA ASTER, 12-20 inches. Of the lavender varieties of this old gar-
    den favorite, so good for midsummer cut flowers, it is safer to
order seed by the color lavender. Mauve varieties are Mauve Queen
and Mauve Gem.

PLANTS DERIVED FROM BULBS OR CORMS

(See Chapter One for Details of Planting)

FEATHER-HYACINTH (*Muscari comosum monstrosum*) 7-12 inches. A
    form of the grape-hyacinth but with much-cut petals. Flowers
light mauve or bluish-purple, in early April. Plant bulbs in autumn.

GLADIOLUS. A beautiful lavender variety is Minuet, 2-3 feet, flower-
    ing in midsummer and fine for cutting. Plant corms in late
May for bloom the same season.

CROCUS. From the many varieties of this spring-flowering bulbous
    plant, it is necessary to order mauve or lavender sorts, as the
names of varieties are uncertain. Among the autumn-flowering *species* of crocus, one of the best is *Crocus longiflorus,* 3-8 inches with
lilac flowers.

AUTUMN CROCUS (*Colchicum autumnale*), 3-8 inches. Beautiful fall-
    flowering bulbous plants, which should be planted in August
for bloom 6-8 weeks hence. There are fine lavender and mauve varieties, but they are best specified by *color.*

PERENNIALS

Most of the early color in the gray and lavender garden will come
from the spring-flowering bulbs already mentioned. Following soon
after, however, is a group of perennials that bloom in April or early
May of which the following are worth growing:

SPRING VETCHLING (*Lathyrus vernus*), 1-2 feet. A delicate little herb,
    not climbing as do some of its relatives, with pea-like bluish-
violet flowers in nodding clusters.

BIRD'S-FOOT VIOLET (*Viola pedata*), 4-6 inches. A beautiful native
    violet with pale lilac flowers. It grows perfectly in open sun-
light and prefers sandy soils.

PRIMROSE. Two of these popular perennials are well suited to the gray
    and lavender garden: *Primula capitata*, 10-15 inches, with
lavender flowers, and *Primula denticulata*, 10-15 inches with lilac
flowers. Both prefer partial shade and a moist site.

PASQUE-FLOWER (*Pulsatilla vulgaris*), 6-12 inches. An anemone-like
    perennial, the showy flowers nearly 2 inches wide. As there
are many color forms it is safer to specify lilac, lavender or mauve
varieties.

Flowering soon after the four just listed are four other perennials
which are generally in flower in May, sometimes a bit earlier southward, and extending into early June as you garden northward or in a
delayed season.

BLUE PHLOX (*Phlox divaricata*), 12-18 inches. In spite of its name
    this native plant is bluish as the flowers open, but becomes
mauve for most of its blooming period. Prefers partial shade.

BEARDTONGUE (*Pentstemon menziesi*), 3-6 feet. A Pacific Coast per-
    ennial, the bluish-violet flowers in showy, terminal clusters.

CRANESBILL (*Geranium grandiflorum*), 8-15 inches. Nothing to do
    with the bedding garden geranium, this Asiatic perennial has
lilac flowers that are purple-veined, about 1½ inches wide.

COLUMBINE (*Aquilegia flabellata*), 8-18 inches. A Japanese peren-
    nial, the showy, lilac flowers often 2 inches wide, its spurs short
and incurved. It often continues to bloom until midsummer.

Following these is a group of perennials that bloom in early summer, approximately from Decoration Day until mid-July.

WILD SWEET WILLIAM (*Phlox maculata*), 1-3 feet. A native perennial
    of the northeastern states, its showy, pinkish-purple flowers
in loose clusters.

IRIS. Among the hybrid tall-bearded (German) iris, 2-3 feet, are
    some of the lavender, purplish, or mauve varieties, best speci-
fied by these colors. In the somewhat taller, later blooming Japanese
iris, 3-4 feet, the following are reddish-purple: Helene von Siebold,
Mahogany, Orion and Paragon. Cassandra has lavender flowers.

PURPLE ROCK CRESS (*Aubrietia deltoidea*), 3-6 inches. This popular
    plant for dry walls, pavement planting and the open border
may be any color unless the variety Lavender Queen is specified.

SHOOTING STAR, 8-12 inches. A beautiful American wild flower,
    suited to the wild garden and the half shady border, has fine
mauve-pink flowers.

HORNED VIOLET or TUFTED PANSY, 12-20 inches. The varieties of this
much planted perennial are legion. To be sure of the color
specify lilac or mauve, both of which are available, but not certainly
from named varieties.

By midsummer, a few more plants are available, but nothing like
the number that one can choose from the other color groups. It is well
to remind the planner of a gray and lavender garden that this de-
ficiency can easily be corrected by consulting the list of plants at the
Blue Garden, particularly those that are pale blue. Among the midsummer perennials suited to the gray and lavender garden may be
mentioned the following:

PLANTS LOW, SCARCELY OVER 15 INCHES HIGH

ROCK ASTER (*Aster alphinus himalaicus*), 4-10 inches. The typical
form has blue or violet flowers and blooms a little earlier than
the variety *himalaicus* which has lilac flowers.
PLANTAIN-LILY (*Hosta japonica*), 10-15 inches. A splendid perennial
for edging walks or drives and covered in summer with its
funnel-shaped, showy lavender-lilac flowers.

PLANTS TALLER, MOSTLY 1–2 FEET HIGH OR HIGHER

STOKE's ASTER (*Stokesia laevis*), 12-30 inches. A showy perennial,
the flower heads 2-4 inches wide, and lavender-blue, which
makes the plant equally at home in the Blue Garden.
PHLOX ARENDSI, 12-20 inches. Several garden forms of this hybrid perennial are common in the garden, but only the variety Louise
has beautiful lavender-mauve flowers.
WILD BERGAMOT (*Monarda fistulosa*), 1-3 feet. A native perennial,
thriving in poor sites, its foliage a little ashy-hairy. Flowers
lilac-purple, in close clusters.
MONKEY-FLOWER (*Mimulus ringens*), 1-4 feet. A native wild flower
of the eastern states, preferring moist sites and some shade.
Flowers irregular about 1 inch long, violet or purplish-violet.
SCABIOUS (*Scabiosa caucasica magnifica*), 2-3 feet. The common
forms of this stout perennial are light blue, but the variety
magnifica has large, deep lavender-blue flower heads, 2-3 inches
wide.
GOAT's RUE (*Galega officinalis*), 2-3 feet. An easily grown, erect
herb, its pea-like flowers purplish-blue and arranged in terminal, rather showy clusters. It was once supposed to increase the flow
of animal's milk.

Toward the end of summer and in early fall, there is a dearth of plants particularly suited to the gray and lavender garden. Again, it would be wise to make up this scarcity from among the late-flowering plants mentioned at the Blue Garden. The only two mentioned here that are readily available are:

MICHAELMAS DAISY. These hybrid derivatives of our common perennial asters are extremely popular in England. Of the varieties carried here King George, 1-2 feet, is bluish-violet, while Climax (already noted at Blue Garden) is nearly 6 feet high and has lavender-blue flowers.

SEA-LAVENDER (*Limonium latifolium*), 15-24 inches. A much-branched perennial, the foliage slightly ashy-hairy. Flowers small, but in a cloud-like cluster, partly white and partly blue, the whole effect misty-bluish-white.

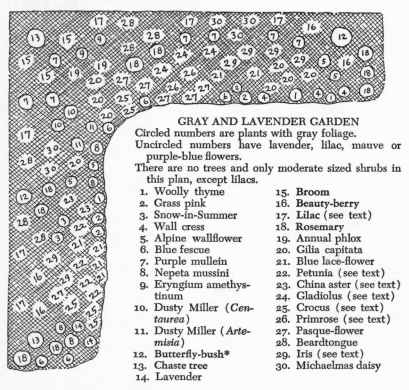

GRAY AND LAVENDER GARDEN

Circled numbers are plants with gray foliage.
Uncircled numbers have lavender, lilac, mauve or
   purple-blue flowers.
There are no trees and only moderate sized shrubs in
   this plan, except lilacs.

1. Woolly thyme	15. **Broom**
2. Grass pink	16. **Beauty-berry**
3. Snow-in-Summer	17. **Lilac** (see text)
4. Wall cress	18. **Rosemary**
5. Alpine wallflower	19. Annual phlox
6. Blue fescue	20. Gilia capitata
7. Purple mullein	21. Blue lace-flower
8. Nepeta mussini	22. Petunia (see text)
9. Eryngium amethystinum	23. China aster (see text)
	24. Gladiolus (see text)
10. Dusty Miller (*Centaurea*)	25. Crocus (see text)
	26. Primrose (see text)
11. Dusty Miller (*Artemisia*)	27. Pasque-flower
	28. Beardtongue
12. **Butterfly-bush***	29. Iris (see text)
13. **Chaste tree**	30. Michaelmas daisy
14. Lavender	

Note: This border is approximately 20 feet long on each angle and about 5 feet wide. Contrasting colors are best found in the chapter on the Blue Garden.

* Those in black-faced type are shrubs.

Book Four

FRAGRANCE
IN THE GARDEN

FRAGRANCE IN THE GARDEN

Nature scatters fragrance with an Olympian disregard for the experts—be they chemists, perfumers, or gardeners. Flower scent is hence so fortuitous that any scheme of arrangement seems hopeless, and would be completely so were it not for the fact that flower odors do conform to basic patterns.

This is not so simple as it sounds. Years of expert research by chemists, botanists, and perfumers finally have permitted us to arrange flower odors, and hence our fragrant gardens, according to the system evolved by Count Kerner von Marilaun, an Austrian botanist, and simplified, as here used, by F. A. Hampton, in his *The Scent of Flowers and Leaves*, first published in 1925.

It is hence urged upon the reader that he look over the first chapter especially. Here will be found the basic arrangement of flower odors, and from it one can plan what to use among the shrubs, trees, and vines in Chapter Two and the annuals or perennials in Chapter Three. Chapter Four is self-explanatory.

In the last three chapters will be found information on how to capture fragrance for the house, how to prepare perfume from flowers, and how to make a potpourri and sachet.

Chapter One

The Nature of Fragrance and How to Identify Some Types of It

Although perfumes are impossible to describe, there are certain *types* of them easily recognized, all of which are derived from the scents of flowers. Most of them, or so the chemists tell us, have been duplicated in the laboratory, to the despair of the discriminating, for natural fragrance is usually a subtle blending of several types of fragrance and the precise mixture baffles the scientist. He can analyze the floral oils, even give us horrendous formulas for the chemical compounds present in them, but no chemical magic or mixing of coal-tar derivatives has ever yet precisely imitated the intoxicating odor of the tuberose or jasmine—those pillars of French perfumery so essential that thousands of acres of southern France are covered with them.

For the gardener these main types of fragrance have more than academic interest. Everyone knows the difference between the scent of mignonette and a rose, even if we cannot describe either one. And the reason is that the mignonette and the rose, as do most garden flowers, belong to definite *types* of fragrance. Skillful gardeners, like skillful perfumers, can, with a few basic facts, blend fragrance for specially alluring or only mildly enticing effects. The trade names of perfumes—Tabu, Toujours Moi, My Sin, Joy, Fleur de Feu, Indiscret, Divine, Vol de Nuit—try desperately to capture the emotional effects produced by the complicated fragrance of a flower as simple as a violet, a rose, or the jasmine.

Nor have the coiners of such colorful names forgotten the basic lure of fragrance, which is sex—delicate or gross as the case may be, for even the vile odor of the skunk cabbage is a lure for those carrion-eaters who will complete its stinking nuptials. Far more subtle is the amazing development of fragrant moths and butterflies, whose scent closely matches the odor of the flowers they fertilize. The insect scent is definitely a sex characteristic, for without it the love life of these particular creatures would be far less enticing. For centuries the flower scent has been known as the lure that attracts the right sort of day-flying or night-flying insect to unite the male and female elements in a floral marriage indescribably fragrant.

Leaving out those scents that are repulsive, or of no interest to anyone, we can list six distinctly different *types* of fragrance that the gardener should know before planning the fragrant garden. Although modern chemistry cannot duplicate any of them exactly, it is to the laboratory that we owe the knowledge that certain chemicals are the basis for these typical flower scents. Those of interest to the gardener can be easily summarized thus:

1. AMINOID, generally having trimethylamine and propylamine as constituents.

This group is rather limited, and its odor is best typified by the hawthorn, pear, spirea, and elder. Many other flowers contain whiffs of it, but none of them is either sweet or heavy. Flowers in this group are fertilized by various species of flies and never by butterflies or night-flying moths. Most of them are spring-flowering.

2. HEAVY, always containing benzyl acetate, indol, and methyl anthranilate.

A large group of extremely sweet-smelling flowers, some of them a little overpowering. The typical odor is that of the jasmine, but it is, in various blends, also found in mock-orange (*Philadelphus* or syringa), many lilies, tuberose, lilac, some honeysuckles, etc. A curious feature of the group is that the indol, which is always present, is also found in the end-products of animal putrefaction. It is the presence of indol in greater or lesser amounts which makes certain flowers in this group, notably *Philadelphus* (mock-orange or syringa), disturbing to some—as though sweetness and decay were mixed by nature as a warning. John Gerard in his famous herbal (1597) found syringa "too sweet, troubling and molesting the head in a strange manner."

Most of this group, which must be used with caution in the garden and especially as cut flowers, are fertilized by butterflies, and many of them, whose odor is perceptible only after dusk, are fertilized by night-flying moths. It is among these moths and butterflies that the extraordinary adaptation is found whereby the fragrance of the flower is almost precisely matched by that of the male insect visitor.

3. AROMATIC. The essential oils of this group contain eugenol, cin-
    namic alcohol, vanilla, and often others. The effect is nearly
always spicy, as why shouldn't it be when the constituents may be
blends of such heavily scented essences as those found in cinnamon,
vanilla, cloves, and anise.

The typical flower of this type is the clove pink, but it contains
many others, where blends of the different main constituents are
pretty complex, particularly when some odors found in Group 2
(Heavy) are mixed with the aromatics. Some flowers are thus hard
to classify as between this group and the last because they contain
elements of both, notably hyacinth, heliotrope, night-scented stock,
and *Nicotiana*. However, since none of the plants in Group 3 contains indol, the flavor of decay, which some find a bit overpowering
in the mock-orange, is avoided.

Other flowers in the aromatic group, often blended with related
essences, are certain species of rose, many pinks (*Dianthus*), primrose, cowslip, some species of *Clematis,* many orchids from the tropics, and the sweet-smelling *Gladiolus tristis.*

All the flowers in the aromatic group are fertilized by butterflies or
moths, and the scent of all of them, with the possible exception of
Nicotiana, is not so heavy nor heady nor sweet-cloying as those
found in Group 2. The aromatics tend to be spicy, lively, and more
cheery—and quite definitely less sensual or downright sexy.

4. VIOLET. The essential oil derived from *Viola odorata* (the florist's
    violet) is characterized by irone, an oily, sweet-smelling com-
pound from which the perfumers derive ionone, the basis of synthetic
violet perfume.

The type flower is the violet, the elusiveness of whose odor is
famous. There is no impact such as comes from the Heavy or Aromatic groups, for the flowers within the violet group are more delicate, and the scent of some of them has the curious faculty of running
out on you. You smell them, and the scent appears to fade—it probably doesn't, but maybe our sense of smell is what really fades.

Outside the true *Viola odorata* and the Parma violet, the scent is
not common, and only extremely faint in most wild violets. It is found
among some species of iris, rather faintly (among other essences)
in mignonette, and in a few tropical acacias.

5. ROSE. The basis of the odor in all fragrant roses is geraniol, a
    highly complex substance containing oil of lemon, oil of
orange, oil of bay leaves, etc.

Only the fragrant roses come within this group, except for one or two species of peony, the Oregon grape, an iris or two, and several tropical plants of little interest to the average northern gardener. The scent is never heavy, but it may be slightly aromatic or fruity.

It should be remembered that the "rose" scent is not found in all roses and that it varies in the roses that are fragrant, especially in some tea roses. The musk rose, the cabbage rose, and the old Provence rose (*Rosa gallica*) are thought by the experts to have a true "rose" perfume, but it may be a complex as difficult to untangle as are some of the hybrid roses that may or may not have any odor at all. It is certainly true that the plants from which the perfumers obtain the famous attar of roses are the damask rose and a variety of *Rosa alba*, known as *suaveolens*, which is much grown in southern France. Some modern roses have practically no scent, and these will be noted later so that we can omit them from the fragrant garden.

6. Lemon. As the name suggests, citral is the active ingredient of this odor, which is found in the lemon and in some other citrus fruits.

Among garden flowers it is not common (in the citrus fruits the odor is in an oil in the rind of the fruit), but some species of *Magnolia* have it as does the four-o'clock and the beautiful, little, white water lily, one of the most fragrant of all our native plants.

The lemon group of flowers has a fragrance a little sharp, somewhat lively, thought by some to be related to the "rose" scent, but scarcely ever heavy. It is rarely found pure in flowers, but is typical in the rind of lemon, the leaves of lemon verbena, and in some species of eucalyptus, balm, etc.

There are perhaps one or two other categories of flower scents, but their chemical constituents are not well known nor are there enough flowers in them to make it worth the gardener's while to clutter up his scheme with them. One of them comprises the musk-scented flowers, which, however, have nothing to do with the true animal musk of the perfumers. Another group is thought to have animal-like odors suggestive of cats, foxes, goats, and other creatures that have no place in the garden.

For the gardener in search of fragrance it will often be helpful to know where the different plants in subsequent chapters fall as to their fragrance. Wherever it is certainly known, each plant is segregated under a group number. These numbers, as outlined previously, will tell the gardener at least what type of fragrance to expect. If further details are wanted, reference should be made to the discussion of the six perfume types. They may be summarized here, together with the flower that typifies each group, as:

1. Aminoid—Hawthorn
2. Heavy—Jasmine
3. Aromatic—Clove pink
4. Violet—Violet
5. Rose—Rose
6. Lemon—Four-o'clock

No gardener should expect to find his favorite fragrance fitting precisely into any one of the six categories. Nature does not work that way. Each of the groups is characterized by some odor. A flower whose odor is nearest to the characteristic is then selected as the type of that group. For each group there are one or more chemical compounds chiefly responsible for the particular odor, and nearly all of these compounds have been chemically isolated from the fresh flowers. But none of this sophistication tells us one helpful word about the true nature of the fragrance of any particular flower, for its odor is a compound of many things. Some are guessed at by the chemists, some are dreamed up by the perfumers, but most of the secrets of fragrance are, one suspects, known only to God.

In spite of our ignorance as to the true nature of fragrance it is still possible for the planner of a fragrant garden to select the plant materials needed to make the garden a delight by day and an alluring intoxication at night. Reference to the key numbers, as outlined above, will help, and it is unfortunate that our knowledge is still too incomplete to supply these data for all the plants in the book. All of them are fragrant in various degrees, but it is not yet possible to assign all of them to the six main types of fragrance.

Concerning the hardiness and availability of the plants discussed in the subsequent chapters, all are perfectly hardy in the area of the United States which stretches from Boston-New York-Philadelphia westward, except those specially noted. The latter, unfortunately containing some of our most sweet-smelling plants, are not certainly hardy northward.

As to their availability, all the shrubs, trees, and woody vines are regularly carried in stock by most of the larger nurseries, and some of them must be sought from such firms, for small roadside stands may not have all the different sorts. For the bulbs, seeds, and plants of the perennials and annuals any good seedman's catalog will list them, and a good many of the plants can be had at most reasonably well-stocked roadside stands.

Cultural notes are omitted except where they are especially needed, for it can usually be assumed that the planner of a fragrant garden is beyond the kindergarten stage of horticulture. If such help is needed, the reader is referred to *Taylor's Encyclopedia of Gardening*, which has complete cultural notes for all the plants in this book and for several thousand others.

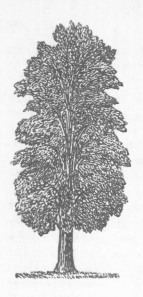

Chapter Two

A Garden of Fragrance from Trees, Shrubs, and Vines

Any permanent fragrance in the garden must come from plants that are themselves relatively permanent, which means trees, shrubs, or woody vines. Grouped either by season of bloom or by the type of perfume they exhale, these woody plants can make any open window, patio, or porch a place of pure enchantment.

Because the plants are permanent, or at least should not be moved without good reason, it is well to study your surroundings rather carefully before planting any of the material to be listed. One of the first things to determine is the direction of prevailing summer winds. If you want fragrance wafted into the house, it is idle to place your plants so that the prevailing wind carries delicious scents toward the garage or across the street.

Once this direction is noted (the summer wind is from the southwest over much of the Atlantic seaboard), it is just as important to know when you want odors from your garden. Some of the shrubs and trees will be in bloom from early in March to late autumn. Do you want continuous perfume in the garden or are some weeks or months of less importance than others? Furthermore, how much fragrance do you want? The answers to these questions you alone can provide, but it is well to remember that fragrance, like color in the garden, can be overdone. It is one of the most charming of experiences to come suddenly upon a sweet-scented plant in a border. But what if the garden were crammed with them to the exclusion of other features? We can get too much fragrance, especially from those that belong to the *Heavy* or *Aromatic* types (as specified in Chapter One).

Furthermore, you should keep in mind when plotting the location of anything as permanent as shrubs and trees, how much fragrance you want from the annuals and perennials treated in Chapter Three and, therefore, how much space must be allowed for them. Many of these herbaceous plants can be scattered in odd places—edges of borders, in the half shade of shrubs and trees, or as edging for foundation plantings.

Generally speaking it is just as sound to make a plan for fragrance as it is for color or for the development of any garden, large or small. The advantages are obvious—if for nothing else, that you can carry it out piecemeal and hence work toward a finished scheme rather than plant haphazardly with all the future adjustments and headaches that a planless garden usually entails. This procedure is necessary for the orderly development of a garden. (I can already hear the protests of some very good gardeners who delight in the wild confusion of some old gardens where color, fragrance, sentiment, and statuary are as delightfully mixed as their minds!)

Because fragrance is our chief object the woody plants below are arranged in the groups outlined in Chapter One, according to the *type* of perfume to be expected. Again it should be emphasized that scarcely any of the plants that belong to any one *type* will give the same fragrance as any other plant in the group. Nature has been lavish in her mixing of the different essences, the total result of which we know and love so much in the fragrance of jasmine, rose, lilac, and scores of others.

To help the reader make a selection, each plant will have notes as to when it will be in flower in the latitude of New York; for places north or south of this latitude, bloom can be expected from a few days to a week or two later or earlier, respectively. Also, proximity to cool seawater, as well as any elevation above 1000 feet, will retard the bloom of spring-flowering shrubs and trees.

Nearly all the most fragrant plants have good, well-known English common names and wherever these are unmistakable they are used. In cases of doubt, and in all for which there are no common names, we must fall back on the Latin names found in the catalogs. Whenever these are used, they must be followed exactly when it comes to ordering seeds or plants, because many large groups (iris, rose, peony, azalea, etc.) contain some fragrant kinds, whereas others are practically odorless.

1. AMINOID–TYPE FLOWER, HAWTHORN

Some time ago the writer was paddling a canoe along the won-drous edge of a tropical forest in the Amazon. Heavy with the scent of orchids and the odor of dank lianes, a new and especially sweet fragrance became dominant and almost overpowering as we rounded a bend in the lagoon—and came upon a dilapidated shed! It was full of tonka beans. One could no more analyze the fascinating odor than he could think up a formula for ambergris. It seemed a mixture of new-mown hay, vanilla, and some of the finest smoking mixtures. What tonka contains is coumarin, a wonderful compound used to flavor good tobaccos for pipe-smokers, to impart an odor to artificial vanilla, and to enhance perfume.

Many of the fragrant plants in this section owe their charm to whiffs of coumarin, which is, in more or less significant concentrations, found in many plants. Without going so far as the Amazon, one can get a hint of it from any freshly cut lawn, the mowing of which seems to release coumarin otherwise locked away in the uncut blades of grass.

Some of the plants below contain minute amounts of this quite magical compound, as well as the others mentioned in Chapter One. None of them has an overpowering scent, such as found in the next section, but the hawthorn was sweet and entrancing enough for Keats to have written:

> So I straightway went to pick a posy,
> Of luxurious May both white and rosy.

While the aminoid type of fragrance is found among quite a few plants, often in seeds, pods, leaves, or roots, the number of garden *flowers* that are in the group is pretty limited. It is found in apple and pear blossoms, and in some cherries, but except for these fruit trees there are only a few shrubs and trees for the fragrant garden. HAWTHORN. A tree 10-20 feet high, blooming in May—hence the other common English name for it of *May*. It comes in white and pink forms and also double-flowered varieties are offered, but these are best avoided if one wants to be certain of fragrance. Not everyone likes the odor of hawthorn and perhaps because of this an old superstition grew up in England that its combination of bitter-almond, coumarin, and faintly fishy smell portended evil. Many sim-ple rustics would never bring cut sprays into their cottages, for it was supposed to be followed by a death in the family. Most modern gardeners prefer to follow Keats, however, although it is certainly

true that neither bees nor butterflies will touch hawthorn, leaving
its fertilization to flies, for bees and butterflies like sweeter odors
than that of the hawthorn. It is, of course, the plant around which
grew up the picturesque rusticity of May Day and the Maypole.

BECHTEL's CRAB. A beautiful, double-flowered crabapple, usually a
shrub 8-10 feet high, but often tree-like, as its ancestor is a
native tree in the central United States. The fruit is inedible; in May
the plant is covered for about ten days with a riot of pink flowers
that seem spicy, or rose-like, and thought by some to have a whiff
of violets. It is, however, neither a heavy nor an overpowering fragrance.

MEADOWSWEET (*Spiraea alba*). A native, almost weedy shrub,
scarcely more than 3-4 feet high, with white flowers in midsummer. The odor is mild, redolent of the wild pastures in which
it usually grows. It should not be confused with the European meadowsweet, which is really an herb (*Filipendula ulmaria*) the odor of
which is unpleasant to some, although Queen Elizabeth I used to
strew the floors of her palace with it.

2. HEAVY—TYPE FLOWER, JASMINE

The heavy, alluring types of perfume immediately conjure up
visions of Cleopatra or the Persians who carried their use to an extravagance and splendor never since attempted. Who today, no matter how prodigal, would drench the sails of a ship with perfume,
as Cleopatra did, so that the very "winds were lovesick." Centuries
later, Saadi, one of the immortal Persian poets, wrote in his *Gulistan:*

> Art Thou, then, musk or ambergris, I said;
> That by thy scent my soul is ravished?

It was the ancient world that brought the art of perfumery to a
perfection it has perhaps never reached since. The Greeks, Romans,
Arabs, Persians, and the Egyptians made such a cult of sweet-
smelling essences that perfumed palaces, princes, kings, queens,
mistresses, baths, and gardens were a commonplace. It is some compensation that we can cultivate some of the very plants used by the
ancients for making fragrant everything from temple worship to the
Bacchanalia.

It is no accident that the chief flower they used in the extraction
of their heavy, languorous, sensual and sex-exciting perfumes should
be a sprawling or half-climbing shrub with perhaps the sweetest-
smelling blooms in the world—the jasmine. It was originally native

in the region from Persia and Arabia to China. We moderns, however, have one advantage over the ancients. Their world did not
know the existence of many other plants that exploration and discovery have added to our gardens, some of which by their fragrance
emphatically belong with the jasmine among the *heavy* or sensuous
types of scent. In addition to the shrubs and trees that will be listed,
there are other heavily scented plants found in Chapter Three (annuals and perennials)—notably the tuberose.

In planting any of them the gardener ought to decide whether he
wants the languorous, seductive scents of some of these plants
wafted into windows, onto the porch, or into some secluded patio.
Or is it better and maybe safer to scatter them in more open places
where allurement will be tempered by wind or the proximity of less
ravishing plants? Only individual tastes can dictate such decisions,
for they are more emotional than horticultural.

With the emotional dangers in view, the reader is now at liberty
to choose these heavily scented plants to suit his mood, for all of
them are of easy culture, and their flowering period stretches from
February to October.

FEBRUARY, MARCH, AND APRIL

The earliest blooming of all fragrant shrubs and trees is a Chinese,
shrubby honeysuckle (*Lonicera fragrantissima*), 8-10 feet high,
evergreen in the South, but losing most of its leaves in winter around
New York, north of which it is not certainly hardy. Its rather small,
white flowers open in greatest profusion in January along the Gulf
Coast, in February in Richmond, and by March in Philadelphia. Its
bloom, which is so sweet-smelling as to be nearly overpowering, is
sometimes blasted by late frosts in the north. If grown north of New
York, it definitely needs protection.

Perhaps even more powerfully scented is the tea olive (*Osmanthus
fragrans*), dear to the hearts of Southern belles, and certainly not
hardy much north of Norfolk or the Eastern Shore of Maryland and
Virginia. It is a lustrous, evergreen shrub or small tree, a native of
southeastern Asia, never more than 25 feet high, and more often
shrub-like. Flowers, inconspicuous, but extraordinarily fragrant, usually bloom about April or earlier southward. A more hardy, but somewhat less fragrant relative, is *Osmanthus ilicifolius* from Japan. It
will stand the climate as far north as Wilmington, Delaware, and
flowers in June or early July.

In the latter part of March or early April, there are two species of *Daphne* that belong in all fragrant gardens from Boston southward. One is the mezereon (*Daphne mezereum*), a shrub 18-36 inches high, covered with rosy-lilac flowers before the leaves unfold. An evergreen relative, sometimes called garland-flower (*Daphne cneorum*), is even lower, forms dense mats and hence is useful as a ground cover. Its flowers are very fragrant and pink. It may need to be covered with leaves in the North, but is generally perfectly hardy as far north as Boston.

Ever since 1902 the garden world has been enchanted with a small shrub from Korea, which in spite of its popularity still has no valid common name. It is or should be known to all gardeners as *Viburnum carlesi* and scarcely exceeds 3-4 feet in height. In April, or in the North in early May, it is covered with a profusion of small, white flowers in dense clusters that are almost dangerously fragrant. It is suited to all soils and all climates up to Canada and blooms with the unfolding of the leaves. Besides its heavy odor there appears to be mixed with the main scent a whiff of aromatic or spicy, almost clove-like, fragrance, making this Korean beauty a match almost for jasmine.

MAY

HONEYSUCKLE. Almost all the common vines of this group are extremely fragrant, most of them a bit rampant and hence to be used with caution in small gardens. For, notwithstanding their perfume, they may become a nuisance. Some of the vines, for instance, may completely smother neighboring shrubs. Since most of the vines will bloom throughout the season, they are valuable, if one curbs their tendency to monopolize too much space. Most of them are pale yellow, merging into orange and red.

Among bush honeysuckles, which never capture too much space, there are two shrubs that should be in any fragrant garden, although neither of them has yet acquired a common name. *Lonicera syringantha*, from China, is 5-8 feet high and bears a profusion of rather small, rosy-lilac flowers, most sweetly smelling, almost hyacinth-like in their perfume. A lower, round-headed relative, *Lonicera thibetica*, from western China, has purplish-rose flowers, just as fragrant and, like *Lonicera syringantha*, perfectly hardy. For other honeysuckles, see *Aromatic* (Section 3 of this chapter).

LILAC. Most old gardens contain the venerable, single-flowered lilac, an original inhabitant of southeastern Europe, but now grown everywhere. It is this flower that has inspired the poets—from the

Persians, who knew it well, on to John Masefield and his "In Lilac Time." Its fragrance is very heavy, and to some distinctly cloying.

This old, single-flowered favorite, mostly 8-15 feet high, has been largely replaced by hundreds of hybrids, because of the genius of Belgian and especially French hybridists. Some are single-flowered, some double, and their color ranges from white to deep lavender-blue. They are undeniably finer plants than their ancestors, but of the hundreds of named sorts, not all are fragrant, and some retain the unpleasant odor of their close relative—the privet.

Among the French hybrid lilacs, it is therefore necessary to choose varieties with care. A dozen of those that are notably fragrant and easily procurable will be all that the average gardener needs, leaving to the lilac specialists the task of sifting out the more than 250 named forms that are offered in the United States. The best (that is, most fragrant and easily procurable from ordinary sources) are:

Lamartine (pink, single-flowered)
Miss Ellen Willmott (white, double-flowered)
Vestal (white, single-flowered)
Congo (deep, purplish-red, single-flowered)
Waldeck Rousseau (rosy-lilac, double-flowered)
Leon Gambetta (rose-salmon, single-flowered)
De Saussure (purple-red, double-flowered)
President Lincoln (blue, single-flowered)
Diderot (claret-purple, single-flowered)
Ludwig Spaeth (red, single-flowered)
President Grevy (blue, double-flowered)

In addition to these fragrant hybrid lilacs there are some species of lilac that ought to be in any fragrant garden, but there are pitfalls in the genus *Syringa* to which all lilacs belong. Not all species are fragrant and some have the objectionable privet odor. Among the available species, which must be ordered by their Latin names, the following are fragrant, and it would be safer to ignore the other nonfragrant or disagreeably scented lilacs. All those below are single-flowered.

Syringa vulgaris, 8-15 feet, lilac-lavender, the original and oldest lilac in cultivation. From it and the next, many of the hybrids have been derived.
Syringa persica, 5-6 feet, pale lilac, often called the Persian lilac, although it is native from Persia to China. The parent of many hybrids.
Syringa oblata, 8-12 feet, pale lilac, and a native of China. Blooms a fortnight before the common lilac.
Syringa chinensis, 8-15 feet, purplish lilac. A hybrid between the first and

second species, developed about 1777 in France long before the modern French hybrids were thought of.

There is, in addition to the honeysuckles and lilacs, a shrub that demands the loyalty of all who seek fragrance in the Southern garden. It is likely to bloom toward the end of May or early in June and is known as *Viburnum odoratissimum*. It is found wild from India to Japan and is a shrub 7-10 feet high. It is closely related to *Viburnum carlesi*, already noted under the shrubs blooming in April, but differs in an important respect. Its fragrance, although very sweet and properly classed with the heavy scents, has also a distinct tincture of the aminoid (see Chapter One). Unfortunately, it is not certainly hardy north of Norfolk or Washington.

JUNE

Three extremely fragrant woody plants bloom in June, and all of them will completely scent any garden, particularly on still, damp days. One is the famous lime tree of Europe, which is really a linden; the other two are shrubs.

LINDEN. Beautiful shade trees, 60-90 feet high, the foliage so dense that little will grow under a full-grown tree. They are always called lime trees in Europe, but our American species are best known as basswood. Toward the first or middle part of June, the trees are covered with greenish-yellow flowers the nectar of which is a favorite of bees.

Their fragrance is famous, but to be sure of the best species it is better to plant the small-leaved European linden, for it is perhaps the most alluringly fragrant of all large trees. Somewhat less fragrant is the native American linden, with much larger leaves. Both trees, besides their heavy, sweet odor, have a dash of the spicy fragrance found among the more aromatic odors in the next section. Both lindens are perfectly hardy.

OLEASTER or RUSSIAN OLIVE (*Elaeagnus angustifolius*). A shrub or small tree 10-20 feet high, of the Mediterranean Region, called by the Portuguese the Tree of Paradise because of its extraordinarily fragrant yellow flowers. These are relatively small and inconspicuous, half hidden by the leaves, but exhaling such a perfume that maidens are said to blush with expectancy and brides with memory. It is one of the hardiest of all shrubs, differing in this respect from a later-flowering relative to be noted later.

MOCK-ORANGE or SYRINGA. There are several different kinds and it is safer to order by the Latin name of *Philadelphus coronarius*.

A native of southeastern Europe and adjacent Asia, it has been famous for its perfume for centuries. The flowers are white and waxy
and suggest orange blossoms both in texture and odor, although many
gardeners are disturbed by its cloying sweetness. Almost no plant in
this book has such conflicting reports as this mock-orange. In addition
to those already cited (Chapter One, in the section on *Heavy* fragrance), various experts have said it smells like a mixture of pineapple and orange blossoms, while one writer likens its odor to that
of cucumbers. Some gardeners will not have the mock-orange at any
price; whether because it is too sweet or too disturbing is not clear.
In any event, it is better planted away from the house. So popular
has it become that there are several named varieties offered. Those
easily available include Golden, Dwarf Sweet, and Double.

MIDSUMMER

Charles Dickens once wrote that the jasmine is "the Isis of flowers," and that we should "crown the jasmine the empress and queen"
of all flowers. Cleopatra thought so, as have the nabobs of India, the
contemplative Persians, and even the staid Dioscorides. As physician
to Anthony and Cleopatra, he found jasmine a symbol of their stormy
passion as it has ever since been endeared to the hearts of countless
millions. Perhaps the most heavily perfumed of all flowers, it is no
wonder that garlands of it were once worn by brides, before orange
blossoms became artificially available. No perfumer has ever exactly
matched its incomparable scent.

Most unfortunately, northern gardeners cannot safely grow the
true jasmine of story, legend, romance, and the perfumers. To distinguish it from the several other species of jasmine grown here, it is
therefore necessary to specify the true jasmine as *Jasminum officinale*
when ordering it, and it will be carried only by southern or California
firms. A native from Persia, through India to China, this most fragrant
of all shrubs is not safe to grow north of the southern part of the
Eastern Shore of Maryland and Virginia, for while it will stand a
little frost it emphatically will not endure protracted cold weather.

The plant is by no means a sturdy shrub, for its rather weak stems
have a tendency to sprawl and, especially in the South, to clamber
up walls. It may grow to 40 feet if given support, and some of it
festoons the balconies of houses near the Battery in Charleston. Late
in June or more likely in July-August, it bears a somewhat scattered
bloom of white, chalice-like flowers.

For those to whom the true jasmine is climatically impossible there are fair compensations among its relatives. Of these *Jasminum nudiflorum,* a low shrub with yellow flowers in February-March, is hardy up to New York, but does not compare with the true jasmine in odor. Somewhat less hardy, but more fragrant species, all with yellow flowers, are *Jasminum floridum* and *Jasminum sambac,* the flowers of the latter used by the Chinese to flavor jasmine tea. Both are not safe to grow north of Washington. There is still another jasmine noted under Aromatic (Section 3 of this chapter).

Another midsummer bloomer is our native sweet pepperbush, (*Clethra alnifolia*), common throughout the eastern United States and easily cultivated. It grows 3-5 feet high and bears terminal, spire-like clusters of deliciously scented white flowers. It can be grown anywhere in a variety of soils. Not so fragrant as jasmine, it suggests the odor of that incomparable plant, although *Clethra* has also a whiff of something aromatic or spicy, and some catch a breath of lilac in its odor.

AUTUMN

Quite naturally autumn is the time of waning fragrance, soon to usher in sere winter. Doubly welcome consequently is an extremely fragrant shrub from Japan, *Elaeagnus pungens,* which grows 10-15 feet high in the South, but less than this as it approaches the northern limit of its possible culture, which is between Washington and Richmond, although it is apparently safe along the Chesapeake coast of the Eastern Shore from Maryland southward. Its quite inconspicuous flowers appear in October and provide a delightful autumnal odor of spicy pungency, mixed with more languorous fragrance.

3. AROMATIC–TYPE FLOWER, CLOVE PINK

When the Dutch once burned a warehouse full of spices, the air over Amsterdam was redolent of the East. For the Dutch East India Company then traded at the Moluccas, Celebes, Java, Sumatra, and Borneo, and some of the group became known as the Spice Islands. Romantic, odorous, and half-savage, the islands became famous as the source of nearly all the spices in the world. Cloves, nutmeg, ginger, pepper, mace, camphor, cinnamon, turmeric, and cardamons —what memories they evoke of rich foods, fine wines, pleasant dinners, and always a haunting sense of places most of us have never seen.

Like so many odors, "spicy" is impossible to describe. Instantly recognized, it defies definition and we fall back upon the known fact that spices are variously aromatic and that many flower scents contain this combination of scents. Many of them are herbs, like the clove pink and some kinds of carnations. All of these will be found in Chapter Three. Here we are concerned only with the trees, shrubs, and woody vines the flowers of which have a definitely aromatic or spicy fragrance.

Unlike those in Section 2 (Heavy) the aromatic fragrance of the plants below is neither sensual nor sex-exciting, except for a few which contain elements of both the heavy and aromatic types of fragrance. They charm rather than allure, and the gardener can plant them accordingly.

TREES

CATALPA. Medium-sized, quick-growing trees with profuse flower clusters in early summer. Of the several sorts grown in this country *Catalpa ovata,* from eastern Asia, is the most fragrant, honey-scented, but with a whiff of heavy odor suggesting the linden. The American *Catalpa speciosa* is considerably less fragrant.

SOURWOOD (*Oxydendrum arboreum*). A native tree, wild from Pennsylvania southward, with curiously bitter leaves and wood —hence its common name, often replaced by sorrel-tree. It reaches 20-30 feet in the wild, but generally less as cultivated, and in mid-summer it is covered by hanging clusters of small, bell-shaped flowers with a decidedly aromatic fragrance. The tree is not well enough known to the garden public, but is carried by many nurserymen.

SHRUBS

Scarcely anyone expects garden fragrance in February, and consequently two shrubs from temperate eastern Asia, of the witch-hazel tribe are most welcome. Both bear yellow flowers like our native witch-hazel, but are much more fragrant, and as in ours have solitary flowers on naked, leafless twigs. As there are several other, and practically scentless, plants in the group, it is best to order them by their Latin names. *Hamamelis mollis* is a true witch-hazel from China; the other, from Japan, is *Corylopsis pauciflora,* a close relative of the witch-hazel. If you have room for only one, it is better to choose the latter.

Another winter-flowering Chinese shrub, very popular in the South, where it may bloom all winter, is *Chimonanthus praecox,* 8-10 feet high and evergreen along the Gulf Coast. Northward it loses most of its leaves and is not hardy above Wilmington, Delaware, and not always there if the winter is severe. Its yellow flowers have a delicious spicy odor, with heavy overtones of a hyacinth-like fragrance.

Shrubs with more usual flowering periods include three that bloom in the spring, and four in midsummer.

SPRING FLOWERING

FLOWERING CURRANT, 6-8 feet high, its reddish-yellow blossoms
    without apparent odor unless cut sprays are taken into the house, when it will be deliciously spicy.

HONEYSUCKLE (*Lonicera heckrotti*), a rather sprawling bush-honey-
    suckle, its extremely fragrant, purple flowers scented only at night. Like the honeysuckles mentioned at Section 2 (Heavy) it has a languorous odor, mixed in this case by a tinge of some aromatic essence; the combination is intoxicating.

CAROLINA ALLSPICE, 4-8 feet, and in June rather sparsely covered by
    deep chocolate or purple-brown flowers, so spicy that the plant has been variously called Sweet-shrub, Sweet-scented Shrub, and Strawberry Shrub. It actually has a combination of fruit scent, especially pineapple, mixed with wine and camphor. No wonder children love to crush it among their clothes.

MIDSUMMER FLOWERING

GARDENIA. Not many gardeners ever think that the gardenia of the
    florists, perhaps the most popular of all corsage flowers, can be grown anywhere in the United States, outside of the greenhouse. But a variety of it, which must be carefully specified as *Gardenia jasminoides fortuniana* (in some catalogs it will be called *Gardenia veitchi*), can be grown outdoors from southern Maryland to the Gulf Coast. It is a handsome, broad-leaved evergreen shrub, 4-10 feet high, and bears its waxy, white, highly spicy blooms nearly all summer. For greatest fragrance and largest blooms it pays to pinch off all but a few blooms from each branch.

ITALIAN JASMINE (*Jasminum humile*). A loosely spreading, half-ever-
    green shrub with handsome, golden-yellow flowers that are nearly, but not quite, as fragrant as the true jasmine, which is noted as *Heavy* (Section 2 of this chapter). The Italian jasmine is a little hardier than the true jasmine, being safe to grow outdoors from Delaware and Cape May to the Gulf Coast. Besides its heavy, sweet odor, there is a spicy or aromatic element in its nearly overpowering fragrance.

BUTTERFLY-BUSH. Of these very showy midsummer-flowering shrubs
the only one worth considering is *Buddleia davidi* from China,
which, besides its aromatic odor, has a mixture of scents allied to
those in hyacinth and lilac. It grows 4-10 feet high and bears handsome spikes of lavender-lilac flowers. In the north, it often is killed
to the ground in winter, but next season's shoots bloom in spite of
this and are just as fragrant.

BUTTON-BUSH, 5-12 feet high and common everywhere in the Eastern
states, especially in swamps. It will grow in any ordinary
garden soil, and its ball-like clusters of small, white flowers have a
spicy or aromatic, but not strong fragrance, which is enticing but
scarcely exciting.

WOODY VINES

One of the surest ways to bring fragrance into the house is to
frame a window or doorway with sweet-smelling vines. Among the
spicy or aromatic group of fragrance only two vines seem of much
significance, but both of them should have a place in any garden.
Clematis, particularly, has a decidedly heady or sultry fragrance.

CLEMATIS. Beautiful and often showy woody vines, most of them so
little known that they have no common names. Of the two-
score species cultivated in the United States, only those below are
fragrant enough to be worth including here. All are readily available.

Clematis recta, 2-5 feet high. Flowers white, in midsummer.

Clematis montana and its variety *rubens,* 10-20 feet high and a showy
vine. Flowers white, except in the variety *rubens* where they are
pink. Both bloom in May.

Clematis paniculata, the Japanese clematis, and a stout climber
which may reach 30 feet. Flowers white. September-October.

Clematis crispa, often called blue jasmine because of its sweet jasmine-like fragrance. It is a shrubby or sprawling vine, 6-9 feet
high, with bluish or bluish-purple flowers in midsummer, and often
into September.

Most of the much more showy clematis hybrids, some of whose
flowers are 4-6 inches across, have no fragrance.

HONEYSUCKLE (*Lonicera periclymenum*). An Old World woodbine
sometimes climbing up to 20 feet, its yellowish-white, sometimes red-tinged flowers fragrant only at night. The scent is indescribably sweet, tinged with a spicy or aromatic odor which makes
its flowers a delight to the young, but as one Englishman said of
another vine "almost too rich and sweet for any respectably middle-

aged liver!" For other honeysuckles, still more intoxicating, see
Heavy (Section 2 of this chapter).

4. VIOLET–TYPE FLOWER, THE FLORIST'S VIOLET

The elusive scent of the violet is practically unknown among
hardy shrubs and trees, although it has been detected in some sub-
tropical acacias. For herbaceous plants that have it, see Chapter
Three.

5. ROSE–TYPE FLOWER, ROSE

The rose type of fragrance, dictated mostly by the compound
geraniol, is found in few other plants, and apparently among no
woody ones, except the rose itself and the Oregon grape. The latter
is a kind of barberry from our Pacific Coast, but perfectly hardy
here. It is a spiny-leaved evergreen shrub, 4-8 feet high, with an
erect cluster of yellow flowers that smell partly of the rose, somewhat
fruity, and some have called it almost animal or musk-like in odor.
Although a useful and handsome broad-leaved evergreen, its scent
does not compare with that queen of all flowers.

The fragrance of the rose is so precious that roses have always
been the most popular plants on earth. So many kinds were known
to the Greeks and Romans that it took books to describe them. Perhaps a better gauge of their love of its scent is found among their
customs, especially among the patricians. For the Bacchanalia they
would strew the floor of their palace with thousands of fresh rose
petals, and release doves to fly above the heads of their guests—the
birds having been sprayed with rose-water. Garlands of roses were
strung along the walls, over statues and fountains, and potted roses
framed such strategic nooks as their love couches.

It did not take the rose twenty centuries to recover from this de-
bauchery, become respectable, and by the Middle Ages a symbol
of purity, beauty, constancy and heaven knows how many other
virtues. Today, judging by the receipts of florists' flowers in all
our large cities, it is demanded more frequently than all other flowers, and in winter by more than all the rest put together.

For the hardy garden of fragrance the rose is a bit of a problem.
Although nearly all wild *species* of rose are more or less fragrant,
some are outstandingly so. Then there are several thousand named
varieties of roses, many of which have lost practically all odor. To
make a reasonable selection from this mass of material demands
drastic restriction, and those mentioned below are among the best

to choose from for fragrance. Other kinds, of course, are fragrant, in varying degrees. With the limited space that most of us can give to them, however, why not confine ourselves to those known to be among the sweetest-smelling varieties?

Not all of them will have the true "rose" scent (see Chapter One), for modern roses have a complex ancestry. Tea roses, for instance, were mostly derived from a Chinese species thought to have the odor of tea leaves—hence a little spicy; others have the blood in them of wild species that have a quite definite fruity fragrance. Others are tinged with lemon, some smell faintly of cinnamon, and should perhaps be classed with *Aromatic* (Section 3 in this chapter). Also, among the hundreds of varieties of hybrid roses, there appears to be some relation between color and fragrance. The deeper the red, the more pronounced the "rose" odor, while fragrance appears to fade as the reds become lighter, and fade still more in the frankly pink roses. Yellow roses are least likely to have a definite odor, while some white roses are very fragrant, especially the Cherokee rose which almost suggests the gardenia. Unfortunately, the Cherokee rose, the state flower of Georgia, is not hardy in the north.

Although not many modern gardeners have space or inclination to grow *species* roses, for the various types of hybrids are so much showier, it should not be forgotten that these species of rose were often the parents of the ancestors of many showy modern roses, some of which have, by gaining size and wonderful texture, lost nearly all their fragrance. Then, too, some of these old species of *Rosa* (which is the generic name of all roses) have a charm, often a dash of elegance; but most of all they have carried the fragrance of the rose for thousands of years without dilution and without the contamination that is inherent in rose genetics.

Of the three dozen species of *Rosa* known to be in cultivation those most worth growing, considering only their fragrance, might be the following. Unfortunately *Rosa alba*, a variety of which is a leading source of attar of roses in France, is all but unknown in this country. All those below, however, are readily available from many nurseries.

ROSE SPECIES

CABBAGE ROSE (*Rosa centifolia*). 4-6 feet high and upright. Flowers double, pink, nearly 3 inches wide. One of the oldest roses in cultivation and a variety of it is the moss rose which has sticky and "mossy" flower stalks.

CHINA ROSE (*Rosa chinensis*). 2-3 feet high and partly evergreen.
Flowers single in the wild type, about 2 inches wide, crimson, pink, or even white in some forms. Not certainly hardy north of Norfolk, Virginia. Its fragrance has been bequeathed to many modern roses, notably the Manetti, Fairy Rose, Green Rose, etc.

DAMASK ROSE (*Rosa damascena*). 4-8 feet high and erect. Flowers double, red or pink, rather small, but in loose clusters, very fragrant. A variety of it is the famous York and Lancaster rose, worn by opposite sides in the "War of the Roses." The damask rose is one of the sources of attar of roses.

PROVENCE or FRENCH ROSE (*Rosa gallica*). 3-4 feet high and upright. Flowers solitary, single, pink or crimson, nearly 3 inches wide. This is one of the roses the petals of which seem to increase their fragrance after drying.

HIMALAYAN MUSK ROSE (*Rosa brunoni*). Partially climbing and very prickly. Flowers white, 2 inches wide, with a musky fragrance, and in many-flowered clusters. Not certainly hardy north of Norfolk, or possibly to Washington, D.C. The true musk rose (*Rosa moschata*) of the Mediterranean region is practically unknown in the United States.

JAPANESE ROSE (*Rosa rugosa*). 4-6 feet high and, if allowed to spread, making clumps 10-20 feet wide. Flowers single, red or white, with a delicious fruity odor. It grows perfectly along the seacoast. Double-flowered forms are known, but are best avoided if one insists on fragrance.

The foregoing, to the experts, may seem a meager list of *species* roses, but it has been deliberately restricted because most gardeners prefer the modern and very beautiful *hybrid* roses, of which the varieties are numbered in thousands, and over 1300 are actually available from the nurseries in the United States. A selection of the fragrant kinds, from such a huge mass of material, would be impossible were it not for the patient records kept by the American Rose Society and by many private growers.

All that space permits here is to list two dozen of these roses that are outstandingly fragrant, giving the class to which they belong, and the color of their flowers. Many fragrant roses, and some that are near-fragrant have had to be omitted, and some favorites may be missing—to the distress of those who for years may have cherished the rare odor of some variety but not always knowing its correct name or its general availability. All those below are to be found in any good nursery catalog, or if not, in those who specialize in roses. Among the latter are Bobbink and Atkins, Rutherford, New Jersey; Jackson and Perkins, Newark, New York; Conard and Pyle, West Grove, Pennsylvania; Kohankie and Son, Painesville, Ohio; C. H. Stocking Co., San José, California; Rosemont Nurseries, Tyler, Texas and A P R Roses, Inc., Tyler, Texas.

TWO DOZEN
FRAGRANT ROSE VARIETIES

Name	Class	Color
Captain Hayward	Hybrid Perpetual	Crimson
Climbing American Beauty	Climbing	Red
*Crimson Glory	Hybrid Tea	Crimson
Donald Prior	Floribunda	Red
*Etoile de Hollande	Hybrid Tea	Red
Florence Izzard	Hybrid Tea	Yellow
General Jacqueminot	Hybrid Perpetual	Crimson
George Arends	Hybrid Perpetual	Pink
Geranium Red	Floribunda	Red
Golden Dawn	Hybrid Tea	Yellow
Horace McFarland	Hybrid Tea	Salmon
Mary Margaret McBride	Hybrid Tea	Dark pink
Mirandy	Hybrid Tea	Red
Mrs. Dunlop Best	Hybrid Tea	Yellow
Mrs. Pierre S. du Pont	Hybrid Tea	Golden yellow
Paul's Lemon Pillar	Climbing	Yellow
*Radiance	Hybrid Tea	Pink
*Red Radiance	Hybrid Tea	Red
Rubaiyat	Hybrid Tea	Crimson
Soleil d'Or	Hybrid Perpetual	Apricot
Signora	Hybrid Tea	Orange-salmon
The Doctor	Hybrid Tea	Pink
Vogue	Floribunda	Cherry-coral

It would, of course, be idle to claim that these were the only two dozen hybrid roses that are fragrant. But they have been chosen because of their availability and their performance as to fragrance. Some of them, particularly among the hybrid tea roses, have a tendency to withhold their fragrance if it is hot, dry, and windy and are hence most charming in the quiet, windless hours. Some, also, are more fragrant just as they open; others only when full-blown. Your local conditions of shelter from winds, soil type, care, etc., will reveal these individual characteristics in a year or two. Also none of the two dozen will have such a consistently fine "rose" scent as the species roses mentioned earlier.

* These varieties also come as climbers.

6. LEMON–TYPE FLOWER, FOUR-O'CLOCK

Lemons from Italy have such a delicious scent that many cooks and some Martini mixers prefer their spicy, lemony flavor, and hence odor, to any other of the citrus tribe. Citral, the dominant compound responsible for their highly pleasing odor, is, however, rather rare among the flowers that can be grown outdoors here. It is prominent in the four-o'clock and a few other herbaceous plants to be found in Chapter Three, as well as in the shrubs, trees, and vines mentioned below.

As in other flower scents this group is impossible to define without referring to something else—the oil found in the rind of a good Italian lemon plus a faint mixture of spicy or even aromatic scents. Orange blossoms may be in this group, but many believe its almost overpowering odor entitles it to inclusion among the *Heavy* scents (see Section 2 of this chapter). In any event, oranges cannot be grown anywhere in the North.

Among the shrubs and trees that are perfectly hardy in the North and certainly have the characteristic odor of the group are certain species of *Magnolia*. Of these the following are available and hardy in the North, except for the evergreen magnolia, which is the finest of the lot.

STAR MAGNOLIA (*Magnolia stellata*). 5-10 feet. A beautiful, rather spreading shrub, covered with star-like white flowers that unfold in early April before the leaves expand and are sometimes caught by late frosts. This, however, does not hurt the plant which will bloom the next year. It is caught by such late frosts about one year in six in the vicinity of New York; more often in Boston.

SWAMP LAUREL (*Magnolia virginiana*). 6-8 feet, but often a tree in the South and one of our most fragrant native shrubs. Flowers white in June. The plant is evergreen in the South, and nearly so in the North. Native in swamps from Rhode Island to Florida, but can be grown in ordinary garden soil.

EVERGREEN MAGNOLIA (*Magnolia grandiflora*). A magnificent tree, 60-80 feet high with showy, dark green, evergreen leaves. In June it bears enormous white flowers (6-8 inches across), and it is by far our most showy tree that is fragrant. Unfortunately it is not certainly hardy north of Washington, D.C. (where there are fine specimens) and up the Eastern Shore (Virginia, Maryland, and Delaware) to Dover, Delaware. There is a large tree of it on a street in

Brooklyn, N.Y.! But that does not mean that it can be grown safely much north of Delaware.

Only two other plants are in this group with lemon-scented flowers.

VIRGINIA WILLOW (*Itea virginica*). 3-5 feet and a native shrub from New Jersey to Florida. In June or early July it bears finger-shaped clusters of small, white, beautifully fragrant flowers. Although it grows naturally in moist or swampy places, it can be grown in any good garden soil from Boston southward.

AKEBIA QUINATA, an Asiatic woody vine, often reaching a height of 15-20 feet with almost evergreen leaves. Flowers purplish-brown, rather inconspicuous, blooming in May at night and magnolia-scented. It is not certainly hardy north of Boston, but often above this along the coast.

For those who like to mix their fragrance in the garden with the fastidious taste that a good cook uses in making a culinary master-piece, the shrubs, trees, and vines in the foregoing six types of fragrance will provide the ingredients. But the odor of some flowers defies classification, perhaps because it is too complicated, but mostly because the scientists have not yet found the ingredients that are responsible for the scent. This needs to deter no one from growing the plants listed below, for all are delightfully fragrant in spite of our ignorance of the cause. Of the many shrubs and trees whose odors have defied the researches of the scientists, the following seem worthy of culture in any fragrant garden:

STORAX (*Styrax japonica*). A tree, 10-30 feet high, but often shrub-like. Flowers, bell-like, white, in finger-shaped clusters in late June or early July.

GORDONIA ALATAMAHA, a shrub or small tree, with evergreen or nearly evergreen leaves, native in Georgia, but now known only in cultivation, for no wild plants have been seen since its discovery, before 1800. Flowers cup-like, white, very fragrant, about 3½ inches across, and blooming in September or October. One of the most interesting of all native shrubs, as it was recently, but erroneously, "re-discovered." Some catalogs use the name *Franklinia* for it.

SWAMP HONEYSUCKLE (*Azalea viscosa*). A shrub, 6-10 feet high, and native in the Eastern states. Flowers white or pink, in June, honey-scented, but not strongly so. Several other native azaleas are similarly fragrant, but a good many of the far more showy hybrid azaleas and their close relatives, the rhododendrons, are not notable for fragrance.

SYMPLOCOS PANICULATUS. A shrub 10-12 feet high and often tree-like. Flowers, small, white, in clusters, and blooming in May, followed by bright blue fruit.

SPANISH BROOM (*Spartium junceum*). An almost leafless, rush-like shrub 6-8 feet high, its very fragrant, pea-like yellow flowers blooming all summer. It is not certainly hardy north of Norfolk, Virginia.

FURZE (*Ulex europaeus*). A low, twiggy and spiny shrub, leafless most of the time, never more than 3 feet high. Flowers pea-like, yellow, spring-blooming, but often lasting into July.

Chapter Three

Fragrant Annuals and Perennials

Although permanent fragrance in the garden must always come from the plants in the chapter just ended, perfume in quantity is best secured by growing the ones discussed in this chapter. From them, except the jasmine and rose, most natural perfumes are extracted, and it is these that make parts of southern France, Italy, and Bulgaria a veritable garden of fragrance. As we shall see in another chapter the professionals have various ways of extracting these intoxicating or elusive perfumes, and some of these methods are applicable to the home perfumer. What they all need is an abundance of fresh flowers, and it is from annuals and perennials that we must get them.

And *abundance* means just that. The perfume of plants comes, in most cases, from an aromatic oil secreted in the petals, ovaries, or nectaries of the flower, usually in almost microscopic amounts, and released a bit at a time so that the flower will be its most ravishing during the whole period of its sexual activity. This may be from a few hours to a week, depending on many factors. It is obvious, then, if we want fragrance in the house, or wish to preserve it in home-made perfume, sachet, or potpourri, we must have a constant supply of fresh flowers at the time when they are at the peak of their fragrance.

The approximate quantities needed will be found in Chapters Six and Seven, and to these must be added those wanted for cutting. The house can be kept constantly perfumed if you plan for it, but again it means growing the annuals and perennials in some quantity. If there is no room in beds or borders, a practical solution is to grow them in rows in the vegetable garden.

Most gardeners will prefer to choose the type of fragrance they want, as was explained in Chapter One, and exemplified in the arrangement of the shrubs and trees in Chapter Two. This, however, is not quite possible in all the herbaceous plants, for many quite fragrant flowers do not conform to any of the six types of fragrance. Some, also, have altogether eluded analysis, and we must fall back on that most important of our organs—the nose. It is the one perfect criterion of fragrance, and it has passed quite critically on the claims of these ten plants.

THE FRAGRANT BUT UNCLASSIFIED TEN

Five of these are annuals, or can be grown as such, and hence one has the opportunity to start as many as the household will need. All except the last one can be sown where wanted.

SWEET PEA. Although all sweet peas are relatively fragrant, the best and most characteristically honey-scented are, among the *purples*, Royal Purple and Perfection; *blues*, Blue Butterfly and Heavenly Blue; *crimsons*, Charity and Unwin's Crimson; *rose-pink*, Empire and Miss Philadelphia. No white varieties are outstandingly fragrant.

SWEET SULTAN. A biennial, but it flowers the first year from seed. Not over 2 feet high, with much cut leaves and a showy head of beautifully musk-scented flowers in midsummer. They may be yellow, red, purple, pink or white.

SWEET ALYSSUM. A popular edging plant, scarcely 8 inches high, the white flowers smelling delightfully of new-mown hay (from coumarin, see Section 1 of Chapter Two). The fragrance is heaviest just after a rain, or in the early morning of heavy dew.

BLISTER CRESS (*Erysimum murale*). 12-18 inches high and leafy. Flowers resembling stocks, golden yellow and with the heavy, sweet odor of orange blossoms.

SWEET SCABIOUS. A tender annual, 2-3 feet high. Flowers in a terminal head, in midsummer, honey-scented. Do not use the many double-flowered varieties. Start seeds in the house and do not plant outdoors until settled warm weather.

Three of these unclassified fragrant plants are very old and favorite perennials, some grown for centuries. All are easily available from dealers in perennial plants.

WALLFLOWER. An ideal plant for the rock wall, as it does not like

wet and slushy soil. It grows about one foot high, and bears
yellow or orange-brown flowers in early spring of a delicate fragrance. Much grown for cut flowers.

MUSK MALLOW (*Malva moschata*). 1-2 feet high, the pink flowers
    of midsummer strongly suggesting the musk used in perfum-
ery. Better and more showy mallows will be found in some related
plants, but none with this exotic scent.

RED VALERIAN (*Centranthus ruber*). A bushy herb, 1-3 feet high with
    a dense cluster of red flowers in June-July, the odor of which
suggests a mixture of honey and lemon.

To provide fragrance both early and late are two bulbous plants
among the unclassified ten. Bulbs for the first must be planted the
fall before bloom is expected, while the bulbs of the second should
be planted in August for bloom the same autumn.

GRAPE HYACINTH. Very early-blooming bulbous plants. The small,
    bell-shaped blue flowers heavily scented with a fruity and
musky odor. Plant in masses (100-200) for fine, fragrant carpeting
effect.

WINTER DAFFODIL (*Sternbergia lutea*). A crocus-like plant with yel-
    low, very fragrant flowers that bloom in late autumn, after
most autumn crocuses are past. Plant in August about 4 inches
deep for bloom in the autumn. They are perfectly hardy as far north
as New York.

All the rest of the annuals and perennials appear to lend themselves to their selection for the *types* of fragrance that the grower
desires. Before making a choice he, and especially she, is strongly
urged to reread most of Chapter One and parts of Chapter Two. For
fragrance can be alluring, or contemplative, charming or titillating,
romantic or passionate, according to one's mood. And to judge by
the literature, some types of fragrance are so close to being an
aphrodisiac that perhaps only science would deny it. Two thousand
years before Galsworthy wrote *The Dark Flower,* Roman girls were
quietly drifting into perdition, not from the comparative innocence
of Galsworthy's dark flower (a clove carnation), but from the haunting sex-charged fragrance of musk, ambergris, and many of the flowers found below. This is especially true of those contained in Groups
2 and 3.

Some will say: "Why bother to grow such plants when I can get
the same effects from a bottle of perfume, with no effort?" The
answer, of course, is that you cannot get the same effects, for perfumery is an art and, however skillful, can never approach the al-

Roses have from time immemorial been the symbol of fragrance. Their uses in the garden are numberless, whether in beds or trailing a picket fence. Though most modern hybrid teas are odorless, there are exceptions and the species roses offer a great variety of fragrance and forms. (*Photo: Gottscho-Schleisner*)

Fragrance and form can be combined in gardens built around roses and flowering trees and shrubs. Hawthorns, the Russian olive, lilac and many other varieties may be used, either as a backdrop to a formal rose garden, complete with pool and statue, or in simpler variations of the sound basic elements pictured here. (Photo: *Genereux*)

Two favorites in fragrant plants are the clematis, shown in hybrid form on the left, and sweet alyssum (on the right). Not all varieties of clematis are fragrant, but of those that are, both small vines like *Clematis recta,* and larger ones like *Clematis paniculata,* are available. The sweet alyssum is a border plant, less than a foot high, particularly fragrant after rain or a heavy dew. (Photo left: *Roche;* right: *Genereux*)

Fragrant gardens for the enjoyment of the blind exist in many parts of the country. The one above is at the Brooklyn Botanic Garden, New York, and is designed with emphasis on fragrance instead of flowers. Its features adapt themselves to home garden usage on a smaller scale. (Photo: *Gottscho-Schleisner*)

chemy of nature. Nor can you make a garden of fragrance out of chemical formulas. It takes patience, love, and a little knowledge to plan for a garden of fragrance, especially if you use annuals or perennials in any quantity. Then, too, one must decide *when* fragrance is most desired. If at night, consult the list in Chapter Four. If daytime fragrance is the chief object, the plants below are the varieties to choose, and the month when they bloom is given for guidance.

Arranged according to their *types* of fragrance, all the rest of the plants in this chapter can be selected or rejected with the knowledge that they will reflect the temperament of the gardener, and the mood you wish to evoke in your friends.

1. AMINOID—TYPE FLOWER, HAWTHORN

While some mistrust the scent of hawthorn (see Chapter Two) most people like it, and many are charmed with the closely related odor of apple blossoms, the pear, and some species of spirea. The scent, however, is found in only a very few annual and perennial plants. Among them are tulips and scilla.

TULIPS. It must be admitted that the finest of all the tulips, the giant Darwins, are all but scentless. However, especially if cut and brought into a warm room, there is much to be said for Cherry Blossom, Joan of Arc, and Pride of Haarlem, all May flowering.

Among the Cottage Tulips there are several that should be in any fragrant garden, notably Dido, Rosabella, Ellen Willmott, and Arethusa. These, particularly indoors, suggest the delicious scent of some tea roses.

In the Early Tulips some are notably fragrant, but usually more so after being cut than in the open. A good choice might include De Wet, Peach Blossom, and Mrs. Van de Hoeff.

There are, of course, hundreds of other varieties of tulips to be found in the catalogs, but most of them are scentless. One cultivates them mostly for their beauty and color, for as that eminent old Dutch bulb grower, Henry van Oosten, wrote in 1703, "Smell gives them no beauty." However, there are at least ten fragrant tulip varieties, although none of them has a strong or sweet odor.

SCILLA. Smelling strongly of hawthorn, but blooming perhaps a fortnight earlier, is the bluebells of England (*Scilla nonscripta*). A low, bulbous plant, very beautiful if planted by the hundreds, it has a delightful, but not strong scent. Meadows at Kew are blue with it. There are pink and white flowered varieties, but for fragrance it is better to select the common blue sort.

PASSION FLOWER (*Passiflora caerulea*). A Brazilian vine, with extraordinary pink flowers nearly 4 inches wide, but with a crown of white and purple. Its fancied resemblance to the Crucifixion so impressed the first Spaniards who saw it that it became a symbol of the ordeal on the Cross, a significance it still holds for many. Its odor resembles the hawthorn, but unfortunately it is not quite hardy north of Washington, D.C., and even precarious there. However, if killed to the ground it usually sends up new growth the following spring. Do not attempt it north of Washington.

2. HEAVY—TYPE FLOWER, JASMINE
(See also Chapter One and Section 2 of Chapter Two)

Judith may have been a jade, but she knew what she was about when she took off to seduce Holofernes, for she "anointed herself with precious ointment, and decked herself bravely, to allure the eyes of all men that should see her." So it reads in the *Book of Judith*, but ever since, and long before, women have understood the lure of fragrance, used it shamelessly or transmuted its indefinable charm into poetry, art, music, or the refinements of feminine coquetry that always tame the male, however crass.

Among annuals and perennials, there are not many that can properly be classed among these *Heavy* and frankly seductive odors, but there are several among the *Aromatic* section which come close to the plants that were in the "precious ointment" of Judith. No gardener should plant these in quantities, near the house, or porch, or patio without realizing that many of them, in spite of exquisite fragrance, have a past steeped in sin. By far the most important is:

THE TUBEROSE

Shelley called it "The daintiest flower for scent that blows," but in India it was, perhaps more realistically, called "Mistress of the Night." Although its odor, particularly in our climate, is perfectly obvious during the daytime, in hot climates its fragrance is enhanced by dusk and becomes intoxicating with darkness. It should perhaps, on this account, have been put among the night-scented flowers in Chapter Four, but it is *the* perfume plant of France, or perhaps second only to the jasmine and the rose. It is certainly more seductive than the latter. With the jasmine it comprises the two most fragrant plants in this book.

Unlike the jasmine, whose culture is restricted in this country by climatic requirements (see Chapter Two, Section 2), the tuberose can be grown anywhere if the autumn months are not afflicted with too early frosts. A native of Mexico, it is not permanently hardy outdoors throughout the country, so that its culture is very like that of gladiolus. In other words, the bulbs cannot be planted until all danger of frost is past and must be lifted before really cold weather. It sends up long, basal leaves, followed by a white, waxy-petalled flower of such incredibly sweet fragrance, in late September and October, that it is all but overpowering. The offsets found when the bulb is dug for winter storage, will not flower the next season, so that if blooms are wanted every year it is better to purchase flowering bulbs each spring. Thousands of acres of it are grown in southern France for perfume.

Quite unrelated to the tuberose, but with a fragrance almost as sweet, is the delicate little lily-of-the-valley which is perfectly hardy and can be grown anywhere in partial or deep shade. Be sure to get the ordinary, single-flowered, white variety, not a double-flowered or pink sort. In early May the beautiful, bell-shaped flowers, much favored for bouquets, are profuse in small clusters. Keats called it "the sweet Lily of the lovely vale," and poets ever since have sung its praises. Once established the plant will make large patches.

Most of the rest of the heavy-scented flowers come from bulbous plants and hence are easily grown, but one of our native woody herbs warrants a place in any fragrant garden—but only if the gardener will provide the specialized conditions it demands. This is the beautiful trailing arbutus or Mayflower, which produces its very sweet-smelling, rather small, white or pinkish flowers in late March or April, depending on its site. It grows naturally in sandy or rocky woods, needs an acid soil, and should be purchased as a potted plant from dealers who specialize in native wild flowers. Few native plants are so sweet-scented as trailing arbutus, but it will not grow in ordinary garden soil. Once established in the right kind of site it will grow and spread—but slowly for it is a shy beauty.

HEAVY-SCENTED BULBOUS PLANTS

The two groups below are easily grown in any ordinary garden soils. Among many relatives in each group, of indifferent odor or none, they have been selected for their outstanding fragrance. In both narcissus and lilies, because of the failure of related species to have any appreciable odor or to have an actually repulsive one, it is important to order them by the names given below. All are perfectly hardy.

LILIES. There are many species and varieties of these gorgeous flowers in cultivation and some authorities credit all of them with fragrance. It may be true under certain conditions, but the average gardener has room only for a small selection and the following five have been chosen because of their undisputed fragrance. All bloom in summer, and their fragrance has been called "brooding and sultry." Other lilies are so stinking that one expert exclaimed, "May dogs devour its hateful bulbs."

MADONNA LILY (*Lilium candidum*). 3-4 feet. Flowers white, waxy and nearly 3 inches long.

WHITE-TRUMPET LILY (*Lilium longiflorum*). 2-3 feet. Flowers trumpet-shaped, pure white, nearly 7 inches long. It is related to the Easter Lily.

LILIUM AURATUM. 4-6 feet, and without a common name, although much cultivated. Flowers nearly 10 inches long, white, but crimson-spotted and with a central yellow band.

ROYAL LILY (*Lilium regale*). 4-5 feet. Flowers about 6 inches long, lilac-purple outside, but yellow at the base and white inside.

JAPANESE LILY (*Lilium speciosum*). 3-4 feet. Flowers about 4 inches long, white or pale pink, rose-spotted. Its scent is too heavily sweet to be liked by all.

NARCISSUS. Most of the common yellow, trumpet narcissus varieties are without enough odor to be worth cultivating for that object. But besides the paper-white narcissus, and its equally fragrant relative the so-called Chinese Sacred Lily, neither of which can be grown outdoors, there are two hardy species of outstanding fragrance.

JONQUIL (*Narcissus jonquilla*). 12-18 inches high. Flowers yellow, about 1 inch long. Do not take double-flowered or color variants.

POET'S NARCISSUS (*Narcissus poeticus*). 12-18 inches high. Flowers white, extremely fragrant, not more than 1 inch long. It is safer to avoid double-flowered varieties, or those of any variety other than the typical form.

3. AROMATIC—TYPE FLOWER, CLOVE PINK
(See also Chapter Two, Section 3)

Many of the flowers in this group could almost as well be classed among the heavily scented plants just discussed; for the aromatics *are* heavily scented, but they have, most of them, a distinctly spicy odor. They are less sultry, seductive, and have fewer sex-linked connotations than cling to jasmine, the tuberose, and those wicked scents of which the debauched Romans were so fond.

On the other hand, no one should dismiss the *Aromatics* as flowers without a past. Such a discriminating gardener as John Galsworthy wove one of his hauntingly beautiful stories around one of them, *The Dark Flower*. And for anyone who reads it, the fragrance of the clove carnation will forever stir a pang for Mark and his pursuit of the unattainable.

One of the completely inexplicable things about fragrance, which baffles all the sciences, is the capacity of odors to bring back memories, clearly and instantly, of things in the past. It may be years ago or it may have happened only yesterday, but a particular scent will bring it back, when mere memory has buried it under layers of other things. It is precisely in this capacity that the *Aromatic* group excel all others, perhaps because of the complexity of the compounds that are chiefly responsible for their fragrance (see Chapter One).

Here, fortunately for the gardener, are many old favorites besides the clove pink or carnation and its relatives, the hyacinth, primrose, stocks, a couple of annuals, and some perennials.

CARNATIONS AND PINKS
"Quaint, gay, sweet and good for nosegays"

When Linnaeus created the genus *Dianthus,* he quite properly included the carnation, all the known pinks, and what were for a century or so known as gilliflowers, a name now nearly obsolete. For the carnation he coined the name *Dianthus caryophyllus,* the latter finally being distilled through the French *giroflee* into our English *Gilliflower*. What matters more than this etymological excursion is that the wise, old Linnaeus called the carnation *caryophyllus* because that was the Latin name for the clove, and as he well knew there is scarcely one of the whole tribe that does not have the rich, spicy odor we know so well in our modern carnation.

All of the original species of *Dianthus* were single-flowered plants with five petals, but the florists and gardeners have developed the multi-petalled forms we see today and incidentally raised the fragrance to a degree of intensity unknown in their wild ancestors.

For the gardener seeking fragrance today it is well to remember that *Dianthus* is a genus of almost 200 species. A selection of them is all that anyone, however enthusiastic over their fragrance, can possibly grow, remembering that of the carnation itself there are over a hundred named forms—some of them grown by the millions by the florists. A reasonable selection might hence include:

CARNATION (*Dianthus caryophyllus*). This, which is also known as the clove pink, cannot be grown continuously outdoors over most of the country, if one is considering only the florist's flower to which the name "carnation" is usually applied.

But there are strains or varieties of it that are reasonably hardy in the South and can be grown outdoors if one can give them a bit of protection over the winter. None of them is as fragrant as the florist's carnation, but they make a very agreeable substitute for it. They are much more commonly grown in England than here, for that island has a better climate for them than ours. Among the varieties of these hardy carnations, the deep red or crimson sorts are the most fragrant.

GRASS PINK (*Dianthus plumarius*). A perfectly hardy, mat-forming perennial, 9-18 inches high, with bluish-gray foliage and single rose-pink flowers (white in some varieties) with fringed petals. May.

CHEDDAR PINK (*Dianthus caesius*). A turf-forming perennial, 3-9 inches high, its matted foliage bluish-green. Flowers rose-red, about 1½ inches wide, with fringed petals. May.

There are several other fragrant species of *Dianthus*, but the Sweet William (*Dianthus barbatus*) is all but scentless.

STOCKS

Perhaps the most fragrant of all stocks is the night-scented or evening stock, which withholds its delicious scent until nightfall and hence is to be found in the chapter devoted to nocturnal fragrance (Chapter Four). Among the day-flowering sort, however, there are several varieties of such sweet, spicy odor that they, too, were once called Gillyflower, because their fragrance is carnation-like. Among them is the Brompton stock, named for a suburb of London, which is a perennial that is inclined to die out in a couple of years. Much more common are the Ten-week stocks which are annuals and have spikes of showy flowers, the blooming of which can be prolonged by sowing a succession of seed. For the earliest lot, start in a cold frame, hotbed, or in a box in the kitchen window, 14 weeks before bloom is wanted. Select a single-flowered variety for best fragrance, although some of the more showy, double-flowered sorts are also acceptable.

It should be remembered that nearly all stocks are predominately spicy or aromatic in their fragrance, but they also contain a tinge, and some think a dangerous tinge, of the heavy odors of the plants in Section 2 of this chapter. So penetrating is the scent that half a dozen sprays will completely dominate the fragrance of a room.

HYACINTH AND CROCUS

Both these bulbous groups contain heavily spiced fragrance, especially the hyacinth, which, besides its balsam-like odor, has a nearly sovereign sweetness, which to some is a bit overpowering. Bulbs of these early-blooming hyacinths should be planted in late October or November for bloom the following May. All of the horticultural varieties are supremely fragrant, and from more than 200 named forms known to be in cultivation here, yellow, blue, white, pink, and deep red sorts can be selected with confidence that they will be fragrant.

Crocus. Practically none of the low, common, spring-flowering varieties of crocus have any odor worth mentioning, but one spring-flowering species and two autumn-blooming sorts are decidedly fragrant. To distinguish them from the common, scentless varieties, the more favored ones are best ordered by their Latin names. The spring-flowering ones should be planted in the fall, while the autumn-blooming kind needs August planting for bloom in October. These are not the usual autumn crocus, which belong to *Colchicum* and are practically scentless.

Crocus imperati, spring-flowering, the flowers lilac or white, with the scent of cowslip.

Crocus longiflorus, autumn-flowering, the lilac flower with a bearded yellow throat and primrose-scented.

Crocus sativus, often called Saffron crocus or vegetable gold. An autumn-flowering crocus with white or lilac-purple flowers having yellow, aromatic stigmas from which commercial saffron is derived in southern Europe where it is grown for the purpose.

THREE AROMATIC PERENNIALS

The lavender, primrose, and our shooting star are the only common garden perennials that are easily available and can be properly put among the *Aromatics*. Not one of them has a tinge of the heavy odor of hyacinth, nor, of course, of the tuberose or jasmine. Each of them is grown for a certain spicy or aromatic scent which is enticing and lively, but has no whiff of seduction about it.

LAVENDER. An old garden favorite grown chiefly for its fragrant foliage which is ashy-gray. The flowers, however, which are lavender-purple, have the same delightful fragrance that is derived from the foliage for making lavender water. Dried flowers retain their odor for months, which is why girls since the days of the Romans like to sprinkle it among their clothes. It is really a low shrub.

PRIMROSES. It is unfortunate that most of the species in the genus *Primula* require moist and especially shady or half-shady sites. It is generally useless to try them in full sun, for they do not like summer heat or dryness. If you have the right conditions all of the following can be grown, and they are delightfully fragrant. All are spring-blooming.

PRIMROSE (*Primula vulgaris*). 3-6 inches high, the flowers yellow. This is *the* primrose of English song and story, which the poets from Spenser to Keats have immortalized. There are today many horticultural varieties, but the common, old-fashioned sort is the safest to use for fragrance.

COWSLIP (*Primula veris*). 4-8 inches high, the yellow flowers with an orange eye. Many varieties are known; some are double-flowered, but are best avoided for surety of fragrance. Like most of the primroses there is a whiff of anise in its scent.

AURICULA (*Primula auricula*). 5-8 inches high, the flowers variously colored, but always with an eye. Among acceptable varieties are Double Red, Rosebud, Scarlet Prince, and White Ensign.

SHOOTING STAR (*Dodecatheon meadia*). A beautiful, native wild flower, 8-12 inches high, its delicate mauve-pink flowers appearing in late May or June, spicy with a cinnamon-like odor. It prefers partial shade.

TWO AROMATIC ANNUALS

The common garden heliotrope and the sand verbena share alike in their delightful almond, or almond plus vanilla, odor, the quantity of which is limited only by how many you grow. Both provide a delicious perfume for a room, while in the case of heliotrope there is also a whiff of the heavy scent of those plants in Section 2 of this chapter.

HELIOTROPE. This is really a perennial, but because it is likely to die out it is best grown as an annual and, for the greatest fragrance, always in the greenhouse. Lacking that, start seed in the cold frame, hotbed, or in the kitchen window in March, transplanting out-

doors when settled warm weather has arrived. They will bloom the
first season from seedlings so started.

SAND VERBENA (*Abronia umbellata*). The verbena-like flower of this
    prostrate, vine-like plant develops its pink bloom in June. It,
like the heliotrope, is really a perennial, but best treated as a tender
annual. Plant seeds indoors in March.

4. VIOLET—TYPE FLOWER, THE FLORIST'S VIOLET

Not many flowers have the scent of violets, and only a handful
of violets themselves have it, for nearly all the American wild kinds
are practically scentless. Even the delightful odor of the florist's violet is little more than a wistful will-o'-the-wisp, fading all too swiftly
as only a memory. Also, the flower is not one for the general amateur,
for it will not grow outdoors over most of the country and hence
needs a cool greenhouse or a hotbed.

The horned violet or tufted pansy, while perfectly hardy, is not
worth cultivating for fragrance, so that the average home grower,
without a hotbed or greenhouse, may well ask himself, is it impossible to produce the wonderful odor of the florist's violet in my garden?

There is a solution to this apparent impasse only because *Viola
odorata* comes in many forms. By far the most fragrant are the double-flowered varieties, bred for odor and for growing under glass by
professionals. These are not for the amateur. But some other forms
of *Viola odorata* can be grown outdoors. One of them is a variety
of the Neapolitan violet known as Marie Louise, which has double-
flowered, beautifully fragrant, reddish-purple bloom. Also, some
single-flowered forms of *Viola odorata* are available from specialists, but if the truth must out, the violet fragrance so well known in
Europe is not easily obtainable here—at least in the average outdoor
garden.

All the more welcome then is the beloved Egyptian weed, with a
violet-like odor, which charmed Paris so much that they called it
immediately *mignonette* (little darling), a name that has pushed
into the background not only its Latin cognomen of *Reseda odorata*
but a dozen others.

When it first reached Paris, about the middle of the eighteenth
century, the ease of its culture soon filled every window box, and a
year or two later London went as mad as that staid city ever becomes
over the enchanting odor of the newcomer which they thought was a
French flower. London markets were soon packed with it, and our

gardens have been ever since. It can be grown anywhere, for it is an annual of the easiest culture. Only a few plants will scent up a whole garden, but it is not for cutting, for once out of the sun it loses its odor rather quickly. Unlike many other fragrant plants, true *Reseda odorata*, is less fragrant than some of the modern varieties the odor of which has been considerably increased, especially in the varieties Machet, Golden Sunset and Red Monarch.

This odor of violets is such a comparatively rare occurrence in the plant world (it is found in some tropical trees) that two widely different bulbous plants that have it are nearly as welcome as the mignonette. They are:

MEXICAN STAR (*Milla biflora*). A bulbous plant with grass-like leaves and a stalk 12-18 inches high, at the end of which is a beautifully fragrant white flower about 2½ inches wide. Blooms in mid-summer and is to be grown exactly as gladiolus.

SNOWFLAKE (*Leucojum vernum*). Whoever named the snowflake *Leucojum* (that is, a white violet) must have smelled the violet-like odor of these beautiful, spring-flowering bulbs. As the name indicates, they are among our first flowers to bloom after snow has gone. Plant in fall for next spring's bloom, and once started they persist for many years.

5. ROSE—TYPE FLOWER, THE FRAGRANT ROSES
(See Section 5 of Chapter Two)

Scarcely any perennials or annuals have the true "rose scent," and as we have seen, not many modern roses have it. But the fragrance of roses, or something very like it, is found among certain irises and in a few peonies.

IRIS

Most modern iris varieties are scentless or nearly so, but *Iris reticulata*, a very early blooming species has a combination of odors including whiffs of violet and rose. It is perhaps the most fragrant of all cultivated irises.

Some enthusiasts, who are a little more ecstatic than factual, would have it that *all* irises are fragrant. Many have a faint odor, but this book is dedicated to providing the amateur gardener with varieties that are fragrant enough to give some compelling reason for cultivating them.

Among thousands of iris varieties generally grouped as tall bearded or German iris, there are a few notably fragrant. These are likely to contain some trace of the blood of *Iris pallida*, a wild species with a delicious odor of vanilla, civet, violet, and rose. Such a combination is as complicated as the genetic history of most horticultural varieties of iris. The following ten seem worth cultivation, considering only their fragrance:

Afterglow	Mary Barnett	Souvenir de Mme.
Aphrodite	Morning Splendor	Gaudichau
Frieda Mohr	Queen Caterina	Zua
Mandalay	Sir Galahad	

PEONY

Many peonies, in spite of their spectacular flower, are all but scentless, and some are downright repulsive. Even among the fragrant sorts listed below, all of which have a tinge of rose scent in them, none is outstandingly fragrant. They are mentioned here because everyone wants to grow these magnificent perennials, and to choose at least a few fragrant varieties seems essential.

Avalanche	John M. Good	Kelway's Queen
Duchess de Nemours	Katherine Havemyer	Lamartine
Frances Shaylor	Nell Shaylor	Marie Lemoine
Jesse Shaylor		

6. LEMON—TYPE FLOWER, FOUR-O'CLOCK
(See Chapter One, and Section 6 of Chapter Two)

No flowers have the characteristic odor found in the rind of the lemon and some other citrus fruits, but some have a fragrance that suggests this highly aromatic odor, because they contain citral, a compound chiefly responsible for the scent of that pungent oil found in most lemon rinds, especially those from Italy. This lemon-like fragrance is found among some magnolias and other trees and shrubs discussed in Chapter Two, but in only a handful of herbaceous plants. Of these the annual and somewhat weedy four-o'clock is paramount, followed by our exquisite native water lily and a prairie evening primrose, which because it is chiefly night-blooming is noted in the next chapter.

FOUR-O'CLOCK. This is a perennial in its native South America, where it is often known as Marvel-of-Peru, and it may often be perennial in our South. But in the North it is best treated as a tender annual, since it blooms the same season from seed if these are sown early in March in boxes set in the kitchen window. The preference in this book for kitchen windows does not mean that the living room is no place for plants. But the kitchen is a work room; hence it is

cooler and usually moister than any living room, especially from the
evaporation from sinks and the steam from cooking. Kitchen windows, therefore, are ideal places to start seedlings.

The four-o'clock, which can be set outdoors as soon as warm
weather is assured, is rather weedy, 14-30 inches high, and will bloom
all summer, especially under partial shade, where it blooms all day.
Its name suggests the fact that in open sunlight it really opens its
typically reddish flowers only as the light begins to fade. Varieties
of it come also in white and yellow shades, but the old-fashioned
red sort is to be preferred for fragrance, which is a delicate combination of lemon and fruit scents.

Water Lily (*Nymphaea odorata*). This beautiful, white-flowered
floating aquatic cannot, of course, be grown unless you have
a pool or can sink a half-barrel in the lawn. It is one of the most
delightfully fragrant of all the native plants in the eastern United
States. The odor is lemony, but mixed with it there are spicy or aromatic elements that make it quite entrancing. Be sure to order by
the Latin name for many of its relatives and even some of its derivative varieties are practically scentless.

Chapter Four

Night Witchery

The Romans, Persians, and Arabs understood the arts of perfumery better than any of us, and they used flowers on such a scale that no rich prodigal of today would dream of like extravagance. Before carpets became general, it was not unusual for a prince to strew with rose petals the floor of a banquet room to the depth of a wine glass.

When the strict and puritanical Christians frowned on perfumes, as well they might considering what had been done with them, the more tolerant *Koran* encouraged perfumes and especially the growing of the flowers that were then the only source of these intoxicating essences.

While the drab Christians of the Middle Ages were plodding a scentless path to the Renaissance, except for incense in the Church, the far more civilized Arabs and Persians were exploring every avenue of sensuous enjoyment. From prince to pauper the love of flowers was a passion, and none knew better than they the far greater impact of fragrance as daylight wanes and dusk turns to darkness. To the witchery of night they added the nocturnal lure of flowers that are scentless by day but, as one poet has said:

> All night incense's sweetest fragrance
> Rises from those perfumed bowers,
> Through the moonlight's silver radiance
> From the yellow jasmine flowers.

Nature, too, seems in league with gardeners who want to capture the enchantment of night fragrance. For then the dusty heat of day is followed by the cool air of evening, and one by one the flowers that were either closed or scentless during sunshine steal into our consciousness, not only by their odor but by their color.

Many night-blooming plants have white flowers, and such an observant poet as Tennyson recorded the sequence of flower visibility as night falls.

Now sleeps the crimson petal, now the white

It is no accident that among these white-flowered, nocturnal blooms are some of the most intoxicating odors known to the seeker of fragrance. This startling whiteness, amid the gloom of night, is one of nature's tricks to guide night-flying moths, so that the nuptials of these fragrant flowers of the dusk may be completed when they are most receptive. There is an extraordinary correlation between the incidence of these night-flying moths and the white floral virgins of the night waiting for a ghostly visitor who will complete their love life.

There is far more to this than the poetic imagery of flower and insect—for it ultimately involves the survival of both. We need not here go into the fascinating by-paths of the marvellously timed operations implied by the nocturnal darting of perfumed moths among perfumed and nocturnal flowers. No one, however, can escape the implications of an atmosphere redolent with the fragrance of sex.

It is precisely this which was so well known to the ancients. And it should be thoroughly understood by any modern gardener who wants either to avoid the perils or to promote the potentialities of night fragrance in the garden. Which you choose will dictate what flowers you select from those mentioned below. Some are as fragrant as any others in this book. Some belong to the "dangerous" scents that the susceptible must use with caution. These are among Groups 2 and 3 of the *types* of fragrance that have been noted in Chapter One and need not be repeated here. To make selection easier each of the plants below, if it is known, will carry a number enclosed in brackets thus: [2], [3], etc. This, of course, means that such plants belong to the same *types* of fragrance as those detailed in the first chapter.

It is urged that before planning a night garden of fragrance, or even planting a few of the species in an existing garden, the reader scan that chapter with this in mind:

Must your night garden of fragrance reflect the mature scents of the middle-aged or do you want it to be a thing of haunting beauty, sex-charged with the mystery of night and perfumed with the intoxicating fragrance which drove Sappho in her ode to Aphrodite to write (about 600 B.C.)

> Its beauties charm the gods above;
> Its fragrance is the breath of Love;
> Its foliage wantons in the air;
> Luxuriant, like the flowing hair.

If hair is no longer flowing, the lady who wrote that shares with her cropped and curled sister of today the universal knowledge that fragrance lures by day but bewitches by night.

PLANT MATERIALS
FOR THE NIGHT-FRAGRANT GARDEN

Scarcely anyone would inflict upon themselves or their guests a garden devoted wholly to nocturnal flowers. The desire to have some near an open window, a porch, in a patio, or in some quiet nook in the garden must dictate what sort of fragrance you want, when it will be available, and if it is to be a shrub, vine, or a perennial or annual herb.

The materials are not copious, for in spite of all the poets the number of plants that both bloom and are fragrant at night is rather limited. This is especially true if one excludes all tropical sorts such as the fabulous Queen-of-the-Night, of which one poet wrote that she

> . . . bares her breast
> Of fragrant scent, a virgin white,
> A pearl amidst the realms of night.

There appear to be no trees with night-fragrant flowers, and among shrubs the honeysuckles are the most likely, and they are among the most heavily scented of all shrubs. Two of them are really both day and night fragrant, or at least the odor from both of them is greater after dark. One is a rather low shrub (*Lonicera heckrotti*) [3]* of unknown origin and without a common name, but of exquisite fragrance. The other is the Old World woodbine (*Lonicera periclymenum*) [3], a scrambling vine up to 20 feet high, with yellowish-white, but red-tinged flowers that bloom most of the summer. For other honeysuckles, all day-blooming, see Chapter Two.

Much less disturbing (for honeysuckles are notoriously that) is a

---

* The numbers in brackets refer to the types of fragrance as detailed in Chapter One. They are important for those who want something more than just any kind of fragrance.

stout woody vine, with the odor of magnolia, but having rather inconspicuous flowers, known as *Akebia quinata* [6], a description of
which will be found in Section 6 of Chapter Two.

If this seems a meagre list of night fragrant shrubs and vines the
gardener should not forget that Nature has been much more prolific
with them in tropical and sub-tropical lands. Scarcely any of these
can be grown here and one must hence leave for more favored gardeners the rich odors of the night that come from many orchids, from
the orange blossom, and scores of tropical shrubs and trees like the
frangipani and ylang-ylang.

NIGHT-FRAGRANT ANNUALS AND PERENNIALS

It is from these, of course, that evening scents must come *en masse*,
particularly in the case of annuals. These can be sown in any quantity, moved from year to year and provide not only fragrance in the
garden but serve as a steady supply for the house.

Before discussing either group it is well to remind the reader that
some plants, noted in Chapters Two and Three, are also night-
fragrant, particularly in the warmer sections of the country. Of these,
two are probably the most fragrant plants in the temperate world
—the jasmine and tuberose. Hence, in planning for night fragrance
these should not be ignored for they are more fragrant and far more
bewitching than the plants below, although some of the annuals
have driven poets and gardeners to the verge of speechlessness!

ANNUALS

All of the seven plants grouped as annuals are not true annuals,
but are best treated as such. Some are tender annuals which should
be started in the greenhouse, hotbed, or in boxes in the kitchen window. Some are biennials and hence need constant renewal. One or
two are short-lived perennials (sometimes permanent in warm sections of the country), but, for continuance of supply, they are best
treated by the constant renewal of annual seed planting.

NIGHT PHLOX (*Zaluzianskya villosa*). A tender annual from South
        Africa, scarcely 12 inches high, related to snapdragon, but
exquisitely night-fragrant from its purplish flowers that are white or
pale lilac on the inside. The seed is sometimes, but incorrectly, offered as *Nycterinia selaginoides*, but under whatever name the plant
demands a place in any garden of night fragrance.

Nicotiana [3] and [2]. When Columbus first saw the Indians in Cuba
        smoking tobacco in November 1492, he little realized that

tobacco would capture the world, and a relative of it equally capture the affections of all gardeners who seek night fragrance. For besides *Nicotiana tabacum,* there are several annual species, of no use for making tobacco, but some of them having flowers that are among the most fragrant ever to scent the night air.

Of these by far the best is *Nicotiana alata grandiflora* [3] and [2], which is really a perennial from Brazil, Uruguay, and Paraguay and is so extraordinarily fragrant that it is often called Jasmine Tobacco. It sometimes seeds itself, but is best treated as a tender annual. It will grow up to 3-4 feet, with long, tubular white flowers that are usually closed (open in the shade) all day, but which expand in the evening and give off an intoxicating scent. There is a related species, *Nicotiana sylvestris* [3] and [2], which is a true perennial, and has a slightly less enticing fragrance.

NIGHT-SCENTED STOCK (*Mathiola bicornis*) [3] and [2]. Often called the evening stock, this annual or biennial herb from the Old World is nothing to rave about by day, for its small, brown-purple flowers are shut tight until sundown. Then they open and give off such a fragrance that if a single cluster is brought into the house it will scent up a whole room. For a succession of its enticing fragrance it is well to make small sowings every ten days up to the middle of July.

EVENING CAMPION (*Lychnis alba*) [2]. An almost weedy roadside herb, naturalized here from Europe. It is not common in usual gardens, for not enough people know about its almost jasmine-like night fragrance. Actually it is a biennial which seeds itself along roadsides and ditches, but can easily be started in the garden from purchased seeds. It is a sticky herb, 1-2 feet high, its white flowers fringed, summer-blooming.

DAME'S ROCKET (*Hesperis matronalis*) [3]. This biennial often called double white rocket, came originally from Europe and Asia, but has been popular in England for centuries. It is a branching plant, 2-3 feet high, the flowers white, purple or lilac, quite open by day, but giving off its spicy fragrance only at night.

SCHIZOPETALON WALKERI [3]. A beautifully night-fragrant Chilean annual, rather sprawling in habit and never over 12 inches high. Its white flowers, which are handsomely fringed and borne in terminal clusters, have an extraordinary odor at night—sweet, but compounded of almond and vanilla. The seed is best sown where wanted, for the plant does not like transplanting, but they should not be started outdoors until settled warm weather.

PRAIRIE LILY (*Mentzelia decapetala*). This very showy prairie bien-

nial, native from South Dakota to Texas is not well known to
Eastern gardeners, but it should be since seeds are available from
dealers in prairie wild flowers. It is scarcely a foot high and has white
or yellow flowers nearly 5 inches wide, the petals velvet-like. Sow
the seeds where wanted and it may persist from self-sown seeds.

PERENNIALS

Only four garden perennials are both night-blooming and night-
fragrant, and even one of these is perennial only in the South. Others
could no doubt be found, and some of them have adherents, but they
are omitted here because of their difficult cultivation or their unavail-
ability to all but the specialists.

One of them has the not inappropriate specific name *tristis*, which
technically means sad, bitter, or dull; or, by extension, that they are
not much to look at by day. But at night how different the story! Shy,
sad, and dull by day, but like some ladies, they put on the raiment of
charm as the sun goes down.

In Chapter Three there is an omission that may have struck the
gardener. Why omit the gorgeous and multi-named varieties of gladiolus? The truth is that practically all of them are scentless, and it is
only among the wild species of *Gladiolus* that we can expect real
fragrance. Of these, *Gladiolus tristis* [3] from South Africa is not only
very fragrant, but does not begin to be so until sundown. It is smaller
than the common horticultural varieties and does not have the usual
sword-shaped leaves. Flowers are yellowish-white, streaked with
purple. It is grown exactly as are its more showy relatives—in other
words its corms must be planted each June and lifted over the winter.
It would be a hardy perennial in its natural climate.

The remaining night-fragrant perennials are:

DAYLILY. These lily-like perennials should, from their common name,
bloom only by day. All belong to the genus *Hemerocallis* and
among them is one species that blooms at night and is deliciously
fragrant after dusk. It is *Hemerocallis thunbergi* [2] from Japan, about
2 feet high with lemon-yellow, lily-like flowers about 2-3 inches long
which bloom in midsummer. Most daylilies are scentless, except one
or two known as lemon lilies, so that this night-fragrant Japanese perennial is a welcome addition to the tribe.

BOUNCING BET (*Saponaria officinalis*) [3]. A decidedly weedy Asiatic
immigrant, naturalized everywhere here, and especially fond
of the cindery wastes along the railroad. No one would think of growing it in the garden were it not for the wonderful, spicy, carnation-

like odor of its flowers, which is obvious only at night. It is a sturdy plant, 1-3 feet high with pinkish-white flowers, and by no means to be despised because it comes from the wrong side of the tracks.

EVENING PRIMROSE (*Oenothera caespitosa*) [6]. From our prairie region come many kinds of evening primroses and their relatives that bloom by day, but nearly all are scentless and some positively repulsive. All the more welcome, then, is this beautiful and, in fact, extremely showy perennial from the prairie states. It is low, has basal leaves, and about sundown it begins to expand a flower that is nearly 4 inches wide, generally white, but tinged with pink. The fragrance is strongly suggestive of some sweet-smelling magnolia.

Chapter Five

Fragrance
in the House

No scientist has ever yet been able to plot on a graph the fragrance of flowers or our emotional response to the widely different *types* of fragrance. We do know something about the intensity of scent—mild in a tulip but ravishing in the jasmine, captivating in the carnation but elusive in the violet, enticing in the mignonette but easily raising quite unholy emotions in the tuberose.

Although scent is just as unmeasurable as our reactions to it, there are a few things we know about flower fragrance that seem warranted by the perfume history of those who have done more than any others to make it an art. It seems clear enough that the *heavy* and *aromatic* (see Chapter One for definitions) types of fragrance were and still are cherished by the Mediterranean, Arabian, Persian, Semitic, and Indian peoples based upon their clear recognition of the fact that the appeal was frankly sensuous and, even more frankly, sexual, especially in fragrance such as jasmine and tuberose. The idea may seem almost repulsive to those who think of fragrance as a symbol of purity. But the evidence points all the other way. Here are the ardent races, passionate and even obsessed by sex, for as one writer has so well put it, "In India the very children are the waifs of sex."

Such people need no graphs to measure fragrance. They know, or think they do, what its significance means. And one of the most scholarly of all writers on flower fragrance has amply confirmed it. He points out, particularly where *heavy* types of fragrance are involved, that these magic flower essences were not created for our enjoyment,

but to complete the sex life of the flower and that of the equally perfumed butterflies or moths which pollinate those flowers.

It is, according to F. A. Hampton,* no accident that these sweetly
heavy odors unconsciously stir the mating instinct, because we too
respond to the very sex-linked factors that have produced that fragrance. Nor is it any accident that from Cleopatra to today all the distilled fragrance of flowers is used by women—if we exclude a coterie
of perfumed dandies ancient and modern. Such heavy odors are perhaps not really aphrodisiac but they come close to it, for as Hampton
says, "A sweet scent is one that can stir the instinct of courtship without evoking the idea of the natural end object of the instinct." So true
is this, and so basic is our response, that it is scarcely surprising that
anthropologists have turned up a primitive tribe in Somaliland in
which girls smear their bodies with a peculiarly sex-excitant kind of
musk extracted from crocodiles.

It is easy to catch the critical chorus of feminine readers who will
be saying, "What's all this to do with Fragrance in the House? My
house is no harem and I'm not trying to imitate Cleopatra or evoke
anything that an imaginative scientist may dream up; all I want is to
give pleasure to myself and guests." To these unimpeachable senti-
ments the answer is so obvious that it scarcely needs laboring. For
whether we know it or not, or will admit it at all, fragrance does affect
the senses just as poor half-crazed Baudelaire knew when he wrote
"My soul hovers over perfumes as the soul of others hovers over
music."

Fragrance in the house, just as in the open, can be arranged and
planned, depending on our mood and the emotions we wish to evoke.
There are, however, a few limitations on bringing flowers indoors
which depend upon the plants themselves and especially on the conditions in the garden that will promote or retard fragrance; whether
their scent will be available during the day or night; how long it will
last; and, particularly, whether an extremely fragrant flower in the
garden will lose it if picked at all—such as mignonette and wall-
flowers.

As to those fit for cutting that are only night-fragrant—the obvious
time to gather them is about or just before sundown because their
fragrance will last all night, and most of them will close up the next

---

* Hampton, F. A., *The Scent of Flowers and Leaves,* London, Dulau and Co.,
1925. See particularly pp. 78-84. The classification of fragrance in this book
has been adapted in part from Mr. Hampton's modification of the older scheme
of Count Kerner von Marilaun, an Austrian botanist.

morning. Many of them will be useless the next evening, with a few
notable exceptions to be stressed presently.

Fragrance in nearly all plants resides mostly in their petals, and
the compounds responsible for the odor are usually rather heavy oils
found in microscopic amounts and of greatly varying capacity to
rouse our senses. In most day-blooming flowers, stillness and moisture definitely releases more scent than wind and dryness. That is
why picking flowers for fragrance is best done in the cool of the morning, while the dew is still on them if possible, or else about sunset.
Even more than in nonfragrant flowers, it is important to keep fragrant cut flowers from withering, and a good precaution is to plunge
the stems in a bucket of water as they are picked. A cloudy or even
a foggy day makes an ideal time for picking because transpiration is
much reduced at such periods.

What has been said applies to most plants that you will be growing
yourself in the open fragrant garden. It is not always true, however,
regarding many greenhouse flowers that are purchased from florists.
For some reason, as yet all but unknown, most greenhouse-raised
flowers have their fragrance markedly increased by bringing them
into a room of ordinary temperature. This is especially true of roses
and carnations and is strikingly so in gardenia, freesia, bouvardia,
stephanotis, stocks, violets, and greenhouse-forced lily-of-the-valley.
Most of these, except roses and violets, belong to the *heavy* or *aromatic* type of fragrance.

But most people with a fragrant garden will want to cut their own
supplies, and before listing the most desirable, it is well to decide
which rooms are to have them and what sort of atmosphere you
wish to create. It is, for instance, almost axiomatic that few fragrant
flowers should be in the dining room, and no heavy or aromatic ones
at all should ever be put on the dining table for the very good reason
that Nature has linked our sense of smell and taste just a bit too
closely.

It is a commonplace that, as a head cold increases, our sense of
taste fades, but it is not so generally known that if you pinch your
nose hard enough you can scarcely "taste" an onion. In other words
our sense of taste and smell is compounded of an intricate biological
association, far too complicated to be enlarged upon here. The end
result, according to some experts, is that, without smell, we can distinguish only a few tastes such as salt, sweet, and sour, especially the
puckery taste of gooseberries.

Nearly all other tastes, especially of the things we like the best,
are thus not pure "taste" at all, but a blend of taste and smell—in

what proportion we can leave to the experts. What it means to the initiated at the dining room table is obvious. Who for instance wants to blend roast beef with bouvardia, or a salad with stephanotis, turkey with a tuberose, or lobster with lily-of-the-valley. If the incongruity seems preposterous the author has suffered acutely from such ignorance enough times to warn the reader against trying to blend flower fragrance and food. If you *must* have flowers on the table choose the scentless kinds or else the milder types of fragrance as listed under 1, 5 and 6 in the first chapter.

As to other rooms in the house there is nothing that needs to restrict the use of fragrant flowers anywhere, except the well-intrenched notion that they should not be left in a sickroom overnight, which is probably a fallacious hangover from the supposed efficacy of flowers as disinfectants! Feminine taste can dispose of fragrance otherwise as she thinks fit, but it should be stressed that of the flowers listed below some are definitely not for the bedroom or boudoir—unless there is still a streak of Cleopatra in her modern sisters. These are all marked [2] or [3] in the list that follows.

FRAGRANT FLOWERS FOR THE HOUSE

We assume that most gardeners will want to use the material they have grown themselves. Hence, all the flowers listed have been already described in Chapters Two, Three, and Four, so that the notes on them will not be repeated here, except as to their utility as cut flowers. No so-called florist's flowers are included, and if the list seems meagre, it should be remembered that only the most outstanding kinds have been included. Wherever known, and for the convenience of those who want to *select* their types of fragrance, each sort has a number written thus [1], [2], etc. Where they are marked with two numbers, it means that they have combined two types of fragrance. Although all these are explained in detail in the first chapter, it is perhaps well to summarize.

TYPES OF FRAGRANCE

1. AMINOID. Type flower, hawthorn. Rather mild, faintly sweet, and disturbing to some.
2. HEAVY. Type flower, jasmine. The heaviest, sweetest, and most seductive of all flower odors.
3. AROMATIC. Type flower, clove pink. Spicy, aromatic, often vanilla-scented, but many of them so sweet as to merge into Group 2.
4. VIOLET. Type flower, *Viola odorata*. Milder, often elusive, found in almost no wild violets.

5. ROSE. Type flower, the fragrant roses. Spicy, fruity, delicate, and often very sweet.

6. LEMON. Type flower, the four-o'clock. Rather lemony, but sometimes very fragrant as in magnolia and our native white water-lily.

The flowers suitable for the house, their type of fragrance, and the chapter in which further notes on them should be sought follow. (Latin names are used only where necessary.)

CARNATION [3]. Chapter Two, Section 3. Fragrance lasts for several days.

Chimonanthus praecox [3]. Chapter Two, Section 3. Cut twigs, unlike a good many other shrubs, are satisfactory as to fragrance in the house.

DAME'S ROCKET [3]. Chapter Four. Night-flowering, and very spicy.

FLOWERING CURRANT (*Ribes sanguineum*) [3]. Chapter Three, Section 3. More spicily fragrant in the house than outdoors.

Gladiolus tristis [3]. Chapter Four. Night-fragrant and summer-flowering.

HYACINTHS [2] and [3]. Chapter Three, Section 3. All of them with a heavy, rich and spicy fragrance.

JASMINE [2]. Chapter Two, Section 2. Probably, with the tuberose, the most fragrant of all flowers, tending to be most fragrant at night.

JONQUIL [2]. Chapter Three, Section 2. Many think this and the poet's narcissus are too sweet, seductive, and "dangerous" for indoor use.

LAVENDER [3]. Chapter Three, Section 3. Flowers keeping their fragrance, as do the leaves, long after they are dried.

LILAC [2]. Chapter Two, Section 2. Beautiful for a day or two, but soon losing its fragrance.

Magnolia virginiana [6]. Chapter Two, Section 6. A sweet-spicy fragrance. A few flowers will scent up a whole room.

Magnolia stellata [6] and [4]. Chapter Two, Section 6. Very early-flowering variety—often in early April.

MOCK-ORANGE (*Philadelphus coronarius*) [2]. Chapter Two, Section 2. One of the most sweet-smelling of all shrubs, entrancing some and obnoxious to others.

NIGHT-SCENTED STOCK [3] and [2]. Chapter Four. Night-fragrant and so much so that a single stalk to a room is enough.

PEONY [5]. As many peonies are scentless and some actually repulsive, it is best to consult details in Section 5 of Chapter Three before selecting any for indoor fragrance.

POET'S NARCISSUS [2]. Chapter Three, Section 2. As with the jonquil, thought to be too sweet for indoor use. However, the Chinese sacred lily, which is a variety of a related species, is grown by the thousands in pebbles and water by those who do not find its odor too disturbing. It is extremely sweet.

ROSES [5] and [3]. Chapter Two, Section 5. Many tea and hybrid perpetual roses may be faintly fragrant outdoors but develop full sweetness in a room. Dried rose petals retain some of the odor for a considerable time.

SWEET PEA. Chapter Three. Many sweet pea varieties are essentially scentless. See Chapter Three for those that are worth cultivating for fragrance. All of these make fine flowers for cutting.

SWEET PEPPERBUSH (*Clethra alnifolia*) [2] and [3]. Chapter Two, Section 3. Sprays of this shrub in August and September are intensely fragrant—aromatic with a whiff of lilac.

TUBEROSE [2]. Chapter Three, Section 2. With the jasmine, the sweetest and most alluring of flower scents, especially in the evening.

TULIP [1]. Chapter Three, Section 1. Many tulips are all but scentless outdoors, especially among the Darwin group. But some varieties, in a closed room, develop a delightful fragrance. See Chapter Three for a list of these.

TEA OLIVE (*Osmanthus fragrans*) [2]. Chapter Two, Section 2. Jasmine-like in fragrance, but otherwise not showy. Found only in warmer regions than New York, and in Norfolk blooming in April.

Viburnum carlesi [1] and [2]. Chapter Two, Section 2. Beautifully fragrant sprays of this, by judicious and careful pruning, add a delightfully spicy and sweet odor to any room in April-May.

VIOLET [4]. Chapter Three, Section 4. Unless you are equipped to grow the florist's violet (*Viola odorata*), one cannot expect much fragrance from any of the wild violets. The florist's violet definitely increases its fragrance indoors.

Any inquisitive and experimental gardener could no doubt find many other plants in Chapters Two, Three, and Four, which are well fitted for cutting and retain their fragrance in a warm room long enough to make them useful. The foregoing list, therefore, does not so much aim at completeness as to suggest basic material for fragrance in the house. Of course, fragrance wafted through open windows is better than any cut flowers, and, for this, certain of the shrubs and vines mentioned in Chapter Two are eminently fitted.

The preservation of fragrant flowers after they have been cut (not pulled or torn loose) is a controversial subject often complicated by considerable chicanery. Various "magic" chemicals are promoted, usually without a formula, doubtfully effective and far too expensive.

If anything better than plain water at room temperature (changed every day or so) is needed, there is some evidence that a bit of charcoal will help to maintain freshness. In the case of tulips, one half ounce of calcium nitrate to about one and one half gallons of water has been recommended, but even this is disputed. Freshness is best enhanced by keeping cut flowers away from a draught, the radiator, and the electric fan.

Chapter Six

Perfume from
Your Garden

There is scarcely a woman in the world who does not yearn for the finest, most choice, and incidentally most expensive perfume made by the masters of the art in Grasse. Within this small section of southern France the finest perfumes, and especially the essential ingredients of them, have been manufactured for generations by a few great houses who guard their secrets better than do some governments.

Those secrets, quite simply, are the extraction of fragrance from many of the flowers already mentioned in earlier chapters, the fixing and blending of them, and, in all but the most costly, adding the necessary amount of synthetic material, as well as various oils, gums, and other odorous products, the very names of which stir memories of far-off places. Musk, civet, ambergris, patouchli, rosewood, olibanum, and neroli oil—what they are and where they come from must be left mostly to the economic botanist, for all but the first three are derived from plants.

Although the basis of all good perfumes is the fragrance of various flowers, very few perfumes consist only of this, partly because it would be fantastically expensive, and mostly because few flower scents are lasting enough to make good perfume without fixatives or enhancements or potentiation of the initial fragrance. These are the secrets of the expert perfumer. The basic principles upon which his mastery is based are well known, but there is no use ignoring the fact that a choice perfume is a combination of rare skills in horticulture, organic and synthetic chemistry, manufacturing processes, and just plain know-how.

Let no amateur gardener think for a moment that she can duplicate such creations from her own garden. What can be done, and it
will be far better than the cheap 100 per cent synthetic perfumes that
flood the market, is to utilize a handful of those basic techniques
which, after centuries of trial and error, have solved the problem of
putting flower fragrance into a bottle.

This may sound simple enough. But, on second thought, is it?
Scents are evanescent, are gone in a day or so, and some, like the
violet, are a will-o'-the-wisp and doubly hard to capture. So true is
this that a true essence of violet flowers is fabulously expensive. So
rare and enchanting is their odor that one easily understands the
enthusiast long ago who told the ladies of his day:

> "Rub thy face with violets and goat's milk and there is not a
> prince in the world who will not follow thee."

Much easier to capture is the heavy, seductive odor of jasmine.
Some women in Persia, Arabia, and India found this out long before
French perfumers were covering thousands of acres with this most
fragrant of all shrubs. The Oriental women rolled up in their well-
oiled hair as many jasmine flowers as convenient, for they knew that
the oil would extract and hold the fragrance. This was gradually released during the night to make of their hair and skin a ravishment
of alluring sweetness.

These Oriental ladies unwittingly discovered a secret that is still
the basis of much French perfumery and, as we shall see presently, is
about the only technique readily applicable to the home gardener
who wants to make her own perfume. Flower scents are captured
and held by various techniques, mostly by distillation, by extraction
with ether and gasoline, by various systems of macerating the flowers, and by the method found so potent by the amorous ladies of the
East.

Distillation is generally impossible for the amateur, and many
flower odors are partly destroyed by the heat unless the process is
carried out by experts. Maceration and extraction by chemical sol-
vents are also for the professionals. But the extraction of odors by
their absorption into oils and fats is perfectly feasible and just as
sure as the absorption of jasmine in the well-oiled hair of the girls in
Persia.

Every housewife knows to her cost that exposed butter in the re-
frigerator will absorb the odor of turnips, fish, cheese, and other unwanted scents. To translate that fact into making perfume seems a

perfectly obvious step to us, but it took many centuries to make it the art that it has become in France where they call it *enfleurage.*

There is, of course, more to enfleurage than the mere absorption of fragrance by fats. The kind of fat and the kinds of flower odors are essential parts of the technique, but more important still is the method of getting the fragrance from the fat or oil into a bottle. Some of this comprises trade secrets, and still more so are the blending and fixing of the odors in the finished perfume.

The typical enfleurage plant in France will have hundreds (or thousands) of sheets of glass, coated both sides with specially prepared fat, and between the sheets of glass (spaced about 2 inches apart) is placed a layer of flower petals (or whole flowers if they are small). The flowers just fill the space between the glass, and a fresh lot of flowers is put in every day or so, until it is obvious that the fat has absorbed all the odor it will contain. What happens in extracting the fragrance from the fat and making the finished perfume is too complicated to include here, but fortunately for the amateur it is perfectly possible to utilize the principle of enfleurage in making an acceptable home-made perfume—at a cost of almost nothing except time.

FLOWER MATERIALS

In home-made enfleurage the choice of material is limited by the fact that some odors are better outdoors than in, and some, like the violet, are all but impossible to capture. Generally those flowers coming within Types 2 and 3 as to fragrance are the most likely to succeed, and it is advisable to look over Sections 2 and 3 of the second, third, and fourth chapters in order to get an over-all picture of fragrance.

By far the best procedure is to go out in the garden and decide for yourself which of the flower odors you want to preserve. Upon that decision will be based your garden practice for the next season, for few except quite extensive gardens will have enough flowers to make anything but a tiny bottle of the finished perfume. After you have decided what perfume you wish to make, the next step will be to increase your plantings of that variety so that there will be an ample supply when fragrance is at its best. Perennials and annuals will always be the best source of perfume material, for they are the easiest to propagate or restrict as tastes vary.

Although a detailed study of Chapters One to Four will be of the greatest help in making a selection for enfleurage, a few notes may be summarized here as to the most desirable flowers for home-made perfume.

ROSES. Choose dark red, crimson, but not white or pale pink varieties mentioned in Chapter Two, Section 5.

VIOLET. There is little use in attempting this. Most "violet" perfume is synthetic, probably because the extraction of true violet fragrance is fabulously expensive.

JASMINE. Probably the most fragrant shrub known, but of use only to those living south of Norfolk.

TUBEROSE. The basis of much French perfumery and easily grown by anyone. See Chapter Three, Section 2.

CARNATION. The ordinary florist's carnation will do, but it is better to grow your own if in a suitable climate. See Chapter Three, Section 3.

LILY-OF-THE-VALLEY. Easy to propagate and will make large patches with hundreds of blooms in a few years.

HYACINTH. Early and spring-flowering and heavily scented.

LAVENDER. Fresh flowers in midsummer. Useful also because the flowers retain a lot of their scent when dried.

NIGHT-SCENTED STOCK. So fragrant that one will scent up a whole room. Night-fragrant, so that the flowers for enfleurage must be picked at night.

JONQUIL AND POET'S NARCISSUS. Both easily grown and extremely fragrant, some think almost insupportably. The trumpet kinds are useless for fragrance.

MIGNONETTE. Must be cut and used at once as it soon loses its fragrance.

Many others will no doubt suggest themselves as you walk about the garden with a nose tuned not only for outdoor fragrance, but to the possibility of preserving it. Almost any flower will do, but it should be remembered in making a choice that the mild and elusive scents are all but impossible to imprison by enfleurage.

It is essential, also, in collecting flowers for this process to keep a few simple rules in mind.

(a) Collect all day-blooming flowers as soon as the dew is off them.

(b) The cut flowers or separate petals must not be dried out.

(c) Generally, the cut flowers should be brought into a room where the heat will often release additional fragrance. But in no case must it be windy or too hot or dry in the room—a kitchen is ideal.

(d) All outer green parts of the flower, and all green leaves, flower stalks, and stems must be removed. To leave them on invites failure because they start decay.

(e) Pick all rose petals from the flower and throw away all the rem-
nants of the flower.

(f) Night-fragrant flowers must be picked only after dark.

HOME-MADE ENFLEURAGE

Since the basis of enfleurage is fat, it is important to choose the
right kinds: it has been found that a mixture of three parts of common
beef suet to one part of lard will be the easiest mixture for the amateur. Both of these have a distinctive odor of their own, and it must
be removed before anything can be done about bringing flowers and
fat together.

To remove the odor it is necessary to put the mixture of lard and
suet into a pot which will be three-quarters filled with water, the
latter being in the proportion of one quart to a teaspoon of alum.
Bring this to a boil and let it boil for a half hour or so. After the fat
and water have separated, put in a new lot of water and alum in the
same proportion, and again bring it to a boil. Keep on repeating this
process until the fat residue is *entirely odorless.*

Then pour off the water and allow the fat to cool, picking out any
impurities that are left from the suet. After this cooling and cleaning
are completed, the fat is ready for the final stage of enfleurage.

Melt the purified and odorless fat so that it can just be poured,
that is, about the consistency of cold molasses. Pour it into soup
plates or, if larger quantities of flowers are to be processed, into bigger platters. The important point is that you must have duplicate
soup plates or platters, which, if placed upside down together, their
rims will engage so that there will be only a minimum of leakage.

While the fat is still soft enough, take a knife and score it, so that
it is ultimately criss-crossed with knife impressions to the depth of the
fat. You then have two (or twenty if you have enough flowers) soup
plates or platters coated on the inside with the scored fat. Allow this
to cool and become hard as it will. You are then, and only then, ready
to use the petals or flowers of your choice.

Place them as thickly as possible, but not more than two layers
deep on one of the fat-lined plates. Upon it, upside down, place the
other fat-lined plate. If they are approximately alike in dimensions,
the two edges ought to make a reasonably tight seal. If they are not
really sealed (that is, if their touching edges permit the escape of too
much flower fragrance), seal them with more fat or tire tape.

In about one or at most two days, nearly all the fragrance from the
flowers will have been absorbed by the fat. The container then

should be opened and a new lot of fresh flowers be put in, with the same precautions to prevent leakage of scent. Repeat the process three or four times, or until it is obvious that the fat has absorbed all the odor it can stand. You are then ready for the next stage of enfleurage.

Remove all the fragrance-impregnated fat from the plates, and chop it up into fine pieces (pea size or smaller). Place them into well-corked or stoppered bottles in the proportion of one half chopped-up fat to one half 90 per cent alcohol by volume. Put the bottle in a dark closet and thoroughly shake it as often as convenient for a period of at least three months. Then strain off the flower-scented alcohol, not with the idea that this is your finished perfume, for it is not. It is only ready for the final stage of the operation.

You are now at the most critical stage of the whole process. Alcohol, being extremely volatile, will if left uncorked evaporate off all the scent it has captured from the fat. To prevent this, and to make your labor produce a first-rate amateur perfume, you must add a fixative. If you are of an experimental turn of mind, any one of several ingredients, none of which comes from your garden, will do.

The best fixatives for the home perfumer are oil of cedar and oil of sandalwood, both of which may be purchased from any good drug store. Whether you use one or the other, and the amount you use of either, will depend on what you want your finished product to smell like. Its initial odor, is, of course, the flower you selected, but both these wood oils have a distinct odor of their own. You can use one or the other, or a combination of both, but the object should be to put in just enough to counteract the volatility of the alcohol without masking the odor of the flowers. Only at this final stage can anyone guess at the right amount of oil of cedar or oil of sandalwood, for it depends on (1) condition of the fragrance when the flower was picked, (2) completely deodorizing the fat before use, and (3) how well it was shaken and stored. A little practice will settle the question. You now have your home-made perfume—except for what the French would consider its most important ingredients.

It should be clearly understood that the amateur perfumer can stop right here and have the fragrance of his choice bottled up in a perfectly acceptable perfume—in fact far better than the plethora of cheap, synthetic substitutes that flood the market. But our home-made product is still far from a blended perfume, and to add the necessary ingredients is both expensive and hazardous. These are civet, musk, and ambergris. We can exclude the last as being so expensive that it is safer to pay the price and buy a bottle of the fine products of France.

Musk and civet, both animal products, are relatively expensive, but they add greatly to any perfume. They can be purchased from dealers in minute amounts and are needed in almost microscopic proportions. The exact amounts only you can tell, for it depends upon the concentration of perfume you have been able to capture and whether it is of the *heavy* or *aromatic* type.

AN EASIER SUBSTITUTE

If all this seems a bit too much trouble and you are satisfied with a somewhat inferior substitute, there is still a way out for the amateur. It involves the same property of fats to absorb odors, but the perfumes made under the process to be noted presently are not as lasting as those prepared by enfleurage. The collection and preparation of the flowers are the same as before, but the operation is much simpler.

Get a good-sized stone or porcelain crock, preferably cylindrical, that is, with straight sides. Put in the bottom a pad of cotton-wool that is soaked in olive oil, or any substitute oil that is essentially odorless. Upon the oil-soaked pad spread a layer of flowers or petals (about three-quarter inch deep) and over them sprinkle a thin layer of common salt (not enough to cover them completely). Put in another oil-soaked pad, which, like the one below and above it, should just touch the sides of the crock. Put in another layer of flowers and salt, and continue the process until the jar is seven-eighths full.

Then press the mass of petals or flowers and oil-soaked pads as much as possible, and leave on the top layer a heavy stone or preferably a piece of lead cut to fit easily inside the crock. After pressing down as much as possible, and leaving the stone or lead to supplement your pressing, tie wax paper over the mouth of the crock and leave it alone, in the shade, for *only two days*.

At the end of the pressing period, open the crock and dump the contents into a porcelain wash basin over which has been stretched a large enough piece of muslin or cheesecloth so that its upturned corners will make a bag holding the entire contents of the crock—of course, suspended over the basin to catch the drops of the fragrant oil. In order to catch all of this oil, it is better to squeeze the bag until there is no more drip.

The basin will then contain your strained and fragrant oil, and in this comparatively simple process you have completed the preparation of your perfume. It will not be so good as that derived from home-made enfleurage, but is an acceptable substitute for it.

Perhaps the amateur perfumer is wondering why no mention has been made of rose water, and attar of roses, which some people prefer to call "otto of roses," although the term *attar* seems more appropriate, since it stems from a Persian word that means perfume, and it was originally from Persia and Arabia that the first attar of roses was produced. Avicenna, a learned Arab physician (A.D. 980-1037) seems to be the first who thought up the idea of *distilling* fragrance, at least three centuries before the distilling of wine to make brandy became common. He was also the first to tell us about coffee.

It is this distilling process which gives us attar of roses. And it takes 180-300 pounds of rose petals to make a single ounce of rose oil which is actually attar of roses. This purest of all rose scents, mostly made from the Damask rose and a variety of *Rosa alba*, is costly and is generally diluted with geranium (*Pelargonium*) and other fragrant leaf oils. In distilling the oil from rose petals there is a large liquid residue, and it is this which is marketed as rose water.

Distilling rose fragrance for attar, and its by-product of rose water is a highly expert job, especially in Bulgaria and France where most of it is produced. Equipment for it is expensive, the amount of petals needed is tremendous, and all this, plus the necessary skills involved, makes attar of roses and rose water a bit impractical for the amateur enthusiast. There are several so-called rose waters concocted by steeping fresh rose petals in wine or alcohol, or by simmering in water, but they are generally rather weak-scented and not worth keeping, for they quickly lose their odor. Oil of rose is precious and gives up its fragrance only to the initiated. Fortunately, however, the oil is not all lost as the petals dry out, which brings us to the preservation of fragrance from dead rose petals and our last chapter.

Potpourri and
How to Make It

Hundreds of years before America bestowed the fragrance of tobacco smoke upon the Old World, the Europeans had discovered that burning fragrant woods and gums was so pleasurable that not only were ordinary houses fragrant with such smoke, but it was used in their temples. No one smoked pipes, for they were unknown before Columbus, but the ancients developed to a high art the practise of inhaling the fragrant smoke of myrrh and frankincense, burned in braziers. And it was apparently the Jews who bequeathed incense to the Roman Church, which to this day makes their ritual a perfumed rapture to the faithful.

Incense, however, was not always so exalted. It figures in many bacchanalian scenes, for, with various scent pots and sachets, it was an easy way to store and use, when wanted, the fragrance in flowers and many other odorous products of the plant and animal world. Smoke seemed to enhance the enchantment of fragrance, especially before the discovery of distillation of perfumes, which did not come until early in the Tenth Century.

Ever since the days of the Greeks, Romans, and Persians, we have sought various ways of holding the dried fragrance of flowers, usually mixed with other things, without burning them. It is this search that has bequeathed us the potpourri. As here understood it will be confined to the capture of rose scent, which is the easiest and most satisfactory, because rose petals hold some of the fragrant oil in their dried petals, although not much.

One rather critical Englishman sniffs at all potpourris just because of the failure of dried rose petals to hold all the fragrance of the fresh flower. A potpourri today, and always in the past, has many other things added to it to enhance or sometimes even mask what should be the predominant odor of the rose. Because the petals do not hold all their fragrance when dry, it is essential to start with only the most fragrant sorts.

Of these the Damask and Provence roses are, by all means, the best. Of the latter there is a variety known as the Apothecary's Rose (*Rosa gallica officinalis*) which is strongly favored by some writers in England where they are especially proficient in the making of potpourri. That variety is all but unknown in this country, so we must fall back on two of the most fragrant of the old-fashioned roses, the Damask and Provence or, as some call it, the French rose. If none of these is available, choose any of the deep red varieties of hybrid perpetual roses listed among the two dozen kinds found in Section 5 of Chapter Two.

A word now as to the amount of rose petals that is necessary, even for a small potpourri of at least one gallon, as it is useless to go to all the trouble for less than this. You will need, but not necessarily all at once, approximately two gallons of fresh rose petals for the moist variety of potpourri and over twice that amount for the dry method. The latter is easier but not so satisfactory.

For both methods the picking of the flowers is the same, and only roses that are nearly or quite fully open should be chosen—none that have passed their prime. Even more important is the time of day. As all are to be fully or partly dried, and as rapidly as possible, the flowers should never be picked when there is any dew clinging to them, and never for at least a day after the last rain, as the petals hold considerable water for longer than one would suspect. Afternoon picking is the best. As the subsequent handling of the flowers is quite different, the details will be deferred until the dry and moist methods are noted specifically.

The purpose of both is the same, and both should be made in very different containers from those ultimately used to perfume a room. The containers are works of art, especially in France and England—often of china, but many of rare woods, or even of gold and silver. All of the better sort should have a double top, the upper one to screw down tight and keep the fragrance in when not wanted, the lower one with holes or criss-crossed open bars to permit the contents to scent the room.

The containers for making the potpourri must be much stouter than this, for their contents will have to be stirred and sometimes rammed, and some of the ingredients, at least in the moist method, will stain. The most practical type of container is the straight-sided crock, such as our ancestors used for butter or cookies, and it must have a fairly tight-fitting crock top. It is quite useless to use any sort of absorbent container such as unbaked clay, as the inner surface must be glazed. Do not use any metal or enamelled container. Also, before starting, provide yourself with a round, heavy stone (8-10 pounds) or a flat piece of lead that will fit the container like a loose piston-head. This will be needed only for the moist method. You will also need a stout, rounded stick to pound down the petals—a rolling pin, with one handle sawn off will do. Also a stout, wooden spoon should be available. Be careful not to use any metal utensils.

DRY POTPOURRI

The ordinary potpourri of the shops is likely to be merely some dried rose petals to which perfume, usually synthetic, has been added. If one is satisfied with such a concoction, there is no use of going to the trouble of making your own—for even the dry potpourri does take time. Also it should be understood that, although much better than the usual store product, it is not as good as the one made by the more difficult moist method.

As the predominant odor is to be rose, the major part of the jar should be filled with dried rose petals—and they should be perfectly dry. To see that they are dried as quickly as possible, spread the petals on cheesecloth-covered frames so arranged that there is a good circulation of air above and below. Lacking such frames, the petals may be spread thickly on clean, unprinted paper. It is absolutely essential that only the petals are used; all green parts of the flower, stem, etc., will only invite the musty odor of decay.

A foggy or humid day is to be avoided, since the object is to dry the petals thoroughly as quickly as possible; in the sun or in a warm, dry room that should not take more than 24-36 hours. If you do not have enough dried rose petals nearly to fill the gallon crock, store some in the crock for a few days until you have accumulated enough.

Before you begin the mixing of your potpourri, there are some other plants from your garden that should also be picked and dried. Leaves, flower clusters, and herbage generally should have been gathered of any of the following: balm, mint, rosemary, lavender, etc. Or, if you fancy it, any other fragrant leaves such as geranium (*Pelargonium*), verbena, lemon verbena, carnations, etc. How you use these will depend upon your taste in odors, especially how much you want to mask the predominant rose scent. It must be confessed

that perfectly dried rose petals do not preserve much of the odor of
the fresh flowers—hence the desirability of having the dried leaves of
the herbs and also the last ingredients that you must have before you
start mixing.

Assuming that you will be starting with about three quarts of dried
rose petals (the extra quart will be taken up with the dried leaves
mentioned above), you will also need the following ingredients, all
of which can be purchased from any good drug or department store.

⅓ ounce of each of the following:
   Powdered mace, cloves, cinnamon and allspice.
⅕ ounce of each of the following:
   Crushed coriander seeds, crushed cardamon seeds.
   Powdered gum storax, powdered gum benzoin.
In addition to these you will need considerable common salt. Some pre-
   fer to use sea salt and common salt mixed half and half, but, if sea
   salt is hard to come by, the common kitchen variety will do.

You are now equipped to mix the potpourri. This is done by putting layers of dried flower petals, leaves, etc., at the bottom of the
crock, sprinkling each layer with a little salt and a pinch or two of
your ground and mixed spices. Keep on repeating the process—
alternate layers of petals, salt, and spices until the crock is filled.
Some then prefer to sprinkle about a third of an ounce of brandy
over the mixture. Put the top on and leave it for about two weeks.
Then give the mixture a thorough stirring, replace the top and stir it
at weekly intervals for at least two months. It is then ready to be put
in any ornate container, a bit at a time, keeping the stock mixture
closely covered.

It must be confessed that such a potpourri, which has been made
for centuries by devoted enthusiasts, somewhat justifies the skepticism of that Englishman who wondered whether we liked the odor
of spices and herbs better than the rose. Dozens of variations of this
recipe from Sir Kenelm Digby's (1603-1665) down to the most recent
"discovery" at last week's meeting of the garden club have been published. All of them, if following the dry method, suffer from the fundamental and inescapable fact that rose petals lose far too much
fragrance when dry.

Some modern, and quite a few old recipes, admit that dried rose
petals are not enough, and to the ingredients already noted they
would add small amounts of bay leaves, orange or jasmine blossoms,
civet, musk, and even attar of roses! This seems a confession that the
dry potpourri with a base of rose petals is very far from providing the
bewitching odors of fresh flowers.

MOIST POTPOURRI

The advocates of this method are likely to be a bit scornful of whatever variation of the dry method you favor. They point out, with unimpeachable truth, that too much of the fragrant oil in rose petals is lost by the complete drying necessary for that process. Hence the moist method, which involves only *partial* drying out of the petals, seems to be preferred. The flowers are picked just as in the dry method, but the plucked, fresh petals are managed so that they hold a good deal more of their fragrance.

The object in the moist method is to dry the rose petals only just enough so that they will have lost about half of their juice by evaporation, without losing at the same time too much of the precious fragrant oil. How to tell this? There is no accurate way to do so, but experience does tell us that they are about half dry when the total *bulk* of the collected petals has been reduced by one half.

To the question "Why not reduce the moisture by artificial heat, under controlled conditions?"—the best answer is provided by Nature. Gradual drying in the shade, and preferably out of the wind, will drive off enough moisture without rapid dissipation of fragrance. Any artificial heat would certainly dissipate the fragrance in a few hours. Generally, with average outdoor drying conditions, the petals should be dry enough to use in two days. A good place to dry them would be on a sheet placed where neither rain nor sunshine can hit it. The petals should be about half their size and feel flabby in two days or less if the humidity is low. Only experience will tell you when the petals have reached the right degree of dryness, for petals vary among themselves, especially the water content of different species.

The important thing is to make a decision as to when they are ready and then to act at once. Put a layer of the half dry petals in the bottom of your crock and sprinkle liberally, but do not cover, with salt. Ram and press down the layer, and keep on putting alternate layers of salt and petals until you have used up the current supply. Ram them all down and weight them down with the stone or piece of lead. Leave them alone until you have another supply of half-dried petals. These may be added every few days, being careful about ramming and the weight. Such a well-stuffed crock can be left all summer, with the lid on, and there will be no danger of spoiling if the rose petals are clean of stems, leaves, etc., and there has been a liberal use of salt. Sometimes, if the petals were not quite dry enough, there will be a small accumulation of liquid at the bottom of the crock, and this should be poured away.

In the meantime you should have been getting together the other ingredients that come from the garden, as well as those from more remote sources. For this you will need another crock, about one-half the size of the one in which the rose petals are brewing. Into this put alternate layers of sweet-smelling herbs and salt, just as with the rose petals, but being careful to see that the leaves, herbage, etc., of thyme, balm, rosemary, geranium, basil, verbena, or whatever fragrant materials you gather is only about one-half dry when put into the crock.

The herbs, with a sprinkling of salt between each layer, will ultimately fill the crock, but while they may be pressed down moderately they must not be rammed tight for the good reason that in between each layer of herbs there is another ingredient to be put in that will not stand ramming. This is orange peel.

If you are fortunate enough to be able to get fresh Seville or bitter oranges (possible only in California and Florida), peel them and cut the rind into strips. While still fresh, stud the outer side of each strip with as many cloves as you can, the shanks pricked into the rind so plentifully that the bulbous tips of the cloves are practically touching. If Seville (which is merely another name for the bitter) oranges are not available, get any variety of the common, sweet orange that has a thick rind with plenty of citrus oil in it.

Between each layer of herbs, put a few strips of these clove-studded orange peels, and leave the crock closed until you are ready for the final mixing of your moist potpourri. If the mixture does not shrink down in the crock, as it should, with absorption of moisture by the salt, it is permissible to press it down *gently;* do not ram it. It should be stated perhaps that the salt can be, as in the dry method, half sea salt and half the common sort, or only the latter if sea salt is not available. Neither has any odor, nor do they enhance the odor of any ingredient. The only virtues of the salt, and they are cardinal, are that it is hygroscopic and hence absorbs some of the excess moisture from your materials, without dwindling its fragrance; it also prevents decay. The latter may be serious if you have not been careful about the correct amount of moisture in petals or herbs as they are finally put into the crocks.

With your two crocks brewing, one with rose petals and the other with fragrant herbs, you are now ready to start the final mixing of your moist potpourri and the stage must be set for this before either crock is opened and actual mixing can start. Both the crocks thus may have been brewing from rose-time to autumn, especially if you have waited for the petals of tuberose which some put into the herb pot to make the final mixture a bit more alluring than most potpourris were ever meant to be. After all, the potpourri is an old invention, mostly for the stylized, aristocratic life of the seventeenth, eighteenth, and nineteenth centuries. But there is no law against making them as seductive as the Greeks and Romans made their sachets or incense.

To finish the job, whether your mixture is elegantly scented or frankly has a touch of what disturbed Socrates twenty-four centuries ago, you must collect and prepare rather carefully the following:

> 1 ounce of each of the following, finely ground: cloves, mace, allspice, and orris root.
> 1 ounce of whole mace and whole cloves.
> 2 ounces of gum benzoin, well pounded.
> 2 ounces of gum storax, well pounded.

Thoroughly mix all the powdered material in a basin, to which can be added the pounded benzoin and storax, which should also be thoroughly mixed with the spices. Keep in a separate dish the whole mace and cloves. It is permissible, if you are affluent, to add to the basin of powdered spices a minute amount (just a pinch or two) of civet, musk, or ambergris, all of them animal products and far more expensive than all the rest of the ingredients combined. Some, also, put in the shavings or sawdust of sandalwood, but these, too, are expensive and not always easy to come by. It is almost axiomatic that this mixture of fragrant spices should not be made until you are actually ready for the final stage of moist potpourri.

By this time the contents of both crocks should have shrunk by about one half, the rose crock, from pounding and the weight, by even more than this. It will also be packed enough so that it needs a stout fork to loosen it up.

Use a large sheet of clean, unprinted paper or a sheet upon which to mix the ingredients, or it can be done on a clean kitchen table (wood or plastic). The mixing should not be hurried, for it involves not only thorough blending of the ingredients, but also a final period of exposure to the air (to reduce some residual moisture) before packing it away for ultimate use.

To ensure a complete mixture of the four ingredients (rose, herbs, ground spices, and whole ones), take 3 cups of rose and spread upon the mixing table, add 1 cup of the herb mixture, spread as evenly as possible. Over this sprinkle a little of the spice mixture, and add at random a few whole mace and cloves. Keep on doing this until all the crocks and basins are empty and you have stratified layers of rose, herbs, spices, etc. Then the whole mass must be mixed with the greatest of care, either by shovelling it first in one direction and then in another, or better yet with your two hands. It is impossible to mix it too much, after which it should be rammed back into the larger crock, or, if there is any left over, into the smaller one. Both should be well covered (not air-tight) and stood in a cool, dry place. Avoid the heat and dryness of an ordinary steamheated room—under the kitchen sink or in a cellar or garage will be ideal.

Some quite expert makers of potpourri prefer the final storage to be in a keg made of cedar or other fragrant wood, with a well-fitted head—not unlike the small, brass-bound kegs sold for keeping ice cubes. The only real argument for these is that, if used year after year, they absorb and hold some of the fragrance of their contents, and perhaps impart to future ingredients the aroma of the past.

It is the fragrance of May and June, of rose-time, lavender-time and thyme-time, with all the other garden scents, which we seek to capture in a potpourri. Let no one ever think that any potpourri, no matter how carefully made, is better than the fresh flowers, but it does raise grateful memories of them on winter evenings, when flowers are scarce and we crave a breath of what Shakespeare called "a strange, invisible perfume"—for a potpourri is just that, hidden in its magic container.

SACHETS

The material for these scented favorites of the wardrobe are usually artificially blended, scented powders, with all the handicaps as to odor and lasting quality that accrue from such products. Herb gardeners and those devoted to fragrance in the garden can easily make better ones at home.

In making a potpourri, whether you use the dry or moist method, your end-product has captured the fragrance of the garden in at least a semi-permanent form. It is this fragrance that you need in a sachet, which is merely a powdered form of potpourri's material put in whatever container you choose, which, of course, must be porous enough to release the scent.

Other combinations can be made by slowly drying the leaves of lavender, rose-geranium, sage, thyme, rosemary and any other of the fragrant-leaved herbs, which are treated in Book Five, *Herbs in the Garden*. To the powdered leaves one can add pinches of such spices as ground allspice, cloves, cinnamon, or ginger to make whatever combination of fragrance you prefer.

Book Five

HERBS
IN
THE GARDEN

HERBS IN THE GARDEN

Since all the plants in this section are annuals, perennials, or low shrubs, there is no need to match the speed of spring with hasty planting. Herb gardeners can move most of their plants, with a little care in watering, almost any time, and the seeds of annuals can be planted whenever there is a reasonable hope of maturity before autumn frosts.

This gives one time for selection, and it is urged that you read Chapter One before deciding what to plant and where to plant it. You can then decide how many annuals or biennials you have room for, and these are all included in Chapter Two, arranged alphabetically under their common names.

In Chapter Three the perennial herbs, which comprise most of the plants in the book, are similarly treated alphabetically for convenience of reference. If you do not know whether the plant is an annual, biennial, or perennial, the index at the end lists all plants both by their common and Latin names. Also, at the beginning of Chapter Two there are definitions of the terms, *annual, biennial,* and *perennial,* with their horticultural implications.

Chapters Four and Five are self-explanatory. Some may wonder why there are no recipes, but that is the function of the cook book, while this one deals with culture. However, the relative frequency of use of the different herbs makes a difference in planning an herb garden. For this reason Chapter Five lists the chief uses of herbs for meats, vegetables, salads, cheeses, eggs, one-dish meals, rice, beverages, desserts, butter, and the vinegars.

Chapter One

Why We Need Them

It seems only yesterday that our grandmothers were saying that to be kissed by a man without a moustache was as insipid as roast lamb without mint sauce, cream cheese without chives, or a salad without leeks. No country in the world has failed to find among plants some essence or flavor that adds piquancy to dishes or even disguises the fact that, quite often, meat or fish, in the days before refrigeration, was often a bit high.

Long before our ancestors landed on that bleak New England shore, the Indians were gathering various aromatic herbs to spice their foods. The drab monotony of hominy they spiked with the native wild ginger, which was also used to kill the flavor of over-tired meat and fish.

The modern urge to grow herbs harks back to the days of the Greeks and Romans who well knew the virtues of rosemary and thyme. Much later, girls of Italy, where herbs are an essential in cookery, succumbed to the traditional lore that surrounds so many of our aromatic herbs. Basil, like the balm, was used not only for flavoring, but also for its heavy fragrance. Like so many perfumes, it became a symbol of love. Hence the placing of a vase of basil on the Italian girl's window-sill when she expected or hoped for her lover—immortalized in *The Pot of Basil.*

Today there are less romantic, and much more practical, reasons for growing herbs. The chemists have not yet been able to imitate the extraordinary galaxy of flavors and essences that Nature has scattered among some plants. We use them in cookery, as we do the tropical spices, because they supply piquancy to food, and sometimes whet the appetite of people whose taste has become jaded by the synthetic commonplaces of the market.

Botanists, however, are a little disturbed by the word "herb" as used by the gardener. To the latter *herb* is generally restricted to fragrant, culinary, medicinal, or other plants of special interest. But to the botanist (and he is right about this) an herb is any plant without a woody stem that dies down to the ground over the winter. To him this is the great distinction between herbs and all the woody plants like shrubs and trees which, instead of hiding their buds below ground during cold weather, leave them exposed on bare twigs.

Hereafter, in this book, the term *herb* will be used in the garden sense—not forgetting, however, that it is a restricted and somewhat vague one. Some heretics have even scoffed at herb gatherers as equally vague but benevolent old gentlemen with glasses, an umbrella, and the unquenchable optimism of the visionary who thinks all plants are good for something if we only knew what.

This optimism has led to some very old fallacies, and the literature of herb gardening is crammed with irrelevant plants once thought to be useful. Even some modern herb books are quite brazenly padded with species long since discredited—holdovers from the days when fearsome potions were brewed from herbs, insects, snakes, and other horrors, upon the theory that such foul concoctions were good for everything from the King's evil to stunting the growth of puppies. Some of these plants have come down to us, not because they yield remedies that are any good, but because around them has grown such a vintage of folklore that scarcely any "old-fashioned garden" would be entitled to the name without them. A few of these are included here, although they have no present medical use, nor are they particularly fragrant, and are of little or no use as culinary herbs. Their inclusion is our last gesture to the past, for really useful herbs are as modern as science.

Historically herbs were grown only for three qualities—fragrance, medicine, or for what they added to cookery. The fragrant-leaved herbs we still treasure, and nearly all the rest of the plants in this book are used in various recipes, but the medicinal herbs require a bit of sifting.

From the Greeks to the Middle Ages there was a vast literature on so-called medicinal plants. Hundreds of different sorts were grown, but scarcely a handful are admitted to the *U. S. Pharmacopoeia* or the *National Formulary,* which are the official repositories of the really useful medicinal plants of today. Growing poppy for morphine, foxglove for digitalis, cinchona for quinine, or monkshood for aconite, all highly important drugs, are specialized operations outside the scope of this book and generally beyond the knowledge of the amateur. Some simples and home-made tonics and teas everyone can make from herbs grown in any garden. But a *simple,* as the word implies, is scarcely a technical remedy, and we grow them today largely because gardeners seem loath to give up the traditions of the past when these storied herbs lined the borders of many old monasteries, the courts of the Saracens, and the gentle knot gardens of Elizabethan England.

A few of the herbs grown for two thousand years as containing "remedies" were ultimately found to have some scientific basis, and this has sometimes led to their indiscriminate culture. It should never be forgotten that growing herbs as a commercial source of drugs is extremely risky, for two excellent reasons. The amateur may be able to raise the herbs with apparent success only to find that the essential ingredient is so sparse as not to be worth extracting. Other people, especially in Europe and Asia Minor, with centuries of experience, a better climate, and carefully selected varieties grow these medicinal herbs better and more cheaply than we can.

Except for the herbs that all old-fashioned gardens grow for sentiment because they once yielded simples, the herb gardener of today specializes in the herbs with fragrant foliage or those which contain the ingredients that no chemist has ever yet imitated—mostly essential oils. It is these that everyone wants to grow, store, and use in a variety of recipes that mark the users of them as among the gastronomically elect.

As to the fragrance that comes from foliage, it is much more available and plentiful than flower fragrance,* and hence more useful, but it never approaches the ravishing odors of jasmine or tuberose. But, as we shall see later, these herbs with fragrant foliage are a boon to the housewife, for their odor may last for years.

---

* Fragrance from flowers, and the perfume and potpourri which the amateur can make for himself, are treated in a companion book of this Garden Guide entitled *Fragrance in the Garden.*

WHERE TO GROW THEM

One beauty of an herb garden is that it can be grown in a small space. Of some varieties you may need only a plant or two because their essence is too strong to be used in any but minute quantities. The average suburban garden will often have all the space one needs for a fairly good showing of herbs, and one must not think he is "sacrificing" space for herbs, because some of them have quite striking flowers. Foliage, roots, and seeds, however, are the main harvest, for it is in these that nature manufactures the fragrant or spicy oils.

Nearly all the herbs need open sunshine, except where especially noted, and hence it is not wise to start an herb garden on the north side of a building or under trees. Some of the herbs, also especially noted, are tender anywhere north of New York, and for these a south-facing slope is the ideal site. If you have a cold frame or hotbed, these are useful for starting seeds of some tender annuals, but a box on the kitchen window-sill will do almost as well.

In the Middle Ages herb gardens were always enclosed. In selecting a site for a modern one, it is well to choose (or make) a partially enclosed area, even with a wall or thick hedge for its boundary. The reason is obvious, for the old monastic gardeners knew that wind would carry off the fragrance of many herbs, because leaf fragrance, without crushing the leaf, is never so pungent as flower fragrance—hence the enclosed herb garden which, as one old writer put it, should be "a sanctuary of sweet and placid pleasure."

A word as to soil preferences. Plant physiologists have found that, within reason, the more difficult the conditions, the greater is the concentration of cell sap, and the more likely is the plant to be a little stunted. It is as though the plant resented the somewhat unfavorable environment, sets up its own defensive mechanism to overcome it, and, to the herb gardener, points an obvious lesson. It is this concentration of cell sap that increases the secretion of the very essences for which we grow them. Also such plants never make weedy and lush growth, which is also what we want to avoid. The implications of this highly complex reaction are, however, quite simple to the herb gardener—avoid heavily manured soil. This does not mean that the soil should be stony, full of ashes, or caked dry in summer. It does mean that most ordinary garden soil will do for herbs. And, except for one or two notable exceptions, which will be mentioned where necessary, the herb garden needs no manure or fertilizer.

The principle upon which this works is one of the reasons why the partly arid Mediterranean region grows so many medicinal plants far better than we. And in our American herb gardens we can, for once, stop preaching about rich soil and the necessity to make it richer, and not be too afraid if summer drought overtakes us as it surely will. In order to prevent too lush a growth the herb garden, when once established, should need no sprinkling (except in desert regions). Of course, young plants just set out should be watered if necessary, like any others, but on the whole the herb gardener should always keep in mind that flavor and fragrance in leaves, seeds, herbage, etc., is most likely to be promoted by a relatively indifferent soil and not too much moisture.

This applies both to the herbs grown chiefly for their fragrant foliage and to that larger and more important group used only for their culinary value. Many hasty cooks, with the modern availability of tropical spices from all over the world, forget that this was not always true. Even the rich in the Middle Ages, and down to Elizabethan England, lacked many spices we now consider as a commonplace. But their tastes were often superior to ours, and they had the advantage of turning to the first-hand knowledge of the monasteries and to the Arabs to spike the insipidity of many foods. This was nearly always done with herbs, just as it is today by that group of gardeners who are among the cognoscenti.

To meet the growing demand for herbs in cookery there are today many commercial firms who advertise them, packaged like spices, ready to use. Some of the products are excellent, but your herb gardener will always want to grow his own, not only for freshness but to be sure that no commercial exploitation has adulterated the mixture. Then, too, some herbs are useful only in the green state. For the cook who demands green herbs, the garden is usually her only resource—unless she lives near an Italian market where quite a few herbs are brought in from the country still fresh and ready to flavor soups, cheeses, and other delectable dainties.

The reflective herb gardener must often wonder at the comparative rarity of plants useful for fragrance or flavor among the huge complex of the plant world. Of the thousands of garden plants grown in America, for food, color, fibers, gums, and many other uses, only a handful are herbs in the restricted sense—that is, savory, fragrant, or yielding what our ancestors called simples. Even more strange is the fact that herbs are not quite wholly, but overwhelmingly, confined to only five plant families. In the order of their importance to the herb gardener these are: (1) Parsley family (Umbelliferae); (2) Mint family (Labiatae); (3) Aster family (Compositae); (4)

Lily family (Liliaceae); and (5) Mustard family (Cruciferae). These botanical families all contain thousands of species, and the enquiring gardener may often wish to explore the possibility of flavors found among the relatives of the plants admitted into this book. For that reason, the plant family of all the plants will be specified. No one, except the most inquisitive of herb gardeners, needs to know the plant family to which his favorite herb belongs, but to those looking to expand the scope of savory herbs it will be a useful guide.

The plant families containing herbs, and the chief ones found in each, are the following:

1. PARSLEY FAMILY (Umbelliferae). An enormous family of plants containing such common vegetables as celery (also an herb), carrot and parsnip, and the beautiful little blue laceflower of the florists' shops. Its flowers are usually minute but grouped in large clusters (umbels), a familiar example being the common, weedy Queen Anne's Lace.

Many plants in it are poisonous, such as the deadly hemlock used to kill Socrates, but many others contain valuable essences much prized by cooks. Among the better known herbs are anise, caraway, celery, chervil, coriander, cumin, dill, the fennels, lovage, parsley, and sweet cicely. We prize them mostly for the flavorful oils secreted in their seeds or herbage.

2. MINT FAMILY (Labiatae). Of over 3,000 species of herbaceous plants, as well as many shrubs and trees in the tropics, only a few are classed as herbs for fragrance or savor, although there is scarcely one of the three thousand that is not aromatic from the oil secreted in their leaves. They have usually small, irregular flowers in often close clusters, generally opposite leaves and a stem square in cross-section. The commonest garden plant is the scarlet salvia, so much grown for bedding and edging. Among the chief herbs in the mint family are balm, basil, catnip, horehound, lavender, the marjorams, mints, rosemary, sage, savory, and thyme.

3. ASTER FAMILY (Compositae). The largest family of plants in the world, comprising over 12,000 species, but only a few are of any interest as herbs. They have daisy-like flowers with ray-like "petals," as in the Shasta daisy, dandelion, and many others, or there are no rays such as in the common garden ageratum. The few herbs in this huge group are useful because of the savory or aromatic oils secreted in their foliage or flowers. The chief herbs are the camomiles, costmary, dandelion, marigolds, mugwort, old woman, south-

ernwood, tansy, tarragon, and wormwood. No doubt many others could be rescued from their obscurity by the enquiring herb gardener, but some care should be used as a few *Compositae* are poisonous.

4. LILY FAMILY (Liliaceae). There are over 2,000 species in this overwhelmingly herbaceous family which includes familiar garden plants, besides the lily itself, such as the asparagus, tulip, lily-of-the-valley, and the well-known dracaena so popular as a house plant. The family is singularly lacking in herbs, but the few are important for they include the onion, chives, leek, shallot, garlic, and the rocambole.

5. MUSTARD FAMILY (Cruciferae). Generally bitter-foliaged but never poisonous plants, comprising nearly 2,000 species, all of which have four petals arranged cross-fashion, hence the name Cruciferae, derived from the crucifer who marched about ancient monastery gardens, heading a procession of monks who sprinkled with holy water many of the species in this book. Not many of the Cruciferae are classed as herbs, and some herb enthusiasts look on them as of only incidental importance. But their pleasant, bitter essence makes them reasonable candidates for inclusion here, especially horse-radish, the mustards, rocket salad, and the watercress.

Of the other families of plants that yield things of interest to the herb gardener, there are a few that would repay the enquiring herb gardener to explore beyond the limit of this book. The plants belonging to them will be listed at the proper place, but, for reference these possibly hopeful sources of other herbs are included in the following families*

Boraginaceae	Borage family
Iridaceae	Iris family
Rosaceae	Rose family
Rubiaceae	Madder family
Rutaceae	Rue family
Solanaceae	Potato family
Verbenaceae	Verbena family

Quite apart from the families of plants into which the botanists have sorted herbs is the wonderful alchemy of nature in producing the fragrance and savories distilled mostly in their foliage, seeds, and roots. No one has ever discovered of what use these fragrant oils and

* In *Taylor's Encyclopedia of Gardening* will be found a full description of all plant families together with a list of all commonly cultivated plants in each family.

essences are to the plant, for many closely related species are without them but still survive. To the easy assertion that pungent odors repel browsing cattle, there is the obvious answer that many quite scentless plants have been able to overcome such an assumed handicap.

For the herb gardener what matters more than a dubious explanation of the secretion of these precious fragrant oils is what we do with them and how to grow the plants that produce them.

There is no doubt that in the Middle Ages and before, when some of our usual garden vegetables were uncommon, herbs provided vitamins for a too-heavy meat diet and, until the discovery of America which gave Europe the potato, sweet potato, corn, tomato, pineapple, peanut, and dozens of other fruits and vegetables, herbs supplied a piquancy to a rather restricted and often dull diet. Some of the very earliest herb gardeners realized this, especially John Evelyn, who carried herb gardening to such great heights that he had little patience with amateur dabblers. Writing in 1699, this prominent member of the Royal Society had this to say: "I can by no means approve of the extravagant fancy of some, who tell us a fool is as fit to be the gatherer of Sallets (salads) as a wise man." And, after pointing out what skill and judgment it really takes, he warns the herb gatherer to choose the materials "not only so as to agree with the Humours of those who eat them, but so that nothing should be suffered to domineer, so should none of them lose their Gust (relish), Savour or Vertue."

Modern herb growers have much to learn from these old writers, for they evolved recipes and used herbs in a period when so many modern aids to flavor were all but unknown or, if known at all, available only to the rich and powerful. From them have come many recipes, but it should be emphasized that piquancy, zest, and what Evelyn called "Gust, Savour and Vertue" are still the main reasons for having an herb garden. No modern chemist has ever made an artificial flavor that compares with the real thing, which is yours if you will grow the plants and, as Evelyn said, use them with skill and judgment.

Today there are more cogent reasons for using herbs than in 1699. The high price of choice cuts of meat forces many thrifty housewives to use cheaper and potentially less palatable ones. For these, various sauces and seasonings made with herbs help enormously to disguise the essential insipidity of many foods, and they have another use that must appeal to anyone anxious to stretch the kitchen budget. In the old days there were many recipes for working various herbs into butter, making it far more tasty than the raw product. Today one can do the same thing with colored oleomargarine, which is already legal in many states and soon may be in all of them. The prejudice against this wholesome product is wholly unwarranted, and the *Journal of the American Medical Association* says that its food value is the same, and even a bit superior, to animal butter. For those whose diet restricts the eating of animal fats, the vegetable oils in oleomargarine are, in fact, a boon, and it can be made even more palatable by using herbs to enhance its flavor.

It will also be found that recipes for rice, nearly all meats, fish, eggs, cheese, and various beverages are more tasty if herbs are used than they would be without them. Think, too, of the delectable soups devised by clever French and Italian cooks, many of whom used herbs centuries before the discovery of America. Our ancestors who landed in New England and at Jamestown soon introduced many of these herbs. The Spaniards in Latin America were even more inventive, for they may have been the first to find such highly flavorable plants as the hot, red peppers (tabasco sauce) and the vanilla, both of which had wide use by the Aztecs, but were unknown before the Conquest.

In the chapters that follow various plants and seeds will be mentioned, some of which cannot always be purchased from roadside stands and even from fairly large nurseries that do not specialize in herbs. To save much time and many disappointments the leading dealers in plants and seeds of herbs are listed alphabetically, chosen geographically for the convenience of widely scattered herb gardeners. It should be remembered that many of the commoner herbs are widely available, but the list below will give a possible source for some items not in general catalogs.

HERB GARDEN DEALERS

George D. Aiken, Putney, Vermont
Armstrong Nurseries, Ontario, California
Greene Herb Gardens, Greene, Rhode Island
Henry Kohankie and Son, Painesville, Ohio
* Laurel Hill Herb Farm, Falls Village, Connecticut
* George W. Park Seed Company, Greenwood, South Carolina
* Rex D. Pearce, Moorestown, New Jersey
Pellett Gardens, Atlantic, Iowa
* Carl Starker Gardens, Jennings Lodge, Oregon

* Seeds only.

The Potters of Baraboo, Baraboo, Wisconsin
Tool Shed Herb Nursery, Salem Center, New York
Village Hill Nursery, Williamsburg, Massachusetts
Wayside Gardens, Mentor, Ohio and Glen Head, Long Island, New York

In the lists to follow the annuals and biennials are best purchased from those who deal only in seeds, although some of the firms offer young seedlings each season for those who do not want to raise their own. All the perennials and shrubs, must come from the dealers in plants, unless you raise your own from seeds, as outlined at the end of Chapter Three.

Chapter Two

Annual and Biennial Herbs
(or best grown as such)

In choosing these one is constantly confronted with the decision of what is an "herb," and when does an herb become a savory vegetable or salad plant. Peppers, celery, the orach, and spinach might be classed as annual herbs, salad plants, or seasonings; the celery has quite certainly a double role— its delicious stalks and its aromatic seeds widely used for flavoring as celery salt.

The twenty-five plants selected for inclusion in this chapter are all annuals, tender annuals, or biennials or perennials best treated as annuals. To save confusion it is better at the outset to define these terms and give general directions as to how each group should be grown, reserving for the individual species any special directions as to culture. Wherever in the list to be given these terms are used, they mean and should be grown in accordance with the following:

1.   ANNUAL. A plant living but a single growing season, flowering and fruiting during the summer and fall, and dying when this is accomplished. Their sole means of perpetuation is by their seeds, which may be self-sown, but it is safer to buy fresh seed each year or save your own. The seeds of annuals should be sown where

wanted after the danger from frost is over and usually thinned out
so that the plants are not too crowded.

2.   TENDER ANNUAL. A plant, often of tropical or subtropical origin,
        which usually will not mature in the North without special
handling—like the tomato. They are true annuals, but their seeds
must be started six to eight weeks before you can safely put the
young seedlings outdoors, that is, after settled, warm weather has
arrived. Plant seeds in flats, pots, or boxes in the greenhouse or hotbed, or, lacking these, in a box on the kitchen window-sill (no es-
caping gas!). Thin out the young seedlings and grow them along
until ready for outdoor planting. Handled carefully such seedlings
of tender annuals can easily be transplanted to the open in late May
or early June in most regions—earlier than this in the area south of
Washington, D.C.

3.   BIENNIAL. A plant that lives only two years, and generally a
        headache to most gardeners. It sprouts from seed the first sea-
son, but usually does not flower or fruit until the second, after which
it dies. Many experienced gardeners sow seeds of biennials every
year to save the trouble and uncertainty of wondering when they
must be planted in order to survive permanently. Seeds of biennials
should be planted where wanted. Fortunately biennials are rare, but
caraway and parsley are among them.

4.   PERENNIALS. The true perennials, treated in the next chapter,
        live more or less indefinitely, coming up each spring from un-
derground bulbs, roots, or rootstocks (underground stems). But a
few herbs are somewhat ephemeral perennials and have a bad habit
of dying off. Their treatment, in the list below, will be specially
noted, but generally such weak-willed perennials must be perpetu-
ated by seeds or cuttings.

In the list that follows the plants are arranged alphabetically by
their best-known common name, followed by their Latin name as
this is often essential for sure identification. The family to which
each belongs will also be noted for those who wish to explore related plants for additional savours or essences. See Chapter One for
a brief account of the chief plant *families* that contain most of the
useful herbs.

Anise (*Pimpinella anisum*)
Parsley Family
(Umbelliferae)

A strong-smelling annual from southern Europe, Egypt, and Asia Minor, well known to the Romans who put its aromatic seeds in a "seed-cake." More modern uses are by "fox" hunters, since their hounds follow, in lieu of a fox, the scent of an anise-seed bag, dragged over the ground.

The plant grows about two feet high, has much divided, toothed leaves, followed by yellowish-white, small flowers. The seed* is highly aromatic and, of course, anise-scented, as is the foliage which is less so. The aroma is so strong that only a very little of the leaves and still less of the crushed seeds can be used without overpowering other flavors. It is very valuable in cottage and bland cheeses, and an anise-seed tea was a favorite two centuries ago.

Anise is one of the best examples of why it pays to grow your own herbs. Because of the medicinal value of the oil extracted from its seeds, many commercial supplies, coming from all over the world are often adulterated with caraway seeds, fine gravel, colored like anise seeds, or coriander. The oil is largely used as a flavoring agent in medicines meant for children, who like it even more than grown-ups. It is one of our oldest and most potent aromatics.

For the ordinary family a row 6-8 feet long would be ample for harvesting leaves for salad and collecting the seeds for cookies, cakes, etc. The seeds should be collected in the late fall, cleaned, and put in tight containers for later use. The oil from the seeds is used for flavoring absinthe and anisette.

Basil (Ocimum basilicum)
Mint Family
(Labiatae)

This annual herb from the Old World tropics is often called Sweet Basil, and is a bushy plant with yellowish-green or often purplish leaves that glisten with the fragrant oil drops which drove Keats to write his exquisite poem, "The Pot of Basil." The odor and, hence, flavor of the dried or fresh leaves are somewhat anise-like, mixed with a dash of spice, liquorice, and lemon. It is this that makes basil such a famous ingredient of French and Italian cookery. Only its foliage is useful, and because it is highly aromatic only a row 4-6 feet long will be needed for the average family. Like all strong-smelling herbs it must be used with discretion, but so used it supplies one of our best herb ingredients for salads, egg or tomato dishes,

---

* Actually, in most plants of this family, the "seed" is the true fruit, but commonly and here called a seed to avoid confusion.

and for many fish and innumerable meat delicacies. It can be used fresh at any time, but most of it will be stored for later use.

When the small white or purplish-tinted flowers are open (late July or August), cut the foliage down to 6-8 inches above the ground, and the plant will put out a new lot of leaves, often after a second or third cutting. Freshly cut leaves should immediately be dried* and the leaves and flower clusters stored in tight containers, but avoid putting in the stems.

Sow the seeds about 1 to 1½ inches apart in the row, and usually the plants will not need a thinning out. There is a lower, more woody and perennial form of this (*Ocimum mininum*), the so-called bush basil, but it is little known here.

Borage (*Borago officinalis*)
Borage Family
(Boraginaceae)

A Mediterranean, rather weedy annual, 1-2 feet high, the beautiful, showy, blue flowers bloom in midsummer. It is not highly regarded by some herbalists, but ibn-al-Baytar, an Arab botanist who lived in Spain in the thirteenth century, thought that the flowers and young leaves in wine "made one jolly" and were supposed to have medicinal qualities, but modern experts call them "feeble." The only reason for including it here is that the tender tops make a little-known flavor for salads, and a few sprigs give an undeniable odor to a claret cup.

Like its close relatives the anchusas, borage is a bristly-hairy herb, the bruised foliage of which suggests the flavor of a mild cucumber. It is easily grown from seed, and a succession should be sown if a continuous supply of the tender terminal foliage and flowers is wanted.

Caraway (*Carum carvi*)
Parsley Family
(Umbelliferae)

With caraway seeds common in every food shop, one wonders why herbalists go to the trouble of growing this biennial plant with its fine thread-like leaves. The only answer is adulteration of commercial sources and the freshness of your own. And adulteration is no figment of the purists, for commercial dealers are warned against

---

* To save needless repetition the drying of foliage of all herbs will be found in Chapter Four.

"large amounts of stems, gravel, sand, dust, weed seeds, and other impurities."

It is a native of Europe and Asia and much loved by the Germans where its oil is the chief flavoring agent of kümmel, one of their favorite liqueurs. And who, as a child, does not cherish fragrant memories of buns, cake, and even bread with plentiful supplies of caraway seeds that were eagerly crunched for the delectable flavor of the oil?

Like several other seeds of the parsley family, caraway seeds are slow to germinate. They should be sown in the spring and allowed to grow all season, but will not bloom nor set seed until the second summer. Generally it prefers a cool climate and hence it is not wise to grow it in the South. During the second summer it will set seed, which should be collected as soon as they have turned brown. Cut the fruiting clusters and dry them thoroughly before picking out the seeds which, after cleaning off bits of stems, leaves, etc., may be kept almost indefinitely in closed containers.

No other part of the plant is of any value except the seeds, and scarcely any cook needs to be reminded of their use in cakes, cookies, cheese by the Dutch, and sauerkraut by the Germans. The plant grows 12-20 inches high and should be spaced about 3 inches apart in the row, which, for the average family need not be over 6 feet long.

Celery (*Apium graveolens dulce*)
Parsley Family
(Umbelliferae)

This salad vegetable, as usually grown for its stalks, is an annual that is never allowed to flower or set seed. As such it would have no place in this book, except that it is derived from a true biennial, and, if left alone and well protected over the winter and not blanched, will flower and fruit the second summer. It is better, however, to get special varieties from the seedsman which are most likely to produce seeds than ordinary blanched celery. Unlike most of the herbs, celery requires a deep, rich, and moist soil. Seeds may be sown directly in place, or it is often better to start them in flats or boxes and transplant them so as to be 4-6 inches apart in the row and the rows at least 25 inches apart. During the first winter they should be mulched with straw or light manure.

The second summer the flowering stalk will be 2-3 feet high, bearing at first many small, white flowers, and ultimately a great mass of seeds. These must be dried and cleaned and, when ground, are the chief ingredient of celery salt (the other is common salt). Celery is perhaps one of the minor herbs, but it does provide seeds which carry over the delicious odor and flavor of the fresh stalk. The plant likes a cool climate.

Chervil (*Anthriscus cerefolium*)
Parsley Family
(Umbelliferae)

This parsley-like annual is much grown by those who are a bit fed up with the ubiquitous parsley and want an herb of milder flavor. Its great use is in salads and it is thus often called salad chervil. Unlike most plants of the family, the seeds germinate readily and should be scattered in a shallow trench (¼ inch deep) not over 6-8 feet long. Chervil resembles parsley in growth and habit, its finely cut, almost lacelike leaves being the only part used in modern times, although Pliny thought that chervil seeds in vinegar would stop hiccough. But its greatest use is in salads, particularly in potato salad, and Pliny, who must have known some pretty ancient Romans, wrote that it was fine "to comfort the cold stomach of the aged." It is slightly anise-flavored, with a touch of a bitter principle like the tarragon.

The chervil, which should not be confused with the turnip-rooted chervil (a biennial vegetable), is a true annual, a native of Europe and Asia, and does better in the North than southward. In Maryland it grows splendidly under the speckled shade of a walnut tree, but northward it prefers full sunshine.

Clary (*Salvia sclarea*)
Mint Family
(Labiatae)

This Mediterranean biennial herb is not one of the really important plants to the herbalist of today since its medicinal virtues are mostly legendary and its foliage of decidedly secondary interest in cookery. However, the beautifully scented oil in its leaves, the clary sage oil of commerce, is used in perfumery and to make sachets. The odor and flavor of clary were once so prized that noted tavern keepers in London, in the seventeenth and eighteenth centuries, gave their avid patrons clary wine, fritters, soups, and heaven knows what other dishes long since obsolete.

Being a biennial, clary (closely related to the true sage which will be found in the next chapter) will not flower until the second season, but its leaves can be harvested at any time and the whole plant is delightfully fragrant—spicily so, as in sage. Unfortunately a good deal of the flavor is lost in cooking, which is probably the reason that clary is now almost a museum piece in most herb gardens. The youngest, and hence uppermost, leaves are those richest in oil.

Coriander (*Coriandrum sativum*)
Parsley Family
(Umbelliferae)

The foliage and unripe seeds of this annual herb smell so bad that they are variously likened to mice or bedbugs, which makes it hard to understand why we import over three million pounds of coriander seed each year. The answer, for the herb gardener, is the most curious fact that as the seeds dry they develop an odor and taste that has a whiff of orange, anise, and cumin. The plant resembles anise, but do not get the two mixed up, for the foliage of anise is delightful in salads, but coriander leaves would ruin anything.

Coriander seed should be planted about one half inch deep, and as the plants become somewhat bushy they are best spaced about 3 inches apart in the row, and the rows 2-3 feet apart. The leaves are thread-like in fineness, followed by minute white or rosy-white flowers, and, about 90 days from sowing, by the seeds. These must not be picked until they have turned distinctly brown, when the fruiting clusters should be cut and dried. If left too long on the plant, many seeds will be lost by shattering out. Keep the cleaned seeds in tightly stoppered bottles. The ordinary family will need only 6-8 feet of coriander.

Coriander is more often used with other herbs and spices than alone. However, the seeds can be added to French dressing and, like anise, used in flavoring cookies. They have no real medicinal value, but were once used to sprinkle over meat to keep it from spoiling. Its chief commercial use is as one of the innumerable ingredients of curry powder. Some modern cooks use coriander seeds to flavor meats, especially the Latin Americans. The flavor is best obtained by crushing the seeds in a mortar, as the ancients nearly always did.

Cumin (*Cuminum Cyminum*)
Parsley Family
(Umbelliferae)

So far as the modern herb gardener is concerned this weedy, little annual plant of the Mediterranean region might almost be ignored. It is, in fact, little grown here, but has been used since the days of Isaiah for a variety of fancied virtues. In the Middle Ages it was supposed to keep "lovers from being fickle," as well as keeping poultry

from straying. Today its greatest use is as an ingredient of curry
powder, while the ground seeds go into sausages, cheeses, and chili
sauce, and some very modern cooks are putting it in soup, meat, fish,
and rice recipes.

The plant needs a fairly long growing season and hence does better in the region south of Philadelphia. Sow the seeds as soon as the
ground is warm, and, as nothing except the seeds is wanted, it is only
necessary to keep it from being smothered by weeds, which is not
too easy as it only grows 4-6 inches high and its much dissected
leaves are thread-like. In the fall, when the seeds are brownish, the
plants should be pulled up, thoroughly dried, and the cleaned seeds
stored in tight containers. They have a bitterish, balsam-like taste.

Dill (Anethum graveolens)
Parsley Family
(Umbelliferae)

Dill pickles would scarcely be pickles without the seeds of this
annual herb from the Mediterranean region, now grown on a large
scale in most of Europe but not much here except in California.
Fresh, home-cured dill seeds, however, are better than the commercial product. This is particularly true of the foliage, which quickly
loses its savor when dried. Because of these reasons and because of
the tasty, aromatic foliage and still more aromatic seeds, this is an
important plant for the herb gardener.

Dill is a rather coarse annual, often 3-4 feet high, with finely divided leaves and a large cluster of small, yellow flowers. The plants
need plenty of room, do not like transplanting, so it is best to sow
the seeds where wanted and thin them out sufficiently to prevent
crowding. The fresh foliage can be harvested at any time and is a
welcome addition to many meat or fish dishes, or in sandwich
spreads, after chopping, and some use it to flavor butter or oleomargarine. For all these uses, the leaves must be fresh. The chief use
commercially is for flavoring dill pickles, the whole fruiting cluster
being utilized, as well as the fresh leaves.

In late August, the ripened seeds should be dried and cleaned and
kept in tight containers to preserve as much of their fragrant oil as
possible. So fragrant is this oil that it is by some considered to be the
true anise of the Bible. Perhaps that is why some of our feminine
ancestors kept one or two seeds in their mouth during church, to kill
the insipidity of long-winded sermons. Equally, they will pep up the
insipidity of many foods.

The Fennels (*Foeniculum*)
Parsley Family
(Umbelliferae)

There are two or three plants known generally as fennel, as well as the fennel-flower, which is the subject of the next entry. All the true fennels belong to the genus *Foeniculum* and should perhaps be treated as perennials in the next chapter, but some are annuals and even the plants that are technically perennials are rather short-lived, and hence best renewed each year from seed—as in the true annuals. To avoid confusion the fennels are best divided thus:

ORDINARY FENNEL (*Foeniculum vulgare*). The common fennel of
commerce, and a tall coarse plant, 4-6 feet high, with much-divided, thread-like leaves and yellowish flowers. Both foliage and seeds used for flavor.

SWEET FENNEL (*Foeniculum vulgare dulce*). Often called Florence
fennel is like the last, but about half the height. It has expanded leaf bases which are used in salads. Called, also, finnochio.

ITALIAN FENNEL (*Foeniculum vulgare piperitum*). Called also Sicil-
ian fennel or carosella by the Italians who eat the fresh stalks. It is not much known here, but it is to be found in Italian markets in the larger cities.

All the fennels are easy to grow as annuals, but they require a long growing season, which is perhaps why the sweet fennel is grown so extensively in California. They should be planted as early in the spring as the land warms up, about ½ inch deep, and thinned out enough to prevent crowding. The leaves of the common fennel are finely divided, but, in the other two varieties, they are not so narrow and have expanded leaf bases. In the carosella or Italian fennel, the young stems are harvested fresh and eaten like celery. Sometimes it will take two years before the flowers appear, followed by the seed which is pleasantly anise-scented but also sweetish like liquorice. It is chiefly from the common fennel that the fragrant oil is extracted to such an extent that nearly half a million pounds of fennel seed are imported annually. The herb gardener should wait until the seed is ripe. Then dry, clean and store it carefully, for it has a tendency to lose its flavor if left in the open air too long. Much of the imported product is badly adulterated by the rascally growers.

The fennels are important herbs in any garden. The foliage of the sweet fennel and the young stalks of carosella have a delightful, faintly anise-scented flavor, very welcome in salads and for the making of tasty *hors d'oeuvres.* Quite apart from the medicinal value, the deliciously flavored seeds of the common fennel are used by discriminating cooks in breads, cakes, and pastries; in all sorts of sauces; in many soups (especially *bortsch*); and as a flavor for teas and more ardent drinks like wines and anisette.

Could it be that the popularity of fennel was fixed for feminine users by Thomas Dawson who wrote in 1585 that a tea made of it "shall swage [slim] him or her."

Fennel-flower (*Nigella sativa*)
Buttercup Family
(Ranunculaceae)

This annual relative of love-in-a-mist is a small, branching herb from the Mediterranean region, the solitary flower surrounded by a lace-like crown. It is not much grown and is decidedly of second-rate importance to the herb gardener, except for its black seeds. These contain a spicy, fragrant oil suggesting nutmeg—hence its other name of nutmeg-flower. Anciently these seeds were put on bread and cakes, but are now wholly supplanted by poppy seeds for this purpose. It has few real uses in cookery, but it was once mixed with a conserve which Moslem women ate to become fat! Although this is not exactly calculated to whip up much enthusiasm for fennel-flower, some herb gardeners and cooks still use its nutmeg-flavored seeds in sauces.

German Camomile (*Matricaria chamomilla*)
Aster Family
(Compositae)

In 1606 William Ram might well have been looking to our more hectic times when he wrote "To comfort the brain, smell camomile, eat sage, wash measurably, sleep reasonably, delight to hear melody and singing." He was almost certainly writing about the true camomile, which is a perennial and hence treated in the next chapter, but both the annual and the perennial have highly aromatic, pungent foliage, unpleasant to some, and in both the chief commercial product is the yellow flower head.

The German or annual camomile, which is largely imported for its dried flower heads, is of secondary importance to the herb gardener. Its crushed, much cut foliage, has a strong, almost stinking odor. Flower heads are about one-inch wide and, when dried, are the source of a medicinal oil used as an emetic. Camomile tea is made from the true camomile, not from this German variant of it

Herbs were among the earliest plants brought to America. In colonial days they were an essential part of the kitchen garden. In George Washington's kitchen garden, maintained now at Mount Vernon much as it was nearly two hundred years ago, herbs border the geometric vegetable beds, giving a utilitarian garden a touch of elegance. Turn the page for the planting list. (Photo: *Mount Vernon Ladies Association*)

The planting list of George Washington's kitchen garden is as follows. The herbs used for bordering are shown in parentheses.

BED NO. 1. Espalier Fruits (Sanctum Basil). 2. Onions • Eggplant • Onions (Lavender). 3. Onion Sets • Beets • Spinach (Germander). 4. French Artichokes (Nasturtiums). 5. Onion Sets • Beets • Spinach (Germander). 6. Onion Sets • Beets • Spinach (Germander). 7. Onion Sets • Beets • Spinach (Germander). 8. Onions • Eggplant • Onions (Lavender). 9. Espalier Fruits (Catmint). 10. Espalier Fruits (Catnip). 11. Lavender (Golden Thyme). 12. Lavender (Golden Thyme). 13. Cauliflower • Carrots & Radishes • Onions (Rosemary). 14. Cabbage • Bush Lima Beans • Spinach (Rosemary). 15. Cabbage • Bush Lima Beans • Spinach (Rosemary). 16. Cauliflower • Carrots & Radishes • Onions (Rosemary). 17. Spinach • Lettuce • Carrots & Radishes (French Thyme). 18. Spinach • Lettuce • Carrots & Radishes (French Thyme). 19. Horseradish (Oregano). 20. Head Lettuce • Spinach • Head Lettuce (Lavender). 21. Horseradish (Oregano). 22. Espalier Fruits (Catnip). 23. Parsley (English Thyme). 24. Salsify (English Thyme). 25. Figs. 26. Caraway (Oregano). 27. Potatoes • Cabbage (Lavender). 28. Cabbage • Potatoes (Lavender) 29. Quince. 30. Nasturtiums (Parsley). 31. Figs. 32. Espalier Fruits (Rue). 33. Head Lettuce • Sweet Potatoes (Chives). 34. Lily-of-the-Valley. 35. Potatoes • Cabbage (Tarragon). 36. Cabbage • Potatoes (Tarragon). 37. Mint & Apple Tree (Boxwood). 38. Broccoli • Lettuce • Beets (Hyssop). 39. Lavender Cotton & Pear Tree (Boxwood). 40. Mint & Silver Thyme. 41. Lovage. 42. Strawberries (English Thyme). 43. Strawberries (English Thyme). 44. Strawberries (English Thyme). 45. Strawberries (English Thyme). 46. Lavender Cotton & Apple Tree (Boxwood). 47. Broccoli • Lettuce • Beets (Hyssop). 48. Mint & Pear Tree (Boxwood). 49. Peas • Summer Squash • Cauliflower (Sweet Marjoram). 50. Head Lettuce • Onion Sets • Kale (Rosemary). 51. Peas • Bush Lima Beans • Spinach (English Thyme). 52. Peas • Pole Lima Beans • Broccoli (English Thyme). 53. Peas • Cucumbers • Cauliflower (Sweet Marjoram). 54. Head Lettuce • Onion Sets • Kale (Rosemary). 55. Parsnips (Lavender Cotton). 56. Okra (Lavender Cotton). 57. Bush Lima Beans • Broccoli (Lemon Balm). 58. Sage. 59. Sage. 60. Asparagus (Lemon Balm). 61. Asparagus (Lemon Balm).

Note: • Indicates "followed by."

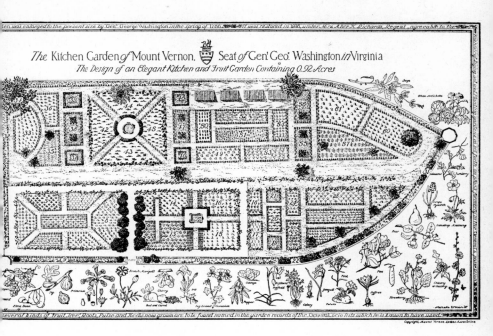

The Kitchen Garden of Mount Vernon, Seat of Gen'l Geo. Washington in Virginia

The Design of an Elegant Kitchen and Fruit Garden Containing 0.92 Acres

Herbs lend themselves to many uses in the small garden, planted either by themselves, or with backgrounds of other plants. Brick walks and staggered brick edgings help to make an attractive setting for even the smallest plot. Here basil and lavender, chives, sage and other herbs are grown with lilies and potted geraniums. (Photo: *Roche*)

Another, less formal, kind of herb garden can be grown close to the kitchen door, with rhubarb and the other perennial plants the cook may need handy for instant use. Stepping stones set in random patterns in the grass walks give form and pattern to the planting scheme. (Photo: *Roche*)

FOUR HERBS FOR FRAGRANCE
Lavender (upper left) is one of the most popular of all perennial herbs, easily grown and used; Sweet Woodruff (upper right) smells of new-mown hay, and can be used also for flavoring; Rosemary (lower left) is a fragrant plant common in legend and song, sometimes linked to Rue (lower right) once valued for many qualities but now grown principally for its decorative aspects. (Photos: *Roche*)

Four Herbs for Flavoring

Pot marjoram (upper left) is much used in salads and in Latin-American cookery, while the common Spearmint (upper right) is part of our own culinary tradition, in salads, mint sauce and juleps. Sage (lower left) is probably the most widely used of all flavoring herbs, followed closely by Thyme (lower right) which since the days of ancient Greece has been, fresh or dried, part of the cook's essential equipment. (Photos: *Roche*)

The drying and storing of herbs is an art in itself, although simple once the principles are learned. Thorough drying is an essential, then crushing (unless you prefer whole leaves) and storage in airtight tins or stoppered bottles. From a few well-grown and selected herbs a family's winter requirements can easily be preserved. (Photo: *Roche*)

which is grown here chiefly for interest but not for its real value in the modern herb garden.

The Mustards (*Brassica*)
Mustard Family
(Cruciferae)

Although mustard is perhaps the most widely used condiment, the source of it threatens to become one of our most pestiferous weeds. Some states have laws framed to eradicate one of the worst weeds the farmer has to cope with—which we call wild mustard.

Actually there are two sorts: white mustard (*Brassica alba*) and black mustard (*Brassica nigra*). Both have yellow, 4-petalled flowers in terminal clusters, and it is the seeds of the latter that are the source of mustard.

It is practically useless to grow either sort of these annual weedy plants for a home-made source of mustard, and the only excuse for growing either one is that their young leaves are used in salads. Being closely related to the cabbage-cauliflower-Brussels sprout tribe, the foliage of mustards is a bit strong-tasting to some, but others think that the young leaves are a pleasant ingredient to be mixed with endive or lettuce. Whichever school you agree with, it should be emphasized that both plants be grown with every precaution to prevent your garden from becoming the center of a fresh eruption of these vigorous and rampant weeds. Since both are annuals, this is easily prevented by seeing to it that all *seeds*, except those saved for planting, under control, are destroyed.

Nasturtium (*Tropaeolum majus* and *minus*)
Nasturtium Family
(Tropaeolaceae)

These popular garden annuals from the high Andes are so widely grown for their flowers that only the herb gardener and children know that the foliage, and especially the unripe seeds, have a delightful, peppery taste.

When nasturtiums were first brought from Peru to England in the sixteenth century, the use of their seeds as a substitute for capers attracted immediate attention, and that is their chief use today. In *The Complete Housewife* (1736) there is a recipe for pickling nasturtium seeds that calls for steeping them three days in salty water. Then horse-radish, pepper, salt, cloves, mace, and nutmeg are soaked in white wine, without boiling, and to this spicy brew is added the nasturtium seeds. Many today prefer the fresh seeds, while still green.

Although the flowers and seeds of the tall, climbing nasturtiums (they scramble over the roof in the Andes) are larger than in the dwarf sorts, it is the latter (*Tropaeolum minus*) which should be used in the herb garden. It flowers more freely than the taller kinds and takes less room. Every gardener knows how easy it is to grow these charming annuals, and there is need here only to point out their uses in the herb garden.

While the leaves and tender, succulent stems are still young, they may be added to salads; the chopped-up leaves are delicious in sandwiches. But it is the plump, but unripe and wrinkled seeds that taste of pepper and spice and can be used as are capers. Do not let them turn brown before harvesting, and don't forget that the young, unopened flower buds have the same flavor.

Opium Poppy (*Papaver somniferum*)
Poppy Family
(Papaveraceae)

No plant has been more properly maligned than this annual herb from the Mediterranean region, the source of opium, morphine, codeine, and heroin, which have caused more misery and corruption than perhaps any other plant product. But to the herb gardener, and to confectioners for two thousand years, poppy seed has been a perfectly innocent addition to buns, rolls, bread, and cake, because the seed is wholly lacking in the dread substances found in opium.

The plant is easily grown, and in reasonably warm summers will flower and set fruit before frost. Growing 2-3 feet high, it has grayish-green leaves and white flowers which are smaller and not so showy as the lovely Oriental poppies of the flower garden. The pod, which is about 2 inches long and half as thick, is filled with the seeds which are dark brown or blackish. They contain an oil, especially in a dark variety of the opium poppy, which is perfectly harmless, and is one of the chief adulterants of olive oil in southern Europe. Apart from its seeds for sprinkling on pastry, the opium poppy has little interest to the herb gardener, and it will not produce opium in any temperate climate.

Parsley (*Petroselinum crispum*)
Parsley Family
(Umbelliferae)

For many years the parsley was known by the name *Petroselinum sativum,* but the modern and best kinds are curly-leaved and hence called *crispum,* meaning crisped or curled. Unfortunately parsley is a biennial and hence a supply of new plants must be raised each year from seed. This is troublesome because they take from 4-6 weeks to germinate and soaking them in tepid water does not hasten matters very much. Since the foliage is the chief harvest, and the plant produces mostly flowers and seeds the second year, it is almost imperative to grow a fresh lot every spring. Some gardeners, especially those in warmer regions, start parsley seed in boxes at the kitchen window long before outdoor planting is possible. The seedlings are then put in the herb garden earlier than they otherwise could be, and make a good growth before intense summer heat, which parsley does not like.

The nearly ubiquitous and rather tiresome use of parsley needs no mention here. The plant, however, has other uses. There is a variety of it, known as Hamburg or turnip-rooted parsley, which has a parsnip-like root, used as a vegetable in soups. And the seeds of the common parsley are even more aromatic than the foliage. Both of them contain an oil which has some medicinal value, but its chief constituent is the flavor—bitter, with a dash of something akin to camphor and turpentine. Incidentally parsley seeds are very rich in carotene and ascorbic acid. These recently discovered attributes of parsley perhaps explain why it has probably been the most popular of all herbs. No one has ever explained its slow sprouting, for, as one old chronicle has it, "Parsley seed goes seven times to the Devil and back before it germinates, and that is why it is so slow in coming up."

Pot Marigold (*Calendula officinalis*)
Aster Family
(Compositae)

This commonly cultivated flower garden favorite, a native of the eastern Mediterranean region, may well be the most showy plant in the herb garden, for it is grown only for its flowers. It is a tender annual and seedlings should not be put outdoors until settled warm weather has arrived. The plant grows about 12-18 inches high, has completely scentless foliage and, in this alone, differs markedly from the French and African marigolds, neither of which has any place in the herb garden.

Some would say "neither does the pot marigold." Its beautifully orange-yellow flower heads have no odor when fresh, but are thought by the faithful to develop one when cooked, while the yellow "petals" (really the rays of the head) are used by the more abject of its devotees to color butter. In either case the fresh flower heads must be collected, the rays all picked off, and the heads dried indoors in the shade. To many herb gardeners the pot marigold will continue to be only one of our more showy flower garden plants. However, it has a colorful history, stretching back to the ancients, and William Turner, writing in 1562, anticipated the feminine desire to change hair color, when he wrote of the marigold, "Some used to make their hair yellow with the flower of this herb, not being content with the natural color which God hath given them."

Red Pepper (*Capsicum frutescens*)
Potato Family
(Solanaceae)

When Cortez landed at Tabasco, on his way to the conquest of Mexico, he found the Mayans using the small, hot, red peppers which have since gone around the world and given us the name "Tabasco" for one of the hottest sauces in the world. Actually, there were, and are, many other kinds of peppers that were revealed by the conquest of America, none of them having anything to do with the common black or white pepper of the East Indies.

The peppers of the New World are the fruits of trees or shrub-like plants which are today grown as tender annuals, as they will mature fruit in a single growing season if started early enough to be a seedling 6-12 inches high when settled warm weather has arrived.

Today we have many varieties of peppers. Among the generally green sorts, fit for slicing and eating in salads, are Chinese giant, Bull Nose, Harris Early Giant, and Ruby King. These are indigestible to some. But the red peppers, especially Small Chili, Long Red Cayenne (fiery hot), and Red Squash, as well as scores more known only in the tropics, are mixed with food to stir sluggish digestion. They must be used with the greatest caution, for some of them promote tears and sneezing immediately.

Red peppers, which have an undeniable value for insipid soups and other dishes without enough flavor to cause comment, can easily be dried and stored over the winter. But as they cannot be adulterated the herb gardener with only a limited area is quite safe in buying the dried fruits from dealers. They hold their fiery hot qualities for years.

Rocket (*Eruca sativa*)
Mustard Family
(Cruciferae)

This mustard-like herb from Europe and Asia has been grown for centuries abroad, but is not so well known here as it might be. It does not like intense summer heat and should hence be started from seed raised in the house. Allow six weeks from planting time until the plants are set outdoors, which should be as early as practical. Some gardeners think of the rocket only as a salad—hence its other name of rocket salad or roquette. The plant grows 18-30 inches high, with large, deeply cut leaves, yellowish-white flowers, and beaked pods. Today only the leaves are used, but the seeds were formerly popular.

Since it is the leaves that are harvested, it is important to produce them as quickly as possible, for the old leaves have a rank odor and taste. It is not one of our most important herb plants, but Gerard's *Herbal* sang its praises in 1597—a song grown somewhat feeble to modern herbalists.

Rose Geranium (*Pelargonium graveolens*)
Geranium Family
(Geraniaceae)

When the botanical sponsors christen a plant *graveolens* it is sure to be strong-smelling and the rose geranium is no exception. The oil from its leaves is so fragrant it is used in France and Italy to perfume soaps, tooth powders, and ointments, and some perfumers with more skill than conscience adulterate attar of roses with the highly aromatic oil of the rose geranium.

Like all the garden geraniums (*Pelargonium*), this one is a native of South Africa and hence tender. It is not a tender annual, but it must be renewed each season from cuttings, or else grown in the greenhouse over the winter. For those without such equipment it is best to grow the rose geranium in pots that are plunged outdoors all the growing season but brought into a sunny window in the fall. From it make a few cuttings about Christmas time, root them in sand, and after well rooted, pot them up for moving outdoors after all danger of frost is over, usually around May 15-20. The rose geranium, in its native home is a woody plant, almost shrubby, but it will not stand frost, so one must carry it through the winter by annually making cuttings. The old plant does not ordinarily do well by being carried over the winter, except in a greenhouse.

Fresh leaves of rose geranium are added to tea. They are more often cooked, their fragrant oil flavoring custards, rice and otherwise stodgy puddings. Perhaps its most delightful feature is the highly aromatic and spicy odor which its crushed leaves give to any room.

Sesame (*Sesamum orientale*)
Sesame Family
(Pedaliaceae)

Far older than the Arabian Nights tale that gave us the legend of "Open Sesame" is the plant itself which has been cultivated throughout the Orient for uncounted centuries. There is, in fact, a huge trade in sesame seeds today, for they are the source of benne (or benny) oil which is much used in Africa and the Orient as food, for cooking, and in medicine.

To the herb gardener sesame is of secondary interest and cultivated only for its seeds, which give a flavor to cookies and soups. The oil is rarely extracted here, for cooking oils are plentiful and cheap. Some recipes call for sesame seeds to be sprinkled on the outside of buns, rolls, and cookies, where their flavor, especially when crunched, will add a pleasing touch.

The plant, which is a rough-hairy tropical annual, can easily be grown here as an ordinary annual. Its flowers are rather showy, rosy or white, followed by a 4-sided pod packed with seeds. These should be cleaned and dried and will then keep indefinitely. The plant will do better and produce more seeds in regions with a long growing season, that is, from Washington southward.

Summer Savory (*Satureia hortensis*)
Mint Family
(Labiatae)

This is one of the most satisfactory and useful of all annual herbs, having also a close relative in the winter savory which is a perennial and hence found in the next chapter. The latter is a little stronger in flavor than the summer savory, which on this account is more widely grown. Only the leaves are used, and it is also easier to get a stock of these for drying in quantities from an annual plant, which can be sown in any amount. It is easily raised from seed, planted about ½ inch deep, and a row 8-10 feet long will supply fresh leaves and enough for drying.

Summer savory grows 12-18 inches high, has oblongish leaves, which unfortunately are none too plentiful, and small, pinkish-lavender or white flowers. Its leaves, dried or fresh, have a delightful odor and taste, and one can understand why Nicholas Culpeper, the English "Physitian," wrote in 1652, "Keep it dry by you all the year, if you love yourself and your ease, and it is a hundred pounds to a penny if you do not." They smell of resinous essences suggestive of spices, camphor, and perhaps a dash of benzoin. It is one of the most widely used herbs in salads, since the fresh leaves add something to spike the monotony of lettuce. And its dried leaves amply support its name of *savory*, for they are used all winter by most cooks worth the name. Over a hundred recipes are available for its use in meats, fish, poultry, sauces, puddings, soups, salads, sandwiches, and in the one-dish meals that have become so popular in servantless America.

Sweet Marjoram (*Majorana hortensis*)
Mint Family
(Labiatae)

This Mediterranean herb is really a perennial in warm regions, but best grown as an annual or tender annual in the North, and is closely related to the pot marjoram which, however, is a true perennial and hence found in the next chapter.

Sweet marjoram is also one of the most popular of all savories, credited of old with every sort of magical virtue, one of them being the power to keep fresh milk sweet—hence its name. More substantial properties are the fragrant and spicy-tasting oil found in its leaf, which is the only part of the plant of any interest to the herb gardener. The oil is of some, but only mild, interest in medicine, chiefly as a tonic and to relieve gas in the digestive tract.

Seed should be sown in a box on the kitchen window-sill about six weeks before settled warm weather is expected, after which they can be planted outdoors, about 6 inches apart in the row, with the rows two or three feet apart. Some dealers will offer seeds under the old, but incorrect name of *Origanum majorana,* but the Latin name *Origanum* belongs to the perennial pot marjoram and is only confusing when applied to the sweet marjoram, which was once called knot marjoram, from the peculiar knot-like swellings from which come the tiny, dirty-white flowers.

The uses of sweet marjoram are truly legion. There is scarcely a recipe that does not contain it, and many very good cooks use it so much that the herb gardener had better grow an ample supply—at least a 10-foot row of it. Ever since the days of the Greeks and Romans it has been one of the most popular herbs.

Chapter Three

Perennial Herbs

In the good old days when igno-
rance was a necessity, superstition a virtue, and belief in magic was
universal, there were literally hundreds of perennial herbs cultivated
for fantastic reasons. Science has exploded many of these ancient
fallacies, adopted and modified a few, and given us today the modern *Pharmacopoeia*. In it, and in one or two basic texts like the
National Formulary and *United States Dispensatory*, are listed *all*
medicinal plants with an accurate appraisal of their medical worth.

It has taken several hundred years to reach this degree of competence in the field of medicinal plants. An ocean of nonsense has
been drained off the mass of knowledge which these investigators
have left to a world eager to know what nature has provided for ill-
ness and how we extract it. Scarcely any other scientific achievement
has meant so much to medical science, for from it has come such
specifics as digitalis, scopolamine, quinine, atropine, morphine, and
aconite, to mention only some of the more important.

It would be nice to be able to record a similar competence among
the herb gardeners. Unhappily they have clung to every rumor of
fancied use and persisted in the cultivation of useless weeds cen-

turies after the advocates of their imaginary virtues have been proved completely wrong. Such all-inclusive gullibility, merely for the sake of growing some plant known to be in cultivation at Tours or Cologne or Rome hundreds of years ago, has had one unfortunate effect upon the literature of herb gardening. Although the medical botanists have purged their modern books of plant dross, modern herb books are too often crammed with plants of no medical value and precious little value in cookery.

The authors of some of these books, having acquired a smattering of the Latin names of plants, think it incumbent to list *all* the species of a genus merely because one of them is of unquestioned value. One of these masterly compilations, open before me as I write, lists, under the genus *Thymus* (thyme), 37 species and varieties, of which only a handful have ever reached this country (most of these being of doubtful value) and only one of which, the true thyme, with its varieties, has any meaning to the modern herb gardener.

It is to spare the reader from this avalanche of the superfluous that there has been a drastic selection of the perennial herbs in this chapter. Only 40 are listed, and this number, to some of the more fanatical, may seem very meagre. All strictly medicinal plants have been excluded, and the aim has been to include those of culinary value only, except for a few old garden favorites the cultivation of which has hallowed associations. The exclusion of medicinal plants like aconite, foxglove (digitalis), and many others has been deliberate because few amateurs are equipped to grow and harvest them.

The exclusion of a few others requires brief explanation, for they are often found in recipes and the herb gardener may wonder why they are not discussed in detail like the admitted forty. The reasons for their exclusion are the following:

BAY (*Laurus nobilis*). A subtropical tree, the unadulterated leaves of which are readily available.

CARNATION (*Dianthus caryophyllus*). A plant, which for proper growth needs several months in a greenhouse.

STRAWBERRIES (*Fragaria*). A garden fruit, unless you collect the smaller and tastier varieties from the wild.

VIOLET (*Viola odorata*). The florist's violet, the only one of value as a flavor, needs special conditions and a hotbed or greenhouse.

WATERCRESS (*Nasturtium officinale*). Can only be grown by those having cool spring or brook water; also, it is available fresh, throughout the year, from markets.

The exclusion of many others will bring a pang to some, but because a desperately tried lady made tea out of New Jersey tea (*Ceanothus americanus*) during the Revolution or that the Mormons made Mormon-tea from an *Ephedra* is no reason for cluttering up the modern herb garden with either plant. Scores of such plants have had to be excluded, hoping thereby to make this book of real use to those who want a list of real culinary herbs.

Perennial herbs will not usually flower from seeds the first year, so you must plan well ahead if you grow your own perennials. Many will prefer to start with well-rooted clumps and this, of course, is far easier—and more expensive. Whichever procedure you follow it will often be necessary to seek the seeds or plants of these herbs outside the regular seedsman or nurseryman. Specialists in herbs will be found in the list in Chapter One.

Balm (*Melissa officinalis*)
Mint Family
(Labiatae)

This lemon-scented herb from southern Europe smells so like the citrus fruit that it is often called Lemon Balm. It will become a bushy, crinkly-leaved plant, 1-2 feet high in a year or two, but makes only a few leaves the first year from seed. Space them 16-18 inches apart because they will ultimately need space and, like other perennials, should not be moved unless necessary.

After the first season the tops, including the small, white flower-clusters, may be clipped back several times during the summer, cutting off 3-5 inches of the top each time and drying* them quickly. When the plants get too bushy and crowded, they should be dug up and divided into smaller clumps for replanting, which ought not to be necessary more than once in three or four years.

There is an old Arabian adage that says, "Balm makes the heart merry and joyful." The scent of balm is a delicious combination of mint and lemon. Balm is little used in cookery, except in teas and as an ingredient of claret cup, both of which require fresh leaves. It can also be used in salads and fruit cups. The bruised foliage, fresh or dried, gives off sufficient scent to perfume a room.

Camomile (*Anthemis nobilis*)
Aster Family
(Compositae)

Long before lawn mowers were invented some gardeners in Eng-

---

* To avoid useless repetition the details of drying and curing herbs will be concentrated in Chapter Four.

land used camomile instead of grass, for its fine thread-like foliage hugs the ground and by cutting off the flowering stalks it made a substitute for turf. As Falstaff most truly observed "the more it is trodden on, the faster it grows." What he didn't mention was the fact that its foliage is highly aromatic and still is today. However, it is not the foliage for which the herb gardener grows it, but for a fragrant oil found in its flower heads.

Camomile, which has been grown for over two thousand years, is a native of southern Europe but has since gone around the temperate world. Normally it grows, or rather its flower stalk will reach a height of 8-12 inches. The flower heads are not particularly striking, having small, whitish rays and a yellow, central disc. It is from the dried flower heads that an oil is extracted that goes into most hair lotions and many shampoo mixtures.

For the herb gardener the plant is grown only for these flower heads, used in making camomile tea, and for its delightful, pungent fragrance. An annual relative of camomile, known as German camomile, will be found in Chapter Two. In regions unfavorable for lawn grasses, camomile has often been used as a fairly acceptable and very fragrant turf that needs little mowing.

Catnip (*Nepeta cataria*)
Mint Family
(Labiatae)

For a plant that has no therapeutic properties and is little used in cookery, catnip has shown a remarkable popularity ever since the Greeks and Romans grew it to please their cats. There is little reason for growing it today except for this, as the plant is rather weedy and is often found wild in fields and thickets here, although its true home is Europe and western Asia.

Catnip owes its value to an aromatic oil in the leaves, which can be easily dried so that cats are not dependent on fresh leaves for their fun. Incidentally another, and much more showy plant beloved by cats, is the silver vine (*Actinidia polygama*) which is very fragrant. Catnip scarcely needs any attention except to keep it within bounds. It grows normally 2-3 feet high, and in New Hampshire is grown commercially because people still think an infusion of its oil in hot water is good for infant colic. The experts insist "there are better remedies."

Chives (*Allium schoenoprasum*)
Lily Family
(Liliaceae)

Chives is really a mild, bulbless onion, of which we use the flat, grass-like but hollow leaves. The "bulb" of chives is little more than the swollen base of the stem, and far smaller than the typical onion, to which it is closely related. It is from these small "bulbs" that chives is started, for it cannot be grown from seed since this is seldom produced. The dealers, however, sell "sets" which are really young bulbs and can be planted like onion sets.

The plant is normally 6-8 inches high, with rather showy, pinkish-lavender, ball-like flower clusters, which, however, are often lacking if the leaves are constantly cut. The plant tends to make dense mats or sods if left alone too long, and these should be dug up, separated into smaller clumps, and replanted in the late fall or early spring.

Scarcely any salad can or should be made without chives. Fresh leaves can be cut at any time and chopped into small bits for flavoring not only salads, omelettes, cheese, soups, and potatoes, and one enthusiast wrote that a "chef who makes a potato salad without chives has no soul." In addition to all of these, chives is widely used to flavor fish, spaghetti, and various vegetables. For related plants, see in this chapter, garlic, leek, rocambole, and shallot.

The leaves of chives are useless when dried and, because of this, some herb gardeners pot up one or two clumps, bring them into the kitchen window, and harvest at least some fresh leaves all winter.

Costmary (*Chrysanthemum balsamita*)
Aster Family
(Compositae)

An Asiatic perennial grown for centuries in Europe but not as well known as it should be in the United States. Like many of its relatives among the garden chrysanthemums, costmary has aromatic leaves—hence its name *balsamita*. Actually the odor is a compound of balsam, mint, lemon, and other unidentifiable odors, and these are strong enough so that some people call it "mint geranium," although it has nothing to do with either. It is also quite incorrectly called "lavender," but it has even less to do with that plant.

The plant is a little weedy and, if left alone, will reach a height of 2-3 feet and become quite bushy. The leaves are toothed or even frilled on the margin, and it is only grown for these, since the August-blooming white and yellow, daisy-like heads are of no use to the herb gardener. It is easily increased by division of the root. The leaves can be stored by cleaning and drying.

Costmary leaves are strong-tasting and should be used with caution. Recipes call, for instance, for only a single leaf in a meat or vegetable stew, and for only one in chicken fricassee. One feminine suggestion of putting a leaf of costmary into an Old-fashioned Cocktail provokes violent masculine shudders, but less controversial is its use in lemonade.

Damask Rose (*Rosa damascena*)
Rose Family
(Rosaceae)

Roses in the herb garden are almost a necessity—but not the fine, showy hybrid tea roses or the hybrid perpetuals. The latter are far more handsome, but it was about the damask, eglantine and Provence roses that the poets have raved for centuries, for these are the plants that have the finest fragrance and flavor of all roses. None, of course, are perennials, for all of them are shrubs, but they are best grown in the perennial herb garden and therefore included here.

The damask and Provence roses are probably the most fragrant in the world and the basis for many perfumes. Both originally were single roses, but often come double, and it is suggested that the herb gardener get these old-fashioned varieties to ensure fragrance and flavor. Once established, both the damask and Provence roses (often called the French rose) are easy to maintain, for they are perfectly hardy over most of the country.

It is important to specify exactly what you need for roses in the herb garden, and as some catalogs are confusing it is well to detail the specifications:

DAMASK ROSE (*Rosa damascena*). A form of it is the York and Lancaster rose, but avoid this. Some old catalog names are *Rosa belgica* and *Rosa polyanthos*, both now incorrect.

PROVENCE ROSE (*Rosa gallica*). Often called the French rose, and one of the sources of attar of roses.

EGLANTINE (*Rosa eglanteria*). This is often called the sweetbrier in this country.

These three are *the* roses for the herb garden. In the first two the petals are used, both fresh and dried for flavoring all sorts of dishes and candies, whereas the eglantine is grown mostly for its "hips." These are the fleshy, swollen flower base that ultimately encloses the fruit. Modern research has shown that rose hips are rich in vitamins.

Once established in the herb garden, these old-fashioned "species" roses (so called because they are not modern hybrids) are far easier to grow than their showy-flowered prototypes. To them the herb gardener and discriminating cook will turn with delight and will echo the old herbalist who wrote in 1525, "Dry roses put to the nose to smell do comfort the brayne and the herte and quickeneth the spyryte."

If any of these roses are grown, also, to supply materials for a potpourri, they must be planted by the dozen as the number of petals needed is far greater than for cooking.*

Dandelion (*Taraxacum officinale*)
Aster Family
(Compositae)

This "tramp with the golden crown," as one imaginative botanist called it, is usually well cursed by gardeners for its pestiferous habit of invading lawns. But herb gardeners, especially if there is a dash of Italian in their ancestry, have several and, in fact, quite kind words to say about dandelion, for they remember that it is first cousin to the chicory, endive, and lettuce.

As everyone knows, the plant develops a strong, thick root and it is still cultivated for this and sold as a remedy for a torpid liver, although the experts agree that it is without therapeutic value. Herb gardeners will not grow it for its roots, but for the young leaves which, growing in the familiar rosette, should be harvested only when young. Like the lettuce to which it is related, the leaves have a milky juice containing a bitter principle that gives it a fine flavor in salads. If the leaves are young enough, the Italians use them alone for salad "greens." Mature leaves are far too bitter to be palatable, but if one wants to harvest the roots this should not be done until late August or September when they contain the most of the assumed medicinal value—now mostly relegated to the old wives' remedies. The root is often used to adulterate chicory, which comes from the root of a related plant. Old-fashioned recipes call for making dandelion wine from the flowers, but it is little made today, for it depends for its flavor mostly on lemon and orange rinds.

---

* In Book 5 of this Garden Guide, *Fragrance in the Garden*, the details for potpourri and the amount of petals for this and for home-made perfume are specified.

Eglantine (*Rosa eglanteria*)
Rose Family
(Rosaceae)

For an account of this, usually called the sweetbrier in this country, see the Damask Rose in this chapter.

Garlic (*Allium sativum*)
Lily Family
(Liliaceae)

This, by far the most pungent of all the onion tribe, must be used by the cook with a fine mixture of restraint and genius. As a faint flavor it can be used with distinction, but its dominating odor and flavor spell disaster to the unwary. Some herb gardeners may wonder why it is included here when commercial supplies are readily available. The answer is that growing your own is more satisfying, and the plant can easily be raised by any amateur if he follows the methods of the professionals.

The plant is a little smaller than the leek, has a ball-like pinkish flower head, and its "bulb" is really a collection of separable parts, the familiar "clove" of garlic. Since seed is rarely available, the cloves are planted in the North in early spring, just as in planting onion sets. Plant the cloves 4-6 inches apart in the row, base downwards, and about 1½ inches deep. By July or August, in the North, the green, onion-like foliage should begin to turn yellow, soon after which the plant should be pulled up and the new cloves, which are surrounded by a papery sheath, should be separated, cleaned, and dried, being careful to remove the roots from the base of each clove.

No cook needs to be reminded of the value of garlic, but it can break up homes and alienate friends if not kept in perfect control. For other, and less pungent relatives of garlic, see in this chapter, chives, leek, shallot, and rocambole.

Gas-Plant (*Dictamnus albus*)
Citrus Family
(Rutaceae)

Centuries ago this curious Eurasian herb was also christened fraxinella and burning-bush, from the fact that the heavy oil in its leaves and flowers is volatile, and on a windless evening the faint exudation of "gas" from them will ignite if a lighted match is held near the leaf and, particularly, the flowers. It was well known to the

Greeks and is cultivated today in the herb garden more for its wonderful odor than for any real culinary or medicinal value.

The plant grows about 2½ feet high, is relatively bushy, having many compound leaves comprising 9-11 rather leathery leaflets, and a terminal cluster of white flowers, although there are also purplish and pink-flowered forms.

It is the leaves and flowers that combine a strong odor of lemon with a dash of almond, vanilla, and perhaps other spicy odors. It deserves a place in any herb garden and, when once planted, should be let alone since it does not like to be moved. It belongs to the same family as the orange and lemon and is, in fact, one of the few temperate zone members of this highly aromatic group. Gas-plant is also known as dittany.

Horehound (*Marrubium vulgare*)
Mint Family
(Labiatae)

Who, as a child, did not love horehound drops, whether they were any good for a cold or not. For centuries they were supposed to be and are still sold in vast quantities for that purpose, or perhaps because people like the taste of them. Unfortunately a good many have synthetic flavor in them, and that is why herb gardeners grow horehound, even if the experts say it "has been abandoned by physicians."

Fortunately no doctor can kill the delightful odor and flavor found in the oil secreted in the leaves and flowering tops of this highly aromatic herb. Originally a native of Europe it has long been grown here and often runs wild in fields and thickets. It grows a little like a weed; 1-2 feet high, with ovalish, white-woolly leaves and small, white flowers in dense clusters. It is easily grown in any garden soil and may become a bit too rampant if not controlled.

The flavor of horehound is predominately bitter, and it is the addition of sugar, until the mixture candies, that makes the drops so popular with those who can't make up their minds whether they are candy or medicine. Only fresh leaves and flowering tops should be used since the dried foliage is nearly worthless.

Horse-radish (*Armoracia rusticana*)
Mustard Family
(Cruciferae)

This most pungent-rooted of all herbs has been cultivated for its root for many centuries. Originally a native of Europe, it was introduced here about 1800 and often runs wild in low, wet places, where it looks not unlike a coarse dock. It grows 2-3 feet high, the leaves long-stalked, notched or cut, very coarse, and often more or less fringed on the edges. Flowers are small and white, in a terminal cluster followed by a pod which usually fails to mature seeds or, if so, they are sterile. In other words seeds of the horse-radish are never available for starting a plantation.

This dilemma is solved by planting sliced pieces of the tremendous root, which are offered by dealers, and should be planted 18-24 inches deep in any garden soil, and once established it will become rampant. The pungent substance in this root is only well developed toward fall, and since the plants are deep-rooted they can stand frost. Also the flavor of horse-radish is quickly lost after digging, so that it should only be dug and grated as wanted. The commercial preparations are soaked with vinegar as a preservative, but this is unnecessary if only freshly dug roots are used. If winter cold makes digging difficult, it is better to dig a supply of roots in late fall and plunge them in sand in a cool, dark cellar, from which they can be harvested as needed. Spring and summer-dug roots are worthless. No one needs to be reminded of the popularity of horse-radish with highly protein foods like beef and oysters.

Hyssop (*Hyssopus officinalis*)

Mint Family

(Labiatae)

The hyssop is so steeped in the history of the Christians and the Jews that it would be nice to think that we grow today in our gardens the hyssop mentioned at the Crucifixion and at the Passover. Unfortunately there is grave doubt that our hyssop ever was the hyssop of the Bible, a curious circumstance, for the genus *Hyssopus* contains only one species, which is certainly the hyssop we grow today. What the hyssop of the Bible may have been must be left to the translators of ancient Hebrew.

The hyssop of today is well worth cultivating in spite of the historical uncertainty, for it contains a pleasant, bitterish oil in its foliage with the odor of camphor, mixed with spicy overtones of sage and an aromatic resin. The oil goes into various liqueurs, particularly those made by the monks in Europe, and furnishes a bitter principle for sauces and soups.

It is a somewhat woody herb, growing 12-18 inches high, with an abundance of narrow leaves and blue, irregular flowers in one-sided spikes. It will stand almost any ordinary garden soil but thrives best in a fairly poor one. Although there are red and white-flowered forms, the herb gardener had better stick to the typical blue-flowered form.

Lavender (*Lavandula spica*)
Mint Family
(Labiatae)

Here's your sweet lavender,
Sixteen sprigs a penny,
Which you will find, my ladies,
Will smell as sweet as any.

That London street cry is the best of all reasons for having in your herb garden a plant without any culinary value, but beloved by all women for the odor it gives to clothes and for lavender water. Neither is lavender of any medicinal value, notwithstanding that a quarter of a million pounds of oil of lavender are imported here annually—mostly for the manufacture of toilet waters. It is the oil distilled from the fresh flowers which is most aromatic, but the whole plant also contains the oil and the herb gardener can preserve it, without extraction, merely by drying the flowering tops and young foliage. The making of lavender water and the extraction of oil of lavender constitute a distilling process too troublesome for the average herb gardener.

The true lavender (costmary occasionally masquerades as "lavender") is really an under-shrub or woody herb, 1-3 feet high, its numerous, small, narrow leaves white-felty, so that the plant is ashy-gray in aspect. Flowers are small, in interrupted clusters, pale lavender in color, and most fragrant. More than most herbs the plant thrives in stony and dry places, perhaps because its original home was in the semi-arid Mediterranean region. It is perfectly hardy here if the site is not too wet and the soil too rich, neither of which it likes, especially in slushy winters.

The foliage and flower clusters are easily dried if they are cut when the plant is in full bloom, on a dry day taking as little of the woody stem as possible. It should be dried in the shade, quickly.

Leek (*Allium porrum*)
Lily Family
(Liliaceae)

A much coarser plant than the onion, of which it is a milder relative, leek, like the onion, bears true bulbs and should be started from young bulbs or "sets" which can be purchased from the dealers. Leaves are nearly flat, about 2½ feet high; the base is swollen and often blanched by heaping up earth over the swollen part. It is this and the bulb that is used in salads and to flavor stews, where the taste of the true onion is too strong. Leeks have never been very popular in America, but they do supply a mild onion flavor not found in most of that highly accented tribe. For other plants of this group see, in this chapter, chives, garlic, rocambole, and shallot.

Lemon Verbena (*Lippia citriodora*)
Verbena Family
(Verbenaceae)

A tropical or sub-tropical shrub from the Argentine would scarcely seem a candidate for a perennial herb garden. But the lemon verbena has such a delightful lemon odor that many northern gardeners grow it in spite of its cultural handicaps. Normally it would be a shrub 6-8 feet high, but by clipping and pinching off its fragrant leaves it can be kept in a pot or tub and carried over the winter in the house—as some people do tubbed orange trees. Its aromatic odor makes it worth the trouble, and, of course, if one has a greenhouse it can be wintered over there better than anywhere else.

Lemon verbena has grayish-green angular leaves 2-3 inches long and small, white flowers in branched spikes. If you live south of Norfolk, Virginia, it can be grown outdoors with a little protection (straw or bagging) in winter. North of this it better be grown in large pots or small tubs, which are plunged in the ground outdoors in the frost-free months and lifted in the winter for storage in the house, or in a (gas-free) cellar. If kept in the cellar, water only about once a week, and this treatment may well result in losing a few leaves. But a fresh crop will come out once it is put outdoors the following spring. While lemon verbena is a favorite pot plant, it has only slight culinary value (teas and fruit drinks) and is grown mostly for its fine lemon odor.

Lovage (*Levisticum officinale*)
Parsley Family
(Umbelliferae)

This celery-scented herb from southern Europe was once very popular among herb gardeners of England and the Continent, but fell into disrepute until more recent times. Now it is a full-fledged member of any good herb garden, for its seeds, stems, roots, and leaves contain an aromatic oil which tastes and smells like celery, but is stronger. Unlike celery, to which it is first cousin, lovage is of easy culture and, when once established, needs little attention. The plant is coarser than celery, grows 2-3 feet high, and has large clusters of very small, greenish-yellow flowers.

Fresh lovage leaves can be used in salads, and some growers earth-up the young stalks to blanch them, when they may be cut like celery. Both the root and seeds contain more of the aromatic oil than the foliage. They have some use as the source of a drug, which, however, is little more than a pleasant, aromatic stomachic. But its celery-like odor and taste are the chief assets of lovage, apart from its charming, old English name.

Mugwort (*Artemisia vulgaris*)
Aster Family
(Compositae)

Legend and history have clung to the mugwort so that it finds a place in many old herb gardens and should be included in many new ones. In the *Great Herball* of 1539 it says: "If this herbe be within a house there shall no wycked Spyryte abide," and a hundred years later William Coles in *The Art of Simpling* (1656) wrote: "If a footman take mugwort and put it into his shoes in the morning, he may go forty miles before noon and not be weary." If science would only agree that mugwort would banish wickedness and fatigue, which are not unknown to moderns, the plant would be grown on a great scale!

As it is, mugwort has "feeble therapeutic action," according to the experts, but it is still grown for its pleasantly aromatic foliage, and because some stick to the old custom of making mugwort tea from its flowering tops. The plant is a sturdy, purplish-stemmed perennial, with segmented leaves and small, yellow flowers in clustered spikes. For related plants in this chapter, see southernwood, tarragon, and wormwood.

Onion (*Allium cepa*)
Lily Family
(Liliaceae)

The onion, being a true vegetable, lies outside the scope of this book. But it is the big, strong brother of many onion-scented herbs, which should be sought in this chapter at Chives, Leek, Shallot, Garlic, and Rocambole.

Peppermint (*Mentha piperita*)
Mint Family
(Labiatae)

There is some confusion among herb gardeners as to the identity of this plant and the spearmint, which is also found in this chapter. Both are true mints, but the peppermint is taller and more straggling than spearmint and has stalked, not stalkless leaves, which in the spearmint are crisped and crinkled. Also peppermint has generally purple flowers, while in the mint they are white or grayish.

Menthol is the main constituent found in the oil of peppermint, and it differs from spearmint in the property of giving one a sense of coolness if the breath is inhaled while chewing peppermint leaves. You do not get this sensation from spearmint, which does not contain any menthol in its fragrant oil.

Peppermint, as a source of menthol, undergoes a commercial distilling operation, and is often now superseded by synthetic substitutes, but that is no reason for not growing it in the herb garden. It is a rampant grower, and its runners, if not controlled by frequent cutting, will monopolize any garden in a few years. Originally a native of Europe, and cultivated since the days of the Greeks, it practically never sets seeds, so that it must be started from rooted parts, which are easily obtainable, for the runners root at the joints, and any neighbor is usually only too glad to get rid of such a rampant spreader.

The peppermint is mostly used, outside its commercial preparations, as a flavor in some drinks, but it is not the plant to use for mint juleps or for mint sauce. Iced tea, lemonade, or even water may have a pleasant, cooling flavor added to them by a few sprigs of peppermint. If one has room for only one mint in the garden it should not be this one, but spearmint, which will be found under that name in this chapter.

Pot Marjoram (*Origanum vulgare*)
Mint Family
(Labiatae)

Culinary experts differ as to the value of the pot marjoram and the sweet marjoram, which is mostly grown as an annual and hence to be found in Chapter Two. Commercially they may be lumped as simply "marjoram," but this hides the fact that there are two quite different plants involved, while many gourmets think they have just as distinct uses. Generally, pot marjoram is favored for Latin American dishes of meat, vegetables, soups, etc., but is, by other and equally gifted cooks, dismissed as "not recommended." As for the sweet marjoram its uses are legion. It enters into dozens of recipes known to all good cooks, and its use in salads was so well known to Shakespeare, that he makes the clown say in *All's Well That Ends Well:*

> "Indeed, Sir, she was the sweet marjoram, of the
> salad, or rather the herb of Grace."

The pot marjoram, or, as it is also called, the wild marjoram, is a true perennial herb of Europe, cultivated since the time of Greece, and like so many fragrant herbs well encrusted with legend and fiction—one of the most colorful being that if wild marjoram was planted on a grave the dead person would be happy. It has creeping roots and the plant tends to sprawl, but the up-curving tips reach a height of 20-30 inches, well clothed with the highly aromatic leaves, followed in July by flat-topped clusters of small, irregular pinkish flowers.

Only the leaves and flowering tops are of value, and, after the first year, these can be cut two or three times during the growing season, and they should be dried and stored as quickly as possible. Fresh leaves can be cut and used at once without drying. As to its manifold uses, modern cook books list it in recipes for salads, stews, soups, meat, and any of the one-dish meals, especially the Spanish and Mexican varieties. The value of pot marjoram is the fragrant oil in its leaves, and, since this oil is strong-tasting, the dried or fresh leaves must be used with discrimination.

Provence Rose (*Rosa gallica*)
Rose Family
(Rosaceae)

Fields of absolutely fragrant delight in southern France are provided by the huge cultivation of this rose, which is the chief source of attar of roses. It is often called the French rose, and its value in the herb garden and its differences from other herb garden roses are treated under *Damask Rose* in this chapter.

Rocambole (*Allium scorodoprasum*)
Lily Family
(Liliaceae)

Often known as the giant garlic, this relative of the onion and garlic

is a native of Asia Minor and southeastern Europe, closely related
to garlic and to be grown the same way. It is milder than garlic and
hence preferred by some. The plant grows nearly three feet high
and needs more space than garlic. Its globular heads of dark purple
flowers are often replaced by miniature bulbs (bulbils). For its culture, see under garlic in this chapter. For other related plants, see
also, in this chapter, chives, leek, and shallot.

Rosemary (*Rosmarinus officinalis*)

Mint Family

(Labiatae)

Rosmarinus means literally sea dew, and it would be hard to find
a more appropriate name for the rosemary, the original home of
which was along the rocky coasts of Spain and France. There it
revels in a mild climate, and its ashy-gray foliage blends with the
mists of the sea. Long after Pliny called it by this fanciful name it
became Rose Mary, for the Virgin, whose pale blue cloak reputedly
gave its flowers their color. No herb plant in the world has ever had
so many legends and stories connected with it as rosemary, although
its culinary value is only moderate, and its once-reputed medicinal
value has been supplanted by better remedies. Why, then, the great
popularity of rosemary from ancient times down to the modern herb
gardener, who is scarcely entitled to the name without at least a plant
or two?

The answer, of course, is its delightful fragrance, both in the foliage
and in the flowers—if you ever get any. That fragrance, haunting
and beautiful, is due to an oil, the extraction of which is large-scale
industry in Europe for the perfumers and manufacturers of *eau de
cologne.*

In "There's rosemary, that's for remembrance," Shakespeare makes
Ophelia add, "Pray, love, remember." It is difficult to forget its odor,
or the ashy gray mass of its tiny leaves if the plant grows to any
size. Ever since Ophelia it has been a symbol of remembrance and
the same sort of steadfastness that the plant exhibits when completely happy.

Unfortunately it seldom or never is hardy in the North, particularly if there are wet and slushy winters. It is actually a low shrub
here, but grows 6-8 feet high along the Mediterranean. For those
who live in the North, rosemary can either be grown by annually
setting out new plants, which will give some harvest of foliage, but
few if any of its pale blue flowers and scarcely any seeds. South of
Philadelphia, especially along the Eastern Shore of Delaware, Mary-

land, and Virginia it thrives. And along Gulf Coast beaches, it has run riotously wild.

If you can leave the plants outdoors without much winter-killing, the shrub may be 2-3 feet high and as wide, so that two or three cuttings can be made of its spicy, aromatic leaves. These are much beloved by women, who dry and store them, not only for their fragrance, but perhaps, like Ophelia, they crave some winter reminder of fidelity and remembrance. Or could its feminine popularity be due to something quite different?

One cynical, old English gardener ascribed to rosemary a property that made it almost distasteful to men—for England two centuries ago was certainly a man's country. One wonders if he had a prophetic vision of modern America when he wrote:

"Where rosemary grows best, the mistress is master."

Rue (*Ruta graveolens*)
Citrus Family
(Rutaceae)

Eighty years before The Great Plague hit London in 1664, *The Goode Housewife's Jewell* gave a sure preventive of this dread disease, the chief constituent of which was rue. That was in the days before rats and lice were known to have anything to do with the disease, and something bitter was a remedy or prophylactic for many other diseases. Rue, however, has modern medical uses, and for this it is widely grown commercially, mostly in Europe, and still is a fairly common plant in American herb gardens.

It has a rather unpleasant odor, some think nauseating if too strong, and this is caused by an oil in its foliage which is much used in the illicit production of an abortion by various European peasants, sometimes fatally. It is a rather pretty perennial from southern Europe, somewhat woody at the base with grayish-green twice-compound leaves that are evergreen in the South, but withering in winter in the North. Flowers are small, yellowish-green in a loose terminal, more or less flat-topped cluster.

Apart from its historical and medicinal associations, rue has no place in the herb garden if only culinary plants are wanted, all the old recipes for it being obsolete.

Saffron Crocus (*Crocus sativus*)
Iris Family
(Iridaceae)

Not many herb plants are so showy as this autumn-blooming crocus, the spicily fragrant blossoms of which do not flower until October. It should not be confused with the common autumn crocus (*Colchicum*), which are equally beautiful, but of no interest to the herb gardener, for some of them are even poisonous. The saffron crocus, on the contrary, has been in active use since the days of the Iliad and even before. The Egyptians strewed palace floors with its heavily scented flowers, which, however, is not the chief interest of the herb gardener. From the center of the flower comes a central shank-like column (the style) divided at the tip into three branches (the stigmas). It is the dried stigmas that are the source of saffron which have been treasured for centuries for their golden yellow color and their flavor.

The corms (modified bulbs) of saffron crocus can be purchased from any bulb dealer, but, as in the autumn crocus, they should be planted in August. They will bloom the same autumn and continue to do so for several years. When they become too crowded, which will stop their blooming, they should be dug up and re-spaced—about 6 inches apart each way. As the harvest is only the stigmas, which usually protrude beyond the chalice-like corolla, these must be picked off carefully soon after the flowers open, being careful not to take the pollen-coated stamens, which are *not* branched. The harvested stigmas should be dried at once and stored in tight bottles.

Saffron was for centuries almost the only yellow dye that could safely be put in food, but there are now perfectly safe synthetic dyes for this purpose. Many herb gardeners, however, prefer the natural yellow of saffron, especially as it has a flavor that, in small quantities, goes well with rice, fish, and some one-dish meals. It is expensive to buy because it still has certain medicinal value, although saffron's chief use in this country is for seasoning and color.

Sage (*Salvia officinalis*)
Mint Family
(Labiatae)

If life really begins at forty, that advance age is quite a landmark in the dietary history of most of us. For it is at about that age of decrepitude that one begins to think that a brisk walk is the best antidote to Thanksgiving turkey with stuffing. The more sage in that stuffing, the brisker will, or should be, the walk. For sage, the most widely used herb in America, has a tendency to cause indigestion, perhaps because we import over two million pounds yearly and some cooks like it so much that enthusiasm runs away with discretion.

Most of it goes into "sage," which is commercially often adulterated, but some is mixed with "allspice" and other condiments, while a little is used for the extraction of its fragrant oil which has some medical appeal here, but much more in Europe.

The herb gardener can easily grow his own, for sage is a readily cultivated woody perennial (a sub-shrub in warm regions) with ovalish or longer leaves and irregular blue flowers that bloom in late June or early July. Leaves and flowering tops should be harvested just as the plant is blooming, and a second cutting can be made in August. It is, however, better not to make a later harvest, thus allowing the last crop of leaves to wither as winter approaches. The leaves, which comprise the sage of commerce and for the cook, should be dried as quickly as possible and put in a tight container.

Sage has been cultivated ever since the earliest of recorded history. It was often credited with magical powers of rejuvenation, and one delightful old fifteenth century herbal wrote that it would

> "Quicken the veins and the mind
> And all thy virtues keep in kind
> Comfort the heart and keep the sight
> No man of earth can tell his might."

Perhaps because of its great popularity sage now comes in several varieties, mostly based on the color of the leaves (red, gray, green, etc.). It does not matter to the herb gardener, for all of them contain the fragrant oil that makes sage what it is. For a related species of *Salvia*, see Clary which is a biennial to be found in Chapter Two.

Shallot (*Allium ascalonicum*)
Lily Family
(Liliaceae)

An onion-like herb grown the same as are onions, but instead of making one large bulb, with offsets, the "bulb" of the mature shallot is a series of separable sections (cloves) like the garlic, but with nothing resembling that flavor. Shallot, sometimes called eschallot, is milder than the onion and is not much grown in this country. It was named for a village in Palestine, Ascalon, as the plant originally came from western Asia. It rarely flowers in cultivation, but if it does bloom there will be small, globular heads of white or violet flowers. The foliage much resembles that of the onion, and the young, mild leaves are often harvested for greens as bunch onions. For related plants, see, in this chapter: chives, leek, garlic, and rocambole.

Southernwood (*Artemisia abrotanum*)
Aster Family
(Compositae)

One scarcely grows southernwood for its culinary or medicinal uses, for these are negligible, but for its historical and imaginative past. For many centuries it was called Lad's Love or Maiden's Ruin, upon the quite unsupported notion that it was an aphrodisiac. Today, perhaps because the scientists have long pricked this erotic bubble, it is more often called Old Man, for the undisputed fact that its foliage is grayish-green. It is also a welcome plant in the herb garden because the foliage is as highly aromatic as its American relative, the sagebrush of our Southwest.

Southernwood is a somewhat woody perennial (a sub-shrub in warm regions) 2-3 feet high, its leaves much divided into fine, thread-like segments, which are aromatic even without crushing. Flowers are very small, the yellowish-white heads scarcely ⅛ inch wide and rather numerous. Perhaps its only real use today is found in the dried leaves which are so aromatic that they scent up closets or chests—not, however, efficacious against moths. For related plants in this chapter see mugwort, tarragon, and wormwood.

Spearmint (*Mentha spicata*)
Mint Family
(Labiatae)

Spearmint, so named to distinguish it from the peppermint, is *the* mint of the kitchen. Scarcely any gardener needs to be told how to grow it, and once started there are many who would rather know how to stop it growing too fast and too far. Nor does any cook need to be told as to its value for mint sauce, in drinks, and in salads.

Mint is a perennial from Europe, cultivated throughout the temperate world and perhaps the only thing about it to confuse the herb gardener is its resemblance to peppermint. The distinctions are important and will be found at *Peppermint* in this chapter.

Sweet Cicely (*Myrrhis odorata*)
Parsley Family
(Umbelliferae)

When the Carthusian monks began to experiment with their famous liqueur, they put into Chartreuse an oil of myrrh, which is today one of the ingredients of this delectable cordial. For them, and for many of us, however, the word *myrrh* is a little confusing. It was and is still applied to the sweet cicely, ignoring the fact that the

myrrh of the Bible is the gum of a tropical tree, whereas the sweet
cicely is a perennial herb from Europe. To compound the confusion
the sweet cicely has a myrrh-like odor, and Linnaeus christened it
with the Latin name *Myrrhis,* apparently because he mistook it for
the source of the biblical myrrh, or perhaps because it smelled like it.

That odor is the only reason for growing the sweet cicely today,
although it is not, as some think, the source of an ingredient of incense, which comes from true myrrh. Sweet cicely is an herb growing 15-30 inches high, with compound leaves and tiny white flowers
in small clusters, on a much branched flowering stalk. By far the
most aromatic part of the plant is the oil in its seeds, which are used
to flavor other drinks besides Chartreuse and some foods. The plant is
not much grown here, but its seeds are thought to have the power
of potentiating other flavors, beyond its own, which suggests anise.

Sweet Flag (*Acorus calamus*)
Jack-in-the-pulpit Family
(Araceae)

This almost weedy inhabitant of marshes throughout the north
temperate zone has so many uses it is unfortunate that most herb
gardeners will not have the right site for its best culture. The plant
will stand ordinary garden soil but does far better with its feet in
the water.

It is a stout perennial with thick rootstocks which are the commercial source of calamus root. This is aromatic and widely used
in perfumery. The fragrance of calamus root (not to be mistaken
for calomel) is also found in the long, grass-like but thick leaves,
which some herb gardeners use to flavor custards and creams. But
the root of the sweet flag had, and still has, a wide use as a home
remedy for colic, especially in the United States, where literally
tons of it are imported yearly. The root may be an inch or two thick
and, in old plants, several feet long. It is easily propagated from
division of the roots, which should be planted 4-6 inches deep and
at least one foot apart.

The powdered roots of the sweet flag have been used for centuries
to protect clothes and furs from moths and other insects, although
its use for this has waned with the advent of synthetic chemicals.

Sweet Woodruff (*Asperula odorata*)
Madder Family
(Rubiaceae)

The smell of new-mown hay is due to the presence of coumarin,

a substance nearly three times as aromatic as vanilla. For that reason
alone the sweet woodruff is worth cultivating, for it is one of the
commercial sources of coumarin. The plant is a native of Europe
and the Orient, but has so long been cultivated here that it has escaped to the woods and is hence not uncommon as a wild plant in
eastern North America.

Sweet woodruff, which is first cousin to our common bedstraw, is
a straggling plant, weak-stemmed, and with 6-8 slender leaves concentrated at each joint (whorled). They are scarcely one inch long,
roughish to the touch, and when cut or crushed as aromatic as spice
or vanilla. It is for this the plant is grown, and it was for this that
the Medieval Germans put it into May Wine, and some Americans
of European ancestry still flavor May Wine with the sweet woodruff.

Other uses are the dried foliage which gives off a scent of new-
mown hay months after they have been cut. The plant is practically
a weed and of the easiest culture, although it does seem to prefer
half shade.

Tansy (*Tanacetum vulgare*)
Aster Family
(Compositae)

What more could a modern, feminine herb gardener desire than
this piece of sound advice from Master Jherom Brunswyke who
wrote in his *Virtuose Boke of Distyllacion* (1527):

> I have heard that if maids will take wild Tansy and lay it to soake
> in Buttermilk for the space of nine days and wash their faces
> therewith, it will make them look very faire.

Not too long after, a certain cook to the Duke of Bolton was re-
galing the ducal table with tansy amber cakes, which reads as though
the Duke would soon need a doctor more than a cook. The history of
tansy is nearly fabulous, for the plant possesses no value medicinally
and, were it not for its odor, would be ignored. Actually, it is a highly
aromatic, weedy European perennial, quite commonly escaped to
roadsides and barnyards here, and grown in many herb gardens for
its odor and associations. Who, after all, wants to ignore a plant that
went into tansy tea, puddings, pancakes, and an apple tansy—not
one of which is known today, except tansy pudding.

The plant is a stiff herb, beautifully dark green, with divided
leaves and many small, button-like heads of yellow flowers. It is of
easy culture almost anywhere.

Tarragon (*Artemisia dracunculus*)
Aster Family
(Compositae)

Not so long ago American cooks, even good ones, had an inferiority complex about tarragon. Perhaps that was because it was then rare here, but most likely because hushed admirers came home from French cooking schools with tales that excited envy and longing for the unattainable. Fortunately that is all over, for anyone can now have tarragon, either imported from France or grown at home. French tarragon will still be better than ours unless we take care to grow it properly, that is, to bring out its greatest flavor. It will grow in any ordinary garden soil, but it will be far stronger if the soil is a bit stony and the season not too wet.

The value of tarragon is the anise-like odor and the bitter tang of the juice. It is this that makes it so popular in various recipes for vinegar, soups, broths, salads, sauces, and vegetables, and it is or should be the chief flavor in Tartar sauce. It is also one of the ingredients in that delightful apéritif Dubonnet, which, however, owes some of its tang to quinine.

Tarragon is a rather sprawling perennial, native from the Caucasus to eastern Asia, and has been so long cultivated that it scarcely ever sets seed. The plants must hence be multiplied by division of their roots. It has fine, unlobed leaves, about one inch long, which are weak. If it flowers, they will be very small, perhaps only ⅛ inch across, and greenish-white. It will do well in partial shade, but the chief thing to look out for is that the soil is not too rich, and, unless in a desert region, never water it. Under these conditions it should produce a maximum of the fragrant oil in its leaves, which is commercially known as estragon, and for which the herb gardener should grow tarragon. Leaves that are to be stored should be dried quickly and put into tight containers.

For other plants related to tarragon, see, in this chapter, mugwort, southernwood, and wormwood.

Thyme (*Thymus vulgaris*)
Mint Family
(Labiatae)

Next to sage, thyme is probably the most widely used herb in cookery, and this has been true ever since the days of Theophrastus, the talented Greek who developed the first botanical garden in the world. Ever since, its praises have been sung by poets and cooks, especially the latter, of whom one old Greek satirist wrote: "A cook is fully as useful as a poet."

Thyme, which is loosely called both English thyme and French thyme, is a somewhat woody herb from the Mediterranean region, sometimes divided into broad-leaved (English) and narrow-leaved (French) varieties. It is doubtful if the active constituent of thyme, a fragrant oil, differs in the two forms, although some connoisseurs profess to a liking for the French variety. Commercially, thyme oil is extracted from the leaves and flowering tops of *Thymus vulgaris*, without regard to its varieties, and the herb gardener may well be guided by this, but it is well, in ordering plants to use the Latin name, as thyme has a bewildering lot of varieties and close relatives.

The plant is scarcely eight inches high, erect and bushy, with white-woolly stems and stalkless leaves, usually less than ½ inch long, gray and glistening. Flowers very tiny, lavender-pink, in cone-shaped, terminal clusters, mostly blooming in early June, and later if the first crop of flowers is harvested with the upper leaves at that time. Two or three cuttings can usually be made during the growing season, and these should be cleaned and dried as soon after cutting as possible. In the North the plant may die down to the ground each winter, but does not suffer, as new shoots come up in the spring. In warmer regions the plant is practically evergreen.

Thyme was once supposed to have a variety of medical uses, but most of these are now obsolete, and its great use is culinary. There is scarcely a cook who does not use it in a wide variety of recipes— mostly in the dried form as found in the markets. Fresh thyme, however, is so fragrant and has such a pleasant bitter tang that it is no wonder that an Oxford University recipe, dated 1600, tells us how to use thyme "to enable one to see the fairies."

Some gardeners may prefer the Lemon Thyme, a related plant with lemon-scented foliage. The plant is carried by dealers under the name *Thymus serpyllum vulgaris*.

Wild Ginger (*Asarum canadense*)
Birthwort Family
(Aristolochiaceae)

In the long history of herb gardening, the plants are overwhelmingly of European or Asiatic origin, as though the flora of the "New Founde World" were either deficient in such species or the natives had not the wit to discover any. At least one exception is the wild ginger, which our New England ancestors found the Indians using for its odor and flavor, as well as for remedies. It is not a plant for the open herb garden, and no one should attempt to grow it unless there is the deep shade of the woods, rich humus, and plenty of moisture.

Given these conditions it will thrive and produce a crop of its curious, spreading, underground rootstocks, which have a delightful, spicy, almost ginger-like flavor. These are now harvested commercially in the Alleghenies, because some people put them in home remedies, but the plant is not in any modern Pharmacopoeia.

Dealers in wild garden material carry the plant which is well worth growing for its handsome, kidney-shaped leaves and curious flowers. These are brownish-purple, borne near the ground level, or below if there is a leafy litter on the forest floor, and well hidden by the luxuriant leaves which may be 5-6 inches wide.

The only culinary value of wild ginger is perhaps the one bequeathed to us by the Indians of New York and New England. They used few seasonings in their food, but one of them was the spicy, aromatic roots of this plant to spike the insipidity of hominy grits.

Wintergreen (*Gaultheria procumbens*)
Heath Family
(Ericaceae)

Another native American perennial herb of the open woodlands, especially the pine-barrens of New Jersey and Long Island, is worthy of a place in the herb garden, but only if the proper conditions are available. It will not grow in ordinary garden soil, and prefers sandy places with a litter of pine needles or oak leaves, so that the site will stay acid. Also it wants the filtered sunlight from a reasonably open canopy of the forest—pine or oak trees—not dense shade.

For two hundred years this plant was the only American source of wintergreen, but when the chemists invented methyl salicylate, wintergreen began to lose its popularity, because the experts agree that the natural oil of wintergreen and the chemical substitute are identical. No herb gardener needs to quarrel with that decision, but a die-hard lot of purists claim that natural wintergreen is better than the synthetic sort, just as vanilla is better than vanilline.

For them, and for any number of wild gardeners, wintergreen will always be a favorite plant to cultivate, and as in the wild ginger, the propagating material must come from dealers in native plants or those for wild gardens. Wintergreen is a low, nearly prostrate, somewhat woody herb with evergreen leaves, and white, waxy, bell-shaped flowers in early July, followed by a bright red berry. It is the oil in the leaves that contain most wintergreen, and during the Revolution the leaves were one of a number of substitutes for British tea that was then anathema.

Winter Savory (*Satureia montana*)
Mint Family
(Labiatae)

This perennial relative of the annual plant, summer savory, looks very different from that plant. Winter savory is an evergreen, woody herb with tiny, very narrow leaves arranged in opposite pairs. Originally native along the coasts of the Mediterranean, it has been grown there for centuries, perhaps because it was long supposed to be an aphrodisiac, which it is not, or more likely for its delightful odor and taste. It is not as widely used for the latter as the summer savory, probably because the latter has larger leaves and hence provide a better supply than the perennial sort with its leaves scarcely $\frac{1}{16}$ inch wide.

The great virtue of winter savory is the fact that it is evergreen and hence available all winter. Also it grows easily and has attractive white or pinkish flowers. Winter-harvested leaves will, of course, have less of the taste and odor found in summer foliage, which should be cut back two or three times, with the flowering clusters. Even the summer foliage of the winter savory will not have so much of the essential oil as the summer savory, and if you have room only for one, it better be the latter, which will be found among the annuals in Chapter Two. Savory is one of the most widely used of all herbs. See Chapter Five.

Wormwood (*Artemisia absinthium*)
Aster Family
(Compositae)

This ashy-gray perennial contains the most bitter oil of any other herb plant, even rue. More important, the young flower heads, from which the oil is extracted, are widely grown in Europe, and the plant has escaped from cultivation to the roadsides of America, where its small, yellow flower heads are harvested in midsummer for commercial extraction of the oil.

That oil is potentially very dangerous, for it is the ingredient in the French liqueur *absinthe*, which, in improper amounts, may lead to epileptiform fits, trembling, nausea, and vomiting, and to death.

Of course, the average herb gardener never will extract this dangerous oil, and the fragrance of the flowers and the foliage make it an attractive herb garden plant. It is, also, one of the most famous, because the Greeks and especially the Romans knew the value of bitter stomachics, of which wormwood is one of the best when taken in proper dilution. Hence the popularity of wormwood teas, wines, and brandies, and the quaint old fifteenth-century herbal, evidently copying lore from the days of the Crusaders, quoted with more truth than spelling:

> Water of wormwoode is gode . . . Grete lords among the Saracenys usen to drinke hitt.

The plant is easy to grow, will reach a height of 2-3 feet, and become quite bushy, although it is a true perennial, dying down to the ground each winter. The leaves are silky-gray, much divided and cut, and the very numerous flower heads, which are a dirty yellow, are scarcely ⅛ inch across. Only these flower heads are used commercially, and neither the flowers nor the leaves have any place in cookery. For plants related to wormwood, which is often called absinthe in Europe, see, in this chapter, mugwort, southernwood, and tarragon.

The word *perennial* is a bit misleading as used in gardening circles. It should mean "living forever," but actually no herbaceous perennial ever does so, and the wise gardener will be on the lookout for signs that a particular plant is failing to maintain itself and take the necessary steps to perpetuate it.

If perennial herbs begin to show signs of dying out, as they may if left alone for a few years, they can often be rejuvenated by digging them up in early spring, dividing the clump, and re-spacing the re-planted parts so they get enough room to thrive. With a good many plants in the foregoing list, this is often all that is necessary to give the plant a new lease of life for quite a few years.

Some perennials, however, have a troublesome tendency to die off at the end of a season or two, probably due to the fundamental fact that ours is not as favorable a climate for them as the one from which they came. These fleeting "perennials," and fortunately there are only a few, are best treated as annuals or tender annuals, and they are hence treated in Chapter Two.

It is, of course, a truism in gardening that the ultimate source of new plants is always by planting their seeds. Most herbs produce a plentiful supply of seeds, and if you do not want to collect your own, there are dealers who always have them. A list of some of these dealers appears at the end of Chapter One.

There are some herbs, however, that, as usually cultivated, never produce seed—notably the horse-radish and tarragon. For these one must rely upon division of the old clumps, and this is also the method of commercial growers.

Raising perennials from seed is the cheapest and most profitable way to start your herb garden and to increase the stock of existing plants. There is nothing difficult about it, and its only drawback is that it takes a little more time. Generally the seeds should be sown in shallow boxes (a cigar box is perfect), in flats if you sow more, or in flower pots if you sow less. All of these seeds should be planted 6-8 weeks before the seedlings are ready for permanent outdoor planting. This means starting them in a cool greenhouse, or lacking this, on the kitchen window-sill (no gas fumes).

In preparing the soil for sowing herb seeds, it is well to remember that they will not stay in the container in which they are started very long. And this means that the soil should not be too rich. A good mixture for most seedlings will be one part of ordinary, good garden loam to two parts of sharp, clean sand (not sea sand unless all salt is washed out of it). Mix the two thoroughly and add a little less than one part of leaf mold (not acid peat). When the whole is completely mixed, see that the boxes, pots, etc., are filled ⅞ full and water thoroughly, so that they will have an initial settling before the seeds are planted. If the soil settles too much, fill up the containers to the required height, which must be so arranged that subsequent watering will *not* overflow the container.

In planting seeds a good rule is not to cover them with more soil than about 2-3 times their own diameter, and for very fine seeds do not make holes or trenches for them at all. Simply scatter such small seeds on the surface, and then sift enough of your soil mixture to barely cover them (as in sowing grass seed). Tamp them down very lightly and give a very gentle but adequate watering, as should, of course, be done with the seeds that have been more deeply planted.

A good watering plan, for the first time or two, is to stand the container, which must, of course, have holes in the bottom, in a pan of water and allow the water to rise by capillarity to the surface, which it will do in a few minutes. Be careful that the water in the pan is not that deep that it will flow over the edge of the container and into it and "drown" the seeds. If this method is too troublesome, the containers can have ordinary overhead watering, but this *must*

be gentle, that is, with an atomizer or a watering pot with a very
fine rose (small perforations). The whole object is to keep the soil
moist (not soaked) without washing out seeds (especially those
shallowly planted) and not to injure the young seedlings which will
soon be showing above ground.

Most of them will be germinating within a week or ten days, but
there are certain seeds, especially in the parsley family, which are
notoriously slow starters. These have already been noted and they
all sprout easier after the "water treatment." This merely involves
soaking the seeds in warm water, kept at about 110-115° for two or
three hours (24 hours for celery) and then sowing in the ordinary
way. For all extremely small seeds, which are hard to pick up and
manipulate, a good plan is to mix them with half their bulk of sand,
and plant seed and sand together. This seed and sand mixture will
be found far easier to handle than trying to plant minute seeds.

When the seedlings become about 1½-3 inches high, they will soon
be crowding each other and must be re-spaced. This is done by
"pricking-out," that is, gently lifting each tiny seedling, roots and
all, preferably with a blunt old kitchen knife, and re-planting them
at once. For this procedure, extra containers must be ready, filled
with the same soil mixture, and the young seedlings planted in them
about 3 inches apart each way. Continue proper watering, and in
about 3-4 weeks you are ready for the final step before the plants
go outdoors.

For this last indoor move the soil mixture should be changed to
consist of one part good garden loam, one part clean sand and one
part of leaf mold (not acid peat). When the seedlings are crowding
each other they should be planted in this richer soil mixture about
6 inches apart each way. Do not use any fertilizer and do not water
them with liquid manure.

When outdoor planting time has arrived, that is, reasonably warm
weather (after at least the last killing frost), the seedlings may be
taken from their final indoor containers and planted where wanted.
Most of them will not flower or set seed the first season, but will be
all ready for the second season. Impatient gardeners, who do not
want to go to all the trouble, can get plants ready rooted from the
dealers. To provide the same number of plants you get from a packet
of seeds will cost from 10-15 times the cost of the packet—and that is
the chief reason for raising your own.

Chapter Four

How to Dry and Store Them

Some of the Antients, and divers Modern writers which have professed
Astrology, have noted a Sympathy between the Sunne, Moon and some
principal Starres, and certain Plants, and so they have denominated som
herbes Solar, and some Lunar, and such toyes put into great words.

Art of Simplina

William Coles, who wrote this gem
of good sense in 1656, had only just escaped the enormous amount
of legend, rumor, magic, and nonsense that surrounded herb culture
throughout the Middle Ages. He fumed against it, well knowing that
some of it was distorted from monkish skills, which were often quite
remarkable, some came from the undoubted knowledge of the Arabs,
and some were survivals of the fabulous, and often untrue, tales
brought to Europe by the Crusaders.

Today it seems incredible that such an essentially simple process
as the harvesting, drying, and storing of herbs should ever have been
surrounded by such hocus-pocus as, when, picking mugwort, it must
be done "before sunrise, but let him first say *'tollam te artemisia ne
lassus sim in via.'*" We now know that no herb should be picked
"before sunrise," for that is when the dew is heaviest upon them, and
it is moisture that the careful herb gardener must try to eliminate.

This moisture is mostly the sap of the plants themselves, together
with any atmospheric moisture that may be clinging to leaves or
flower clusters from dew, fog, or left-over raindrops. Hence all herbs,

of which the foliage is harvested, should not be picked until free of atmospheric moisture, which means on a bright, sunny day, preferably before noon. Late afternoon picking is to be avoided, for reasons not too well known, but late picking appears to decrease the fragrant oils found in nearly all herbs and hence diminishes their flavor.

These oils, especially those found in foliage and flower clusters, are not found in greatest quantity at all stages of the plant's growth, so that it is important to harvest these at the most advantageous time. In practically all of them the oil content of foliage and flowering tops is greatest just before the first flowers expand. A day or two (or even a few hours) before blooming is the ideal time for harvesting all those that are to be dried and stored. In many herbs, as noted in the lists, more than one cutting can be made, since taking off the flower cluster and upper leaves often induces fresh growth and a second or even a third crop of flowers.

Generally it does not pay to pick old leaves, nor those near the base of the plant, unless the latter are part of the first growth of spring, when basal leaves often contain considerable oil.

All cut foliage and flowering tops should be brought immediately into the house, and only if they are dirty (that is, sand, soot, or soil) should they be washed under the tap. The latter delays drying, and some herb gardeners, who are unfortunate enough to have to wash herbs, dry off this water in the oven at once. This is an operation needing great care, as artificial heat will inevitably drive off not only extraneous water, but some of the precious oil that it is your prime object to preserve. If you use the oven, see that it is turned low and leave the oven door open. Most commercial herbs are artificially dried and can never approach the flavor of those you dry yourself—if you use ordinary care and keep in mind a few simple facts.

Leaves and flowering tops were once tied in bunches and hung, head down, from the rafters of a shed. That was almost universal practice, and it made redolent mysteries of many an old garden tool house. It is far better, and quicker, and prevents dust from accumulating, to spread your herbs on a wire netting (an old window screen or a chicken-wired frame is excellent) over which cheesecloth is spread. All stems must be removed before drying, for they hold too much sap and very little oil.

Spread the plucked leaves and flowering tops on the cheesecloth, and cover with another piece of cheesecloth, never having more than a single layer of leaves on the rack if possible. The screens must be so arranged that the air will reach them from above and below. If, for lack of equipment, you are forced to put leaves in two or three layers deep, it is essential to stir them up gently each morning until dry.

The racks must be in the shade, and it helps drying if there is cross ventilation. In any event, keep the windows open from 10 A.M. to 5 P.M., but close them at night to keep out dew, rain, or fog. In about three days most herbs will be dry, but it is important to see that they are as *dry as you can get them* before storing. Some plants of Mediterranean origin have felty or gray-green, silky foliage and will need more time to dry. "Dryness" can usually be determined by crushing a leaf. If it is crisp and falls to bits, it is dry enough to store. If you try to store them before they are dry, mildew, fermentation, and a musty flavor are inevitable.

Some herb gardeners crush their leaves to powder before storing, but others prefer the whole leaf, or as much of it as can be rescued. Generally, if the herbs are dry, they are so brittle that few whole leaves will survive handling. It is largely a matter of preference, and how much trouble you will give to preserving whole leaves—for the flavor will be the same. The essential point is that the herbs must be gotten as quickly as possible into air-tight tins or still better into stoppered bottles. In the drying process you have inevitably lost some of the precious oil, and closed containers, in a reasonably cool place, are the best method of holding the residue.

In those herbs of which the flowers comprise the harvest, such as camomile, lavender, pot marigold, etc., the flowers should, of course, be cut when in full bloom, not when just opening, as in the flowering tops of herbs where the leaves are the chief object. The flowers, however, should be dried and stored as already noted except that the flowers of roses require somewhat different handling.

All green parts of the rose flower must be pulled off and thrown away before attempting to dry the petals. These should all be picked apart, and the base or claw of each petal, which is usually lighter in color than the exposed part, should be clipped off with scissors. The petals can then be dried and stored as previously described.

Where seeds are the harvest, it is only needful to see that they are thoroughly ripe, which is usually indicated by their becoming darker and of a fixed (not greenish) color. They can then be harvested and all withered bits of flower parts, stems, etc., should be cleaned away. They are then ready for storage in tight containers. But they should not be stored until all surface moisture has dried off, and if there is any doubt about this, it is safer to leave them on the drying rack for a few days. Their loss of oil is neglible, but putting away moist seeds will surely ruin them.

Chapter Five

Herbs in the Kitchen

No man, unless he be an incipient Brillat-Savarin or an Auguste Escoffier, would dare to suggest to a large feminine audience what to do with herbs. Being neither, and having considerable awe of kitchen mysteries, the author has not rehashed a lot of recipes for this book—and a good many recipes appear to be just this—a rehash of something done before.

There are notable exceptions, and to give the reader adequate browsing in this esoteric field, the following books are recommended —not arranged in the order of their importance, although Mrs. Fox's book is highly recommended. Only those herb books that contain recipes are included.

* *Gardening with Herbs for Flavor and Fragrance.* Helen Morgenthau Fox. Macmillan, 1933.

A Garden of Herbs. Eleanour Sinclair Rohde. Herbert Jenkins, Ltd., London, 1927.

Magic in Herbs. Leonie de Sounin. M. Barrows, 1941.

Herbs: How to Grow Them and How to Use Them. Helen Noyes Webster. Ralph T. Hale Co., 1939.

* Especially recommended for recipes.

* *Herbs for the Kitchen*. Irma Goodrich Mazza. Little, Brown and Co., 1939.

Herb-lore for Housewives. C. Romanné-James. Herbert Jenkins, Ltd., 1938.

* *Herbs, Their Culture and Uses*. Rosetta E. Clarkson. Macmillan, 1946.

* *The Art of Cooking with Herbs and Spices*. Milo Miloradovich. Doubleday, 1950.

Herbs, as far as their use in cookery is concerned are classified into *fine* and *robust* herbs, depending on their chief uses. The term *fine herbs,* usually and by the cognoscenti always Gallicized as *fines herbs,* does not in the least mean that the herbs comprising it are any finer than the others. It is simply a convention by which the term has come to mean a *blend* of certain herbs used in combination instead of singly. The most ordinary combinations of fine herbs include:

> Chervil, Chives, and Parsley
> Chives, Parsley, and Basil
> Basil, Chervil, and Thyme
> Rosemary, Tarragon, and Parsley

When used in the restricted sense often applied to *fine herbs,* these or other combinations that the herb gardeners will invent for themselves are mixed together, chopped very fine, and added to whatever dish they are to flavor at the last moment. Some will omit rosemary, and many ban tarragon altogether. Both must be used with caution in fine herb combinations. Fine herbs go chiefly into salads, sauces, herb butters, omelettes, cheeses, and soups; much more rarely into meat and fish dishes. If fresh herbs can be had, so much the better, but you may often have to use some of your stored supply to make the desired combination.

The *robust* herbs are the standby of the cook, for they do not need to be, but often are, mixed with other herbs. The outstanding robust herbs are horse-radish, dill, fennel, caraway, winter and summer savory, mint, sage, the marjorams, coriander, and anise. They enter into hundreds of recipes, and the relative importance of them to the cook is a good indication of how much of each the gardener should grow. A check of many of the books mentioned and some others indicates that, whether fine or robust, herbs may be arranged in something like the following order as to their chief use in cookery:

* Especially recommended for recipes.

CHIEF HERBS USED IN COOKERY

(Arranged in the order of their importance)

1. Parsley	7. Chervil	13. Winter savory
2. Basil	8. Thyme	14. Cumin
3. Summer savory	9. Rosemary	15. Fennel
4. Sweet marjoram	10. Tarragon	16. Coriander
5. Chives	11. Pot marjoram	17. Anise
6. Mint	12. Caraway	18. Dill

Naturally there are many others, but their use has usually been restricted to a few experts or specialists in herb cookery. Some will be found among the annuals in Chapter Two, or the Perennials in Chapter Three, but some will perhaps be looked for in vain. This book contains only 25 annuals and biennials and 40 perennials, practically all of them of culinary value. To the herb gardener these 65 different plants will provide endless herb combinations. Not the least of the pleasures of herb gardening is being able to go outdoors and collect fresh material whenever it is ready for harvesting. And to the beginner it is of some advantage to know what *not* to grow.

While this book shuns recipes, a useful summary of hundreds of them ought to tell the amateur what the best chefs have demanded in the dishes that are most common. A check of a good many sources reveals many conflicting recommendations—especially among those favoring French, Italian, Spanish, American and, Heaven help us, even English cooking, which is almost the worst in the world. But in spite of much conflict of ideas, there is a surprising agreement on some fundamentals, and they are epitomized here for those who wish to start with the basic rules of herb cookery.

A Selection of Herbs to Use in Various Dishes

MEATS

POULTRY: Sage, sweet marjoram, summer savory, thyme, and tarragon.
VEAL: Same as poultry with possible addition of rosemary.
PORK: Rosemary, anise, sage, chives, basil, and sweet marjoram.
BEEF: Summer savory, thyme, coriander, sweet marjoram, and basil.
LAMB: Garlic, rosemary, dill, mint, and summer savory.
FISH: Parsley and chives (as garnish); also fennel, chervil, basil, thyme, saffron, and sweet marjoram.

VEGETABLES

BEET: Tarragon, caraway, coriander, and sweet marjoram.
CABBAGE: Caraway and fennel.

CARROT: Parsley, tarragon, chives, rosemary.

ONION: Basil, thyme, parsley, celery, and tarragon.

PEAS: Thyme, mint, basil, and summer savory.

POTATO: Thyme, sweet marjoram, parsley, chives, mint, and basil.

STRING BEANS: Rosemary, celery, summer savory, sweet marjoram, and sage.

TOMATO: Red pepper (not the spice), basil, garlic, sage, and sweet marjoram.

SALADS: Almost any herb of which the leaves are used, but they must, of course, be fresh. Notable ones are borage, chervil and chives, summer savory, thyme, leek, tarragon, rose geranium, and anise.

CHEESES: Chives, caraway, sesame, cumin, sweet marjoram, anise, basil, thyme, mint, dill, and sage.

EGGS: Basil, thyme, tarragon (garlic, thyme, and parsley for Eggs in Hell!).

ONE DISH MEALS: Sweet marjoram, thyme, coriander, saffron, caraway, cumin, garlic, pot marjoram, celery, and rosemary.

RICE: Rose geranium, parsley, sweet marjoram, saffron, chives, thyme, basil, and rosemary.

BREAD, PASTRIES, COOKIES: Anise, caraway, poppy, sesame, fennel, coriander, cumin, saffron, and mint.

SPAGHETTI, MARCARONI, ETC.: Basil, chives, parsley, rosemary, and sweet marjoram.

DESSERTS: Anise, sesame, sweet marjoram, mint, and rose geranium.

BEVERAGES

COLD TEAS, LEMONADE, ETC.: Mint, summer savory, costmary, and rose geranium.

HOT TEAS: Sweet marjoram, hyssop, anise, lavender, camomile, costmary, mint, and eglantine.

Alcoholic:

OLD-FASHIONED COCKTAIL: Costmary, but see page 364.

CLARET CUP: Borage and balm.

SAUTERNE CUP: Mint.

JULEP: Mint.

BUTTER OR OLEOMARGARINE: Seeds* of coriander, anise and caraway; leaves of chives.

VINEGAR: Tarragon, mint, garlic, caraway, dill and balm.

Final Caution: If you want the family to be converted or enthusiastic over the use of herbs in cookery, *use them sparingly.* Many are strong-tasting, and it is far better strategy to have people say

* In some recipes calling for seeds, these should be bruised or crushed before mixing. A small stone mortar and pestle make the best equipment for this, and they are the only ones the herb gardener will need beyond ordinary kitchen utensils.

"How good this is" and wonder what made it so, than to venture the suggestion, "Isn't this salad divine, flavored with . . . ?" People like dietary surprises, and your herb garden is your armamentarium for thousands of them. Robert Burns knew it when he wrote:

> Some hae meat and canna eat,
> And some wad eat that want it;
> But we hae meat and we can eat;
> Sae let the Lord be thankit.

Book Six

FRUIT IN THE GARDEN

FRUIT IN THE GARDEN

WHETHER you have room for an extensive fruit garden or space for only a few trees, it is urged that you read the first and last chapters before anything else. The first contains the basic principles upon which all fruit culture depends, while the last deals with its hazards.

Having read them you are ready to decide what fruits to grow and how many to plant. Special chapters, on each of the important ones, will tell you how, and why the choice of varieties is so important.

No other fruit book that comes to mind has separated the five major fruit districts of the region east of the Rocky Mountains. They are important because each reflects certain climatic controls to successful fruit culture. At the outset determine in which one you live.

Every plant is keyed to whatever fruit districts it is suited. Turn to whatever is the fruit of your choice and pick one or more of the varieties suited to your own district, generally avoiding the others.

Finally, for those who have only the most limited space, Chapters Eight and Nine suggest both attractive and abundant alternatives in dwarf and trained fruit trees.

Why Grow Your Own?

CHAPTER I   *A*NY traveler on the truck route from Florida to New York is struck by the occasional dumping of apparently good fruit. This is not because it is bad but because the driver has been told by telephone that the market price will not pay for further transportation.

Thereby hangs a tale for all home fruit growers. It is well known to the experts that commercial fruit growing must be based upon varieties that will stand long hauls and that they must be picked long before true ripening to further this transit. Consequently one never gets really *fresh* tree-ripened fruit in any market. In almost everything, except pears and bananas, we are thus forced to accept not the best varieties but those best adapted to market handling—with all the loss of aroma, flavor, and possibly vitamins that such delay implies.

Recommendations of varieties in many nursery catalogs and in some Experiment Station bulletins naturally favor the commercial grower, for the fruit business in the United States runs into hundreds of millions of dollars. Such recommendations will be ignored in this book, for it is assumed that the home grower will not be a commercial shipper and can avail himself of varieties that are much better than those dictated by long transportation. Also, as many discriminating fruit store patrons have found out to their cost, it is not always the most beautifully colored and shiniest fruit that is the finest tasting. Some commercial varieties, however, have never been improved upon, and one can use them with perfect confidence. They will be better than the same variety from the market simply because you give them what nature asks—a chance to ripen on the tree!

Some gardeners wonder if home-grown fruit is possible on a small plot. Others have, very likely, heard of the difficulties of pest control. Still others are bothered by such terms as whips, stocks, cions, espalier, cordon, spurs, and a dozen others—all of them necessary to the professional fruit grower, but admittedly confusing to the amateur. If any of these terms are used here they will be defined where first used, and if you happen to skip the definition in the text, the term will be found in the index, cross-referenced to a definition.

One feature of fruit growing must be decided at the outset. Fruit and berry plants take more care than most ornamental shrubs and trees. Unless one has the time and inclination to give them that care it is better not to start—for failure follows neglect with unerring regularity. Not only must they get this care at planting time, but there is a yearly program of pruning, spraying, thinning, and harvesting. Each operation is a heavy expense to commercial growers, but if your home fruit garden is not too large, each of the yearly tasks can be a pleasurable use of leisure time. Then, too, some varieties need little spraying, and that saves one from a yearly chore.

Another point that must be decided before you plan the home fruit garden is how much space you can afford to give to it. Fruit trees are roughly divided, according to the room they need, into *standard* and *dwarf*. The former is the natural height and spread of a mature tree. But dwarfs and semi-dwarfs are much lower, usually grafted on slow-growing and often worthless stocks chosen because they dwarf the top. Some idea of the difference between them is shown in the table.

	Height	Spread	Planting Distance Between Trees in Feet	Years Before Fruiting*
	in Feet			
Standard apple	30-40	30	35	6-8
Dwarf apple	6-8	10	10-12	2-4
Standard pear	35-45	30	30	5-7
Dwarf pear	6-10	8-10	10-12	3-5

If you have sufficient room, at least 50 x 50 feet, by all means choose *standard* trees. If your fruit area is much less than this, you may have to omit all standard fruit trees. But fortunately there are dwarf and semi-dwarf varieties of many common fruits, and, for those where space is still more restricted, there are the espaliers, cordons, etc., which are based on the techniques of French orchardists who are perhaps the most skillful in the world. The exact significance of dwarf fruit trees, espaliers, cordons, etc., that are available in this country, and the cultural directions for them, are all grouped in Chapters Eight and Nine. Formerly little more than a fad or an expensive hobby, these dwarfed and trained fruit trees have become a boon to those with limited space. They will never supplant standard trees, except in Normandy and Brittany where commercial orchards of this type are amazingly productive. Labor costs here make it commercially

---

* This figure varies greatly depending on soil, season, care, and the variety chosen. The figures are hence guides rather than a horticultural timetable.

impossible, even if the necessary skills were generally available, which they are not. But the home grower can easily conquer the details, and with patience and care may some day reach the perfection of French orchardists. For all those with limited space, Chapters Eight and Nine should hence be read first—before you plan your fruit garden.

Another important feature of fruit growing is where you live. All temperate-zone tree fruits need a period of dormancy during the winter. So important is this winter chilling of dormant fruit trees that it is impossible to grow satisfactory crops of apples, pears, peaches, cherries, or plums where the winters are too warm. Generally speaking (there are exceptions in highlands), our ordinary fruits should not be attempted south of the coastal plain regions of Georgia, and along the Gulf Coast to eastern Texas (Georgia peaches do not come from the coastal plain). Some of the more southerly of these localities have orange and grapefruit orchards—neither of which can be treated here. Nor can the peculiar and enormously productive orchard practice of California be considered here, because the varieties, climate, and procedure differ too much from that of any other region in the country.

Although winter cold is thus necessary, and winter warmth a barrier, there are parts of the northern United States where winter cold is too severe for peaches, and for many varieties of other fruits. If there is likely to be even moderately prolonged periods of temperatures 10-20° below zero, many varieties cannot be grown. In the discussion of the different fruits these climatic hazards will be given according to the fruit districts outlined below. If you live in northern New England, New York, and in the upper peninsula of Michigan it is safer to consult these lists of varieties before planting.

The only other climatic barriers to the successful home growing of fruit are dryness, summer winds, and deficient rainfall. Over much of the region west of the states of Iowa, Missouri, and Arkansas to the escarpment of the Rocky Mountains, summer rainfall and drying winds make fruit growing hazardous enough so that few amateurs should try it. There are, of course, favorably situated regions within this huge tract, such as the Ozarks, where delicious fruit is produced. But, generally, if you live in this area, you must study the varieties mentioned later, as they are the only ones likely to thrive in these unfavorable places.

In addition to these main climatic factors the experts are fond of the term *micro-climate*. This is the purely local condition dictated by topography, site, proximity to bodies of water, protection (by planting or buildings) from cold north winds or hot drying ones—all of which may exert a beneficial or baneful influence.

In a rolling country where spring frosts are common, such frosts settle in the depressions, but often avoid the higher parts of a site. With very early-flowering fruit trees, like the peach for instance, this may dictate whether the blossoms are blasted by a late spring frost or not.

If your site is sloping, it is better if it inclines toward the south, for this will be warmer than a north-facing slope, and in certain varieties this is often a distinct advantage. In some cases, however, this is also a disadvantage, for it may hasten the flowering of certain trees so that they, too, will be caught by an erratic late frost—which means, of course, no fruit that year.

One of the most favorable factors is proximity to large bodies of water which tends to moderate climatic extremes. This is why the most successful grape vineyards in the East are scattered along Lake Ontario and Lake Erie. Similarly favorable sites along the Coast, near the sea or Chesapeake Bay, and in the Hudson Valley, have dictated the large commercial orchards in these regions.

FRUIT DISTRICTS
(See map, p. 484)

If all this sounds rather forbidding it should be remembered that the science or art of pomology (fruit growing) is so advanced in this country that geneticists have developed thousands of varieties dictated by the varied conditions found within our country. If you live anywhere within the areas noted below, fruit for home use is a climatically possible enterprise. Students of this preferred fruit-growing region have divided it into several sections, and it is well to look these over before planning your fruit garden. So far as the area covered by this book is concerned, these fruit regions are the following:

DISTRICT ONE

Winter cold is the chief factor, and it limits the cultivation of some varieties.

Area: Extreme Northern New England, Eastern Canada (except Nova Scotia), northeastern New York, and the northern peninsula of Michigan and adjacent Canada.

DISTRICT TWO

This comprises the region where most commercial orchards in the East are located.

Area: All of New England and New York that are not in district one (see above), northern New Jersey, Pennsylvania (except the southern border), northern Ohio and Indiana, northeastern Illinois, and all of Michigan (except the northern part of the peninsula).

DISTRICT THREE

In this region, which tends to merge with the southern part of district two there are huge commercial fruit orchards (apples in the Shenandoah Valley, for instance).

Area: Southern New Jersey and Pennsylvania, Maryland (except the eastern shore), southern Ohio and Indiana, all of West Virginia and Kentucky, most of Tennessee (except the Mississippi Valley region), those parts of Virginia and North Carolina that are *not* on the coastal plain (this is roughly the area north and west of a line stretching from Alexandria, Charlottesville, and Danville, Va., to Winston-Salem and Gastonia, N.C.), and finally the hilly and mountainous sections of Georgia and Alabama.

DISTRICT FOUR

The Coastal Plain region. This is warmer than districts one, two, and three, not only because it is further south, but on account of the proximity of the Atlantic and a deeply indented shore line (Delaware Bay, Chesapeake Bay, Albemarle Sound, Pamlico Sound, etc.).

Area: All of Delaware, the eastern shore of Maryland, all of Virginia that is not in district three, coastal North Carolina and South Carolina, and all of Georgia except the mountainous north and a strip along the Atlantic from Savannah to Brunswick, which may be too warm in winter for temperate fruit trees that demand a winter chilling. South of this zone many bush fruits and strawberries thrive.

DISTRICT FIVE

Central Valley region. Within the drainage area of the Mississippi River, fruit growing is possible, but regions south of Arkansas are apt to be too hot, whereas Minnesota has such cold winters that only the varieties in district one are likely to be hardy. On the southern edge of this zone many bush fruits are grown, some of them thriving in areas too warm for tree fruits.

Area: Minnesota (see above). Wisconsin (only the southern part), Iowa, Illinois (southern and western parts), Missouri and Arkansas (mostly in the Ozarks). South of this, large areas are occupied by dewberries and blackberries. See bush fruits in Chapter Two.

District five is not very well defined, because it merges with areas to the westward where fruit growing is not likely to be satisfactory for the amateur, except for apples. As pointed out earlier in this chapter, these western states have too much drying wind, great summer heat, and deficient rainfall—not to speak of icy winters. All of these hazards can be overcome by shelter-belt planting, irrigation, and careful selection of varieties, but this is too expensive to warrant the outlay.

Note: All the fruit varieties in this book that need it will be keyed to one or more of these five main fruit districts, depending on their adaptability to the different regions. No individual could ever accumulate enough data to make such a scheme of value, and it should be emphasized that the plan is the result of years of study by the United States Department of Agriculture, and of records of hardiness and performance by all the experiment stations in the states involved. Thousands of varieties have been studied, but only those of interest to the home grower are included here. It should scarcely be necessary to remind the user of this scheme that the boundaries of the different districts must overlap, due to topography, mountains especially, and to other local conditions. In other words, the scheme is a *guide* rather than an attempt at strict delineation of each area. If you live close to any of the boundaries, it is safe to use varieties common to your own district and the adjoining one.

Throughout the book, therefore, you will find a varietal name, like McIntosh apple for instance, with one or more numbers in parentheses—written thus, McIntosh (2, 3). This means that the variety is most suited to districts two and three, as defined above, but not so well to others. For the amateur it is much safer to pick a variety that is known to perform well in his vicinity rather than one that is uncertain. In other words, look out for the numbers, as ignoring them may invite failure.

SOILS

There is scarcely a soil type in this country that will not grow satisfactory fruit. The only possible exceptions are sands that are too porous to hold enough water for growth, and layers of clayey hardpan below the surface, which hold too much water. Notably acid or alkali soils are best avoided, and if you do not know how to determine this your county agent will do it.* Nor will most fruits grow in swamps.

* In *Taylor's Encyclopedia of Gardening*, at the article on Acid and Alkali soils, there is a full description of these tests and their significance.

Generally speaking, any soil that will grow potatoes or a vegetable garden will grow good fruit. Of course the soil must not be too thin, *i.e.*, a skimpy layer on a flat rock. That would be dooming the tree to be blown down at the first gale. Nor should very stony land be chosen if it is possible to avoid it. All that is needed is a reasonably rich soil, deep enough to dig the necessary hole for planting. As most orchards should be started from *whips,* which are yearling, single-stemmed, slender young trees, the hole for planting may not need to be more than a foot deep.

As to whether or not to add commercial fertilizer or manure, there is still some controversy. It will no doubt induce lush growth, but it may be mostly leafy twigs rather than fruit. This is to be avoided in standard trees, but among dwarfs, espaliers, and cordons, which are rigorously pruned for fruit production, manure or fertilizer is more than justified. The experts in Normandy and Brittany heavily manure their trees, but pruning for fruit production is drastic.

Some commercial growers think it pays to put about half a pound of nitrate of soda around each tree that is 1-2 years old, and 2-3 pounds for a tree 8-10 years old, annually. Others that are equally successful use only stable manure, about 2 inches deep and dug into the soil around the tree. Still others, who believe that available food is sufficient in most soil, see that the humus content of it is kept up by digging in grass-cuttings, leaves, corn-stalks or any other green refuse that will, when decomposed, help the moisture-holding capacity of any soil. And, finally, there are those who think that *any* kind of fertilizer or manure is unnecessary for fruit culture, except on the poorest and sandiest soils.

For the home fruit grower the only sensible plan, which will be dictated by the kind of soil you have, is to try a little (not more than one-half pound) of a commercial fertilizer, to each young tree and watch the result. The writer prefers a little stable manure, not more than once in three years, or none at all if the the soil is reasonably rich, *i.e.*, if the soil will grow a good lawn or crop of vegetables. Humus content of the soil is perhaps the most important single factor in plant growth. Manure or vegetable refuse adds this, but none is added by the application of commercial fertilizer.

The amateur should also be especially warned against various nostrums, widely advertised as "wonder soil conditioners," "magic fertilizers," etc. These are generally profuse in promises but scanty in scientific details. Some of them may be justified for a small vegetable garden where the owner is as well equipped with gullibility as with cash. But they should have no lure for the intelligent amateur fruit grower—as it is not at all sure that his trees need *any* commercial fertilizer, and certainly no nostrums. There is no indication that fruit trees are helped in the least by an application of lime which seems to have a peculiar fascination for the amateur. Lime has a legitimate place in the garden and farm, but fruit trees appear never to need it, unless the soil is acid.

In other words, the normal tolerance of most fruit trees for a slightly alkaline or slightly acid soil, as well as for neutral ones, make the application of lime a useless expense, and in the case of the blueberry it invites certain failure.

FERTILE OR INFERTILE?

It is high time to talk about another sort of fertility far more important to fruit growers than the controversial maintenance of soil fertility. This is the ability of any particular fruit blossom to produce a fruit. Many, left to themselves, would provide a splendid spring show of color, but no fruit at all. The reason is a bit complicated, but should be understood by all fruit growers. It involves the sex life of all plants, and especially the showy, but often unproductive blossoms of fruit trees.

The normally functioning sex life of plants is that, in most flowers, there is a central column (the style) with a usually slightly swollen base (the ovary) and a forked, branched or knobby tip (the stigma or stigmas). These are all, collectively, called the pistil. Within the ovary are unfertilized ovules, which should ultimately become seeds, as the swollen and much modified ovary should become a fruit. (There are technical variations of this which we can ignore here.) This stigma, style, ovary, and ovules (the pistil) comprise the female organs of reproduction—as yet quite virgin.

The male elements comprise a number of tiny thread-like organs (the stamens) which in all fruit trees are found in the same flower as the pistil and usually surround it. Stamens have a minute knob-like tip (the anther) which at the proper time produces a dust-like mass of usually yellow powder (pollen). The latter is the sole male fertilizing element in all flowering plants.

At the climax of the sexual rhythm of the ovary, its stigma becomes sticky, and hence receptive to the grain of pollen which has the capacity to transform the hitherto virgin female into a sexually mature fruit. The growth of the pollen tube down through the style and the ultimate fertilization of the waiting ovule is, in ordinary plants, a

marvelously timed operation, far more complicated and even romantic than this simple outline of its drama.

But Nature works in devious ways to make the process of fertilization still more difficult. She apparently hit upon the principle that
steady fertilization of a flower with its own pollen might lead to
sterility, and it would quite certainly retard the production of hybrids,
with their supposed greater vigor and their undoubted capacity to
produce interesting new strains or even species. Whatever the motive,
if there was one, there grew up in the plant world a wilderness of
flowers that became perfectly sterile to their own pollen, thus depending for their survival upon pollen coming from a different flower
of the same species—a process, commonly, but not quite correctly,
called cross-fertilization. This happens to so many plants, and the
methods of ensuring cross-fertilization are so intricate and fascinating,
that Darwin devoted one of his volumes to it. *The Effects of Cross-
and Self-Fertilization in the Vegetable Kingdom* (1876) is still worthwhile reading for any inquisitive fruit grower. For here are the
fundamentals of cross- and self-fertilization that modern genetics has
changed very little since Darwin first announced his theory.

It is precisely this self-sterility that afflicts many fruit trees. In
order to produce fruit they *must* get pollen from another tree of the
same species. In fruit blossoms this is a fairly simple operation, although the timing of it has to be precise. When the stigma is receptive,
which may last only a few hours, rarely a few days, the foreign pollen
must be available, and must be carried from the flower that produces
it to the one waiting to receive it.

This always happens if there is a favorable wind or, most important
of all, if there are plenty of insects. These busy creatures, especially
bees, are constantly at work visiting all the blossoms they need for
a load of nectar. In such traffic they become coated with pollen and
cannot help rubbing some of it off on the receptive stigma. Only a
single pollen grain is necessary for ultimate fertilization, for the ovule
is quite literally monogamous, and there is thus a prodigal wastage of
the male units of reproduction. But Nature has accomplished her purpose—the production of a fruit with foreign pollen and within which
will be seeds that are not the result of self-fertilization. Sometimes
during storms, pelting rain, or unseasonable cold during blossom-
time, there will be no chance for insects to ensure cross-fertilization.
Such unhappy accidents result in a poor yield of fruit that year, or
none at all if the conditions are severe. It also accounts for the so-called
"off-year" habit of some trees, although other factors are often involved in this intermittent production of fruit.

The implications of all this are obvious to any fruit grower. Not all varieties are self-sterile, but many are, and for them we must provide other, closely related trees so that pollen will be available when needed. The terms *self-sterile* and *self-fertile* will hence be used throughout this book. They must be understood *before* you plan a fruit garden, although as far as possible self-fertile varieties will be selected. But it is impossible in many highly desirable fruits to find *all* self-fertile varieties, notably among pears, plums, cherries, strawberries, etc. Most peaches, however, and many apples are self-fertile.

Notes of self-sterility and self-fertility will be found in all the chapters on the different fruits, whenever necessary, and they must be followed carefully to ensure a good crop. If there is no mention of either it means that the tree is self-fertile, which most amateurs take for granted, but as we have seen this is by no means a safe assumption.

PLANNING THE FRUIT GARDEN

If the space you can devote to fruit is about 50 x 50 feet, you can grow sufficient fruit to keep the average family well supplied during the season, give some away, and have enough left over for storage, canning and deep-freezing, if you have the equipment.

Planning a fruit garden is primarily dictated by the tastes of the family, and by the capacity to save surplus fruit for later use. Hence an "average" plan is impossible. But, as a guide in planning a fruit garden, it is safe to assume that it should contain the following:

3 apples
3 pears*
3 peaches
2 cherries
2 plums*
1 nectarine
2 varieties of raspberry
1 variety of blackberry   Low or bush fruits, of which
3 varieties of strawberry   several or dozens of plants will
2 varieties of currant   be needed. See the chapter on
1 variety of gooseberry   Bush Fruits and the one on
3 varieties of blueberry   Strawberry
3 varieties of grapes to be grown
   on wires, fences or arbors.

* Pears and plums are not safe in certain of the fruit districts mentioned above. See the chapter on Apple, Pear and Quince, and the one on Stone Fruits for details. If one or both are impossible in your vicinity, you can increase the planting of other kinds—apples and peaches, for instance.

This will mean 6 large trees (apples and pears), 2 medium-sized trees (cherries), and 6 smaller trees (peaches, plums, and nectarine) —making a total of 14 trees, all of which will be standards (not dwarf or trained). It is quite obvious that such a plantation cannot be crowded into a space 50 x 50 feet unless you can plant some of the larger trees along the edges or corners of the plot. If this is impossible, due to proximity of the street (a fruit orchard is a constant temptation to vandals), or your neighbor objects to shade encroachment, you will have to reduce the number of large trees (apples and pears), or replace them with dwarf varieties (see Chapter Eight).

Generally, if you have as much as 50 x 50 feet for fruit, your grounds are large enough to permit the planting of nearly all the fourteen trees on the edges and corners, allowing shade encroachment to take care of itself. All the large trees, particularly the apples, are apt to spread in age, and this must be provided for.

In addition to the fourteen trees, space must be provided for the low or bush fruits. These comprise the bramble fruits (raspberry and blackberry), the currant and gooseberry, the blueberry, and finally the strawberry, which some prefer to grow in the vegetable garden.

In commercial orchards the ground between the fruit trees will be cultivated once or twice during the growing season, and often a cover crop of vetch or the clovers will be sown broadcast, and plowed under in spring or fall. In the home fruit garden this is unnecessary, and sod or a lawn is the only ground cover needed for the taller trees. Either should be mown, when necessary, for neatness and to keep down weeds.

The accompanying plan of a 50 x 50 fruit garden shows how the trees should be spaced, and where the low bush fruits and strawberries may be put. The largest and most permanent of the trees are apples and pears, and the peaches and nectarine are the shortest-lived (8-10 years). No plan will fit every need, and this one is presented with the idea that you can modify it to suit local conditions of topography, adjacent buildings, the family's preference for certain fruits, or any other factor that demands changes.

PLANTING AND AFTER CARE

The planting of fruit trees is the same as for ornamental ones. All fruit trees are grafted or budded on to a vigorous rootstock; and this union, having been made by the nurseryman, generally at ground level, you may not notice unless you look sharp. Its only significance

FRUIT GARDEN 50 X 50 FEET

1.	Apple	3 trees	
2.	*Pear	3 "	Standard Trees
3.	Cherry	2 "	(If your area is less than 50 x 50
4.	Peach	3 "	feet you must use dwarf or semi-
5.	Nectarine	1 "	dwarf trees. See Chapter Eight)
6.	*Plum	2 "	

7.	Currant	4 plants	
8.	Blueberry	6 "	Bush Fruits
9.	Gooseberry	3 "	

10. Raspberry, 2 varieties, 5 plants
     each   Bramble Fruits
11. Blackberry, 1 variety, 4 plants

12. Strawberry, 3 varieties, a double row of about 18 plants each, mak-
     ing 36 plants in all, depending on variety. See Chapter Three.

For the actual varieties to go in each space, see the details in the chapters on each group of fruits. It is impossible to specify them here because of the diversity of climate in different regions. See *Fruit Districts* earlier in this chapter. No grapes are shown as their use depends upon an available trellis or fence—there is no room for a grape arbor.

* See the footnote on page 408. If you live in a region unsuited to either or both of these fruits you can increase the number of peaches or apples or perhaps add a quince.

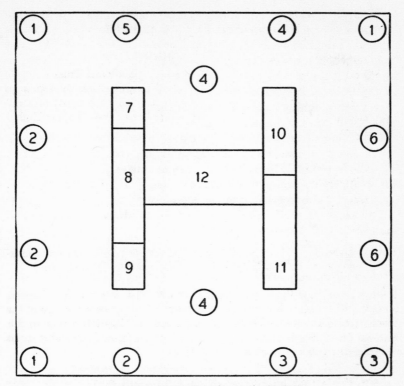

FRUIT GARDEN 50 X 50 FEET

to the fruit grower is to see to it that no shoots spring up from the rootstock, which sometimes happens; and, if they do, cut such shoots (usually called suckers) off at or just below ground level. The need to do this is obvious, because, if the sucker were allowed to grow, it might well replace the grafted top (cion), and ultimately the tree would be as worthless as the stock from which it sprang. In other words you purchase fruit trees only for the grafted (or budded) cion which will develop into the tree of your choice.

In starting a fruit garden it is far better to purchase 1- to 2-year-old whips (slender, often unbranched and usually yearling trees), rather than older, probably branched, and much more expensive ones. From the whip, which will grow surprisingly fast, you can guide the future branching of the tree, as explained later, and the chances of loss from the shock of planting are far less with young trees than with older ones.

In getting trees from a nursery it is well to study the catalogs of several rival firms before placing an order. While it would be unfair to say that nurserymen are more unscrupulous than other business-men, it is a fact that the catalogs of some of them suggest precisely this. Lurid color, wildly improbable claims, many so-called letters of approval from satisfied customers—all are the stock-in-trade of the patent medicine barker of fifty years ago. Throughout this book there are definite named varieties of fruit, all of them tried and tested over a period of years. The amateur would do well to insist upon these varieties, see that he gets them, and leave all expensive novelties (some of them are even patented!) to the appraisal of the experts.

In planting standard fruit trees, put them in at about the same level they occupied at the nursery. You can easily see this by noticing the difference in the color of the exposed and formerly buried stem. Dig a hole deep enough to plant the tree at the proper level (i.e., the old one), and wide enough to take care of its present root-spread. If there are any broken roots cut them off at the break with a sharp knife or pruning shears. Then fill in the hole with the best soil you have (avoiding or breaking up lumps) until it is about two-thirds full. Then shake the whip gently to filter the soil down close to the buried roots, and tramp down the soil firmly, with the feet or a stout piece of timber. When thoroughly packed down, fill up the hole with water, and after this has settled, put in enough more soil to fill the hole up to within an inch or so of the ground level. This will leave a shallow well for subsequent watering if the tree needs it. If there is normal rainfall, the tree will not need watering.

When the whip is planted, it will probably be 4-5 feet high. From the whip cut off about one third of the tip, and no other pruning should be done the first year. For the subsequent pruning of standard fruit trees and ultimate spacing and direction of the main branches, see the drawings on pages 415–417.

All that has been written above applies only to the planting of standard fruit trees. For special handling of dwarfs and trained espalier or cordon trees, see Chapters Eight and Nine. Also the planting of berry bushes, strawberries, blueberry, and grapes should be sought in the chapters devoted to those fruits.

Nor is it possible here to deal generally with the control of pests, for they vary greatly and control methods will be found in Chapter Ten.

Before turning to the chapters on the different kinds of fruits it is perhaps well to epitomize some of the main factors that dictate success.

1. Be sure of the fruit district you live in. See that section of this chapter.

2. Know definitely whether the fruit you wish to plant is self-sterile or self-fertile. See that section of this chapter.

3. Make at least a rough plan of what you want to plant, several weeks before actual planting time, estimating the amount and varieties of trees necessary for your needs.

4. Do not buy unnamed, unspecified fruit trees from irresponsible salesmen or roadside stands. Reputable dealers issue catalogs, their stock is government-inspected for pests, and their varieties, at least among the better dealers, are apt to be true to name.

5. Every year or two various firms advertise fruit "novelties," usually with a fanfare of publicity. Shun such offers unless your purse is long and you can give them the scientific appraisal that the Experiment Stations will certainly do in a few years. Until then they are apt to be expensive and untried variants of some well-known and tested variety. Some novelties are even patented which permits the sponsor to be the sole distributor and charge whatever a gullible public will pay. Don't be one of them.

6. Beware of advertising clamor over "miracle soil conditioners," "magic fertilizer mixtures," and other nostrums with lurid claims of fertility. Re-read the section on soils in this chapter—*caveat emptor*.

PRUNING

The object of pruning is to so set the pattern of branching (scaffold) of the young tree that the mature one will not have too many main branches, and that the foliage crown will not be too dense. This can be done in the first year or two so much the better than later, that nearly all the illustrations are of the management of young trees. Subsequent thinning of mature trees is obvious enough, as the object is to permit light and air to get into the center of the foliage canopy. Light thinning every year or two will accomplish this.

APPLES AND PEARS

1. Heading back a 1-year-old apple whip, immediately after planting. It is always better to start with such trees. Cut at dotted line.
2. A two-year-old, unpruned apple tree. The dotted lines show where cuts should be made to balance the branches. A should be removed entirely.
3. An older apple tree in need of pruning.
4. The same tree, as in 3, after pruning, the object of which is to thin out enough wood to prevent crowding of ultimate branches.
5. This is the type of branching to avoid by early pruning. Crotch is weak and such trees are apt to split in storms.

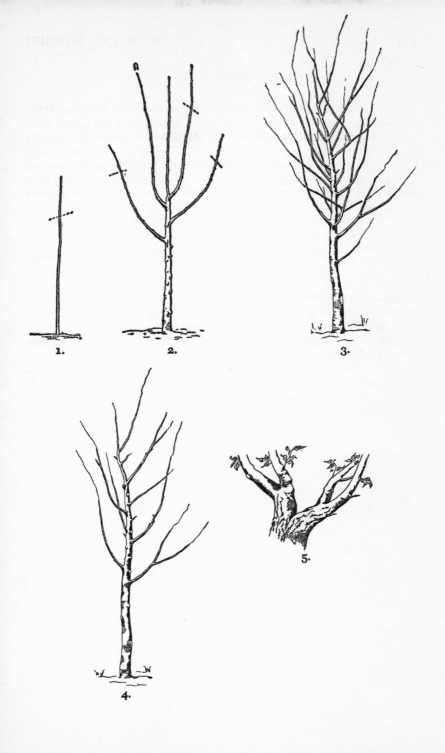

1. 2. 3.

4. 5.

PRUNING

1. Peach whip as it comes from the nursery and after it has been headed back to about 40 inches.
2. Same tree, one month later, showing that it will produce too many branches if left unpruned.
3. Same tree with all branches removed except those that will make the permanent scaffold of the tree.
4. Midsummer aspect of peach tree, started as a whip (see Fig. 1), after it has branched in accordance with the pruning shown in Fig. 3. This will be the permanent form of the tree, and only enough subsequent pruning is necessary to keep the tree open enough so that sunlight may get into the interior of the foliage crown.

Cherries and Plums

5. Sweet Cherry tree 2 years old, unpruned.
6. Same tree as in Fig. 5, pruned so that there will be no weak crotches, and the head of the future tree will not be too crowded.
7. What happens to fruit trees when pruning was neglected the first year or two. Weak crotches invite wind destruction.

The pruning or thinning of grapes, strawberries, and bush fruits will be found at the account of each fruit. For the specialized pruning of espaliers, see Chapter Nine.

Raspberries (above) are best grown on wires, and may reach a height of six or seven feet. Fruiting is from second year growth, and culture in a single row makes heading back and pruning easier. (Photo: *Genereux*)

Cultivated blueberries (below) are a relatively new fruit, having been developed first in New Jersey around 1910. For gardens with acid soil they are both decorative and productive. (Photo: *Genereux*)

The espaliered fruit tree (above) can be used in many planting plans. In the foundation planting of this house young espaliers add the necessary accents to a clipped hedge of uniform height. (Photo: *Genereux*)

Carefully espaliered apple trees, trained over a dome of iron rods, make the green summer house (below) typical of the unusual garden uses to which espaliers lend themselves. (Photo: *Genereux*)

Dwarf trees make possible a bearing orchard in a fraction of the space normal trees would need. These pear trees are of fruiting size and can be kept under ten feet in height. (Photo: *Genereux*)

The crops on dwarf trees are disproportionate to the size of the tree, and a few specimens will keep a family well supplied. The apple tree (right) is part of a mixed planting of dwarf apples, pears and peaches.
(Photo: *Genereux*)

Mature fruit trees can be an integral part of the garden picture. This pear tree is the focus of a group of forsythia and spring-flowering bulbs. (Photo: *Genereux*)

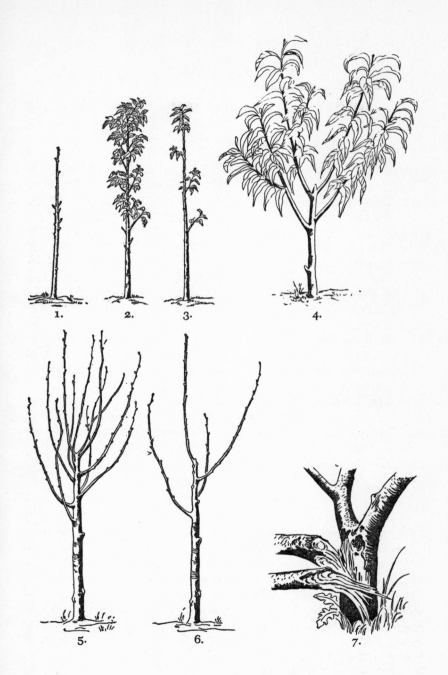

1.   2.   3.   4.

5.   6.   7.

Bush Fruits

*F*ORTUNATELY all the bush fruits except certain blackberries are self-fertile so that the grower does not have to worry about planting possibly unwanted varieties to ensure cross-fertilization. These shrubby fruits are a boon to those who have no room for standard fruit trees, for the bush fruits take relatively little space, especially the currants and gooseberries. These produce rather long-keeping fruit; but in all the blackberries, and especially the raspberries, the fruit keeps poorly and hence is better suited to the home garden than to shipping.

As here restricted the term "bush fruits" includes the currant and gooseberry, which are relatively unimportant in America, but much prized in England, and the far more important blackberry and raspberry, which are usually called *bramble fruits,* from their descent from wild brambles that are common all over the United States and many other parts of the world.

All the bush fruits are best grown in cultivated soil, not in sod or on a lawn; they all need to be weeded. Some of them need stakes or wire trellises, and a few kinds of blackberry and some raspberries are such rampant growers that drastic digging out of too vigorous intruders is all that keeps them within bounds.

RASPBERRY

The raspberries are inclined to be weak-stemmed, usually prickly plants that often sprawl, so that most home growers prefer to tie them to stakes or to tightly strung wires. They all fruit only on the canes (stems) that were produced last year, so that no fruit is borne on the canes of the current year. This biennial habit has a profound effect upon the handling of a raspberry plantation.

When the plant arrives from the nursery it will be little more than a mass of roots and maybe only one or two short stems or none. No fruit is to be expected the first year, but the plant will send up several canes, usually 4-6 feet high, which should be allowed to grow as long as they will. Early the following spring, before the leaves appear, this cane (which will produce fruit this second year) should be cut back to not more than 3-5 feet in height, depending on its vigor. Four or five such fruiting canes can be left at each plant, but all weak ones should be cut down to the ground to conserve nourishment for the fruiting canes.

During this second year, and in all successive ones, there will also spring up, in the red raspberry, a new crop of nonfruiting canes, which should be allowed to grow as they will, but will be headed back the next spring, just as was done with the initial plants. In other words, all raspberry plants will have one set of fruiting canes and another set of nonfruiting ones that will bear fruit next year.

After the fruit has been picked, the fruit-bearing canes should be cut to the ground level, for they will otherwise use nourishment that should be channeled into the new canes of the current year. Another and most cogent reason for cutting down the fruiting canes after picking is that such fruiting canes will never again bear any fruit and will, in any case, be dead by the spring of the next year.

Raspberries are inclined to send up many unwanted shoots (suckers) in all sorts of inconvenient places. If left alone a raspberry patch may well become a weedy thicket with little fruit due to overcrowding. It is this habit that has dictated the two most usual ways of growing raspberries. You can choose either, depending on the space you have.

The first method puts the plants 5 x 5 feet apart each way for the red raspberries, and 6 x 6 feet apart for the purple and black varieties. The ground is kept cultivated all around each plant, and all unwanted shoots are dug out. This is essential in order to keep the planting free of weeds. Each plant is usually tied to a stout stake to prevent sprawling.

The other method grows raspberries in rows which are at least 7 feet apart, but the plants may be only 3½ feet from each other in the row. Quite soon such a row of raspberry plants will be almost hedge-like and must have support. This is best done by heavy stakes put down every 20 feet, each with a stout cross-arm about 20 inches long. From the ends of the cross-arms strong wires are stretched, and when the two wires are strung all the plants will be between them. If tied to the nearest wire, the plants will be more secure. The wires should be about 4 feet from the ground.

Under this linear system of growing raspberries, all shoots that spring up between the rows of plants should be dug up, and the area thoroughly cultivated to keep down weeds and to prevent the area from becoming an impassable thicket.

There is no particular trouble about planting. Set the young plants from the nursery about an inch deeper than they formerly were, and give each of them a little water if the soil is dry. They must, of course, be set out when dormant, and this means as early in the spring as you can work the ground.

The raspberry does not like extreme cold, nor will it thrive in great summer heat, especially if it is moist heat as occurs along the coast from Delaware southward. Hence, pay particular attention to the numbers in parentheses after each varietal name. They apply to fruit districts as outlined in Chapter One.

There are three main types of raspberry, the red, the black, and hybrids between them which are known as purple raspberries. Which you prefer is wholly a matter of personal taste, but if you have only a small amount of space, it is probably better to stick to the red sorts.

In the lists below only those are included which are best suited for home consumption. The fruit is so perishable that other varieties must be used by commercial growers to permit long-haul shipping.

RED-FRUITED VARIETIES

CHIEF (1,2,3,5),* an early variety, resistant to disease; fruit is rather small, but firm and of good quality.

LATHAM (2,3,5), an old and very popular sort, with larger fruit than Chief, but the plants are less resistant to disease in some localities.

JUNE (1,2), has large fruit that keeps better than most, is very early, and comparatively free from disease.

RANERE (3), sometimes called St. Regis. A valuable sort because it is later fruiting than June, and in favorable sites may also fruit again later in the summer. Fruit not so good as Latham or June.

CUTHBERT (2,3), has bright red, medium-sized fruit of good quality. Moderately susceptible to disease.

NEWBURGH (1,2), a vigorous grower with large firm fruit; nearly immune to disease.

VAN FLEET (4), only a moderately good bearer, and the fruit does not compare with June, Latham, or Newburgh, but valuable as it will grow in fruit district four, which is unfit for most red raspberries.

PURPLE-FRUITED VARIETIES

COLUMBIAN (2,3,5), fruit large, late, dark purple to blackish, of good quality, and profusely borne. Plants susceptible to disease.

* For the significance of these numbers see the section on Fruit Districts in Chapter One. It is not safe to choose a variety until you have done so.

SHAFFER (2,3,5), perhaps not superior to Columbian, but more productive, suitable especially for canning, and less susceptible to disease.

SODUS (2,3), resembling Columbian, but even more productive. Fruit more acid than Columbian, and not of such good quality. It is almost free of disease.

BLACK-FRUITED VARIETIES

CUMBERLAND (2,3,5), a midseason variety with a large berry of good quality; quite subject to disease.

PLUM FARMER (2,5), fruit large, with a bloom, and of the best quality. Somewhat subject to disease in some localities, but nearly immune in central New York State.

BLACK PEARL (2,3,5), not unlike Plum Farmer, the fruit, however, glossy; the plant nearly immune to disease.

NAPLES (2), fruit large, glossy, rather late, mildly acid; the plant nearly immune to disease.

There is one rooting habit of the purple and black varieties that needs attention. Late in the season the current canes are apt to get long, somewhat weak, and if left alone will arch over so that their tips touch the ground. Whenever this happens the tip will catch root if the soil is loose and mellow. In fact, commercial growers encourage this tipping by slightly burying such tips, thus helping them to root thoroughly. After which (the next spring) such tipped plants are cut free of the old one, and this habit thus becomes the source of new plants.

Such tipped plants ensure propagation of these black and purple varieties, but they need to be watched by the amateur, because their production is erratic and, unless ruthlessly removed from between the rows, they make cultivation impossible. In such cases the black or purple raspberry patch becomes an unmanageable thicket.

In cultivating all raspberries, remember that they are rather shallow-rooted, and whether you use a hoe or a wheel cultivator, do not cultivate deeper than 4 inches. All that is really necessary is to keep the berry patch free of weeds and prevent the soil from caking.

The number of plants needed for the average family can be estimated from the yield. In well-established plants, properly pruned, the annual yield of fruit ought to be about two pints per plant—but much less if the season is dry. By choosing early and late varieties the fruiting season can be extended for several weeks. It will need about twenty plants to give you such a long-continued crop. If you

plant only one variety and hence concentrate your crop, ten or fifteen plants will be ample both for eating and canning or the deep
freeze.

For the pests of the raspberry, see Chapter Ten.

BLACKBERRY

Gloves are needed to handle this most prickly of all the bramble
fruits—especially when pruning the canes or picking the crop. The
blackberry is closely allied to the raspberry and has the same habit
of sending up suckers. Like the raspberry, it can be tied to a stake
or grown between wires stretched between posts. It is even more
rampant than the raspberry, and thus all suckers that come up between the rows must be ruthlessly destroyed. The penalty for failure
to do this will inevitably be a jungle of extremely prickly and unmanageable growth. The only way to prevent this is constant, clean
cultivation, by machine if the plantation is extensive, or by hoeing
if you have only a few plants.

More than almost any other fruit in this book the blackberry has
acquired a bad reputation from the tartness of the commercially
available fruit. The blackberry is not ripe merely because it turns
black. After this happens it begins to develop its sweetness and flavor,
but becomes risky to ship because of danger of spoilage. Practically all
store blackberries are picked to avoid this hazard, and the home
grower is almost the only one who knows what a good ripe blackberry
tastes like.

Because blackberries are more rampant than raspberries they
should not be planted closer than 7 feet apart each way if tied to
stakes. And if tied to wires the plants should not be nearer than 4
feet apart in the row, and the rows at least 7 feet apart.

It is absolutely essential to keep down weeds in the row, in addition to constant cultivation between the rows. If weeds get a good
start among the plants in the row they are difficult to get out because
the plant is so prickly. The remedy is hoeing out all weeds while they
are very young. But care must be used in cultivating and hoeing, because the blackberry is shallow-rooted; do not cultivate deeper than
3½ to 4 inches. Badly weed-infested blackberry plantations might
as well be destroyed, as it is cheaper to start fresh on weed-free soil
than attempt to clean out a weedy row of blackberries. To do so
means gloves and a leather jacket—the prickles are so ferocious!

All erect blackberries tend to sprawl and would become unmanageable without being tied to some support—to stakes if you have

only a few plants, but between tightly stretched wires if you have more. The latter method must be used for some varieties that are semi-trailing and for the frankly trailing sorts, such as the dewberry and youngberry. The boysenberry and loganberry, both originating in California, are trailing sorts not well suited to our area. The dewberries are not suited to all sections of the country, as will be noted below. Nor are all erect blackberries hardy everywhere, although the whole group has a wider range of adaptability than most fruits. However, it is essential to determine the fruit district in which you live before planting any variety. Those below have been selected only for home consumption. The numbers in parentheses refer to the fruit districts described in Chapter One.

VARIETIES

BLACKBERRIES

ALFRED (1,2). An erect plant, and early fruiting, the berries sweet and firm.

ELDORADO (2,3,5). Erect, and a very satisfactory variety for home use. Fruit medium-sized, sweet, and produced in midseason.

SNYDER (1,2). Chiefly of value because of hardiness to cold. Berries medium-sized, rather seedy, but produced in large quantity. Plant erect.

BRAINARD (3,4). Semi-trailing, and must be trained on wires. It is a hybrid developed by the United States Department of Agriculture between Himalaya and an eastern blackberry, to provide a plant of the semi-trailing habit with the fine fruit of Himalaya, which should not be grown in our area.

EARLY HARVEST (4,5). Erect, fairly vigorous, and with not so many suckers as some others. Fruit medium-sized, of good quality.

NANTICOKE (3,4). A late-fruiting variety, the fruit sweet, soft, and of fine quality. Plant erect, very prickly, and drought-resistant.

McDONALD (4,5). Semi-erect and needing wires. Fruit very early, of good quality. Plant is self-sterile,* and another variety must be planted with it. Use Early Harvest for this at the rate of one Early Harvest to five McDonald. Not recommended for the northern part of district five.

DEWBERRY

None of these is fit to grow in fruit districts one and two, and only three are suggested for the remainder of our area. Most of them are

* See section on Fertile or Infertile? in Chapter One.

best grown in California. The dewberries are always trailing plants
needing wire supports.

LUCRETIA (3,4,5 [southern part only]). This is sometimes called the
        dingleberry. Fruit sweet if left on for 2-3 days after turning
black. If local conditions are rigorous in winter, the plants need a protective mulch of straw or soil.

MAYES (4,5). Sometimes known as Austin Mayes. A fine variety for
        the home grower, and fruiting at least a week earlier than
Lucretia. Stands drought well and largely grown in Texas. Not suited
to northern part of district 5.

YOUNG (4,5). Generally called Youngberry, and originated at Morgan
        City, Louisiana, by B. M. Young, from a cross-pollination of
Mayes and another variety. It has better fruit than Lucretia, deep
wine-colored, sweeter than the loganberry or boysenberry. Not quite
safe north of Washington, D.C., in the east, and not at all fit for
northern part of district 5.

The erect blackberries and the trailing sorts are best planted in
early spring and behave like the raspberry. See that section of this
chapter for planting directions and care for the first season. If the
plants arrive from the nursery with long canes, cut them down to 6-8
inches before planting. When it comes time to reduce the length of
the fruiting canes of erect blackberries at the beginning of the second
season they are best cut down to about 3 feet high. If left much longer
the weight of the fruit may break down the cane.

Most trailing blackberries and the dewberries tend to root at the
tip of the cane. This makes propagation easy, but it also makes it
imperative to control this root-tipping tendency because, if left to
itself, your dewberry plantation will become a dense low thicket
of inextricable vines. Dewberries are not easy to manage unless you
can confine them to the wires to which they must be tied. For the
pests of blackberry and dewberry, see Chapter Ten. They are far
less susceptible to diseases than the raspberry.

CURRANT AND GOOSEBERRY

These closely related fruits have never been very popular in this
country, perhaps because we do not generally grow the varieties
found in England where they are much appreciated. Another and
much more serious reason for curtailing the planting of either of these
shrubs is that both of them, especially the gooseberry, harbor a
microscopic parasite which lives the other half of its life on a white
pine tree, which it usually kills.

Once this white pine blister rust infects the tree, nothing can be done to save it, and so serious is this to forest and ornamental plantings of white pine that the U. S. Government passed stringent quarantine laws that forbid the planting of currants and gooseberries in critical areas. This prevents the organism from completing its life cycle on these bush fruits, and saves the immensely more valuable white pine forests of the country.

If you live in any of the following states you *must* apply to the Experiment Station in your state to find out whether you can plant currants or gooseberries. Do this before ordering plants from the nursery.

WHITE PINE BLISTER RUST STATES

(in our area)

Connecticut	Maryland	New York	Vermont
Delaware	Massachusetts	North Carolina	Virginia
Georgia	Michigan	Ohio	West Virginia
Illinois	Minnesota	Pennsylvania	Wisconsin
Kentucky	New Hampshire	Rhode Island	
Maine	New Jersey	Tennessee	

Not all parts of every one of these states are under the ban—only where the danger to white pine is critical. In other words, you cannot have white pines and gooseberries or currants in the same vicinity. But in many sections of at least some of the states you will be free to grow them.

Gooseberries and currants are all derived from relatively northern ancestors and hence stand more cold than many other fruits. But not liking heat, particularly for long periods, all except certain heat-tolerant varieties are quite unsuited to the south, except in mountainous areas.

The culture and handling of both gooseberry and currant are easy and similar. The only real difference is the larger, tarter fruit of the gooseberry, and the fact that the plants are bristly or even quite spiny, whereas currant bushes are perfectly smooth.

They should be grown in cultivated land, spaced 5 x 5 feet apart for currants and 6 x 6 feet apart for gooseberries. Both are erect plants that need no staking, and both of them do better if planted in the fall rather than in the spring. In ordinary garden soil they rarely need fertilizer, but a mulch of stable manure during the winter is helpful.

Subsequent care is the same for both. Flowers and fruit are most plentiful on stems that are only 1, 2, or 3 years old. Hence a regular thinning out of old stems is essential to continuous fruit production.

You do not need to tag the stems in order to know how old they are, because a little observation will soon show by the color and texture of bark which are the old and which the new stems. All the currants and gooseberries are self-fertile.

In choosing varieties to grow it is essential to know the fruit area in which you live. All those below are numbered (in parentheses) according to the fruit districts defined in Chapter One.

VARIETIES

GOOSEBERRY

CHAUTAUQUA (1,2,3). One of the best of the European varieties, with medium early, greenish-yellow, rather large fruit, of fine quality. Plants small (3-4 feet).

POORMAN (1,2,3). Later fruiting than Chautauqua, the fruit red, medium-sized. Plant larger (4-5 feet).

DOWNING (1,2). An American hybrid gooseberry, derived from crossing a European sort with a wild American plant, by Charles Downing at Newburgh, New York, about 1855. It has ever since been a favorite with both amateur and commercial growers. Fruit silvery-green, aromatic, medium-sized, and apt to spoil if left on the plant a few days after it is perfectly ripe.

It will be noticed that gooseberries are not suited to fruit districts four and five, unless you happen to be in a mountainous section.

CURRANT

Red Varieties

PERFECTION (1,2, and northern part of 3). Perhaps the best in flavor of all red currants, the fruit borne in long clusters so that picking is easy. Pick as soon as ripe because the fruit may be sun-scalded if left on too long. Plant medium-height (3-4 feet), vigorous but not dense. Fruit early to midseason.

RED LAKE (1,2, and northern part only of 3 and 5). A fairly new variety, with a larger fruit cluster than in Perfection, and a later variety. Originating in Minnesota it will stand any amount of cold, but it does not like summer heat. Fruit large, light red.

LONDON MARKET (5, northern part only). Fruit deep red, somewhat acid, midseason to late. One of the best varieties for the northern part of the Middle West.

DIPLOMA (1,2, and northern part of 5). One of the best for the home grower, the fruit glossy, bright red, mildly acid, so transparent that the seeds show through the skin. A midseason variety.

CHERRY. Another red currant that might be considered is known as
Cherry. Its fruit is fine, but the plant tends to become unproductive in age. The varieties above will last for years.

White Variety

WHITE IMPERIAL (1,2, and northern parts only of 3 and 5). The only
white-fruited variety to be considered by the home grower.
Fruit glistening white, the dark seeds showing through, sweet to
mildly acid. A choice dessert fruit, for this purpose perhaps better
than all other currants.

Black Variety

NAPLES (1,2, and northern part only of 3). A favorite of those of
English ancestry, as they like its peculiar aromatic, almost
smoky flavor. Introduced from England in 1852, and the leading
black currant ever since. Not everyone likes its peculiar flavor.

Pests and their control will be found in Chapter Ten.

Another bush fruit that might be placed in this chapter is the blueberry. But its culture differs so much from all other bush fruits that
a separate chapter is devoted to it. See Chapter Seven.

Strawberry

CHAPTER III   *F*RAGARIA, from the Latin *fragrum,* fragrant.

Few strawberries of today live up to their Latin name of *Fragaria* which Linnaeus gave them just two hundred years ago (1753). He knew the common wood strawberry of Europe, which had already been cultivated for three hundred years, and the common strawberry of eastern North America which he christened *Fragaria virginiana.* Both these wild strawberries were and still are deliciously fragrant.

Earlier, there was introduced into France another American strawberry, found first in Chile and named *Fragaria chiloense,* but subsequently known to grow along the Pacific Coast from Chile to Oregon. From these three sorts have come the hundreds of varieties known here today, many of their ancestors being produced by French hybridists. The French were so enthusiastic about the garden possibilities of the Chilean sort that to this day their word for strawberry is *fraisien,* taken from the name of Captain Frazier, a young French officer who first brought the plant from Chile to France in 1712.

Before this the only strawberries in cultivation were variants of the common wild strawberries so that the fruit as we know it today is a fairly modern one—nearly all the others in this book having been cultivated for two thousand years and some of them much longer.

In the course of the breeding which has produced the modern strawberry, we have enormously increased the size, juiciness and keeping qualities of the berry, but lost much of its fragrance. And somewhere along the line of its brief history the strawberry has lost, in some varieties, its normal sex life. These plants are self-sterile, not because they are infertile to their own pollen, but for the much more serious reason that some varieties produce no male flowers (anthers and pollen) at all and hence depend upon other varieties that do. Such self-sterile varieties must be interplanted with normal-flowered sorts, generally at the rate of 3 normal-flowered sorts to 10 self-sterile kinds, or there will be no fruit.

The varieties listed below will not need this treatment but some

good local varieties, offered by nurserymen, are self-sterile and should
be so designated by the dealer. If you purchase any varieties other
than those listed below, be sure to ask whether or not they are self-
fertile. Often purely local varieties, unknown beyond the range of
their immediate use, and too numerous to list here, are excellent.
The only catch is to be sure they are self-fertile.

The strawberry is, as grown, a biennial herb that produces many
runners, which root at the joints and upon which we depend for the
propagation of new plants. These are needed constantly, because
the newly set out plants do not or should not produce any fruit the
first year, an abundant crop the second year, and a dwindling one
or none at all the third. The home grower will be wise to purchase a
few plants each year, unless he has the time and space to propagate
new plants from the runners that will be freely produced during the
life of the "mother" plant, *i.e.*, the one which he has set out and will
produce fruit only in the second season.

Purchased plants will or should have a few leaves, all but two or
three of which should be pinched off before planting. It is well,
also, to shear off about one quarter of the root mass at the lower end.
The plants must be kept moist if there is any interval between their
arrival from the nursery and actual planting. They will grow in any
good garden soil—slightly acid, if possible—which preferably should
have been cultivated for a year or two and *must be kept free of weeds*.
If weedy, the runners and the weeds will soon make an inextricable
mat which makes cultivation difficult or impossible. The area between the rows must also be free of weeds, or mulching with straw
will be equally impossible, and this is an essential feature of all good
strawberry culture.

Two methods of handling strawberries are available to the home
grower—in hills or rows. If you have room for only a few plants they
are best isolated in hills (*i.e.*, isolated patches), so that cultivation
can go on all around them. If your planting is more extensive it is probably better to grow them in rows. Hills should be about 12 inches
apart each way, with one plant in each hill. Rows ought to be at
least 30 inches apart, and the plants set about 12 inches apart in the
rows. If, as will often happen, the newly set plants bear a few flowers
the first season, they should all be picked off, because no fruit should
be allowed to mature until the second season.

In planting, see that the new plants are set at the same level
as they were when in the nursery—not buried too deep, or with their
roots exposed because of too shallow planting. This is important in

regions of frost, as plants not set deep enough are often frost-heaved and will then die if not immediately replanted.

Being a true herb, the strawberry has a much wider geographical range than the fruits that have woody stems, so that there are few regions, except the deserts, where some variety cannot be grown, at least by the home planter. Commercially, they are limited by such factors as keeping quality, which do not affect the home grower.

VARIETIES

It should be noted that all the varieties specified as useful in fruit district* 4 and the southern part of district 5 are also good in southern Florida and along the Gulf Coast to eastern Texas. Some of the varieties are everbearing, the significance of which will be noted presently. While strawberries are widely distributed, they do not like extremely cold winters, and it will be noted that only a few varieties are suited to fruit district one.

BELT. See William Belt.

BLAKEMORE (3,4,5). Early ripening, with a medium-sized, somewhat tart berry, good for preserving.

CATSKILL (2,3). Late ripening, or midseason variety, the berries large, of good quality. Does better in the northern parts of both fruit districts.

CHESAPEAKE (2,3,4). Late variety, the fruit large, scarlet, firm and of very good quality.

DORSETT (2,3,4). An early variety, the berries large, lighter in color than some, very juicy and sweet. Apt to flower early and may be caught by late frosts in the northern part of the area.

DUNLAP (1,2). Valuable as one of the few varieties suited to cool regions. Berries medium-sized, red, and excellent for preserving.

FAIRFAX (2,3,4). An early variety and an old favorite. Fruit dark red, sweet, and does not keep well, so should not be left on the plant when ripe. Many consider this the finest strawberry in cultivation.

GEM (2,3). Everbearing. Useful mostly for late summer and fall fruit; is on the tart side. Useless for spring fruit.

HOWARD 17 (2,3,4). This is often incorrectly listed in the catalogs as Premier, but by whatever name, it is one of the best strawberries for the home grower, for productiveness, and its medium-

---

* See the fruit districts as defined in Chapter One, as it is unsafe to select varieties without knowing their suitability for your vicinity.

large berries. The latter are better in the northern than in the southern part of their range.

KLONDIKE (southern part of 5, and along the Gulf Coast). Useful in regions of great heat. Berry slightly acid, the quality only fair, although it is one of the chief varieties to reach the New York market in February-March.

KLONMORE (southern part of 5 and near the Gulf Coast). Useful in the South, in a narrow belt about 100 miles north of the Gulf of Mexico. Fruit not up to other varieties.

MASTODON (2,3). Everbearing. Unlike most everbearing varieties this also produces berries in the spring, and many fail to do so in the autumn but it usually fruits also in fall. Berries of fair quality, somewhat acid.

PREMIER. See Howard 17.

PROGRESSIVE (1,2). Everbearing. Useful chiefly because it is one of the few everbearing types fit for the north. Fruit conical, dark glossy red, mild and only slightly acid.

ROCKHILL (1,2). Everbearing, but often failing to produce fall fruit. Berries similar to Progressive and perhaps not superior, but the plant is very hardy to cold.

SPARKLE (3,4). Late fruiting and one of the best varieties for the home grower. Berries medium to large, very attractive as to looks and flavor. It was originated by scientists at New Jersey Agricultural Experiment Station at New Brunswick.

TEMPLE (3,4). Midseason variety, equal to Sparkle in quality, and originated at Maryland Agricultural Experiment Station at College Park.

WILLIAM BELT (2,3). A late-fruiting variety often listed in the catalogs as Belt. Fruit early to midseason, large, apt to be irregular in shape, deep red, juicy; for the northern home grower, but it does not like drought.

Sixteen varieties make up only a fraction of the hundreds of named sorts that are known, and of the scores offered by various nurserymen. Many of the claims of the latter are exaggerated, and the home grower should be on his guard against too lavish promotion (colored pictures and unverified statements of quality). The varieties selected above have been tested over a period of many years. If you are offered some spellbinding strawberry "novelty," write to your local experiment station for a report on its performance. It may save you money.

Some of the varieties are marked *everbearing*. The term is really a misnomer, for no strawberry is actually everbearing. The plant is normally spring flowering, and May and June the usual time of fruit ripening, depending on the season and your locality. A few aberrant plants have in the past shown a tendency to prolong fruiting into summer and even into the autumn, often at the expense of spring fruiting. Over the years several varieties have been isolated with this tendency, and those who want to have strawberries in the late summer and fall will always choose such varieties, perhaps not knowing and maybe not caring that they do not compare with spring-fruiting kinds.

CARE OF THE STRAWBERRY

Once your so-called "mother plants" have been set out as early in the spring as the ground can be worked, you must cultivate your plants and watch for the development of new leaves. Each plant will at first have only two or three if you followed the directions given earlier, but by one month from planting time it should have 6-7 leaves, and in two months about a dozen. Also in two months it will send out its first runner, of which it may well produce nearly a dozen before the end of the summer. Unless you intend to propagate from these long, prostrate runners, they should all be cut off, in order to produce the greatest crop of leaves possible this first season. If all runners are cut off the plant may well produce 60-80 leaves, but half this number or less if the runners are left on.

The importance of getting a good crop of leaves the first season is realized only when it is known that, from near the base of leaf stalks, the plant matures the buds that will produce flowers and fruit next season. Hence, the value of cutting off all runners if you want maximum yields next year. For those who grow their plants in rows it is often advisable to leave one or two runners on the mother plant. These may be used to propagate the young plants that inevitably root from the tips or joints of all runners. Such a procedure is to be recommended, if you use the matted row method. This permits enough runners to root, so that your original row of spaced mother plants becomes a matted row of constantly renewed new ones. From such a row all plants that have fruited should be dug out. The matted row method is preferred by many home growers, although it needs constant attention to remove old plants, keep the mat free of weeds, and especially to prevent too many runners from rooting, which will ultimately make the row too crowded.

Because the strawberry is really a biennial, the mother plant should be destroyed as soon as it has finished fruiting. If you want to propagate your own plants separately, take the cut-off runners to a separate bed, and so get the young plants ready for spring planting the next year.

As cautioned earlier, cut off all flowers that bloom the first year. Your plants at this stage will hence be denuded of all flowers and runners and in prime shape to produce (hidden) fruit buds for next year's crop. They will go through the winter in the south without protection, but in fruit districts 1, 2, and 3, and the northern parts of districts 4 and 5, some protection must be provided, which brings us to the question of why the plant was ever called a strawberry.

Wheat, rye, or barley straw make the best winter mulch for strawberries, put on about 4 inches deep. In fruit district one, it should go on about October 20; in district two, about November 1; and in district three, about November 15. It need not go on until Thanksgiving in the northern part of district four, while it should be on by November first in the northern part of district five. In some sections snow cover may be all the plants need for protection from winter cold, but it is not always safe to rely on this.

In the spring, as soon as frosts are no longer expected, pull the straw from the crowns of the plants and leave it in the row between them. Add some more if the mulch around and between the plants is too skimpy. There should be enough to keep the fruit from getting mud-spattered when it is "teeming." You cannot, of course, cultivate the mulched row.

This use of straw in strawberry culture is, however, not the reason why the plant is so called. A couple of centuries ago boys in London used to peddle the berries, a few of which were pierced on a straw—hence straw berry. But a more erudite explanation goes back to Saxon times when the plant was called streouberrie, i.e., a berry that was strahen or scattered, as the runners will always do if not kept under control. As far as most of us are concerned we can take our choice, so long as the name has nothing to do with the straw mulch.

The subsequent management of a strawberry bed is really a matter of your own choice. Some professional growers plow under all plants that have fruited, well knowing that if left for a third year the yield will be poor or none. In other words they put out fresh stock each year, so that they always have a crop of (a) freshly set out plants that will not bloom until next year, and (b) a current bearing crop, which will be destroyed after fruiting.

The amateur grower, without space or time to propagate his own, unless he uses the matted row method already mentioned, will likely buy fresh plants each year from a reliable nursery. You can judge the number of plants you will need by the fact that a single plant (counting its runner-progeny) may produce a quart of berries. This means that a matted row of strawberries should produce about 2 quarts of berries for each 3 feet of row. Isolated plants in hills will yield more than this, but there is, of course, the loss of space needed for cultivation all around the individual hills. The hill method will always produce the largest and finest fruit, but not as many berries as the row culture.

For most home growers the pest problem is negligible, especially if new plants have been purchased. Any exception will be noted in Chapter Ten.

Stone Fruits
Peach, Plum, Cherry

CHAPTER IV   ONFUCIUS, writing five centuries before Christ, compiled a selection of still more ancient poetry wherein the peach and plum were mentioned by several different poets—so well known were these fruits even at that time. One of these poems goes back to 1800 B.C., and cultivation of at least the peach is probably much older. In other words, the peach is a Chinese fruit, unknown in America until brought by the Spaniards, and Portuguese after the conquest. The Indians eagerly adopted the peach which soon ran wild all over the South, came to be called "Indian Peach" and misled many into thinking it was a native American tree.

The stone fruits differ from the apple, pear, and quince in that the ovary develops only a single ovule, the husk of which becomes the pit of a peach, cherry, or plum, inside which is the kernel or seed. The pits are variously sculptured in the peach, usually grooved in the plums, and generally smooth in the cherries. All of them develop from spring-blooming and often very showy flowers, especially the peach and plum. Closely related to all of them is the apricot and almond which do better in California, and are hence outside the scope of this book.

PEACH

This is a medium-sized tree useful for the home grounds because it needs less space than some of the larger fruit trees. It can be planted 20 feet apart, each way, and is fairly tolerant of a variety of soils, so long as they are not too wet. The tree will not thrive if its "feet are in the water." More than almost any other fruit tree it thrives in sandy or stony loams, and there is good evidence that fertilizers or manure may provide lush growth of leaves and twigs, often at the expense of fruit production. For the average home grower any light sandy loam that will grow vegetables will be good for peaches.

The tree is short-lived (10-15 years) and highly intolerant of bitter cold, and late frosts often kill its blossoms and the fruit crop of that year. Such late spring frosts do not, however, do the tree any harm; they simply stop all or a good part of the fruit crop that season.

This sensitiveness to winter cold and the occasional loss of the fruit from late spring frosts make it most important to choose only the varieties suited to your fruit district.* There are some regions where cultivation of the peach is impossible, generally because they are too cold. But like most fruit trees, the peach does need a winter chilling. Some regions in the southern part of the coastal plain are too warm and moist for most varieties of it, not only because they do not provide winter-chilling sufficient for healthy growth, but also because warm humid summers promote some dangerous peach diseases.

The ideal site is thus one with a well-drained soil, good summer heat (with little humidity), reasonably mild winters, and an absence of erratic and unpredictable frosts when the tree is in bloom. This is not so easy, for the peach is one of the earliest of all the common fruit trees to bloom—often as soon as April 15 near New York, and earlier than this further south. Proximity to large bodies of water is a help, as they ameliorate winter cold, and often prevent late frosts from doing appreciable damage. The shores of Lake Erie and Lake Ontario are good peach areas, as are Long Island and southern New Jersey, while much of central New York State is somewhat hazardous, except near the Finger Lakes.

All peach varieties are divided into clingstone and freestone, the latter being best for eating out of hand, while clingstone is preferred by commercial canners. The flesh of the fruit clings to the stone, and such varieties scarcely need to bother the home grower, except for the fact that some of these clingstone varieties are hardier and more productive than freestone kinds. All the varieties below are freestone unless designated otherwise.

VARIETIES

Choosing peach varieties is rather difficult. There are hundreds of them, the climatic requirements are elastic, and their season of fruiting varies. Also different growers have preferences as to yellow or white-fleshed sorts. There are, too, a bewildering number of "new" peaches, widely advertised "novelties," and the legitimate production of new sorts by reliable hybridists. From this mass the following will

---

* See Chapter One for detailed discussion of the fruit districts, and follow the numbers in parentheses in the list below.

provide a choice of well-tested varieties that should cover the wants of any home gardener who lives within the area where peach growing is wise and safe.

ANGEL (south of 4, and southern part of 5). Not a very good sort, but standing the heat of northern Florida. Fruit with white flesh, but reddish near the pit, ripening June 15-July 1 in Florida.

ARP (2,3,4,5) Clingstone. A very early variety with fine yellow flesh, originating in Texas but of great climatic adaptability.

BELLE (3,4). Universally called, except by the experts, Belle of Georgia and probably the finest-tasting white-fleshed peach in existence; midseason. Also available in dwarf form. See Chapter Eight.

CARMAN (2,3,4,5). Almost Clingstone. A white-fleshed peach of wide adaptability, an early ripener, and pleasantly mild, although it is considered a trifle tart by some. Also available in dwarf form. See Chapter Eight.

CHAMPION (3,4,5). A white-fleshed peach of very superior flavor, but the fruits are apt to be small on poor soils. The taste is as fine as in Belle; midseason. Also available in dwarf form. See Chapter Eight.

EARLY CRAWFORD (3,4,5). Early to midseason. A superior yellow-fleshed peach, with almost unsurpassed flavor. Its only fault is a tendency to unproductiveness in some seasons. Also available in dwarf form. See Chapter Eight.

ELBERTA (2,3,4). The most widely grown peach in America and one of the distinctly poorer varieties. Its great virtues are the gorgeous reddish-orange skin, juicy yellow flesh, and fine keeping qualities when shipped. But even when allowed to ripen on the tree its fruit is "scarcely edible by those who know good peaches"! Not recommended for the home grower, although nearly 90 per cent of all store peaches are of this variety. Also available in dwarf form. See Chapter Eight.

GOLDEN JUBILEE (2,3,4). A fine yellow-fleshed variety, maturing in midseason, the fruit large, and bruising easily. Tree productive and vigorous. Also available in dwarf form. See Chapter Eight.

GREENSBORO (2,3, and northern part of 5). A white-fleshed, very early peach, of chief use because of its adaptability to the cooler parts of the range of peach culture.

HALEHAVEN (2,3,4). Midseason. A fine, yellow-fleshed variety, with a vigorous, productive tree, and considerable climatic adaptability. Also available in dwarf form. See Chapter Eight.

HALL YELLOW (south of 4 and southern part of 5). An early, yellow-
fleshed peach, with an agreeable flavor. Suited only to areas
of summer heat and humidity.

HONEY (4 and southern part of 5). Midseason, its creamy-white flesh
aromatic, rich, and sweet. It was a direct importation from
China, via France, and brought a spicy tang to peach blood.

J. H. HALE (3,4). Self-sterile* and must be interplanted with other
varieties. Midseason, the flesh yellow of better flavor than most
commercial varieties, and the fruit larger than almost any other.
Also available in dwarf form. See Chapter Eight.

MARIGOLD (3,4). Clingstone. Medium-sized, yellow-fleshed fruit maturing in midseason. Quality good and the tree vigorous.

MAYFLOWER (3,4, and southern part of 5). Clingstone. A medium-
sized fruit with greenish-white flesh, maturing very early, and
with only slightly acid juice.

MIKADO (2,3,4). Self-sterile* and must be interplanted with other
varieties. Similar to Marigold, but freestone and maturing
among the earliest of all yellow-fleshed varieties—about five days
earlier than Marigold.

ORIOLE (2,3,4). Midseason, the yellow-fleshed fruit not so large as
Elberta, but of much better flavor. Tree hardy and productive.

SOUTH HAVEN (2,3,4). A fine, very late peach, often not ripening until
mid-September. Fruit medium-sized, yellow-fleshed, juicy, and
sweet.

SOUTHLAND (3,4, and southern part of 5). A variety developed by the
United States Department of Agriculture in 1946 and now
widely spread in the south. Flesh yellow, the skin light blush. Suitable for home garden, but also keeps well.

There is perhaps no field of horticultural advertising so beset with
pitfalls for the amateur as the peach section of the lurid catalogs
of the more sensational nurseryman. There are several hundred
varieties in cultivation in the United States, and all the really good
ones have been tested by the experiment stations for many years.
The list above has been culled from these expert records of performance. While it is obvious that no one will want to grow all the
varieties in the list, it is a simple matter to determine your fruit
district, decide whether you want a clingstone or freestone variety,
or whether you want to extend your peach season from the earliest
to the latest weeks of it. You will then be in the position to choose as

* See Chapter One for the significance of this, in the section entitled Fertile or
Infertile?

many of the varieties as you have room for, without much reference to the exaggerated claims of highly competitive nurserymen. It will not have escaped the reader that no varieties are recommended for fruit district one.

CARE OF PEACH TREES

Assuming that you started with a one- or two-year-old whip, and that you have pruned it in accordance with the figures in Chapter One, when can you expect fruit? In most varieties there should be some by the second year, quite a lot more the third, and a full crop thereafter. Which brings us to an essential of peach culture.

Left to itself nearly any peach tree will bear so much fruit that its branches will break off with the weight of it, or the fruits will be so crowded as to stunt their growth. The remedy is thinning out the fruit. There will, in any case, occur what the professionals call "June drop," which is a natural shedding of a small amount of immature fruit. But this is not enough.

Just after June drop, deliberately pick off enough unripe fruit so that no peach is nearer than 5 to 6 inches to any other. This will lessen the load on the branches, not exhaust the tree, and increase the size of the individual fruit. It also obviates the propping up of branches which one often sees in orchards where they have neglected to thin the fruit in June.

NECTARINE

Some people call the nectarine the peach without the fuzz. It is a smooth-skinned and hairless peach, with the general flavor of that fruit and grown in exactly the same way. No one knows its origin, although it has been in existence for more than 2000 years, and occasionally occurs today as a bud sport. It grows better on the Pacific Coast than east of the Rocky Mountains, but the following varieties are worth a trial if you have the space for an unusual fruit and live in fruit district 2 or 3: Sure Crop, Hunter, and Quetta.

The diseases of the nectarine and its insect pests are the same as those of the peach, and detailed instructions for combating these pests will be found in Chapter Ten. The nectarine is not a fruit to be grown anywhere in the East if space is limited, and is mentioned here only because the flavor is like a very aromatic peach and most unusual among cultivated, temperate zone fruits.

PLUM

More than almost any other fruit tree, plums are apt to be self-sterile, especially the Japanese varieties. This means that they must scarcely ever be planted alone, and the home grower who does not have room for at least two different varieties had better leave plums out of his fruit garden. For the significance of self-sterility, see the section of Chapter One headed "Fertile or Infertile?". Some plums are self-fertile, especially the European varieties, and in the list of recommended varieties those that are self-sterile will be so designated. All others are self-fertile. It is especially important in those that are self-sterile to see to it that the variety selected for cross-fertilization belongs to the same *group* of plums—otherwise there will be no fruit.

Plums, so far as commonly cultivated, are naturally divided into four groups, three of which comprise most of the worthwhile varieties. These are:

EUROPEAN PLUMS, often called domesticas, the best known varieties of which are the green gage (Reine Claude) and its relatives. But many others have dark skins. All varieties are freestone, and generally pointed. Most cultivated plums are in this group.

DAMSON PLUMS, sometimes called insititias, considered by some as a mere variety of the European plum, but the fruits are all clingstone, seldom more than an inch in diameter, and generally round.

JAPANESE PLUMS are nearly all self-sterile, but they have a wider range of climatic adaptability than others, and are valued especially for resistance to some plum pests. Their original home was China. Fruit round or conical, pointed, generally clingstone, and considered inferior to the European sorts.

NATIVE AMERICAN PLUMS. These comprise varieties that have originated from the wild plums of the United States, or have been crossed with Japanese varieties. Some of them have fine flavor, but their great virtue is that they can be grown in parts of the Middle West where plum culture would otherwise be impossible. Scarcely known in the eastern states.

The origin of these different groups rather complicates plum culture, besides the necessity of interplanting only with trees of the same group where self-sterility occurs. Their original native habitat dictates the size of the trees, the shape of the fruit, its flavor and especially the ability of the tree to stand what is frankly the unsuitable climate of eastern North America for many desirable plums. Of these some occur within the European group of plums, and all of these, while thriving in California, do not like the extremes of heat and cold found elsewhere. That is why they are mostly confined to areas near Lakes Erie and Ontario, do well in Nova Scotia, and in the Finger Lakes region of New York. Proximity to large bodies of water helps to temper climatic extremes.

Proximity to the eastern sea coast is, however, an entirely different matter especially in the South, for humidity is generally unfavorable, especially as some plum pests thrive so well as to make plum culture almost impossible. It is completely so over large sections of the South, except for a few special varieties. Hence, in no other group of fruits is it more important to know and study your fruit district than in the plums.

In the lists below, each recommended variety will not only have its preference for certain fruit districts indicated, but also the group to which it belongs on account of the necessity of choosing another variety within its own group (and only such) to provide foreign pollen in case the variety is self-sterile.

Plums differ also in their soil preferences. Most varieties within the European and Damson groups, grow best on heavy loams, and an admixture of clay will do no harm. But the Japanese varieties do better on light sandy loams, while the native American kinds are tolerant of a variety of soils.

Next to the peach, the plum is the earliest flowering of our fruit trees and hence most likely to be blasted by an erratic spring frost. Such a hazard can be combated by planting the trees on a north-facing slope if this is possible, as that may retard the opening of flower buds beyond the period of such frosts.

Plums, like peaches, tend to set more fruit than it is wise to let them carry to maturity. They, too, are subject to "June-drop" of fruit, but this is not enough, and immature fruits should be picked off in late June so that no fruit is nearer to any other (when full grown) than 2½ to 4 inches—depending on the variety. The Damsons should be spaced at the smaller interval.

Although everyone would like to have a few plum trees in the fruit garden, it is generally a difficult matter to grow them along the Atlantic Coast. It is no accident that practically all the plums grown in New York State come only from counties bordering Lake Ontario, Lake Erie, the Finger Lakes, and the upper part of the Hudson Valley, near Albany. Anywhere else there is either too severe winter cold or too much humidity in the summer.

High humidity favors the growth of parasitic fungi that have deci-mated commercial plum cultures on the coastal plain. Although the home grower has remedies for the control of these pests, they are relatively troublesome and expensive. A good many amateurs, therefore, decide to abandon plum culture in regions that no expert can recommend. This is not necessary if you will take the trouble to combat these difficulties. For pests of the plum, see Chapter Ten.

VARIETIES

EUROPEAN

Often called Domesticas. All are self-fertile.

ARCHDUKE (2,3). A late plum, the fruit nearly round, reddish-purple at first, becoming dark blue.

ARCTIC (1, and northern part of 5). A midseason plum, nearly round, dark purple or black; one of the hardiest to winter cold, often called Moore's Arctic. Also available in dwarf form. See Chapter Eight.

BRADSHAW (2,3). A midseason, ovalish fruit, dark purple, covered with a bloom. The tree is relatively free of serious fungous pests. Also available in dwarf form. See Chapter Eight.

GRAND DUKE (2,3). Late-fruiting variety, and one of the largest of European plums. Fruit elongate-oval, nearly 2 inches long, purple, and with a bloom.

GREEN GAGE. See *Reine Claude.*

IMPERIAL EPINEUSE (2,3). Fruit purplish-red, very sweet and of delicious flavor; midseason to late.

ITALIAN PRUNE* (2,3, and northern part of 5). Sometimes listed as Fellenberg. A splendid variety for culinary use, the fruit purpleblack. Also available in dwarf form. See Chapter Eight.

REINE CLAUDE (2,3, and northern part of 5). This is *the* green gage plum, although the fruit is actually yellow. It was so called by an English gardener who worked for a family named Gage. They imported a lot of plums from a monastery in France in the eighteenth century, all of which were labeled except one. To this the gardener applied the name Green Gage, and so it has been called ever since. It was actually the variety Reine Claude, named for Queen Claude when brought from Italy to France about 1500. Also available in dwarf form. See Chapter Eight.

STANLEY (2,3). Fruit deep blue, with a bloom, nearly 2 inches long

* This and many other plums are sun-dried on the Pacific Coast to make prunes. This cannot be done in the East without artificial heat, and great care is required to produce satisfactory results.

and of fine flavor; midseason. Also available in dwarf form. See Chapter Eight.

WASHINGTON (2). Fruit light yellow, ovalish, rather sweet; midseason.

DAMSONS

Both self-fertile

FRENCH (2,3). The best of the damson varieties, the fruit purple-black with a bloom. Not so productive as Shropshire, but the fruit larger and of better quality.

SHROPSHIRE (2,3, and northern part of 5). Similar to the above, but with somewhat inferior flavor. Its chief virtues are its tremendous production of fruit and ability to stand more winter cold. Also available as a dwarf tree. See Chapter Eight.

JAPANESE PLUMS

All are clingstone fruits and all are self-sterile and must be interplanted with varieties that are also in this group.

ABUNDANCE (2,3, and northern part of 5). Fruit red, with a bloom and matures early. Its best flavor is ensured by picking it a day or so before it is ripe and allowing it to ripen at room temperature. Also available as a dwarf tree. See Chapter Eight.

BEAUTY (2,3). Fruit deep red, the flesh also tinged with red, more or less conical; midseason. Tree large and productive.

BURBANK (2,3, and northern part of 5). An early plum, nearly round in outline, the skin red, the flesh reddish and of good quality. Also available in dwarf form. See Chapter Eight.

FORMOSA (2,3, and northern part of 5). One of the largest fruits among the Japanese plums, oval, the skin yellowish-red, the flesh pale yellow; midseason. Also available in dwarf form. See Chapter Eight.

RED JUNE (3, and northern part of 5). An early plum, the fruit roundish-oval to heart-shaped, pointed, bright red, and with a bloom. Also available as a dwarf tree. See Chapter Eight.

NATIVE AMERICAN PLUMS

These are mostly derived from wild plums or have been crossed with other sorts, often with Japanese plums. All the fruits in those below are in some shade of red, and all of the group are self-sterile and must be interplanted with related varieties of the native group. In the catalogs they are sometimes called *native, American,* or *hybrid* plums. All are freestone, except those mentioned as clingstone. None of them provide as good fruit as the European group, but they can be grown in parts of the Middle West where most European Plums will not thrive.

AMERICA (3). An early or midseason plum, roundish-oval, and with a bloom.

GOLDEN (2, and northern part of 5). One of the showiest of all red plums, nearly round and quite large, but the flavor is inferior to some other native sorts; early.

DE SOTO (1, and northern part of 5). A midseason plum, nearly spherical or ovalish, and about 1½ inches in diameter; nearly clingstone.

SURPRISE (1, and northern part of 5). Clingstone, deep red and of fine flavor; midseason.

POTTAWATTOMIE (1, and northern part of 5). Clingstone, early plum the fruit currant red. Tree dwarf and apt to straggle.

WILD GOOSE (3, and northern part of 5). Fruit red and with a bloom, round-oval and slightly pointed. One of the best of the native plums; midseason.

WOLF (2, and northern part of 5). Fruit dull red, roundish, small, but of fine flavor; midseason.

There are two dozen plum varieties scattered among the four groups in the above lists, and the home grower may well wonder which to choose. Because of the diversity of their habitats and their preference for specialized places, it is impossible to reduce the number of recommended varieties.

If, however, you have room for only a few trees, it is better to choose from the European and Damson groups, for they are all self-fertile. But if you live within the area where plums are risky, the native American sorts are safer.

Plums may be spaced 18 feet apart each way for the Damson, native American, and the Japanese sorts; but the European varieties should be at least 20 feet apart on reasonably good soils, and on richer soils they should be at least 22 or 24 feet apart. Most professional growers keep plum orchards free of weeds by constant cultivation, but if you have room for only a few trees they can be spotted on the lawn.

There is one native plum that is in the process of becoming a garden subject in the region where it is native. It is the beach plum, which grows wild from Maine to Virginia almost exclusively in coastal dunes, the downs at Montauk, Long Island, and among rocky pastures near the sea in New England.

It is a low or medium-sized shrub with a profusion of white flowers, followed by dark, purple fruit which has a musky or guava-like flavor that makes it very popular for beach plum jelly. Attempts to improve this wildling are practically confined to Cape Cod, where the plant is very common. It can scarcely be recommended as a garden plant unless you have sandy dunes available.

CHERRY

For the home grower cherries are in much the same category as the plums—they will not thrive in all parts of the country. To save needless repetition look over the climatic preference outlined above for plums, as they also apply very generally to cherries.

There are three main groups: sweet cherries that are fine for eating raw; sour cherries that are good only in pies and preserves, and the Dukes, which are hybrids between the sweet and sour groups and combine some of the characteristics of both.

All sour cherries are self-fertile, but some of the Dukes are self-sterile and must be interplanted with other Dukes or with sour or sweet cherries which will ensure cross-fertilization. All sweet cherries are self-sterile and must be interplanted only with other sweet cherry varieties. For the significance of self-sterility and self-fertility, see the section of Chapter One entitled "Fertile or Infertile?".

Cherries, more than most tree fruits, are particular about their soil preferences. Sweet cherries demand a friable, warm soil, do well in a sandy loam, but not so well on gravelly soil. The sour cherries should have heavier soils, even with an admixture of clay, and the moisture-holding capacity of the soils should be higher than in those chosen for the sweet varieties. The Dukes fall between, and most garden soils will be suitable for them. None of the three groups will tolerate standing water on the surface, nor at their roots; in other words, they must not be grown where the underground water table is too near the surface.

Take special care in planting cherries, because they need it. See that all broken roots are pruned off, that the hole is big enough for the roots, and that the best soil (no subsoil) is used to fill the hole. Sweet cherries and the Dukes should be 25-30 feet apart each way, while the sour varieties will need about 20 feet. At planting time, which should be in spring, the young trees need almost no pruning or heading back, as in nearly all other fruit trees. Their subsequent pruning will be found in the discussion of that subject in the first chapter, and their pests in the final one.

VARIETIES

SWEET CHERRIES

All varieties are self-sterile so that two or more other sweet cherry varieties must be planted to ensure cross-fertilization. There are scores of varieties of sweet cherries of which the following six may be chosen, depending on your locality. The trees are larger than in any other group, but most of them are available as dwarfs.

BING (2,3,5).* Fruit dark red or nearly black, late, juicy and sweet, but apt to crack if ripening coincides with heavy rains.

BLACK TARTARIAN (2,3,5). Fruit purplish-black, early or midseason, of fine quality. Tree vigorous and productive.

SCHMIDT (2,3). Fruit black, midseason, rather firm and hence keeps well after picking when ripe; does not crack in rainy spells.

WINDSOR (2,3). Fruit purplish-red, crisp, sweet and keeps well; the latest and hardiest of all sweet cherries. It is also a commercial variety but excellent for the house if allowed to ripen.

WOOD (2,3). Also called Governor Wood. Fruit yellow, early, not large but very sweet. A fine home variety, but not always productive.

YELLOW SPANISH (2,3). Fruit yellow with a red cheek, large, the tree hardy and vigorous.

SOUR CHERRIES

There are only two suited to the home garden, both self-fertile. The fruits are too tart for eating raw, but delicious in pies and preserves. Both are available as dwarf trees. See Chapter Eight.

EARLY RICHMOND (2,3, the northern part of 4 and 5). Fruit rather small, early, profuse and light red.

MONTMORENCY (2,3, the northern part of 4 and 5). Fruit large, bright red, midseason. The standard commercial sour cherry, but often picked too early for its best flavor.

DUKE CHERRIES

Intermediate between the sour and sweet cherries, but generally the fruit tends to tartness. Especially good for the home garden, the juicy fruit being too soft for shipping. Both the varieties are self-sterile, but are fertile to each other, and with any sweet or sour variety.

REINE HORTENSE (2,3, and northern part of 5). Fruit early, large, red,

* For the key to these numbers, see "Fruit Districts" in Chapter One. It is unsafe to plant cherry varieties until you have determined in which fruit district you live. No cherries are suitable for district four, except two sour varieties.

delicious and borne on a hardy, vigorous but sometimes un-productive tree.

ROYAL DUKE (2,3, and northern part of 5). Fruit later, large, dark red, borne on a very productive tree, which is not quite so hardy as Reine Hortense.

Three things should be remembered by all home growers of cherries. Birds may and often do ravage the fruit crop, the only remedy for which is to pick earlier than complete ripeness, or to plant enough for you and the birds. The second hazard is the tendency of some cherry fruits to crack or split when heavy rains coincide with ripening. There is, of course, no control for this except picking before the fruit is really ripe, which no home grower wants to do.

The third factor may be within your control. All cherry trees are grown upon stock of two wild varieties, upon which the varieties above have been budded by the nurseryman. One of these stocks is known as *Mahaleb*. It is cheap and easy to handle and many nurserymen are hence tempted to use it. The other, and much superior stock is the *Mazzard*. Try to insist that your trees are on the latter stock, and if the nurseryman tries to make you accept the inferior stock, change nurseryman. No experienced expert will tolerate anything but Mazzard understock.

You may find, in some old books and in a few catalogs, certain terms that are confusing and have been omitted from the lists above. "Heart" cherries are simply soft-fleshed varieties of sweet cherries, which are also sometimes known as "Geans." "Bigarreau" cherries are merely sweet cherries with a somewhat firmer flesh. Among the sour cherries some are called "amarelles" because the fruit is pale red (Early Richmond), others "morellos" because the fruit is darker red (Montmorency). Such terms are unnecessary here.

For the pests of the cherry, see Chapter Ten.

Pome Fruits
Apple, Pear, Quince

CHAPTER V   ℭHE *ANCIENT* Romans coined the word *poma* for a fruit, which may or may not have been an apple, but it certainly gave us the word *pome*, which includes the apple, pear, and quince. All agree in being pomes, which are fleshy fruits that, unlike the peach, plum and cherry, never bear stones or pits. Instead their seeds are enclosed by a papery or membranous envelope (the core of the apple) embedded in the juicy flesh.

In the apple this is smooth and firm, while in nearly all pears the flesh is softer and has a few or many tiny "grit cells" embedded in it, so that the fruit, however juicy, is always faintly gritty. The quince differs from both of them in being useful only when cooked, but it has a flavor unlike any other temperate-zone fruit—more like a tropical guava.

Of these three the apple is the most popular, the pear the most luxurious, and the quince the most exotic, for the latter is emphatically, and maybe exclusively, only for the connoisseur. Hence, more apples are grown than any other fruit, pears are much more rare and are more difficult to grow, and far too few people know anything about the aroma and flavor of the quince.

APPLE

The apple is variously described as the king of fruits, perhaps because it is so popular, and it might also be for the reason that it has greater climatic adaptability than any fruit in this book and is the easiest to grow. Except for deserts, there is scarcely a state that cannot grow some variety of apple, and in most of the fruit districts it is possible to grow many kinds. The only exception is the coastal plain region comprising fruit district four. If you have space enough for several trees, it is possible to have apples practically throughout the year, because late, keeping sorts can be stored over the winter nearly until the earliest varieties come into bearing the following summer.

Not all varieties, however, will grow everywhere, so it is necessary to look out for the numbers of the fruit districts best suited to a particular variety. This is especially true of the Great Plains regions, which is west of fruit district five, and most varieties will do poorly in all but the northern part of fruit district four.

If you have only a limited space you can get trees upon which several varieties have been grafted, called "Five-in-one" apple trees. With even less space, you can use only dwarf trees that are noted in Chapter Eight. And, if you have only a wall, you can get espaliered apples, but they are inclined to be expensive (see Chapter Nine).

Not only are apples tolerant of a wide range of climate, but they are equally tolerant of many types of soil. They will not thrive on sand or muck, but almost any reasonably good garden soil will grow apples. Nor is there any good reason for the home grower to put on commercial fertilizer or stable manure. If, as most home growers are apt to do, you grow your apples in the sod, it may pay to mulch each tree with stable manure, put on in late fall, not more than 2 inches thick. On poor soils, evidenced by poor leaf color, small or badly colored fruit, and short shoot growth, it is wise to put around each young tree a heavier mulch of manure. If this is not available, about 2 pounds of ammonium nitrate may be scattered near the trunk of each tree annually. Ammonium nitrate is sold by all fertilizer dealers.

All commercial orchards are kept cultivated; and, if you have more than a few trees, it will be better to keep your orchard cultivated throughout the growing season, not so much for the good of the apple trees as to keep your orchard from becoming a weedy thicket.

If you happen to have a place with old or over-mature apple trees you will have to come to a decision as to what to do about them. They are picturesque or even beautiful in blossom, but generally not much good for fruit. A process known as renovation involves cutting back the old branches as much as one third or even one half, in order to force out a new crop of young wood upon which fruit is more plentiful than on old wood. Few commercial orchardists think the labor is worth while and generally cut down such trees. But the home grower, with only one or a few such over-mature trees, may wish to save them by renovation.

If you decide to renovate, cut back all old branches at least one third of their length, and in old trees practically one half of all old wood should come out. For a year or two the tree will look mutilated, but new growth will ultimately make it more sightly. It will speed renovation to dig up the soil around the trunk, making a circle at least 12 feet in diameter, and mulch the soil with a layer of manure about 3 inches deep. Whether to renovate or not depends upon the value you put upon the tree and its age. If quite old and with many dead branches, renovation is too costly of time, especially for a tree that in any case will not be worth much in a few years.

That brings us to the age of apple trees and, especially, when you should expect the first fruit crop. Most apple varieties should have some fruit 6 to 8 years after you plant them. They should soon after bear a full crop, and go on doing so for 40 or 50 years. Then they become what the foresters call overmature, heralded by slower growth, less fruit, and the apples much reduced in size and flavor. As a practical matter such trees should be cut down to make room for younger stock. The only alternative, which is frankly a temporary expedient, is renovation.

VARIETIES

More than one thousand apple varieties are listed in the catalogs of commercial nurserymen in this country. Most of them are known only to a few specialists, and many of them differ little from older and well-tested sorts. Geographically, the apple is more widely grown than any other fruit, and some varieties have been developed to meet the requirements of special regions—as, for instance, the irrigated orchards of Washington, Oregon, and California. Nearly continuous sunshine makes such fruit beautifully colored, but often at the expense of flavor.

For the home grower, within the region covered by this book, the apple varieties can be divided into three categories. (1) Early, (2) Midseason, and (3) Late, which are mostly for winter storage. Some of the varieties are self-sterile and must be interplanted with other sorts, as explained in the section "Fertile or Infertile?" in Chapter One. Such are marked self-sterile, and all the rest are self-fertile.

Some of the varieties are excellent both as dessert fruit and for cooking. If you do not have much space, it is better to omit varieties good only for cooking, as such are easily and cheaply available from the shops, whereas good eating apples, ripened on the tree, are available only to the home grower.

A few of the varieties below have given rise to bud sports, differing from the parent, usually in being brighter colored. It is these that some nurserymen feature as novelties, often with lurid colored pictures. Unless you have plenty of space and are willing to pay fancy prices, it is better to avoid such innovations. If they are superior to the parent they will ultimately become generally available. Most of the varieties below are available as dwarfs or as espaliers. See Chapters Eight and Nine.

Ripening in the vicinity of New York in mid-July or early August

YELLOW TRANSPARENT (1,2,3,5). Self-sterile. Fruit yellow, conical, slightly acid and one of the first to ripen. Tree shorter-lived than most apples, but very hardy to winter cold.

RED ASTRACHAN (1,2,3, and northern part of 4 and 5).* Self-sterile. Fruit nearly round, crimson and of delicious flavor, but slightly acid. Tree not long-lived.

EARLY McINTOSH (2,3,5). Very like its famous parent, McIntosh, but earlier. One of the best early red apples.

DUCHESS OF OLDENBERG (1,2,3,5). Self-sterile. Fruit streaked with red, round-oval, of fine flavor as dessert fruit, but also a good cooking apple. Often listed as Oldenberg or Duchess.

GRAVENSTEIN (2,3,5). Self-sterile. Fruit nearly round, streaked with crimson, good for eating and cooking. Tree hardy and very productive.

RED JUNE (3, northern part of 4 and 5). Fruit conical to oblong, crimson or yellowish-red, not very large but of fine flavor.

Ripening in the vicinity of New York from early August to mid-September

WEALTHY (1,2,3,5). Fruit ovalish to round, medium-sized or larger, bright red and of good flavor. It does not keep well.

TWENTY-OUNCE (2,3,5). One of the largest apples, the fruit round or slightly conical, red-striped but greenish-yellow, and excellent also for cooking.

FAMEUSE (1,2,3,5). Often listed as Snow, Snow Queen, or Snow Apple. Fruit nearly round but slightly oval, greenish-yellow, flushed with red or crimson, the flesh extremely good.

McINTOSH (1,2,3,5). Self-sterile. A famous old variety with basically whitish-yellow fruit, overlaid crimson or red, the flavor superb for those who want a slightly acid apple.

SWEET McINTOSH (1,2,3,5). Similar to McIntosh, but the fruit sweet and thought by many to be the finest of all sweet apples.

---

* For the significance of these numbers, see "Fruit Districts" in Chapter One. In the case of the apple those marked 5 may also be grown west of fruit district 5, up to the limit of where all fruit trees are grown only under irrigation. Many of the varieties can also be grown in the upland parts of the South.

DELICIOUS (3, northern part of 4 and 5). One of the latest of the
    midseason varieties, the fruit yellow, but striped with red, al-
most oblong, faintly acid but mildly sweet.

Fall ripening, and most of the varieties can be stored for use in
winter or even up to May first of the following spring. The dates
after the fruit district numbers indicate the time they can be kept in
storage if the latter is properly provided for. Directions for storage
are included at the end of the list. In some regions, early autumn frosts
may hasten picking in order to avoid frozen fruit.

GRIMES GOLDEN (1,3, northern part of 4 and 5). February first. Self-
    sterile. Fruit yellow, roundish-oval, aromatic, rich, slightly
acid. Tree not so large as most varieties.

JONATHAN (3,5). March first. Fruit bright red, often yellow-striped,
    round or round-conical, the flesh mildly acid. Tree very pro-
ductive.

ROME BEAUTY (3,5). May first. Fruit red, striped with yellow, the
    flesh pleasantly flavored, aromatic, slightly acid. A medium-
sized tree but bearing one of the larger apples.

WINESAP (3, northern part of 4 and 5). April first. Self-sterile. This
    and its derivative, Stayman Winesap, are among the latest of
apples, particularly good for cider. Fruit red, often somewhat striped,
the flesh finely flavored, mildly acid, excellent as a dessert fruit and
a good keeper in storage. Stayman Winesap is yellowish-red, ripens a
little earlier, and does not keep so well in storage.

YELLOW NEWTON (2,3,5). Often called Newtown Pippin. Fruit medi-
    um-sized, round-oblong, greenish-yellow, the flesh crisp, mild
and of excellent quality. The tree tends to be a shy bearer.

RHODE ISLAND GREENING (2,3,5). April first. Self-sterile. A good dessert
    fruit if allowed to ripen on the tree, but it has become one of
the best known varieties for cooking. Fruit large, greenish-yellow,
nearly round, mildly acid. Bears poorly in the off-years.

Winter storage of apples, without refrigeration, is not easy for the
average home grower. An ordinary cellar with a heating furnace or
a hot water tank is useless, because the air is too warm and dry.
Root cellars are ideal, because they generally take the temperature of
the ground (about 50° at New York) and hence are cool, dark, and
damp. They must not, however, be wet, and there should be no drip
from moisture condensed on the sides or top. Also they must be free
of frost. Such conditions are hard to come by. A possible alternative,

but not so satisfactory, is a bin in a garage that is kept at about 50° all winter.

Whenever you store winter apples, each fruit should be picked when almost ripe and wrapped in paper, so that no fruit touches another. Fruit stored in bulk, without wrapping, needs a constant temperature of 33-35°. Without such a temperature, and with the fruit touching each other, spoilage is practically certain, especially if the fruit is intended to be kept until the dates indicated on the list of late apples above.

CARE OF APPLE TREES

The apple is the largest of the fruit trees in this book. Hence it needs space. Commercial orchardists usually plant the trees 40-45 feet apart each way, but the home grower can reduce this to 30-40 feet. If you do not have space enough, a possible remedy is to use only dwarf varieties, which are dealt with in Chapter Eight, or, if there is still less room, the espaliered trees mentioned in Chapter Nine.

Many apple varieties are plagued with what the orchardists call "off-years." An "off-year" usually follows a year with a heavy crop of fruit, as though the tree wanted a rest after maturing too much fruit for its strength. This may well be the explanation, especially if the fruit has not been thinned, which should always be done if there is too large a crop. Thinning should be done while the apples are still green, and no fruit, when mature, should be nearer than 3-4 inches to any other.

Another explanation of an apparently "off-year" has nothing to do with over-bearing one year and under-bearing the next, but is caused by factors over which we have no control. If, at blossom time, the weather is cold, or if there are hard rains, bees will not be about the business of pollinating apple blossoms, or only sporadically so, and the consequent crop reduction is often blamed on the inherent off-year tendency of some apples. And if there is an erratic late frost at blossom time, there will be practically no fruit that year, although some trees will put out a small, secondary lot of blossoms if the first bloom is frost-blasted.

In regions where the ground can be worked late in the fall, it is better to plant apple trees then, but in the north they should be spring-planted, as early as frost will permit. Most growers will do best with one- or two-year-old whips—all of which have been grafted or budded by the nurseryman. This is essential, as few apples will come true from seed, which explains the futility of the efforts of

"Appleseed Johnny," who scattered apple seeds all over Ohio and Indiana, few of which ever amounted to anything.

Apples, especially the late varieties have an annoying habit of dropping some of their fruit a few days before ripening. The only remedy is to pick such varieties in time to anticipate this fruit drop. Fortunately it does not occur in all varieties, nor every year, and some authorities attribute it to too liberal use of commercial fertilizers. Little is really known as to its cause.

If your apple orchard is sizable and you keep it in sod (which most professionals never do), it is better to keep such sod mown—at least three times during the growing season. This reduces the hazard of fire, and discourages the mice or rabbits which often gnaw bark. If the place is infested with either animal, wire guards around the trunk or poison bait are correctives. In the average home orchard, which is near buildings, this trouble is not likely to be serious.

For the pruning of apple trees, see Chapter One; and for the pests, see the last chapter.

PEAR

This is the aristocrat of all pomaceous fruits, but unhappily it is difficult to grow in the East, fickle as to site and climate, and worst of all prone to a deadly disease, fire blight, for which there is no real cure. This is true, especially in fruit district four, and in all the coastal parts of fruit districts two and three, except for one or two pear varieties that are immune to fire blight, or very nearly so.

This is a scourge. It is a bacterial disease which attacks the young twigs, blossoms, branches, or trunks, making them look, in a few days, as though they had been burned—hence the name fire blight. Pruning such twigs off, well below the infestation, may delay the death of the tree, but this is often inevitable, because there is no known spray program that will control, much less eradicate, fire blight. Some nurserymen occasionally advertise novelties that are said to be immune to fire blight. Such claims are seldom verified by experiment stations who test such varieties over a longer period than the home grower can afford to give to dubious innovations.

The plain fact is that for most of us in the East, the luscious and magnificent pears of Oregon and California are impossible. This does not mean that we cannot grow any pears, but it emphatically does mean that only carefully chosen varieties, in favorable sites, are likely to be satisfactory.

Pears, also, are nearly universally self-sterile, and must be interplanted with compatible varieties.* To further complicate the problem two of the varieties that we can grow here, Bartlett and Seckel, are inter-sterile and hence will not cross-fertilize each other. If you grow them alone or together there will be no fruit—a third variety must be interplanted. This may not be so simple, for the interplanted variety may be cut off by fire blight, which means no fruit from either Seckel, which is practically immune to fire blight, or Bartlett, which is not always so, especially in unfavorable regions.

If all these hazards sound rather discouraging, there also are some compensations. Some of the varieties to be listed presently are delicious fruits, which can be grown in any of the fruit districts specified, and the further away from the humid Atlantic Coast you are the better chance you have of avoiding the dreaded fire blight. Some commercial orchards have been all but exterminated by it, even when fully mature, in a few weeks. Generally, however, it attacks young growth with most virulence, and a partial control is sometimes effective by cutting off affected twigs and burning them immediately.

Constant watchfulness is needed to accomplish this. At least twice a week, daily in most periods, you must inspect your trees, and at the first sign of trouble (a few "scorched" leaves or tips of twigs) cut out the affected part, and disinfect your pruning shears by dipping them in alcohol or a corrosive sublimate solution. Fire blight is a purely American scourge, having been first recorded from the Hudson Valley in 1780. It never reached the continent or England where most of our pears originated, but many fine French varieties are difficult or impossible to grow in the Eastern States because of it.

Control of fire blight should also include watchfulness for insect pests that make punctures in twigs, etc., because it is reasonably certain that fire blight enters the plant through such openings or others caused by injuries. All twigs, from which diseased portions have been cut, should be washed with corrosive sublimate solution, and when dry the cut end should be covered with tar. For insect pests of the pear, see the last chapter.

The pear is also demanding as to soil, preferring a relatively heavy loam. If you have good garden soil, not too sandy, it will, however, grow good pear trees. The ground under the trees should be kept cultivated, because grass, weeds, or trash favor the entrance of insects or disease. No commercial fertilizer or manure should be used, for it may produce a lush growth of leaves and young twigs which are especially vulnerable to fire blight. The only exception to this is if your

* See Chapter One, the section on "Fertile or Infertile?" for the significance of self-sterility and self-fertility.

soil is relatively poor, fertilizer at the rate of one pound per tree, or a light mulch of stable manure may be tried with caution—*i.e.*, do not encourage too lush a growth on young trees.

The tree does not like extremes of temperature, being impossible in very cold regions, and scorching badly in very hot ones. The equable climate of northern France and southern England is ideal for it, and we have no such places here except the northern half of the Pacific Coast. Because the climate of the eastern states is relatively unfavorable for most pears, and impossible for the best varieties, it is essential that we give the young trees the best of care. This means rigorous spraying for pests, clean cultivation, and constant watchfulness for fire blight. Because the latter is the most important limiting factor in pear culture in the East, the varieties mentioned below will be specified as to their degree of resistance to this baffling hazard of all pear growers.

VARIETIES

French, Belgian, and British pomologists, and some in Japan, have produced hundreds of varieties of pears, but only a handful are suited to the East. A few were developed here, two of them partially or wholly resistant to fire blight, but one of these is a distinctly inferior sort. All are self-sterile and must be interplanted with other varieties.

Recommendations as to fruit districts (as outlined in Chapter One) must be followed rigorously with the pear. Also, wherever fruit districts two and three are mentioned, it means only that part of each district that is at least 100 miles from the Atlantic Coast. If you live nearer than this, except for immune or partially immune varieties, fire blight will almost certainly be dangerous. Some very good pear varieties are omitted, because of their great susceptibility to fire blight in the East. Many of the varieties below are available as dwarfs or espaliers. See Chapters Eight and Nine.

KIEFFER (all fruit districts). Nearly immune. A comparatively worthless pear, so gritty and hard as to be used only for canning. Its great virtue is resistance to fire blight and wide climatic adaptability. Ninety per cent of all canned pears are Kieffer. When ripe it is a large, roughish fruit, brownish-red, and almost useless as a dessert fruit. Ripening in October.

SECKEL (2,3, northern part of 4 and 5). Nearly immune. One of the finest flavored pears in existence, but the fruit small, russet colored, only slightly gritty, buttery, juicy, and sweet, ripening in October. It cannot be fertilized by Bartlett, so a third variety must be provided if you grow both. The best and safest variety for the home grower.

BARTLETT (2,3). Somewhat susceptible to fire blight, especially near the Atlantic Coast. The most popular pear in America, the fruit typically pear-shaped, quite large, yellow, blushed with red, and faintly russet-dotted, ripening in September. It is cross-sterile with Seckel (see above), and is a fair gamble for the home grower. It is known in Europe, where it originated, as Bon Chretien.

TYSON (2,3). Practically immune to fire blight. Resembling a cross between Bartlett and Seckel, although it is actually derived from a wildling that originated in Pennsylvania in 1794. Fruit medium-sized, russet-yellow or blush, juicy, sweet and aromatic, ripening in August.

CONFERENCE (2,3). Partially immune. A pear developed in England and introduced in 1894. Fruit medium-sized, somewhat gourd-shaped, green but russet-dotted, juicy sweet, and only slightly gritty. Ripening in October or later. A winter pear.

BEURRE BOSC (2,3). Susceptible to fire blight near the Atlantic Coast and often inland. Included here because it is the only long-necked, russet pear that can be grown in the East with any chance of success. Fruit large, tapering into a long neck, brown-russet, juicy, aromatic and sweet, ripening in October or later. A winter pear.

ELIZABETH (2,3). Nearly immune. A small but productive tree, more nearly immune to fire blight than any other Belgian pear. Fruit medium-sized, yellow, but the cheek blush-pink faintly russet, the flesh slightly gritty, sweet, and aromatic. Ripening in August.

WINTER NELIS (2,3). Nearly immune. Fruit yellowish-green, over-laid with russet, the flesh yellowish-white, juicy, aromatic, and sweet. Ripening in October-November. A winter pear. The tree is straggling and the branches are often zigzag making it a hard tree to train.

GORHAM (2,3). Practically immune. Resembling the Bartlett but a little inferior to it, the fruit ripening two weeks later. Its chief virtue is that it is less susceptible to fire blight than Bartlett, and in some sections away from the Atlantic Coast it is essentially immune.

Unlike most fruits, except the banana, pears develop their best flavor only when allowed to ripen off the tree. Fruit should be picked from a week to ten days before it is ripe, and all summer-fruiting varieties can be ripened in the house at ordinary room temperature. If you wish to delay ripening they can be treated as described below for winter pears. Fruit allowed to ripen on the tree, with the exception of Seckel, develop more grit cells than if matured off it.

Those varieties marked winter pears in the list above will never ripen on the tree in our climate, as they will be cut off by frost. They should stay on the tree and be picked just before hard frost is due. Their subsequent handling, each wrapped separately in paper, is exactly the same as already described for winter storage of apples.

While the pear is not so large a tree as the apple, most varieties should not be planted closer than 30 x 30 feet apart. Dwarf varieties can be closer together, and the trained espalier or cordon pear trees, which are nearly universal in Normandy, can be grown against walls or even in rows like nursery stock. Both dwarf and espaliered trees are treated separately in Chapters Eight and Nine.

QUINCE

Closely related to the apple and pear, the quince is like neither, for it has a spicy, aromatic flavor unlike its better known relatives. Because the fruit is inedible without cooking, it is little grown, although those who know it deplore this neglect, because its flavor is like no other temperate-zone fruit.

The tree is medium-sized, should be planted about 20 feet apart each way, but most home gardeners will need only a single tree. It should begin to bear 3 or 4 years after planting, and last about 30 years. The fruit is more or less pear-shaped, very hard and gritty when green but delicious when stewed. Its aroma is so strong and distinctive that fresh fruit should not be stored with apples or pears. It is easier to store than either the apple or pear.

The quince prefers a heavy, almost clayey soil and can be grown wherever apples thrive. It is inclined to be shallow-rooted, so deep cultivation is risky. Ordinarily they can be grown as a lawn or field specimen, as the flowers are showy. Of the few varieties offered by nurserymen one called Orange is the best, followed by Champion. Both can be had as dwarfs if you cannot spare space for a standard quince tree.

Grapes for Eating and Wine

CHAPTER VI   *HE GRAPE* of history, the classics, and Bacchus came only from the *vine*. Ever since they have been called *vinifera* grapes, because they stem from a European or Persian species known as *Vitis vinifera*, the latter name meaning wine-bearing. This is *the* grape of California, now found in scores of varieties, and produces wine, table grapes and raisins, but it cannot safely be grown east of the Rocky Mountains.

This limits the home grower (and all the professionals) in the East to grape varieties that have been mostly developed from native wild species and their hybridized progeny. Among them are old favorites like the Concord and Catawba, and these, with other varieties to be mentioned presently, must be our compensation for not being able to grow the admittedly superior varieties that have made California the greatest grape-growing region in the New World. Very superior table grapes and some of our driest sherries are produced from those grape varieties that can be grown in the East, and New York State Champagne is not inferior to many French products.

The grape, in nature, is an immense woody vine, often climbing to the top of the tallest trees, and producing a woody stem almost trunk-like in age. All garden varieties for the East have been derived from such vines, but we must control this vegetative exuberance for the very good reason that fruit is borne only on *canes* that are 2 years old, which should then be removed after fruiting.

It is the annual production of these 2-year old canes that make grape pruning a necessity, whether you train the vines on wires, which is the best method, or grow them on arbors, which is decidedly next best, but dear to the hearts of youngsters and many oldsters with nostalgic memories. Keep in mind that grapes are never produced on old wood, so that long, woody vines may give shade (on an arbor), but will produce only as many grapes as there happen to be 2-year old canes on such an old and neglected vine.

Whether you train them on wires or on an arbor, grapes should not be planted less than 8 feet apart; and, if grown on wires, the rows should be at least that distance apart, or even more. Neither wires nor arbor need to be constructed the first year, because the vines are allowed to sprawl for one growing season, and no grapes will be harvested until the third growing season.

When the plants arrive from the nursery and have been planted in early spring, select only one or two of the thickest stems to leave, cutting off all weak and spindling ones. During the following winter select the best cane you have, cutting it back to about 5 feet in length if you grow it on wires, or 7 feet if on arbors. This will ultimately make the permanent stem or "trunk" of your vine. All other canes should be cut off, except one other which may be allowed to grow for a year or two as a possible substitute in case the main stem fails. Later such substitute canes should be removed, if the permanent one is thrifty, as the ultimate aim is to produce only one main stem for each plant.

As soon as possible tie this to the lowest wire (which should be 2½ feet above the ground) and later to the top wire (which is 5 feet from the ground). If you grow them on an arbor 7 feet high, let the main stem (and only this one) grow to that height. Both wires (which should be stretched tightly between posts set 20 feet apart) and arbors should be put up in the late summer or autumn of the second year.

It is in the winter of the second year that pruning is most important, because you then begin the production of canes that will produce fruit the third year. The trunk should by that time have reached the topmost wire (or the top of the arbor) and should be securely tied. It will, in the meantime, have produced several or many lateral canes, all but four of which should be removed. Let these grow laterally, one on each wire, to the left and right of the trunk. Tie the four to the wires (or arms of the arbor) but do not let these laterals interfere with the laterals that come from neighboring trunks. Cut them back so that they have 10-12 buds per cane and no more. From these buds shoots will spring and bear grapes that season, but not again.

After the canes have borne fruit they should be removed, and new young canes be allowed to take their place for fruiting next year. You must, to get the best fruit, be constantly cutting off old fruiting canes so that they can be replaced with new ones. Left to itself any grapevine will produce far more canes than it needs, but by proper pruning you can keep it to the four-cane method, which is universally used by most professionals and is by far the easiest method for the home grower. It is known as the 4-cane Kniffen system and without it, or some modification of it, grapevines become unmanageable or overbear with inferior fruit.

The writer has seen many old-fashioned grape arbors where neither this 4-cane system nor any other has been followed. The plants are jungle-like in thickness, produce inferior fruit, and cast too much shade, which encourages disease; their only virtue is that one can walk under them and pick the fruit. If you insist on an arbor, keep in mind that the pruning method outlined above must be followed; but grape canes on an arbor are far harder to manage than on wires, because old canes must be untied and new canes tied to it each year.

The grape is quite adaptable to many sorts of climate, and thus some variety can be found for all fruit districts except the extreme north. In the coastal plain and southeastern states most of the best varieties cannot be grown. But from wild grapes of this region several varieties have been developed, notably the Scuppernong, which is good eating and produces a rather sweet musky wine.

In the home garden, assuming you have a reasonably good soil, fertilizers or manures should not be used—they merely promote a lush, vegetative growth which you are trying to reduce by pruning. The plant wants plenty of summer heat, a sandy or even a gravelly loam, and not too much humidity. These conditions, which prevail in France and California, are impossible to imitate in the East, but our ideal grape regions and culture methods approach them. That is why grapes grow better in the Middle West than along the Atlantic seaboard, especially south of Delaware.

One thing grapes will not tolerate is too much moisture at their roots. That is why so many commercially successful vineyards are on well-drained hillsides.

All the varieties to be mentioned presently are self-fertile, but many grapes are self-sterile. If you plant a variety not in the list below (there are scores to choose from), always inquire from the nurseryman whether or not it is a self-fertile sort. If not, it must be interplanted with some other variety.

VARIETIES

No true *vinifera* grapes can be recommended for the eastern states, although experimental planting of them in warm, dry sections of the South is perhaps justified. Nor can any of fruit district one be recommended for the varieties suitable for the East. The growing season (the time between the last killing frost in spring and the first in the autumn) is too short for proper maturity of fruit, and early spring frosts often do damage.

For the remainder of the East the selection of varieties suffers from a plethora of material. Many native American grapes were sent to

France years ago because they were more immune to the dreaded
phylloxera disease than the *vinifera* varieties of that country. The
American sorts were used as stocks upon which to grow *vinifera*
grapes, and were sometimes crossed with the latter. Back-crosses of
some of these French hybrids were made with native American varieties, so that today the parentage of many grape varieties is decidedly mixed. All those below are of purely American origin in the
sense that they were developed here, but some have *vinifera* blood
in them, and will be so designated, as it is important culturally.

It is impossible, also, to know how many readers prefer a wine
grape to a table sort, but fortunately some varieties are suitable for
both. In the list below it will be specified whether the variety is
best for white or red wines.

CONCORD (2,3, northern part of 4).* The most popular grape in cultivation for the home garden. Fruit black, with a bloom, large,
foxy and aromatic, midseason, the skin thick and somewhat tough.
Not a wine grape.

FREDONIA (2,3, northern part of 4). A black-fruited variety originating
in New York in 1915, covered with a heavy bloom. Juice somewhat foxy, sweet, aromatic. An early grape, good for eating and for
red wine.

IVES (2,3, and northern part of 5). Originated in Ohio in 1841 (?).
Fruit blue-black, not so good for table, but one of the best for
red wine.

CATAWBA (2,3, northern part of 4, and central part of 5). Known in
the District of Columbia as early as 1823 and contains some
vinifera blood. Fruit purplish-red, with a bloom, aromatic, reasonably
sweet, late-season, and fine for dessert. It is one of the best, also, for
all white wines.

BROCTON (2,3, and northern part of 5). A medium-sized fruit, green
to amber-colored, the pulp juicy, sweet, delicately flavored,
the skin rather thin and tender. Midseason. Very good, also, for white
wines. Has *vinifera* blood in it.

ONTARIO (2,3, and northern part of 5). Fruit medium-sized, amber to
greenish, with a light bloom, the pulp juicy, sweet. An early
variety with *vinifera* blood in it and especially good for dessert. Not
a wine grape.

DELAWARE (2,3, and northern part of 4). Known in Ohio as early as
1849. Fruit light red, with a thin pale bloom, the pulp juicy,
above the average in sweetness, aromatic and vinous. One of the best

---

* For the significance of these numbers see Fruit Districts in Chapter One.

for table use and a good grape for white wines. Has *vinifera* blood in it.

GOLDEN MUSCAT (3, and northern part of 4). Fruit green to amber-colored, larger than most, the pulp tender, juicy, sweet, and distinctly tinctured with the flavor of muscatel (a musky wine of France), although it is not a wine grape. Its only drawback is that the vine is not very vigorous. Has *vinifera* blood in it.

SHERIDAN (2,3, and northern part of 4). One of the earliest of black table grapes, the skin thick and somewhat tough, the pulp juicy, aromatic, and medium-sweet. Good, also, for all red wines. A vigorous, hardy, and productive grape with *vinifera* blood in it.

CLINTON (2,3, and northern part of 4). Fruit somewhat small, but very numerous, black, with a bluish bloom. Not a table grape but one of the best for grape jelly and for all red wines.

Of the ten varieties, selected from literally scores, six have *vinifera* blood in them, which means that somewhere in their ancestry they were crossed with a *vinifera* variety. Having the blood in them of the finest grapes in the world, however dilute, they are especially welcome in a region unfit for true *vinifera* varieties. But such blood carries a hazard which should be guarded against.

A century or more ago the grape vineyards of France, Spain, and Italy were all but decimated by the phylloxera disease (a microscopic parasite). Quite by chance some vineyards near Bordeaux were sprayed with copper sulfate to keep boys from stealing the grapes. It was found that the spray, while it discolored the vines, helped to check disease. This was the origin of Bordeaux mixture, which became a world-wide spray solution.

But neither Bordeaux mixture nor anything else really controlled the disease, and disease-free American varieties were imported into France. Upon these the *vinifera* varieties were grown, but incidentally many of the French grapes were crossed with American stocks as explained above.

Hence the *vinifera* strain in some of the varieties listed above. With it came not only better flavor, but somewhat lessened resistance to disease. It is for this reason that all those with *vinifera* blood in them should have the greatest care, the best, well-drained sites, and a thorough spraying program as noted below, or bagging the fruit clusters, or sometimes both.

The plants should be sprayed with a prepared Bordeaux mixture put on with care to follow exactly the dilution stated on the container, as follows:

1. When spring shoots are 8-12 inches long
2. Just before blossoms open

3. Just after blooming
4. Ten days after No. 3
5. When fruit is pea-sized, and to each 5 gallons of Bordeaux add ½ cup of wettable DDT
6. In July, spray only with ¼ cup of wettable DDT in 5 gallons of water.

If this sounds formidable, some growers omit numbers five and six, or substitute bagging the fruit after it has had four sprayings and the fruit is pea-sized. Slip a paper bag over the cluster and pinch it around the stem, fastening it with pins or paper clips. Prick a small hole in the bottom of the bag to permit rain water to escape. Many bagged clusters will avoid any further disease and the insect pests that attack the grape, which are also controlled with the spray program outlined above.

No one can advise omitting this spraying ordeal at least for those varieties with *vinifera* blood in them, and for practically all varieties if you live near the humid Atlantic Coast.

All varieties contain varying amounts of grape sugar (dextrose), upon which depend the sweetness of the juice and its ability to ferment. The amount of dextrose increases rapidly as the fruit ripens, so that thoroughly ripe grapes, fresh from the vine, are a luxury that only the home grower can enjoy. All commercially produced fruit must be picked days before ripening, because ripe fruit would spoil in transit.

For dessert use and for wine, it is better to allow complete ripening before picking. Some varieties, especially the Clinton, contain, also, various amounts of pectin, upon which jelly-making depends. If picked for jelly-making it is better to harvest the fruit a few days before complete ripeness, even if the dextrose is not up to maximum, as cane sugar can easily be added, and the pectin appears to be best developed a few days before maturity.

Blueberry

*A*N ANTHROPOLOGIST recently announced that, for thousands of years, man has not rescued from wild vegetation a single major food crop—all the Old World fruits, vegetables, and cereals being very ancient. New varieties have, of course, been developed, but they all stem from old basic stocks, the origin of which is usually prehistoric, certainly very old, and often lost in the mists of time.

The statement is so generally true that it is a source of some satisfaction that the state of New Jersey was the scene of actually rescuing from the wild vegetation one of our most delicious fruits, the blueberry, all of which has happened since 1910. At that time Frederic V. Coville, of the United States Department of Agriculture, began the work upon the highbush blueberry that is common in the bogs of New Jersey (and many other states). Methods of propagation and much hybridizing have developed the fruit far beyond its wild relatives which had always been harvested by itinerant berry pickers. But the idea of cultivating it never occurred to anyone, except a few amateurs in the deep South, until Coville and his associates actually transformed the wildling highbush blueberry into the fruit it has become in the last thirty years.

It was not an easy conquest, because the blueberry is exacting in its soil preferences and should not be grown in any ordinary garden soil. It demands an acid soil, well aerated, and the underground water table should be nearer the surface than for most fruits.

Native blueberries of the eastern United States can be roughly divided into two groups: the highbush kinds which are naturally acid-bog plants, or at least grow in low places; and the lowbush sorts which inhabit sandy or rocky acid wastes from Maine to Florida and westward. The highbush kinds have larger and better berries than the low sorts and all of the cultivated varieties are of the highbush type.

Also, blueberries must be distinguished from the closely related huckleberry which is an inferior fruit and often confused by amateurs.

Blueberries all belong to the genus *Vaccinum*, which has many small
seeds and often has a bloom on the fruit; the huckleberries belong to
Gaylussacia, have ten rather bony seeds and are usually black, without
a bloom. No huckleberries are cultivated.

SOILS

No one should attempt the culture of the highbush blueberry
(hereafter called simply the blueberry) unless he can give it the
conditions it demands, or is lucky enough to have them on the place.
For best results it must be grown in a soil with a pH of 4.3 to 4.8.
Above pH 5.00 and below pH 4.00, it will not generally thrive. If
you are not equipped to make such tests, your county agent may do
it for you, or if you really mean to grow blueberries it is better to
get the necessary equipment and learn how to use it.*

Few gardens having such sites, the next step is to create them. If
you have ordinary garden loam, dig it all out 18 inches deep, and put
in the following mixture: two parts clean sharp sand (not sea sand
unless it has been thoroughly washed), one part loam, and two parts
acid peat. The latter can be bought in bales from dealers if you cannot get it from a peat bog. Mix these ingredients thoroughly and
test them for acidity. If they are above pH 5 add enough aluminum
sulfate, again thoroughly mixed, to bring the whole down to pH 4.5.
This may take about ¾ pound of aluminum sulfate to each bushel
of the total mixture. It is difficult to know the exact amount of aluminum sulfate, for less is needed on sandy soils and more on heavy
ones to bring the mixture to about pH 4.5.

If, on the other hand, you live in a region with naturally acid soils
and your mixture is below pH 4.00, a very little lime can be added
gradually to bring the mixture to as near pH 4.5 as you can get it.

For most home gardeners, who will probably need only a few plants,
it is easier to dig a trench 18 inches deep, 3 feet wide, and as long as
you need to take care of your plants. These should be set 4-5 feet
apart in the row; and, if you have more than one row, there should
be 8 feet between rows. Fill the trench with your tested soil mixture
and test it once a year. If it loses acidity it may be top-dressed with
as little aluminum sulfate as is necessary to keep the mixture at
about pH 4.5. Some growers use sulfur instead of aluminum sulfate

---

* One of the best soil testing devices for acidity and alkalinity is the Hellige
Soil Tester, a description of which and its use in gardening will be found in
Taylor's Encyclopedia of Gardening. The tester is inexpensive and accurate
enough for all practical purposes.

for correcting acidity, broadcasting it over the existing soil at the rate of 1 ounce for each 16 square feet of surface and raking it in. No manure or commercial fertilizer should ever be put on blueberry plants—at least by the home gardener.

Young plants should be set in the trench very early in the spring (or even in winter in the South), and watered at first, preferably with rain water. Do not use tap water for this initial watering if it tests pH 7.0 or 7.5, as many hard waters may do. Ordinary rainfall should take care of subsequent needs.

In estimating the number of plants you need, it is safe to figure that each mature bush will yield 8-10 pints per year, but much less during the first few years and more in later years. The plant is hard-wooded, slow-growing and will not reach maturity until 6-8 years old. It should then bear indefinitely. A few berries may be harvested after the third year.

Because the blueberry is a little difficult to transplant, careful nurserymen wrap shipped plants in moist peat moss, or sometimes dig with a ball of earth. It is well to insist on one or the other method, because the roots never should be exposed to the wind or allowed to dry out.

Much of the improvement of wild blueberries has come from hybridization, mostly in the direction of increasing the size of the berry. Being relatively young as a cultivated plant, berry size is not yet wholly standardized, and it can be controlled by pruning. The plant, or at least some of the varieties, is variable as to berry size. You may have to decide whether you want a greater number of relatively moderate-sized berries, or fewer of considerably greater diameter.

If you want the latter it is well to cut out too vigorous fruit branches, which will reduce the total yield but increase the size of the fruit. Such pruning can be done when fruit-set is completed, well before final harvest.

Blueberries in the home garden do not need to be cultivated. To keep down weeds and conserve soil moisture, it is a good plan to mulch the area between the rows, or around the plants if they are not in rows, with 4-5 inches of sawdust, woodpile chips, or straw— never with strawy manure. Do not smother the stems with this mulch, leaving a clear space of 6-8 inches around each plant.

VARIETIES

The home grower should have at least three plants, an early, mid-season, and late sort. Also, while the blueberry is not wholly self-sterile, it is apt to fruit much better if cross-fertilized. It will hence be better to have 6-8 plants, of at least three different varieties.

Because the fruit is relatively new to cultivation it is impossible to assign certain fruit districts where a particular variety is expected to do better than another. Such recommendations are based on years of testing, and there has not been sufficient time in the case of the blueberry.

The varieties below, therefore, have been taken from the latest official report on performance, with the understanding that it is the best that can be done in this comparatively new culture. All the varieties have been tested for at least a few years and are reported upon by the U. S. Department of Agriculture.

ATLANTIC. A late or midseason variety suitable for the region east of Michigan and south to North Carolina. Fruit large, not cracking in wet weather, and of fine flavor. Bush vigorous, a little over-productive, and pruning is necessary to increase size of berry.

JUNE. An early variety with medium-sized berries, not much subject to cracking in wet weather. Bush below average size and vigor, but valuable as one of the first available blueberries. Can be grown anywhere in the East, especially along the Atlantic seaboard.

RANCOCAS. A midseason variety, the bush erect, vigorous, and pro- ductive. Fruit flat-spherical, medium-sized unless pruned, of more than fair flavor, but cracking badly in rainy spells. Can be grown from Michigan eastward, and south to North Carolina.

STANLEY. A midseason variety the fruit inclined to be small, but of the finest flavor, and very aromatic. Best suited to the Coastal plain from Virginia to New York. Considered by many as the finest flavored of all cultivated blueberries.

BURLINGTON. Next to Stanley considered the best-flavored of culti- vated blueberries and superior to it in vigor. It is late-fruiting, medium to large in size, and resistant to cracking in rainy seasons. Suited for all regions east of Michigan.

COVILLE. One of the largest and latest of cultivated blueberries, the fruit aromatic, pleasant only when fully ripe, as it is tart when picked before this. Bush vigorous, productive, suited mostly to the Atlantic coastal plain.

Many other varieties are already available, but their acceptance must wait for more extensive tests. The habit of some blueberries to crack in wet weather has not yet been conquered. And some varieties adhere too firmly to the stalk so that their skin is torn in picking or they leave too big a scar at the point of attachment. One of the best for this particular trouble is the Burlington which has only a small, clean scar after picking.

From South Carolina to Florida and along the Gulf Coast the best varieties are derived from the rabbiteye blueberries, which were developed from a southern wild species that is twice the height of those in the list above. They are unsuited to the North, but are heavy yielders in the South. There are at least 10 varieties of rabbiteye, the most notable being Coastal, Callaway, Ethel, and Walker.

Blueberries for the eastern states reach a height of 6-8 feet, and the berries are ripe from June 15-28 (early), June 29-July 20 (mid-season), and July 25-August 9 (late). Most cultivated berries should be at least one-half inch in diameter. In good years and with moderate thinning to increase size, the largest fruits may be three quarters of an inch in diameter.

In most home plantations of small size the pests of the blueberry can be ignored. In more extensive commercial operations there are a few diseases and insects, for which spraying is necessary.

If any twigs or shoots show discoloration or there are scab-like patches on the leaves, cut out the infected parts and burn them. Most of the varieties above are relatively immune to the diseases of the blueberry, especially in small home plantings.

Birds love blueberry fruits and are often such a local nuisance that some growers keep their plants under temporary nets at fruiting time.

Dwarf and Semi-Dwarf
Fruit Trees

*I*N CHAPTER *I* it was noted that many standard (*i.e.*, full sized) fruit trees were apt to be too large for the small place, particularly apple, pear, and cherry trees. Plum and peach trees are smaller and will fit into most gardens, but even plum trees now come in dwarf or semi-dwarf form.

It is well for the grower to understand not only the exact significance of the terms *dwarf* and *semi-dwarf*, but how they are produced, and why some unscrupulous dealers palm off mere runts as dwarfs, when they are really only ill-thriven, stunted specimens of standard trees, and will never bear anything but inferior fruit.

Dwarfing depends upon grafting the desired variety upon a stock which is naturally dwarf or semi-dwarf. In the case of apples, an experiment station near Maidstone, Kent, England, known as the East Malling Research Station, worked for years upon many dwarfing stocks and practically all those today are derivatives of these. They produced at least a dozen different dwarfing stocks, known in America as Malling I, Malling II, etc. For our purposes Malling IX is used for dwarf apple trees (5-6 feet high) and Malling I, II, IV, and VII for semi-dwarfs which should be 8-10 feet high. As dwarf trees are relatively expensive, it is well to insist that your dwarf or semi-dwarf apples meet these specifications. Failure to do so may mean that years hence, when it is too late to correct the error, your "dwarf" may be a full- or half-grown standard.

Dwarf pear trees are not grafted upon Malling stock, but upon the Anger quince. Not all pear varieties will grow upon quince stock, so that after a pear that *will* grow on it has made a strong union, the first pear cion (upper part of the graft) acts as the *stock* for the variety of pear that is finally desired. Such pears are known as double-worked or double-grafted. It is well to have the nurseryman specify whether the dwarf pear is simply grafted on quince or is double-worked, as it makes a difference in how it is treated in the years to come. The second graft, if there is one, may be 18-24 inches above the lower, which is essentially at ground level.

From central North America comes a small wild tree or shrub known as the sand cherry (*Prunus besseyi*). Its fruit does not amount to much, but it has been found to be one of the best stocks upon which to dwarf plums. Another dwarfing stock for plums is *Prunus tomentosa* from China. Neither of these are quite so satisfactory as Malling stock for apples, but it is well to have your nurseryman specify which he uses, as they are the best available for plums.

Cherries are usually dwarfed upon a low-growing variety of another sort of cherry and are apt to be less satisfactory, as dwarfs, than apples or pears. Peaches, if you need dwarf varieties, are dwarfed on the same stock as plums, using mostly *Prunus besseyi*. There is little real need for dwarf peach trees, for they are naturally small trees and too short-lived to be worth the expense of dwarfing.

Dwarf trees cost from three to four times the price of young standard trees, and the home grower should buy them with care, from a reliable nurseryman, and keep in mind the relative value of the understocks outlined above. Real dwarf trees take time to produce, expert grafting skills, *i.e.*, compatibility of stock and cion, and we must pay accordingly. Almost any good nursery carries some dwarfs and semi-dwarfs.

The advantages of them on the small place are several. They take up less room, usually begin fruiting earlier, are far easier to prune and spray, and picking the fruit of dwarfs does not ordinarily require a ladder, and only a stepladder is needed for semi-dwarfs. Watching out for pests is so much easier than with standard trees that for most small gardens dwarfs seem the only solution.

It would be quite so were there not a disadvantage to all dwarf trees, especially apples. The Malling stocks are shallow-rooted, and both dwarf and even some semi-dwarf apple trees are prone to be blown down in a wind. For that reason all dwarf apples, and many semi-dwarfs should be fastened to a stout stake, driven into the ground at planting time, especially if the site happens to be windy. If the dwarf trees are protected from winds it may be safe to omit the stake.

Also all dwarf trees, because they are grafted a little higher than standards, are apt to snap off in a wind at the union of the graft, especially when they are young and the union has not completely "set"—something like a newly set fracture. It is consequently safer to stake all dwarfs and semi-dwarfs for the first three years, and permanently if they are on Malling stocks. Double-grafted pear trees are particularly subject to this danger.

It is for these reasons that few commercial fruit growers have ever made a success of dwarf fruit trees in this country, as open orchards are too vulnerable to the wind hazard, and large growers have found other faults with them such as much decreased yield.

These need not restrain the home grower, nor have they affected the commercial growers in France. Dwarf trees fill a useful niche, and, with the hazards understood and the understocks carefully specified, the home orchardist is usually willing and eager to pick his own fruit from a tree sometimes one fifth the size of a standard.

PLANTING AND CARE

Dwarf apple trees must be planted with more care than ordinary fruit trees. Follow the usual procedure for planting as outlined in Chapter One, but with an important, and in fact an essential, difference. Standard trees are planted at the same depth as they were in the nursery, but no dwarf or semi-dwarf apple tree should ever be.

Find out the exact place of the union between the understock and cion, which can usually be felt as a slight swelling, even if there is no difference in the color of the bark. In planting see that this union is as near 2 inches above permanent ground level as possible, allowing for some settling of the tree in its hole. If the tree settles too much, from failure to pack the soil properly, or because of heavy rains soon after planting, scrape away enough soil so that the union of understock and top is just 2 inches above any soil.

This precaution is so essential because the grafted base of your tree, if actually in, or too near the soil, may send down roots of its own. When that happens, especially if it passes notice for a year or two, your "dwarf" tree may shoot up because it is thriving on its own roots instead of being dwarfed by its proper understock. In other words inspect your dwarf trees once or twice a year and cut off all unwanted roots. Also, of course, cut off all suckers from the understock which may spring up from any fruit rootstock as explained in Chapter One. What you want is the variety you are paying for and only this, properly dwarfed by its understock. It cannot be without watchfulness.

In the case of double-grafted dwarf pear trees there is also an additional contingency to be looked out for. All that is stated above is true of pear trees, and should be followed strictly, also, with those that have been double-worked. But the stem between the lowest graft (2 inches above ground) and the upper graft (18-24 inches above the lower one) is a variety that you do not want. Hence see that all leaves, twigs, or branches that spring from that part of the stem between the upper and lower grafts are permanently suppressed.

Generally, because grafted dwarf trees take more time to grow than the whips of standard trees, you will be planting a dwarf that is already 2-3 years old. Its general pattern or skeleton will have been fixed by the nurseryman. This means that dwarf trees need little or no pruning the first year or two after you plant them. Later all you need to do is to cut off straggling branches, and keep the crown of the tree open enough to let the sunlight ripen the fruit.

The intensive production of fruit, such as is common in France, requires much attention by the grower. Its technique is mostly applicable to espalier and other trained fruit trees, but it can be done to dwarf trees if you follow the pruning directions in the next chapter. Such a procedure cannot be recommended for dwarf trees because their branches are unsupported and might easily break if overloaded, while all trained fruit trees are supported on wires or trellises.

Dwarf and semi-dwarf fruit trees may be planted much closer together than standards. It will depend a little on the variety, but a safe general guide may be as follows:

	Dwarf	Semi-Dwarf
Apples	10-12 feet	12-18 feet
Pears	10-12 feet	12-18 feet
Plums	10-12 feet	12-18 feet
Quince	10-12 feet	12-18 feet
Cherry	12-15 feet	15-20 feet

Trees should not be closer than these intervals, and if you have the space they should be a little further apart. Because cherries do not dwarf as well as apples, they need more space than the latter both in dwarf and semi-dwarf form.

All the varieties to be mentioned presently are subjected to the same pests as their standard relatives, and the control of them will be found in the last chapter. Also, before deciding to plant dwarf or semi-dwarf trees it is suggested that you re-read the account of the standard forms in earlier chapters.

FRUIT VARIETIES

Not all the varieties listed in earlier chapters can be had in dwarf and semi-dwarf form, and some varieties are available as dwarfs that have not been noted heretofore. In the lists below all varieties have already been described, so that descriptions of them need not be repeated here and should be sought in the various chapters devoted

to these fruits. In these earlier pages will be found a description of
the fruit, whether or not it is self-sterile, and to what fruit districts
it is suited. Such information is just as essential for dwarfs as for
standards. For the significance of "self-sterility" and "fruit districts,"
see Chapter One.

Not all the varieties mentioned below will be available at any one
nursery, so that it will be well to get the catalogs of half a dozen of
the leading dealers in fruit trees before placing an order. Dwarf and
semi-dwarf trees are emphatically not items to be picked up at any
roadside stand, the risks are too great and the cost is too high. Some
very reputable dealers charge as much as $5.00 for a 3-year-old dwarf,
and five times that for a 5-year-old specimen.

The following varieties are available both as dwarfs and semi-
dwarfs, either as 2- or 3-year-old trees. Average price $4.00-$5.00
each, for 3-year specimens. Cheaper stock is offered but is not always
safe as to variety, and especially as to the skill of the grafter.

APPLES

Early: Yellow Transparent, Red Astrachan, Duchess of Oldenberg,
   Gravenstein, Red June.
Midseason: Wealthy, Fameuse, Delicious.
Late: Jonathan, Rome Beauty, Winesap, Yellow Newton, Rhode
   Island Greening.

PEARS

Before planting any variety read over the section on fire blight
   in the account of pears in Chapter Five.
Kieffer (but scarcely worth it), Seckel, Bartlett, Conference, Beurre
   Bosc, Winter Nelis, Gorham.

QUINCES

Orange, Champion.

PLUMS

European or Domesticas: Bradshaw, Arctic (Moore's Arctic),
   Italian Prune, Reine Claude (Green Gage), Stanley.
Damsons: Shropshire.
Japanese: Abundance, Burbank, Formosa, Red June.
American or hybrid: None.

CHERRIES

Sweet: Black Tartarian, Bing, Schmidt, Windsor, Yellow Spanish.
Sour: Early Richmond, Montmorency.
Duke: None.

PEACHES

Because peach trees are short-lived and relatively small trees, the expense of dwarfs does not seem justified. The following varieties, however, are available:

Belle (Belle of Georgia), Carman, Champion, Early Crawford, Crawford, Elberta, Golden Jubilee, Halehaven, J. H. Hale.

NECTARINES

Sure Crop, Hunter.

Many other varieties of dwarf or semi-dwarf fruit trees are available, but have been excluded here because it seems safer for the amateur to stick to varieties the performance of which is known. If you are in an experimental frame of mind by far the best collection in America is at the nursery of Henry Leuthardt, Port Chester, New York. Some of his rare and choice apple and pear varieties sell for as much as $8.00-$10.00 for a 2-year-old dwarf.

Trained Fruit Trees

ESPALIERS, CORDONS, PALMETTE VERRIER, FANS, ETC.

CHAPTER IX   EVERYONE who has ever wandered through France is astounded at the profusion, productivity and beauty of trained fruit trees, most of which are pear and apple trees. In Normandy it seems as though every farm house and barn has fastened to it a magnificently trained fruit tree, and in April this makes an unforgettable picture of loveliness. If one adds to this mile after mile of trees trained as cordons in the fields, it is no wonder the French became the greatest growers of fine pears in the world.

So completely French is the whole concept of trained fruit trees that we have inherited their terms for them, and these need definition, now that they are available in the United States.

Espalier: French for an epaulet or shoulder strap, in allusion to the fact that the branches of such trees are trained to be more or less at right angles to the main stem. There are many modifications of the espalier, one the Palmette Verrier (French), another the Fan, which with the Gridiron, is British.

Cordon: French for cord or rope, in allusion to the fact that such trees are trained along parallel wires and look like leafy ropes. This is the type grown mostly in the open, and often they are trained so that the wires are a foot or two apart and stretch from post to post much as in the Kniffen system for grape growing here (see Chapter Six on grapes).

All such trained fruit trees, which are a fraction of the size of standards, are grafted on dwarfing understocks, just as are dwarf and semi-dwarf fruit trees. But, in addition to dwarfing, the French orchardists have developed a technique of bending young growth in the proper manner so that the food supply is partially cut off, and this helps in training the tree into the almost architecturally symmetrical forms shown in the illustrations.

The European reason for such trees was twofold. As all other branches or twigs are cut off, except those in a single plane, the trees could be trained flat against a south-facing wall, to capture the heat absorbed by brick or stone, as this was often needed to ripen the fruit. Such is never the case here, and in fact espaliers should almost never be put on a south wall because the heat would be too intense for most fruits. The other reason was to increase fruit production in a limited space. That is perfectly possible only by an intensive and continuous system of summer pruning which will be dealt with presently. Without it espaliers and cordons are merely interesting examples of training fruit trees into flat architectural patterns.

It is this that made trained fruit trees in this country an expensive horticultural fad, and it is still not much beyond this, except for a few growers willing to take the time and patience to conquer the rudiments of French perfection. There the method of pruning and manuring trained trees produces so much, and such superior fruit, that the plants must be anchored firmly to wall or wire or they would collapse with the weight.

No amateur grower, and very few nurserymen here can produce an espalier or cordon. It takes from three to four years and often longer to make the more elaborate sorts. Only two nurseries in this country are especially interested in them and know how to make them. It is strongly advised that the home grower deal only with one or both. They are Henry Leuthardt, Port Chester, New York, and the U. S. Espalier Nursery Company, Sherwood, Oregon. Their prices range from $6.00 to $30.00 per tree according to the complexity of the trained specimen and the time required to produce it. Trained fruit trees are hence so expensive in this country that no one would dream of using them as an economical method of fruit production.

Their great use in the home garden is that they take practically no space. In flower, especially if pruned in the way to be outlined presently, they make strikingly beautiful and unusual pictures. Their fruit depends upon the variety chosen, but it is often superior to the same variety grown as a standard or even as a dwarf. To cover a wall with trained fruit trees or line a drive or path with a triple-tiered cordon of apples or pears is, while expensive, an interesting and unusual method of producing fruit where there is perhaps no room for a semi-dwarf or even a dwarf.

But no one should attempt to grow them who is not willing to give them almost constant attention, particularly through the summer. Unlike most fruit trees they need rich soil and an annual application of stable manure. The soil around them should be kept cultivated, and the easiest way of applying the manure is to mulch the plants in the fall with a 3-inch layer of well-rotted manure, and dig it in the following spring. The whole theory of feeding trained fruit trees is to encourage the utmost vigor and then, by drastic pruning, force this added strength into fruit production. The plants are grown on dwarfing stocks, their limit of growth is rigidly controlled, and what would be a lush growth of branches, twigs, and leaves in such an over-fed standard tree, produces more fruit in a small area than any known method of orchard practice.

The size of trained fruit trees is usually fixed by the nurseryman who trains them. Ordinarily they should be kept to this size by cutting off terminal buds or twigs so that there shall be no increase in length of arms or branches. Most specimens offered by the dealers, no matter how complex their branching, will be from 5 to 8 feet in height for erect forms like the Palmette Verrier or espalier, and from 7 to 10 feet long for the cordon types.

If you decide to increase the height or length of your trained fruit tree it can be done by allowing terminal twigs to grow that should otherwise be cut off. Unless this is done with a good deal of skill and patience, you may well lose the symmetry of your specimen, and hence the chief charm of trained fruit trees.

The ultimate production of blossoms and later of fruit is so tremendous that in April such trees seem to be clothed with a white sheet of bloom, hiding most twigs and branches, and looking for all the world like the most extravagant picture in the catalogs. Such plenty, however, can only be secured by meticulous pruning.

PRUNING TRAINED FRUIT TREES

The ordinary winter pruning of fruit trees, which is usually followed for standards, semi-dwarfs or dwarfs, will not do for trained trees. In ordinary trees the fruit is borne mostly at the periphery of the plant, but the object is to make practically *all* branches of the trained tree fruit producing branches.

To accomplish this needs careful study. The tree, as it arrives from the nursery, will have a number of main branches from which, during the first season, other twigs, leaves, and blossoms will spring. Observe them closely, and get to distinguish the sort of buds from which leaves, twigs, and blossoms actually arise. Do no pruning the first growing season, as the dealer will deliver the plant properly pruned for that season.

You will notice that blossoms and fruit are almost never produced by leafy twigs, but come from stubby spurs on older wood (*i.e.*, not the current season's growth). It is the object of pruning, not only to take advantage of this fact, but to force the production of such fruiting spurs by removing current growths that produce none. There is, however, some danger in removing too many leafy twigs for a very good reason that owners of trained fruit trees should understand.

All trees, especially these trained dwarfs, have only two sources of food. One is the nutriment from their roots, and the other is the food manufactured by the green coloring matter (chlorophyll) in all leaves. This leaf-manufactured food is so important to trees that without it they would die. This leaf-food is drained by downward moving sap to the roots, which cannot function without it.

It is the nice understanding of the amount of safe summer pruning, in order to maintain food balance, which has resulted in the method outlined below. It was devised years ago by Louis Lorette, and has ever since, and with some modifications, been called the Lorette system of pruning. He was perhaps the most skillful orchardist in France, and practically all French fruit growers, but few here, have used it. Labor costs here make it impossible, commercially, but any amateur can follow it if he practices patience and care.

The first pruning of lateral leafy shoots should be done about mid-June. Many of them will by that time be 12-15 inches long, or more on some varieties. Cut these, and only these, back to the branch from which they sprang, but be careful to leave the pair of leaves (or it may be a tuft of them) usually found on the branch at the point of emergence of the cut twig. This preliminary cut is cardinal to the whole scheme, for near this basal pair or tuft of leaves there is, or may be, an incipient fruiting spur from which fruit may be expected next year. It will, however, be most unlikely to develop, unless you remove the leafy twig which will otherwise rob the spur of so much food that it may be suppressed. It is, of course, of the utmost importance that you do not injure any *mature fruiting* spur that may also be at the base of the cut twig.

At this stage your plant will be denuded of all leafy twigs that were 12-15 inches long, but you must allow *all shorter twigs to grow on,* also you must leave all terminal leafy shoots alone. This is for the maintenance of the balance between root food and leaf food, mentioned above.

During the rest of the summer keep on removing all leafy shoots, except the terminal ones, from whatever source, when they reach a length of 12-15 inches, but not before. At the end of the summer cut off all leafy twigs that have not reached that length, but still do no

TRAINED FRUIT TREES

The various forms of trained fruit trees on the following page illustrate those most likely to be available in this country.

1. Espalier. This is a single U-form type, not usually over 5-7 feet high and from 15-24 inches wide.

2. A 4-armed Palmette Verrier espalier. These are also found in 6-armed form. The 4-armed type will be about 4 feet wide and 6-8 feet high.

3. Fan-espalier. These may be 5 feet high and spread nearly 6 feet.

4. Gridiron espalier. Not over 5 feet high, and about 6 feet wide.

5. Simple cordon. A single horizontal tier of branches trained on wires about 18 inches above ground. Total spread not over 10 feet, usually 6 feet.

6. Triple cordon. Three tiers of branches trained on three fence-like wires. Dimensions as in Number five. The top wire 4-5 feet above ground.

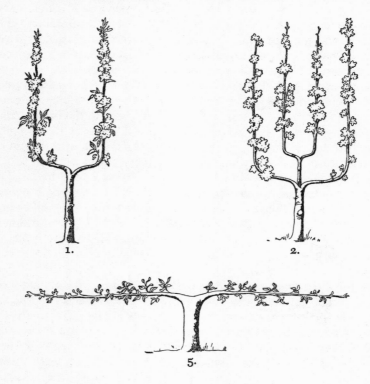

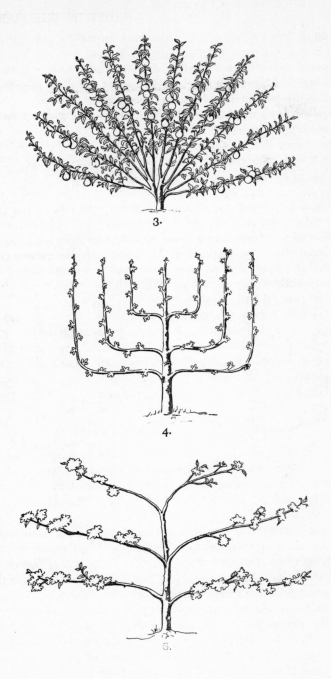

3.

4.

6.

cutting of *terminal* twigs, i.e., those that increase the length of any main branch.

These terminal shoots should be pruned back to the point where they originated, but not until the following April. If you decide to increase the size of your espalier, these terminal shoots should be cut back only so much as to give you the desired increase in height for espaliers, or in length for cordons.

The theory behind this constant summer pruning, which should be done with care and very sharp clipping shears, is that each leafy twig has at its base one or more incipient fruiting spurs that may be forced into growth by diversion of food to them that would be otherwise going to the leafy shoot. You may not force these fruiting spurs out the second year, and it may be the third or fourth, but ultimately you will have your trained fruit tree with far more blossoms than leaves, for which you will be leaving only the young growths (4-8 inches). Some French orchards appear to have almost no leaves, so drastic is this summer pruning, although they must, of course, have enough to keep the tree healthy.

Trained fruit trees, due to this pruning system, are likely to produce too much fruit. It is necessary, especially on young trees to thin them out so that there is a little air space between each mature fruit. This will greatly increase the size of those left on the tree. Thinning should be done soon after the young fruit begins to swell. Also it is not good for the tree to hold all the fruit it will produce.

PLANTING AND AFTER-CARE

As all trained trees are on dwarfing stock it is necessary to follow the same directions for planting as were noted in Chapter Eight on Dwarf and Semi-Dwarf trees. In planting espaliers, fans, or any other type against a wall, see that the main stem is at least 8-10 inches away from it.

All main lateral and upright branches against a wall must be securely tied to it. Ring bolts or some device like them must be sunk into brick walls and the branches tied to these with raffia or loose-fitting string. Old leather shoelaces are fine for tying. Leave the tie loose enough so that it will not bind any stem. If you have shingle or clapboard it is better to erect a trellis upon which to tie your tree.

Cordons need stretched wires. For single cordons the wire can be 15-18 inches above the ground. For double cordons a second wire must be strung 15 inches above the lower one, and so on up to about four wires. Not many cordons will be more than four tiers high. Each must be securely tied to its wire, usually at intervals of 2 feet—less if there is much wind.

Some modifications of the espalier, such as the Belgian espalier fence, which is very expensive, need ironwork support made by a blacksmith. It is almost a "trick" feature that most of us will be glad to omit.

For the pests that attack trained fruit trees, see the last chapter. However, the plants are relatively so small and so easily watched that pest control is much easier than with larger trees. Scale insects, for instance, can often be brushed off by mild rubbing with a coarse cloth.

VARIETIES OF TRAINED FRUIT TREES

Not all varieties of fruit are to be found in espaliers, cordons, etc. Before ordering any of them it is wise to study the space you have to fit and the form and symmetry of the available types (see the illustration in this chapter).

Apples and pears make the most satisfactory espaliers and cordons, followed by peaches, plums, and the nectarine. The following varieties are available, all of which have been described at the different chapters devoted to each fruit, and such notes will not be repeated here. It is, however, important to determine the question of self-sterility and to what fruit district the variety is suited. All such notes will be found at the account of each fruit in the earlier chapters.

APPLES
Early: Yellow Transparent, Gravenstein.
Midseason: Fameuse, Delicious.
Late: Rhode Island Greening, Winesap.

PEARS
Before planting any variety look at the section on fire blight in pears in Chapter Five.
Seckel, Bartlett, Beurre Bosc, Winter Nelis.

PLUMS
European or Domesticas: Reine Claude (Green Gage), Italian Prune.
Damsons: None.
Japanese: Abundance.
American or hybrid: None.

PEACHES
Elberta, Champion, J. H. Hale, Golden Jubilee.

NECTARINES
Sure Crop.

Fruit Districts of the eastern United States
(For essential details of these zones see text, pp. 402 to 404)

1. Winter cold limits the cultivation of some varieties.
2. Favorable conditions for most temperate zone fruits.
3. Large commercial orchards indicate favorable conditions, especially for apples, pears and some peach varieties.
4. Coastal Plain region. Care is needed and selected varieties only should be used.
5. Central Valley region. Winter cold in the north and lack of winter chilling in the south restrict this zone to certain varieties.

Do not use this map without consulting pages 402 to 404

What to Do about Pests

HE AVERAGE home grower should avoid the literature of the experiment stations on pests just as most sensible people shun medical literature on diseases. Both are addressed to professionals, and, in the case of fruit-tree pests, directions are so horrendous and complicated that most amateurs are likely to say: "Why try to grow your own?" If all the things that *might* happen actually materialized, your trees would be mere blackened stumps and the fruit only a withered shroud.

Furthermore, to understand completely the literature of plant pathology (diseases) and entomological terms (insects), one needs to be what no amateur and few professional fruit growers can ever hope to be—a technician in two widely different scientific disciplines. It is to spare the reader this feeling of incompetence, on the one hand, and frustration, on the other, that the following simplified program of pest control is presented. It can be used by anyone with average intelligence, without pretending to knowledge few of us have and with the reasonable certainty that it will protect you from most of the hazards of fruit growing.

It is presented with profound gratitude to that army of pathologists and entomologists who, by their researches over the years, have pointed the way to pest control, even if their terminology is a little terrifying and their specific recommendations much too complicated.

Insecticides for insect control, and fungicides for disease control call for a long list of pretty messy chemicals, mixed according to definite formulas. If you try to do it in the kitchen it may well lead to Reno, not to speak of residual poisons that may contaminate utensils. Fortunately alert manufacturers have foreseen such domestic crises, because you can now buy from any good supply house, from most country hardware stores, and from the mail-order titans, concentrated mixtures that need only added water to make them ready to use.

These, in other words, are combined insecticides and fungicides, in one mixture, which cuts the spraying program in half. They are necessarily complicated formulas, highly poisonous, and must be used *precisely in the dilution stated* on the package. To increase the strength beyond the recommended dilution is to court disaster to the current season's fruit crop, and in extreme cases, the death of your tree.

While it is perhaps unnecessary to know all the constituents of these mixtures, which are available from many manufacturers, the targets at which they are aimed need a little explanation. Fruit trees are plagued by at least three different types of attack which it is far better to prevent than to cure, especially if infestation is likely to become serious.

1. *Scale insects.* They include the famous San José scale and many others, all of whom suck their food through the bark of young branches and twigs. They are generally about pinhead sized, and all of them are easily controlled by a dormant spray, put on in late March. Some sucking insects are not scales and have to be controlled by other means.

2. *Chewing insects.* These are legion and some, like the Japanese beetle and codling-moth, very destructive. They can only be controlled by poisons containing arsenate of lead, or the newer chemicals that are included in the combined mixtures mentioned below.

3. *Fungous and bacterial diseases.* These cause various blights, scabs, molds, and one of them is the notorious fire blight of pears, already discussed in the chapter on pome fruits. The control for most of these diseases was for years secured by Bordeaux mixture (which comes ready mixed for use with added water), but now by the combination mixtures already mentioned.

It would be idle to assume that these comprise all the things that can happen to fruit trees, but they do include the main targets at which spray programs are aimed, and if the directions given below are followed carefully, it will eliminate other infestations that need not concern the home grower.

Fruit trees do have some capacity to resist disease, although they are relatively helpless against a plague of insects. It will help to combat both, if the home grower keeps his trees clean. All trash, dropped fruit, broken branches, twigs, etc., should be removed and burned to kill the spores of disease or the eggs or larvae of insects. Keep the area around each tree cultivated and free of weeds. Diseases flourish in warm, moist and windless places. You may not be able to do much about two of them, but it is often possible to plant a tree so that it gets a fair amount of breeze.

Another factor in helping to prevent pests is agreed upon by all the experts. A vigorous, quickly growing tree is much more likely to resist infection than a starved or slow growing one. Unfortunately most diseases and insects attack the young growth of the current growing season, and become less destructive as leaves, twigs, etc., approach maturity. That is why so much of the spray program is concentrated in the first weeks of the growing season. It is also one of the reasons that has prompted the caution to use fertilizers and manure with care. Such stimulation, especially if it promotes lush vegetative growth, may be inviting trouble that more moderate growth would avoid.

MIXTURES TO USE

It will save useless repetition, in the program that follows, to understand some of the terms used in them and what they signify. The main chemicals used to combat pests will be found in the combined mixtures, and need not be discussed specifically. But some chemicals used separately, or combined with the mixtures for special effects, need discussion.

BORDEAUX MIXTURE comes ready prepared in powdered form. It is a mixture of copper sulfate (bluestone) and hydrated lime. It must be used only in the concentrations stated on the package.

DINITRO OR DN OR DNC. These are collective terms for salts of dinitro ortho cresol. Various trade names for these compounds are Ortazol powder, Elgetol, Krenite, etc. They can only be used as a dormant spray applied in late March.

LIME-SULFUR. One of the best for dormant sprays against scale insects, but it generally cannot be used after leaves expand. It comes in liquid and dry form and must be diluted with great care and in accordance with the directions on the container.

WETTABLE SULFUR. A dry, but wettable, very finely ground sulfur, without the lime. Use only in the strength recommended.

DDT AND MARLATE. Get 50 per cent wettable powder of DDT and dilute as directed. DDT in oil (kerosene) solution as used by householders for flies and mosquitoes should never be used on fruit trees or any other plants. A variant, methoxychlor, is known in its trade name as Marlate, and is used as directed on the package.

FERBAM. A collective term for fungicides that contain ferric dimethyl dithio-carbamate. A very useful compound and sold under several trade names, among them being Fermate, Coromate, Niagara Carbamate, Nu Leaf, etc. They have largely replaced Bordeaux mixture.

BLACK LEAF 40. A nicotine insecticide useful against sucking insects that attack foliage and twigs. Use only according to directions on the package.

OIL SPRAYS. A combination of miscible oil and water, used only for dormant spray. It comes ready to mix with water. Preferred by some to a dormant spray of lime-sulfur.

Not all home growers will need all these, for most of us will not have all the fruits, and some may be lucky enough to escape attacks. The latter, however, is not safe to gamble on, especially if you live near the humid Atlantic Coast where diseases are virulent. In other words, it is far better to play safe and follow the spray programs below.

It scarcely needs emphasis that all the above materials are violent poisons and should be treated as such. All reserve stocks should be kept out of the reach of children, pets, etc., and all utensils used in their mixing or spraying should be thoroughly washed. Never leave unlabeled containers with insecticides in them that, months later, you may be unable to identify.

Depending on the number of the trees you have to care for, spray pumps range in effectiveness from a mere Flit gun to power sprayers for high trees. A convenient sort for the home grower is a knapsack sprayer, holding 4-5 gallons, which has a compressed-air pump, and can be operated by yourself. Barrel sprayers, holding 30-40 gallons, need two persons and a wheel carrier. All except the largest spray outfits are stocked by all regular dealers and at many roadside stands.

In putting on spray mixtures it is essential to cover the plant thoroughly. There is considerable wastage of spray material in doing so, especially if there is a wind, and it is better to choose a quiet day. Keep yourself out of the spray or mist, as many of them are dangerous to inhale and none of them good for the eyes. In other words, try to spray down wind, not against it.

SPRAY PROGRAM

In all of the mixtures below, the total amount of the finished solution is *five gallons.* This is about enough for a medium-sized tree when covered with leaves and young fruit. Much less will do for dormant sprays, where there are no leaves. Remember, also, that the *time* when the spray is recommended is most important. Use ordinary tap water for diluting all 5-gallon mixtures.

APPLE, PEAR, QUINCE

1. *Dormant Spray.* Use on frostless day in late March, or earlier, never when any leaves are expanded.

Dinitro (DN or DNC) according to directions on package; or lime-sulfur, in dry form, 6 cups.

2. *Pink.* Just before leaf and flower buds show that they are about to open, i.e., pink; not after.

1 cup of dry lime-sulfur

1 cup of DDT

3. *Petal Fall.* See that all petals have fallen, or you may poison indispensable bees.

Ferbam, according to directions on package, but not more than ⅔ cup.

4. *First Cover.* Five weeks after petal fall.

Ferbam as in No. 3.

Continue No. 4 at fortnightly intervals until about three weeks before fruit is expected to be ripe.

Unless there has been plenty of rain between last spraying and harvest, the fruit should be washed before eating.

If, after any of the fortnightly sprayings, it is obvious that the tree has escaped further infestation some of the later spraying may be omitted.

PEACHES, NECTARINES, PLUMS, AND CHERRIES

1. *Dormant.* Before any green growth is obvious. Spray on windless day if possible, and it must be frostless.

8 cups dry lime-sulfur (on peach, plum and nectarine only) plus 2 tablespoonsful of Dinitro (for cherries only).

2. *Pre-blossom.* Just before blossoms open.

1½ cups of dry wettable sulfur.

3. *Full Bloom.* When blossoms are all out.

1½ cups of dry wettable sulfur.

4. *Petal-fall.* When nearly all blossoms have fallen.

1 cup dry wettable sulfur, plus ½ cup Marlate.

For cherries only add 1½ tablespoonsful of Black-leaf 40.

5. *Shuck*-fall.* Repeat number 4, but omit Black-leaf 40 on cherries.

6. *Cover Spray.* About 2½ weeks after No. 5. Repeat No. 4.

7. *Pre-harvest.* About 4 weeks before picking.

Peach and Nectarine, repeat No. 4.

Cherry and Plum, 1 cup dry wettable sulfur.

After the last cherries have been harvested a spray containing 1½

* In peaches the withered calyx, which is the remnant of the flower, and is just below the developing fruit, is known as a shuck.

cups of wettable sulfur and ½ cup of Marlate to the 5-gallon solution should be used.

In peach trees a serious borer is often found at or just below ground level, which must be exterminated. On a few trees, find the tunnel-like hole and kill the borer with a soft wire. To prevent infestation spray the trunk and ground with a solution of 2 cups Marlate to 5 gallons of water about July 20 and a month later. Spray the trunk only up to the first branch with this solution, keeping it away from leaves.

STRAWBERRY

As mentioned in the account of that fruit, the home grower is not likely to be bothered very much by pests, especially if he buys fresh plants each year. If, however, as many home growers prefer, the plants are grown in more or less permanent matted rows, there are some things to be looked out for.

Ants in a strawberry bed may carry below the surface of the soil small insects that attack the roots. Kill ants by dusting the soil, but not the plants, with dry DDT powder.

Sometimes, especially on old matted rows, there may be trouble from two diseases. For prevention, spray the plants with a Ferbam solution (used according to directions), once just before the blossoms open, the other three weeks later. Also, some growers use Bordeaux mixture, every two weeks from early spring until the opening of the flowers. Both of these applications may be unnecessary in the home garden, and whether they are or not, no spray should ever be put on while the plants are in flower.

RASPBERRY AND BLACKBERRY

While the old canes are dormant, or just when the new canes begin growth use 1 cup Ferbam to 5 gallons of water. Repeat this once more just before the blossoms open.

After all petals have fallen, and *before* any fruit has changed color use ½ cup Marlate to 5 gallons of water. Use no spray when fruit is partly or wholly ripe, as it is difficult to wash it out of the fruit.

After all fruits are harvested give a last spraying of one cup Ferbam to 5 gallons of water.

CURRANT AND GOOSEBERRY

Note: See the discussion of the white pine blister rust in the chapter on bush fruits.

The currant and gooseberry will both profit by a spray of prepared Bordeaux mixture (diluted according to directions on the package). Use this once before the plants are in bloom, and again just after all blossoms have fallen.

BIBLIOGRAPHY

GENERAL

BAILEY, L. H.
  Hortus II. 778 pages.
  The Macmillan Co., New York. 1941.
HUBBARD, H. V. AND THEODORA KIMBALL
  An introduction to the study of landscape design. 406 pages.
  The Macmillan Co., New York. 1924.
LEVISON, J. J.
  The home book of trees and shrubs. 524 pages.
  Alfred A. Knopf, Inc., New York. 1949.
REHDER, ALFRED
  Manual of Cultivated trees and shrubs. 996 pages.
  The Macmillan Co., New York. 1940.
TAYLOR, NORMAN
  Taylor's encyclopedia of gardening. 1225 pages.
  Houghton Mifflin Co., Boston. 1948.
U. S. DEPARTMENT OF AGRICULTURE
  Atlas of American agriculture; Precipitation, Temperature, Frost Data
  and Natural vegetation. 1920-1928.
  U. S. Government Printing Office, Washington, D.C.
METEOROLOGICAL SUMMARIES, 1925-1952.
  U. S. Government Printing Office, Washington, D.C.
WESTCOTT, CYNTHIA
  The gardener's bug book. 579 pages.
  Doubleday & Company, Inc., New York. 1956.
  Plant disease handbook. 764 pages.
  D. Van Nostrand Co., Princeton. 1951.
WYMAN, DONALD
  Shrubs and vines for American gardens.
  The Macmillan Co., New York. 1949.

THE PERMANENT GARDEN

BOTTOMLEY, M. E.
  The design of small properties. 233 pages.
  The Macmillan Co., New York. 1926.
ELLIOT, JOHN

65 practical garden plans.
D. Van Nostrand Co., Inc., New York. 1950.

HALL, G. W.
Garden plans and designs. 226 pages.
W. H. & L. Collingridge, London. 1947.

JOHNSON, L. R.
How to landscape your grounds. 221 pages.
A. T. De La Mare Co., Inc., New York. 1941.

LAMSON, MARY D.
Gardening with shrubs and small flowering trees. 295 pages.
M. Barrows & Co., Inc., New York. 1946.

RAMSEY, L. W.
Landscaping the home grounds. 169 pages.
The Macmillan Co., New York. 1930.

THE EVERBLOOMING GARDEN

LEVISON, J. J.
The home book of trees and shrubs. 524 pages.
Alfred A. Knopf, Inc., New York. 1949.

MATSCHAT, CECILE H.
The Garden calendar. 118 pages.
Houghton Mifflin Co., Boston. 1936.

ORTLOFF, H. S. AND H. B. RAYMORE
Color and succession of bloom in the flower border. 256 pages.
Doubleday, Doran and Co., Garden City. 1935.

WILDER, LOUISE B.
Colour in my garden. 410 pages.
Doubleday Page and Co., Garden City. 1927.

WYMAN, DONALD
Shrubs and vines for American gardens. 442 pages.
The Macmillan Co., New York. 1949.

COLOR IN THE GARDEN

BRITISH COLOUR COUNCIL
Horticultural colour chart. 100 colored plates.
Henry Stone & Son, London. 1939-1942.

FOLEY, D. J.
Garden flowers in color. 349 pages.
The Macmillan Co., New York. 1943.

KOSTER, P. M.
Koster's color guide. 100 colored plates.

A. T. De La Mare Co., Inc., New York. 1931.
ORTLOFF, H. S. & HENRY B. RAYMORE
   Color and design for every garden. 301 pages.
   M. Barrows & Co., Inc., New York. 1951.
   Color and succession of bloom in the flower border. 256 pages.
   Doubleday, Doran & Co., Garden City. 1935.
RIDGWAY, ROBERT
   Color standards and color nomenclature. 53 colored plates.
   Published by the author, Washington, D.C. 1912.
SEYMOUR, E. L. D.
   Favorite flowers in color. 634 pages.
   W. H. Wise & Co., Inc., New York. 1949.
STEBBING, MAUD E.
   Colour in the garden. 300 drawings + 53 colour plates.
   Thomas Nelson & Sons, New York. 1934.
TINLEY, G. F.
   Colour planning of the garden. 288 pages.
   T. C. & E. C. Jack, London. 1924.
WILDER, LOUISE B.
   Colour in my garden. 410 pages.
   Doubleday Page & Co., Garden City. 1927.

FRAGRANCE IN THE GARDEN

FOX, HELEN M.
   Gardening with herbs for flavor and fragrance. 334 pages.
   The Macmillan Co., New York. 1933.
HAMPTON, F. A.
   The scent of flowers and leaves. 135 pages.
   Dulau and Co., London. 1925.
MCDONALD, DONALD
   Fragrant flowers and leaves. 136 pages.
   Frederick Warne and Co., London. 1905.
ROHDE, ELEANOR S.
   The scented garden. 311 pages.
   Hale, Cushman and Flint, Boston. 1932.
THOMPSON, C. J. S.
   The mystery and lure of perfume. 247 pages.
   John Lane the Bodley Head, London. 1927.
VERILL, A. H.
   Perfumes and spices. 304 pages.
   L. C. Page and Co., Boston. 1940.
WILDER, LOUISE B.
   The Fragrant Path. 407 pages.
   The Macmillan Co., New York. 1932.

HERBS IN THE GARDEN

CLARKSON, ROSETTA E.
   Herbs, their culture and uses. 226 pages.
   The Macmillan Co., New York. 1942.
FOX, HELEN M.
   Gardening with herbs. 334 pages.
   The Macmillan Co., New York. 1933.
   Gardening for good eating. 262 pages.
   The Macmillan Co., New York. 1943.
SEYEL, HILDA
   The magic of herbs. 320 pages.
   Jonathan Cape, London. 1926.
MARIL, LEE
   Spice and scent. 63 pages.
   Coward-McCann, New York. 1943.
MAZZA, IRMA
   Herbs for the kitchen. 312 pages.
   Little, Brown and Co., Boston. 1939.
MILORADOVICH, MILO
   The home garden book of herbs and spices. 236 pages.
   Doubleday, Garden City. 1952.
ROHDE, ELEANOR S.
   A garden of herbs. 300 pages.
   H. Jenkins, Ltd., London. 1926.
   Herbs and herb gardening. 130 pages.
   The Macmillan Co., New York. 1937.
ROMANÉ-JAMES, C.
   Herb lore for housewives. 264 pages.
   Herbert Jenkins, Ltd., London. 1938.
SOUNIN, LEONIE DE
   Magic in herbs. 208 pages.
   M. Barrows Co., New York. 1941.
WEBSTER, HELEN M.
   Herbs; how to grow them and how to use them. 69 pages.
   Published by the author, Boston. 1934.

FRUIT IN THE GARDEN

ABJORNSON, E.
   Ornamental dwarf fruit trees. 65 pages.
   A. T. De La Mare Co., New York. 1929.

CHANDLER, H. H.
Deciduous orchards. 436 pages (2nd edition).
Lea and Febiger, Philadelphia. 1951.
HEDRICK, U. P.
The plums of New York. 616 pages.
State of New York, Albany. 1911.
The peaches of New York. 541 pages.
State of New York, Albany. 1917.
The pears of New York. 636 pages.
State of New York, Albany. 1921.
The small fruits of New York. 614 pages.
State of New York, Albany. 1925.
Fruits for the home garden. 171 pages.
Oxford University Press, New York. 1944.
KAINS, M. G.
Grow your own fruit. 434 pages.
Charles Scribner's Sons, New York. 1940.
MELADY, J. H.
Better fruits for your home garden. 156 pages.
Grossett and Dunlap, New York. 1952.
SHOEMAKER, J. S.
Small fruit culture. 433 pages.
The Blakiston Co., Philadelphia. 1948.
TALBERT, T. J. AND A. E. MURNEEK
Fruit crops. 345 pages.
Lea and Febiger, Philadelphia. 1945.
WILKINSON, A. E.
Encyclopedia of fruits, berries and nuts. 271 pages.
The Blakiston Co., Philadelphia. 1945.

INDEX

Generally look for **oak,** *red* or **spruce,** *white,* not for **red** *oak* or **white** *spruce,* etc. There are hundreds of cross-references in the index to make it easy to find things, but the plan of it is to make the main entry word at iris, chrysanthemum, pear, etc.— not at the adjective red, blue, etc.

As in all other indexes of plant names, the Latin names of genera and species are in *italic* type, while the horticultural varieties and English names are in ordinary Roman type.

Abelia
  chinensis, 170
  grandiflora, 170, 221
Abies, 81-82
Abronia, 297
absinthe, 379
accents and vistas, 36-47
  evergreen accent plants, 86
Achillea
  ptarmica, 160, 237
  tomentosa, 211
aconite, 159, 203, 204
Aconitum, 159, 203, 204
Acorus calamus, 380
acre, dimensions of, 17
Actinidia, 363
Adam's needle, 235
Adenophora, 201
Adonis, 133, 210, 211
Aesculus, 92
ageratum, 202
Ailanthus, 52, 67
Akebia, 304
alder, 93
alkanet, 201
Allium
  ascalonicum, 378
  cepa, 372
  porrum, 370
  sativum, 367
  scboenoprasum, 364
  scorodoprasum, 374
Alyssum, 212

amarelle cherry, 447
aminoid fragrance, 262
Anchusa, 201
Anemone
  japonica, 170
  sylvestris, 234
Anethum, 350
anise, 344
annuals, culture of, 182, 343
Anthemis, 362
Anthriscus, 348
Apium, 347
apple, 448-454
  renovation of old trees, 449
  Early apples, 451
  Mid-season apples, 451
  Late apples, 452
Appleseed, Johnny, 454
Aquilegia
  chrysantha, 212
  coerulea, 199
  flabellata, 256
Arabis, 251
arborvitae, 40, 82
Arbutus, 174
Armeria, 222
Armoracia, 368
Arnold Arboretum, 228
aromatic fragrance, 262
Artemisia
  abrotanum, 379
  absinthium, 385
  dracunculus, 382

stelleriana, 252
vulgaris, 252, 372
Aruncus, 235
Asarum, 383
ash
  European, 62
  flowering, 50, 59
  mountain, 23, 57
  white, 62
Asperula, 380
Aster
  acris, 171
  alpinus, 222, 257
  amellus, 166, 172
  China, 191, 225
  ericoides, 171, 238
  frikarti, 171
  Italian, 166
  ptarmicoides, 238
  rock, 222, 257
  Stokes, 165, 257
Astilbe, 226
attar of roses, 280
Aubrietia, 144, 223, 256
Auricula, 296
autumn color
  foliage, 25
  fruits and berries, 93
autumn crocus, 173, 255
autumn snowflake, 172
avens, 191
Azalea, 99, 140, 187, 220, 231, 284

B & B, definition of, 103
baby blue-eyes, 202
baby's-breath, 222, 235
Baccharis, 170
bald cypress, 73
balloon-flower, 252
balm, 362
balsam, 81
barberry
  evergreen, 97-98
  Japanese, 50, 89
  wintergreen, 208
barrenwort, 189
Bartram's garden, 169
basil, 345
basswood, 61
bay, 361
beach plum, 444
beardtongue, 226, 256
beauty-berry, 92, 94, 253
beauty-bush, 91, 220
beebalm, 192
beech, 23, 95

American, 95
  copper, 242
  European, 242
  weeping, 242
bedstraw, 380
bellflower, 152, 159, 199, 200
benne oil, 358
Berberis
  julianae, 208
  sargentiana, 208
  verruculosa, 208
bergamot, wild, 257
Bergenia, 122
berries, colored, 93
biennial, definition of, 344
birch
  gray, 66
  white, 66
blackberry, 422-425
  fruit, tartness of, 422
black currant, 427
bladder senna, 208
blanket-flower, annual, 191
bleeding-heart, 222
blister cress, 287
blister rust, 425
bluebell
  California, 201
  of England, 126, 198, 221
  Spanish, 126, 221
blueberry, 465-469
  acid soil for, 466
bluebottle, 201
blue garden plan, 205
blue myrtle, 198
blue sage, 203
blue spirea, 169, 196
blue succory, 204
Boltonia, 227
borage, 201, 346
Borago officinalis, 346
bouncing bet, 306
box, 97
boysenberry, 423
Brassica, 353
bramble fruits, 418
bread, herbs in, 395
bridal wreath, 129, 231
broad-leaved evergreens, 96-101
  planting and care, 104-105
broom, 253, 285
  bush, 215
  Scotch, 208
Brunnera macrophylla, 199
Buddleia, 92, 155, 252
Bulbocodium vernum, 124

bulbs, culture of, 183
bush broom, 215
bush clover, 164, 175, 221
bush fruits, 418
butter, herbs in, 395
butterfly-bush, 38, 92, 155, 252, 278
button-bush, 156, 278

cabbage rose, 280
cactus dahlia, 158
Calendula, 355
Callicarpa, 93
Callistephus, 191
Calluna vulgaris, 163
camomile, 362
 false, 227
 German, 352
Campanula
 garganica, 199
 medium, 159, 200
 portenschlagiana, 152
 pyramidalis, 159, 200
 trachelium, 159, 200
candytuft, 225, 235
canna, 193
Canterbury bells, 159
Capsicum, 356
Caragana, 95
caraway, 346
cardinal-flower, 192
carnation, 293, 312, 361
Carolina allspice, 277
carosella, 351
Carpinus betulus, 64
Carum, 346
Caryopteris, 92, 169
Catalpa, 50, 58, 276
catchfly, 223, 235
catnip, 363
Ceanothus, 198
cedar, 76
 red, 40, 76
 white, 82
celery, 347
Celtis, 64
Centaurea, 252
Centranthus, 288
Cephalanthus, 156
Cerastium tomentosum, 251
Ceratostigma plumbaginoides, 171, 204
Cercis, 130, 219
Chaenomeles, 120, 187
Chamaecyparis, 84
chaste tree, 91, 155, 196, 252
cheddar pink, 142, 294
cheeses, herbs in, 395

Cheiranthus cheiri, 142
Chelone lyoni, 168, 226
Cherokee rose, 279
cherry, 445-448
 Duke cherry varieties, 446
 sour cherry varieties, 446
 sweet cherry varieties, 446
cherry
 Cornelian, 119
 Japanese flowering, 219
 rosebud, 219
chervil, 348
chief herbs, list of, 394
chimney bellflower, 159
Chimonanthus praecox, 114, 276, 312
Chinese
 honeysuckle, 114
 houses, 254
 redbud, 130
 sacred lily, 153, 292
Chionodoxa, 123, 198
chives, 364
chlorophyll, 240
Christmas rose, 115
Chrysanthemum, 165, 172, 175, 193,
  216, 227, 238
Cladrastis, 154
claret cup, herbs in, 395
Clarkia, 191, 225
clary, 348
Clematis, 96
 crispa, 198, 253, 278
 montana, 278
 montana rubens, 220, 233
 recta, 233, 278
 texensis, 166, 187
Clethra, 163, 275
cockspur thorn, 90
Colchicum
 autumnale, 173, 255
 bornmuelleri, 173
Collinsia bicolor, 254
colored fruits, 93
COLOR IN THE GARDEN, 181-258
columbine, 199, 212, 256
coltsfoot, 122
compost, 32
Confederate violet, 134
coral bells, 152, 224
cordon fruit trees, 476, 480
Coreopsis
 grandiflora, 215
 tinctoria, 214
coriander, 349
Coriandrum sativum, 349
corms, culture of, 183

Cornelian cherry, 89, 207
cornflower, 201
Cornus, 93
Corylopsis, 114, 207
cosmos, 216, 238
costmary, 364
Cotoneaster, 93, 98
coumarin, 268
Coventry bells, 159
cowslip, 199, 296
crabapple, 38, 56, 137, 220
cranberry tree, 90
cranesbill, 256
crape myrtle, 92, 163, 221
Crataegus
  oxyacantha, 58
  phaenopyrum, 58
  tomentosa, 89
Crocus, 116, 125, 198
  aureus, 125, 209
  imperati, 117, 295
  longiflorus, 173
  nudiflorus, 173
  pulchellus, 117
  speciosus, 117, 173
  susianus, 125, 209
  tomassinianus, 117
crown imperial, 189
Cryptomeria, 244
cucumber tree, 57
cumin, 349
Cuminum Cyminum, 349
Cupressus, 83
currant, 424
  flowering, 277
cut flowers, preservation of, 313
Cynoglossum, 201
cypress
  American, 73
  bald, 73
  Italian, 40, 83
  Sawara, 41, 83
Cytisus
  nigricans, 208
  purpureus, 253
  scoparius, 208

daffodil, winter, 175, 215
dahlia, 157, 193, 213, 224, 236
daisy, English, 223
daisy, Shasta, 158, 237
dandelion, 366
damask rose, 148, 365
dame's rocket, 305, 312
Daphne, 98, 120, 219, 253, 271
Darwin tulip, 144, 210, 234

daylily, 150, 211, 306
dealers in herb plants, 341
decorative dahlia, 158
Delphinium, 150, 191, 200
desserts, herbs in, 395
Deutzia, 90, 139, 220, 231
  gracilis, 90, 139
  lemoinei, 90, 139, 231
  scabra, 147
dewberry, 423
Dianthus, 142, 189, 251, 293
Dicentra, 222
Dictamnus, 367
dill, 350
dittany, 367
Dodecatheon, 296
dogwood, 39, 58, 89, 138
  red-flowering, 138
  white, 230
double-flowered peach, 128, 187
Douglas fir, 244
dropwort, 237
drying herbs, 389-391
dust-resistant trees, 66
dusty miller, 252
Dutchman's-pipe, 95
Dutch Yellow crocus, 125
dwarf fruit trees, 470-475

Echinops, 203
egg dishes, herbs in, 395
eglantine, 365
Elaeagnus
  angustifolius, 273
  pungens, 275
Elm
  American, 23, 63, 242
  Chinese, 52, 63
Elsholtzia stauntoni, 92, 170
Elymus, 252
Emmenanthe, 213
enfleurage, 317, 319
English hawthorn, 58
English primrose, 134
Epimedium alpinum rubrum, 189
Eranthis hyemalis, 209
Eremurus
  bungei, 215
  elwesi, 226
  robustus, 226
Erigeron, 211
Eruca, 357
Eryngium, 252
Erysimum, 251, 287
espalier fruit trees, 476
Euonymus, 95

European meadowsweet, 269
evening campion, 305
evening fragrance, 301-307
evening primrose, 307
evening stock, 305
EVERBLOOMING GARDEN, 109-177
everbearing strawberry, 431
evergreen magnolia, 230
evergreens, 69-86, 243
  advantages and objections, 21, 22
  accent plants, 86
  for suburbs, 86
  planting, 103
  weeping, 86

fall planting, 102
false indigo, blue, 203
fan espalier fruit trees, 480
Father Hugo's rose, 149
feather hyacinth, 255
fennel, 351
fennel-flower, 351
fescue, blue, 251
Festuca ovina glauca, 251
Filipendula, 269
fine herbs, 393
finnochio, 351
fir, 81-82, 244
  American, 81
  Nordmann, 82
  veitch's, 82
  white, 81
fire-pink, 189
fire thorn, 98
flame azalea, 208
flax
  (blue), 198
  flowering, 191
  golden, 215
flowering almond, 50, 90, 219
flowering currant, 187, 312
flowering quince, 120, 187
flowering trees, 56-59
flowers for the house, 308
Foeniculum, 351
forget-me-not, 198, 202
formal vista, 44
Forsythia, 89, 121, 208
foundation planting, 34, 35
  shrubs for, 88
four-o'-clock, 283, 299
foxglove, 152
foxtail lily, 215, 228
Fragaria, 429
FRAGRANCE IN THE GARDEN, 262-330
franklinia, 169, 284
Frau O. Bracht dahlia, 193
French rose, 149, 365
French tarragon, 382
fresh fruit, importance of, 399
fringe tree, 230
fruit districts, 402
FRUIT IN THE GARDEN, 398-491
furze, 285

Gaillardia, 213
Galega, 257
Galanthus, 116
garden
  frame, 15
  plans, 26-31, 51
Gardenia, 277
garland flower, 98
garlic, 367
gas plant, 367
Gaultheria, 384
gay-feather, 171
Gaylussacia, 466
Genista, 156
gentian, 204
Geranium
  grandiflorum, 256
  platypetalum, 201
German camomile, 352
Geum, 191
Ghent azalea, 140
Gilia
  capitata, 201, 254
  rubra, 190
gilliflower, 293
ginkgo, 23, 50, 52, 72
gladiolus, 157, 192, 213, 224, 236
Gladiolus tristis, 157, 306, 312
globe candytuft, 225
globe-shaped evergreens, 86
globe thistle, 203
Globularia, 199
glory-of-the-snow, 123, 198
goatsbeard, 235
goat's rue, 257
Godetia grandiflora, 191
gold-dust, 210
golden bell, 121
golden chain, 39, 59, 147, 208
golden glow, 216
gooseberry, 424
Gordonia, 169, 284
grape, 459-464
  arbors vs. wires, 460
  Kniffen system of pruning, 460

varieties, 461
grape-hyacinth, 132, 198, 234, 288
grass pink, 142, 251, 294
gray garden plan, 258
gridiron espalier, 480
ground covers, 85, 98
ground pink, 135, 222, 234
groundsel bush, 170
gum tree, 64

hackberry, 23, 64
Halesia, 58
Hamamelis, 113, 207, 276
Hamburg parsley, 354
hardy ageratum, 204
hawthorn, 39, 58, 220, 268
heart cherry, 447
heather, 163
heavy fragrance, 262
hedges
    evergreen, 86
    plants for, 94, 95
    tree hedges, 95
heeling-in, 102
Helenium, 165, 175, 193, 216
heliotrope, 296
Hemerocallis, 150, 211, 306
hemlock, 79
herb, definition of, 334
herb garden dealers, 341
HERBS IN THE GARDEN, 333-396
herbs in the kitchen, 392-395
Hesperis, 305
Heuchera, 224
Hibiscus, 253
hickory, 63
highbush blueberry, 466
Hippophae rhamnoides, 94
holly, 39, 97
    sea, 252
hollyhock, 159, 192, 225
    wild, 227
home-made perfume, 315-322
honey locust, 59
honeysuckle, 278
    bush, 253
    Chinese, 38, 88, 230, 270, 271
    for vines, 96
horehound, 368
hornbeam, 23, 64
horse-chestnut, 23, 50, 58, 242
horse-radish, 368
Hortensia, 91
Hosta, 257
house fragrance, 308-314
houseleek, 191, 211

huckleberry, 466
hyacinth, 145, 189, 198, 210, 222, 234,
    295, 312
hybrid tea rose, 148
Hydrangea
    climbing, 96, 233
    Hortensia, 91
    paniculata grandiflora, 91
    petiolaris, 96
Hypericum, 91, 92, 215
hyssop, 369
Hyssopus officinalis, 369

Iberis, 225
Ilex crenata, 97
Indian currant, 91
informal vista, 44
insects in pollination, 407
Iris, 211
    cristata, 134
    German, 143
    Japanese, 143
    missouriensis, 199
    netted, 122
    pallida, 298
    pumila, 134
    reticulata, 122, 298
    tall bearded, 143
    versicolor, 199
ironweed, 171
Italian aster, 166
Italian fennel, 351
Italian jasmine, 277
Itea virginica, 284
ivy, 95

jacinth, Spanish, 126
Jacob's ladder, 199
Japanese anemone, 170
Japanese flowering cherry, 56, 89, 128,
    131, 219
Japanese flowering quince, 89, 95
Japanese iris, 152
Japanese lily, 225, 292
Japanese pagoda tree, 162
Japanese rose, 208
    Jasione, 201
jasmine, 274, 312
Jasmine iris, 211
jasmine tobacco, 305
jasmine, winter, 89, 119
Jasminum
    floridum, 275
    humile, 277
    nudiflorum, 274
    officinale, 274

sambac, 275
jetbead, 232
jonquil, 132, 292, 312
juniper, 244
    Chinese, 75
    common, 42, 75
    Irish, 40, 75
Juniperus, 42, 75-76

Kerria, 208
Kew Gardens, 289
Kniffen system of pruning, 460
Kniphofia uvaria grandiflora, 192
Kurume azalea, 141

Laburnum, 59, 147
lace-flower, blue, 254
Lacinaria, 171
ladybell, 201
Lagerstroemia, 163
lamb's-ears, 251
larch, 73
larkspur, 150, 191
Lathyrus, 255
laurel, mountain, 101, 149, 220
Laurus, 361
Lavandula, 370
Lavatera, 225
lavender, 252, 296, 312, 370
lavender cotton, 252
lavender garden plan, 258
lawn, making and keeping, 245-248
lead plant, 196
leek, 370
lemon fragrance, 264
lemon verbena, 371
length of day, 118
Lespedeza thunbergi, 175, 221
Leucojum
    autumnale, 172
    vernum, 124, 298
Levisticum, 371
Liatris spicata, 171
lilac, 50, 90, 139, 187, 231, 271, 312
Lilium
    auratum, 159, 236, 291
    browni, 151
    canadense, 151
    candidum, 151, 236, 292
    chalcedonicum, 159
    concolor, 151
    elegans, 151
    martagon, 151, 236
    monadelphum, 151
    pardalinum, 159
    parryi, 159

regale, 159, 291
sargentiae, 159
speciosum, 167, 225, 291
superbum, 167
tigrinum, 167
lily, 151, 159, 167, 236, 291
lily-of-the-valley, 142, 234
lily, toad, 176
lime tree, SEE linden
Limonium, 258
linden, 23, 61, 242, 273
    American, 61
    small-leaved European, 52, 61
Linum
    flavum, 215
    narbonnense, 198
    perenne, 198
Lippia, 371
lobelia, 204, 205
locust, 57
locust, honey, 59
loganberry, 423
London plane, 52, 67
Lonicera
    fragrantissima, 114, 230, 270
    heckrotti, 303
    periclymenum, 278, 303
    syringantha, 253, 271
    thibetica, 253
Lorette system of pruning, 479
lovage, 371
love-in-a-mist, 202
lowbush blueberry, 465
lungwort, 134, 190, 198
lupine, 152, 201, 215, 237
Lychnis
    alba, 305
    chalcedonica, 190
    coronaria, 252
    haageana, 190

Macleaya, 235
Madonna lily, 292
magnolia
    cucumber tree, 57
    denudata, 57, 130
    evergreen, 283
    macrophylla, 57
    star, 38, 89, 231, 283
    soulangeana, 131
    stellata, 120, 231, 283, 312
    virginiana, 90, 232, 283, 312
    yulan, 57, 130
Mahaleb cherry, 447
maidenhair-tree, 23, 50, 52, 72
maiden pink, 142, 222

Malling dwarfing stock, 470
mallow, 225, 227, 288
Maltese cross, 190
Malus, 137, 231
Malva, 288
maple
  Japanese, 62
  Norway, 23, 50, 62, 242
  red, 62
  sugar, 23, 62
marigold, 214, 355
marjoram
  pot, 373
  sweet, 359
Majorana hortensis, 359
Marrubium, 368
Mathiola, 305
Matricaria, 352
May (a tree), 58, 268
May wine, 380
Mazzard cherry, 447
meadow saffron, 124
meadowsweet, 269
meat dishes, herbs in, 394
Meconopsis
  cambrica, 215
  wallichi, 203
Melissa officinalis, 362
Mentha
  piperita, 373
  spicata, 379
Mentzelia, 305
Meratia fragrans, 276
Mexican star, 298
mezereon, 120, 253
Michaelmas daisy, 166, 172, 205, 227, 258
mignonette, 297
Milla, 298
Mimulus, 257
miniature dahlia, 158
mint, 379
mock-orange, 50, 91, 95, 232, 273, 312
Mollis azalea, 140
Monarda, 192, 257
monkey-flower, 257
monkshood, 158, 203, 204
montbretia, 167, 192
morning-glory, 202
moss rose, 280
mountain ash, 23, 57
mountain camellia, 91, 163
mountain laurel, 101, 149, 220
moving shrubs and trees, 102
mugwort, 372
mullein, purple, 251

Muscari, 132, 255
musk mallow, 227, 288
musk rose, 280
mustard, 353
myrrh, 380
Myrrhis odorata, 379
Myosotis, 198
myrtle
  blue, 196

Narcissus, 132, 210, 234, 292
nasturtium, 190, 211, 353
Nasturtium, 361
nature of fragrance, 262
navelwort, 199
nectarine, 439
Neapolitan violet, 297
nemesia, 202
Nepeta, 251, 363
netted iris, 122, 298
New Year's gift, 209
Nicotiana
  alata grandiflora, 305
  sylvestris, 237, 305
  tabacum, 305
Nigella, 351
night-fragrant flowers, 301-307
night phlox, 304
night-scented stock, 305, 312
night witchery, 301-307
nocturnal flowers, 301-307
Nycterinia selaginoides, 304
Nymphaea odorata, 300

oak
  live, 61
  pin, 23, 50, 60
  red, 23, 60
  scarlet, 23, 52, 60, 243
  white, 23, 61
Ocimum, 345
Oenothera, 307
"off year" fruiting, 407, 453
oleaster, 273
oleomargarine, herbs in, 395
onion, 372
Ononis, 226
opium poppy, 354
Oriental poppy, 190, 237
Origanum
  majorana, 359
  vulgare, 373
osier, green, 90
Osmanthus
  fragrans, 270
  ilicifolius, 270

oxlip, 134, 210
Oxydendrum, 276

Pachysandra, 98
Paeonia, 142
pagoda tree, 38, 59, 162
painted tongue, 255
Palmette Verrier fruit trees, 480
pansy, tufted, 199, 256
Papaver, 354
paper white narcissus, 133
parsley, 354
pasque-flower, 133, 256
Passiflora caerulea, 290
passion flower, 290
pastries, herbs in, 395
Paulownia, 23, 59
peach, 435-439
  varieties, 436
peach, double-flowered, 89, 128, 187
pear, 454-458
  fire blight, its critical importance, 454
  varieties, 456
pear haw, 89
Pelargonium, 357
Pentstemon
  barbatus, 226
  menziesi, 256
  torreyi, 192
peony, 142, 190, 211, 234, 299, 312
peppermint, 373
perennials, culture of, 182, 344, 386
perfume, 315-322
periwinkle, 199
PERMANENT GARDEN, 13-86
Persian lilac, 272
pests of fruit trees, 485
Petroselinum, 354
petunia, 191, 201, 225, 236, 255
pheasant's-eye, 210
Philadelphus, SEE mock-orange
Phlox
  arendsi, 257
  blue, 203, 256
  divaricata, 256
  lavender, 254
  pink, 224, 225
  red, 192
  subulata, 222
Picea, 80-81
Pieris japonica, 98, 231
Pimpinella, 344
pine
  Austrian, 78
  Japanese black, 78

Japanese red, 78
Japanese umbrella, 78
Scotch, 78
Swiss mountain, 78
Tanyosho, 78
white, 77
pink, 142, 222, 251, 293
pink dogwood, 187
pink garden plan, 228
plane tree, 242
plan of fruit garden, 411
plantain-lily, 257
planting shrubs and trees, 102-105
plant names, 185
Platycodon, 252
pleached trees, 46
plum, 440-445
  Damson varieties, 443
  European varieties, 442
  Japanese varieties, 443
  Native American varieties, 440
Plumbago, 171, 204
poet's narcissus, 133, 292, 312
Polianthes tuberosa, 176
pome fruits, 448-458
pomegranate, 90
pompon dahlia, 158
poplar, 66
poppy, 153
  California, 213
  Iceland, 223
  Oriental, 153, 190, 224, 237
  plume, 235
  satin, 203
  Welsh, 215
Potentilla
  pyrenaica, 212
  red, 192
potpourri, 323-330
prairie lily, 305
preservation of cut flowers, 313
primrose, 134, 198, 210, 256, 296
Primula
  capitata, 256, 296
  denticulata, 256
  elatior, 134, 210
  vulgaris, 134, 198, 210
Provence rose, 149, 365
prunes, 442
pruning fruit trees, 414
Prunus
  bessyi, 470
  glandulosa rosea, 219
  subhirtella, 174, 219
  tomentosa, 231
  triloba, 219

Pulmonaria
  angustifolia, 134, 198
  officinalis, 190
Pulsatilla, 133, 256
purple rock cress, 144, 256
Puschkinia scilloides, 132
Pyracantha, 98
pyrethrum, 226

queen-of-the-meadow, 237
quick-growing trees, 65
quince, 458
quince, flowering, 187

ragged sailor, 201
raspberry, 418-422
  varieties
    black-fruited, 421
    purple-fruited, 420
    red-fruited, 420
redbud, 57, 130, 219
red currant, 424
red dogwood, 187
red garden plan, 194
red-hot poker, 165, 192
red pepper, 356
red valerian, 190, 288
renovation of apple trees, 449
Reseda, 297
restharrow, 226
Retinospora, 84
rhododendron, 38, 100, 149, 188, 220,
  232, 254
Rhodotypos, 232
Ribes, 187
Robinia, 57
robust herbs, 393
rocambole, 374
rock cress, purple, 223
rocket, 357
room fragrance, 308-314
roquette, 357
Rosa, 90, 281
  damascena, 148, 281, 365
  eglanteria, 365
  gallica, 149, 281
  hugonis, 149
  rugosa, 50, 90, 281
rose, 90, 148, 188, 208, 220, 280
rosebud cherry, 219
rose fragrance, 263
rose geranium, 357
rosemary, 375
rose-of-Sharon, 92, 164, 196, 253
Rosmarinus, 375
royal lily, 292

rue, 376
Russell's lupines, SEE lupine
Russian olive, 273
Ruta, 376

sachet, 333
saffron crocus, 295, 376
sage, 166, 192, 203, 377
salads, herbs in, 395
Salpiglossis, 255
Salvia, 166, 203, 348, 377
sand verbena, 297
Santolina, 252
Saponaria, 223, 306
sassafras, 23, 64
Satureia
  hortensis, 358
  montana, 385
savory
  summer, 358
  winter, 385
Saxifraga, 122
scabious, 203, 257
Schizopetalon, 305
Scilla
  hispanica, 126, 198, 221
  nonscripta, 126, 198, 221, 289
  siberica, 124, 198
sea buckthorn, 94
sea lavender, 258
Sedum
  acre, 212
  album, 158, 235
  reflexum, 212
  spectabile, 167, 227
  spurium, 158, 226
semi-dwarf fruit trees, 480-482
Sempervivum
  arenarium, 211
  tectorum, 191, 211
Senecio cineraria, 252
senna, 208
sesame, 358
sex life of fruit trees, 406
shade trees, 60-66
shallot, 378
Shasta daisy, 158, 237
shepherd's scabious, 201
shooting star, 256, 296
shrub, definition of, 55
shrubs, 87-101
shrubs, fragrant, 266-286
Siberian
  squill, 124
  tea, 122
Sidalcea, 227

Silene
    alpestris, 235
    pendula rosea, 223
    virginica, 189
silver-bell tree, 230
silver vine, 363
simple, definition of, 335
small place, 48-54
small vista, 42
smoke-resistant trees, 66
snapdragon, 191, 214, 225
sneezeweed, 175
sneezewort, 160, 237
snowball, 231
snowberry, 50, 91, 94
snowdrop, 116
snowdrop tree, 58
snowflake, 124, 298
snow-in-summer, 251
Sophora, 162
Sorbus, 230
sour gum, 23, 64
sourwood, 276
southernwood, 379
spaghetti, herbs in, 395
Spanish
    bluebell, 126
    jacinth, 126
Spartium, 285
spearmint, 379
speedwell, 158, 200, 204, 223
Spiraea, 90, 91, 129, 155, 188, 269
spirea, 155
    blue, 92
    bridal wreath, 50, 89, 129
    Japanese, 90
spray program, fruit trees, 488
spring frosts, 401
spring meadow saffron, 124
spring planting, 102
spruce
    blue, 81
    Engelmann's, 80
    Koster's, 81
    Norway, 41, 80
    tigertail, 80
squill, 124, 126, 198, 221
Stachys, 251
standard fruit trees, 400
star magnolia, 120, 283
star, yellow, 193
Sternbergia lutea, 175, 215, 288
Stewartia, 91, 163
stock, ten-weeks, 191, 223, 294
Stoke's Aster, 165, 204
Stokesia laevis, 165, 204, 257

stonecrop, 158, 167, 212, 226, 227
stone fruits, 435-447
storax, 284
storing herbs, 389-391
strawberry 361, 428-434
    everbearing types, 431
    self-sterility, 430
    varieties, 430
strawberry shrub, 277
strawberry tree, 174
striped squill, 132
Styrax, 284
succory, blue, 204
summer savory, 358
swamp honeysuckle, 284
swamp laurel, 90, 232
sweet alyssum, 287
sweet bay, 232
sweetbells, 231
sweet cicely, 379
sweet fennel, 351
sweet flag, 380
sweet gum, 23, 64, 243
sweet pea, 190, 223, 235, 254, 287, 313
sweet pepperbush, 163, 275, 313
sweet scabious, 287
sweet-scented shrub, 277
sweet sultan, 287
sweet william, 223, 234
sweet woodruff, 380
sycamore, 23
Symplocos paniculatus, 93, 285
syringa (mock-orange), 232
Syringa, 272

Tabasco, 356
Tamarix, 92, 163, 221
Tanacetum vulgare, 381
Tansy, 381
Taraxacum, 366
tarragon, 382
Taxus, 74
tea olive, 270, 313
tea rose, 148
teas, herbs in, 395
tea, Siberian, 122
tender annuals, culture of, 182, 344
ten-week stock, 191
thistle, globe, 203
thrift, 222
Thuja, 82-83
thyme, 251, 382
Tilia, 61
toad lily, 176
tobacco, 305
Torenia, 202

trained fruit trees, 476-483
tree cypress, 190
tree, definition of, 55
trees
  fragrant, 266
  quick-growing, 65
  ten most popular, 64
tree of paradise, 273
Tricyrtis, 176
Tropaeolum, 353
trumpet-creeper, 188
trumpet narcissus, 133
tuberose, 176, 238, 290, 313
tulip
  cottage, 144, 210, 234, 288
  Darwin, 144, 210, 221, 234, 288, 313
  water lily, 124
Tulipa
  kaufmaniana, 124
tulip-tree, 23, 59, 243
Tunica, 222
turnip-rooted parsley, 354
turtlehead, 166, 226
Tussilago, 122
types of fragrance, 262

Ulex, 285

Vaccinium, 466
valerian, red, 190, 288
vegetable dishes, herbs in, 394
vegetable gold, 295
verbascum, 251
verbena, 237
verbena, lemon, 371
Vernonia, 171
Veronica
  gentianoides, 200
  incana, 200
  spicata, 158, 200, 204, 223
  spuria, 200
vervain, blue, 204
vetchling, spring, 255
Viburnum
  carlesi, 89, 129, 231, 271, 313
  lantana, 232
  odoratissimum, 273
  trilobum, 93
vinegar, herbs in, 395
vines, 95, 96
vinifera grape, 461
Viola, 134, 211, 256, 297, 361
violet, 134, 211, 313, 361
  bird's-foot, 256
  Confederate, 134
  fragrance, 263

horned, 256
yellow, 211
Virginia cowslip, 199
Virginia willow, 284
vistas, 41
  evergreen, 44
  how to plan one, 41-46
Vitex, 91, 155, 196, 252

wall cress, 251
wallflower, 142, 251, 287
walnut, 63
Washington thorn, 58
watercress, 361
water lily, 200
water lily tulip, 124
wayfaring tree, 232
weeping Japanese cherry, 89, 128, 131
weeping trees or shrubs
  evergreens, 86
weeping willow, 65
Weigela, 90, 220, 232
whitebeam, 230
white currant, 424
white garden plan, 239
white pine blister rust, 425
white-trumpet lily, 292
wild ginger, 383
wild marjoram, 373
wild Sweet William, 256
willow, 65
windbreaks, evergreen, 85
windflower, snowdrop, 234
wind-resistant trees, 66
wine grapes, 459-464
wing-flower, blue, 202
winter
  aconite, 209
  daffodil, 175, 288
  fragrance, 114
  jasmine, 119
  rose, 115
  savory, 385
  storage, apples, 453
    pears, 458
wintergreen, 384
Wistaria, 96, 139, 253
witch-hazel, 88, 113, 208
woadwaxen, 156
worm-grass, 235
wormwood, 385

yarrow, 190
yellow bells, 213
yellow garden plan, 217
yellow star, 165, 216

yellow tuft, 212
yellow-wood, 154
Yew
   American, 74
   English, 41, 73
   Irish, 40
   Japanese, 74

youngberry, 423
Yucca, 235
yulan, 57, 130

Zaluzianskya, 304
zinnia, 191, 214